POLITICS AND THE CHURCHES
IN GREAT BRITAIN
1869 TO 1921

Politics and the Churches in Great Britain 1869 to 1921

G. I. T. MACHIN

'It is certain that the Church of England will, some day or other, cease as an establishment to exist.'

The Radical Programme, 1885

'Considering the great mass of social reform that both great parties in the State had set themselves to deal with, it could not be thought for one moment that the vast problem of the disendowment and disestablishment of the Church of England was practical politics.'

Speech by Stephen Walsh in the House of Commons, Feb. 1908

CLARENDON PRESS · OXFORD

1987

Oxford University Press, Walton Street, Oxford OX2 6DP

Oxford New York Toronto Melbourne Auckland
Delhi Bombay Calcutta Madras Karachi
Petaling Jaya Singapore Hong Kong Tokyo
Nairobi Dar es Salaam Cape Town

Associated companies in Beirut Berlin Ibadan Nicosia

OXFORD is a trade mark of Oxford University Press

Published in the United States
by Oxford University Press, New York

British Library Cataloguing in Publication Data
Machin, G. I. T.
Politics and the churches in Great Britain
1869–1921.
1. Church and state—Great Britain—
History—19th century 2. Church and
state—Great Britain—History—20th
century 3. Great Britain—Church history
—19th century 4. Great Britain—Church
history—20th century
I. Title
322'.1'0941 BR759
ISBN 0-19-820106-0

Library of Congress Cataloging-in-Publication Data
Machin, G. I. T.
Politics and the churches in Great Britain,
1869 to 1921.
Bibliography: p.
Includes index.
1. Church and state—Great Britain—History—19th
century. 2. Church and state—Great Britain—History—
20th century. 3. Great Britain—Church history—
19th century. 4. Great Britain—Church history—
20th century. 5. Great Britain—Politics and
government—1837-1901. 6. Great Britain—Politics and
government—1901-1936. I. Title.
BR759.M27   1987   322'.1'0941   87-1620
ISBN 0-19-820106-0

Phototypeset by Cotswold Typesetting Ltd, Gloucester
Printed in Great Britain
at the University Printing House, Oxford
by David Stanford
Printer to the University

TO JANE, JONATHAN, AND RAOUL

AND

IN MEMORY OF ANNA

Preface and Acknowledgements

IN 1869 occurred the greatest single nineteenth-century triumph for the forces of religious equality in the United Kingdom, the disestablishment of the Irish Church. Many thought this would lead to greater victories until nothing was left of religious privilege or State support of a particular Church. To some extent these hopes were realized. Yet by 1921, while Welsh disestablishment had been attained, support for English disestablishment was dwindling and most of the voluntary pressure in Scotland had been diverted into a quest for reunion with the established Church. Ecclesiastical issues, weakened by declining church membership, were leaving the political scene.

In studying this process and trying to explain it, I have concentrated, as before, on issues concerning the position of the Churches *vis-à-vis* the State within Great Britain. These issues included disestablishment, Nonconformist and Catholic relief, Ritualism, education, and Church reform. Opinions and pressure groups are dealt with as well as Parliamentary proceedings. My method is generally chronological rather than thematic because the repeated interaction of different ecclesiastical demands and tendencies was important in explaining the responses of politicians.

I have accumulated many debts during a decade of reasearch on this book. I have received two generous grants from the British Academy; numerous subsidies from the Carnegie Travel Fund of the University of Dundee; and grants from the Research Fund of the Faculty of Arts and Social Sciences in the same university. Many librarians and archivists have enabled me to see material, especially in the British Library, National Library of Scotland, Dundee University Library, Bodleian Library, Scottish Record Office, National Library of Wales, Lambeth Palace Library, House of Lords Record Office, and Dundee Local History Library. Mention should be made of Mr John Barker and his unfailingly helpful staff in Dundee University Library; Dr Brenda Hough, Archivist to the General Synod of the Church of England; Miss Joan Coburn, Head Archivist to the Greater London Council; Miss Elizabeth Poyser, Archivist at Archbishop's House, Westminster; Mr R. H. Harcourt Williams, Librarian and Archivist at Hatfield House; Mr Robert Smart, Keeper of Manuscripts at St Andrews University; Mr Michael Moss, Archivist at Glasgow University; Dr B. S. Benedikz, Sub-librarian at Birmingham University; Mr Alistair Elliot of Newcastle upon Tyne University Library; Dr Peter Anderson, Registrar of the National Registry of Archives (Scotland); and Mr D. W. Riley of the John Rylands Library, Manchester University.

My colleagues and students have been a constant help and stimulus. I am especially appreciative of Dr Donald Southgate's generous gifts of books. Mrs Jessie Young, who typed my manuscript, has proved an ever-present help in time of academic demand. I am also grateful to the custodians and authors of unpublished theses, and to the staff of Oxford University Press. Others who have helped in various ways include Lord Balfour of Burleigh, Mr Mark Bonham Carter, the Hon. Mrs Crispin Gascoigne, Mr J. R. Wynter Bee, Dr Clyde Binfield, the Revd Prof. A. Chapeau, Dr Pauline Dower and the Trevelyan family, Miss Valerie Cromwell, Dr Catriona Levy, and Dr J. P. Parry. Grateful mention should also be made of Cdr. E. R. Dawson, sometime Lecturer in Mathematics at Dundee University, who presented an extensive run of *Annual Registers* to the University Library. Last but first, my heartfelt thanks go to my wife and family for putting up with a historian's preoccupations.

G. I. T. MACHIN
Dundee University
June 1986

Contents

Abbreviations

AP	Asquith Papers
AR	*Annual Register*
BLP	Bonar Law Papers
BP	A. J. Balfour Papers
CBP	Campbell-Bannerman Papers
CCDI	Church Committee for Defence and Instruction
CDI	Church Defence Institution
C. of S.	Church of Scotland
CP	Chamberlain Papers
CR	*Contemporary Review*
CRL	Church Reform League
CU	Church Union
DN	*Daily News*
DP	Disraeli Papers
ECU	English Church Union
EHR	*English Historical Review*
FR	*Fortnightly Review*
GP	W. E. Gladstone Papers
H	Hansard's *Parliamentary Debates*
HGP	Herbert Gladstone Papers
HJ	*Historical Journal*
ILP	Independent Labour Party
INLGB	Irish National League of Great Britain
JEH	*Journal of Ecclesiastical History*
LGP	Lloyd George Papers
LS	Liberation Society Minutes (executive committee)
NLF	National Liberal Federation
NUCA	National Union of Conservative Associations
RP	Rosebery Papers
SHR	*Scottish Historical Review*
SP	Salisbury Papers
T	*The Times*
UP	United Presbyterian
VS	*Victorian Studies*
WHR	*Welsh History Review*

CHAPTER I

Introductory

AN almost unprecedented challenge faced the established Churches in the United Kingdom at the beginning of 1869. Gladstone had just been returned to power with a large majority of 110, uniting Protestant Dissent and Irish Catholicism behind disestablishment of the Church of Ireland. This cause had already received the sanction of the House of Commons and had aroused tremendous controversy in public opinion.[1] The voluntaries (advocates of disestablishment) hoped that the imminent passage of this reform would lead to disestablishment of the Churches of England and Scotland. Behind this hope lay other encouraging events. There had been the recent resumption, after a lull since the 1830s, of important concessions to Dissent, including the settlement of the lengthy Church Rates dispute in 1868. This had been conceded by a Conservative Government to a Liberal majority in the Commons. In the previous year the second Reform Act, carried by the same Government with radical support, had enfranchised many Dissenters.

So strong did the liberalizing tendency appear that even some supporters of the English establishment seemed ready to yield it up to the march of history. It was not only Karl Marx—obviously no friend of the establishment—who believed that 'with its overthrow in Ireland the Established Church will collapse in England'.[2] A politician of a far paler leftish hue, the Whig Earl of Clarendon, thought the established Church in England would 'perhaps last till the end of the century'.[3] The liberal Dean of Canterbury, Henry Alford, wrote in the *Contemporary Review* that the severance of Church from State was practically inevitable: 'History has for ages been preparing its way . . . God's arm is thrusting it on and man's power cannot keep it back . . . There is hardly a reflecting man among us who looks forward to the existence of a State Establishment in this land a century hence'.[4] The new premier might be a staunch Churchman who now preached that liberal concessions were the only way to strengthen the Church of England. But his attitude was ambiguous, and it was feared that his idea of concessions might even extend, in the future, to English disestablishment. He told his son in 1865 that the main duty of

---

[1] G. I. T. Machin, *Politics and the Churches in Great Britain, 1832 to 1868* (Oxford, 1977), 355–79.

[2] Marx to Ludwig Kugelmann, 6 Apr. 1868; K. Marx, *The First International and After: Political Writings*, iii, ed. D. Fernbach (Harmondsworth, 1974), 162.

[4] Clarendon to Earl Russell, 14 Nov. 1868; Sir Herbert Maxwell, *The Life and Letters of George William Frederick, Fourth Earl of Clarendon* (2 vols., London, 1913), ii. 351.

[4] 'The Church of the Future', *CR* ix (Sept.–Dec. 1868), 165 f.

Churchmen should be 'to secure the Church in her spiritual office', and that 'if temporal sacrifices can promote this purpose, they should be made as freely as the shipmaster throws cargo overboard to save the lives of passengers and crew'.[5] To Matthew Arnold he wrote in March 1869 that voluntary (i.e. non-established) religion, while not 'absolutely good', might be 'the best and safest of the alternatives before us . . . to keep in a state of freshness the heart and conscience of man'.[6]

The question of disestablishment was an important one up to about 1920, the period covered in this book. But the strength of the question differed widely between countries within the United Kingdom and between phases within the long period from 1869 to 1921. Only Wales at length emulated Ireland in actually receiving disestablishment. In Scotland the question was eventually diverted into a successful search for reunion between the major Presbyterian bodies; while in England the strength of the movement in the 1870s and early 1880s was followed by recession and the fading of prospects. Besides the aim of disestablishment promoted by 'political Dissenters', there were other Nonconformist objects concerning religious equality, limited for the most part to England and Wales. These were the abolition of university tests, freedom to hold nonconformist burial services in parish churchyards, the removal of inequality over Dissenting marriages, and the extension of an undenominational system of education. All these questions were alive and seeking a solution in 1869. While some were resolved quite soon—university tests being abolished in 1871, and burials being generally settled in 1880—the controversy over education was a persistent one which only lessened towards the end of the period. This question involved a Dissenting challenge to Anglican interests which was closely allied to disestablishment. The voluntary movement might hinder the lesser Dissenting claims because of the Church defence fervour it evoked. But the settlement of most of these claims probably hindered disestablishment in turn, by removing practical objects from the arena and leaving a more theoretical grievance with less support.

Anglicans reacted in different ways to the prospect of disestablishment. Some were prepared to welcome it, but among many others of varied theological complexions the prospect caused determined resistance. Not all of these could be so confident of the future as Archbishop Tait, who announced in June 1880: 'Ever since I was a boy . . . the Church of England has been passing through a crisis. It has got out of all these crises, and it will get out of all others'.[7] To Dean Stanley, a prominent Broad-Churchman, the connection of Church and State was 'the nearest approach which . . . can be made to the original and essential

---

[5] W. E. to W. H. Gladstone, 16 Apr. 1865; D. C. Lathbury (ed.), *Correspondence on Church and Religion of William Ewart Gladstone* (2 vols., London, 1910), ii. 172.

[6] Quoted Machin, op. cit. 382.

[7] R. T. Davidson and W. Benham, *The Life of Archibald Campbell Tait, Archbishop of Canterbury* (2 vols., London, 1891), ii. 486.

idea of the Christian Church'; to James Fitzjames Stephen, disestablishment would be an act of 'covert unbelief' by the State and an admission of failure by the Church; to J. C. Ryle, well-known Evangelical and first Bishop of Liverpool, good relations between Church and Dissent were being obstructed by 'the senseless bitter crusade of liberationists against the Establishment, which if successful can only paganize the rural districts'.[8] Voluntaries naturally thought the opposite: the essential idea of a Christian Church could only be realized independently of intervention and control by a secular State; the Churches would flourish better under a voluntary system which required more effort of them; cordial relations between Church and Dissent could only come about when the former had lost its privileged status.[9]

Added to these religious opinions, however, was a class conflict—also, to some extent, a financial grievance. The established Church was still a symbol of aristocratic domination, though a diminishing one as a result of contracting clerical incomes caused by the agricultural decline which started in the 1870s— a fact which weakened the demand for disendowment of the Church. The advance of the middle classes following industrialization had indeed blurred the social differences between Nonconformists and the establishment. But these differences remained significant, especially in Wales where a linguistic barrier was helping to produce a nationalist one: 'Allegiance to the chapels was an additional way of drawing a line between the lower orders, Welsh speaking and economically subjugated, and the elite of landowners, who were . . . English-speaking Anglicans'.[10] Scotland had a more relaxed socio-religious situation, the Presbyterian establishment being much less aristocratic than the Church of England, partly because so many of the nobility were Episcopalians and therefore officially Nonconformist. Throughout Britain, however, further socio-religious tensions had resulted from large-scale Irish Catholic immigration.

The defence of the English Church as an establishment was shown not least by the activities of the Church Defence Institution (as it was called from 1871), a body originally formed in 1859, having a central council and numerous local branches.[11] Church defence may sometimes have appeared to be lacking in constructiveness. But a Church Reform Union was founded in 1870 and, much later, a Church Reform League in November 1895. An article in the *Nineteenth Century* magazine in 1896 advised that Church reform was the best means of

---

[8] D. Nicholls (ed.), *Church and State in Britain since 1820* (London, 1967), 208, 130; J. C. Ryle, *Churchmen and Dissenters*, paper read at Church Congress, Leicester (London, 1880), 9.

[9] Cf. Machin, op. cit. 100–2. The arguments for and against disestablishment were exhaustively listed in S. Buxton, *A Handbook to the Political Questions of the Day*, 9th edn. (London, 1892), 41–63.

[10] G. Day and M. Fitton, 'Religion and Social Status in Rural Wales', *Sociological Review*, NS xxiii (1975), 885.

[11] M. J. D. Roberts, 'Pressure-group Politics and the Church of England: The Church Defence Institution, 1859–1896', *JEH* xxxv (1984), 560 ff.

defence;[12] it might also attract Dissenters into the established fold. Reform and extension of the Anglican establishment was a leading theme of the period, seen in various demands—more self-government for the Church and more voice for the laity in Church councils; reform of the patronage system in clerical appointments; the creation of additional sees; and better financial provision for Church schools.[13] These aims all had a certain amount of success, though in some cases only after a long struggle. Reform of patronage, for example, was much discussed both inside and outside the Church of England for thirty years. After many attempts a degree of success was reached in the Benefices Act of 1898.[14] Patronage had already been abolished in the Church of Scotland, after considerable discussion, in 1874.[15] Such measures would probably have been achieved eventually without the threat of disestablishment, but this did act as a spur, in Gladstone's phrase, to the aim of 'weakening the invading army'.

The attempts to reform the Church of England were sometimes contradictory, or at least supported by conflicting parties in the Church. Unity in the establishment, indeed, was notably lacking in the face of Dissenting criticism. Serious divisions had become well entrenched. Not only did Evangelicals, Broad-Churchmen, and High-Churchmen differ markedly, but the reasons for opposition to the High section were increasing because it was getting Higher. Old High-Churchmanship had been partly superseded by Tractarianism, and Tractarian doctrines were, in logical sequence, expressed by Ritualism—the general adoption of Catholic ceremonies and vestments, the practice of confession, and the founding of convents and monasteries. Ritualism had begun to arouse popular hostility in the 1840s. In the 1860s Ritualism was gathering force and becoming a major issue of the time, as it remained until the 1930s. Ritualist churches came to be distinguished by the practice of 'six points' in their liturgy, a kind of 'charter' of Anglo-Catholicism—taking the eastward position at the Eucharist; wearing the full Eucharistic vestments; mixing water with wine in the chalice; using lighted candles on the altar, unleavened or 'wafer' bread in the Eucharist, and incense during the service.[16]

The organization of opinion both for and against Ritualism was becoming prominent in the 1860s. The English Church Union was formed by High-Churchmen in May 1860 with a council of twenty-four, consisting half of clergy and half of laity. By the end of 1865 it had forty-seven local branches and 2,300

[12] Augustus Jessopp, 'Church Defence or Church Reform', *Nineteenth Century*, xxxix (Jan.–June 1896), 132–49.
[13] e.g. reform of Convocation was demanded by J. C. Ryle, *Church and State* (London, 1877), and by G. H. Curteis in *CR* xxxi (Feb. 1878), 594–5.
[14] M. J. D. Roberts, 'Private Patronage and the Church of England, 1800–1900', *JEH* xxxii (1981), 199–223.
[15] F. Lyall, *Of Presbyters and Kings: Church and State in the Law of Scotland* (Aberdeen, 1980), 59–62.
[16] N. Yates, *The Oxford Movement and Anglican Ritualism*, Historical Association (London, 1983), 26; O. Chadwick, *The Victorian Church*, ii (London, 1970), 308 ff.

members; by 1876 it had 13,877 members.[17] From 1868 until 1919, and again from 1930 to 1934, its devoted president was Charles Wood, second Viscount Halifax. Its views were defended and propagated by the *Church Times*, commenced in 1863. Although the ECU supported Church defence in general (and sought to co-operate with Evangelicals for this purpose), it was particularly concerned with repelling attacks on Tractarian doctrine and Ritualist practice. The ECU resorted to law in 1862 in a fruitless attempt to prosecute the Evangelical Bishop of Carlisle for heresy.[18] But its example was contagious, and it soon had to defend Ritualists from similar action. The Church Association was a rival Evangelical body formed in 1865 with a veteran anti-Catholic campaigner, J. C. Colquhoun, as chairman, and 7,000 members by 1869. There were many other anti-Catholic societies, either national or local in scope, and there was much overlapping in membership between the Church Association and, say, the forty-year-old Protestant Reformation Society. The Church Association raised £42,000 by 1868 to sue Ritualist clergy, through the action of aggrieved parishioners, for practices which were held to be illegal as going beyond the directions of the Prayer Book. The prosecutions which they sponsored, including the notable ones of A. H. Mackonochie, W. J. E. Bennett, John Purchas and others, became a regular feature of the national scene for many years.[19]

Growing anxiety over Ritualism was also shown in Convocation and Parliament. Ritualism was debated in the Convocation of the Canterbury province in 1866, and a committee was appointed to consider it. Convocation agreed in February 1867 that clergy should not make ritualistic innovations without the consent of their Bishop. In the House of Lords the Earl of Shaftesbury, a leading Evangelical, had been trying unsuccessfully for several years to pass a bill restraining Ritualism. The Government announced in 1867 that a Royal Commission would investigate Ritualism. But Shaftesbury insisted on introducing his Clerical Vestments Bill, only to see it postponed for two months on a small vote in May; and the bill was not brought forward again.[20] The Royal Commission began to sit in June, and soon issued the first of four reports. In February 1868 Convocation again debated the problem. Bishop Tait of London, who had long been troubled by Ritualism in his diocese, complained that Ritualists were tending to reject episcopal authority, said 'this evil exists unchecked', and strongly hinted that Parliamentary legislation might be needed

[17] G. B. Roberts, *The History of the English Church Union, 1859–1894* (London, 1895), 9 ff., 67, 183. Cf. M. J. D. Roberts, 'The Role of the Laity in the Church of England, *c*.1850–1885', D.Phil. thesis (Oxford, 1974), 109 ff.

[18] J. Bentley, *Ritualism and Politics in Victorian Britain: The Attempt to Legislate for Belief* (Oxford, 1978), 37.

[19] L. E. Ellsworth, *Charles Lowder and the Ritualist Movement* (London, 1982), 80–1. For details of the Mackonochie case and its effects see ibid. 91 ff., and M. Reynolds, *Martyr of Ritualism: Father Mackonochie of St Alban's, Holborn* (London, 1965), 129–48.

[20] Davidson and Benham, op. cit. i. 402–8; G. B. A. M. Finlayson, *The Seventh Earl of Shaftesbury, 1801–1885* (London, 1981), 519–20; Ellsworth, op. cit. 81–2.

to secure greater discipline.[21] In the following July Shaftesbury introduced his Uniformity of Public Worship Bill, which was wider than its predecessor but was not put to a vote. Ritualism caused some stir in the 1868 election. In the Buckingham contest the president of the Evangelical Alliance, who won the seat, said of his opponent J. G. Hubbard (who had presented A. H. Mackonochie to his living): 'if you [the voters] are Protestants you will not return a Ritualist'.[22]

With the trials of Ritualist clergy taking place in the courts, debates occurring in Convocation, bills being presented in the Lords, and reports being issued by the Royal Commission, the Ritualist dispute gathered strength without finding a solution. The Church of England was increasingly divided by the question, but the division was a theological and constitutional one which, unlike disestablishment, had little trace of social conflict. Both the Evangelical and High-Church parties had aristocratic leaders and a middle- and lower-class following, though the High-Churchmen were smaller in number at all social levels. By no means all High-Churchmen, moreover, were Ritualists, though most of them probably sympathized with Ritualism. The conflict was very deeply rooted: it was 'waged by Satan on the one hand, and Jesus on the other', said a speaker at a Church Association conference in 1867.[23] 'Except Ritualism is resisted, repudiated, and cast out of our communion', said J. C. Ryle in 1869, 'the days of the Church of England are numbered'.[24] The battle took many forms, and not the differences alone but similar methods of proselytization caused rivalry. Two Anglo-Catholic missions in London and elsewhere in 1869 and 1874 helped to produce the Evangelical fervour at Moody and Sankey's famous visit in 1875.[25] Nor was the controversy limited to Anglicans. Nonconformists, as Evangelicals, naturally disliked Ritualism as a religious practice but also appreciated its value as weakening the Church establishment. The weakening occurred because the establishment could be depicted as increasingly and treacherously Romanist, abandoning the Protestantism it was supposed to represent, and because Ritualists were extremely restless under State control. The final court of appeal in ecclesiastical cases, the Judicial Committee of the Privy Council, was a secular body which repeatedly condemned Ritualist practice. Hence many Ritualists wanted more freedom from the State, and some (including Mackonochie) were prepared even to advocate disestablishment for this purpose. A leading Congregationalist was to

---

[21] Davidson and Benham, op. cit. i. 411–12. He wrote to Bishop Wilberforce: 'I think the Ritual difficulty must be met by an amended Church discipline Bill' (1 Dec. 1868; Samuel Wilberforce Papers, d. 47, fo. 106).

[22] R. W. Davis, *Political Change and Continuity, 1760–1885: a Buckinghamshire Study* (Newton Abbot, 1972), 214.

[23] Church Association: *Annual Reports, The Report of the Conference of the Church Association held in Willis's Rooms, London, 26 and 27 Nov. 1867* (London, 1867), 45.

[24] Church Association: *Lectures in St James's Hall, London* (London, 1869), 170.

[25] J. Kent, *Holding the Fort: Studies in Victorian Revivalism* (London, 1978), 236, 273.

say in 1912: 'Every true Nonconformist is a High Churchman, in the sense that he resents the connection of the State in regard to the creeds he holds, and the forms of worship he follows'.[26]

Perhaps some Dissenters abandoned their support of disestablishment because they feared that Ritualism would spread more freely in a Church released from Erastian control.[27] This was indeed a likely danger, and disestablishment was of course desired by some Ritualists in order to promote it. But it was generally discounted in favour of using the encouragement given by Ritualism to disestablishment to support the voluntary movement. Most Dissenters who saw the danger doubtless prepared to face it, hoping that, in a disestablished Church, Evangelicalism would be strong enough to overcome it.

Ritualists were disliked particularly because of their commonly supposed desire to 'romanize' the Anglican Church and return it to the papal fold—though this was an allegation that Ritualists denied.[28] Romanization seemed especially dangerous at a time of increasing Ultramontane illiberalism in the Roman Church, shown by the adoption of the Syllabus of Errors in 1864 and the definition of papal infallibility at the first Vatican Council in 1870. British anti-Catholicism was sustained by these developments, and by others—a long and unsuccessful campaign in Parliament by Charles Newdegate for the State investigation of convents;[29] the uproar over Irish disestablishment in 1868–9; and continuing friction with the large body of Irish Catholic immigrants and their offspring. Rioting between Catholics and Protestants was already familiar. A notable spate of it resulted from the inflammatory outdoor tirades of William Murphy in 1868. Rioting was to occur again, for example at Tredegar, Monmouthshire, in July 1882 and at Liverpool in July 1889, and frequently thereafter in that turbulent city, as also occasionally in Glasgow.[30] The antagonism was bolstered both by anti-Ritualism and by the organization of Irish Catholic immigrants in favour of Irish Home Rule.

These questions of Disestablishment, Education, and Ritualism formed the main ecclesiastical disputes of the period, together with associated matters such as Roman Catholicism and Church reform. Other developments—secularization, party political changes, and increasing concentration on social reform—could not remove the disputes, though in time they greatly weakened their force. The controversies were conducted with an intensity of passion which is

[26] W. B. Selbie, *The Life of Charles Silvester Horne, MA, MP* (London, 1920), 232.

[27] J. P. Parry, 'Religion and the Collapse of Gladstone's First Government, 1870–1874', *HJ* xxv (1982), 75. Cf. Mrs Melly to George Melly (n.d.); George Melly Papers, 2nd ser. xiii (1), fos. 3230–1.

[28] Church Association: *Annual Reports*, op. cit. 79.

[29] W. L. Arnstein, *Protestant versus Catholic in Mid-Victorian England: Mr Newdegate and the Nuns* (Columbia and London, 1982), 64 ff.

[30] J. Denvir, *The Irish in Britain* (London, 1882), 306–13; *T*, 8 July 1889, p. 6; P. J. Waller, *Democracy and Sectarianism: A Political and Social History of Liverpool, 1868–1939* (Liverpool, 1981), 188 ff.; I. Wood, 'Irish Immigrants and Scottish Radicalism, 1880–1906', in I. MacDougall (ed.), *Essays in Scottish Labour History* (Edinburgh, 1978), 69.

not always displayed in the documentation but was very real because it could reach the inmost recesses of human thought and emotion.

In this study we are concerned not only with the disputes but with their relationship to politics. To achieve success, the contending parties had to convince a majority in Parliament in order to pass, or reject, legislation. For the purpose of convincing Parliament each section appeared as a political pressure group. This was even true, to some extent, of Church assemblies. But the political role of strictly Church bodies was ambiguous. There was a widespread feeling that the Churches as such, being spiritual associations, should not involve themselves directly in secular politics but should view them *sub specie aeternitatis*. Political preaching from the pulpit, while many found it unexceptionable or even desirable, brought its mead of protest—and not only from those who disagreed with the political views expressed. 'We share your views, but politics are not what we come to hear from the pulpit', was the complaint of a deputation to a London Nonconformist minister.[31] A small but 'highly respectable and influential' group in the Scottish United Presbyterian Church objected to the discussion of public questions in the Church's assemblies.[32] Too much political activity, it was feared, might mean too little energy to spare for spiritual concerns.

But the issues were such that it was very difficult to separate the religious from the political. Overt political commitment by clergy and ministers could easily be defended on religious grounds, as an essential vindication of spiritual standpoints. Roman Catholic priests were sure they were championing spiritual values by urging their flocks to vote in the interest of their Church. The great Baptist preacher C. H. Spurgeon defended his own political involvement on the ground that disestablishment was 'a divine and not a party cause'.[33] Probably a large majority of Congregationalists and Baptists supported disestablishment; this and other political aims were frequently urged in their local chapel meetings and national assemblies. At the autumn assemblies of the Congregational Union of England and Wales in both 1868 and 1872, for example, the chairmen's addresses dwelt on the merits of disestablishment.[34] Even the 'no politics' tradition (or veiled Toryism) of the Wesleyan leadership was breaking down by mid-century in face of a growing tendency to align with the political radicalism of most Nonconformists. This tendency, though resisted by an 'old guard' of ministers and checked by the Home Rule crisis of 1886, was illustrated by the fact that all the Wesleyan MPs between 1868 and

[31] D. W. Bebbington, *The Nonconformist Conscience: Chapel and Politics, 1870–1914* (London, 1982), 7. Cf. ibid. 80–3.

[32] *United Presbyterian Magazine*, N.S. xiii (1869), 284.

[33] Patricia S. Kruppa, *Charles Haddon Spurgeon: A Preacher's Progress* (New York and London, 1982), 291.

[34] *Congregational Year-book* (1869), 61–7; (1872), 71–84. Cf. *Baptish Handbook* (1869), 162–5.

1886 were Liberals, also by the growing influence of the Revd Hugh Price Hughes, who began to edit a new radical paper, *The Methodist Times*, in 1885.[35]

But the Church assemblies themselves did not assume the propagandist role of political pressure groups. This part was taken by other bodies, some specially formed for the purpose but others only functioning in this way as an addition to primarily religious activities. Some of these associations were markedly denominational, like the Church Defence Institution or the Catholic Union of Great Britain (founded in 1871); some represented a particular Church party, as in the case of the English Church Union or the Church Association; and some were broadly undenominational like the Liberation Society (originally the Anti-State Church Association), the Protestant Alliance, or (more restrictedly) the Protestant Dissenting Deputies.

The political concerns which might occupy these associations included the registration of electors, efforts to influence votes in Parliamentary elections, and attempts to guide the attitude of MPs to bills of ecclesiastical interest. The Liberation Society and the Protestant Dissenting Deputies jointly held the first of a long series of 'Parliamentary breakfasts' in 1866, attended by MPs and other notabilities.[36] Ecclesiastical opinions were also brought to bear on the party political organizations which grew rapidly after the enfranchisement of 1867—the National Union of Conservative Associations, the National Liberal Federation, and their numerous constituent societies.[37] The introduction of the secret ballot in 1872 forbids from that date the comparison of poll-books with church membership lists in order to connect denominational membership with party voting. So we are left with the not unreasonable assumption that comparative denominational strength in a constituency was an important factor influencing elections. Detailed studies have indicated the validity of this assumption.[38] The political effect of denominational strength depended, of course, on the extent of the franchise and the distribution of constituencies. For example, reasonably full opportunities for Nonconformists to influence the composition of the House of Commons were not provided until the Reform and Redistribution of Seats Acts of 1884 and 1885. Ironically this was a triumph the expected fruits of which were immediately snatched from them.

The ecclesiastical movements and parties behind these organizations had their own distinct aims, so that it was difficult to form a complete political alliance with other groups. Dissenting voluntaries might sympathize with some

---

[35] R. F. Wearmouth, *Methodism and the Struggle of the Working Classes, 1850–1900* (Leicester, 1954), 212–16; I. Sellers, *Nineteenth-century Nonconformity* (London, 1977), 16; Bebbington, op. cit. 8; id. 'Nonconformity and Electoral Sociology, 1867–1918', *HJ* xxvii (1984), 638.

[36] B. L. Manning, *The Protestant Dissenting Deputies* (Cambridge, 1952), 394–5.

[37] H. J. Hanham, *Elections and Party Management: Politics in the Time of Disraeli and Gladstone* (London, 1959), 93 ff., 106.

[38] H. Pelling, *Social Geography of British elections, 1885–1910* (London, 1967), 432–3 and *passim;* F. Bealey and H. Pelling, *Labour and Politics, 1900–1906* (London, 1958), 3–8; J. Bochel and D. T. Denver, 'Religion and Voting: A Critical Review and a New Analysis', *Political Studies*, xviii (1970).

Ritualists in their desire for disestablishment, but could not agree with their religious doctrines and practices. Voluntaries might share much common religious ground with Anglican Evangelicals (and even more with Church of Scotland Evangelicals), but were at odds with them over establishment. Voluntaries could co-operate with Roman Catholics over Irish disestablishment and other matters of Catholic relief, but not over the maintenance of denominational schools. The liberal ideals of Broad-Churchmen might attract some Nonconformists, but not the Broad-Churchmen's desire for an all-embracing National Church.

The different viewpoints were firmly held, but party political interest sometimes demanded that they be muted or modified. Politics and ecclesiastical issues were parts of a two-way process in which party interests sometimes supervened; and party interest involved the consideration of many other matters besides the ecclesiastical. Political parties were loose combinations of different views in which sectional interests had often to be submerged for the sake of general unity. Both the Conservative and Liberal parties contained anti-Ritalists, for example, but these were usually disappointed in their desire to enforce liturgical uniformity. Most Nonconformists might vote Liberal, but their quest for general disestablishment was not taken up by the Liberal party. This was for reasons of political strategy and because the party was a non-denominational one which contained many Erastian Churchmen, especially among the Whigs. Political Dissenters were frequently restive in their imprisoning Liberal allegiance, but never attempted the hazardous task of forming their own party—perhaps because they believed, with good reason, that they would be weaker outside the Liberal party than inside. The Conservative party was, in general, a firm defender of the established Churches, and at least ninety per cent of Conservative MPs are said to have been Anglican in 1911.[39] But the Public Worship Regulation Act of 1874, passed by a Conservative Government, annoyed Conservative Ritualists; and ardent Churchmen among MPs thought it necessary to form a Church Parliamentary Committee (officially non-party) in 1893 to pay special attention to Church protection and advance. The Dissenting reply on the Liberal side was a Nonconformist Parliamentary Council formed in 1898. Irish Catholics had to face two ways in politics, looking to Liberals for Home Rule but to Conservatives for assured defence of their denominational schools.

The political parties, in fact, were non-confessional organizations, and no ecclesiastical viewpoint became an essential feature of a party creed. Ecclesiastical solutions in politics were therefore reached on pragmatic and non-theoretical grounds, and for a common pragmatic reason—that they were seen as a desirable response to a convincing majority demand. This explains why no Act was passed against Ritualism in the early twentieth century, and

[39] J. Ramsden, *The Age of Balfour and Baldwin, 1902–1940* (London, 1978), 99–100. For Nonconformity and Liberalism cf. Bebbington, 'Nonconformity and Electoral Sociology', 634–40.

why disestablishment came in Ireland and Wales but not in England and Scotland.

Structural changes in party politics also contributed to the fortunes of ecclesiastical questions. Just when Nonconformity had received apparent encouragement from the enfranchisement and redistribution of 1884–5, and when, if the Liberal party were to be split, it seemed that Joseph Chamberlain's disestablishment campaign might do it, the Irish Home Rule issue intervened to divide the party instead. The prospect of disestablishment was lessened for many years by the Liberal disruption and the adhesion of many Nonconformists to Liberal Unionism, and by the long period of Conservative rule which followed the Liberal split. Another new departure, the formation of a separate Labour party, reflected the increased working-class electoral strength since 1885. This organization was concerned with social and economic reform, and paid very little attention to ecclesiastical questions such as disestablishment and anti-Ritualism, though it was more concerned with educational reform. Social and economic aims were the predominant concerns of working-class electors of whom probably a majority were non-churchgoers. The growing importance of social questions, both inside and outside the Labour party—and, for that matter, inside the Churches—progressively diminished the importance of the old ecclesiastical issues, to the general relief of the establishment. A Labour MP asserted in a debate on the Prayer Book in 1928: 'The working man is not interested in the Prayer Book but in the Rent Book.'[40] The rise of the Labour party helped, somewhat ironically, to speed the decline of disestablishment.

Political changes were an important but secondary reason for the lessening interest in ecclesiastical matters by the early twentieth century. The fundamental reason was a decline in church membership and attendance which gave the Churches a diminishing pool of human resources to support their religious, political, and social aims. The large church attendance figures revealed by the Religious Census of 1851 probably held up quite well, in proportion to population growth, for the next thirty years—although there was no subsequent national religious census, and one is dependent on the results of various local investigations for making perhaps dubious wider assumptions. But a slackening seems to have begun in the 1880s and has not been effectively reversed in the succeeding century. This was in extraordinary contrast to immense church growth in the expanding overseas Empire, commencing about the same time as the onset of comparative decline in Great Britain. Abroad, Christian efforts were richly successful; at home, while still being made in abundance, their reward was much less.

'Declining membership' is usually a general statement which does not take account of widely differing denominational and local experiences. But it is a

[40] C. Garbett, *Church and State in England* (London, 1950), 215.

statement which generally holds true for the Protestant Churches. Until the early twentieth century the decline was obscured by the fact that numbers were still rising, though not usually so much as the population as a whole. Figures for Anglican Easter Day communicants did in fact rise more rapidly than the population, from 1,384,000 in 1885 to well over two millions by 1908. Nonconformist membership also rose, though not as rapidly as population growth, during this period. But in the years 1906–8 several major Nonconformist denominations began to experience an absolute drop in numbers. This was a remarkable coincidence, and was in striking contrast to the return of the highest ever number of Nonconformist MPs in the 1906 election. It was not long before a leading Baptist minister said that his world seemed to have become twenty degrees colder.

The Wesleyans reached their highest membership level in England (447,476) in 1906, though they almost reached this level again in 1932, just before the Methodist union. Congregationalism had its highest membership in Wales in 1905, and in England in 1908. Baptist membership reached its peak in England in 1907, and in Wales in 1906. Primitive Methodism attained its peak of British membership in 1908. The numbers of Sunday school attendants in these four large Nonconformist Churches all reached their highest points in 1906. Nonconformist statistical trends after these dates generally went downwards, though at varying denominational rates. It is worth noting, however, that the Quakers reached a high point of British membership in 1908 and remained stable (at about 20,000) until 1970. The Nonconformist figures, though declining, held up fairly well until the 1930s. The Church of England figures are not strictly comparable, but Anglicanism was statistically more successful than Nonconformity—a fact which contributed to the decline of the disestablishment challenge. Annual confirmations were at their highest in 1911 (244,030) and Sunday scholars in 1913; Easter Day communicants remained at over two millions until 1940, and temporarily exceeded this number again in the 1950s and early 1960s.

The Scottish Protestant statistical experience differed significantly from the English. Membership growth did not keep pace with the population, but Church of Scotland membership increased from 422,357 in 1868 to a high point of 762,774 in 1925. After the union of this Church with most of the other major Presbyterian body, the United Free Church, in 1929, the enlarged membership remained stable until 1953 and rose to a fresh peak of 1,319,574 in 1956, followed by a slow decline. Methodist membership in Scotland also reached its peak in 1956.[41] The United Free Church grew from its foundation in 1900 until union with the Church of Scotland. The communicants in the Scottish Episcopal Church rose steadily from 1883 to 1940. Finally, the Roman Catholic Church in Great Britain differed strikingly from the general pattern by growing

[41] Carol Fry, 'The Demographic Status of Methodism in Scotland', *Journal of the Scottish Branch of the Wesley Historical Society*, xii (1979), 7.

faster than the population from 1,680,000 in 1887 to 2,813,244 in 1931 and 4,963,854 in 1969, though decline commenced just after this.[42]

There was a wealth of worried contemporary comment, either about the growth of Catholicism or the relative general decline in attendance from the 1880s.[43] 'The crying need of the hour in Wesleyan Methodism is a replenishment of its membership', said the *Wesleyan Methodist Magazine* in 1910, before making suggestions how to meet it.[44] Prominent among such comments were references to the majority working-class absence which had been noted by Horace Mann in his report on the 1851 Religious Census and was a continuous source of concern thereafter.[45] There was considerable working-class membership, but this had a strong tendency to be denominationally selective, limited in its concentrated form to the Roman Catholics, the Primitive Methodists, the Salvation Army, and a few smaller sects. All of these were particularly attractive, for different reasons, to sections of the working class. The Catholic Church was a natural home for immigrant Irish workers who were isolated in their adopted society. The Primitive Methodists had a strong tradition of working-class participation and government, though this was probably becoming less marked by the early twentieth century.[46]

In spite of vigorous home missionary efforts in the late nineteenth century,[47] a stubborn mass of working-class indifference persisted and, indeed, was spreading. From the 1880s there also appears to have been a slow middle-class drift away from regular attendance—the beginning of shrinkage of the Victorian religious backbone. This is not to say that the Churches went into immediate or very obvious decline as a result. The Welsh revival of 1904–5 showed that the Churches could still be given a marked expansive impulse.[48] In the Church of England, if not yet among Nonconformists, there were signs of decline in the number of candidates for ordination: the days when there could appear a statistic like that of 1880–2, placing England second only to Spain in its

---

[42] These statistics are taken from R. Currie, A. Gilbert, and L. Horsley (eds.), *Churches and Churchgoers: Patterns of Church Growth in the British Isles since 1700* (Oxford, 1977), 128–91.

[43] K. S. Inglis, *Churches and the Working Classes in Victorian England* (London, 1963), 22–3, 56, 66, 86, 102–3; J. Clifford, *The Non-attendance of Professed Christians at Public Worship* (London, 1868); *Primitive Methodist Magazine* (1877) 126, (1882) 63–4; Dean F. W. Farrar in *FR*, lviii (Oct. 1895), 557–65; R. Mudie-Smith (ed.), *The Religious Life of London* (London, 1904), 15–17.

[44] *Wesleyan Methodist Magazine* (1910), 414.

[45] For elaboration of this matter see É. Halévy, *Imperialism and the Rise of Labour*, trans. E. I. Watkin, 2nd edn. (London, 1951), 380–1; E. R. Wickham, *Church and People in an Industrial City* (London, 1957), 150–9; D. Martin, *A Sociology of English Religion* (London, 1967), 27–33; S. Mayor, *The Churches and the Labour Movement* (London, 1967), 25ff.; C. D. Field, 'Methodism in Metropolitan London, 1850–1920: A Social and Sociological Study', D. Phil. Thesis (Oxford, 1974), 358–60.

[46] H. Pelling, *Popular Politics and Society in Late Victorian Britain* (London, 1968), 20–36; C. D. Field, 'The Social Structure of English Methodism, Eighteenth to Twentieth Centuries', *British Journal of Sociology*, xxviii (1977), 205–16.

[47] K. S. Inglis, op. cit. 143 ff.

[48] D. B. Rees, *Chapels in the Valley: A Study in the Sociology of Welsh Nonconformity* (Upton, Wirral, 1975), 71, 154–7; K. O. Morgan, *Rebirth of a Nation: Wales, 1880–1980* (Oxford, 1981), 134–7.

proportion of clergy and ministers, seemed to be numbered.[49] None the less the Churches remained prosperous, popular, and very influential until at least the 1920s and, in the case of some denominations, long afterwards.[50] But the combination of failure to attract most workers and decline of middle-class support produced, in the end, contraction of the Churches' role on all fronts— religious, social, and political. It has been convincingly suggested that changing political circumstances can have a sensitive effect on religious allegiance.[51] As the Churches lost influence in politics, their numbers may have declined further because they lost supporters who had seen them mainly as vehicles for political expression.

The question why the Churches lost members invites a multiplicity of answers, and it is doubtful whether a satisfactory reply can be given. Doubt and unorthodoxy, and outright unbelief, were clearly spreading from the mid-nineteenth century, under the influence of biblical criticism, the theory of evolution, and the rejection of belief in hell.[52] 'Only too clearly the times are unbelieving times', said the president of the General Baptist Association in 1886.[53] Gladstone, presenting the prizes at Liverpool College in 1872, proclaimed that 'the spirit of denial is abroad, and has challenged all religion, but especially the religion we profess, to a combat of life and death'.[54] The Marxist Ernest Belfort Bax wrote in *Justice*, the organ of the Social Democratic Federation, in 1895: 'The old dogmatic basis as such has collapsed, with few exceptions, among all classes of society'.[55] The erosion of doctrinal landmarks caused fierce controversy over a wide denominational spectrum, especially amongst Evangelicals.[56] Spurgeon left the Baptist Union in 1887 because he was convinced that increasing liberal thought had put the denomination 'on the downgrade'.[57] Scriptural criticism by a brilliant young professor, the Revd

---

[49] M. G. Mulhall, *The Dictionary of Statistics*, 4th edn. (London, 1899); O. Chadwick, *The Victorian Church*, ii (London, 1970), 248.

[50] Cf. J. Kent, 'A Late Nineteenth-century Nonconformist Renaissance', in D. Baker (ed.), *Studies in Church History*, xiv (Oxford, 1977), 352–4; C. Binfield, *So Down to Prayers: Studies in English Nonconformity, 1780–1920* (London, 1977).

[51] A. D. Gilbert, *Religion and Society in Industrial England: Church, Chapel, and Social Change, 1740–1914* (London, 1976), 206; Currie, Gilbert, and Horsley, op. cit. 109 f.

[52] A. D. Gilbert, *The Making of Post-Christian Britain* (London, 1980), 120; G. Rowell, *Hell and the Victorians* (Oxford, 1974), 212–13; R. Currie, *Methodism Divided: A Study in the Sociology of Ecumenicalism* (London, 1968), 112–25; M. R. Watts, ' "The Hateful Mystery": Nonconformists and Hell', *Journal of United Reformed Church History Society*, ii (1978–82), 248–58; R. F. Horton, *An Autobiography* (London, 1917), 30–2; Beatrice Webb, *My Apprenticeship*, 2nd edn. (London, 1946), 47, 71–2; H. McLeod, *Class and Religion in the Late Victorian City* (London, 1974), 214–27; D. Lyon, 'The Eclipse of Christian Religious Assumptions: England in the 1870s', Ph.D. thesis (Bradford, 1976).

[53] *General Baptist Year-book* (1886), 7.

[54] *AR* cxiv (1872), 143.

[55] *Justice*, 8 June 1895.

[56] W. B. Glover, *Evangelical Nonconformists and Higher Criticism in the Nineteenth Century* (London, 1954); Anne Bentley, 'The Transformation of the Evangelical Party in the Church of England in the Late Nineteenth Century', Ph.D. thesis (Durham, 1971), 11.

[57] Patricia Kruppa, op. cit. 404–33.

William Robertson Smith, embroiled the Scottish Free Church in dispute from 1875 to 1881.[58] Congregationalists were much disturbed by proposals for relaxing Evangelical standards of belief at the time of their Leicester assembly in 1877.[59] In the Catholic Church, Ultramontanes battled with Modernist thought.[60]

But doubt and unorthodoxy had always been present, though their influence grew towards the end of the nineteenth century. Eighteenth-century scepticism had not prevented the religious expansion of the early nineteenth century, and late nineteenth-century agnosticism would not necessarily prevent a revival again. In any case, intellectual doubt affected only a small minority, and often produced 'unorthodoxy' rather than unbelief. An investigation into reasons for adopting secularism has shown that moral revulsion from the Bible or from the preaching of a particular minister was more important than intellectual questioning: 'the many men who saw intellectual errors in religious dogma probably became liberal Christians or syncretists rather than atheists'.[61] The Churches could accommodate unorthodoxy, at the price of internal uproar. This accommodation was shown, for example, by the acceptance of biblical criticism in *Lux Mundi*, essays published by High-Church clergymen in 1889, and by Bishop Frederick Temple's statement in 1884: 'We cannot find that Science, in teaching Evolution, has yet asserted anything that is inconsistent with Revelation'.[62] The ultimate in Christian non-theology was probably the Revd R. J. Campbell's 'New Theology' of 1907, abandoning traditional beliefs in favour of 'divine immanence' in nature and mankind. The various possibilities for belief within the Churches had grown greatly, and the young D. H. Lawrence may well have written bemusedly to his Congregational minister in 1907: 'I do not think Campbell solves any problems . . . But I should like to know whether the Churches are with him . . . I would like to know, because I am absolutely in ignorance, what is precisely the orthodox attitude . . . It is essential that we should understand the precise position of the Church of today.'[63]

The Churches could not, of course, accommodate determined unbelief. But unbelief made a comparatively small contribution to declining interest in the Churches. Indifference made a much greater contribution, and this was

---

[58] P. Carnegie Simpson, *The Life of Principal Rainy* (2 vols., London, 1909), i. 306–403.

[59] M. D. Johnson, 'Thomas Gasquoine and the origins of the Leicester Conference', *Journal of United Reformed Church History Society*, ii (1978–82), 346–8.

[60] E. R. Norman, *The English Catholic Church in the Nineteenth Century* (Oxford, 1984), 333–44.

[61] Susan Budd, *Varieties of Unbelief: Atheists and Agnostics in English Society, 1850–1960* (London, 1977), 106–12. Cf. Chadwick, op. cit. ii. 112–18.

[62] A. O. J. Cockshut (ed.) *Religious Controversies of the Nineteenth Century: Selected Documents* (London, 1966), 265. Cf. St G. Mivart, 'The Catholic Church and Biblical Criticism', *Nineteenth Century*, xxii (1887), 31–51; D. Bowen, *The Idea of the Victorian Church* (Montreal, 1968), 173–80; Chadwick op. cit. ii. 97–111.

[63] Lawrence to Revd Robert Reid, 15 Oct. 1907; J. T. Boulton (ed.), *The Letters of D. H. Lawrence*, i (Cambridge, 1979), 36–7.

associated with the spread of 'popular materialism', the beginning of the great expansion of leisure activities produced by decreasing hours of labour, gradually increasing prosperity, and technological advance. Even worse than intellectual scepticism, said the president of the General Baptist Association in 1886, was 'practical unbelief. Indifference and worldliness abound.'[64] The Churches made notable efforts to satisfy the thirst for leisure pursuits, as was shown by the formation of cycling, football, literary, and many other clubs as church auxiliaries.[65] But leisure was often in competition with the churches and perhaps led people away from them. Secular pleasure, at least on Sundays, was in conflict with a still thriving puritanism. When the Leicester Secular Club started Sunday cricket in 1885, 'the opponents of the practice stormed the wickets and seized the bats'.[66]

On the other hand, popular materialism does not necessarily lead to abandonment of church-going. The twentieth-century experience of the United States shows that large-scale church-going (much higher than in this country) and the abundant enjoyment of leisure opportunities are not mutually exclusive. An additional reason, perhaps peculiarly marked in Britain, was a reaction against formal church-going—a tendency to abandon the forms of religion though not, in most cases, the beliefs. This occurred most notably among the middle classes, which gradually relaxed their formal observance. Exactly why they did so is doubtless a result of multifarious personal motives which defy rigid analysis.

Reduced Church allegiance naturally weakened the general influence of Churches in society and the strength of their political voice. Another reason for the decline of Church questions in politics, as already mentioned, was the growing interest in social reform and the increasing demand for this from the enlarged electorate. By the 1880s, when several Socialist groups appeared, the commitment of many Church leaders to social reform had become clear. The moral fervour which inspired successful campaigning in the 1870s and early 1880s for repeal of the Contagious Diseases Acts (held by many to encourage prostitution), was also directed to reforming the living conditions of the majority.[67] In 1883 a famous penny pamphlet, *The Bitter Cry of Outcast London,* was produced by two Congregational ministers. In 1884 began the religious 'settlements' in slum areas, zealously idealistic if without much obvious effect on the workers, and by 1914 forty had been established. The Christian Social Union was founded by Anglicans in 1889, and its influence rapidly expanded: by 1913 sixteen of its members had become Bishops. Cardinal Manning was celebrated for his intervention in the London Dock

---

[64] *General Baptist Year-book* (1886), 7.

[65] J. Cox, *The English Churches in a Secular Society: Lambeth, 1870–1930* (Oxford, 1982), 83, 85–6; Sir James Marchant, *Dr John Clifford, CH: Life, Letters, and Reminiscences* (London, 1924), 63.

[66] *AR* cxxvii (1885), Chronicle section, 38.

[67] Bebbington, *The Nonconformist Conscience*, 38–45.

Strike of 1889; and Pope Leo XIII's encyclical *Rerum Novarum,* sympathetic to some of the workers' aspirations but emphatically not to Socialism, was produced in 1891 partly under Manning's influence. Commitment to Socialism was much more restricted than a broad sympathetic interest in social improvement. But many clergy and ministers became Socialists of the mild Fabian variety, such as Stewart Headlam and John Clifford, and a few even joined the Marxist Social Democratic Federation in spite of H. M. Hyndman's outspoken hostility to Christianity. Anglicans formed the Church Socialist League in 1906, and there were Socialist associations in other denominations.[68] In 1891 the Congregational Union of England and Wales formed a Social Questions Committee which later conferred with Labour MPs about specific questions of social improvement.[69] Altogether, the Churches did a good deal to initiate and sustain the interest in social reform which marked the age. In so doing they bore some responsibility for the displacement of ecclesiastical issues from politics by social ones. Such a displacement was in fact welcomed by some people in all Churches.

The spread of common interest in social reform assisted another tendency of the period, that of growing understanding between the Churches which led to some interdenominational unions. There was much discussion in Convocation and Church Congress about the possible reunion of Nonconformists, and especially Wesleyans, with the Church of England, and a Home Reunion Association was formed in 1870.[70] But the religious obstacles to such a reunion were very great, especially at a time when disestablishment was a flourishing issue and Ritualism was growing. Even Nonconformists who were lukewarm about disestablishment did not want to join an established Church in which Ritualism was expanding. Ritualists, for their part, did not want an enlarged Evangelical element in their Church. If they hoped for a reunion themselves, it was one between the Church of England and the Church of Rome.

Conferences took place between Anglicans and Nonconformists: Archbishop Tait caused a stir by arranging one at Lambeth Palace with about twenty leading Dissenting ministers in 1876.[71] Anglicans first attended a Congregational Union assembly in 1882.[72] Anglican clergy sometimes accepted invitations to preach in Nonconformist churches, but this practice was censured by Convocation in 1887.[73] Goodwill was often expressed between Anglicans

---

[68] Mayor, op. cit. 50–66, 196 ff.; Inglis, op. cit. 143–74, 250–321; P. d'A. Jones, *The Christian Socialist Revival, 1877–1914* (Princeton, 1968); Norman, *Church and Society in England, 1770–1970* (Oxford, 1976), 161–6, 221–60.

[69] A. Peel, *These Hundred Years: A History of the Congregational Union of England and Wales, 1831–1931* (London, 1931), 332–3.

[70] G. F. Nuttall and O. Chadwick (eds.), *From Uniformity to Unity, 1662–1962* (London, 1962), 330–8. Cf. P. T. Marsh, *The Victorian Church in Decline: Archbishop Tait and the Church of England, 1868–1882* (London, 1969), 246–51.

[71] Davidson and Benham, *Tait,* ii. 491.

[72] L. E. Elliott-Binns, *Religion in the Victorian Era* (London, 1936), 475; A. Peel, op. cit. 290.

[73] Nuttall and Chadwick, op. cit. 338–41.

and Nonconformists, and there was some co-operation, for example over the revision of the Bible and in the temperance movement. But religious and political differences were too pronounced for hopes of corporate reunion to flourish. Even co-operation was sometimes difficult. Writing of the position in 1889, a Congregational minister did not unduly exaggerate when he said that 'real fellowship between Anglicans and Free Churchmen . . . was practically non-existent. They confronted one another in opposite camps.'[74]

Co-operation was much easier between Nonconformists of different denominations, and the unions achieved were all between Dissenters who acknowledged the same roots. Bodies of Presbyterians combined to form the Presbyterian Church of England in 1876. The Particular and the General Baptists united in 1891. The Free Methodists, the New Connexion, and the Bible Christians formed the United Methodist Church in 1907. In Scotland most of the Reformed Presbyterians joined the Free Church in 1876; Congregationalists and the Evangelical Union combined in 1897; and union between most of the Free Church and the United Presbyterians was attained in 1900. Discussions also took place on other denominational combinations, and some eventually succeeded.[75]

As well as some unions, there was organizational co-operation between Dissenters. Conferences in Switzerland between British Free Churchmen in 1892 led to the foundation of the National Free Church Council in 1896,[76] and this was a powerful body over the next ten years. If in the early nineteenth century the British religious denominations had been characterized by division and multiplication, by the early twentieth century they were marked by unification and contraction.

In spite of greater interdenominational understanding, however, ecclesiastical divisions and contentions remained strongly marked. Various tendencies were acting to diminish them—the removal of most of the 'religious equality' grievances, leaving disestablishment high and dry; declining support for the Churches, reducing their strength to fight political battles; changes in the shape of party politics, affecting the Churches' political interests; growing working-class demands for social reform, and greater concentration on this, not least by the Churches, at the expense of ecclesiastical issues. All these trends were in evidence by the early twentieth century. The result was that, while some issues were still being settled as late as 1920, and some were still matters of contention at that date, others declined into comparative insignificance.

---

[74] J. D. Jones, *Three Score Years and Ten* (London, 1940), 198.
[75] Currie, *Methodism Divided*, 239 ff.
[76] J. S. Drummond, *Charles A. Berry, DD: A Memoir* (London, 1899), 111–12.

CHAPTER II

Gladstone and the Churches, 1869–1874

I. INTRODUCTORY

GLADSTONE'S first ministry, formed in December 1868 after a resounding electoral victory, consisted of Whigs, former Peelites, and one or two radicals. It was an unwieldy alliance, and Gladstone had great difficulty in holding it together—a familiar problem for Liberal premiers. The various radical demands caused resistance from the Whigs, who were still the predominant element in both the ministry and the Liberal party. Ecclesiastical issues were foremost among the causes of disruption, and were linked to educational, democratic, and Irish Home Rule questions. The Whigs were Erastian upholders of established Churches, but they were asked to agree to disestablishment in Ireland if not yet in Britain. They believed in aristocratic landed influence, but had to meet demands for the secret ballot and Irish land reform. They wanted to maintain Parliamentary supremacy over the United Kingdom but were challenged by a growing demand for Irish Home Rule. Gladstone was too enthusiastic a reformer to please the Whigs on such matters, though he was conscious of having to hold the balance in his party and consequently did not satisfy the radicals or Home Rulers either. Nonconformists and Catholics, though agreeing in 1869 over Irish disestablishment, became divided over education and religion. The strong Government formed in 1868 managed to carry many important reforms, but at the price of growing contention within the ranks of its followers. Well before it ended in 1874 it was exhausted and disrupted. Its story was one of failure through success.

The religious minorities still had only small numbers in the Parliament elected in 1868. Thirty-six Roman Catholics were returned, all of them from Ireland. A maximum of sixty-four Nonconformists is said to have been returned (only five of them Wesleyans), a larger number than ever before.[1] But this was still a very inadequate force with which to obtain great changes, even though—as the Liberation Society justifiably claimed—a fair number of Anglican Liberal MPs was also ready to support general disestablishment.[2]

---

[1] Dr J. F. Glaser's figures, quoted P. T. Marsh, *The Victorian Church in Decline: Archbishop Tait and the Church of England, 1868–1882* (London, 1969), 141 and n. Only fifty-three Nonconformists appeared on a Whip's list of Dissenting MPs, in Gladstone Papers, 44612, fos. 138–9; but this list is probably incomplete and perhaps inaccurate.

[2] Marsh, op. cit. 28.

Even in Wales, where the 1868 election was quite a notable advance for radicalism, only four of the thirty-three MPs were Nonconformists compared with seventy-five per cent of the churchgoers (who were probably about half the population). Nonconformist politicians, moreover, were divided in attitude, some being militant like the veteran voluntary leader Edward Miall, others increasingly moderate like Samuel Morley, Miall's fellow-Congregationalist who resigned from the Liberation Society in December 1868. Certain aims of the more extreme Nonconformist politicians, notably disestablishment and purely secular education, were opposed by the Government. After Irish disestablishment, the only Dissenting aim which succeeded in this Parliament was the abolition of nearly all the remaining university tests in 1871, and even this settlement was not entirely satisfactory to Nonconformists. Other Dissenting questions—burial services in parish churchyards, and British disestablishment—were aired several times but remained unresolved.

Also unresolved was the question of Ritualism, which continued to distract the Church of England. A Church Association lawsuit against the Revd W. J. E. Bennett on account of his Eucharistic beliefs finally failed in June 1872. But A. H. Mackonochie had been successfully prosecuted for Ritualistic practices in December 1868, when he was condemned by the Judicial Committee of the Privy Council. This court also condemned John Purchas of St James's, Brighton, in February 1871 for his use of vestments and wafer bread, taking the eastward position, and mixing water with wine. High-Churchmen were outraged by the Purchas judgment, especially the condemnation of the eastward position because this seemed to place a fresh restriction on the Church of England.[3] The judgments, which were execrated by the English Church Union,[4] led only to an increase of Ritualist practice and of confession. Some High-Churchmen called for disestablishment in order to be rid of the judgments of a secular court.

As Ritualism grew, so did demands for its suppression. According to the Hon. and Revd E. V. Bligh, speaking in the Brighton Pavilion in December 1870, Ritualism was 'eating like a canker into the very heart of the National Church', and only outright expulsion would serve as a remedy.[5] The promulgation of Papal Infallibility at the Vatican Council in July 1870 strengthened anti-Ritualism by defining more clearly the 'romanism' to which Ritualism was supposed to lead.[6] Infallibility emphasized, however, not only the religious division between Catholics and Nonconformists but also between Catholics and Gladstone. A High-Churchman who supported the Ritualists,

[3] Ibid. 125–8.
[4] ECU Minutes, 13 Dec. 1870; CU Dep. 4, pp. 127–8.
[5] E. V. Bligh, *Lord Ebury as a Church Reformer* (London, 1891), 275.
[6] For the proceedings of the Council, the decrees and the reaction to them, see E. Cuthbert Butler, *The Vatican Council, 1869–1870, based on Bishop Ullathorne's Letters*, ed. Christopher H. Butler (London, 1962); also Cuthbert Butler, *The Life and Times of Bishop Ullathorne* (2 vols., London, 1926), ii. 40–122.

Gladstone was strongly opposed to the new Vatican Decrees for political and religious reasons, though he did not publicize his views until he was out of office. Politically he opposed the decrees because he was against the temporal power of the Pope in Italy; spiritually, because he disliked the growing Ultramontanism which was taking Catholicism further away from union with the English Church. Ironically, Ritualists would now find it more difficult to lead the Church of England back to Rome, though they were increasingly accused of trying to do so.

As prime minister at a time of intense controversy in the Church of England, Gladstone tried to encourage calmness by treading delicately when making episcopal appointments. His method was to appoint moderate men from all sections of the Church, fulfilling the desire of Thomas Hughes, a leading Broad-Churchman, that he would 'have the courage to promote strong men of all the schools, else I doubt how the Church will hold together much longer'.[7] Gladstone was hampered only by the difficulty of finding enough men of calibre and weight among the Evangelicals, who, the High-Church Bishop Wilberforce told him, were a party 'in utter decadence'.[8] The appointments were to avoid a marked bias towards Gladstone's own High-Churchmanship, though several High-Churchmen were appointed. But the weakness of the Government in the House of Lords required that most new Bishops should be Liberals. As he told the Queen in January 1874, he had never been guided in this matter by 'so poor and unworthy a standard as my own impressions or belief in Religion'.[9] A special consideration for Wales was that Bishops proficient in Welsh should be appointed, in a belated attempt to win back Nonconformists for the Church. Although one or two recent Bishops had learnt and used Welsh while occupying their sees, the first appointment of a Welsh speaker since 1715 was that of Joshua Hughes to St Asaph in 1870.

Because a Bishop's Resignation Bill was passed in 1869, there was a flood of episcopal vacancies that year. Seven new Bishops were appointed and one Bishop translated. In October Frederick Temple, a prominent Broad-Churchman who had contributed to the famous *Essays and Reviews* in 1860, was incongruously appointed to succeed old Henry Phillpotts, a doughty High-Churchman, at Exeter.[10] The appointment was heartily welcomed by Broad-Churchmen such as Dean Stanley, who said it 'may yet be the salvation of the Church of England'.[11] But it was opposed by a coalition (up to a point) of Pusey and Shaftesbury, the Church Association and the English Church

[7] Hughes to Bishop Temple, 9 Oct. 1869; E. G. Sandford (ed.), *Memoirs of Archbishop Temple* (2 vols., London, 1906), i. 277.

[8] Wilberforce to Gladstone, 24 Nov. 1869; quoted D. Bahlman, 'The Queen, Mr Gladstone, and Church Patronage', *VS*, iii (1959–60), 358.

[9] Quoted P. Magnus, *Gladstone* (London, 1954), 227.

[10] Marsh, op. cit. 148–52.

[11] Stanley to Temple, 6 Oct. 1869; Sandford, op. cit. i. 277.

Union—though this alliance included by no means all Evangelicals or High-Churchmen. An English Church Union memorial, signed by the representatives of eighty-two branches, was presented to Archbishop Tait, urging that 'explanations and assurances' should be obtained from Temple before his consecration, and the president and council of the ECU asked that the Church should have more say in episcopal appointments.[12] There were complaints that the appointment might promote the demand for disestablishment from within the Church.[13] A rumour in August that Dean Stanley might become Bishop of Oxford had caused Pusey to tell Gladstone that 'a more mischievous appointment could not easily be made', and that Anglican disruption must surely ensue.[14] Temple's appointment he thought equally mischievous, and it caused a breakdown in Pusey's relations with Gladstone, a man of Pusey's school of thought who persisted—incomprehensibly to Pusey—in taking liberal ecclesiastical measures. In a bitterly extreme letter Pusey expressed his amazement that Gladstone 'should try to force one so stained with criminality and with blood upon us as one of our bishops'. 'And now', he added, 'comes the end, unless we should live to see the time when, the Church being disestablished, you will act not as a politician but as a Christian'.[15]

The storm over Temple's appointment soon died down when the new Bishop showed great powers of winning trust and conciliating former opponents. Over this appointment Gladstone, in spite of his desire to be equitable, had increased the friction between different sections in the Church of England. The Temple affair fitly took its place between the two major ecclesiastical controversies of this Government, Irish Church disestablishment in 1869 and the educational reform of 1870.

II. IRISH DISESTABLISHMENT

Disestablishment of the Church of Ireland had been the main topic of Gladstone's successful election, and was to be the first of a trio of reforms—succeeded by land tenure and education—which he hoped would pacify Ireland. Several other religious equality measures were debated in the Parliamentary session of 1869, and one was passed—W. E. Forster's Endowed Schools Bill to remove Church control from many secondary schools. But the Irish Church Bill was by far the most important and controversial measure of the session. Immediately after forming his ministry, Gladstone began to prepare the way for the bill. He saw the Queen about it on 13 December 1868, though she later told him that she disliked it and feared that it might bring

---

[12] ECU Minutes, 14 Dec. 1869; CU Dep. 4, p. 110.
[13] Very Revd H. L. Mansel to Earl of Carnarvon, 21 Oct. 1869; Carnarvon Papers.
[14] Pusey to Gladstone, 20 Aug. 1869; GP, 44281, fos. 349–50.
[15] Pusey to Gladstone, 12 Oct. 1869; ibid. fo. 360.

similar treatment on the Church of England.[16] He enthusiastically began to write a draft of the measure on Christmas Eve, continuing over the festive season and well into January.[17] Cabinet first discussed the bill on 8 February, and settled the basis of the measure then and on the next day without serious disagreement. The bill was then referred to a committee of six Ministers, who discussed it at three sittings on 18, 19, and 22 February, finally settling its form on the last of these dates.[18] The bill was ready to be brought into Parliament on 1 March.

But it was already clear that the measure would encounter much opposition, not least because it was feared that Irish disestablishment might lead to English. Resistance would come not merely from obvious sources—Gladstone's Conservative opponents and most of the Church of Ireland clergy and laity— but also from some Whigs who favoured concurrent endowment (for Catholics and Presbyterians as well as the Church of Ireland) rather than complete disendowment.[19] Sir Roundell Palmer had indeed refused office in the Government because he objected to disendowment. But Nonconformists were strongly against concurrent endowment, and the Irish Catholic hierarchy agreed with them—not on the same voluntary principle, but in order to avoid the dependence on a Protestant State which acceptance of a grant might cause. As Gladstone told the Queen on 13 February, concurrent endowment was 'the very thing that the Parliament was elected not to do'.[20] Gladstone's scheme was tilted much more towards radical opinion than Whig, and the pressure for complete disendowment which Edward Miall exerted on Gladstone during January was unnecessary, for the premier had already decided that this was the essential solution.[21] When the bill was brought into Parliament the Liberation Society and the Congregational Union found it very satisfactory. Indeed the Earl of Harrowby, a Conservative, said in the Lords that the bill was the Liberation Society's scheme 'as part of a campaign against Church establishments, and not a measure for purely Irish objects'.[22] But this was of course denied by the Government.

On 1 March Gladstone successfully sought leave to introduce his bill in one of his best speeches, three and a half hours long and taking up fifty-four columns of Hansard but none the less concise and to the point, 'avoiding his

[16] Queen Victoria to Gladstone, 31 Jan. 1869; G. E. Buckle (ed.), *The Letters of Queen Victoria, 2nd ser., 1862–1885* (3 vols., London, 1926–8), i. 578.
[17] J. Morley, *Life of W. E. Gladstone* (3 vols., London, 1903), ii. 259–60; H. C. G. Matthew (ed.), *The Gladstone Diaries*, vi (Oxford, 1978), 647–54; vii (Oxford, 1982), 1–13.
[18] First Earl of Kimberley, *A Journal of Events during the Gladstone Ministry, 1868–1874*, ed. Ethel Drus; *Camden Miscellany*, xxi (London, 1958), 2.
[19] D. Southgate, *The Passing of the Whigs, 1832–1886* (London, 1962), 340–2.
[20] Morley, op. cit. ii. 262.
[21] e.g. Miall to Gladstone, 23 Jan. 1869; GP, 44418, fos. 198–9; J. S. Newton, 'The Political Career of Edward Miall', Ph.D. thesis (Durham, 1975), 325.
[22] LS, 5 Mar. 1869, cxxvii. 131–2; *Congregational Year-book* (1870), 35–6; H 3rd ser. cxcvii. 27–9.

usual diffuseness' as a colleague noted.[23] Much of the speech explained the dry details of the intended disposal of Church property, but there were also general statements about the benefits of an equitable measure which would strengthen the Union and weaken sectarian animosity.[24] By no means all of the House agreed with this argument; and there was extensive dispute over the measure's principles, especially in the four nights' debate on the second reading (18 to 23 March). Disraeli denounced disendowment as spoliation which would be similarly applied to the English Church; R. A. Cross complained that the bill, if logically extended, would lead to establishment of the Roman Catholic Church in Ireland; Sir Stafford Northcote condemned the proposed abolition of the Maynooth Grant and the Presbyterian *Regium Donum* as pandering to the voluntaries; Lord Claud Hamilton said the bill would encourage dissolution of the Union by treating Ireland separately; and Sir Roundell Palmer, while ready to accept disestablishment, could not countenance the removal of any Church property. John Bright, on the other hand, defended the bill as helping to maintain the Union, and Robert Lowe said that disestablishment merely recognized the true religious situation in Ireland. In a large House of 622 the second reading was carried by a majority of 118, and there was little cross-voting, only six Liberals opposing the bill and four Conservatives supporting it.[25]

The committee stage began on 15 April. An attempt by C. N. Newdegate to defer the committee for six months (i.e. to kill the bill) on the grounds that the measure tried to please the Ultramontanes and threatened to establish popery in Ireland, was defeated in spite of winning the support of 229 members.[26] Many evenings were consumed in committee, and a few minor alterations were conceded, but all the important amendments were defeated and the bill emerged almost in its original shape.[27] A brief but vigorous debate preceded the third reading, which was carried on 31 May.[28]

The bill's passage in the Commons had been smooth, thanks to the large Government majority. But it was quite otherwise in the Lords with their large Conservative majority, and a serious constitutional clash almost developed between the Houses. Even in the country, though it was fairly quiet in face of an apparent *fait accompli*, there was some repetition of the rioting over the issue in the previous year. William Murphy, the ultra-Protestant lecturer, was again the focus of a riot at Tynemouth in March, when some 250 Irish immigrants marched on a hall where he was holding a meeting. The police managed to debar them while the audience fled, and Murphy and some followers seized chair-legs to defend themselves, but the windows were smashed by the

[23] Kimberley, op. cit. 3.
[24] *AR* cxi (1869), 24–9; H cxciv. 412–66.
[25] *AR* cxi (1869), 30–47; H cxciv. 1662 ff.
[26] H cxcv. 847 ff.
[27] *AR* cxi (1869), 53–65.
[28] Ibid. 65–9.

attackers. Murphy was arrested in June in order to prevent his attending a meeting on the bill in Birmingham Town Hall, addressed by Joseph Chamberlain; and though Murphy sued the mayor and the chief of police he secured only forty shillings in damages. The denial of free speech to Murphy, even though said to be necessary to preserve the peace, caused complaints by Conservatives. Newdegate presided at a protest meeting of 1,400 in St James's Hall, London, and tried to censure the Home Secretary in an unsuccessful resolution in the Commons in July.[29] In south Lancashire there was a campaign of meetings against the bill from March to July, and a consequent growth of Orange lodges.[30]

The storms within their Lordships' chamber were naturally more muted, but also more important, and the Conservative peers were doubtless encouraged by the feeling that they had a large section of public opinion behind them, even if they disliked its more strident manifestations. Meetings, petitions, and deputations against the bill, particularly a large gathering in St James's Hall on 3 May and an Irish Protestant deputation which met Conservative peers on 29 May, were aimed at persuading the Lords to reject the measure and so force another election. The radicals were well aware, however, that the Lords might not want to risk a rejection, and John Bright warned the peers that if they flouted the national will 'they might meet with accidents not pleasant for them to think of'.[31]

Among the Conservative peers there was moderate and influential counsel that the second reading should be allowed to pass, and then amendments adopted to mitigate the disendowment clauses. Archbishop Tait, encouraged by the Queen, assiduously urged this course in order to prevent an inter-House collision.[32] However, Salisbury and Carnarvon were unable to persuade a meeting of about 130 Conservative peers on 5 June to agree to pass the bill; Derby and Cairns (Opposition Leader in the Lords and a devoted member of the Church of Ireland) carried the majority in favour of rejection. It was therefore somewhat surprising that after a four days' debate of very high quality—a brilliant speech for rejection by Bishop Magee of Peterborough, formerly Dean of Cork, marked him out as probably the greatest episcopal orator of his generation—the House voted in favour of the second reading in the early hours of 19 June by a majority of thirty-three.[33] The speeches of Lord Granville (a Liberal Minister), Tait, and Salisbury had evidently carried much

[29] W. L. Arnstein, *Protestant versus Catholic in Mid-Victorian England: Mr Newdegate and the Nuns* (Columbia and London, 1982), 100–5.

[30] R. L. Greenall, 'Popular Conservatism in Salford, 1868–1886', *Northern History*, ix (1974), 135–6.

[31] Quoted R. B. McDowell, *The Church of Ireland, 1869–1969* (London, 1975), 45.

[32] R. T. Davidson and W. Benham, *The Life of Archibald Campbell Tait, Archbishop of Canterbury* (2 vols., London, 1891), iii. 20 ff. Cf. Sir Stafford Northcote to Disraeli, 14 May 1869; Iddesleigh Papers, Add. MS 50016, fos. 74–5.

[33] *AR* cxi (1869), 72–92.

influence, holding out the hope that important amendments might be made.[34] Thirty-two Conservative peers voted for the bill, two Liberals against, and many (mostly Conservatives) abstained.[35] Only one Bishop, Thirlwall of St David's, voted in favour, sixteen opposed, and several (including Tait) abstained.

Next, however, the peers carried sixty-two amendments, most of them minor but some shattering the disendowment provisions. The amount of property and money to be kept by the disestablished Church was greatly increased.[36] The preamble was rewritten so that the remaining surplus should not be spent on purposes specified by the Government but left to be applied later by Parliament. Concurrent endowment crept into the bill when, after a failure in committee, a motion was narrowly carried on the third reading—with the help of forty-nine Whigs[37]—providing that glebe-houses and lands should be given to Catholic and Presbyterian clergy out of the surplus funds of the Church of Ireland.[38] The date of disestablishment was postponed from 1 January to 1 May 1871. Altogether, while disestablishment remained in the bill, little was left of disendowment, and the Irish Church would receive about £2,800,000 more than was originally planned, plus a share of the unintended concurrent endowment. Clarendon said that, as a result of this 'lordly disfigurement', the deadlock 'may be quite as bad as if the second reading had been rejected'.[39] On 12 July the amended bill was read a third time and sent back to the Commons.

The changes were far greater than the Cabinet could accept, and when they met on 10 July they agreed to make only limited concessions towards them. Concurrent endowment was emphatically rejected again. The Liberation Society held a joint meeting with the Dissenting Deputies about the amendments on 2 July, which adopted resolutions moved by members of seven denominations.[40] Resistance to the concurrent endowment and other amendments came from Scottish Dissenters as well as English and Welsh, and many of the protests were sent to Gladstone.[41] The Irish Catholics were no more prepared than before to accept State endowment at the anticipated price of State direction. Archbishop Manning wrote forcibly to Gladstone in this sense,

[34] P. M. H. Bell, *Disestablishment in Ireland and Wales* (London, 1969), 146–7.

[35] Kimberley, op. cit. 5; J. E. Denison, *Notes from my Journal* (London, 1899), 245.

[36] For details see Bell, op. cit. 48–9.

[37] J. P. Parry, 'Religion and the Collapse of Gladstone's First Government, 1870–1874', *HJ* xxv (1982), 78.

[38] *AR* cxi (1869), 98–9, 103–4.

[39] Clarendon to Lady Salisbury, 26 June 1869; Sir Herbert Maxwell, *The Life and Letters of George William Frederick, Fourth Earl of Clarendon* (2 vols., London, 1913), ii. 360.

[40] LS, 9 July 1859 (iv. 156).

[41] Minutes of Edinburgh United Presbyterian Presbytery, 14 July 1869 (vol. 34, pp. 68–71); Dundee Free Presbytery, 14 July 1869 (vol. ii, p. 183); Edinburgh Free Presbytery, 19 July 1869 (vol. 29, p. 178). C. H. Spurgeon to Gladstone, 13 July 1869; Patricia S. Kruppa, *Charles Haddon Spurgeon: A Preacher's Progress* (New York and London, 1982), 317–18.

and, at the premier's request, interviewed Irish Catholic MPs who might have been tempted to welcome the offer of glebes for their Church.[42]

The Commons rejected the more important amendments on 16 July before returning the bill to the Lords.[43] The peers, however, seemed determined to stand by their changes in a hot debate on the 20th. Gladstone, who said the Lords were 'living in a balloon', out of touch with the real world, was impulsively inclined to throw up his bill and try another in the next session. But Granville reacted more calmly and merely accepted an adjournment.[44] This provided a breathing-space for a compromise to be attempted. There was genuine desire on both sides to avoid a crisis, and the result of feverish negotiations between 18 and 22 July was agreement between Granville and Cairns. The Government made financial concessions but carried most of its points, and there was to be no reference to concurrent endowment. When Granville shook Cairns' hand it was 'trembling with nervousness', and no wonder. The terms were announced by Cairns in the Lords on the evening of the 22nd, and accepted then by the peers and next day by the Commons.[45] On 26 July the bill became law.

Irish disestablishment was a most significant event. It was the first permanent break in the traditional link between Church and State in the United Kingdom. It had important implications for the political relationship of Ireland and Great Britain, for further Irish reforms, and for the future position of other established Churches. Many allusions had been made in the Lords' debates to the possibility that disestablishment of the Church of England would follow that of its Irish wing. Opponents of the bill had given this as a reason for resistance, while supporters had denied the possibility. Bishop Magee had said that religious equality would now demand either a Roman Catholic establishment in Ireland or no establishment in England. Replying to him, Earl de Grey and Ripon gave (somewhat ironically for one who was to be a notable convert to Catholicism) a strong vindication of the national strength of the Church of England, and said that Irish disestablishment would remove the best weapon of the Liberation Society.[46] A protest signed by forty-five peers after the passage of the bill in the Lords said that the measure 'cannot but give great encouragement to the designs of those who desire its extension to every part of the United Kingdon'.[47] A speaker at a council meeting of the Church

---

[42] Manning to Gladstone, 13 and 14 July 1869; GP, 44249, fos. 84–9; Bell, op. cit. 151.

[43] AR cxi (1869), 107–12.

[44] Ibid. 112–14; Morley, Gladstone, ii. 272 ff.; Kimberley, op. cit. 7; Lord Edmond Fitzmaurice, The Life of Granville Leveson Gower, Second Earl Granville (2 vols., London, 1905), ii. 11–12.

[45] Bell, op. cit. 152–3; D. H. Akenson, The Church of Ireland: Ecclesiastical Reform and Revolution, 1800–1885 (New Haven and London, 1971), 271–3; J. D. Fair, British Interparty Conferences: A Study of the Procedure of Conciliation in British Politics, 1867–1921 (Oxford, 1980), 31–4; AR cxi (1869), 114–20.

[46] H cxcvi. 1859, 1882.

[47] AR cxi (1869), 105.

Institution, supporting a motion for propaganda efforts against the bill, said: 'If the Church in Ireland was knocked down and plundered, the Church of England was not safe for ten years. The supporters of the Liberation Society scrupled not to assert this and he quite agreed with them.'[48] That it was not only the Church of England which felt its established status to be threatened is shown by petitions from the Church of Scotland against the bill.[49].

Church reform received much support, largely as a means of Church defence as it had in the perilous 1830s. Members of the Church of Scotland looked to the abolition of patronage in ministerial appointments, and its replacement by much wider participation in the election of ministers, as a means of increasing popular involvement in the Church and gradually regaining the allegiance of Dissenters. A Scottish anti-patronage deputation went to London in June and interviewed Gladstone, but received no encouragement for its aim.[50] Abolition of patronage had to await the coming of a Conservative Government which was not dependent on Dissenting votes in Scotland. In the Church of England it was argued that popular support must increase if the Church was to avoid the fate of the Church of Ireland, disestablished because it embraced only a small minority of the population. 'Unless the Church of England becomes much more than it is now the Church of the people', wrote the Revd W. H. Fremantle, 'its claim to be a National Church will be less and less allowed.'[51] He wanted 'real and legal power' for the laity in Church affairs, not limited to mere consultation with the vicar or Bishop. Church councils should be formed in each parish, comprising members who were avowed worshippers in the parish church but who could be elected by all the parishioners (including Nonconformists and others outside the Church). The councils should be able, within important limits, to decide on policy. Such a development, he hoped, would speed the return of Nonconformists to the Church.[52] A Liberal MP, Thomas Chambers, said he intended to raise in the next Parliamentary session the matter of how the Church of England could be brought 'more into harmony with the opinions and feelings of the laity' and made 'a more effective instrument for the evangelization and improvement of the whole community'.[53] Behind this concern lay a growing conviction that the Church, if it was to deserve its status as a national establishment, must become more attractive to the body of the people in an increasingly democratic age.

Current fears about the English and Scottish establishments were no doubt magnified by Nonconformist rejoicing over Irish disestablishment. To

[48] CDI, Central Council Minutes, vol. 206 (9 June 1869).

[49] e.g. Minutes of Edinburgh Presbytery of Church of Scotland, 11 June 1869 (vol. 27, pp. 70–1).

[50] D. Macleod, *Memoir of Norman Macleod, DD* (2 vols., London, 1876), ii. 305–10; A. L. Drummond and J. Bulloch, *The Church in Late Victorian Scotland, 1874–1900* (Edinburgh, 1978), 91.

[51] W. H. Fremantle, *Lay Power in Parishes: The Most Needed Church Reform* (London, 1869), 4.

[52] Ibid. 28–39.

[53] *Nonconformist*, 18 Aug. 1869; xxix. 779.

Dissenters this was significant as the first major victory in an already long voluntary campaign, though other considerations sometimes broke in—the Congregational Union, for example, hoped that the reconstituted Church of Ireland 'will be blessed by God to promote the union of Protestant Christians and Churches, and the evangelization of Ireland'.[54] Efforts to achieve disestablishment in England, Wales, and Scotland had been stimulated, as had the desire to remove Bishops from the House of Lords, which was expressed for example by George Hadfield (a veteran Nonconformist campaigner) when he opposed the Bishops' Resignation Bill in the Commons.[55] The *Nonconformist* journal, after expressing amazement at the 'legislative miracle' of Irish disestablishment and its currently unbounded admiration for Gladstone,[56] was seized with fresh zeal for 'The Work Before Us'—the title of a series of articles in September and October 1869. The first of these stated that the completion of the 'revolution' was as morally certain 'as that the sun will rise tomorrow morning'.[57] A speaker at a Perthshire Liberal meeting at the end of August hoped that 'the principles of the Irish Church Bill would soon be applied throughout the British dominions'.[58] Archdeacon G. A. Denison, a leading High-Churchman and former fierce Church defender who had recently espoused voluntaryism because of the latitudinarianism in the Church, said that the 1869 Act had virtually destroyed the principle of a national Church in England.[59]

The Liberation Society's Parliamentary committee reviewed the prospects for disestablishment and surprisingly found them more favourable in England than in Wales or Scotland—the opposite of what would have been expected from the relative strength of the established Churches in the three countries. In Scotland events were tending 'in the right direction', but the establishment did not seem enough of a practical grievance to prompt an immediate campaign; in Wales, raising the issue might only cause Liberal losses until the secret ballot had been won. England was suggested as a field for the practical pursuit of disestablishment, but only on a preparatory basis, even though disestablishment was 'an event which is rapidly approaching'.[60]

But circumstances were even less ripe for proposing disestablishment than the committee suggested. In Scotland discussions were indeed proceeding on union between the Free Church and the United Presbyterian Church, which indicated the likely strengthening of the voluntary cause. But by 1873 the very failure to agree on voluntaryism ended the discussions. Notice of a motion for

---

[54] *Congregational Year-book* (1870), 79.
[55] 5 Aug. 1869; H cxcviii. 1306–7.
[56] *Nonconformist*, 28 July 1869; xxix. 705.
[57] Ibid. 15 Sept. 1869; vol. xxix.
[58] Ibid. 1 Sept. 1869; xxix. 826–7.
[59] G. A. Denison, *The Church of England in 1869* (London and Leeds, 1869), 4.
[60] LS, 1 Oct. 1869; iv. 177–80.

Welsh disestablishment in the 1870 session was given by Watkin Williams, an Anglican who was Liberal MP for the Denbigh boroughs. Williams had said during the Irish disestablishment campaign in 1868 that Wales too should strike while the iron was hot. But in giving notice of his motion he acted independently of the other Welsh radical MPs, and he was accused by some of his colleagues of a rash disregard for political tactics. He was also opposed by the Liberation Society on the ground that Welsh disestablishment should not be separated from English.[61] But this contention was dubious in its turn. In England the establishment was less of a practical grievance than in Wales, commanding in the former country considerable popular respect and not being susceptible to the nationalist opposition which caused Wales to bear something of an ecclesiastical resemblance to Ireland. In May 1870 Williams' motion was strongly opposed by Gladstone and heavily defeated, obtaining only forty-seven votes (seven from Welsh members). The eventually powerful cause of Welsh disestablishment was still weak, awaiting the stimulus of the ballot in 1872 and a wider franchise and redistribution of seats in 1884–5.

Disestablishment in one part or another of Great Britain might be raised in Parliament, but it could expect no help from the Government because Liberal disunity would be magnified. Radical Nonconformity was only a section of the Liberal Parliamentary party and Whig Erastianism was the dominant force. Irish disestablishment had succeeded because Gladstone had persuaded the Whigs to support it, and because Irish Catholics were allied to British Nonconformists. In any further attempt at disestablishment not only would Whiggism reject Nonconformity's proposal, but Nonconformity could not count on the support of Catholics. Despite fears expressed by the *Bulwark* (the journal of the Scottish Reformation Society),[62] Catholics did not consistently take up disestablishment as a political cause in Britain; though there were later occasions when their political interests caused Irish Catholic MPs to support disestablishment motions. Manning was in favour of maintaining the English establishment as a hedge against secularism,[63] and Catholics became alienated from their Nonconformist allies in 1870 and after on account of a radically different attitude to education. The education crisis of 1870 shattered the rare Liberal consensus which had prevailed in 1869.

[61] Henry Richard to Thomas Gee, 17 Aug. 1869; Gee Papers, 8308D, fo. 297; Evan Richards to Gee, 21 Aug. 1869; ibid. 307; 'Gohebydd' to Gee, 9 and 11 Aug. 1869; ibid. 8310D, 507, 508; Carvell Williams to Gee, 30 Sept. 1869; ibid. 8311D, 584; K. O. Morgan, *Wales in British Politics, 1868–1922*, 2nd edn. (Cardiff, 1970), 29–32; J. W. Roberts, 'Sir George Osborne Morgan, 1826–1897', MA thesis (Wales, 1979), 39–40. Williams' intention was, however, supported by Scots Dissenters because of the example it would provide for the Scottish Disestablishment movement; *United Presbyterian Magazine*, NS xiii (1869), 495 ff.

[62] *Bulwark, or Reformation Journal*, 1 Sept. 1869; xix. 64.

[63] D. E. Selby, 'Henry Edward Manning and the Education Bill of 1870', *British Journal of Educational Studies*, xviii (1970), 198–9.

III. THE EDUCATION CONFLICT, 1870 AND AFTER

The question of extending elementary education had been second only to Irish disestablishment in the 1868 election,[64] and was a major concern of the Liberal Government. Various considerations—humanitarian, economic, democratic, and patriotic—combined in the late 1860s to urge the introduction of a national education system. The movement was strong in Scotland as elsewhere, and the second report of the Argyll Commission in 1867 was followed by a Parochial Schools (Scotland) Bill in 1869. The bill proposed to create a dual system of grant-aided denominational schools and rate-aided State schools. But the bill failed, and Scotland obtained in 1872 a different and reasonably acceptable solution of her education question, placing all parochial schools and many others in a national rate-aided system with scope for religious education.[65] England and Wales, however, obtained in their Education Act of 1870 a measure similar to the Scottish bill of 1869, for the Government decided both to maintain denominational, Church-controlled schools and to create an unsectarian, popularly controlled State sector.

Whereas the education issue was largely removed from ecclesiastical contention in Scotland, in England it became much more of a contributor to religious disputes. The education conflict joined the contentions between Church and Dissent over disestablishment, university tests, and churchyard burials, and these other differences exacerbated the education dispute. The growth of Ritualism contributed to the fear of an Anglican dominated educational system and provided another reason for diminishing it. The Church of England's control over education was regarded as an important symbol of established status; hence the education quarrel became largely integrated with the conflict over establishment. Catholics, however, firmly defended their own denominational education and, not least because Vaticanism was emphasizing the distinctiveness of Roman Catholicism, they were opposed by the majority of Nonconformists who wanted an unsectarian system. Thus, while Nonconformists were able to draw closer to the 'unsectarian' Whigs over education, they became politically divided from the Catholics until, in the mid-1880s, the Irish Home Rule question brought most Dissenters closer to the Catholics while taking them further away from the Whigs.

The Government was confronted by pressure groups advocating radically different educational ideas. The National Education League, launched at Birmingham in February 1869 by the Unitarian Joseph Chamberlain and

---

[64] Marsh, *Victorian Church in Decline*, 67.

[65] D. J. Withrington, 'Towards a National System, 1867–1872: The Last Years in the Struggle for a Scottish Education Act', *Scottish Educational Studies*, iv (1972), 15–17; *United Presbyterian Magazine*, NS xiii (Apr. and May 1869), 186–8, 239–40; Minutes of Church of Scotland Presbytery of Edinburgh, 16 Mar. 1869 (vol. 27, pp. 27–8); Minutes of UP Presbytery of Dundee, 11 May 1869 (vii. 1, (1847–75), pp. 203–4).

others, wanted a national system of rate-aided schools, unsectarian and free, providing compulsory education. It was a wealthy and rapidly expanding organization, having 1400 members by September 1869 and over a hundred branches by the end of 1870. It gained the support of secular radicals and trade unionists as well as Nonconformists and some Liberal Anglicans, and posed a strong challenge to denominational education. 'Our choice', said Chamberlain in October 1869, 'is between the education of the people and the interests of the Church. Education to be national must be unsectarian.'[66] When the Cabinet was preparing its education bill at the end of the year, Chamberlain warned the Government against compromise over the League's principles, even though the League was not unanimous over what these principles should be: 'tinkering legislation is not expected from a Cabinet of which Mr. Bright is a member'.[67]

Birmingham clergy and lay Churchmen responded to the League by forming the Birmingham Education Union in August 1869, defending the ability of an extended denominational system (with a 'conscience clause') to supply educational needs. This organization and a similar society combined in November to form the National Education Union at Manchester. Far less wealthy than the League, the Union was none the less an important counter-instrument. Local rating and free education were condemned, unsectarian teaching declared impossible to realize. The Union's members were mostly Conservative Churchmen, but they also included Roman Catholics and some leading Nonconformists—the Wesleyan J. H. Rigg and the Congregationalist MPs Edward Baines and Samuel Morley.[68] Some Dissenters, indeed, could not accept unsectarian education. Even more Dissenters could not accept the purely secular education (i.e. exclusion of all religious teaching) advocated by the Welsh Educational Alliance, by Edward Miall, and by a minority of the National Education League including the Revd R. W. Dale, a leading Birmingham Congregationalist.[69] Gladstone himself was favourable to this idea, but only seventeen Nonconformist MPs voted for a motion for purely secular education during debates on the bill.[70] Such divisions among Nonconformists weakened their challenge to the Government, as Gladstone well appreciated.

The National Education League was accused of aiming to disestablish the Church, and though this was not the League's stated objective many of its supporters wanted it. The Liberation Society saw the benefits of allying with

[66] J. L. Garvin, *The Life of Joseph Chamberlain*, i (London, 1935), 96; A. F. Taylor, 'Birmingham and the Movement for National Education, 1867–1877', Ph.D thesis (Leicester, 1960), 76–7.

[67] Garvin, op. cit. i. 100.

[68] Marjorie Cruickshank, *Church and State in English Education, 1870 to the Present Day* (London, 1964), 17; D. Roland, 'The Struggle for the Elementary Education Act and its Implementation, 1870–1873', B. Litt. thesis (Oxford, 1957), 164–7.

[69] For the Welsh Educational Alliance see L. Hargest, 'The Welsh Educational Alliance and the 1870 Elementary Education Act'. *WHR* x. 2 (1980), 172–205.

[70] Parry, 'Religion', 77. Cf. M. R. Temmel, 'Gladstone's Resignation of the Liberal Leadership, 1874–5', *Journal of British Studies*, xvi. 1 (1976), 169.

the League, and another Nonconformist organization, the Central Nonconformist Committee, was formed at Birmingham to support the League.
Catholics, on the other hand, firmly opposed the League's objects. In June 1869
Archbishop Manning had issued a circular to his diocese urging that, in view of
'the certainty that in the next Session of Parliament a scheme of National
Education will be attempted', Catholic schools should be preserved and
extended: 'in the interval of time still remaining to us, our efforts to extend our
system of education should be redoubled'.[71] By October, when the Cabinet
Ministers were beginning to discuss an education measure, Manning was
seeking to influence them.[72] He hoped that Catholics, allied to Anglicans and to
Nonconformists who joined the National Education Union, would 'render our
Christian Education safe for many a day'.[73] Manning was initially unfavourable
to a dual educational system, but accepted it partly for financial reasons when
the bill was published. He insisted, however, that Catholic schools should be
immune from any State interference, and sought increased Government grants
for them.[74] Gladstone was sympathetic to Manning's desires, but warned him
that they might be difficult to obtain, particularly in view of the current attempt
to adopt Papal Infallibility at Rome.[75] This was already causing a stiffening of
Protestant opinion in Parliament, seen for example in the temporary success of
Newdegate's motion of March 1870 to enquire into convents and monasteries.[76]

When the Education Bill emerged from the Cabinet early in 1870 it was a
compromise between the conflicting policies of the League and the Union, and
so could be entirely pleasing to neither group. The Ministers chiefly responsible
for the bill were W. E. Forster, a former Quaker (now an Anglican) who was
vice-president of the council outside the Cabinet, and Earl de Grey and Ripon,
president of the council and Cabinet Minister responsible for education. They
were supported by Gladstone who, however, played a far less central role in this
question than in Irish disestablishment and Irish land legislation. Forster had
indicated publicly early in 1869 that he did not wish to destroy but to
supplement existing educational provisions. This was the gist of his original
memorandum of October 1869 (building on de Grey's similar ideas). It also
formed the core of the bill which got through Cabinet (after objections) on 4
February 1870 and which Forster introduced in the Commons with a masterly

---

[71] Manning Papers (Oblates of St Charles, Bayswater, London).

[72] Gladstone to Earl de Grey and Ripon, 27 Oct. 1869; Ripon Papers, Add. MS 43513, fo. 279; de
Grey to Gladstone, 28 Oct. 1869; ibid. fo. 281.

[73] Manning to Gladstone, 8 Nov. 1869; GP 44249, fos. 110–11.

[74] Selby, op. cit. 198–207; G. A. Beck (ed.) *The English Catholics, 1850–1950* (London, 1950), 158–9,
374–5; Manning to Gladstone, 20 Mar. 1870; GP 44249, fos. 146–7.

[75] Gladstone to Lord Acton, 28 Mar. 1870; GP, 44093, fo. 133.

[76] Gladstone to Manning, 16 Apr. 1870 quoted D. C. Lathbury (ed.), *Correspondence on Church and
Religion of William Ewart Gladstone* (2 vols., London, 1910), ii. 52–4; E. R. Norman (ed.), *Anti-
Catholicism in Victorian England* (London, 1968), 83–4; Arnstein, *Protestant versus Catholic*, 124–47. For
Catholic reactions see also Montagu Corry to Disraeli, 21 Apr. 1870; DP, B/XX/Co/59.

speech on 17 February, two days after the controversial Irish land bill.[77] The bill proposed to give voluntary schools (with the help of Government building grants) a year to expand, and then to fill the gaps by means of new schools established and managed by school boards and maintained partly out of the local rates. A dual system—in one aspect, it might be argued, establishing concurrent endowment at last[78]—would thus be permanently instituted. The voluntary (i.e. denominational) schools would be financed by direct Government grants as a supplement to voluntary contributions, also from the rates if the school boards so decided. Education in the board schools was not to be free, as this would be far too expensive, though fees could be waived in particular cases. Education in these schools would be compulsory, however, if the school boards decided to make it so.

If the National Education Union and other bodies were disappointed that it had been thought necessary to supplement denominational schools with another system, the National Education League was even more disappointed that its own principles had been very largely ignored. It had wanted either to abolish the voluntary schools by absorbing them into a rate-aided scheme, or to leave them entirely without grants, but they were now to be confirmed as a permanent, protected segment under the Government's wing, and could receive rate aid to boot. Not only would denominational education continue in voluntary schools (subject to a conscience clause) but it could also be given in the new schools if the school boards so decided.

Reactions to the bill in the Commons were at first fairly mild but they soon became stronger, some impassioned radical denunciations being made. On 15 March Henry Winterbotham, a Baptist MP who attained Government office before his early death in 1873, widely condemned the extension of establishment privilege and the depression of Dissenting hopes of equality which he found in the measure.[79] In many rural districts, he said, 'Dissent is treated like the cattle plague, to be stamped out', though many Dissenters (himself included) did not desire the downfall of the Church of England.[80] He was supported by William Vernon Harcourt who said the bill would hand over to the Church an absolute monopoly of education in rural districts.[81]

Outside Parliament storms of opposition soon gathered, propelled by the League, the Welsh Educational Alliance, and the Central Nonconformist Committee which was formed on 3 March with Francis Schnadhorst as secretary and with delegates returned by congregations. The Liberation

---

[77] *AR* cxii (1870), 50–6; T. Wemyss Reid, *Life of the R. Hon. W. E. Forster*, 3rd edn. 2 vols. in one (Bath, 1888), i. 459–80; L. Wolf, *Life of the First Marquess of Ripon* (2 vols., London, 1921), i. 231–4; Roland, op. cit. 227 ff.; F. Adams, *History of the Elementary School Contest*, ed. A. Briggs (Brighton, 1972), 208ff.; Cruickshank, op. cit., 22–4.

[78] *Nonconformist*, 23 Feb. 1870, xxx. 169.

[79] H cxix. 1963–80.

[80] Ibid. 1974–6.

[81] Ibid. cc. 224.

Society, though slow to take action, gave some support to these organizations.[82] The National Education League sent a deputation of forty-six MPs to Gladstone on 9 March, when Chamberlain stated the League's objections; and the Welsh Educational Alliance sent its own deputation on the same day.[83] Nonconformists were divided over the matter, as has been mentioned, with some supporting denominational education.[84] But the weight of Dissenting reaction came from the undenominational angle, as was shown in meetings, petitions, and deputations. After recently obtaining two major victories, the abolition of compulsory Church Rates and Irish disestablishment, militant Dissenters were in no mood to accept the set-back given to them by the bill. 'If this is the Liberalism of the men for whom the Dissenters fought tooth and nail', wrote one Nonconformist minister perceptively, 'I think we made a terrible blunder . . . the passing of this Bill in anything like the form it now has will end in the break-up of the Liberal party and the return of Dizzy to power.'[85] Forms of petition against the measure were widely distributed in the chapels for signature, and one petition was signed by 5,173 ministers within four days; even a majority of Wesleyan ministers signed it.[86] On 11 April this protest was presented to Gladstone by a deputation led by R. W. Dale and H. W. Crosskey, both Birmingham ministers and honorary secretaries of the Central Nonconformist Committee. On the other side, Anglican and Catholic protests were not lacking against the challenge to denominational education.[87] St James's Hall in London was the venue for large rival meetings, the League using it on 25 March and the Union on 8 April.[88] A Catholic demonstration against the bill was held in Liverpool on St Patrick's Day in March.[89]

Amid the uproar the bill slowly made its way through the Commons, Liberal defections from Government policy being outweighed by Conservative support. The second reading passed without division on 18 March. There was then a lengthy delay of three months before the Committee stage while the Cabinet, realizing the strength of radical opposition, decided to make some changes. Some new proposals were made available in the House on 26 May.[90] The main alterations were announced in the Commons by Gladstone on 16 June, just before the Committee debates. The conscience clause was to be made more effective by timetabling arrangements. Other changes signified that the

[82] LS 7 and 11 Mar. 1870; iv. 227–31.

[83] Adams, op. cit. 215–17.

[84] Roland, op. cit. 372–80; J. Guinness Rogers, *An Autobiography* (London, 1903),200–1; Edith H. Fowler, *The Life of Henry Hartley Fowler, First Viscount Wolverhampton* (London, 1912), 548–9.

[85] Revd G. S. Reaney to R. Rylands; L. G. Rylands, *Correspondence and Speeches of Mr Peter Rylands, MP* (2 vols., Manchester and London, 1890), i. 111.

[86] A. W. W. Dale, *The Life of R. W. Dale of Birmingham* (London, 1898), 276.

[87] ECU Minutes, 29 Mar. 1870; CU dep. 4, pp. 119–20; meeting of Catholic clergy and laity, 22 and 23 Feb. 1870; Manning Papers.

[88] Roland, op. cit. 350–4.

[89] T. Burke, *A Catholic History of Liverpool* (Liverpool, 1910), 187–8.

[90] Adams, op. cit. 223.

denominational and rate-aided spheres were to be divided more clearly. Government had accepted an amendment by William Cowper-Temple, a Liberal MP, an Anglican and president of the National Education Union, that religious education in board schools (which could be given at the discretion of the board) should exclude all denominational catechisms and formularies. School boards would not be allowed to give rate aid directly to voluntary schools, but in compensation the Government grant to these schools would be increased up to a maximum of fifty per cent.[91]

But these attempts to separate the two systems still left both sides complaining, and in any case the separation remained incomplete. Clause 25 quietly kept its position in the bill, its importance being temporarily overlooked: it enabled school boards to pay the fees of needy children at voluntary schools out of the rates. The Cowper-Temple clause was regarded by the bill's opponents, notably Harcourt, as an inadequate protection against denominational bias; and naturally the increased grant to voluntary schools was disliked. Several amendments were moved in Committee but defeated. Henry Richard, a Congregational minister who sat for Merthyr Tydfil, obtained only sixty votes on 24 June for a motion which included a demand for purely secular education in board schools; and he aroused considerable Nonconformist protest against his action.[92] Similarly Jacob Bright, brother of John, moved with Harcourt's support to toughen the Cowper-Temple clause in order to make sure of eliminating denominational teaching in board schools. But only 130 Liberals supported him, and 121 Liberals joined 132 Conservatives in opposition, so the motion was easily defeated.[93] Some amendments were successful, however, including a provision that voluntary schools should have a period of only six months for extension purposes (instead of the original year) before school boards could be elected to compete with them. The cumulative vote was introduced for the first time as the method of election to school boards, in order to assist different educational interests to secure representation on them.[94]

The third reading passed without a division on 22 July. But in the preceding debate the worsening relations between Government and militant Nonconformists was clearly shown. Miall was disappointed not only by the education measure but by the failure of burial and university test bills that session—though Gladstone had spoken for the first time in favour of abolishing university tests.[95] Miall bitterly attacked Ministers for betraying the wishes of Nonconformity, thus arousing 'the suspicion, distrust, and antagonism of some of their most earnest supporters'. Gladstone's almost Cromwellian retort was

[91] H ccii. 266–85; *AR* cxii (1870), 63–4; Cruickshank, op. cit. 29–31.
[92] *AR* cxii. 64–7; Dale, op. cit. 278–80.
[93] *AR* cxii. 67; Harcourt to Gladstone, 25 May 1870; GP, 44196, fos. 16–19.
[94] *AR* cxii. 68–9; Cruickshank, op. cit. 32.
[95] *Nonconformist*, 25 May 1870 (xxx. 485); W. R. Ward, *Victorian Oxford* (London, 1965), 258–9.

that Miall had entertained quite unjustified expectations, and that his support 'ceased to be of value when accompanied by reproaches such as these'. 'I hope my honourable friend will not continue that support to the Government one moment longer than he deems it consistent with his sense of duty and right. For God's sake, Sir, let him withdraw it the moment he thinks it better for the cause he has at heart that he should do so.' Gladstone was rebuking what he thought was the overweening sectionalism growing in his party: 'when we think he [Miall] looks too much to the section of the community he adorns, and too little to the interests of the people at large, we must then recollect that we are the Government of the Queen, and that those who have assumed the high responsibility of administering the affairs of this empire, must endeavour to forget the parts in the whole'.[96] This was the natural reaction of the leader of a Government which, for all its impressive numerical strength, was beset by internal disputes. Gladstone could be confident in making these remarks, for Nonconformity, while fairly effective as a portion of the Liberal party, could scarcely muster the strength to become a permanently independent political organization. Such a heated clash was not likely to disappear overnight, and it signalized the beginning of a lengthy political struggle which only diminished when Gladstone was out of office.

The Education Bill passed smoothly through the Lords, which contained a large majority of Conservatives and no Nonconformists, and the much-debated measure became law on 9 August.[97]

The Act, whose provisions lasted until 1903, was an important recognition of the religious plurality in society, and the penalty for adopting it was the opposition of different parts of the plurality. Not only Nonconformists but many Anglicans resented the Act. Staunch Churchmen and Catholics did not welcome rival new schools teaching undenominational education, which was considered by many a danger to faith. Reactions to the Act took several forms. First, there were competing efforts to expand in each part of the dual system. Within the few months up to the end of 1870, the voluntary sector raised £1,290,716 and used this to provide accommodation for an extra 1,096,712 children.[98] Even though the new school boards, first elected in November 1870, began energetically to build schools after the brief period of grace had elapsed, the voluntary schools remained a powerful rival. In some rural districts there was no scope to challenge the church school with a board school, and when these single-school areas were also heavily Dissenting districts there was complaint about Church monopoly of education. In time it became clear that the school boards had the advantage in financial resources, and could afford to staff and

[96] *AR* cxii. 70; H cciii. 741–5.
[97] *AR* cxii. 70–2.
[98] M. J. Wilkinson, 'Educational Controversies in British Politics, 1895–1914', Ph.D thesis (Newcastle upon Tyne, 1977), 28. Cf Sister Joan Bland, 'The Impact of Government on English Catholic Education, 1870–1902', *Catholic Historical Review*, lxii (1976), 45.

equip their schools more effectively. This was largely, the denominationalists complained, because they had rate aid, which came partly from the pockets of denominationalists who also supported the voluntary schools. Moreover, the exchequer grants to the latter were found to be insufficient, and many poorer Church schools transferred themselves to board control.[99] Despite this, voluntary schools (most of them Anglican) still educated a clear majority of children in 1902.

Apart from the rivalry of building and maintenance, the school boards pioneered a number of political features—female voting and membership, the cumulative vote, and the secret ballot—and provided a great new forum for the expression and application of educational and religious opinions. School board elections, taking place triennially in November, were often hotly contested between groups with different religious motives. It was important to gain power on school boards in order to protect or undermine the denominational system. New voluntary schools had to be recognized by the school boards before they could obtain Government grants, and in one celebrated case the Swansea board refused to recognize a new Catholic school for four years.[1] On the other hand, at Stockport in 1879 the school board was suspended by the denominationalists who controlled it. It was also important to control a school board in order to secure or prevent the teaching of religion in board schools and to extend or limit expenditure on them. The elections could decide such policies, and educational conditions consequently differed widely from district to district.[2]

At Birmingham, an extraordinary tactical lapse by the Liberal Association enabled denominationalists to win the 1870 election, gaining the first eight seats on the new board with a Roman Catholic leading and Chamberlain coming only thirteenth. There were similar results at Merthyr Tydfil and Newport, also heavily Nonconformist areas. Clause 25 was used by the Birmingham board to pay fees at voluntary schools, though there was a fierce legal struggle with the town council to obtain the money from the rates. At the next election in 1873 the Birmingham Liberals managed to triumph and head the polls. 'One reverend gentleman said the question really was "whether the Lord God should rule in the land" ', Chamberlain told John Morley, 'and enquiries are being freely made to-day as to whether the Almighty has sent in his resignation.'[3] The policies of the board were consequently changed, only to be altered again in later years.[4] At Salford, on the other hand, the board's composition and policies

[99] Marsh, *Victorian Church in Decline*, 78.

[1] Gillian Sutherland, *Policy-making in Elementary Education, 1870–1895* (Oxford, 1973), 108.

[2] J. Murphy, *Church, State, and Schools in Britain, 1800–1970* (London, 1971), 66; Cruickshank, op. cit. 41–6; N. J. Richards, 'Religious Controversy and the School Boards, 1870–1902', *British Journal of Educational Studies*, xviii (1970), 180–96; Angela Gill, 'The Leicester School Board, 1871–1903', in B. Simon (ed.), *Education in Leicestershire, 1540–1940* (Leicester, 1968), 156–68; J. H. Bingham, *The Period of the Sheffield School Board* (Sheffield, 1949), 160–1.

[3] Chamberlain to Morley, 19 Nov. 1873; Garvin, op. cit. i. 127.

[4] Dale, op. cit. 476–83; Taylor, op. cit. 158 ff.; *Religious Instruction in Board Schools: Report of a Debate in the Birmingham School Board, 1872* (Birmingham, 1872), 3–11.

were more stable, since Churchmen and Catholics controlled the board for its entire thirty-three years, to the benefit of voluntary education.[5] In Liverpool, sectarian strife caused electoral contests not only between Orangemen and the Catholic Club but also between Anglican Evangelicals and Ritualists.[6] In London a Voluntary Schools Defence Union intervened in school board elections.[7] There were cases of refusal to pay rates through fear that the proceeds would be used to apply Clause 25. Some refusals in Sheffield had the support of the local Nonconformist Committee, and distraint of goods took place which was reminiscent of the old church rate contests.[8] Religious teaching was introduced in the great majority of board schools. By 1894 out of 2,392 school boards in England and Wales only ninety-one provided a purely secular education, seventy of them being in Wales.[9]

Many issues were involved in the election and conduct of school boards, and ecclesiastical warfare was chief among them. Underlying much of the turmoil was the contest over the established position of the Church. Lord Shaftesbury, addressing the National Society (the Church of England elementary education society) in 1875, stated: 'If the time ever arrives when the clergy are driven from the schoolroom and confined to the functions of the pulpit, one-half of the argument for maintaining the Established Church will have been destroyed'.[10] A defender of the church school was usually also a defender of the State Church.

The National Education League declared itself in favour of purely secular education in 1872, and increased its branches and agents, reaching a peak by the end of that year. The League remained in being until 1877, though well before this Chamberlain was looking for a wider field and hoping to transform the League into a broader reforming organization. With the Anglican George Dixon as its main spokesman in the Commons, the League made several unsuccessful attempts in 1872 and 1873 (and later) to amend the 1870 Act. The reformers were particularly anxious to repeal Clause 25. This they tried to do with the support of Nonconformist meetings such as a conference of 1,885 chapel representatives at Manchester on 24 and 25 January 1872, and the Congregational Union assembly which resolved in May 1871 to oppose the clause as 'a species of concurrent endowment'.[11]

[5] R. L. Greenall, 'Popular Conservatism in Salford, 1868–1886', *Northern History*, ix (1974), 136–7. Cf. T. C. Tyson, 'The Church and School Education', in W. S. F. Pickering (ed.), *A Social History of the Diocese of Newcastle, 1882–1982* (Stocksfield, 1981), 282.

[6] P. B. Pritchard, 'The Churches and the Liverpool School Board, 1870–1903', Ph.D thesis (Liverpool, 1981), 93–204; P. J. Waller, *Democracy and Sectarianism: A Political and Social History of Liverpool, 1868–1939* (Liverpool, 1981), 28–30, 123.

[7] *T* 28 Aug. 1894, p. 5.

[8] W. S. Fowler, *A Study in Radicalism and Dissent: The Life and Times of Henry Joseph Wilson, 1833–1914* (London, 1961), 39–41.

[9] J. E. B. Munson, 'The London School Board Election in 1894', *British Journal of Educational Studies*, xxiii (1975), 8.

[10] Quoted W. H. Mackintosh, *Disestablishment and Liberation* (London, 1972), 251.

[11] *Congregational Year-book*, 1872; Adams, op. cit. 255 ff.

Unsuccessful in Parliament, the League could claim to have better fortunes outside, if on dubious grounds. It challenged the Government in several by-elections in which Liberal fragmentation was clearly revealed. Other issues were also involved in these contests between Liberal and Liberal. But the League claimed electoral success for its principles when a recalcitrant Liberal candidate was persuaded to yield to them, and even when competition between Liberal candidates or abstention of Liberal voters produced a Conservative victory. Chamberlain did not heed Dissenting warnings that a Tory victory would mean that Nonconformist interests, instead of being advanced inadequately as at present, would not be advanced at all. 'What is that to us?', he asked in March 1872. 'What matters it . . . whether a Tory Government sits on the Cabinet benches or a Liberal Government passing Tory measures?'[12] R. W. Dale fully supported him: 'When the Liberal party is false to its noblest principles, it is time that it should be broken up.'[13] At a meeting of the Cambridgeshire and Huntingdonshire Nonconformists in October 1871, some speakers said that if the Government did not administer the Education Act more satisfactorily, they would do all they could to replace it with a Tory administration.[14]

This approach was intended to persuade the Ministry to amend the Education Act in accordance with the League's wishes. Failing to achieve this, its only result was to weaken the Government by helping (along with other issues) to produce a ministerial loss of no fewer than thirty-one seats at by-elections between April 1870 and January 1874. These included seven Home Rule gains in Ireland. The rest were all Conservative successes, with the Government making only three gains to offset them. Attempts were made to pledge the Liberal candidates to try and repeal Clause 25. But this policy could also cause Liberal defections: Liberal Churchmen were not always prepared to tolerate the radical clamour and the support given by some Liberal candidates to disestablishment.[15] The pitch of by-election fever was reached in 1873,[16] when the Government was rapidly weakening and a general election seemed close.

IV. DISESTABLISHMENT EFFORTS AND CHURCH DEFENCE,
1870–1872

While the education issue absorbed much ecclesiastical and political energy between 1870 and the end of Gladstone's ministry, other Dissenting questions were partly settled and helped somewhat to reduce Nonconformist hostility to the Government. The abolition of university tests, a topic of Parliamentary

[12] Quoted Garvin, op. cit. i. 132.
[13] Quoted D. A. Hamer, *Liberal Politics in the Age of Gladstone and Rosebery* (Oxford, 1972), 6–7.
[14] D. A. Hamer, *The Politics of Electoral Pressure* (Hassocks, Sussex, 1977), 123 and ff.
[15] Ibid. 127.
[16] See below. p. 57.

debate since 1834, was again the subject of a bill in 1870. Passing the Commons, this measure was amended by the Lords and then side-tracked by reference to a select committee. The year 1871, however, saw the matter largely settled. Gladstone adopted the previous year's bill as a ministerial measure and introduced it on the first day of the session. Degrees and offices still subject to restriction at Oxford, Cambridge, and Durham universities were to be opened to non-Anglicans (except divinity degrees). Clerical fellowships would not be abolished, however: Gladstone told a Nonconformist deputation on 18 January, to its displeasure, that these would remain in order to ease the bill's prospects in the Lords.[17]

The bill passed swiftly through the Commons in February, amendments to open divinity degrees and clerical fellowships being defeated with Conservative aid. In the Lords, Salisbury obtained the reappointment of the select committee and there was a delay until the committee reported. The report was indecisive enough to encourage Salisbury to try and amend the bill. In a contentious debate on 8 May Salisbury (whose views were perhaps influenced by the leading Tractarian H. P. Liddon, with whom he was intimate)[18] insisted that orthodox Christian teaching should be protected in the universities: 'the question raised by the bill is not a question between Church and Dissent but between Christianity and infidelity'. He carried various 'safeguards' by a majority of five, including a declaration by tutors that they would teach nothing contrary to the doctrine and authority of Scripture, and the prevention of any alteration in college statutes which imposed clerical restrictions.[19] Lord Houghton (Richard Monckton Milnes) claimed that no one who expressed hostility to the Bible would be allowed to hold 'any office connected with moral or religious teaching' in this country, but Salisbury refused to withdraw his declaration. Nonconformists objected strongly to the amendments, however, and the Commons would not accept them. Bishop Ellicott of Gloucester and Bristol supported Salisbury in wanting to resist the 'dictation' of the lower House.[20] But when the bill returned to the Lords the amendment imposing a tutors' declaration failed by forty votes on 13 June, the other amendments were abandoned, and the bill passed.[21] The Liberation Society recognized that, apart from the retention of clerical fellowships and headships, the Act was satisfactory. But occasions arose, leading to lawsuits, when reformers claimed the Act was being disregarded. Compulsory clerical headships in most colleges, and compulsory clerical fellowships except in the case of college chaplains, were abolished in 1882.[22]

[17] J. S. Newton, 'The Political Career of Edward Miall', Ph.D. thesis (Durham, 1975), 153–4; Ward, op. cit. 260.

[18] Liddon to Salisbury, 1 Mar. 1871; SP.

[19] H ccvi. 338–84; Mackintosh, op. cit. 265–6.

[20] Ellicott to Salisbury, 7 and 8 June 1871; SP.

[21] H ccvi. 602–5, 705–14, 1181–209, 1962–73; Ward, op. cit. 261.

[22] Mackintosh, op. cit. 269–72. See also A. Peel and J. A. R. Marriott, *Robert Forman Horton* (London, 1937), 110–12; H. Richards, 'The Church of England and the Universities', *FR*, xviii (1875), 443–8.

Anti-papists like Newdegate had opposed the bill because it opened university degrees and posts to Catholics. But the attendance of Catholics at the same universities as Protestants, already firmly condemned (though not formally banned) by Propaganda, was further discouraged by the passing of the bill. This was because the official Catholic view was that the universities affected would become even less religious than before. The Catholic policy of boycott remained until 1895, when it was alleged that moral improvement at the universities had made them safer.[23]

With the university tests question largely resolved, only the burial issue remained as a major practical grievance of Nonconformity. This had become a subject of annual Parliamentary debate. On the invitation of a joint committee of the Dissenting Deputies and Liberation Society, the Anglican George Osborne Morgan (MP for Denbighshire) succeeded George Hadfield as chief Parliamentary advocate in 1870. Morgan's advocacy symbolized the importance of the question to Wales: most Welshmen were not only Dissenters but dwellers in rural parishes without the convenient alternative of public cemeteries. Morgan's bill of 1870, to permit Dissenting burial services in parish churchyards, got no further than the committee stage in the Commons, and another attempt in 1871 ended in the same way. Further efforts in 1872 and 1873 were similarly abortive. In December 1872 Gladstone refused, on account of the pressure of other Parliamentary business, an appeal from 154 Liberal MPs to take up the matter as a Government question—a refusal which cannot have eased his strained relations with Nonconformists.[24] But Morgan persevered under the next ministry.

At a time when disestablishment was being much discussed, it was not surprising that the burial bills should be opposed as a possible encouragement to the severing of Church from State—that such legislation should be described, for instance, as 'one further step towards destroying the Church of England, and seizing its property'.[25] An annual meeting of the English Church Union in June 1870 resolved that success for the bill would be 'the admission of a principle which, if carried out to its conclusion, would throw open churches as well as churchyards to all the parishioners, whatever their creed or religious profession'.[26] It was argued to the contrary, however, that burial relief would strengthen the establishment by removing an important Dissenting grievance against it.[27]

If burials remained stubbonly alive, another religious equality issue was laid to rest in July 1871, after a failure the previous year. The Ecclesiastical Titles Act of 1851 was repealed, despite the opposition of some ultra-Protestant

[23] Arnstein, *Protestant versus Catholic*, 157; E. R. Norman, *The English Catholic Church in the Nineteenth Century* (Oxford, 1984), 295–300, 367.

[24] Mackintosh, op. cit. 277.

[25] H cciv. 1136–40 (speeches of Beresford Hope and R. A. Cross).

[26] G. B. Roberts, *The History of the English Church Union, 1859–1894* (London, 1895), 126.

[27] H cciv. 1122–3.

societies and MPs, and Catholic clerics were thenceforth legally allowed to use their territorial titles. The repeal was partly a result of Irish disestablishment, which had made the Church of Ireland clergy subject to the Titles Act. For this reason the Lords were probably persuaded more easily to pass the bill.[28] But the main function of the measure was to make a concession to Catholicism. It was important for the Government to emphasize that antipathy to the Vatican decrees would not lead them to abandon the cause of Catholic relief. Gladstone's own stated readiness to protect the independence, for spiritual purposes, of the Pope in Rome—which duly produced some protests in the country—doubtless had a similar object.[29]

The Liberation Society had been encouraged by Irish disestablishment to try and hasten English, and voluntaries were further urged in this direction by disappointment with the Education Act. Many Anglicans might have viewed the Act as State encroachment on their rightful sphere, but voluntaries regarded it as recognizing, in important ways, the establishment's educational ascendancy. Chamberlain had written to George Dixon on 3 March 1870 that 'if Forster forces his Bill through the House there will be a tremendous revival of the agitation for disestablishment of the English Church', and he repeated the warning in a speech in Birmingham Town Hall four days later.[30] The Congregational Union assembly in October 1870 carried a unanimous resolution against the Education Act and for disestablishment, though a minority disliked the inclusion of disestablishment and left the hall before the vote.[31]

Contemporary debate for and against an established Church was quite voluminous, as shown in the *Contemporary Review* and other periodicals.[32] In Scotland it still seemed possible that a union of the Free Church and the United Presbyterians would occur and strengthen disestablishment. But the union was effectively resisted by a Free Church minority led by Dr James Begg, on grounds both of theological conservatism and of opposition to disestablishment. The prospect of union faded by 1873 and did not revive for many years.[33] In the Church of England, the anger of High-Churchmen such as Pusey and Liddon over anti-Ritualist decisions by the Judicial Committee, and their desire to retain the complete Athanasian Creed in church services against the wishes of

[28] Arnstein, op. cit. 159; H cciv. 273–4, 780–808, ccvii. 1332.
[29] e.g. Minutes of Aberdeen Free Presbytery, 3 Jan. 1871 (vol. 7, p. 65); Edinburgh Church of Scotland Presbytery, 25 Jan. 1871 (vol. 27, pp. 258–9).
[30] Garvin, op. cit. i. 110; C. W. Boyd (ed.), *Mr Chamberlain's Speeches* (2 vols., London, 1914), i. 13; D. Nicholls (ed.), *Church and State in Britain since 1820* (London, 1967), 81.
[31] A. Peel, *These Hundred Years: A History of the Congregational Union of England and Wales, 1831–1931* (London, 1931), 187; S. M. Ingham, 'The Disestablishment Movement in England, 1868–1874', *Journal of Religious History*, iii (1964), 44.
[32] e.g. *CR* xvi (1871), 298–320, xvii (1871), 15–31, 282–98, 365–98.
[33] e.g. Minutes of Edinburgh Free Presbytery, 8 Nov. 1870 (vol. 29, pp. 236–9); J. Kennedy, *Unionism and its Last Phase* (Edinburgh 1873); id. *Disestablishment and Disendowment of the Established Churches* (Edinburgh, 1873).

Broad-Churchmen such as Stanley and Tait, increased their suspicion of State control and promoted talk of secession.[34] A High-Church plea for disestablishment was read to the Liverpool branch of the English Church Union in January 1871; and the ECU's annual meeting in June resolved that 'the inherent right of the Church of England, as a spiritual community, to declare and to determine all matters and things affecting her doctrine and discipline' should be recognized as a fundamental condition of the union of Church and State.[35] In December 1870 the *Nonconformist* had stated that the Ritualist Society of the Holy Cross could be reckoned as a valuable coadjutor of the Liberation Society in the quest for disestablishment: 'the two societies will work to the same end, but by different paths'. But, it was hoped, Evangelicalism would revive rather than Ritualism flourish when the Church was freed. In such a revival, the Ritualists will find a hindrance of a hundredfold more potency in the way of their insidious attempts at perversion than all the shackles of the law'.[36]

Against this background Miall made three attempts to get disestablishment motions accepted in the Commons, in the sessions of 1871, 1872, and 1873. In July 1870 he had decided to introduce a resolution the following year, and the Liberation Society had begun to try and obtain public support for it. On the recommendation of the Society's Parliamentary committee, it was decided to put pressure on constituencies whose MPs might be induced to support such a motion; to issue an address, handbills, and tracts; to hold public meetings in London and other cities; and to organize visits by members of the executive committee in order to stimulate agitation far and wide.[37] In December it was resolved that the motion should seek to apply the policy of the Irish Church Act 'to the other established Churches of the Kingdom', and Miall adopted these terms.[38] By the end of November the Society's secretary, Carvell Williams, reported that Miall's proposed motion had been unanimously approved at conferences at Manchester, Bradford, and Hanley, though he also said that at Stalybridge in Cheshire he was prevented from speaking 'by the riotous proceedings of a body of persons, who had obtained admission by means of forged tickets'.[39] Chamberlain, Dale, Jesse Collings, and Carvell Williams spoke at a Liberation Society meeting in the lecture room at Dale's church in

[34] For the Athanasian Creed controversy, eventually settled by the adoption of an 'explanatory rubric' by Convocation, see Marsh, *Victorian Church in Decline*, 40–51; H. P. Liddon, *Life of E. B. Pusey*, ed. J. O. Johnston and R. J. Wilson (4 vols., 1893–7) iv. 228–60; Liddon to Salisbury, 10 and 14 Mar. 1871, and to Lady Salisbury, 8 and 16 Mar. 1872; SP; A. J. Beresford Hope to Gladstone, 26 May 1871; GP, 44213, fos. 339–42; Lord Carnarvon to Gathorne Hardy, 21 Oct. 1872; Carnarvon Papers.

[35] H. Clark, *Disestablishment Necessary for the Well-being of the Church of England*; English Church Union (London, 1871); Roberts, op. cit. 134–5.

[36] *Nonconformist*, 21 Dec. 1870 (vol. xxx), also 7 Dec. 1870 (ibid.)

[37] LS, 21 July and 8 Sept. 1870 (iv. 261, 270–4); Newton, op. cit. 490.

[38] LS, 9 Dec. 1870; iv. 293–4.

[39] Ibid. 25 Nov. 1870 (iv. 292); Ingham op. cit. 44.

Birmingham on 13 December, when Chamberlain and Collings said that disestablishment should be made a test question in Parliamentary elections.[40]

The Society's newspaper, *The Liberator*, noted that seventeen large meetings were held in December (eleven of them in Yorkshire and Lancashire) and 150 meetings between January and May 1871, mostly in the Midlands and North of England.[41] Miall also received, as expected, the support of the Congregational Union committee, the annual session of the Baptist Union in April, and the Dissenting Deputies.[42] Some indirect support might also have been gained from a noisy meeting held in St James's Hall on 3 April to protest against the House of Lords' rejection of bills repeatedly passed by the Commons, and to call for 'the immediate removal of the Bishops' from the Lords. Called by persons who had become frustrated by the Lords' rejection of bills permitting marriage with a deceased wife's sister (a Parliamentary question of twenty-two years' duration and not to be settled until 1907), the meeting was invaded by republicans, and the speeches were interrupted by shouts of 'We want a Republic!' A resolution was put, suggesting that the Lords' veto be limited. But to this an amendment was moved, seconded by the trade union leader George Odger, that the upper House should be abolished altogether. The chairman, Thomas Chambers (a Liberal MP), declared the amendment lost. Uproar followed, but the meeting quietened down and carried a resolution opposing the Lords' rejection of deceased wife's sister bills. Another resolution was put, to remove Bishops from the Lords, but an amendment was moved to this also, seeking to establish a new legislative chamber 'responsible to the people'. The chairman tried to block this, but it clearly had the support of a large majority and was declared carried.[43] The champions of marriage with a deceased wife's sister had got a lot more than they bargained for.

Miall moved his resolution on 9 May in a moderate speech. He disclaimed any immediate hope of disestablishment but nevertheless thought the subject should be promoted. The Church of England should be disestablished. It had the allegiance of no more than half the population; as a rich establishment it added to social tensions; it would be more effective without the cramping conditions of State control; and it would be all the safer for being disestablished when (with a side-glance at the recent Paris Commune) the attempts at revolution came.[44] Among the speakers supporting Miall were Henry Richard and Watkin Williams, who stressed the existence of the large Nonconformist majority in Wales, and E. A. Leatham (member for Huddersfield) who emphasized the importance of Nonconformists to the Liberal party and the small rewards they had so far received: 'we are sick of these doles of compassion

---

[40] *Nonconformist*, 21 Dec. 1870 (vol. xxx).

[41] Ingham, op. cit. 45.

[42] *Congregational Year-book* (1872), 26–7; *Baptist Handbook* (1872), 27–8; B. L. Manning, *The Protestant Dissenting Deputies* (Cambridge, 1952), 396.

[43] *AR* cxiii (1871), 43–4.

[44] H ccvi. 474–97; *AR* cxiii (1871), 92–3.

flung to us with supercilious hesitation'.[45] Speakers against included Sir Roundell Palmer, the Home Secretary H. A. Bruce, and finally Gladstone, who defended the Church of England on account of its great religious and social work.[46] Disraeli also opposed, speaking scathingly of 'revolutionary' Dissenters and their 'sacerdotal' allies, and saying that, though Miall's policy might be a logical sequel to Irish disestablishment, 'fortunately this country is not governed by logic'.[47] The motion was lost by 374 votes to eighty-nine. A majority of the Nonconformist MPs, approximately thirty-six, supported Miall, and only three of his supporters were Roman Catholics—a reflection of the notable Catholic lack of interest, partly no doubt because of the educational dispute, in transferring their empirical support of Irish disestablishment to broader theoretical support of the voluntary principle.[48] As many as 144 Liberals were absent unpaired, which was doubtless more encouraging to Miall than to the ministry.

Despite the defeat, voluntaries showed every sign of optimism. The Liberation Society claimed to have received 'the strongest incentive to renewed exertions', and ordered 30,000 copies of Miall's speech to be circulated. The *Beehive*, urging working-class interests, wanted disestablishment to become less of a sectarian conflict and more concerned with 'the proper disposition and use of national property'. Even *The Times* said that 'this century will see the consummation Mr. Miall so devoutly wishes'.[49] The Liberation Society had begun definitely to woo workers' support by appointing George Potter, a trade union leader, to its executive committee at the triennial conference in May; and by forming a 'Working Men's Committee for promoting the separation of Church and State', with George Howell as chairman, Potter as secretary, and Robert Applegarth and Henry Broadhurst among the other nine members, all of them skilled workers. The Society's minutes noted that more freedom should be allowed to speakers at working-men's meetings than 'to the Society's better trained and disciplined advocates', and that the Working-men's Committee should not be blamed 'for occasional acts of indiscretion which may be distasteful to some of the party's supporters'.[50] This body, nominally separate from the Liberation Society but financially dependent on it, issued an address to working men in October, stressing the social advantages which might come from disestablishment. An inaugural conference was held in November at the Cannon Street Hotel in London, with Miall present. It was resolved to extend the local working-men's committees which already existed.

[45] H ccvi. 520–9, 531–5, 538–48.

[46] Ibid. 500–18, 559–71.

[47] Ibid. 550–1.

[48] Cf. Norman, op. cit. 364 and n.

[49] Newton, op. cit. 496–8; C. Binfield, *So Down to Prayers: Studies in English Nonconformity, 1780–1920* (London, 1977), 117; LS, 15 May, 5 June, and 3 July 1871 (iv. 336–7, 343–4, 354–6); *The Bee-hive*, 6 May, p. 9; 13 May, pp. 8–9.

[50] LS, 17 July 1871 (iv. 363).

Although their connection with the Liberation Society was not always smooth, Howell and Potter gave the voluntary message to many meetings during the winter of 1871–2. Sometimes they met opposition. Howell had to dodge an egg at Liverpool and chair-legs at Wigan, and started taking a precautionary walking-stick to meetings. He encountered loud interruptions at Sheffield, and Potter said an assembly at Leeds was broken up by middle-class Churchmen. Nevertheless it was decided that the meetings had been generally successful, and more were financed. In May 1872 it was agreed to continue the arrangement for a further year. But by early 1873 the scheme petered out, and the Working-men's Committee ceased to function. Howell and Potter remained on the Society's executive committee for some years, and the link between the Society and some working-class organizations persisted for a long time.[51] But this could not disguise the fact that the anticipated popular movement against the established Church had generally failed to materialize. Urban workers in general showed little positive zeal either for or against the establishment. Most of them did not attend church, were little touched by organized religion, and were scarcely affected by any 'social oppression' which might be attributed to the established Church. It was not clear what material or religious benefit disestablishment could give them.

The rural areas, however, had a different religious and social character, the clergyman having a much more intimate role in the day-to-day life of the labourer. In the 1860s some agricultural workers' unions were formed and led by clergymen, which showed the community of feeling which could exist between clergy and worker.[52] But there was also a good deal of strain in the relationship between the labourer and the Church. The obligation of farmers to pay tithes could be seen as holding down labourers' wages, and the parson, with his often elevated social background and large role in local government and the execution of the law, often seemed an extension of irritating landlord domination. Such reasons contributed to the strength of Nonconformity in many rural areas. The burial grievance was stronger in the countryside because, unlike the towns with their public cemeteries, the parish churchyard was the only convenient place of interment.[53]

In April 1872 the National Agricultural Labourers' Union was founded and led by Joseph Arch, a Primitive Methodist lay preacher with unpleasant youthful memories of the established Church. By June 1873 the Union had 72,000 members and 982 branches in twenty-four counties.[54] The influence on many farm workers of Primitive Methodism, and to a lesser extent of Wesleyanism, was shown in the organization and propaganda of the union.

[51] Newton, op. cit. 499–503; Ingham, op. cit. 47–51; LS, 3 and 17 July 1871, 18 Sept. 1871, 3 June 1872 (iv. 356, 382–3, 452–3); D. E. Fletcher, 'Aspects of Sheffield Liberalism, 1849–1886', Ph.D. thesis (Sheffield, 1972), 108–9.

[52] D. Bowen, *The Idea of the Victorian Church* (Montreal, 1968), 247.

[53] O. Chadwick, *The Victorian Church*, ii (London, 1970), 202–3.

[54] LS, 9 June 1873 (v. 33–4), also 29 Sept. 1873 (v. 60).

There was some noticeable Baptist influence, but little from other Nonconformist denominations. Support from the Anglican clergy was limited to a few individuals. Archbishop Manning (Cardinal from 1875) was a strong supporter.[55] The *Nonconformist* gave a big welcome to the union, and Carvell Williams, on behalf of the Liberation Society, attended its conference at Leamington in June 1873. The union clearly had important possibilities as a means of advancing the voluntary cause. The demand for disestablishment appeared in the speeches of Joseph Arch and other union leaders, as it did in the *Primitive Methodist Magazine*. In 1873 even a clergyman who had been highly sympathetic to the union, Canon E. D. Girdlestone, left it because its leaders were 'meddling with the resources of our clergy and . . . with the connection of Church and State'.[56] The Liberation Society executive had reservations about Arch and his social aims—it decided in 1879 to employ him 'occasionally only' as a lecturer[57]—but there is no doubt that enthusiasm for disestablishment among rural workers nourished hopes of what might be done when they received the Parliamentary franchise. Economic depression greatly weakened the Agricultural Labourers' Union in the mid-1870s, but it also made tithe rent more difficult to pay and this sustained the desire for disestablishment.

Miall's motion and the public support for it deepened the concern of Church defenders. There were increased efforts to arouse support for the establishment. 'We must buckle on our armour, and do battle for the Establishment principle', said J. C. Ryle at the Church Congress in October 1871, and many similar sentiments were expressed in speeches and pamphlets at this time.[58] The Church Institution, founded in 1859, was renamed the Church Defence Institution in 1871. With Bishops and clergy now admitted to its governing bodies, and an enlarged membership of its general council, it issued many publications including (from 1872) a monthly newspaper, *The National Church*. From about 100 in 1871, the number of branches quadrupled in the next four years.[59] There were some separate organizations such as the Northern Church Defence Association at Manchester and the Yorkshire Union of Church Institutes. In competition with the Liberation Society's efforts to obtain working-class support, the Church Defence Institution formed in 1871 a

---

[55] J. P. D. Dunbabin, 'The Revolt of the Field: The Agricultural Labourers' Movement in the 1870s', *Past and Present*, xxvi (1963), 69–71; N. Scotland, *Methodism and the Revolt of the Field: A Study of the Methodist Contribution to Agricultural Trade Unionism in East Anglia, 1872–1896* (Gloucester, 1981), esp. 22, 34–58, 68–84, 100–9; J. Arch, *The Autobiography of Joseph Arch*, ed. J. G. O'Leary (London, 1966), 57, 66; Bowen, op. cit. 247–8; J. C. MacDonnell, *The Life and Correspondence of William Connor Magee* (2 vols., London, 1896) i. 277.

[56] Quoted Bowen, op. cit. 249.

[57] Ingham, op. cit. 49–50.

[58] J. C. Ryle, *Yes or No! Is the Union of Church and State Worth Preserving?*, CDI (London, 1871); M. J. Mayers, *Establishment and Voluntaryism Contrasted, in Answer to Mr Miall* (London, 1871).

[59] *The Church Defence Institution: List of Associations in Union Throughout the Country* (Westminster, 1872); *National Church*, Oct. 1872; M. J. D. Roberts, 'Pressure-group Politics and the Church of England: The Church Defence Institution, 1859–1896', *JEH* xxxv (1984), 568–71.

London Working-men's Council. This comprised twenty-two craftsmen, who countered the propaganda of the Liberation Society's Working-men's Committee and urged that Church defence should be made a test for Parliamentary candidates.[60] Similarly the Revd Dr Alfred T. Lee, secretary of the Institution, said at a meeting in June 1872 that Nonconformist efforts to increase their Parliamentary strength must be met by the counter-efforts of Church defenders. The Institution's annual income (only £1,200 in 1871) must rise to equal the £6,000 to £7,000 of the Liberation Society.[61] Some working-men's councils were established in other towns besides London, but the London council did not prosper, having only ten struggling branches and annual receipts of £46 in 1875.[62]

Many believed that Church defence must be accompanied by reform in order to be effective. 'We must set our own house in order' said Ryle in his address of October 1871; division of large dioceses, reform of Convocation and other matters must be considered.[63] Shaftesbury noted in February 1872 that in order to resist disestablishment he would 'admit any wide reforms, certainly to the extent of excluding the Bishops from the House of Lords'.[64] Some proposals for reform displayed the differences between Church parties: a pamphlet of 1873 advised giving laity a voice in the election of clergy in order to diminish Ritualism.[65] A Church Reform Union was founded in late 1870 by William Cowper-Temple and others; its aims included giving a share in Church government (initially at parish level) to the laity.[66]

Lord Sandon, an Evangelical, had brought into the Commons in 1870 a bill to provide for the compulsory formation of parochial councils. This bill had made no progress, and Sandon introduced another in 1871 for councils only to be formed when the parishioners so desired. But the bill aroused considerable opposition, especially among High-Churchmen who feared that nominal parishioners might control the council and rule the incumbent. Beresford Hope, a noted High-Churchman and brother-in-law of Lord Salisbury, opposed the measure in the Commons, pointing out that some church councils already existed on an informal basis and arguing that these should be allowed to increase by natural volition. Gladstone also argued that the measure should be deferred until public opinion had had time to mature on the subject. The bill was given a second reading, but was then postponed, and it was to be many years before the bill's object was realized.[67]

---

[60] *Addresses of the London Working-men's Council to their Brethren of Great Britain* (London, [1872]).

[61] *Minutes of Proceedings at the Church Defence Meeting at Cheam, Surrey, 29 June 1872*, CDI (London, 1872), 8.

[62] Ingham, op. cit. 51.

[63] Ryle, op. cit. 5–6.

[64] E. Hodder, *The Life and Work of the Seventh Earl of Shaftesbury* (London, 1888), 660.

[65] *The Church of England: Reform or Disestablishment, Which? By One of her Presbyters* (London, 1873), 25 ff.

[66] *Nonconformist*, 28 Dec. 1870 (vol. xxx).

[67] H ccv. 822–75.

Sandon also tried to reform the system of patronage by supporting a bill of R. A. Cross (a moderate High-Churchman), in 1870 to prevent the sale of next presentations (i.e. the next occasion when a clergyman was presented to a living). The bill passed the Commons without a division, but was successfully opposed in the upper House, Lord Cairns arguing that it infringed property rights.[68] In the following year a joint committee of the Convocations of Canterbury and York decided that the sale of next presentations should be banned and that parishioners should be allowed to object formally to a patron's nominee.[69] But there was no further Parliamentary attempt to reform patronage until the next Government was in office.

The abolition of patronage in the establishment was currently a larger issue in Scotland. There it was seen by reforming members of the Church of Scotland such as Alexander Whitelaw (later Conservative MP for Glasgow) as an important means of strengthening that Church against voluntaryism and attracting Dissenters back to it. One reformer noted in 1870 that patronage, imposed in 1712 in violation of the Treaty of Union, had caused all the secessions from the Church of Scotland since then.[70] The abolition of patronage had been debated in the General Assembly of the Church of Scotland since 1863, and in 1869 a resolution was carried against the law of patronage and a petition to Parliament was adopted requesting its repeal. Similar resolutions were passed at the Assemblies in each of the next three years. But the Liberal Government was most unlikely to abolish patronage because of the opposition of its numerous Scottish Dissenting supporters. These had disestablishment in mind rather than the strengthening of the established Church.[71]

Miall's disestablishment motion of 1871 had stimulated both voluntary efforts and Church defence. His next motion in 1872 helped to maintain the tension. Support for voluntaryism was sustained by developments already discussed and by additional ones. Though clinging to some faith in Gladstone, Nonconformists remained discontented with the ministry's education policy and expected no adequate improvement in it as long as the 'traitorous' Forster remained vice-president of the council.[72] In a lecture for the Manchester Nonconformist Association in November 1871, R. W. Dale had been much applauded when he said 'it seems probable that we shall be driven into open hostility, and shall be compelled to form a separate and independent party in the State'.[73] The Manchester Nonconformist conference in January 1872, chaired

[68] M. J. D. Roberts, 'Private Patronage and the Church of England, 1800–1900', *JEH* xxxii (1981), 215.

[69] Ibid.

[70] 'H. A. Page' (i.e. A. H. Japp), 'Church Tendencies in Scotland', *CR* xiv (1870), 387.

[71] Macleod, *Memoir of Norman Macleod*, ii. 322. Reasons for Free Church opposition were stated, e.g., in Edinburgh Free Presbytery Minutes, 4 Apr. 1870 (vol. 29, pp. 207–8).

[72] Dale to Newman Hall, 7 and 16 Nov. 1871; GP, 44188, fos. 101–3, 107–8; Bright to Gladstone, 24 and 28 Nov. 1871; GP, 44112, fos. 193–4, 200.

[73] R. W. Dale, *The Politics of Nonconformity* (Manchester, 1871), 11.

by Henry Richard and addressed by Chamberlain, affirmed the principle of purely secular education, though it was still disputed among Nonconformists and caused the resignation of the treasurer of the Liberation Society.[74] A vote of censure on the 1870 Act, moved by George Dixon in the Commons in March, was crushingly defeated.[75]

Dale and other advocates of secular education found further cause for complaint in the Scottish Education Act of 1872 because it permitted school boards to provide denominational education in the schools taken under their control, which would be rate-supported. There were protests against this and other provisions from Scottish and English Dissenters, and Dale was delegated to stimulate opposition in Scotland. But he undertook the task against the advice of prominent Scottish Dissenters, who were divided over the bill and were anxious about the delicate negotiations still proceeding between the Free Church and the United Presbyterians. Although Dale addressed meetings in Edinburgh, Glasgow, and Aberdeen he received insufficient support, mainly because most Scots were Presbyterians even though divided denominationally and did not disagree a great deal over the Presbyterian education which would be offered.[76] A conscience clause was included, but Catholic schools and a small number of Episcopalian schools remained outside the board system and received Government grants. Catholic schools were vigorously extended, and by 1908 provided accommodation for about ten per cent of Scotland's pupils. As in England Catholics stood for election to school boards in order to protect their denominational interests, and were often returned.[77]

Miall's second motion helped to express the continuing Nonconformist irritation over such matters. The Liberation Society's Parliamentary committee conferred with Miall at the end of 1871, and it was decided that he would move for a Royal Commission to examine the amount and application of the Church of England's property and revenues.[78] This was a more general approach than in 1871, and the emphasis on property was perhaps designed to appeal to potential working-class supporters. Miall gave notice of his motion on 29 February 1872, but it was not introduced until 2 July. During the interval, opposition came from the Church Defence Institution and from important public speeches by Disraeli in April and June. Support came from Nonconformist denominational bodies; and there was the additional encouragement of a growing voluntary movement in Scotland, including the formation

---

[74] *General Conference of Nonconformists: Authorized Report of Proceedings*, 2nd edn. (Manchester and London, 1872), 154; Mackintosh, *Disestablishment and Liberation*, 215; J. Guinnes Rogers, *Why Ought Not the State to Give Religious Education?* (London, 1872).

[75] H ccix. 1395–485.

[76] Minutes of Dundee UP Presbytery, 20 Feb. 1872 (vol. 1, 264–5); *Congregational Year-book* (1873), 8–9; *The Congregationalist*, i (1872), 193–201; A. W. W. Dale, *Life of R. W. Dale*, 289–95; A. R. MacEwen, *The Life and Letters of John Cairns, DD, Ll D* (London, 1895), 545–9.

[77] J. E. Handley, *The Irish in Scotland* (Glasgow, 1964), 309–20; B. Lenman and J. Stocks, 'The Beginnings of State Education in Scotland, 1872–1885', *Scottish Educational Studies*, iv (1972), 95.

[78] Newton, op. cit. 504.

of a Scottish Disestablishment and Disendowment Association in December 1871 to complement the activities of the Liberation Society.[79]

In the Commons' debate Gladstone said that Miall's motion must be opposed because of his ultimate aim of disestablishment.[80] Ninety-four MPs voted for Miall, and sixty-one of these had voted in April to repeal Clause 25. The day after the debate a Conservative noted that '[the Church's] enemies represented by Miall & Co. are not strong, and the attack of last night was unreal and feeble'; and *The Times* reversed its 1871 reaction, now saying that Miall was leading a lost cause.[81] Nevertheless, though opposed by 295 MPs and losing by a majority of 201, Miall had slightly increased his support. Six members who had voted against him in 1871 had now supported him, and although there were more Liberal absentees only a third of the Liberal MPs had opposed him.[82] Bishop Magee professed to be not at all optimistic for the establishment: 'I think that . . . disestablishment is postponed for five or even ten years by Miall's defeat, but that is supposing that no great pressure for war or taxes on the working and shopkeeper classes sets them hungering for confiscation'.[83]

On 19 July the Liberation Society decided, on Miall's suggestion, to introduce the question again next session and to hold an autumn and winter campaign. Nonconformist meetings gave anticipated backing to a new attempt.[84] As the time of a general election drew nearer it seemed important to keep the issue to the forefront.

V. CHURCH ISSUES AND THE GOVERNMENT IN 1873

Not only the sectionalism of Dissent, but also that of Irish Home Rule, was proving troublesome to the Government. Isaac Butt's Home Government Association was founded in May 1870, and during the next three years Irish immigrants in large British towns began to form societies affiliated to it. The first of these branches was formed in Glasgow by John Ferguson, a Protestant immigrant, after a visit by Butt in 1871; and one existed in Dundee by March 1872, when another Home Rule MP, John Martin, was welcomed there. These associations became active in local politics and aspired to return Homer Rulers to Westminster. A Home Rule candidate was put up by the local association in a Liverpool by-election in February 1873, but withdrew in order to assist the

---

[79] Drummond and Bulloch, *The Church in Late Victorian Scotland*, 94–100; A. Oliver, *Life of George Clark Hutton, DD* (Paisley, 1910), 233–5.

[80] H ccxii. 575, 578 (527–81 for whole debate).

[81] Gathorne Hardy's diary, 3 July 1872; Nancy E. Johnson (ed.), *The Diary of Gathorne Hardy, Later Lord Cranbrook* (Oxford, 1981), 163; Newton, op. cit. 507.

[82] LS, 3 June 1872 (iv. 460–1); Binfield, op. cit. 117.

[83] Magee to Dean MacDonnell, 7 July 1872; MacDonnell, op. cit. i. 276.

[84] LS, 3 June 1872 (iv. 467–8, 479, 483, 493–4); Disestablishment conference at Birmingham, 1 Oct. 1872; *AR* cxiv (1872), 89–90; Baptist Union autumn session, 9 Oct. 1872; *Baptist Handbook* (1873), 64; Newton, op. cit. 507–9.

Liberal candidate against an anti-Catholic Conservative; the latter, however, held the seat.

Isaac Butt visited a Home Rule convention at Manchester on 8 January 1873, organized by John Barry and attended by delegates from about twenty local associations. At this meeting it was decided to establish a union of the British societies, to be named the Home Rule Confederation of Great Britain. The final form of the union was settled at a conference at Birmingham in February. The organization then developed additional branches. Butt was president until 1877 and was succeeded by Parnell, who was followed in turn by T. P. O'Connor in 1883. By this time the union had been placed on a new basis as the Irish National League of Great Britain. The headquarters were at Manchester for two years until 1875, and were then moved to Liverpool because the publishing office of *United Irishman,* the Confederation's recently established mouthpiece, was in that city. Later the headquarters were transferred to London.[85] The Confederation aimed at using its force independently of the two British parties, but its members were torn between the Liberals, who seemed likelier to adopt desirable Irish legislation, and the Conservatives, who defended Catholic educational interests.

The Irish thus appeared to be less and less pacified despite Gladstone's notable efforts over Church and land in 1869 and 1870. Support for Home Rule was only increased by Gladstone's third attempt at conciliatory legislation, the Irish University Bill of 1873.[86] This was intended to carry out a thorough reform of Irish university education. The existence of only the Protestant Trinity College, Dublin, and the undenominational Queen's Colleges at Belfast, Cork, and Galway was an impediment to conscientious Catholics seeking university education, and few Catholics attended these institutions. The Catholic hierarchy wanted a State-endowed university under Catholic control, but this had no chance of winning the consent of a mainly Protestant Parliament. Only a secular university might win Parliamentary acceptance. The Cabinet discussed a bill in the autumn of 1872, and on 21 November accepted Gladstone's proposal. This was to create a new Dublin University and give it an 'undenominational' governing body and a purely secular curriculum. The teaching of theology, philosophy, and modern history was to be excluded because of the scope they provided for religious controversy. Trinity College and the Belfast and Cork colleges would be affiliated to the new university, but the Galway college would be closed. Catholic and Presbyterian colleges could also affiliate, but would receive no State endowment.

Like previous conciliatory efforts in this field, the scheme only aroused fresh

[85] J. Denvir, *The Irish in Britain* (London, 1892), 263 ff.; I. Wood, 'Irish Immigrants and Scottish Radicalism, 1880–1906', in I. MacDougall (ed.), *Essays in Scottish Labour History* (Edinburgh, 1978), 70; E. P. M. Wollaston, 'The Irish Nationalist Movement in Great Britain, 1886–1908', MA thesis (London, 1957), 7 ff.; T. Burke, *Catholic History of Liverpool* (Liverpool 1910), 211.

[86] Cf. Parry, 'Religion', 90–1.

dispute. Many advocates of secular education, such as Miall, were quite pleased with the plan because the State would not be supporting any religious education—the principle they were striving to establish in Britain.[87] About forty-four Nonconformist MPs voted for the second reading of the bill. But Whigs would have preferred a more decidedly undenominational measure;[88] and some other Liberals disliked the bill on academic grounds, especially because of the exclusion of the aforementioned subjects—a proposal which caused Harcourt to describe the measure in the Commons as 'the most hideous deformity ever laid by an English Government upon the table of an English parliament'.[89] Among Catholics, Manning praised the plan to Gladstone because it excluded 'mixed' or undenominational religious education;[90] and he urged Cardinal Cullen, the Irish Catholic primate, that it should be accepted. But the Irish Catholic Bishops almost unanimously opposed it at a meeting on 27 February.[91] This decision was fatal to the bill, because it was now condemned as unsatisfactory by the group it was mainly intended to please. Most Roman Catholic MPs opposed the second reading and only five supported it.

The premier unfolded his intricate scheme to the Commons in a three-hour speech on 3 March. The plan was supported by Miall and Osborne Morgan but sharply criticized by some other Liberals—Henry Fawcett, Harcourt, and Edward Horsman. Disraeli chimed in, perhaps scenting Conservative victory through Liberal division, and echoed the dissident Liberals' denunciation with his own: the bill was 'monstrous in its general principles, pernicious in many of its details, and utterly futile as a measure of practical legislation'. Although Gladstone held out the hope of ministerial agreement to amendments in committee, the second reading was thrown out on a big vote at 2.30 a.m. on 12 March, by a majority of three (287–284).[92] The adverse Catholic vote was largely responsible, and Home Rule was strengthened. But if twenty British Liberals had not opposed or abstained, the Government would have won.

The ministry had lost its grip on the Commons it had dominated so long. Following his intended course if divisions went against him, Gladstone resigned. But Disraeli, not wishing to lead another minority Government and hoping that the Liberal disintegration would spread in the ensuing months, refused to succeed him.[93] On 20 March the discomfited Ministers were back in their places.

In this situation it was difficult for the Government to retain its former

[87] Cf. LS, 17 Feb. 1873 (v. 10); *Primitive Methodist Magazine*, ix (1873), 190.

[88] Parry, op. cit. 92–3.

[89] Quoted B. Holland, *The Life of Spencer Compton, Eighth Duke of Devonshire* (2 vols., London, 1911), i. 114.

[90] Manning to Gladstone, 14 and 15 Feb., 5 and 7 Mar. 1873; GP, 44250, fos. 83–7, 109–14.

[91] E. R. Norman, *The Catholic Church and Ireland in the Age of Rebellion 1859–1873* (London, 1965) 451.

[92] *AR* cxv (1873), 8–33; Morley, *Gladstone*, ii. 437–44.

[93] Sir Stafford Northcote to Disraeli, 14 Mar. 1873; Iddesleigh Papers, Add. MS 50016, fos. 144–7.

authority, already much reduced by internal division. The Liberal disagreements continued, as did the stream of Conservative by-election victories. The differences between Nonconformists and the ministry came to the fore again when Miall introduced another disestablishment motion, supported by the usual apparatus of Liberation Society meetings since the autumn, by denominational assemblies in England and Scotland, and by a Nonconformist Conference held on 11 February to inaugurate the Parliamentary session.[94] There were also signs that more Wesleyans were turning to disestablishment in reaction to the spread of Ritualism. A Wesleyan speaker at Bolton on 20 January had said that the Church of England was no longer a bulwark of Protestantism when 'thousands of Ritualists . . . [were] doing the work of Popery in Protestant pulpits'. The Congregational Union's annual assembly in May declared that the English Church had become part rationalist and part romanist. Some additional confidence for Dissent, though not necessarily for voluntaryism, may have been gained from the renewed passage of the second reading of Osborne Morgan's Burials Bill on 26 March. This followed the largest division so far on the issue, and the debate had been overshadowed by disestablishment.[95]

Even if failure was tacitly pre-admitted, Miall presented a bold and straightforward motion on 16 May, calling for disestablishment of the Churches of England and Scotland in the name of religious equality and ecclesiastical self-government. He appealed not only to Nonconformists but to Church reformers: 'the Church [of England] is hampered and shackled by the State in the prosecution of her spiritual enterprise. She cannot organize her own machinery; she cannot increase the number of her episcopate; she cannot select her own chief rulers . . . she cannot remove the scandals of patronage . . . without having recourse to a secular legislature in which all shades of religious belief and non-belief are represented'.[96] As befitted a motion which specifically included Scotland, the seconder was a Scottish MP, Duncan McLaren, a United Presbyterian who stressed that voluntaryism was growing north of the border. However, the motion was soon defeated. If Miall's task was now familiar, so was Gladstone's in refuting him. The premier threw Miall's comparative lack of eloquence into the shade by a trenchant rebuttal, asserting that most of the population showed no desire for disestablishment: the question was really one for 'the indefinite and remote future'.[97] Gladstone's oration seemed too decisive to merit Bishop Magee's comment that 'it leaves him free to bring in a Disestablishment Bill any day that suits him';[98] though this remark clearly indicates the suspicion of Gladstone held by many Churchmen.

[94] LS, 17 Feb. 1873 (v. 9); Minutes of Dundee UP Presbytery, 22 Apr. 1873 (vol. 1, 289).
[95] J. Barlow, *The Wesleyans and Disestablishment: A Speech Delivered at Bolton*, Nonconformist Association of Bolton and Neighbourhood, (Bolton, 1873), 3; *Congregational Year-book* (1874), 14; H ccxv. 158–217.
[96] H ccxvi. 26.
[97] Ibid. 37–49.
[98] Magee to J. C. MacDonnell, 17 May 1873; MacDonnell, op. cit. i. 287.

Soon after Gladstone had spoken the debate suddenly ended. The division was called when many of Miall's supporters, not thinking they would be summoned to vote so early, were out of the House. As a result Miall obtained the smallest backing of all his three efforts—only sixty-one votes (forty-eight of them from supporters of the previous year) against 356. Miall considered preparing another motion for the next session, but decided against this in December because of the likelihood of a general election. When the election came he did not stand, and his Parliamentary career thus ended in disappointment.

Miall's motion, said Gathorne Hardy (a Conservative MP and ex-Minister), had been 'crushed by Gladstone admirably: his speech was delightful to hear'.[99] Gladstone's Dissenting 'supporters' had a very different view of his performance, and some of them openly expressed their pain. The Revd Henry Allon, a Congregationalist and editor of the *British Quarterly Review*, wrote to Gladstone that the schism between Government and Dissent was 'becoming hopeless' and was 'much wider than it was a few weeks ago'. This was owing not so much to Gladstone's argument in the debate as to the 'tone of asperity and apparent intolerance' in which it was delivered. Nonconformists, moreover, were still very dissatisfied with the Education Act, which Bright had just called 'the worst act passed by any Liberal administration since the Reform Act of 1832'. Dissenters, indeed, were 'ready to welcome the accession to power of the Tory party for a while in order to compel what they think a more fruitful adherence to Liberal principles on the part of their opponents'.[1] In reply Gladstone denied any offensive intentions in his speech, and said he contemplated 'with repugnance' the idea of a breach with Nonconformity.[2] But there was no suggestion of anything definite to ease the Dissenting grievance, and the premier soon began to consider an entirely different way of trying to reunite his party.

Nonconformist frustration was increased by the Government's failure to attempt a satisfactory amendment of the Education Act. Early in April Chamberlain led a Birmingham deputation to Bright and asked him to put their views to Ministers about the need for change in education policy. Bright, after seeing Forster, held out some hope that education would 'wear a more cheerful aspect before long'. The repeal of Clause 25 was a foremost desire of the National Education League, and Bright urged Gladstone that, since the clause had a very limited application, 'harmony on the Education question would be cheaply gained' by getting rid of it. Some alternative arrangement could be made to educate the small number of children who benefited from it. Bright enclosed a letter from Chamberlain, 'an able young man . . . [who] will before long I doubt not be in the House'. But Gladstone said that Parliament would

[99] Diary of Gathorne Hardy, 17 May 1873 (Johnson, op. cit. 180).
[1] Allon to Gladstone, 2 July 1873; GP, 44095, fos. 325–6.
[2] Gladstone to Allon, 5 July 1873; ibid. fo. 327.

not repeal the clause merely to satisfy some radicals, and in any case the matter was too small for the Government to worry about.[3] Ministers had promised an amending bill at the start of the session, but when this was at length brought in by Forster on 12 June it was totally unsatisfactory to the League. Rate aid under Clause 25 for poor children at voluntary schools was not abolished but transferred to the authority of the poor law guardians, and it was to be compulsory. The Liberation Society's executive committee condemned the bill because it reaffirmed this matter 'in a still more objectionable form' and did not provide for the establishment of school boards in every district. The *Nonconformist* described it as 'the expiring effort of an effete and palsied administration'.[4]

The bill was withdrawn, and the transference of fee payments to the authority of poor law guardians was postponed until a Conservative Government enacted it in 1876. But the National Education League was now plunging more fully into the chaotic Liberal electoral situation. In June 1873, in the second of three by-elections at Bath in that year, a League candidate (J. C. Cox, a member of the executive) was put up—the first time this independent line was taken—because the official Liberal candidate (A. D. Hayter) had refused to express views on educational policy. Cox's nomination paper contained the names of two Conservatives, thus adding to the excitement which broke out into rioting. Hayter yielded, making even larger concessions to the League's demands than had originally been asked. Cox withdrew from the poll after obtaining thirteen votes, but the seat was lost to the Conservatives.[5] At the same time another member of the League's executive, Edward Jenkins, stood at Dundee, where all three candidates were Liberals. Although education featured very little in the contest Jenkins polled three times as many votes as the Government Liberal, even though a third candidate (the only local man among them) won the seat.[6]

However, the League's electoral policy depended precariously on the behaviour of voters (mainly Nonconformists) who were divided and uncertain in their attitude to education, disestablishment, and the question of loyalty to the Liberal party. It was also difficult to find suitable and willing radicals to stand only to help a Conservative to be returned. In July Chamberlain asked Sir Charles Dilke whether there were any 'fanatics willing to join the Forlorn Hope and help in smashing up that whited sepulchre called the Liberal party'.[7] Chamberlain had seen that educational reform had limited value as a popular

---

[3] Bright to Chamberlain, 10 Apr. 1873; CP, JC 5/7/2; Bright to Gladstone, 16 Apr. 1873; GP, 44113, fos. 34–8; Gladstone to Bright, 17 Apr. 1873; Bright Papers, Add. MS 43385, fos. 211–14.

[4] LS, 7 July 1873 (v. 45); Mackintosh, op. cit. 257.

[5] Adams, *The Elementary School Contest*, 291–4; Hamer, *The Politics of Electoral Pressure*, 131–3.

[6] *Dundee Advertiser*, 5 and 12 Aug. 1873.

[7] S. Gwynn and Gertrude Tuckwell, *The Life of the Rt. Hon. Sir Charles W. Dilke* (2 vols., London, 1917), i. 165. Cf. Chamberlain to John Morley, 19 July 1873; CP, JC 5/54/3, and Aug. (undated) 1873; ibid. 54/7.

cause, and was looking for wider social concerns on which to found a broad
radical party with strong working–class support.[8] So it was not entirely
surprising that the League, after consulting representatives of Nonconformist
committees, decided to suspend its electoral policy in August. Next month it
appeared to be given some solid reason for doing this by the return of the
Quaker John Bright to the Cabinet, which possibly indicated a change in
Government policy.[9]

Gladstone of course intended that Bright's readmission would mollify the
Nonconformists, but Chamberlain and John Morley (now firm allies in the
radical battle) were justly sceptical that anything tangible would come of it.
Bright repeatedly denounced the Education Act, but when interviewed by
Chamberlain and Dale it was clear he had obtained no promise that ministerial
policy would change.[10] Morley said that 'the old tribune' had been made a
'catspaw' by Gladstone who wanted to paralyse the League's electoral action.[11]

Gladstone defended voluntary schools at a parish meeting at Hawarden in
August. He had frankly told Bright that the education issue could not give the
Liberal party a 'positive force' but only a weakening and divisive one. Finance
alone, it seemed, might 'raise us to a higher and firmer level', and once this level
was reached education might be tackled again.[12] Gladstone might have thought
that finance was the highest common factor between the otherwise conflicting
views of Bright and Forster, for if Bright was condemning the Act Forster was
trying to operate it. Forster told Gladstone in October that a speech by Bright at
Birmingham had greatly increased his difficulties: 'with the League trusting
and the Voluntaries [i.e. denominationalists] fearing, by reason of this speech,
that the Educational Policy of the Government will be changed, the
Department will be almost powerless and my position will be hardly tenable'.
To Bright himself Forster complained about 'such a speech spoken by a Cabinet
Minister, and especially by you, with your power and influence in the country'.
Gladstone told Bright that his speech wrongly hinted that a new policy might be
introduced next Session.[13] Nevertheless, a result of Bright's speech which

[8] Garvin, *Life of Joseph Chamberlain*, i. 159–60; Chamberlain to Morley, 19 Aug. 1873; CP JC
5/54/13.

[9] Hamer, op. cit. 134–7; Adams, op. cit. 296 f.; R. W. Dale, 'The Nonconformists and the Education
Policy',*CR* xxii (1873), 643–4; Patricia Auspos, 'Radicalism, Pressure Groups, and Party Politics: from
the National Education League to the National Liberal Federation', *Journal of British Studies*, xx. 1
(1980), 191–4.

[10] Chamberlain to Morley, Aug. (undated) 1873; CP, JC 5/54/7; Morley to Chamberlain, 11 Aug.
1873; ibid. 54/9; Chamberlain to Morley, 14 Aug. 1873; ibid. 54/10; Garvin, op. cit. i. 139–40.

[11] Morley to Frederic Harrison, 17 Aug. 1873; F. W. Hirst, *Early Life and Letters of John Morley* (2
vols., London, 1927), i. 279; Morley to Chamberlain, 18 Aug. 1873; CP, JC 5/54/12.

[12] Garvin, op. cit. i. 139 n. ; Gladstone to Bright, 14 and 27 Aug. 1873; Bright Papers, 43385, fos. 220,
228.

[13] Forster to Gladstone, 25 Oct. 1873; GP, 44157, fos. 87–8; Forster to Bright, 25 Oct. 1873, copy
ibid. fos. 89–91; Gladstone to Bright, 30 Oct. 1873; Bright Papers, 43385, fos. 241–3; Forster to
Gladstone, 12 Nov. 1873; GP, 44157, fos. 94–5.

gratified Gladstone was that the League decided to continue its suspension of electoral action until the following year.[14] The Prime Minister had now to consolidate this advantage by producing an election manifesto which would distract Liberals from their quarrels.

Educational and Nonconformist questions had now provided the Government's foremost religious problems for four years. Other religious difficulties existed but had not yet obtained a large share of the political limelight. During 1873, however, there was another demonstration of anti-popery in Parliament when Newdegate received ninety-six votes (including twenty-six Liberal ones) in support of his revived, but again unsuccessful, motion to investigate convents.[15] High-Churchmen scored a small victory in this year, when legal reform in the Judicature Bill opened the prospect of removing Bishops from the consideration of ecclesiastical appeals. High-Churchmen wanted this change because, they argued, it would make judgments more impartial and therefore more likely to be obeyed. But opponents of the removal said that Ritualists only wanted it because they could more easily disobey the judgments of an entirely secular tribunal whose right to adjudicate in spiritual matters they could more forcefully deny.

Suggested by Bishop Wilberforce, an amendment to achieve this reform was moved by Salisbury in the Lords, but then withdrawn. But the amendment was moved again on 4 July by Gathorne Hardy, another Conservative High-Churchman, in the Commons' committee. The move was supported by members with diverse religious opinions. Gladstone accepted it for the Government, ostensibly on administrative grounds alone. The Commons unanimously agreed to it, to the fury of Archbishop Tait who immediately protested to Gladstone, Gathorne Hardy, and Disraeli. To Gathorne Hardy he wrote: 'To alter the Constitution of the Church . . . without any consultation with the Heads of the Church . . . is itself a very serious matter. I doubt whether any step so grave in the way of disestablishment has yet been taken; for, if the amendment is adopted in its present state, an ecclesiastical cause . . . may be decided, from its first to its last stage, without any ecclesiastic having the power of giving his advice on it.'[16] He told Disraeli that the amendment must have been inspired by influences 'not friendly to the maintenance of the connexion between Church and State'.[17] Tait's attitude, which was shared by other leading Churchmen, had a marked effect. When the Judicature Bill returned to the Lords, a different amendment was substituted, to which Tait had already agreed. Subject to arrangements to be made by the Privy Council, Bishops would still attend the appeal court when ecclesiastical appeals were being

[14] Hamer, op. cit. 137.

[15] Arnstein, *Protestant versus Catholic*, 174–5.

[16] Tait to Gathorne Hardy, 7 July 1873; Cross Papers, Add. MS 51267, fo. 4; Davidson and Benham, *Tait*, ii. 117–22.

[17] Tait to Disraeli, 7 July 1873; DP, B/XXI/T/13.

considered, but only as assessors with an advisory role and not as judges.[18] This policy was suspended when the Conservatives took office and did not become law until 1876. Ecclesiastical appeals, which the 1873 bill had proposed to allocate to the new Court of Appeal, were then transferred back to the Judicial Committee of the Privy Council, with Bishops acting only as assessors. The new system was rather more satisfactory to High-Churchmen but it did nothing to lessen the dispute over judgments on doctrine and ritual.

The Ritualist controversy was indeed rising to a new pitch. On 5 May 1873 the Church Association presented to the two Archbishops a memorial, signed by 60,000 laymen, wanting 'the entire suppression of ceremonies and practices adjudged to be illegal'. As if in defiant reply to this, four days later a petition was presented to the upper (i.e. episcopal) House of the Convocation of Canterbury, signed by 483 clergymen, asking it to consider providing for the education and licensing of 'duly qualified confessors'. The ensuing debate, in which Tait denounced the 'evil' of confession, was not at all favourable to the request. But in their official response the Bishops were restrained, merely referring the petition to a committee. A lengthy delay followed, during which Evangelical indignation was shown at numerous meetings. Lord Shaftesbury chaired one at Exeter Hall in London on 30 June, when he denounced the Bishops for not rejecting the petition out of hand. He was supported in speeches by Newdegate and the Liberal Sir Thomas Chambers, who said 'the peril [to the Church] from Mr. Miall was very little; the peril from this petition was serious and great'.[19] When an episcopal declaration appeared on 23 July it was nothing like as strong as the opponents of confession desired. It said that the Church of England knew nothing of 'sacramental confession', but that the practice of auricular confession, while it should be regarded as exceptional, was not illegal.[20]

Similar caution had marked the reply of Archbishops Tait and Thomson on 16 June to the Church Association memorial. The law should of course be obeyed, but endless litigation should be discouraged. The Bishops should not be 'dragged into an unlimited number of judicial investigations founded upon charges and countercharges made by contending theological parties against their opponents'. Rather should the unfortunate Ritualist developments be checked by 'kindly personal influence in our several families and neighbourhoods'.[21] This was far too mild for the memorialists. Not only did the Church Association demand immediate legislation to enforce liturgical uniformity, but *The Times* said that the Bishops should adopt 'exceptional

---

[18] Marsh, *Victorian Church in Decline,* 129–32; M. D. Stephen, 'Gladstone and the Composition of the Final Court in Ecclesiastical Causes, 1850–1873', *HJ* ix (1966), 198–9.

[19] *The Confessional in the Church of England: A Full Report of the Meeting Held at Exeter Hall,* repr. from *The Rock* (London, 1873); Marsh, op. cit. 132–3; Davidson and Benham, op. cit. ii. 165 ff.; H. H. Maughan, *Some Brighton Churches* (London, 1922), 28–9.

[20] Davidson and Benham, op. cit. ii. 169–70.

[21] Ibid. 116.

measures to repress an exceptional abuse'.[22] Tait, urged on by the Queen, decided to bow to the strength of anti-Ritualist feeling, and at the beginning of 1874 he launched a new legislative attempt to suppress Ritualist practices. Gladstone, being sympathetic to Ritualists, disliked this turn of events. But his electoral defeat, soon after learning of the Bishops' decision to introduce legislation, relieved him of having to oppose the ensuing bill as Prime Minister.

VI. THE 1874 ELECTION

Gladstone's decision to dissolve Parliament was suddenly announced in the press on 24 January. The Government was bidding to reunite its bitterly divided following and obtain a second term in office through the 'positive force' of finance. Gladstone wished to abolish the income tax and reduce local taxation. In order to do this it was necessary to lower Government expenditure, but some ministers resisted economies in their departments, so the Cabinet decided to appeal to the country.[23]

The announcement caught the various Liberal sections unawares, and they were unable to enter the election with the full force of their organizations. The National Education League, the strongest of the dissident pressure groups, had already suspended its electoral activities; it could not suddenly marshal its resources and resume the onslaught of mid-1873. But the League advised its associate organizations to question candidates on their views about educational reform before deciding whether to grant or withhold support. This policy elicited some kind of promise from 300 out of 425 candidates to support the repeal of Clause 25.[24] Other pressure groups, such as the Home Rule organizations, behaved similarly: some Home Rulers of London met in Grafton Hall, Soho, and called on electors to return candidates 'who will support Home Rule for Ireland and amnesty to the political prisoners'.[25]

So the Government's attempt to distract attention from Liberal fissures by a diversion into domestic economy had little success. The aim of extending the franchise to the counties had the support of most Liberals, but education and disestablishment, temperance and foreign policy, Home Rule and trade union demands were divisive issues among Liberals in the election. Unofficial Liberal candidates stood against official ones in thirty-four constituencies, and thirteen Liberal seats were said to have been lost in consequence.[26] 'If the scale be turned against us', Gladstone wrote to Bright, 'it will be by the cases in which undue multiplication of Liberal candidates, or their egotistical or crotchety obtrusion, will have been the means of introducing [i.e. returning] a

[22] Quoted Marsh, op. cit. 133.
[23] W. H. Maehl, 'Gladstone, the Liberals, and the Election of 1874', *Bulletin of the Institute of Historical Research*, xxxvi (1963), 53–65.
[24] Ibid. 66; Adams, op. cit. 300.
[25] *DN*, 26 Jan. 1874.   [26] Maehl, op. cit. 67.

Conservative'.[27] Liberal seats were also lost through the abstention of Liberal voters, or even through their positive support of Conservative candidates. Disraeli's manifesto made the most of the Liberal divisions, accusing some Liberals of voluntaryism, some of republicanism, and some of wanting to thrust religion out of national education.[28]

The electoral activity of the Liberation Society in pursuit of disestablishment paralleled that of the United Kingdom Alliance in support of the Permissive Bill to restrict drink sales.[29] A committee of the Baptist Union called for disestablishment as well as educational and burials reform.[30] The Liberation Society executive committee had decided on the broad lines of electoral policy as early as June, and had appointed an electoral committee in July.[31] In January the Society issued a circular saying that candidates should be pressed to espouse burial reform, abolition of clerical fellowships at the universities, repeal of Clause 25, universal establishment of school boards, and disestablishment.[32] Such demands for religious equality had been ignored in Gladstone's address, as Nonconformist committees repeatedly noted. Nonconformist division, however, was still very clear, and radically different views were expressed by leading Dissenters on whether or not to heed Gladstone's call for unity. Guinness Rogers, a prominent Congregationalist, might say that in the absence of adequate assurances from Gladstone there would be many Nonconformist abstentions from the polls, but Baldwin Brown (another leading Congregationalist) thought the Education Act liberal on the whole and was 'profoundly thankful that the Government was able to do so much'.[33]

Where the Liberation Society trod the Church Defence Institution was not slow to follow, even if it had much less money than its rival to prosecute campaigns. During the election the Institution circulated a list of 126 MPs who had supported at least one of Miall's motions, and who were therefore to be opposed. There was also issued an address of the London Working-men's Council for Church Defence, urging a 'right' use of the franchise.[34]

Anti-Ritualism was considerably in evidence in the election. A conference of Nonconformist committees at Crewe on 27 January noted that 'the sacerdotal pretensions of a large section of the Established Church are provoking the utmost distrust, hostility and indignation'.[35] On the other hand, defence of the established Church was sometimes linked with defence of Protestantism.

---

[27] Gladstone to Bright, 5 Feb. 1874; Bright Papers, 43385, fos. 249–50.

[28] *DN*, 26 Jan. 1874, p. 5.

[29] A. E. Dingle, *The Campaign for Prohibition in England: The United Kingdom Alliance, 1872–1895* (London, 1980), 50–2.

[30] *Baptist Handbook* (1875), 38.

[31] LS, 9 June, 14 July 1873; v. 36, 39, 49–50.

[32] *Pall Mall Gazette*, 22 Jan. 1874, p. 7.

[33] Correspondence of Guinness Rogers, Baldwin Brown, and others in *DN*, 30 Jan. 1874, p. 5, 31 Jan., p. 5, 2 Feb., p. 3.

[34] Tracts of CDI (London, 1874).

[35] *DN*, 28 Jan. 1874, p. 3.

Viscount Sandon, for example, told the Liverpool electors that, while he was firmly attached to the established Church, he was also convinced that 'obedience to law on the part of the clergy, and faithfulness to the principles of the Reformation, are absolutely essential to the maintenance of her position'.[36] Branches of the Church Association asked candidates whether they would support legislation to suppress confession and expel 'Romish doctrines and practices from the Church of England', and a gratifying response was claimed.[37] Meetings in London at St James's Hall and Exeter Hall on 27 January condemned Ultramontanism and praised Bismarck's anti-Catholic drive. Newdegate, seconding one of the resolutions, said the Pope was 'endeavouring to enforce slavery on mankind'. An answering Roman Catholic meeting was held on 6 February.[38] The Protestant Evangelical Mission and Electoral Union, the body which had sponsored William Murphy, recommended that candidates should only be supported if they promised to protect Catholics from 'tyranny and fraud' by the Pope's agents, to give full legal protection to nuns kept in convents against their will, and to support the repeal of the Relief Act of 1829.[39]

There was considerable rioting during the elections. Outbreaks occurred in Glamorgan, Wolverhampton, Sunderland, Stalybridge, Chesterfield, and Stoke-on-Trent, with much damage to property and injury to the public and police.[40] But brief demonstrations of physical violence were less of a worry to the Government than divisions among those whose votes they wanted in order to stay in office. Differences over the issues already noted were frequently displayed in the constituencies. The Liberal candidate for Brecon Boroughs could not, as an Anglican, bring himself to support disestablishment but condemned the disruptive tendencies of the Ritualists who were 'unconsciously doing their best to destroy the hold of the Church upon the nation'. The Conservative candidates for Middlesex were closely questioned on their attitude to Ritualism.[41] The concern over Ultramontanism was shown on many occasions, sometimes in association with antipathy to Home Rule. Edward Ellice, Liberal candidate for the St Andrews Burghs, distrusted 'the encroaching pretensions of the Church of Rome', and was prepared to resist concessions to that Church 'whether in educational measures or in the more open form of the demand for a separate Irish legislature'.[42] Sir Thomas Chambers, standing as a Liberal at Marylebone, was convinced that 'our liberty, both civil and religious, depends on the emphatic repudiation of Ultramontane pretensions'. W. H. Gladstone, the premier's eldest son,

[36] Ibid. 3 Feb. 1874, p. 7.

[37] Lida E. Ellsworth, *Charles Lowder and the Ritualist Movement* (London, 1982), 128.

[38] *DN*, 28 Jan. 1874, p. 3; *T*, 7 Feb. 1874, p. 9; J. L. Altholz, 'The Vatican Decrees Controversy, 1874–1875', *Catholic Historical Review*, lvii (1971–2), 596.

[39] Arnstein, op. cit. 176.

[40] *AR* cxvi (1874), 10; *T*, 5 Feb. 1874, p. 9; *DN*, 4 Feb. 1874, p. 3, 6 Feb. 1874, p. 2.

[41] *DN*, 30 Jan. 1874, p.7, 9 Feb. 1874, p. 2.

[42] *Dundee Advertiser*, 27 Jan. 1874, p. 1.

speaking in support of a Perthshire candidate, strongly denied that his father had Roman Catholic sympathies and, for good measure, said that the premier's character was 'like polished marble, to which neither dust nor dirt could stick'.[43]

In some areas with sizeable Catholic populations, Liberal disunity was illustrated by division over Catholic interests in Home Rule and denominational education. In Glasgow, added to the five Liberal candidates was an independent Catholic candidate, the Hon. Francis Kerr, who supported Home Rule. There were between four and five thousand Catholic electors (about ten per cent of the total), and most of their support was given to Kerr, who received 4,003 plumpers and 4,444 total votes. Priests were said to have intervened openly and this may have lent support to Bright's comment to Gladstone that Catholic electors 'vote as the Priests tell them, and the Priests are for public money for Catholic schools, and they have no politics apart from the Church'.[44] Kerr did not come near being elected, but he removed some support from the Liberals and helped one Conservative to be returned—Alexander Whitelaw, a firm defender of the established Church and the first of his party to succeed in 'radical Glasgow' since 1832. This indirect Catholic aid to the Conservatives was ironic, for an Orange propagandist had urged Protestant voters to support the Conservative candidates against 'secularism, mammon, and Popery'.[45] A Liberal paper commented on the result: 'the evil effects of want of union and proper organization among the Liberals have been strikingly exemplified at Glasgow. With good management the three seats might have been secured; but from the first the Liberals have been hopelessly divided.[46]

In Liverpool dissension broke out in the Catholic Club when younger Irish members proposed to put up a Catholic and Home Rule candidate against the Liberals, William Rathbone and W. S. Caine. These were both Nonconformists and were being pressed to pledge their support to the repeal of Clause 25. Catholics wanted to keep the clause because it gave rate aid towards the fees of poor children at Catholic schools. A Catholic deputation was dissatisfied with an interview with the local Liberal Association leaders, and in the Catholic Club it was decided by a vote of thirty-nine to thirty-seven to nominate a Catholic candidate. Another deputation was sent to the Liberal candidates, and many Catholics—particularly those who belonged to the Home Rule Association— were still dissatisfied with the answers they received. An attempt to sponsor a Home Rule candidate failed, whereupon the Home Rule Association advised its supporters to abstain, and this counsel was partially successful. In the Scotland ward, containing a high proportion of Irish, only sixty-three per cent of the

[43] DN, 27 Jan. 1874, p. 2, 7 Feb. 1874, p. 2.
[44] Catriona Levy, 'Conservatism and Liberal Unionism in Glasgow, 1874–1912', Ph.D. thesis (Dundee, 1983), 45 ff. Bright to Gladstone, 26 Jan. 1874; Quoted John P. Rossi, 'English Catholics, the Liberal Party, and the General Election of 1880', Catholic Historical Review, lxiii (1977), 412.
[45] Scotsman, 5 Feb. 1874, p. 4.
[46] Dundee Advertiser, 6 Feb. 1874, p. 2.

Irish electors voted, and W. S. Caine was defeated though Rathbone was returned as the minority Liberal member along with two Conservatives. Lord Sandon, a firm defender of the establishment and of denominational schools, received the largest number of votes ever yet obtained by a borough member. No doubt some Catholics supported him for educational reasons.[47]

At other places—Edinburgh, Manchester, Salford, and Wigan—there were signs of Catholic support for the Conservatives, either on educational grounds or to give Liberals a sharp demonstration of Home Rule strength.[48] In Cardiff priests urged the Catholic electorate of 520 (out of 6,500) to vote Conservative, but the local Home Rule Association none the less supported the Liberal after he had declared belatedly for their cause. The Catholic vote was split, but the Liberal squeezed home by nine votes.[49]

Liberal fragmentation was also shown by the behaviour of Nonconformist voters, reacting to the education, disestablishment, and temperance issues. The Liberal Edward Baines lost his seat at Leeds because he supported the 1870 Education Act and because of the intervention of an extreme temperance candidate.[50] The Central Nonconformist Committee called on Dissenters not to support a candidate who refused to pledge himself to repeal of Clause 25, to universal school boards, and to denial of Parliamentary grants to new denominational schools.[51] The Liberal Ministers made some vague conciliatory gestures during the election, and Robert Lowe even advocated repeal of the 25th clause, but these moves were too late to save Liberal disruption. Numerous Liberal candidates, sometimes at the request of Nonconformist committees, declared themselves in favour of repealing Clause 25 and for other changes desired by the League.[52] Some declared for English and Scottish disestablishment and the burials bill, either together with the educational demands or separately.[53] Others supported repeal of the 25th clause and a burials bill but could not stretch to support of disestablishment.[54]

Conservative candidates usually defended the 1870 Education Act and the union between Church and State, though some also wanted reform of the Church in order to make her more 'the Church of the people'.[55] The

---

[47] Burke, *Liverpool*, 211–14; *DN*, 7 Feb. 1874, p. 2.

[48] *Scotsman*, 7 Feb. 1874, p. 4; *Dundee Advertiser*, 6 Feb. 1874, p. 2; Greenall, 'Popular Conservatism in Salford', 137.

[49] *DN*, 14 Feb. 1874, p. 2.

[50] A. W. Roberts, 'Leeds Liberalism and Late Victorian Politics', *Northern History*, v (1970), 132.

[51] Taylor, 'National Education, 1867–1877', 223.

[52] e.g. Sir John Lubbock (Maidstone), *DN*, 27 Jan. 1874, p. 2; Edward Marjoribanks (West Kent), ibid. 28 Jan., p. 7; Address of South Essex Nonconformist Committee, ibid. 3 Feb., p. 3; Hargest, 'The Welsh Educational Alliance', 203.

[53] e.g. Henry Labouchere (Southwark), *DN*, 27 Jan. 1874, p. 2; B. Whitworth (Monmouthshire), ibid. 16 Jan., p. 3; George Odger and Andrew Dunn (Southwark), ibid. 28 Jan., p. 7; J. Fortescue-Harrison (Kilmarnock Burghs), *Scotsman*, 2 Feb., p. 2.

[54] e.g. Viscount Enfield (Middlesex), *DN*, 10 Feb. 1874, p. 2.

[55] e.g. William Grantham (E. Surrey), ibid. 27 Jan. 1874, p. 7; Thomas Halsey and Abel Smith (Herts.), ibid. 29 Jan., p. 7.

Conservative candidates for South Essex promised 'a most uncompromising opposition to the disestablishment of our National Church, believing that it would involve the downfall of our Monarchy and the destruction of the Constitution, besides removing one of the greatest safeguards against infidelity and communism.'[56] The Scottish establishment, like the English, was defended by Conservative candidates. Some of these advocated Church reform through the abolition of patronage and some also condemned the reduced security of religious education under the Scottish Education Act of 1872.[57]

The contests in which the great rivals Forster and Chamberlain stood—at Bradford and Sheffield respectively—were fiercely fought. At Bradford there was no Conservative candidate but four Liberals competed for the two seats. The moderates Forster and Ripley were supported by Anglicans and Catholics who were anxious to preserve denominational education, but opposed by militant Dissenters and Catholic Home Rulers who gave their support to J. V. Godwin and James Hardaker, who were for disestablishment and Home Rule. The moderates won, though perhaps only with Tory votes.[58] At Sheffield there was a similar division of Liberal forces, and again no Conservative candidate unless J. A. Roebuck (formerly a radical but now practically a Tory) be counted as such. Henry Joseph Wilson, a Congregationalist and very active radical, had formed the Sheffield Reform Association in March 1873 as a breakaway group from the Sheffield Liberal Association. The new body's programme included disestablishment, universal school boards, and compulsory attendance, and the Parliamentary vote for all female householders. Chamberlain was sponsored as a candidate by this body, and he wanted to broaden his campaign from a purely educational one in order to gain working-class support. He had told John Morley in August: 'I have long felt that there is not enough force in the Education question to make it the sole fighting issue for our friends. From the commencement it has failed to evoke any great popular enthusiasm. Education for the ignorant cannot have the meaning that belonged to "Bread for the Starving".'[59] He expected a Conservative victory in the country as a whole, but said: 'if we can only break the power of the "moderates"—the respectable Whigs—and leave Toryism and Radicalism face to face, there will soon be an end of reaction'.[60] However, despite having a broad programme which included 'free land' and better conditions for trade unions as well as disestablishment, Chamberlain was defeated by Roebuck and Mundella who were supported by Anglican and Catholic voters.[61]

[56] Ibid. 27 Jan. 1874, p. 7.

[57] e.g. R. Baillie Hamilton (Berwick-on-Tweed), *Scotsman*, 2 Feb. 1874, p. 2; G. H. S. Douglas (Roxburghshire), ibid.

[58] D. G. Wright, 'Politics and Opinion in Nineteenth-century Bradford, 1832–1880', Ph.D. thesis (Leeds, 1966), 912 ff., 932–3.

[59] M. Hurst, 'Liberal versus Liberal: The General Election of 1874 in Bradford and Sheffield', *HJ* xv (1972), 685–9; Garvin, op. cit. i. 146.

[60] Garvin, op. cit. i. 161.

[61] Fletcher, 'Sheffield Liberalism, 1849–1886', 119–28; Fowler, *Radicalism and Dissent*, 42–6.

So it was that Liberal disunity over education, disestablishment, Home Rule, the drink trade and other questions helped to bring about a Conservative victory by an overall majority of fifty. The enormous inequalities in representation meant that there was no relation between the number of votes and seats obtained: in England and Wales the Liberals had a majority of the votes while the Conservatives had a majority of 105 seats.[62] The radical reaction against moderate Liberals—indicated by the fact that in thirty-four constituencies more Liberals stood than there were seats available[63]—added to a drift of right-wing Liberals towards Conservatism to produce the election result. Calls for Liberal unity had been made—the *Daily News,* for example, had urged that Forster's education policy should be temporarily forgotten in order to avert the worse evil of a Conservative Government[64]—but these had been far from adequately heeded. Even Scotland and Wales, while retaining Liberal majorities, had Conservative gains of twelve and four respectively. In Ireland the return of fifty-seven Home Rulers displeased Conservatives and Liberals alike, and only twelve Liberals were returned from Ireland.

The Conservative victory gratified Church defenders such as Canon Ryle, who said the House of Commons was now more friendly to the Church establishment since there had last been a Conservative majority in 1846. Ryle also asserted that while the immediate peril had gone, the Church could not afford to be complacent: 'As long as that restless and gifted Statesman lives who planned and executed the Disestablishment of the Irish Church, so long we are never safe'.[65] To Chamberlain, on the other hand, the Liberals' fall had come directly from 'the meanest manifesto that has ever proceeded from a great minister'.[66] But the radical sections of the party had done better than the Whigs, most of the Conservative gains having been from the latter.[67] The *Nonconformist* did not consider the result as necessarily a set-back for disestablishment since Gladstone had not only declined to champion this cause but had seriously impeded it. Five years of Tory rule, said this paper, might serve religious equality better than five years of a Liberal administration having no sympathy with disestablishment: 'we are no longer linked to allies anxious to disarm us'.[68] Three more dissenters were returned for Welsh constituencies, and the total number of Nonconformist MPs showed no diminution. The Liberation Society claimed that ninety MPs in the new House were favourable to disestablishment.[69] The National Education League was also not without success. Of the 300 candidates who had pledged support to the repeal of Clause

[62] John Jenkins to Gladstone, 8 Apr. 1874; GP, 44443, fos. 131–2.
[63] W. H. Maehl, op. cit. 67.
[64] *DN,* 28 Jan. 1874, p. 4.
[65] J. C. Ryle, *Disestablishment: What Would Come of It?* (London, 1874), 30 f.
[66] Chamberlain to Revd Henry Allon, 13 Feb. 1874; quoted Newton, op. cit. 99. Cf. John P. Rossi, *The Transformation of the British Liberal Party, 1874–1880* (Philadelphia, 1978), 10.
[67] Southgate, *Passing of the Whigs,* 353–4; Adams, *The Elementary School Contest,* 301.
[68] *Nonconformist,* 18 Feb. 1874 (xxxiv. 145), 25 Feb. (ibid. 169).
[69] Morgan, *Wales in British Politics,* 38.

25, 167 were elected, though only about a third of these accepted the full League aims of secular, free, and compulsory education, and universal school boards.[70]

The League, the Liberation Society, and the temperance United Kingdom Alliance could claim to have taught the Liberal Government a lesson. But it has been pointed out that the efforts of all of the pressure groups combined supporting their own candidates, are not enough by themselves to explain the Liberal defeat.[71] There were further reasons for the Conservative success, including a reaction against radical demands for reform, and in any case a Conservative victory was a very hollow triumph for radicals. In the contest over education, disestablishment, and other questions neither the Liberal leadership nor their radical opponents had won, and their relationship had to be worked out afresh during the new Conservative ministry.

[70] P. C. Griffiths, 'The Origins and Development of the National Liberal Federation to 1886', B.Litt. thesis (Oxford, 1973), 77.

[71] Dingle, op. cit. 53. Cf. Hamer, *Electoral Pressure*, 137–8.

CHAPTER III

Disraeli and the Churches, 1874–1880

I. INTRODUCTORY

GLADSTONE resigned on 17 February after his defeat, and Disraeli kissed hands the following day. A Conservative Government might have seemed likely to stabilize the ecclesiastical situation but this did not happen. It was true that voluntaries and radical educationalists could hope for little during Conservative rule, and it was five years before the Liberals were able to attain unity and proceed to regain power. On the other hand the Churches of England and Scotland gained nothing but trouble from the Government's main ecclesiastical measures, though these were intended to help them.

The new Government had a much more united following than its predecessor. But divisions were marked at the outset, even if they lessened later on, and the dissensions were caused mainly by religion. Disraeli managed to persuade Salisbury and Carnarvon, who had resigned from the previous Conservative ministry over Parliamentary reform in 1867, to take office in the new one. But both were High-Churchmen, and they were concerned about prospective legislation against Ritualism. Not only the political past but the religious future affected Salisbury, who had made a speech advocating considerable Ritualist liberty at the Church Congress in 1873.[1] He told his wife that for seven years he had been determined not to serve under Disraeli, and was still most unwilling to do so. But he was pressed to take office not only by Carnarvon but by Sir William Heathcote, 'almost the only man in England whose political judgement in party questions I much respect—and who hates D[israeli] as much as I do'.[2] On 15 February he wrote: 'the prospect of having to serve with this man again is like a nightmare'.[3] But the previous day he had told Lord Derby that he was satisfied with the prospective Government's policies, except on 'the religious point', about which he had to ask Disraeli.[4] Regarding the Ritualists he had 'no fancy for the idiots themselves', but 'any attack on them would certainly break up the Church of England'.[5]

---

[1] *Popery in the Church of England: A Joint Letter by Five Wesleyan Ministers* (London, 1873).

[2] Salisbury to Lady Salisbury, 10 Feb. 1874; Lady Gwendolen Cecil, *Life of Robert, Marquess of Salisbury* (4 vols., London, 1921–32), ii. 44.

[3] Salisbury to Lady Salisbury, 15 Feb. 1874; ibid. 46.

[4] Ibid. 47; Salisbury to Carnarvon, 15 Feb. 1874; Carnarvon Papers, Add. MS 60758, fos. 127–8.

[5] Salisbury to Lady Salisbury, 15 Feb. 1874; Cecil, op. cit. ii. 47. Cf. E. J. Feuchtwanger, *Disraeli, Democracy, and the Tory Party* (Oxford, 1968), 41–2.

Salisbury had a decisive interview with Disraeli on 17 February and accepted office. 'As far as words went', he told Lady Salisbury, 'he [Disraeli] pledged himself that the Government would introduce or, as a Government, support no measure against the Ritualists. He . . . professed himself a High-Churchman, but said he intended in his patronage to give fair representation to all schools in the Church.' Salisbury added that the only Cabinet colleagues he could depend on in religious matters were Carnarvon and Gathorne Hardy.[6]

Besides the admission of these High-Churchmen to the Cabinet, two High-Church peers (Lords Bath and Beauchamp) were given royal household appointments in spite of Queen Victoria's well-known antipathy to Ritualism. 'I am sure they will feel it a matter of duty not to put themselves forward in Church matters in a sense disapproved of by the Queen', Salisbury assured the premier. The Queen herself might be dissuaded from advocating an anti-Ritualist measure by the adverse implications: 'the Ritualist party . . . if driven by any act of serious aggression, will listen to its most reckless advisers, and throw itself on the Free Church side'. The Bishops, he added, 'are at some work which may be dangerous'.[7] This 'work' was their decision to introduce a measure of the very kind which Ritualists would think an 'act of serious aggression', namely the Public Worship Regulation Bill. If Disraeli was a High-Churchman, as he told Salisbury, he was able to conceal it very effectively; and the Government's eventual support for this bill greatly strained relations again between Salisbury and his leader.

II. PUBLIC WORSHIP REGULATION, 1874 AND AFTER

Lord Shaftesbury had failed to pass a bill controlling Ritualism, and Archbishop Tait had long talked of the need for such a measure. It was finally the Queen who gave the initial impetus to a bill which got through Parliament. While receiving a discouraging reply from Gladstone about anti-Ritualist legislation,[8] she was having much more success with Tait. The Archbishop was with her at Osborne early in January, and on the 15th she wrote to him that something must be done to check Ritualism. Other influences, for example a Church Association petition to the Bishops for legislation 'against changes which tend to obscure the work of the Reformation', probably also helped Tait to decide that a bill should be brought in. He announced this proposal at a large meeting of Bishops of both provinces of the Church of England at Lambeth Palace on 13 and 14 January, and nearly all present agreed. News of this decision was soon conveyed by Bishop Ellicott to Disraeli and later to

---

[6] Salisbury to Lady Salisbury, 18 Feb. 1874 (Cecil, op. cit. ii. 50); Sir A. Hardinge, *The Life of Henry H. M. Herbert, Fourth Earl of Carnarvon* (3 vols., London, 1925), ii. 61–2.

[7] Salisbury to Disraeli, 22 Feb. 1874; DP, B/XX/Ce/170.

[8] Gladstone to the Queen, 22 Jan. 1874; D. C. Lathbury (ed.), *Correspondence on Church and Religion of William Ewart Gladstone* (2 vols., London, 1910), i. 383–4.

Salisbury.[9] The bill which emerged was Tait's work, but it was to be greatly changed before it passed and consequently lost some episcopal support. At the end of Disraeli's first week as premier Tait sent him a memorandum, dated 24 February, making some moderate suggestions for increased discipline. Diocesan boards should be created, composed of equal numbers of clergy and laity, to advise the Bishop in disputes over ceremonial. If the Bishop's monition to a clergyman was not obeyed, the incumbent could lose his benefice, subject to appeal to the Archbishop of the province.

Tait's proposal, accompanied by a request for Government support, was most embarrassing to Disraeli. He told Lady Bradford that the matter was 'the hardest nut to crack that ever was the lot of a Minister'. The members of his Cabinet were of diverse religious views, and, as already seen, he had obtained the service of some High-Churchmen partly by saying that the Government would not introduce or support an anti-Ritualist measure. Disraeli's colleagues therefore reacted in different ways when consulted about Tait's intention. The Earl of Derby supported Tait, but Salisbury, Gathorne Hardy, and Carnarvon were firmly opposed. Although Disraeli did eventually support a modified measure, at this stage he was carefully neutral and (though anti-Ritualist himself) only barely inclined to support legislation.[10]

Tait did not introduce his bill in Parliament until 20 April, but his intentions became public knowledge well before then, and there was considerable time for attitudes to form outside Parliament before the bill was debated within. Tait asked *The Times* to inform the public, and this paper produced articles on 10 and 13 March explaining and commending the measure. Response was immediate, especially from High-Churchmen who disliked the proposals. H. P. Liddon saw Salisbury, Gladstone, and Sir Robert Phillimore, and all three expressed opposition. Liddon then wrote on 14 March to Hon. Charles Wood, president of the English Church Union, trying to stir up resistance. Opponents should not wait, he said, until the bill was drafted, as it was 'easier to destroy such a creature in the embryonic stage than after birth'. But he also stressed the need to check excessive Ritualist practice lest it be used to support the bill.[11] Liddon and Pusey wrote jointly on 14 March to A. H. Mackonochie about the need to restrain ritual in order to disarm the attack, but Mackonochie refused to give up any of his own elaborate practice at St Alban's.[12] Mackonochie was

[9] Notes on Bishops' meeting in Tait Papers, 203, fos. 113–20 (Cf. ibid. 123–4); C. J. Ellicott to Disraeli, 24 Jan. 1874; DP, B/XII/F/1a; Ellicott to Salisbury, 21 and 23 Feb. 1874; SP.

[10] P. T. Marsh, *The Victorian Church in Decline: Archbishop Tait and the Church of England, 1868–1882* (London, 1969), 159–65; G. E. Buckle, *The Life of Benjamin Disraeli, Earl of Beaconsfield*, v (London, 1920), 315–17; memo of Tait to Disraeli, 24 Feb. 1874; DP, B/XII/F/3; Note by Salisbury on Tait's memo, 2 Mar. 1874; ibid. B/XII/Ce/178; undated memo in Carnarvon Papers; Derby to Disraeli, 3 Mar. 1874; DP, B/XII/F/34; A. E. Gathorne-Hardy, *Gathorne Hardy, First Earl of Cranbrook* (2 vols., London, 1910), i. 338–42.

[11] J. O. Johnston, *Life and Letters of Henry Parry Liddon* (London, 1904), 176–8.

[12] H. P. Liddon, *The Life of Edward Bouverie Pusey*, ed. J. O. Johnston and R. J. Wilson (4 vols., London, 1893–7), iv. 273–4.

particularly defiant at this time because the Church Association was prosecuting him again: this later resulted in his condemnation on most of the contested points and suspension for six weeks in 1875. Pusey, who disliked extreme Ritualism but wanted to protect the doctrine which lay behind it, wrote three long letters to *The Times*, appearing on 19, 24, and 30 March. He made a conciliatory proposal: instead of the diocesan board suggested by Tait, the joint wishes of incumbent and congregation should guide the Bishop in making a decision.[13] Less conciliatory, however, was Mackonochie. He knew from experience, he wrote to *The Times*, that compromise would not prevent attack. 'Low' ceremonial annoyed Ritualists as much as Ritualism annoyed Low-Churchmen, and all he could advocate was mutual toleration.[14]

In late March and early April Tait corresponded frequently with Disraeli about his Bill. Lord Chancellor Cairns, with Disraeli's support, made important alterations to the measure. The diocesan board composed equally of clergy and laity became a board of assessors consisting of the Dean, an Archdeacon, and a lawyer. Complaints about illegalities alone would be considered by the board, and only if the Bishop authorized it to do so. Appeals would go not to the Archbishop but to the Judicial Committee of the Privy Council.[15] The Bishops accepted the revised bill at a meeting on 17 April.

In the Lords the bill was to be changed more fundamentally by Lord Shaftesbury, aided by Cairns. Tait's speech introducing the bill on 20 April gave examples of extreme Ritualist practice and made it clear that suppression of Ritualism was the main intention, thus ensuring that the controversy intensified outside Parliament. The second reading was postponed until 11 May so that the Convocations would have time to express their opinions. Both Convocations disapproved of the bill, and the Lower House of the Canterbury Convocation suggested numerous alterations. Some of these Tait accepted. Three parishioners instead of one were to be required to make a complaint, and the Bishop's advisory board was replaced by the diocesan chancellor or one assessor.

Shaftesbury, Salisbury, and others objected to the second reading on diverse grounds, but the reading was allowed to pass without division so that the changes could be incorporated.[16] The committee stage was therefore the crucial one in the Lords. After a motion by the Duke of Marlborough to reject the measure was crushed by 137 votes to twenty-nine, the bill went into committee on 4 June. Shaftesbury had previously expressed his dislike of the power given to Bishops by the bill, on the ground that Bishops could not be impartial judges. He now had an important amendment accepted, by a vote of 112 to thirteen, to

[13] Marsh, op. cit. 166.

[14] Ibid.

[15] Ibid. 172; Tait to Disraeli, 4 and 14 Apr. 1874; DP, B/XII/F/8; L. E. Ellsworth, *Charles Lowder and the Ritualist Movement* (London, 1982), 128.

[16] *AR* cxvi (1874), 69–76; H ccxviii. 786–808, ccxix. 2–65; Bishop W. C. Magee to Revd J. C. MacDonnell, 14 May 1874; Macdonnell, *Magee*, ii. 5–8.

substitute for the Bishops a single well-paid lay judge, to be appointed by the two Archbishops and to act in both provinces. Each case of complaint, unless it was vetoed by the Bishop or it was determined that the latter should settle it, would be decided by this judge. Secular authority was thus replacing ecclesiastical, and the Erastian tendency seemed to be confirmed by the allocation of appeals to the Judicial Committee. A process of monition and suspension would follow and—if disobedience persisted after three years— deprivation of the living. Archbishops Tait and Thomson and thirteen Bishops reluctantly voted for the amendment rather than abandon the bill. If the bill was given up a more drastic anti-Ritualist measure, now before the Commons and promoted by the Church Association, might be swept through by ultra-Protestant feeling, and the Church would be much more disturbed. But Tait refused to abandon the episcopal veto, which Shaftesbury would have liked to remove.[17]

On the third reading on 25 June, further criticism came from Salisbury, Bath, Marlborough, Bishop Wordsworth of Lincoln, and others. But none of these attempted the seemingly hopeless task of trying to defeat the bill. The third reading was therefore carried without division and the bill—which to at least one observer seemed no longer Tait's but Shaftesbury's—was sent down to the Commons.[18]

Meanwhile High-Church opposition was abundantly shown. The president of the English Church Union complained to Gladstone about the bill and likened it to the contemporary German measures in the *Kulturkampf*. W. F. Hook, the old Dean of Chichester, also complained to the ex-premier about a bill which, he alleged, was 'supported by the Ministers of a Presbyterian Queen . . . introduced by the Primate, a Scotch Presbyterian, and ammended [*sic*] by a bitter Dissenter like Lord Shaftesbury'. Liddon told Malcolm MacColl that the bill was 'a cheap and easy method of crushing the High Church School', and that 'we may look forward to the worst'.[19] The English Church Union circulated petitions, held meetings and arranged for a deputation led by the Duke of Marlborough to see the Prime Minister.[20] A large gathering, together with an overflow meeting, was held by the Union in St James's Hall on 16 June. Meetings at 167 places sent delegates to this assembly, which was addressed by Pusey, Liddon, and Archdeacon G. A. Denison amongst others. Four resolutions were adopted, one of which protested against 'any Parliamentary legislation on the subject of Ritual, apart from the previous

[17] *AR* cxvi. 76; H ccxix. 920–65; R. T. Davidson and W. Benham, *The Life of Archibald Campbell Tait, Archbishop of Canterbury* (2 vols., London, 1891), ii. 211; Marsh, op. cit. 177–9.
[18] H ccxx. 390–413; Ellsworth, op. cit. 130; Marsh, op. cit. 181.
[19] Hon. C. L. Wood to Gladstone, 7 June 1874; GP, 44187, fos. 1–4; Wood to Tait, 5 May 1874; Tait Papers, 204, fos. 71–2; Hook to Gladstone, 10 June 1874; ibid. 44213, fo. 206; G. W. E. Russell (ed.), *Malcolm MacColl: Memoirs and Correspondence* (London, 1914), 337.
[20] ECU Minutes, 7 and 12 May 1874; CU dep. 12, pp. 14–16; J. Bentley, *Ritualism and Politics in Victorian Britain: The Attempt to Legislate for Belief* (Oxford, 1978), 52.

consent of the Church given after due deliberation in her Synods'.[21] The bill,
said Charles Wood at an ECU anniversary meeting on the same day, transferred
'from the Church to the State the supreme authority in matters of faith'.

Conservative Ritualists threatened to vote Liberal and press for
disestablishment.[22] Malcolm MacColl, a Liberal High-Churchman, told
Gladstone that the Bishops through their ill-advised bill had brought
disestablishment nearer, and it was essential to try and remove them from the
House of Lords.[23] Liddon, MacColl, and others were anxious that Gladstone
should attack the bill in the Commons.[24] All this High-Church opposition was
of course countered by support for the bill. Bishop Magee wrote to *The Times*
against Pusey's letters, and the 202 local branches of the Church Association
were urged to oppose the tactics of the ECU.[25]

When the bill entered the Commons its lengthy progress became hurried as
the session would end in a month. Tait told Disraeli that if the bill did not pass
that session the disputes would become much greater.[26] But the bitter
controversy which had been growing outside Parliament now sharply
penetrated its walls. Fierce intra-party clashes took place, showing that, with
religion transcending politics, Ritualism could cause deep divisions regardless
of party political ties.

The second reading in the Commons was moved on 9 July, and an
amendment was proposed that the bill be rescinded. Gladstone then spoke—
three days after he had emerged from his semi-retirement to denounce the
Scottish Church Patronage Bill. He had shown great interest in Tait's bill for a
long time, and expressed dislike of it in a letter to Lord Granville on 7 May.[27]
High-Churchmen had, as already mentioned, been urging him to attack the bill
in the Commons. Like Pusey and Salisbury, Gladstone did not think that
elaborate ritual was a necessary demonstration of doctrine. But he came to
sympathize more with Ritualism, especially when he scented persecution. 'My
sympathy with the Ritualists', he said in 1878, 'is founded entirely on the one-
sided, shabby, cruel treatment of them'.[28] In a speech of fiery eloquence which

[21] *Report of Speeches Made at the Meeting of the English Church Union, 16 June 1874* (London, 1874),
43 (speeches repr. from *Guardian*, 17 June 1874); *Church Union Gazette*, suppl. 1 July 1874, p. 206; ECU
Minutes, 16 June 1874; CU dep. 4, 177–8.
[22] Revd. G. D. Tinling to H. Drummond Wolff, 26 June 1874; DP, B/XII/F/51a; Revd
J. M. Rodwell to Gladstone, 27 June 1874; GP, 44443, fo. 316; J. E. Gorst to Disraeli, 29 July 1874,
with enclosure; DP, B/XII/F/66. Cf. Revd W. J. Tracey to Tait, 4 May 1874; Tait Papers, 204, fos.
61–2.
[23] MacColl to Gladstone, 11 June 1874; GP, 44243, fos. 322–3.
[24] G. W. E. Russell, op. cit. 338; MacColl to Gladstone, 8 July 1874; GP, 44243, fos. 327–30; Sir
Robert Phillimore to Gladstone, 26 June 1874, ibid. 44278, fo. 143; Revd J. M. Rodwell to Gladstone, 27
June 1874, ibid. 44443, fo. 315.
[25] J. Bentley, op. cit. 52.
[26] Tait to Disraeli, 8 July 1874; DP, B/XII/F/16.
[27] Agatha Ramm (ed.), *The Political Correspondence of Mr Gladstone and Lord Granville, 1868–1876*,
Camden 3rd ser. (2 vols., London, 1952), ii. 451–3.
[28] Quoted Lathbury, op. cit. i. 376.

won praise for its ability even from strong opponents (though Shaftesbury condemned it as 'an ultramontane address'),[29] Gladstone denounced the bill for attempting to establish rigid liturgical uniformity. In the name of freedom he pleaded for the retention of diversity of ritual based on local tradition, and could not agree that 'in the services of the Church of England all unlawful omissions and commissions shall be deliberately and advisedly put down'.

Gladstone concluded by reading six long resolutions containing the principles which he thought should guide legislation. The resolutions were probably meant to provoke debates long enough to 'talk out' the bill for that session.[30] But the House, led by Sir William Harcourt (Gladstone's ex-ministerial colleague) would have none of this. Harcourt's Whig, Protestant, and Erastian approach to religion differed completely from Gladstone's Tractarian love of spiritual independence. Their religious difference had already led to conflict between them over the 1870 Education Act.[31] Gladstone, said Harcourt, had rejected uniformity in his speech, but the Church of England was founded on successive Acts of Uniformity. The diversity which Gladstone upheld—'the individual judgement and personal license of particular priests'—could not be reconciled with the principle of a national Church. Parliament must regulate the unhappy situation by reasserting 'the unalterable attachment of the English people to the principles of the English Reformation . . . we must not set up the dangerous doctrine of optional conformity, which would allow any priest to do what he pleased and to set at defiance those principles of the Reformation which for three centuries have been established by the law of England'.[32] Harcourt's sentiments (which he also expressed in letters to *The Times*) obviously appealed strongly to the Commons and to many Protestants outside.[33] When Gathorne Hardy opposed the bill in the next speech he met loud disapproval from his own side of the House. Later speeches confirmed the division of opinion among both Conservatives and Liberals. Also divided were Nonconformists, some of whom followed an anti-Ritualist line while others defended religious liberty and diversity against the measure.[34]

Towards the end of the debate on 15 July, Disraeli spoke clearly in the bill's favour. This followed an agreement in Cabinet four days before (with Salisbury reluctantly adhering) to give the bill every facility in what was left of the session.[35] The bill's primary object, said Disraeli, was 'to put down Ritualism'.

[29] Shaftesbury's diary, 18 July 1874; E. Hodder, *The Life and Work of the Seventh Earl of Shaftesbury*, one vol. ed. (London 1888), 683.

[30] *AR* cxvi (1874), 78–84; H ccxx. 1372–92; Bentley, op. cit. 61–4.

[31] A. G. Gardiner, *The Life of Sir William Harcourt* (2 vols., London, 1923), i. 273 ff.

[32] *AR* cxvi (1874), 84–5; H ccxx. 1414–23.

[33] Louisa E. King to Harcourt, 26 July 1874; Harcourt Papers, 205, fo. 73; Carr J. Glyn to Harcourt, 1 Aug. 1874; ibid. 77–8; Richard Nugent to Harcourt, 28 Aug. 1874; ibid. 84–5.

[34] Henry Richard made a strong anti-Ritualist defence of the bill; H ccxxi. 56–67. But E. A. Leatham denounced it as unjustly restrictive; H ccxx. 1431–7.

[35] Marsh, op. cit. 185.

Gladstone might say he did not know what Ritualism was, but the House and country clearly understood it as 'practices by a portion of the clergy, avowedly symbolic of doctrines which the same clergy are bound in the most solemn manner to refute and repudiate'. Catholic doctrines should be respected when held by Roman Catholics, but condemned when held by Anglican clergy who liked to perform 'the Mass in Masquerade'.[36] Soon after the premier's speech the second reading was carried without a division. A relieved Queen commented: 'If my faithful Commons had not supported me, I should have been fain to give up my heavy crown to some of my Italian Cousins—the representatives of the Stuarts'.[37]

On the following day Gladstone said he would not move his resolutions, as the House obviously wanted to go straight into Committee. Viscount Cardwell had already asked Granville to persuade him not to move them, in order to avoid a display of Liberal division.[38] In Committee some significant amendments were made. The date when the bill would come into operation was postponed from January to July 1875 in order to allow Convocation to revise the rubrics and Parliament to legislate accordingly. More important, the House adopted an amendment by J. M. Holt, a Conservative MP and spokesman for the Church Association, to allow complainants to appeal to the Archbishop in cases where the Bishop vetoed proceedings. Gladstone moved to rescind it, but this caused another clash with Harcourt and the motion was defeated. The bill was read a third time and passed on 3 August.[39]

Returning to the Lords with its amendments, the bill was shorn of its appeal to the Archbishop by a majority of twelve, the Archbishops supporting the clause but nine Bishops opposing.[40] Another intra-party conflict occurred, this time on the Conservative side. Salisbury denounced the proposed appeal as being potentially damaging to the interests of the clergy, and scorned as 'bluster' any plea that the Lords should yield to it in order to avoid a collision with the Commons. When the Lower House debated the Lords' action on 5 August, the inclination was to submit to it rather than risk losing the whole bill in the minimal time left. Harcourt, while accepting this argument, castigated the Lords for weakening the measure. He lauded Disraeli as a Protestant champion (Gladstone called this 'his slimy, fulsome, loathsome eulogies upon Dizzy . . . aimed at me');[41] and summoned the premier to uphold the dignity of the Lower House against the 'rash and rancorous tongue' of his own colleague, Lord Salisbury. Disraeli caused a sensation by actually obliging,

[36] *AR* cxvi (1874) 87–9; H ccxxi. 76–82.

[37] Quoted Marsh, op. cit. 187.

[38] Granville to Gladstone, 14 July 1874; A. Ramm (ed.), *The Political Correspondence of Mr Gladstone and Lord Granville, 1876–1886* (2 vols., Oxford, 1962), ii. 456.

[39] H ccxxi. 200–6, 247–68, 873–918, 1043–95, 1152–7; *AR* cxvi (1874), 92.

[40] H ccxxi. 1232–65; *AR* cxvi (1874), 92–3; Hardinge, op. cit. ii. 70–3; Marsh, op. cit. 189–91; Bentley, op. cit. 69–71.

[41] Gladstone to Granville, 7 Aug. 1874; Ramm, op. cit. ii. 457.

saying of his colleague: 'He is not a man who measures his phrases. He is a great master of gibes and flouts and jeers'—though he added: 'I do not suppose there is any one who is prejudiced against a Member of Parliament on account of such qualifications'. Nevertheless Disraeli asked the House to accept the Lords' decision in order to save the bill, and this point was carried without division.[42] Thus the contentious measure at last became law. Meanwhile the tiff between leading Conservatives was smoothed over when Salisbury readily accepted Disraeli's assurance that he had been trying to protect him from the Commons' wrath by means of a 'playful' defence.[43] The rift between Gladstone and Harcourt, however, lasted five years.

Not only did the Public Worship Regulation Bill get through, but in order to allow its passage the Government had abandoned or diluted some of its own legislation. Among this was the Endowed Schools Amendment Bill. This measure—the one attempt by the ministry to revise its predecessor's legislation—had been intended to return to the Church of England control of schools removed from its authority by the Liberals' Act of 1869. But this proposal aroused intense controversy. Although having majority support in the Commons it was vigorously opposed by Forster, Gladstone, Fawcett, and Lowe. In order to avoid a protracted dispute which might have prevented the passage of the Public Worship Bill and consolidated the Opposition, the Cabinet decided, towards the end of July, to abandon its contentious proposal. So the bill passed with only the mild provision that the Endowed Schools Commission would be abolished and its work transferred to an enlarged Charity Commission.[44] This was another blow to Salisbury, who had found himself alone in resisting the dilution at a Cabinet meeting. But the reverse was one which, like the Public Worship Act, he did not allow to drive him from the Government. 'My position is very disagreeable', he told Carnarvon on 24 July, but 'I feel the matter is too small to resign upon'.[45] Later his relations with Disraeli, which had come perilously near to breakdown, began to improve through the determination of both of them.

The Public Worship Regulation Act provided for the appointment, by the two Archbishops, or failing them the Crown, of a barrister or ex-judge (who had to declare himself an Anglican) as judge of the provincial courts of Canterbury and York. The judge would be Dean of the Arches court of Canterbury, Master of Faculties, and official principal of the Chancery Court of York. A Bishop, on receiving complaint of a liturgical illegality from an Archdeacon, church-warden, or three parishioners, could either veto proceedings (provided he stated

[42] *AR* cxvi (1874), 92–6; H ccxxi. 1337–72.

[43] A. L. Kennedy, *Salisbury, 1830–1903: Portrait of a Statesman* (London, 1953), 89; Salisbury to Disraeli, 5 Aug. 1874; DP, B/XX/Ce/173; Hardinge, op. cit. ii. 73–5.

[44] *AR* cxvi (1874), 53–9; *Primitive Methodist Magazine*, NS xii (1874), 576; Marsh, op cit. 187–8; S. Maccoby, *English Radicalism, 1853–1886* (London, 1938), 198–200.

[45] Salisbury to Carnarvon, 23 July 1874; Carnarvon Papers, 60758, fos. 133–5, 1 and 24 July 1874; Cecil, op. cit. ii. 63; Carnarvon to Salisbury, 25 July 1874; SP.

his reasons), decide the case himself with the consent of the parties involved, or transmit it for decision by the judge. The latter's decision could be enforced by inhibition of clerical functions, and eventually by loss of benefice, but an appeal could be made to the Judicial Committee of the Privy Council.

The offensiveness of these provisions to Ritualists and their High-Church sympathizers was increased because the appointed judge, James Plaisted Wilde, Baron Penzance, though a staunch Churchman had been a judge in the divorce court under the Act of 1857 which legalized divorce for adultery. High-Church indignation cannot have been alleviated by the remark of the Nonconformist *Examiner* that Penzance would be responsible for dissolving yet another adulterous union, that of Church and State.[46] Moreover, Penzance underlined the secularity of his position by refusing to qualify himself as an ecclesiastical judge. The stage seemed set for a long and turbulent contest not only between different religious opinions but, more importantly, between civil authority and religious conscience. Penzance took on his new role after retiring from his former judicial duties because of ill health; Disraeli doubtless supported the bill because he thought it would consolidate and strengthen the Conservatives; Archbishop Tait hoped the measure would unify the English Church and protect it from disestablishment, and had said that it would bring 'one of those peaceful revolutions for which England is famous among nations—revolutions which have quietly removed proved abuses, and have saved many a venerable institution which might otherwise have been destroyed'.[47] But if Penzance expected an untroubled semi-retirement job he was disappointed; the premier found himself threatened with defection by Conservative High-Churchmen; and to Tait the Act proved anything but the peaceful and integrating solution he had envisaged.

Before the Act came into operation on 1 July 1875 the controversial atmosphere surrounding it was intensified by dispute not only over Ritualism but over the Ultramontanism to which many feared Ritualism would lead. At the centre of the storm over 'Vaticanism' in later 1874 and early 1875 was Gladstone, who was currently (and appropriately) retreating from the political leadership which he officially relinquished in January 1875. Gladstone was greatly perturbed by the startling and much discussed conversion to Roman Catholicism of his ex-colleague the Marquess of Ripon—ex-Evangelical, Christian Socialist, and Grand Master of the English Freemasons. The conversion was announced at the beginning of September 1874.[48] *The Times* expressed a popular view by saying that Ripon had 'renounced his mental and moral freedom' and that 'a statesman who becomes a convert to Roman Catholicism forfeits at once the confidence of the English people . . . To become

---

[46] Marsh, op. cit. 189.

[47] Quoted Davidson and Benham, op. cit. ii. 202.

[48] See L. Wolf, *Life of the First Marquess of Ripon* (2 vols., London, 1921), i. 286 ff.; A. Denholm, *Lord Ripon, 1827–1909: A Political Biography* (London, 1982), 105 ff.

a Roman Catholic and remain a thorough Englishman are—it cannot be disguised—almost incompatible conditions.'[49] Gladstone's reaction probably influenced his article on 'Ritualism and Ritual' in the October *Contemporary Review*. In this he demanded spiritual proportion in ritual and the avoidance of excess—'no ritual is too much, provided it is subsidiary to the inner work of worship: and all ritual is too much, unless it ministers to that purpose'. He played down the danger that Ritualists would romanize the Church of England, however; for romanization had become impossible 'when Rome has substituted for the proud boast of *semper eadem* a policy of violence and change in faith; when she has refurbished and paraded anew every rusty tool she was fondly thought to have disused'—and (more to the point, *vis-à-vis* Ripon) 'when no one can become her convert without renouncing his moral and mental freedom, and placing his civil loyalty and duty at the mercy of another'.[50]

Catholics who were Liberals and close to Gladstone were naturally pained. William Monsell, Lord Emly, an Irish convert who had been a member of the late Government, wrote to Ripon suggesting that a protest be made to the ex-premier about his 'calumnious rhetoric' and especially his allegations about the civil loyalty of converts.[51] Both of them complained to Gladstone, and a lengthy correspondence took place between Gladstone and Ripon in which the former said he had not been referring to the marquess in his article, and did not doubt his civil loyalty; nevertheless he could no longer believe that Roman Catholicism 'as expounded by competent authority imported nothing disparaging to civil loyalty'.[52] In 1878 Gladstone added to a reprinting of his article the belief that 'some, at least' of the converts to Rome since the Vatican Council would 'adhere under all circumstances to their civil loyalty and duty'.[53] Ripon remained a loyal Liberal but was not prominent as a political leader again until 1878.[54]

Gladstone had got himself into a mood for writing heated religious essays, and political caution was cast to the winds. His questioning of the civil loyalty of Catholics was justified at length in his celebrated diatribe, *The Vatican Decrees in their Bearing on Civil Allegiance*, published on 4 November; 145,000 copies were sold by the end of the year and Bismarck had a German translation distributed. The Vatican decrees with their firm assertion of Papal Infallibility were deeply hurtful to Gladstone and other Anglo-Catholics who hoped for the reunion of Canterbury and Rome but now found a solid dogmatic obstacle in

---

[49] Quoted Wolf, op. cit. i. 293; Denholm, op. cit. 119; W. W. Arnstein, *Protestant versus Catholic in Mid-Victorian England; Mr Newdegate and the Nuns* (Columbia and London, 1982), 185.

[50] *CR* xxiv (1874), 673–5; repr. in W. E. Gladstone, *Gleanings of Past Years, 1843–1878* (7 vols., London, 1879), vi. 127.

[51] Emly to Ripon, 29 Sept. 1874; Ripon Papers, Add. MS 43625, fos. 202–3.

[52] Wolf, op. cit. i. 297–310; Emly to Gladstone, 3 Oct. 1874; GP, 44152, fos. 235–8.

[53] Gladstone, op. cit. vi. 127 n.

[54] Denholm, op. cit. 121–8; John P. Rossi, 'Lord Ripon's Resumption of Political Activity, 1878–1880', *Recusant History*, xi (1971–2).

their path. Ultramontanism, moreover, challenged the liberal development of the United Kingdom by not accepting toleration and freedom of speech as essential civil virtues.[55] Gladstone told Granville, with apparent sincerity, that he believed the Catholics were 'waiting in one vast conspiracy for an opportunity to direct European war to the re-establishment by force of the temporal power'.[56] The ex-premier was also still smarting from the treatment given to his Irish University Bill by the hierarchy.[57] At any rate, Ripon's conversion seems to have let loose the expression of deep feelings which had been smouldering for several years in the hitherto busy statesman.[58]

Some political gain Gladstone might have hoped to make from his pamphlet—in particular, to help reconcile disaffected Nonconformists to the Liberal party. The *Nonconformist* and the *British Quarterly Review* (another Dissenting journal) did indeed welcome the pamphlet.[59] At the same time, of course, it outraged many Catholics;[60] and aroused, in at least some Whigs and the more secular radicals, mere ridicule that a party leader should be deeply and publicly concerned with such an issue. Harcourt was generally hostile to Gladstone at this time, but he was not untypical of Liberals in saying that the party's troubles could not be overcome 'by blazing rhetoric and sensational pamphleteering', and that Catholic support in Parliament would be lost.[61] Chamberlain said that 'an ex-Minister of the first rank who devotes his leisure to a critical examination of the querulousness of an aged priest is hardly in sympathy with the robust common sense of English Liberalism'.[62]

The pamphlet, in fact, was more likely to divide Liberals further than to unite them. After a spate of divergent replies from Newman, Acton, Manning, and other Catholics, and a rejoinder from Gladstone, public interest died away early in 1875. If some had hoped for a revival of the great anti-popish demonstrations of 1850–1, and perhaps even for new legislation along the lines of the Ecclesiastical Titles Act, they were disappointed. But of course the circumstances were very different; in particular, the union with Ireland was

[55] Cf. H. C. G. Matthew, 'Gladstone, Vaticanism, and the Question of the East', in D. Baker (ed.), *Studies in Church History*, xv (Oxford, 1978), 420–5; Malcolm MacColl to Gladstone, 10 Aug. 1877; GP, 44243, fo. 249; M. R. Temmel, 'Gladstone's Resignation of the Liberal Leadership, 1874–1875', *Journal of British Studies*, xvi. 1 (1976), 164–5.

[56] Ramm, ii. 458.

[57] W. E. Gladstone, *The Vatican Decrees in their Bearing on Civil Allegiance: A Political Expostulation* (London, 1874), 27–8; E. R. Norman, *Anti-Catholicism in Victorian England* (London, 1968), 218.

[58] Norman, op. cit. 86 ff.

[59] Ibid. 96; J. L. Altholz, 'The Vatican Decrees Controversy, 1874–1875', *Catholic Historical Review*, lvii (1971–2), 602.

[60] Norman, op. cit. 98–104; H. Jenkins, 'The Irish Dimension of the British Kulturkampf: Vaticanism and Civil Allegiance, 1870–1875', *JEH* xxx (1979), 356–7; John P. Rossi, *The Transformation of the Liberal Party, 1874–1880* (Philadelphia, 1978), 14.

[61] Gardiner, op. cit. i. 281, also 285, 289–90; Harcourt to George Melly, MP, 7 Jan. 1875; G. Melly, *Recollections of Sixty Years, 1833–1893* (Coventry, 1893), 33; Granville to Gladstone, 10 Nov. 1874; Ramm, ii. 458–9.

[62] J. L. Garvin and J. Amery, *The Life of Joseph Chamberlain* (4 vols., London, 1933–51), i. 221–2.

now much more under threat. However, the political revulsion of Catholics (similar to that of the 1850s) remained for some years and was still present in the election of 1880.

Vaticanism had stirred up anti-Catholic feeling—displayed, for example, in the formation of a new Protestant society, the Metropolitan and General Protestant Defence Association, in February 1874.[63] But apart from the Public Worship Regulation Act this feeling bore no Parliamentary fruit. Newdegate, Thomas Chambers, and J. M. Holt had no success in their continued efforts from 1874 to 1877 to obtain a committee of enquiry into monasteries and convents.[64] By the later 1870s the recent phase of anti-Catholicism seemed to be abating. One probable reason was considerable public reaction against the effects of the Public Worship Act. This measure, by leading unexpectedly to the imprisonment of clergy, seemed too strong a deterrent to conscientious expression for an age which prided itself on its toleration.

Indeed it proved very hard to discipline determined characters who wished to be advanced Ritualists yet to remain in the Church of England. From July 1875 until 1882, only eighteen suits were commenced under the Act, and eight of them were vetoed by Bishops.[65] Nevertheless, some of the suits were long and bitter, and between 1877 and 1882 four clergy were imprisoned—a development which made the Act generally more unpopular and strengthened the hands of Bishops in using the veto.[66] A fifth imprisonment came in 1887. Instead of quietening the ritual controversy, the new Act ensured it would last for a long time to come.

Two weeks after the Act became effective three parishioners of St Peter's, Folkestone, encouraged by the Church Association, complained about twelve examples of Ritualist practice by the vicar, the Revd C. J. Ridsdale. These included eucharistic vestments and the eastward position. Tait, in whose diocese the case occurred, did not use his veto but attempted personal conciliation in order to achieve settlement without resort to law. The attempt failed, the suit went before Lord Penzance's court, and Ridsdale was condemned on all twelve points. Ridsdale, who was supported financially for part of the way by the English Church Union, said he would disregard the monition while he appealed on four of the points to the Judicial Committee. His case was heard by the reconstituted final appeal court of 1876, with some Bishops sitting as assessors but all the judges being laymen. The judgment, delivered on 18 May 1877, found by a majority of seven to three that Ridsdale was guilty on two charges (including vestments) but acquitted him with important qualifications on two others, including the eastward position.

---

[63] *DN*, 18 Feb. 1874, p. 5.
[64] Arnstein, op. cit. 178–81, 198–200.
[65] S. L. Ollard, G. Crosse, and M. F. Bond (eds.), *A Dictionary of English Church History*, 3rd edn. (London, 1948), 492. Cf. W. H. Hutchings, *Life and Letters of T. T. Carter* (London, 1903), 173–5.
[66] Ibid. Cf. D. C. Lathbury, *Dean Church* (Oxford and London, 1905), 116 ff.

Ridsdale eventually complied with the judgment, after Tait agreed to give him a dispensation from obeying the ornaments rubric according to his own interpretation of it. The *Church Times* condemned the verdict, and militant Ritualists were prepared to ignore its declarations; but this protracted case had ended satisfactorily within its own personal limits.[67]

It was quite otherwise, however, with a suit heard by Penzance in 1876 and financed by the Church Association. This concerned the Revd Arthur Tooth, Vicar of St James's at Hatcham, Surrey. Some of the charges against Tooth were *sub judice* in the Ridsdale case, and Penzance condemned him only for other practices previously condemned by the Judicial Committee. Tooth entirely disregarded his monition, and was consequently inhibited from serving in his church for three months. Tooth, supported by the English Church Union,[68] disregarded the inhibition as well, and refused to appeal to the Judicial Committee since he denied the authority of a secular body just as he had denied Lord Penzance's. The Bishop of Rochester ordered the church to be closed. But Tooth and his churchwardens kept it open, and a crowd estimated at 8,000 (many arriving by train) surrounded the church on 13 January 1877; it took 300 police to disperse them. Tooth was cited for contempt but, to the dismay of Tait and Penzance, the only penalty for contempt of an ecclesiastical court was the forgotten one of imprisonment. Accordingly, Tooth was arrested on 22 January and lodged in gaol.

This was a sensational result of complaints about ritual, and reaction was intense. A Jesuit preacher at Oxford insisted that the Church of England lacked spiritual liberty; Charles Wood, president of the ECU, resigned his post of groom of the bedchamber to the Prince of Wales; and the Church Association lost members. Things were not turning out at all as Tait had hoped. But at least Tooth was soon out of gaol. At first he had tried to control his church *in absentia* by appointing a substitute clergyman; but police barred the substitute from the church, and a nominee of the Bishop obtained entry and conducted worship in a strictly legal manner. The law was thus vindicated and, on application to Penzance, Tooth was released on 17 February. But he was still subject to inhibition.

After a holiday in Italy the intractable Tooth exhibited fresh contempt by breaking into his church on Sunday 13 May, admitting 300 supporters, and celebrating communion dressed in a eucharistic vestment. He informed Tait, who was now administering the diocese of Rochester because of an episcopal vacancy, that he would not defer to Penzance's court, the Judicial Committee, or his Bishop. Tooth could be imprisoned again or, in three years, deprived of his benefice. But suddenly he scored a legal victory. Lawyers acting for the ECU applied to the Court of Queen's Bench, on a legal technicality, for

---

[67] *AR* cxix (1877), ii, 169–73; Marsh, op. cit. 219–25; D. B. Swinfen, 'The Single Judgment in the Privy Council, 1833–1966', *The Juridical Review* ii (1975), 161–3.

[68] Unanimous resolution of ECU meeting, 7 Dec. 1876; ECU Minutes, CU dep. 4, 197–8.

restraint of further proceedings. They were successful. The judgment in Queen's Bench stated, moreover, that Penzance's court was purely a creation of Parliament without the ecclesiastical authority of the Court of Arches which it had superseded. The judgment did not destroy the Public Worship Act but its authority was shaken, and Bishops had been encouraged to make greater use of the veto power. Seven of the eight suits commenced in 1878 were vetoed.

The Tooth case ended with the vicar resigning his benefice in November 1877 in a triumphant letter to Tait, in which he generously waived his entitlement to sue his prosecutors and Lord Penzance for wrongful imprisonment. He claimed his health was broken but lived on for fifty-four years, directing an orphanage, a nunnery, and a home for drunkards.[69] Further prosecutions resulted in the imprisonment in 1880 of the Revd T. Pelham Dale, Rector of St Vedast's, Foster Lane, London, and the Revd R. W. Enraght, Vicar of Holy Trinity, Bordesley, Birmingham; and, in 1881, of the Revd S. F. Green, Rector of St John's, Miles Platting, Manchester, who was held for eighteen months in by far the longest of these incarcerations.[70] Mackonochie came near to experiencing a similar fate after another lengthy suit against him, starting in March 1878; leaders of the Church Association prepared to seek imprisonment for contempt, but their agent refused to take the necessary action.[71] Anti-Ritualists who were frustrated by the Bishops' veto could always sue the Bishop. In 1878 a parishioner of Canon T. T. Carter sued the Bishop of Oxford, J. F. Mackarness, for not agreeing to Carter's prosecution. The Court of Queen's Bench found against Mackarness, but he was acquitted on appeal in 1879. This outcome no doubt encouraged use of the veto.[72]

The creation of several martyrs for Ritualism was not the only cause of excitement among these matters, for confession was also creating a stir. A copy of the second part of *The Priest in Absolution,* a frank and detailed confession manual written for the Society of the Holy Cross, fell into hostile hands in 1877 and was passed to the Earl of Redesdale. He complained about the book in the House of Lords in June and read out extracts from it. He was supported by Tait and Harrowby, and the matter was raised several times in the Commons and debated in Convocation.[73] There was uproar in the press; a *Times* leader said that Ritualism as represented by the Society of the Holy Cross was a conspiracy against public morals.[74] The ultra-Protestant *Rock* produced a list of 2,700 clergy who were supposedly involved in the 'ritualistic conspiracy'; and a pamphlet denounced the ECU as a 'romanizing confederacy' on many counts

[69] Marsh, op. cit. 225–9; *AR* cxix (1877), Chronicle, 6–18, 46.

[70] Bentley, op. cit. 102–12; Marsh, op. cit. 231–2, 275–9; Ellsworth, *Lowder,* 138–58.

[71] M. Reynolds, *Martyr of Ritualism: Father Mackonochie of St Alban's Holborn* (London, 1965), 228–37.

[72] O. Chadwick, *The Victorian Church,* ii (London, 1970), 350–1.

[73] H ccxxxiv. 1741–53, ccxxxv. 83–5, 884, 946, 1174–5.

[74] Reynolds, op. cit. 219; Liddon, *Pusey,* iv. 303 ff. For a detailed account see Ellsworth, op. cit. 138–46.

including defiance of the law, promotion of reunion with Rome, sympathy with the Jesuits, support of confession, and voluntaryism.[75] Many localities must have been affected by Ritualist dispute and tension. For instance, controversy accompanied the opening of the huge church of St Bartholomew at Brighton in September 1874. A local journalist claimed to have discovered a lot of sinister little 'cells' off a dark spiral staircase, but these were stated to be only a 'structural feature' together with accommodation for the heating system.[76]

Archbishop Tait was alarmed by the troubled and disintegrating effects of his 'peaceful' and 'unifying' solution, and in the later half of 1877 he sought a new way to peace by holding large meetings of clergymen of diverse opinions for united prayer and discussion of their differences.[77] Some individuals representing different viewpoints disagreed with this method. In any case the differences were too deeply rooted to disappear, and they involved much more than the details of ritual cases. The outrage of High-Churchmen at State interference with the spiritual concerns of the Church enlivened the struggle for ecclesiastical autonomy against secular encroachment which had been prominent since the early 1830s. The Judicial Committee had been condemned as an organ of secular interference for twenty-five years, and now it was joined by Lord Penzance's court. Indeed Parliament itself, a body containing any and no kind of Christian, which had created these courts, was condemned in the same way. The ECU resolved at a large meeting at the Westminster Palace Hotel in January 1877 that, while the courts should be obeyed in matters temporal, the secular power had no authority in matters spiritual; only synods had the power to decree ceremonies and settle disputes over belief.[78]

It was urged (and not only by High-Churchmen) that the Church should be given more self-government, including the right to appoint Bishops, hold Convocations without State sanction, and enact canons in Convocation without reference to Parliament. A familiar claim was made that the English Church should be allowed 'as much independence of State control as now appertains, without questioning, to the Presbyterian Establishment in Scotland'.[79] The Revd A. D. Wagner, who had built several churches in Brighton (including St Bartholomew's) published a plea for Church autonomy entitled *Christ or Caesar?* He wrote that concession of the State's claim to decide spiritual questions in the last resort and to pass Acts affecting religion without consulting

[75] *The Ritualistic Conspiracy, Comprising Lists of Priests Reprinted from the Rock* (London, 1877); 'Presbyter Protestans', *The English Church Union Proved from its Official Publications and Other Documents to be a Romanizing Confederacy* (London, 1877).

[76] H. H. Maughan, *Some Brighton Churches* (London, 1922), 51–63.

[77] Marsh, op. cit. 235–6.

[78] G. B. Roberts, *The History of the English Church Union, 1859–1894* (London, 1895), 187–8; Liddon, op. cit. iv. 287.

[79] Resolutions of Exeter branch of ECU, adopted 13 Nov. 1874; ECU Council Minutes, CU dep. 12, p. 45. Cf. Charles Wood to Gladstone, 28 Feb. 1877: 'Why, people ask, is the Church of England to be kept in a worse condition than [the Church of Scotland]?'; GP, 44187, fos. 13–14.

the Church, was a denial of the Church's divine authority and an admission that she was a mere department of State. He gave fifteen reasons why the ecclesiastical decisions of the Judicial Committee of the Privy Council should be disobeyed.[80] Charles Wood similarly stated that 'we cannot admit the right of the Privy Council to be the supreme arbiter of the destinies of the Church of England'; Archdeacon Denison contended that 'it is not for Parliament, nor for the courts created by Parliament irrespectively of the voice of the Church in her Synods, to so much as touch . . . the faith and worship of the Church'; and Canon T. T. Carter maintained that, by a relentless process of encroachment, the Church was being placed 'in complete subjection to the State'.[81]

Was disestablishment the answer to these abundant complaints? Several leading High-Churchmen, including Pusey, Wood, Carter, and C. F. Lowder, discouraged this course. Not the dissolution of the Church-State link but the inauguration of better relations, through the ending of 'unconstitutional aggression' by the civil power, was advocated by Carter at an ECU meeting in December 1876.[82] Gladstone was said to be more eager for disestablishment after the failure of his resolutions in 1874, but he was still far from adopting this policy. He did not dread disestablishment, he said, but wished to avert it.[83] Some High-churchmen, however, were convinced that disestablishment was needed before an acceptable degree of self-government could be obtained. A speaker at the Clifton branch of the ECU claimed that all Ritualist clergy would prefer disestablishment to complete surrender of the Church's spiritual power to the State.

There was indeed some evidence that voluntary opinions were spreading among Ritualists. A resolution for disestablishment at a meeting of the Society of the Holy Cross was overwhelmed by twenty-six votes to four in September 1874, but lost by only twenty-two to twenty in May 1876, and by another small margin a year later. Liddon, Mackonochie, and Denison favoured disestablishment. Mackonochie, who (with Arthur Stanton, one of his curates) had belonged to Miall's Liberation Society for a short time, became president of a new 'Church League for promoting the separation of Church and State', founded in 1877. Resolutions adopted by this body could easily have been passed by the Liberation Society. Mackonochie explained his voluntary views in articles in the *Nineteenth Century* in June 1877 and October 1878, and included in the later of these a suggested bill, containing a preamble and thirty

[80] A. D. Wagner, *Christ or Caesar? A Letter to the Archbishop of Canterbury* (London, 1874), 9, 19–22.

[81] J. G. Lockhart, *Viscount Halifax* (2 vols., London, 1935–6), i. 236; G. A. Denison, *The Charge of the Archdeacon of Taunton at his Visitation, April 1877* (Oxford and London, 1877), 11; T. T. Carter, 'The Present Crisis in the Church of England', *Nineteenth Century*, i (Mar.–July 1877), 433. Cf. Marsh, op. cit. 214–16.

[82] Carter, *The Position and Duty of Churchmen at the Present Time*, ECU publ. (London, 1877).

[83] Gladstone to Earl of Harrowby, 1 Oct. 1874; Lathbury, *Correspondence*, i. 396. Cf. J. Guinness Rogers, *An Autobiography* (London, 1903), 223–4.

clauses, to disestablish the Church of England from 1 January 1881.[84] But there was High-Church opposition to this proposal, even from the rather extreme *Church Times*, and Nonconformists must have had mixed feelings about Mackonochie's initiative. As an aid to the disestablishment campaign it was welcomed, but not as an aid to the extension of Ritualism which Mackonochie desired. The *Primitive Methodist Magazine* wanted Evangelicals to prove their love of 'pure doctrine and simple worship' by leaving the contaminated establishment. Guinness Rogers wanted Ritualism to be reduced not by legal restrictions but by disestablishment, which would deprive it of the 'protection' it was receiving (he claimed) from a State Church.[85]

The 1874 Act had stimulated the call for disestablishment, even from within the establishment, and this was embarrassing to a Conservative Government pledged to maintain established Churches. The ministry risked losing the electoral support of High-Churchmen. Among the numerous letters to Disraeli from clergymen about the Public Worship Bill, a few threatened to abandon Conservatism.[86] These were in contrast to the far more representative letter which said that the Church would have been 'destroyed . . . by a batch of boobies and bigots—Maconochies, Denisons, and Carters, and Puseys—if their unprincipled and unjustifiable anticks had not been put down by the strong hand of law'.[87] John Gorst, the chief Conservative party organizer, told Disraeli that the Government might be in danger of 'being broken up by the High-Church party, as Gladstone's was by the Dissenters';[88] defecting clergy might well influence other defections. A paper written in 1877 said that three-quarters of the Ritualist clergy were now Liberals because of Gladstone's stand against the bill, and suggested that, to counteract this, more High-Churchmen be given preferment.[89] But no appointments of extreme High-Churchmen were made by Disraeli.[90] Malcolm MacColl, on the other hand, warned the editor of the *Daily News* that the tendency of Ritualists to become Liberals would be stifled if the Liberal press did not show more favour to Ritualism. The Ritualists and their sympathizers, he claimed, were 'strong enough to turn the scales' at a general election.[91]

[84] J. Dunn, *The Honesty of our Position* (London, 1878), 6; Ellsworth, op. cit. 136; Marsh, op. cit. 212; Bentley, op. cit. 93–4; Reynolds, op. cit. 206–9; *AR* cxix (1877), Chronicle, 65; G. A. Denison, *Notes of My Life, 1805–1878*, (3rd edn. (Oxford and London, 1879), 367; *Nineteenth Century*, iv (July–Dec. 1878), 627–42.

[85] *Primitive Methodist Magazine*, NS xv (1877), 447–8; J. Guinness Rogers, 'Some Aspects of Disestablishment', *Nineteenth Century*, i (Mar.–July 1877), 439, and 'Political Dissent', *Fortnightly Review*, xxii (July–Dec. 1877), 825–6.

[86] DP, B/XII/F/68, 77, 79, 80a, 81b, 90.

[87] Revd W. G. Cooke to Disraeli, 7 Aug. 1874; ibid. 74.

[88] Quoted Feuchtwanger, *Disraeli*, 217, and Marsh, op. cit. 194.

[89] Col. Edward Nevill to Montagu Corry, 11 Apr. 1877; DP, C/111/B/i/28b; D. Bahlman, 'Politics and Church Patronage in the Victorian Age', *VS* xxii (1979), 266–7.

[90] Chadwick, op. cit. ii. 337.

[91] Russell, *Malcolm MacColl*, 43–4.

III. SCOTLAND: PATRONAGE REPEAL AND VOLUNTARYISM, 1874

The legislative attempt to bring peace to the Church of England, encouraged by the Government, proved a failure. Similarly, a ministerial effort in the same year to encourage the union of Scottish Presbyterians did not have the desired effect. For several years a majority in the General Assembly of the Church of Scotland had supported resolutions to abolish patronage in that Church, and what had been refused by Gladstone's ministry was enacted by Disraeli's in its first session. But such a measure, proposing to remove a factor which had played a large part in causing the Disruption of 1843, was naturally suspected by the major Presbyterian Dissenting bodies (the Free Church and United Presbyterians) of seeking to lure them back into the establishment. Their suspicions were sustained when supporters of the bill said there should now be no need for disunity to persist. Both bodies were determined not to be lured back, for the abolition of patronage left intact their fundamental and different reasons for opposing the establishment—United Presbyterians objected to a State Church on principle, Free-Churchmen to the existing establishment because it did not have spiritual independence from civil authority. The majority of the Free Church General Assembly, led by Professor Robert Rainy, was frustrated by the recent failure of negotiations to combine the Free Church with the United Presbyterian Church on account of anti-voluntary opposition by a Free Church minority led by James Begg and John Kennedy. This failure had left the Free Church majority all the readier to campaign for disestablishment. Even the minority party would not consent to reunite with the Church of Scotland when its spiritual independence had not been gained, and when liberal theology was preached from many of its pulpits.[92]

Several Scottish Conservative MPs (Alexander Whitelaw, Charles Dalrymple, A. Orr Ewing, Sir W. Stirling-Maxwell) and some leading Church of Scotland ministers urged the new Government to pass a bill abolishing patronage. The Cabinet was willing to satisfy them, and much consultation took place. The Revd Archibald Charteris, for example, paid five visits to London concerning the measure.[93] On 16 May Charteris was told it had been decided that, as a substitute for the patronage system, communicants would elect the ministers. The Government bill, drafted by Lord Advocate E. S. Gordon, was introduced in the Lords on 18 May by the Duke of Richmond and Lennox, lord president of the council, and read a first time. Richmond's speech was described as 'rambling and hazy' but none the less comprehensible to a House which was

[92] Cf. A. Drummond and J. Bulloch, *The Church in Late Victorian Scotland, 1874–1900* (Edinburgh, 1978), 104 ff.; T. Smith, *Memoirs of James Begg, DD* (2 vols., Edinburgh, 1885–8), ii. 518–19; P. Carnegie Simpson, *The Life of Principal Rainy* (2 vols., London, 1909), i. 254–73; A. Stewart and J. Kennedy Cameron, *The Free Church of Scotland, 1843–1910: A Vindication* (Edinburgh and Glasgow, [1910], 58–9.

[93] Revd the Hon. A. Gordon, *The Life of Archibald Hamilton Charteris, DD, LL D* (London, 1912), 228–30; Alexander Whitelaw to Duke of Richmond, 16 May 1874; Whitelaw Papers, Letter-books, D101 1/3, 196.

largely unfamiliar with the Presbyterian details involved.[94] The private patrons (but not the Crown and corporations) were to be offered compensation for the loss of patronage—the amount being equivalent to the annual ministerial stipend taken as the average of the last three years. The bill provisionally proposed that only male communicants should be able to elect, but it was recognized that the General Assembly meeting in a week's time would be consulted over this. The presbytery (the local Church court) would confirm or decline the elected person as minister, and would itself appoint the minister if one was not elected within six months. The civil courts could intervene in cases of conflict between the congregation and the presbytery.

The bill was welcomed in speeches by the Liberal Earls of Aberdeen and Rosebery; the latter regretted that the late Government had not dealt with the question. But Richmond's statement that the measure would 'give renewed strength and vitality to the Establishment' was provocative to voluntary opinion, and the Earl of Dalhousie (a Free Churchman) warned that the bill would cause much dispute and probably not aid the interests of the establishment.[95]

In the Church of Scotland General Assembly a motion approving of the bill, moved by Professor William Pirie and seconded by Lord Balfour of Burleigh, was adopted unanimously. The Assembly then examined the bill in committee. A proposal by Sir Robert Anstruther that the minister should be elected by all inhabitants in a parish who were in communion with a Protestant church was not accepted, but it was decided that female as well as male communicants of the established Church should form the electorate. Compensation for private patrons was opposed, but the Assembly decided to retain it by 127 votes to thirty-nine. A suggestion that the bill be used to grant self-government to the Church, on the grounds that this might attract Dissenters towards the establishment, was rejected, after it was stated to be inadvisable at this juncture to raise the whole question of spiritual independence in Parliament.[96]

On 2 June the second reading in the Lords passed without division, after an amendment against it was defeated and the Duke of Argyll had criticized the opposition of Free Churchmen and United Presbyterians. In committee it was decided that female communicants and other adult members of congregations would have the right to vote, subject to regulations to be drawn up by the General Assembly. A complaint was later made that female electors would have too great a preponderance.[97] The Lords finally passed the measure on 16 June and sent it down to the Commons.[98]

Meanwhile Dissenting opposition was being amply displayed. 'We regard Church Establishments as an evil', said the *United Presbyterian Magazine* in

[94] Gordon, op. cit. 230.

[95] Ibid. 230–2, 237–8; H ccxix. 368–90; *AR* cxvi (1874), 46–7.

[96] Gordon, op. cit. 233–4; G. W. T. Omond, *The Lord Advocates of Scotland*, 2nd ser. 1834–80 (London, 1914), 301.

[97] By Earl of Minto in Lords, 15 June 1877; H ccxxxiv. 1826–7.

[98] H ccxix. 809–46, 1226–59, 1568–9.

June, 'and surely what requires to be done with an evil is not to seek to improve it, but to sweep it away.' The UP presbytery of Edinburgh petitioned the House of Commons against the bill as tending to strengthen and perpetuate the establishment.[99] On 29 May the Free Church General Assembly opposed the bill by a majority of 433 votes to sixty-six and supported disestablishment by 298 to ninety-eight. Alexander Whitelaw, who thought the bill granted too much popular power, feared it would encourage disestablishment.[1] Carvell Williams communicated with several supporters of the Liberation Society in Scotland, where a branch had been formed in 1871. With the approval of the Society's executive committee he attended an Edinburgh conference on 2 June arranged by the Scottish Disestablishment Association. United Presbyterians, Free Churchmen, and other dissenters were present at this meeting, which Carvell Williams addressed. As well as resolving against the bill and for disestablishment, it was decided to raise a fund of £10,000 to continue the agitation. Williams also attended meetings at Greenock and Aberdeen. Conversely, a deputation of two United Presbyterian ministers reported to the Liberation Society committee that they had been trying to influence MPs against the bill.[2]

Liberals were divided over the measure, and the opposition could not hope to succeed even though Gladstone joined it. Attempts to sway Gladstone were made by Liberals on both sides before the bill was debated in the Commons. Argyll, a long-standing colleague of Gladstone, believed (as he told Richmond on 22 June, and as Richmond then informed Disraeli) that he knew 'beyond doubt' that Gladstone was opposed to the bill and would probably speak strongly against it.[3] None the less he tried in several letters to persuade Gladstone to change his mind. 'I think it hard and unjust', he told him, 'that when the leading Patrons in Scotland have come to see the uselessness and evil of their "Property" as it stands, others should step in to prevent them from accomplishing what is a great act of justice to their countrymen'. He knew a UP minister who refused to oppose the measure, and he insisted that abolition of patronage in the Scottish Church would not affect patronage in the English.[4] The Glasgow town council, 'full of Dissenting members', had declined by twenty-eight votes to twelve to oppose the bill, despite the fact that the council would lose its patronage.[5] Argyll saw that his appeals were not bearing fruit, however, and wrote on 6 July (when the bill was to be debated in the Commons) that he hoped Gladstone and his 'Voluntary and other Radical allies' would be

[99] *UP Magazine*, NS xviii (1874), 287–8; Minutes of Edinburgh UP Presbytery, 30 June 1874; CH3/111/34, pp. 445–8. Cf. Resolution of Dundee UP Presbytery, 23 June 1874; Minutes, i. 322.

[1] Whitelaw to Dr Cook of Haddington, 3 June 1874; Whitelaw Papers, Letter-books, D101 1/3, 215–17; Whitelaw to Andrew McGeorge, 8 June 1874; ibid. 221–2.

[2] LS, 1 and 11 June 1874; A/LIB/5, 117–18, 120; *United Presbyterian Magazine*, NS xviii (1874), 332.

[3] Argyll to Richmond, 22 June 1874; encl. in Richmond to Disraeli, 25 June 1874; DP, B/XX/Le/51, 51a.

[4] Argyll to Gladstone, 27 June 1874; GP, 44103, fos. 137–41; Eighth Duke of Argyll, *Autobiography and Memoirs*, ed. Dowager Duchess of Argyll (2 vols., London, 1906), ii. 314–16.

[5] Argyll to Gladstone, 23 June 1874; GP, 44103, fos. 133–6.

well beaten.[6] Also disappointed was Sir Robert Anstruther, Liberal MP for Fife, who told Gladstone that many Liberals would support the bill and that its opponents were strongly moved by voluntaryism.[7]

Among Liberals who were against the reform, Gladstone heard from Robert Rainy; from Taylor Innes, a prominent Free Church lawyer, who assured him that the bill was planned 'to restore the balance in Scotland in favour of Conservatism'; from Carvell Williams, who suggested ways of opposing the bill and later sent a 'statement of objections' prepared for the benefit of English Liberal members and indicting the measure as one of sectarian privilege; and from Samuel Laing, Liberal MP for Orkney and Shetland, who urged the importance of trying to unite Liberals against the bill.[8] Such opinions were much more acceptable to Gladstone than Argyll's. The ex-premier favoured the view that the bill was a stimulus to voluntaryism, and told Lord Selborne that 'if it passes it will lead to a movement for Disestablishment in Scotland more serious than any that has been known there, and likely to spread its influence into England'.[9]

It seemed just as likely, however, that voluntaryism would be boosted if Dissenters scored a victory over the establishment by defeating the bill. The interests of political Dissent might gain as much from defeat of the bill as from its passage. From this point of view, there was little reason for supporters of the establishment to oppose the bill.

Carvell Williams settled with W. E. Baxter, a Congregationalist who sat for Montrose Burghs, the terms of an amendment which Baxter would move on the second reading in the Commons, to the effect that legislation should not take place without further enquiry.[10] To Gladstone, Williams wrote that 'your anticipated contribution to the debate will have a decided effect on some who are now hesitating'.[11] When the second reading was moved by the Lord Advocate on 6 July, Baxter introduced his amendment and Gladstone rose to support him, to the vociferous delight of Liberal MPs who welcomed (as did Disraeli more formally) his reappearance after a long absence from the House. Gladstone argued that the measure was unjust to Free Churchmen, who had left the establishment because they objected to patronage. The abolition of patronage would only be fair if it were accompanied by a generous effort by the Church of Scotland, 'on terms of fraternal equality', to reunite with the Dissenters. The bill was arousing Dissenting militancy; and (he claimed with some exaggeration) there was scarcely any disestablishment movement in

---

[6] Argyll to Gladstone, 6 July 1874; ibid. fo. 146.

[7] Anstruther to Gladstone, 26 June 1874; GP, 44443, fos. 310–11.

[8] A. Taylor Innes to Gladstone, 3 June 1874; GP 44443, fos. 260–1; J. Carvell Williams to Gladstone, 13 June 1874; ibid. fos. 294–5, and 4 July 1874; GP, 44444, fo. 12; S. Lang to Gladstone, 17 June 1874; GP, 44443, fos. 298–9.

[9] Quoted Lathbury, i. 167.

[10] Williams to Gladstone, 4 July 1874; GP, 44444, fo. 10; LS, 2 July 1874; A/LIB/5, 133.

[11] Williams to Gladstone, 4 July (see last note).

Scotland until the introduction of this '. . . crude, premature, and insufficiently considered bill'. The enactment of the measure would only provoke 'a fierce and probably a prolonged and bitter controversy' over the question of establishment.[12]

Thus Gladstone countered the Government's appeal to its establishment supporters by appealing to the separatism of Free Churchmen and United Presbyterians. Rainy, while not agreeing with all of Gladstone's speech, thanked him for it and said it would 'greatly confirm the confidence and attachment felt towards you in Scotland'.[13] But Gladstone's opposition failed, as it was to do over the Public Worship Regulation Bill a few days later. Disraeli, Gathorne Hardy, and others spoke in favour of the patronage bill; Dr Charles Cameron, Henry Campbell-Bannerman, and Duncan McLaren spoke against it in the interests of Scottish Dissent; and the second reading passed by 307 votes to 109 on 13 July. Sixty-five Liberals voted in favour, including at least two Scottish Free Churchmen, but many Scottish, English, and Welsh Nonconformists voted against.[14] Scottish MPs supported the bill by thirty-two to twenty-four, with fifteen Scottish Liberals voting for and twenty-four against.[15] The bill was much discussed in committee at the end of July. An amendment was adopted definitely extending electoral rights to all adult members of the congregation, though other moves failed to give these rights to members of non-established Protestant churches. The bill was read a third time on 3 August and became law four days later.[16]

The Act's preamble stated that the measure was intended to ease the reunion of Scottish Presbyterians, but the hostile reactions of United Presbyterians and most Free Churchmen ensured that this aim would not be realized. The first tract in a series issued by the Scottish Disestablishment Association said the bill was a half-measure intended to preserve Erastian control and to 'weaken and arrest the progress of the Disestablished Churches'. A speaker at the United Presbyterian Synod in December 1874 said that no efforts could 'bring an Established Church into harmony with the law of Christ . . . You cannot keep Christianity in the old bottles of Constantine'. Most of the Aberdeen Free Church presbytery in January 1875 voted for a motion stating that the Patronage Act did not touch the spiritual independence issue on which the Free Church had separated from the State, and this was repeated in a pamphlet by Taylor Innes.[17] The Liberation Society committee condemned the Act for

[12] *AR* cxiv (1874), 49–52; H ccxx. 1086–130.
[13] Rainy to Gladstone, 7 July 1874; GP, 44444, fos. 25–6.
[14] H ccxx. 1130–85, 1527–604; Gordon, op. cit. 240.
[15] LS, 30 July 1874; A/LIB/5, 149.
[16] H ccxxi. 684–703, 837–44.
[17] *The New Patronage Act and the Scottish Churches* (Church Disestablishment Association: Tract No. 1, n.p., n.d.), 3; G. C. Hutton, *State Churchism in Scotland* (Edinburgh, 1875), 5; Aberdeen Free Church Presbytery Minutes, 5 Jan. 1875; CH3/2/7, 210–11; A. Taylor Innes, *The Scotch Law of Patronage* (Edinburgh, 1875), 11 ff. Cf. D. Ogilvy, *The Present Importance of Free Church Principles* (Edinburgh, 1875), 18–19, 24–31.

giving the Church of Scotland 'both the freedom of a sect and the advantages of an Establishment'. The opportunity should now be taken, decided the committee, to develop the voluntary campaign in Scotland, and a Scottish agent was appointed by the Society at a salary of £250 p.a.[18]

Thus, whatever the fond hopes of encouraging peaceful reunion and the strengthening of the establishment, only a hardening of ecclesiastical divisions resulted. Over the next few years intense controversy developed over disestablishment, which became the leading political question in Scotland. There were numerous well attended public meetings, debates, and resolutions in presbyteries and General Assemblies, and arguments in pamphlets and articles between prominent and less prominent figures—including Principal John Tulloch for the establishment; Rainy for the Free Church majority supporting disestablishment; James Begg and John Kennedy for the Free Church minority, which had its main support in the northern and western Highlands.[19] Voluntary propaganda was issued by the Scottish Disestablishment Association. The Liberation Society took a constant interest in the dispute, and a Scottish Council of the Society was formed in 1877.[20] Carvell Williams visited several Scottish towns in September 1874, and again in December.

The voluntary arguments, given varying emphases by different Dissenting sections, were based on ideals of spiritual independence, religious equality, and financial equity, and held that disestablishment was necessary before Presbyterian reunion could take place. Church defence invoked the benefits of a State-supported national religion with a firm territorial organization, and said that the 1874 Act was an adequate basis for Presbyterian reunion. The dispute tended to become a battle over membership figures. 'The Liberationists are busy spreading cooked statistics', wrote Principal Tulloch in 1878.[21] In statistical warfare the voluntaries seemed at a disadvantage, for though they disputed the establishment's figures it was confidently stated that the Church of Scotland was gaining relatively in strength. An estimate in 1874 gave the Free

[18] LS, 13 Aug. 1874; A/LIB/5, 152, 156–7.

[19] e.g. J. Begg, *The Principles, Position, and prospects of the Free Church of Scotland* (Edinburgh, 1875); J. Kennedy, *Letter to the Members of the Free Church in the Highlands* (Edinburgh, 1876); J. Tulloch, *Position and Prospects of the Church of Scotland* (Edinburgh, 1878), and *A Plea in Self-defence Addressed to Leaders of the Disestablishment Party in the Free Church* (Edinburgh, 1878); *The National Church: An Appeal Against Disestablishment* (London and Edinburgh, 1878); *Some Facts About the Scottish Establishment*, Liberation Society tract (London, n.d.); *United Presbyterian Magazine*, June 1878; NS xxii (1878), 263–4, 314, 384; Duke of Argyll, 'Disestablishment', *CR* xxxi (1878), 217–55; R. Rainy, 'Disestablishment in Scotland: *CR* xli (1882), 431–44; J. Tulloch, 'Disestablishment in Scotland: A Reply', ibid. 749–67. Cf. J. Fleming, *A History of the Church in Scotland, 1875–1929* (Edinburgh, 1933), 26–7; Drummond and Bulloch, op. cit. 109; Simpson, op. cit. ii. 1 ff.; G. I. T. Machin, 'Voluntaryism and Reunion, 1874–1929', in N. Macdougall (ed.), *Church, Politics, and Society: Scotland, 1408–1929* (Edinburgh, 1983), 222–3.

[20] *Primitive Methodist Magazine*, NS xii (1874), 640; *Dundee Advertiser*, 11 Dec. 1874; LS, 17 Dec. 1874; A/LIB/5, 194.

[21] Tulloch to Revd Dr R. Story, 2 July 1878; M. Oliphant, *A Memoir of the Life of John Tulloch* (Edinburgh, 1888), 326.

and United Presbyterian Churches combined a slight numerical lead over the establishment in total membership.[22] But in 1882 John Tulloch claimed that the number of communicants in the Church of Scotland was considerably higher than in the other two Churches together, and that Church of Scotland communicants were increasing much more quickly.[23] Comparative figures published recently, however, suggest that Tulloch's figures for the Church of Scotland were rather exaggerated.[24] Tulloch wanted funds to be raised, literature to be issued, and support to be given to the Association for the Maintenance of National Religion—'a good pull and a pull altogether, to increase the majority against disestablishment'.[25] As the establishment was growing more rapidly than Dissenting Churches the voluntary claim to have a decided majority was weakened.

The numerical support for voluntaryism naturally affected its political strength. The Parliamentary careers of politicians might be governed by their ability to satisfy most of their constituents; hence the majority view on disestablishment had an important bearing on how politicians approached that question. Scottish Dissenters naturally wanted the Liberal party to adopt disestablishment as a policy. But apart from comparative Church statistics the existence of many 'Church Liberals' indicated that party unity would probably be destroyed if disestablishment was adopted. Unlike the clear-cut case of Ireland, therefore, Scottish disestablishment found Liberal leaders avoiding any commitment. They said the matter could be resolved when the opinions of the Scottish people had matured on the subject—an impeccably Liberal sentiment which, by postponing the issue, had the additional benefit of maintaining Liberal party unity. Such, not surprisingly, was the tactic of the Whig Lord Hartington (leader of the party after Gladstone's retirement in January 1875) when speaking in Edinburgh on 6 November 1877 to inaugurate the moderate and Whig-dominated East and North of Scotland Liberal Association. 'It will . . . be necessary that I should be extremely careful', he had told Gladstone, 'and certainly that I should not at the present time commit myself either for or against disestablishment . . . [but] it will probably be as well that I should . . . indicate it as one of the subjects to be dealt with some day by the Liberal party.'[26] Accordingly he said in Scotland that, when Liberal opinion had been sufficiently formed, the party would deal with the matter, irrespective of possible consequences to the English establishment.[27] The emphasis was on postponement, while admitting that some time the subject might have to be

[22] J. Johnston, *The Ecclesiastical and Religious Statistics of Scotland* (Glasgow, 1874), 28.
[23] J. Tulloch, 'Disestablishment in Scotland: A Reply', *CR* xli (1882), 765–7: Church of Scotland communicants 550,000, Free Church and United Presbyterian communicants together only 407,000. Cf. Anon., *The Distribution and Statistics of the Scottish Churches* (n.p., 1886), 55.
[24] R. Currie, A. Gilbert, and L. Horsley (eds.) *Churches and Churchgoers: Patterns of Church Growth in the British Isles since 1700* (Oxford, 1977), 132–3.
[25] Oliphant, op. cit. 325–7, 338–9; see also 345–7.
[26] Hartington to Gladstone, 31 Oct. 1877; GP, 44144, fos. 245–7.
[27] LS, 17 Nov. 1877; A/LIB/6; 18.

tackled as a political question. Gladstone told Argyll: 'I am not able to see the very great moment of the question for Scotland, one way or the other . . . there is no crying grievance or mischief, and I have no desire to make one'.[28] Such statements showed the difficulty of the question, not least for party unity. When another general election approached it became even more important, for the sake of unity, to keep the matter quiet.

IV. NONCONFORMITY AND THE LIBERAL PARTY, 1874–1879

English Nonconformists who wanted disestablishment hoped that anti-Ritualism would help their cause. An assembly of the Congregational Union in October 1877 carried unanimously, on the motion of Guinness Rogers, a resolution that 'it is the duty of all who desire the maintenance of a scriptural faith, and of Christian simplicity in worship . . . to use their influence as citizens to bring about the disestablishment and disendowment of the Church, that they may be freed from complicity in the dissemination of errors which they abhor'.[29] R. W. Dale said in a *Fortnightly Review* article in March 1876: 'The development of Ritualism is kindling excitement in many who have been indifferent to the Liberation Movement till now'.[30] At the same time the desire of some Ritualists for disestablishment was an encouragement to voluntaries: the *Primitive Methodist Magazine* said that 'the members of the Church of England have had new evidence of the complete dependence of that Church on the will of the Legislature, in regard to its most important concerns'.[31] A more direct stimulus was the growth of the Scottish movement for disestablishment; and a further, if waning, reason for Nonconformist political action was continued opposition to the 1870 Education Act. This was shown by unsuccessful attempts in mid-1874 to repeal Clause 25 and introduce compulsory attendance.

While a Conservative Government was in power Nonconformist objects were unlikely to be realized, so hope was placed in rebuilding the shattered alliance with the Liberal party. In order to do this, however, voluntaries would have to join their cause with others and it might lose distinctiveness and force. 'The next page of the Liberal programme', an article by Chamberlain in the *Fortnightly Review* (edited by John Morley) for October 1874, surprisingly chose disestablishment as the only question of immediate importance which might succeed in uniting Liberals. Chamberlain gave secular and social (not religious) arguments for disestablishment and disendowment.[32] Disestablishment really only interested Chamberlain as part of a broad radical programme including social and franchise reforms. When attending a Liberation Society

[28] Gladstone to Argyll, 9 Sept. 1878; Lathbury, op. cit. i. 172–3.
[29] *Congregational Year-book* (1878), 108.
[30] *FR* xix. 338.
[31] *Primitive Methodist Magazine*, NS xii (1874), 638.
[32] *FR* xvi. 405–29; D. A. Hamer, *John Morley, Liberal Intellectual in Politics* (Oxford, 1968), 106 ff.

meeting at Manchester with Morley in November, he was disappointed not to persuade that body to join forces with the National Education League and play a more central, if less distinctive, role in radicalism.[33] After this meeting Morley, an agnostic, suggested to Chamberlain that disestablishment should be made the subject of 'a purely political agitation', to be launched at a great Birmingham meeting: 'R. W. Dale will be the only pastor on the platform, and not a word to be said about "the freedom which is in Christ Jesus" . . . The Liberation Society is even now not national, not political enough'.[34] Morley later complained that he found the Society's leaders 'a weak band: vague, slow, crude'.[35] Both he and Chamberlain continued to support the Society, however. Chamberlain sat on its executive committee and in May 1876 chaired one of its meetings at Spurgeon's Tabernacle: 'Ye Gods, think of a Unitarian in the seat of the Prophet'.[36]

In order to strengthen its appeal to the Liberal party the Society tried to win more support in the country. Its council resolved in February 1874 that exertions be doubled 'for the instruction of the whole community respecting its principle aims'.[37] The Triennial Conference in May decided to raise a campaign fund of £100,000 over five years. A figure of £84,000 was obtained by 1879, some large subscriptions and legacies coming from wealthy businessmen like Sir Titus Salt and Samuel Courtauld. It was also decided to enlarge the executive committee. In June a new 'organizing and travelling agent', the Revd John Fisher, was appointed to supervise district agents and encourage the formation of local committees. By mid-1875 thirty district and local agents were at work.[38] The number of lectures sponsored rose steeply, from 699 in 1874–5 to 957 in 1875–6.[39] The Society had links with the Central Nonconformist Committee and its associated local organizations; with the rapidly spreading Liberal associations; and with Scottish disestablishment bodies. Attention was given to the special aspects of Welsh disestablishment, conferences being held in Wales and publications issued in Welsh.[40] Some leaflets were aimed at converting more Wesleyans to voluntaryism; there were already some committed voluntaries among Wesleyan ministers, challenging the Wesleyan tradition that ministers should not engage in politics.[41] The Triennial Conference in 1877, with Chamberlain chairing the public session, was

[33] R. Jay, *Joseph Chamberlain: A Political Study* (Oxford, 1981), 32.
[34] Morley to Chamberlain, 16 Nov. 1874; CP, JC5/54/40.
[35] Morley to Frederic Harrison, 29 Mar. 1876; F. W. Hirst, *Early Life and Letters of John Morley* (2 vols., London, 1927), ii. 1–9.
[36] Chamberlain to Jesse Collings, 13 Feb. 1876; quoted Garvin, op. cit. i. 226.
[37] LS, 9 Mar. 1874; A/LIB/5, 94. Cf. D. A. Hamer, *The Politics of Electoral Pressure* (Hassocks, Sussex, 1977), 141 ff.
[38] LS, 10 Feb., 20 July 1876; A/LIB/5, 321, 375–8.
[39] Ibid. 20 May, 17 June 1874; 7 Jan., 4 May 1875; 18 May 1876; A/LIB/5, 108, 125–6, 200–6, 248–50, 352; W. H. Mackintosh, *Disestablishment and Liberation* (London, 1972), 217–19.
[40] LS, 13 Aug. 1874; A/LIB/5, 154–5.
[41] Ibid. 12 Oct. 1877; A/LIB/6, 8; D. W. Bebbington, *The Nonconformist Conscience: Chapel and Politics, 1870–1914* (London, 1982), 32.

attended by delegates from 100 groups throughout the United Kingdom. At the conference some 'Practical Suggestions' regarding disestablishment and disendowment were announced. The Positivist Frederic Harrison, who lectured for the Society, prepared a disestablishment bill in 1878.[42]

Church defenders were worried by the current Liberationist activity. The council of the Church Defence Institution resolved in June 1876 that the 'organized dissemination of Voluntary opinions required equally strong counter-action by Churchmen' and that much more money was needed.[43] A new Church of England Working-men's Society was formed in August 1876 and had 184 branches and ninety-four agencies by 1885.[44]

There was a growing prominence of secularists in the Liberation Society not entirely pleasing to those who championed voluntaryism primarily on religious grounds. The annual report of the Congregational Union for 1875 said that 'the sacred work of the Church's emancipation' could not be left to 'the influence of forces, some of which are hostile to the doctrines, and others inimical to the spirit, of the Christian faith'.[45] Two leading Congregationalists and staunch evangelicals, R. W. Dale and Guinness Rogers, went without the Society's official sponsorship (but with its blessing) to preach voluntary principles to the nation in two lecture tours in the winters of 1875–6 and 1876–7. Their work, they both agreed, was 'a part of the service to which Christ has called us—with the one object present to us always of getting His will done on earth as it is in Heaven'.[46] Somewhat appropriately the tours coincided with the purely Evangelical mission of Moody and Sankey, but Dale and Rogers' Evangelism had an emphatic voluntary bias. Their first tour included Bradford, Liverpool, Leeds, Manchester, Norwich, Derby, and London; the second took them to Hull, Bristol, Plymouth, Newcastle upon Tyne, Swansea, Cardiff, Caernarvon, and elsewhere. Their reception was sometimes appreciative, but opposition was not lacking—at Liverpool there were loud interruptions, and rotten eggs were thrown at Bristol. *The Times* was sufficiently impressed with the tours to declare that resolute men were at war with the establishment.[47]

The voluntaries were naturally hoping, through a display of increased popular support, to gain more influence in the Liberal party. The Central Nonconformist Committee instigated a conference of ministers at Crewe at the beginning of 1875, which expressed the hope that the new Liberal leader would

[42] Mackintosh, op. cit. 220, 226–9; F. Harrison, *Autobiographic Memoirs* (2 vols., London, 1911), ii. 294–5.

[43] CDI Central Council Minutes, 26 June 1876 (Vol. 306).

[44] *Constitution and Rules of the Church of England Working-men's Society*, rev. 1884 (London, 1885), 1, 27–8.

[45] *Congregational Year-book* (1876), 44–5.

[46] Quoted Bebbington, op. cit. 27. Cf. A. W. W. Dale, *The Life of R. W. Dale of Birmingham* (London, 1898), 377–8.

[47] J. Guinness Rogers, *An Autobiography* (London, 1903), 176–80; Dale, op. cit. 379; LS, 3 and 24 June, 23 Sept., 5 Nov., 2 and 16 Dec. 1875, 6 Jan., 17 Feb. 1876; A/LIB/5, 260, 264, 282, 294, 301, 308, 315, 324–5.

'terminate the alienation of the nonconformists from their former allies'.[48] This was a detrimental reference to Forster's candidature for the leadership, and Forster's withdrawal was seen as defeat of an old enemy. Lord Hartington, who became leader, was (although a Whig) at least milder and more elusive in his attitude to radical Nonconformist claims, and had voted the previous June for the repeal of Clause 25.[49] Though no longer leader, Gladstone remained a very important figure in the party with much potentiality left in him, and Dissenters continued to cultivate his acquaintance and woo his support. His Vatican pamphlets provided a congenial means of approach. Newman Hall, a leading Congregational minister and an old hand at these matters, arranged a meeting between Gladstone and about twenty eminent Nonconformists of different denominations at his house on 16 February.[50] 'For two hours we discussed Papal decrees and Disestablishment', noted Hall. 'His courtesy and marked attention to every question and remark won all hearts.'[51] Gladstone, in a letter to the *Nonconformist* of 22 March 1876, said he could not promise concurrence in the voluntary plea: he thought 'the Establishment of England (not of Scotland) represents the religion of a considerable majority of the people'.[52] But a further meeting was held at Hall's house on 12 July 1876;[53] and in the meantime Gladstone had received invitations from another leading Congregationalist, the Revd Henry Allon.[54] It was not surprising that Gladstone wrote to his friend Dr Ignaz Döllinger: 'There is a preparation of mind going on for disestablishment, and I do not say it may not be precipitated by events'. But he was cautious as ever about the subject: 'the work is tremendous, there are millions of fibres to tear away'.[55]

Given the differing attitudes to disestablishment among Liberals, voluntaries had also to be cautious when seeking a closer bond with the Liberal party. Moderate and extreme voluntaries expressed different views at meetings, the moderates paying attention to the importance of political issues apart from disestablishment when deciding on electoral action. The moderate approach, advocating integration in the 'broad Church' of the Liberal party, tended to prevail. When an electoral policy was suggested by Charles Miall, brother of Edward, in the *Nonconformist* and at the Liberation Society's Triennial Conference in 1877, he advised that disestablishment should not be aggressively or prematurely urged. Rather should there be patient efforts by voluntaries to influence the choice of candidates in popular constituencies where they

[48] P. C. Griffiths, 'The Origins and Development of the National Liberal Federation to 1886', B.Litt. thesis (Oxford, 1973), 267.

[49] Ibis. 79.

[50] Newman Hall to Gladstone, 15 and 18 Feb. 1875; GP, 44188, fos. 120–1, 122–8.

[51] Hall's diary, 16 Feb. 1875; N. Hall, *An Autobiography* (London, 1898), 271.

[52] D. Schreuder, 'Gladstone and the Conscience of the State', in P. Marsh (ed.), *The Conscience of the Victorian State* (Syracuse, NY, 1979), 116.

[53] Hall to Gladstone, 12 July 1876; GP, 44188, fos. 140–1.

[54] Henry Allon to Gladstone, 22 Apr. 1875, 3 Feb. 1876; GP, 44095, fos. 336–9.

[55] Gladstone to Döllinger, 8 Dec. 1874; GP, 44140, fo. 405.

commanded substantial weight. George Baines of Leicester also wrote to the
Nonconformist in April 1877 that voluntary electoral efforts should not conflict
with 'the regular action of the Liberal party, or become the occasion of
disunion'. The Liberal party must be persuaded rather than threatened, its
unity succoured rather than weakened.[56] This gentle approach was a natural
reaction from the dissensions of 1870–4, and a result of the *rapprochement*
between Gladstone and Nonconformity reached through the Bulgarian
agitation in 1876.[57]

While voluntaries were working to establish better relations with the Liberal
party, and the question of disestablishment was being considered as one of long-
term, gradual development, some more practical Nonconformist claims had
still to be resolved. The chief of these was the claim for burial with Dissenting
services in parish churchyards. Over this issue the Liberal leaders were allied
with Nonconformists. There was still some determined resistance, but
Churchmen were divided over the matter. Some leading Evangelicals such as
Lord Shaftesbury believed that concession would strengthen the establishment, but other Churchmen thought it would only encourage the voluntary cry.
J. C. Ryle was as opposed as Pusey to surrender, arguing that if Nonconformists were allowed to hold burial services in the churchyard they would be
permitted to share the church building itself 'on the first rainy day'.[58] The
National Church said that Churchmen 'must defeat this premeditated invasion
of their sacred burial places'.[59] Many High-Churchmen were against the
reform, and the English Church Union passed numerous resolutions against
it.[60] But Malcolm MacColl wanted concession on religious grounds: 'Almost
anything's better than a law which compels a parish priest to bury, with the rites
of the Church, every legal parishioner, though he may possibly be an avowed
Atheist'.[61]

In 1875 the Dissenting Deputies proposed that a fresh burials bill be brought
in. Osborne Morgan agreed to introduce the measure, which gave to
parishioners in general the right to use the churchyard for burial services,
without the Prayer Book or the clergyman. Gladstone, Bright, and Forster
spoke for the bill. Though the Government was opposed, several Conservatives
voted for the measure and the second reading was lost by only fourteen votes on
21 April. On 13 July the Court of Arches declared against allowing a Wesleyan
minister at Owston Ferry in Lincolnshire, the Revd Henry Keet, the right to

---

[56] D. A. Hamer, op. cit. 139–45; H. J. Hanham, *Elections and Party Management: Politics in the Time
of Disraeli and Gladstone* (London, 1959), 123.
[57] See below, p. 105.
[58] J. C. Ryle, *Shall We Surrender?* (London, 1876), Cf. W. H. Mackintosh, op. cit. 277–8.
[59] *The National Church*, Dec. 1875 (iv. 285–6), also Aug. 1876 (v. 151). Cf. *Report of the London
Working-men's Council for Church Defence for the Year 1875* (London, 1876), 5.
[60] G. B. Roberts, *History of the English Church Union, 1859–1894*, 126 ff., 179.
[61] Letter of Malcolm MacColl to *Church Times*, enclosed in MacColl to Gladstone, 14 Sept. 1874;
GP, 44243, fos. 53–5.

erect a tombstone to his daughter's memory on which the inscription described him as 'Reverend'. Although the issue was not that of burials, it helped to sustain Nonconformist irritation over the matter of churchyards. The *Watchman*, a Wesleyan newspaper, said the judgment revealed 'one more of the foul abuses of the Established Church' and would drive Wesleyans to voluntaryism.[62] The Judicial Committee of the Privy Council, however, allowed Keet's appeal on the matter in January 1876.[63]

In the 1876 session Morgan obtained only a late position for his bill, so instead of introducing it he moved a resolution on 3 March allowing burials with any Christian service or with no service. This was defeated in a large House by a majority of thirty-one although thirteen Conservatives supported it. Morgan's speech denied that the burial issue was connected with disestablishment, but Disraeli declared uncompromising opposition on religious grounds.[64] A similar resolution was moved by Lord Granville, Liberal leader in the Lords, on 15 May; but this limited the concession to Christian services and excluded the right to have no service. Granville said that the exclusive churchyards of England and Wales had no parallel in the world. But the Duke of Richmond opposed the resolution on the Government's behalf, saying that many supporters of the reform regarded it as a first step to disestablishment; and the Bishop of Lincoln, Christopher Wordsworth, said that the demand challenged 'the very existence of the English Church'. Lord Salisbury, though favourable to an attempt at settlement by the Government, made an effective point by quoting a verse from a Secularist hymn book in which the doctrine of immortality was repudiated, and asking how they could provide against such hymns being sung in the churchyard. Frederick Temple of Exeter was the only Bishop to support the resolution, which was defeated by 148 votes to ninety-two, sixteen bishops voting against and the two Archbishops abstaining.[65]

In March 1877 the Government fulfilled its promise to propose a settlement by introducing its Burial Acts Consolidation Bill in the Lords. Dissenters thought the bill unsatisfactory because its main object seemed not to meet their claim but merely to close some burial grounds for sanitary reasons and open others. A clause allowing silent burials was the sole overt concession to the Dissenting grievance, but this clause was dropped under pressure from two High-Churchmen in the Cabinet, Salisbury and Gathorne Hardy. The Congregational Union passed a long resolution against the measure; the newly

[62] Quoted in *Wesleyan Connexional Record and Year-book for 1875* (London, 1875), 241–2. The Bishop of Lincoln, Christopher Wordsworth, had opposed Keet's plea, and *The National Church* supported Wordsworth (Sept. 1875; iv. 214).
[63] *AR* cxvii (1875), Chronicle section, 198–208.
[64] H ccxxvii. 1296–398; *AR* cxviii (1876), 42–4; Nancy E. Johnson (ed.), *The Diary of Gathorne Hardy, Later Lord Cranbrook* (Oxford, 1981), 264.
[65] *AR* cxviii (1876), 44–7; H ccxxix. 588–666; Davidson and Benham, *Tait*, ii. 383–5; E. G. Sandford (ed.), *Memoirs of Archbishop Temple* (2 vols., London, 1906), i. 579; Cross Papers, Add. MS 51265, fo. 128 (Provisional nos.).

founded Presbyterian Church of England adopted an overture opposing it; and the Liberation Society and Dissenting Deputies held a conference to protest.[66] The Lords passed the second reading on 26 April, after rejecting an amendment by Granville to allow Dissenters to conduct burials in churchyards with their own services. Salisbury said the Dissenters' burial claim would be a step to disestablishment: 'If I were pursued by a lion it would be no use for me to present him with one of my legs and expect him to be satisfied'. Selborne, however, argued to the contrary that concession of the burials claim would prevent disestablishment.[67]

The Government announced the removal of the clause permitting silent burial, and this annoyed Archbishops Tait and Thomson because they had declared in the Lords that the religious problem over burials should be settled. This had caused Gathorne Hardy to note that 'the archbishops as usual betray their clergy'.[68] The Earl of Harroway proposed in committee an amendment conceding the Dissenters' case by allowing them to hold their own burial services. After first obtaining a tie vote, and being rejected on a casting vote (given by Lord Redesdale), this proposal was carried at the report stage on 18 June by sixteen votes. Archbishops Tait and Thomson, three Bishops and twenty-one Conservative lay peers supported the amendment. However, after a strong protest signed by 13,770 clergy (about two-thirds of the clerical strength of the Church of England) had been sent to the Government, Ministers withdrew the transformed bill. So the burial question remained unresolved, but the Lords' acceptance of the Dissenters' claim seemed to promise a satisfactory settlement. 'As to the future', wrote Bishop Magee regretfully, 'it is clear that the game is up'.[69]

Besides proposing an unacceptable solution of the burial issue and forming a barrier against disestablishment, the Conservative ministry also annoyed Nonconformists by aiding Anglican interests over education and Church extension. Lord Sandon, vice-president of the committee of council on education, circulated a memorandum to his colleagues in 1875 stigmatizing board schools as nurseries of radical and Dissenting agitation. He wished to make church schools more equally competitive with board schools.[70] After a bill of George Dixon for compulsory attendance and universal school boards had been defeated on 5 April 1876, Sandon introduced a measure which was read a first time in the Commons on 18 May.[71] The bill provided higher Government

[66] *Congregational Year-book* (1878), 39–40; *Digest of the Proceedings of the Synod of the Presbyterian Church of England, 1876–1905* (London, 1907), 611.

[67] H ccxxxiii. 1869–940.

[68] Diary, 18 May 1877; Johnson, op. cit. 322; Marsh, op. cit. 251–6.

[69] *AR* cxix (1877), 52; Davidson and Benham, op. cit. ii. 387–8; MacDonnell, *Magee*, ii. 67–9.

[70] M. J. Wilkinson, 'Educational Controversies in British Politics, 1895–1914', Ph.D thesis (Newcastle upon Tyne, 1978), 219–20; Gillian Sutherland, *Policy-making in Elementary Education, 1870–1895* (Oxford, 1973), 130 ff.

[71] H ccxxix. 929–65.

grants for voluntary schools, allowing them to earn up to 17s. 6d. per child without having to match this amount from private contributions (a departure from previous practice); additional amounts would be supplied if these could be equalled by private receipts. Powers to make attendance compulsory (for children under eleven years of age) were given to town councils and the Poor Law boards of guardians. This implied that in areas where there was no board school the children of Nonconformists might be compelled to attend church schools by law, rather than just by desire for education which probably motivated nearly all of them to attend anyway.[72] Clause 25 was repealed; the payment of fees for poor children at voluntary schools was not abandoned, however, but transferred from school boards to the boards of guardians.

A storm of Dissenting criticism met the bill—from the National Education League meeting on 24 May, the Central Nonconformist Committee on 26 May, and the joint committees of the Liberation Society and Dissenting Deputies on 12 June. Many petitions came from Nonconformist bodies condemning the bill as a blatantly reactionary measure.[73] Strong opposition was also shown during the second reading debates in the Commons on 15 and 19 June and the protracted committee stage in July. But the Government easily succeeded. The second reading passed by the huge majority of 278, an amendment by A. J. Mundella for direct compulsion being lost by 146, and one by Henry Richard to place all elementary schools under State management by 218. On the other hand, an amendment to dissolve school boards which did not have schools to manage or sites to build them on was carried—but only after opposition by Disraeli, after stringent conditions had been inserted, and after five nights' debate.[74]

Liberal divisions were clearly revealed over the bill, and many Liberals helped the Conservatives to get it through. Fifty-five Liberals voted against Richard's motion, and many Liberals abstained. Disraeli claimed to see in the debates 'the utter demoralisation and rancorous breaking up of the Liberal party'. The revival of educational controversy had certainly given a blow to Nonconformist hopes of unity with the Liberal party, even if the hindrance was only temporary. After a third reading in the Commons on 5 August, the bill slid quickly through the Lords in the next few days.[75]

In spite of their new assistance, the voluntary schools were still likely to be the underdogs of elementary education, finding it increasingly hard to compete with the wealthier board schools which could afford to provide better buildings, wider curricula, and higher standards—even, in some cases, more than

[72] Cf. R. W. Dale to Henry Richard, 25 May 1876; Henry Richard Papers, 5503C, 41.

[73] Mackintosh, op. cit. 259.

[74] E. J. Feuchtwanger, *Disraeli*, 18–19; Lord John Manners to Disraeli, 22 July 1876; DP, B/XX/M/192.

[75] *AR* cxviii (1876), 65–9; Sutherland, op. cit. 138–44; Griffiths, op. cit. 78; Disraeli to Lady Bradford, 5 Aug. 1876; Marquess of Zetland (ed.), *The Letters of Disraeli to Lady Bradford and Lady Chesterfield* (2 vols., London 1929), ii. 61–2.

elementary education.[76] In the future, voluntary schools were to provide further political controversy by wanting more assistance from the Conservatives to offset the advantages of the board schools backed by Liberals.

The 1876 Education Act caused differing reactions. There was some Anglican expression of disappointment, and a chorus of Nonconformist denunciation. The Parliamentary committee of the Liberation Society, the autumn Baptist and Congregational assemblies, and the *Nonconformist* all condemned the Act as favouring denominational schools at the expense of board schools, and advised Dissenters to fight hard at school board elections.[77] Nevertheless the National Education League decided that the repeal of Clause 25 and the surprisingly capacious provisions for compulsory attendance were sufficient reason for it to dissolve, and its last meeting was held on 28 March 1877. Not only was Chamberlain anxious to widen his radical movement beyond the limited and not very popular cause of education, and even beyond disestablishment, but the Bulgarian agitation had made overseas policy a new focus for Liberal attacks on the Government.

Apart from the educational reform, Ministers encouraged Church interests by establishing new Bishoprics. Lord Salisbury and R. A. Cross, the Home Secretary, were convinced of the need for these, and the Conservative *Quarterly Review* said in July 1874 that the extension of Church government was the best means of Church defence.[78] Cross and others introduced bills to increase the episcopate, and most of these were enacted in spite of opposition from voluntaries and some objections from anti-Ritualists who feared that more Bishoprics might lead to the advancement of Ritualists.[79] In May 1875 the second reading of a bill to create a diocese of St Albans was opposed by Henry Richard, who (like the Liberation Society executive) did not want the extension of 'a class of politico-ecclesiastical State officials'. He claimed that few Anglicans wanted more Bishops, and quoted some comments deprecating Bishops from both High-Church and Evangelical newspapers. Only disestablishment, he predictably said, could give the Church of England the freedom necessary to develop its forces. The bill was supported, however, by Harcourt who said that it vindicated the true principles of Church legislation by asserting 'the absolute authority of Parliament', which could deal with Church affairs 'without consulting the clergy or anybody else'. Richard only mustered sixty-one votes against 273; and the bill sailed through both Houses.[80] A bill of 1876

---

[76] Marjorie Cruickshank, *Church and State in English Education, 1870 to the Present Day* (London, 1964), 55 ff.

[77] *Nonconformist*, 3 Jan. 1877, p. 25; *Liberator*, Sept. 1876, p. 157; quoted Mackintosh, op. cit. 260; *Primitive Methodist Magazine*, NS xiv (1876), 512; Baptist Union resolution, 5 Oct. 1876; *Baptist Handbook* (1877), 91–2; Congregational Union resolution, 10 Oct. 1876; *Congregational Year-book* (1877), 129.

[78] Salisbury to R. A. Cross, Feb. 1874; Cross Papers, Add. MS 51263, fos. 6–7, provisional nos.; Marsh, *Victorian Church in Decline*, 200.

[79] 'Telegonus', *The Increase of the Episcopate: Is it Desirable at the Present Time?* (London, 1877), 19.

[80] H ccxxiv. 489–509; LS, 15 Mar. 1875; A/LIB/5,228–9.

(which had already passed the Lords the previous year) enabling the Ecclesiastical Commission to propose the creation of many new sees, was opposed by Cross and others and was eventually withdrawn.[81] But a measure introduced in the same session by Cross, to establish a Bishopric for Cornwall, succeeded against voluntary opposition.[82]

The sees of St Albans and Truro were duly inaugurated in 1877. In that year Cross presented a Bishoprics Bill providing four new sees in the North and Midlands. The bill did not obtain enough Parliamentary time in 1877, but passed the following year under 'strong private pressure' from Bishops (according to Magee), and against strong opposition especially from Joseph Cowen, radical MP for Newcastle where the bill proposed to establish a new see.[83] The *Primitive Methodist Magazine* commented that a better way to relieve the work of Bishops would be to remove them from the House of Lords.[84] In accordance with the new Act, sees were established over the next decade at Liverpool, Newcastle upon Tyne, Southwell, and Wakefield.[85] Some of the finance for the new sees came from the dioceses out of which they were carved, but most of it came from private contributions. There was to be no increase of Bishops in the Lords, since most Bishops would sit there in rotation.

Attempts to reform the patronage system were less successful. Bishop Magee obtained in 1874 the appointment of a select committee on patronage, and this reported in favour of modest changes. Radical desires for the abolition of the sale of patronage were ignored.[86] It was merely proposed that sales be subjected to certain publicity and registration requirements and that the Bishops and parishioners could object to presentees on the grounds of physical incapacity or moral unfitness. Magee introduced a bill in the Lords early in 1875 to meet the committee's recommendations, stressing its restrained nature and its object of strengthening the establishment; Bishop Temple indeed wished the bill were stronger.[87] The Lords passed the bill, but this was an inopportune time to urge such a reform because the anti-Ritualist agitation was at a height, and supposed clerical pretensions against the rights of laymen were at a discount. The mild and well-meaning bill was represented as an attack on property and even on Protestantism. Pamphlets and petitions opposed it, and at a protest meeting Bishops were accused of wanting to confiscate the property of lay patrons.[88]

[81] H ccxxvii. 337–71, ccxxx. 1020–7.

[82] Marsh, op. cit. 203.

[83] MacDonnell, op. cit. ii. 97; H ccxlii. 829–42; P. J. Jagger, 'The Formation of the Diocese of Newcastle', in W. S. F. Pickering (ed.), *A Social History of the Diocese of Newcastle, 1882–1982* (Stocksfield, 1981), 39–42; E. R. Jones, *The Life and Speeches of Joseph Cowen, MP* (London, 1885), 326–35.

[84] NS i (1878), 255.

[85] Marsh, op. cit. 205–7.

[86] Cf. Hon. A. Elliot, *The State and the Church* (London, 1882), 117–18, 121; Bishop C. J. Ellicott, 'The Church of England, Present and Future', *Nineteenth Century*, i (Mar.–July 1877), 59 ff.

[87] H ccxxii. 808–36; MacDonnell, op. cit. ii. 18–22.

[88] M. J. D. Roberts, 'Private Patronage and the Church of England, 1800–1900' *JEH* xxxii (1981), 215–17.

The Liberation Society found the bill inadequate from an opposite angle, and said that 'what is declared to be a sacred trust will still be a marketable property ... Promotion by purchase ... will continue to be a characteristic of the Establishment.' Disestablishment was required to initiate satisfactory reforms in the Church. [89] Salisbury, Cross, and even Cairns favoured the bill, but it was withdrawn from the Commons on 27 July before it could be debated there.[90] E. A. Leatham, a Quaker who was MP for Huddersfield, brought in a motion for strong remedial action in June 1877, which was withdrawn, and another in 1878 which was talked out.[91] The Government, which Magee claimed was 'sick of all Church questions',[92] appointed a Royal Commission in 1878 which repeated most of the select committee's findings. But no further legislative attempt was made before the Liberals returned to office.

In June 1876 early reports of the massacres in Bulgaria began to arouse shocked reactions. These gathered force and were expressed in numerous protest meetings, notably a gathering of the League in Aid of the Christians of Turkey on 27 July, presided over by Lord Shaftesbury, and a National Conference in St James's Hall on 8 December. The Government's pro-Turkish policy was strongly challenged in this affair, which was aggravated by early sceptical comments by Disraeli and fomented by radicals like Auberon Herbert, W. T. Stead, and H. J. Wilson. Eventually, after some prodding, Gladstone intervened spectacularly with his passionate best-selling pamphlet, *The Bulgarian Horrors and the Question of the East*—called by Disraeli 'of all the Bulgarian horrors, perhaps the greatest'—which appeared on 5 September.[93]

No revolution in foreign policy resulted from this upheaval, but other political effects occurred. Religious bodies were particularly involved in the moral fervour of the agitation, not only for its own sake but for their own political purposes. Mutual religious sympathies played no part in deciding the alignment of forces; Anglican Evangelicals were usually divided from Nonconformists, and Anglo-Catholics from Roman Catholics. Those who were already inclined to support Gladstone and oppose the Government now found an additional reason for doing so. Nonconformists looking for reintegration in Liberal politics, High-Churchmen strongly opposed to the Public Worship Regulation Act, were prominent in the Bulgarian agitation and eulogized Gladstone. He 'has pursued an enlightened and noble course, unmoved by opposition, uninjured though not unassailed by the shafts of calumny', was the praise given to the ex-premier by the Revd Dr T. W. B. Aveling, chairman of

[89] LS, 15 Mar. 1875; A/LIB/5, 228–9.

[90] MacDonnell, op. cit. ii. 32–3.

[91] H ccxxxv. 298–318, ccxxxvii. 1540–67.

[92] MacDonnell, op. cit. ii. 22.

[93] R. T. Shannon, *Gladstone and the Bulgarian Agitation, 1876*, 2nd edn. (Hassocks, Sussex, 1975), 38 ff.; Rossi, *Transformation*, 28–49; Estelle W. Stead, *My Father: Personal and Spiritual Reminiscences of W. T. Stead* (London, 1913), 57 ff.

the Congregational Union, whose son Edward became the lover of Karl Marx's daughter Eleanor.[94] Against the agitation were leading Roman Catholic clerics who were opposed to Russia, and Conservative Catholic nobility; many Evangelicals and Broad-Churchmen who defended the establishment and disliked Ritualists and their pro-Russian sympathies; and supporters of the Church establishment in Scotland.[95]

The country was only temporarily swept by the moral power of the agitation. The lasting significance of the upheaval was that it emphasized existing political inclinations and revived or confirmed political alliances. It also brought Gladstone back to the centre of the political stage and made him a strong contender for a future Liberal premiership. A certain amount of consolidation was achieved in the centre and left of the Liberal party. This was partly because of the desire of Nonconformists to become reattached to Gladstone, and Gladstone's desire to reattach them. 'With lively pleasure I witness from day to day the exertions made by the Nonconformists in the cause of humanity and justice for the East', Gladstone told Newman Hall.[96] But many Whigs disdained the agitation, suspected its implied popular powers, and disagreed with its foreign aims. Even a few radicals were also, for varying reasons, out of sympathy with the movement.[97]

In 1877 Liberal disputes over the Balkan crisis continued. Government support of Turkey, in the Russo-Turkish war which broke out in April, was challenged by Gladstone's proposal to move resolutions against it—a repeat performance of his ill-fated resolutions against the Public Worship Regulation Bill three years before. The official Liberal leaders found the resolutions too strong, and Harcourt was 'boiling over with rage'. Chamberlain addressed a Liberation Society meeting in favour of Gladstone's move, however, and various Liberal associations supported it; but some radicals opposed the resolutions, as they had opposed the Bulgarian agitation. Gladstone introduced and defended his five resolutions in an impressive two-and-a-half-hour speech in the Commons on 7 May, and a five-day debate followed. The resolutions were easily defeated, not least because over seventy Liberals and Home Rulers did not vote with Gladstone. Six Liberals and nineteen Home Rulers voted against him, and only one Conservative for him.[98] Many Home Rulers, noted Chamberlain (now in Parliament), were anti-Russian because of the interests of

[94] Autumnal Assembly of Congregational Union, 10 Oct. 1876; *Congregational Year-book* (1877), 122.
[95] R. T. Shannon, op. cit. 147–201; Bentley, *Ritualism and Politics*, 87–9; Matthew, 'Gladstone', 440; M. D. Johnson, 'Thomas Gasquoine and the Origins of the Leicester Conference', *Journal of United Reformed Church History Society*, ii (1978–82), 349–50; H. St C. Cunningham, 'British Public Opinion and the Eastern Question, 1877–1878', D.Phil. thesis (Sussex, 1969), 280–2.
[96] Gladstone to N. Hall, 12 Oct. 1876; C. Newman Hall, *Autobiography* (London, 1898), 272.
[97] Shannon, op. cit. 226–31; D. Southgate, *The Passing of the Whigs, 1832–1886* (London, 1962), 356–9; Newman Hall to Gladstone, 24 Oct. 1876; GP, 44188, fo. 157.
[98] Rossi, op. cit. 50–5. Cf. Southgate, op. cit. 358.

the Catholic Church—they were 'a scurvy lot', he reflected, and 'a most embarrassing element in all party politics'.[99]

Whig disapproval of Gladstone's views on foreign policy probably helped to account for his support of the National Liberal Federation. This was a wide radical body suggested by William Harris, vice-president of the Birmingham Liberal Association, and founded by Chamberlain at a national Liberal conference of nearly 100 delegates from local bodies which opened at Birmingham on 31 May 1877. This was part of a tendency to radical organization already shown, for example, by the formation of the West and South of Scotland Liberal Association at Glasgow the previous autumn.[1] Gladstone went to stay at Chamberlain's house and delivered the main speech at the inauguration of the NLF. Gladstone spoke mostly about the Balkan question, but Chamberlain raised the cry of 'Free Church, Free Schools, Free Land'. Robert Spence Watson, Quaker president of the Newcastle upon Tyne Liberal Association and later president of the NLF, said the advantage of such a federation would be mainly felt in future agitations, including efforts for disestablishment.[2]

The Federation was bound to emphasize the gap between Whigs and radicals. It was intended to be a delegate forum of the numerous local Liberal associations which were run largely by middle-class Nonconformists and others who were a standing challenge to the traditional aristocratic leadership of the party.[3] Chamberlain had told Morley in February that he hoped the new Federation would be 'very powerful . . . and proportionately detested by all Whigs and Whips'.[4] The radical energy of the National Education League was infused into the new body, as the League was formally dissolved in March 1877. A lot less was heard of the Central Nonconformist Committee, and it seems the NLF was intended to speak for Nonconformity. Even the Liberation Society, though far from dissolving itself, muted its independent political action for many years.[5]

Towards the end of 1877 public sympathy swung to the Turks as they came under increasing pressure from Russia in the conflict. Disraeli (now Earl of Beaconsfield) benefited from this, and Gladstone became temporarily less popular with the public. The NLF also encountered resistance in some Liberal associations, including those of Manchester and Sheffield, where the strength of Birmingham influence was resented. But radical domestic aims remained very

[99] Chamberlain to J. T. Bunce, 16 Feb. 1877; CP, JC5/8/25, quoted Cunningham, op. cit. 102.

[1] J. G. Kellas, 'The Liberal Party in Scotland, 1876–1895', *SHR* xliv (1965), 2.

[2] *Proceedings Attending the Formation of the National Federation of Liberal Associations, with Report of Conference held in Birmingham, 31 May 1877* (Birmingham, 1877), 29.

[3] Griffiths, 'Origins', 87–95; F. H. Herrick, 'The Origins of the National Liberal Federation', *Journal of Modern History*, xvii (1945), 125–6; *Proceedings*, 14 ff.; Hanham, *Elections and Party Management*, 137–54; Southgate, op. cit. 360; T. Lloyd, *The General Election of 1880* (Oxford, 1968), 89.

[4] Chamberlain to Morley, 6 Feb. 1877; CP, JC5/54/158.

[5] Bebbington, *Nonconformist Conscience*, 23.

much alive. Advocates of disestablishment would find support in the address of Henry Richard, chairman of the Congregational Union, at the Union's annual assembly in May 1877; in a vigorous article by Frederic Harrison in the *Fortnightly Review* of the same month; and in a contribution by Guinness Rogers to the new *Nineteenth Century* in November.[6] Alarmist or pseudo-alarmist reactions came from the other side. 'We are fighting for the very life of the Church', said the *Church Times* in March; 'disestablished in some form she must clearly be'.[7] The demand for Scots disestablishment continued to grow, many disestablishment resolutions being passed in Dissenting presbyteries—though resolutions in the Free Church presbyteries were often opposed by a minority.[8] How far disestablishment would be aided by the formation of the National Liberal Federation remained to be seen. The formation emphasized the current desire of voluntaries to combine with the Liberal party; but the hope that the Liberal party would adopt disestablishment might be disappointed by the submergence of the issue in other party considerations.

Foreign affairs during 1878 and the rise of jingoism gave triumph to Beaconsfield and continued division and humiliation to the Opposition. Nonconformist leaders continued to communicate with Gladstone and to raise the question of disestablishment with him.[9] But public obsession with the Near Eastern conflict caused Dale and Rogers to abandon arrangements for further disestablishment meetings;[10] and the *National Church* claimed that some Nonconformists were becoming Church defenders.[11] The Government's good fortune culminated at the end of July when Liberal resolutions against the Treaty of Berlin were crushed, only ten Home Rulers supporting them and forty-seven Liberals abstaining. The turn of the tide was near, however. Within six months a decline in trade, a poor harvest, and disastrous colonial wars put new heart in the Liberals and gave them temporarily a united appearance.[12]

A development which caused remarkably little protest, considering the great upheaval over a similar event twenty-eight years before, was the restoration of a Roman Catholic hierarchy in Scotland on 4 March 1878 by the bull *Ex Supremo Apostolatus Apice*. Two Archbishoprics and four Bishoprics were created, making a total of ten new sees (including the four Anglican ones) authorized in

---

[6] *Congregational Year-book* (1878), 71; *FR* xxi (Jan.–June 1877), 653–75 (part quoted D. Nicholls (ed.), *Church and State in Britain since 1820*, London 1967, 92–104); *Nineteenth Century*, ii (Aug.–Dec. 1877), 632–46.

[7] Quoted D. Bowen, *The Idea of the Victorian Church* (Montreal, 1968), 126.

[8] e.g. Glasgow Free Church Presbytery Minutes, 21 Feb. 1877, CH3/146/39, pp. 67–9; Edinburgh Free Church Presbytery Minutes, 27 and 28 Mar. 1878; CH3/111/30, pp. 10–12. Cf. discussion and voting on the issue, at Dundee Town Council meeting, 5 Apr. 1877 (newspaper extract in Lamb Collection, 176 (11), Dundee Local History Library).

[9] Henry Allon to Gladstone, 13 and 15 Apr. 1878, 3 July 1878; GP, 44095, fos. 332–3, 353–6; Newman Hall, op. cit. 275.

[10] LS, 28 Jan. 1878; A/LIB/6, 38.

[11] Leading article, Jan. 1878; vii. 2.

[12] Rossi, op. cit. 63–77.

Britain in 1878. Six months before the restoration the Whig *Glasgow Herald* had anticipated it with tolerant nonchalance: 'Since it pleases the Pope to call the bishops who hold spiritual sway over the Roman Catholics sojourning in her midst, by titles taken from her ancient cities, [Scotland] . . . will allow him to do so, since it gives him pleasure, and does her no harm. Scotland will not for a moment deem that her liberties, civil or religious, are endangered.'[13] In November 1877 the *Scotsman* rebuked Dr James Begg, author of the *Handbook of Popery*, for his hostility to the expected measure; and *The Times* said the proposal was purely an internal matter of papal administration.[14] The current disputes of Presbyterians perhaps distracted their attention, but some presbyteries petitioned against the hierarchy.[15] Serious rioting occurred on 14 April on Glasgow Green, where 20,000 people assembled, many of them being addressed by an anti-popish lecturer.[16] A protest came from the Bishops of the Scottish Episcopal Church who complained that some of their own territorial titles were being duplicated by Rome.[17] A document by prominent lawyers published in the *Scotsman* argued that, while the assumption of the episcopal titles could not be legally prevented, they could not be legally recognized.[18]

Another question particularly concerning Catholics was that of a new university for Ireland. In May 1879 the O'Conor Don, MP for Roscommon, introduced a bill to establish a University of St Patrick, to which certain denominational colleges would be affiliated. The necessary funds were expected to come from the Church of Ireland surplus after disendowment, and strong protests were made by the Liberation Society and Dissenting Deputies who feared that the funds of a former establishment would be used again for the State endowment of religion. Several Liberals, however did not share this attitude and gave strong support to the bill.[19] But the Government opposed the measure, which failed in June. On 30 June a Government bill to deal with the question was brought into the Upper House by Lord Cairns. This proposed to replace the Queen's University with the Royal University, a purely examining body which would deal only with secular subjects and confer degrees on all successful candidates, whatever their place of education. The bill passed

[13] Quoted A. Bellesheim, *History of the Catholic Church in Scotland*, trans. O. Hunter Blair (4 vols., Edinburgh and London, 1890), iv. 312, and P. F. Anson, *Underground Catholicism in Scotland 1622–1878* (Montrose, 1970), 333.

[14] Bellesheim, op. cit. iv. 312–13.

[15] e.g. Dundee Free Presbytery Minutes, 13 Feb. 1878; CH3/91/4, vol. 2, p. 329; Edinburgh Church of Scotland Presbytery Minutes, 13 Feb. 1878; CH2/121/28, p. 331. Cf. *United Presbyterian Magazine*, NS xxii (1878), 53–8, 109–14.

[16] *AR* cxx (1878), 38.

[17] Bellesheim, op. cit. iv. 315–17.

[18] Ibid. 315.

[19] *AR* cxxi (1879), 66–7; J. Phillips, 'The Irish University Question, 1873–1908', Ph.D. thesis (Cambridge, 1978), 103; Denholm, *Lord Ripon*, 131; Henry Richard to Thomas Gee, 23 May 1879; Gee Papers, 8308D, fo. 302; Carvell Williams to Gee, 24 May 1879; ibid. 8309D, 368; Watkin Williams to Gee, 29 May 1879; ibid. 8309D, 411; Sir George Bowyer to Cardinal Manning, 20 Feb. 1879; copy, DP, B/XXI/B/769a.

through both Houses and was enacted after modification, but it still left Catholics and others seeking a satisfactory university.[20]

Meanwhile one large practical grievance, that of burials, remained to concern Nonconformists. The passage of a favourable amendment in the Lords in 1877 encouraged Osborne Morgan to make fresh attempts, and on 15 February 1878 he intervened with an amendment on the order for committee of supply that 'the time has arrived when the long-pending controversy as to interments in parish churchyards ought to be closed' by means of allowing such interments either without a service, or with the service preferred by the deceased relatives or friends and performed by a chosen person. To continue refusing the concession, he said, would only goad the voluntaries. In the debate it was argued to the contrary that concession would encourage encroachments on the established Church and lead to its destruction. The young A. J. Balfour tried, with his uncle Salisbury's approval, to compromise by suggesting that a restricted concession should be temporarily granted until other burial grounds had been provided for the parish. Morgan's motion was lost by only fifteen votes.[21] The Liberation Society executive committee thought that the matter should not be raised again in that Parliament but should be publicized with a view to the next election.[22] Carvell Williams wrote that the die-hards who were 'making the burials question their Plevna' were waning, and said that 'a dissolution will bring the subject before the people as it has never been brought before them at any previous election'.[23] But Members of Parliament did not agree that the question should be rested, and in the next session no fewer than six bills relating to burials were presented.

From late August 1878 the burial question received fresh publicity from the Akenham case in Suffolk. The rector, the Revd George Drury, was a pronounced Ritualist in a heavily Dissenting area. He objected to the reading of a burial service over the body of the unbaptized child of Baptist parents. The Congregational minister who was reading the service outside the churchyard (it was not, of course, legal to read it within) became involved in a fierce altercation with Drury—though the minister was, somewhat ironically, in favour of an established Church. The rector prosecuted the editor and proprietor of the *East Anglian Daily Times* for publishing what he claimed was a libellous account of the quarrel written by the minister—it said, amongst other things, that Drury was 'pacing the graveyard, attired in indescribable petticoats and inconceivable headgear'. In March 1879 the Court of Common Pleas found for Drury, but awarded him only forty shillings damages.[24] The storm in a hamlet had aggravated great topical issues—Ritualism and disestablishment as well as

---

[20] *AR* cxxi (1879), 67–8.
[21] H ccxxxvii. 1736–839.
[22] LS, 25 Feb. 1878; A/LIB/6, 50.
[23] J. Carvell Williams, *The New Position of the Burials Question* (London, 1878), 46 ff.
[24] R. Fletcher, *The Akenham Burial Case* (London, 1974), 13 ff.

burials. Carvell Williams, in a speech on the affair, said that unless a general settlement was reached the battle for disestablishment might have to be fought over the tombstones.[25]

The Akenham case helps to explain the large amount of attention given to burials in the 1878–9 session of Parliament. Of the six bills introduced (all by private members) two had little relevance to the Dissenters' grievance. One of the remainder proposed that the incumbent could permit Dissenting burial services if he wished, and another suggested that unconsecrated ground should be fenced off for Dissenters. The two other bills were those of Morgan and Balfour, the former proposing equal rights as before and the latter that certain churchyards only (not those, for example, within three miles of a public cemetery) should be opened to non-Anglicans. Neither of these bills reached a second reading. Only Morgan's measure was acceptable to Dissenters, but this was withdrawn.[26] Balfour's compromise bill was talked out on 19 February. Opposition was shown to it in this debate by Church defenders (led by Balfour's uncle, Beresford Hope) on the grounds that its concession would only promote disendowment and disestablishment—which Balfour explicitly said his concession was meant to avoid. The churchyards were already used quite enough for burials, said Hope when moving to reject the bill, and if used a lot more on account of this concession they would become a menace to health. Hope's seconder said there was 'nothing more repulsive to right feeling than that people should go to the house of God surrounded by all the foul and decaying elements of humanity'. The increase of public cemeteries was still, to many, the only acceptable ecclesiastical, hygienic and aesthetic solution.[27]

From the autumn of 1878 ministerial fortunes waned. There was commercial and agricultural depression, growing unemployment, and disaster in Zululand and Afghanistan. If previous overseas success had told in the Government's favour, the Liberals were now able to capitalize on the ministry's colonial reverses, even though these were followed by better fortune.[28] Not only was the nation's money being squandered on imperial ventures but these ventures came to grief—so radicals and Whigs at last had something on which they could unite. The colonial controversies gave Nonconformists an additional approach to Gladstone. Newman Hall congratulated him in December for being 'the most forcible utterer of the protest of the best part of the Nation, against the atrocious wickedness our rulers are perpetrating in Afghanistan'.[29] In 1879 the autumn meeting of the Baptist Union resolved unanimously that Government

[25] Ibid. 245.

[26] H ccxliii. 206–9, 217, 1791–822; *Primitive Methodist Magazine*, NS ii (1879), 126–7.

[27] H ccxliii. 1447–99; *AR* cxxi (1879), 35–6; Arthur James, First Earl Balfour, *Chapters of Autobiography*, ed. Mrs E. Dugdale (London, 1930), 118–20; B. L. Manning, *The Protestant Dissenting Deputies* (Cambridge, 1952), 319–20.

[28] Rossi, op. cit. 77–9; Hanham, op. cit. 228–9. Cf. T. A. Jenkins, 'Gladstone, the Whigs, and the Leadership of the Liberal Party, 1879–1880', *HJ* xxvii (1984), 337–43.

[29] Hall to Gladstone, 27 Dec. 1878; GP, 44188, fos. 176–7.

policy 'had been the cause of endless wars, had involved the nation in grave financial difficulties, and had done nothing to relieve by home legislation the evils under which the nation suffers'.[30] An article by Guinness Rogers in the *Nineteenth Century* said Liberals must unite in order to win the next election against 'the present worthless Tory government, which has squandered the national resources in order to pursue a showy and dangerous foreign policy'. Once the Liberals were in they would have to deal with burials and, perhaps, Scottish disestablishment.[31]

Scottish voluntaryism currently had stronger teeth than English or Welsh. Indeed the strength of the Scottish disestablishment demand was embarrassing to those Nonconformists who were prepared to delay voluntary claims in order to improve Liberal election chances. The Liberation Society executive might complain that Scotland ran away with far more of the Society's funds than it gave back in subscriptions,[32] but Scotland was after all the brightest star in the Liberationist firmament—a position later usurped by Wales. The Society's Scottish Council was growing in numbers and activity, and reported that disestablishment was becoming the primary question in Scotland.[33] The ubiquitous Carvell Williams continued to speak at Scottish disestablishment meetings. A Nonconformist conference at Leeds in January 1879 resolved that Scots disestablishment was 'ripe for immediate practical action' and told the Liberal leaders, Hartington and Granville, that it should be included in the party programme.[34] A leading United Presbyterian, the Revd G. C. Hutton, threatened withdrawal of UP support from the Liberals unless their demand was adopted.[35] But electoral moderation prevailed in the Scottish Council of the Liberation Society. At a conference held by this body in November 1879, Hutton tried to urge abstention from voting if a Liberal candidate refused to promise support for disestablishment. But he was opposed by another United Presbyterian, Duncan McLaren (MP for Edinburgh); and the main resolution, while saying that every effort should be made to obtain voluntary candidates, ruled against prescribing 'a uniform course of action in regard to the choice or the support of candidates'.[36]

The Liberal leaders would offer Scottish voluntaries only hope for the future and non-commitment for the present. In June 1878, when Scots disestablishment was debated in the Commons, Gladstone endorsed Hartington's statement in 1877 that the question would be taken up when Scottish Liberal opinion was 'fully formed' on it.[37] In September Gladstone assured the Whig

[30] *AR* cxxi (1879), 90.
[31] *Nineteenth Century*, vi (July–Dec. 1879), 367, 374.
[32] LS, 18 Nov. 1878; A/LIB/6, 113.
[33] Ibid. 8 Apr. 1878; A/LIB/6, 64.
[34] Ibid. 27 Jan. 1879; A/LIB/6, 133–4; Omond, *Lord Advocates of Scotland*, 2nd ser. 330.
[35] *United Presbyterian Magazine*, Nov. 1878; NS xxii. 492–6.
[36] Hamer, *Electoral Pressure*, 147.
[37] J. Fleming, *A History of the Church in Scotland, 1875–1929* (Edinburgh, 1933), 27–8.

Duke of Argyll that he could not 'see any great moment in the question for Scotland, one way or the other . . . there is no crying grievance or mischief, and I have no desire to make one'. As for disestablishment in England, he added, 'even were the question ripe and my mind made up in favour of the change, neither of which is the case, I should contemplate with pleasure and relief the high improbability of its becoming a practical question during the short remainder of my political life'.[38]

Principal Rainy tried to impress on Gladstone in May 1879 that disestablishment was more important than Liberal party unity, but Gladstone only stressed the importance of imperial questions, repeated his adhesion to Hartington's statement, and said it was not his duty 'either to urge the question forward or to keep it backward'.[39] When W. E. Forster was urged by Alfred Illingworth, treasurer of the Liberation Society, to stand in partnership with him at Bradford and rejoin Liberals who had opposed him over the now much quieter education issue, he affirmed that he took the Hartington-Gladstone line on Scots disestablishment.[40]

There was certainly good reason to believe that, for the sake of Liberal unity in Scotland, the disestablishment issue should be put off. Several prominent 'Church Liberals'—Church of Scotland Liberals wishing to preserve the establishment—remonstrated with W. P. Adam, the Liberal Whip, that most Scots did not want disestablishment, and their insistence had a marked influence on Liberal policy.[41] In six Scottish by-elections in 1878, the leading issue of Church defence versus voluntaryism found Conservatives united but Liberals split.[42] It was clear, therefore, that Liberal fortunes would hardly benefit by adopting disestablishment.

That the Liberals should not commit themselves on the matter of Scottish disestablishment was stressed at a Liberal delegate conference at Glasgow on 16 October 1879. It was then declared that a mature opinion on the question should only be reached after the election.[43] The need for this approach was confirmed by Gladstone who, having agreed early in the year to stand for Midlothian in the general election, undertook his first superlatively oratorical 'Midlothian campaign' from 24 November to 9 December. His copious denunciation of the Government was mainly concerned with foreign and colonial policy, but he explained his position on the Church question in the Corn Exchange at Dalkeith on 26 November. There must be full consideration by the people before Parliament dealt with the question. He accused his opponents of being the main agitators over the issue. The Conservatives, for

[38] Gladstone to Argyll, 9 Sept. 1878; Lathbury, *Correspondence*, i. 172–3.
[39] Rainy to Gladstone, 8 May 1879; Gladstone to Rainy, 24 May 1879; Simpson, *Rainy*, ii 5–8.
[40] *Bradford Observer*, 10 Aug. 1878.
[41] C. N. Johnston, *Handbook of Scottish Church Defence* (Edinburgh, 1892), 57–8; *AR* cxxi (1879), 61, 81–2; G. W. T. Omond, *The Lord Advocates of Scotland*, 2nd ser. 1834–80 (1914), 330.
[42] H. Cunningham, op. cit. 297–302.
[43] Typescript in RP 10148, fo. 83.

example in Salisbury's speeches, were trying to exploit the issue in order to divide Liberals and benefit themselves. Quietude was the Liberals' best policy. It was strongly implied that 'full consideration' could only occur after the general election, though perhaps before the next one. At Glasgow on 5 December he said that, in order to achieve unity, Liberals had to 'make great sacrifices' of their own 'personal and sectional views'. Church Liberals were still worried, however, and sent a memorial to W. P. Adam expressing reservations about supporting Liberal candidates, lest 'the votes of the Scottish Members might be held to represent the wishes of the Scottish people'. But Adam replied that he could not understand 'what madness of suspicion' possessed them.[44]

The economic recession and recent failures of Government policy assisted Liberal unity, and the Opposition approached the election fairly optimistically. Gladstone's acclaimed attacks on the ministry had placed him at the head of the Liberal revival and made him a strong candidate for the premiership if the Liberals won. Nonconformists had become more closely bound to the party, and they naturally hoped that another Liberal Government would benefit them. But both Gladstone and the voluntaries clearly understood that the Liberals would not go to the country with a programme that included disestablishment.

V. CONSERVATIVE DEFEAT, 1880

Ministers delayed the dissolution of Parliament until March 1880. Doubtless they hoped that postponement would benefit them; indeed, by-election results in the winter of 1879–80 were in their favour and lifted their spirits.[45] But delay worked more to the advantage of the Opposition because the Liberals were developing their organization and held the attacking initiative over policy, especially through Gladstone's speeches. Both sides, however, fought in a negative way. The Conservatives defended their record in foreign and imperial affairs and condemned Home Rule. The Liberals sought unity in attacking the Government rather than making constructive proposals which might only divide them. So they condemned the ministry's imperial record without adopting Home Rule, lamented the depression without suggesting an alternative economic policy, and lauded religious equality while saying that consideration of disestablishment would have to wait. They did promise, however, to raise the county franchise to the level of the boroughs, despite the opposition of a few Liberals. They also said they intended to meet the burial claim, and it became clear again during the election that they would have some Conservative support in doing so.

[44] Omond, op. cit. 331; W. E. Gladstone, *Midlothian Speeches, 1879* (Leicester, 1971), 76–80, 189; D. Brooks, 'Gladstone and Midlothian: The Background to the First Campaign', *SHR* lxiv (1985), 59–65.
[45] Rossi, op. cit. 110–14; D. E. Fletcher, 'Aspects of Sheffield Liberalism, 1849–1886', Ph.D. thesis (Sheffield, 1972), 149–53.

The coming dissolution was announced on 8 March, and took place on the 24th. On 9 March a manifesto appeared in the newspapers from the Earl of Beaconsfield, addressed to the Lord Lieutenant of Ireland, the Duke of Marlborough. The Government's overseas policy was defended, but the main thrust of the manifesto concerned Ireland. It was clear that, whatever aid Ministers hoped to gain from Roman Catholics on educational grounds, they were not seeking any over Home Rule. Perhaps building too much on the recent defeat in a Liverpool by-election of a Liberal candidate who had promised to support Home Rule, the manifesto vehemently denounced the Irish nationalist movement as 'a danger, in its ultimate results, scarcely less disastrous than pestilence and famine'. Further, it was to be hoped (in a phrase soon condemned as ungrammatical) that 'all men of light and leading will resist this destructive doctrine'.[46] The reply of the Home Rule Confederation of Great Britain was clear and forthright: 'the vicious manifesto of Lord Beaconsfield directly appeals to the worst passions and prejudices in order to stir up the English people against Irish nationality . . . Vote against Benjamin Disraeli as you should against the mortal enemy of your country and your race.'[47] Hartington and Gladstone said in addresses to their constituents that they did not want to abandon the Empire but to liberalize it, not to dissolve the union with Ireland but to reform that country.[48] Conservative attempts to brand the Liberals as Home Rulers were effectively resisted.

The highlight of the election was another display of rhetorical virtuosity by Gladstone in a second Midlothian campaign. At every place where he stopped to speak on his journey North, the Liberals gained a seat.[49] The election as a whole was very active, as many as 352 seats being contested compared with 277 in 1868 and only 199 in 1874.[50]

The election found Catholics facing in opposite directions, both away from the Liberal party. Some eminent Catholics had recently been turning from Whiggism to Conservatism. Cardinal Manning was currently inclined to the Tories. The Duke of Norfolk voted with the Conservatives in the Lords in 1879 and his brother-in-law Lord Edmund Talbot stood unsuccessfully as a Conservative in the election—the sole Catholic candidate in Great Britain. Two Catholic landowners who had previously supported the Liberals, Thomas Weld-Blundell and Lord Beaumont, switched allegiance to the Tories. Gladstone's anti-Vatican pamphlets helped to account for this move to the right, as did the Conservative defence of voluntary schools and fears that a Liberal Government might threaten them; also the Catholics' support of Government foreign policy on the ground that their Church's influence would

[46] AR cxxii (1880), 32.
[47] Manifesto printed in *Dundee Advertiser*, 11 Mar. 1880, 6; AR cxxii (1880), 33–5, 43–4; T. Lloyd, *The General Election of 1880* (Oxford, 1968), 19.
[48] AR cxxii (1880), 33–4.
[49] T. O. Lloyd, op. cit. 25.
[50] AR cxxii (1880), 50.

suffer from an extension of Russian authority. But probably just as important in affecting the attitude of British Catholics of the upper and middle classes (who were unmoved by their Irish co-religionists' demand for Home Rule) was the gradual tendency of wealthier people to swell the Conservative ranks.[51] This was a feature of the later nineteenth century which found a particularly tempting outlet in the Home Rule split of 1886.

Lord Ripon, who had recently resumed his political career, tried to stem the Catholic drift to Conservatism, for example by publishing a letter in the *Tablet* of 20 March and distributing it as Liberal propaganda. As well as regretting Beaconsfield's hostility to Home Rule, Ripon said that nothing in recent events would 'induce me, as a Catholic, to abandon . . . the Party to which English and Scotch Catholics owe a long series of measures of justice and relief'. Ripon's plea was countered by some Catholic Conservatives, notably Viscount Bury, a junior Minister who defended his leader's manifesto in the *Tablet* and asked if Ripon was really urging Catholics to support Gladstone, the author of pamphlets 'fiercely denunciatory of Catholics and Catholicism'. Bury also exploited the Liberals' educational weakness: 'The Conservatives have at least this in common with the Catholics, that they dread the complete secularization of education'. Ripon, chairman of the Catholic Poor Schools Committee, well understood Catholic fears about Liberal education policy. He could only assert in the *Tablet* that a Liberal ministry would leave the 1870 Education Act alone; and in a letter intended to aid Sir Charles Dilke's campaign in Chelsea he wrote: 'I, who am Chairman of . . . the principal Catholic educational body, am perfectly convinced that Catholics have nothing to fear for their educational interests from the establishment of a Liberal Government'. Lord Hartington gave the same assurance when speaking at Blackburn on 26 March.[52]

If the Liberal allegiance of 'native' British Catholics was dubious, Beaconsfield's manifesto had at least ensured that Liberals could count on the support of Irish Catholics in Britain who were attached to Home Rule. The strength of Home Rulers had already been shown in some municipal elections, especially in Liverpool where the cause was led by Dr Andrew Commins, a lawyer in the city who became Parnellite MP for Roscommon in the 1880 election.[53] The importance of Home Rulers as Parliamentary voters in areas where they were a numerous minority was displayed in the Liverpool by-election of January 1880. The Liberal candidate, Lord Ramsay, opposing a Conservative Orangeman, at first refused to support a call for an enquiry into the need for a separate Irish Parliament. This caused the local Home Rule committee to advise the Irish Catholics (accounting for 9,000 to 11,000 votes

---

[51] Rossi, 'English Catholics, the Liberal Party, and the General Election of 1880', *Catholic Historical Review*, lxiii (1977), 414–17.

[52] Ibid. 419–27. Cf. E. R. Norman, *The English Catholic Church in the Nineteenth Century* (Oxford, 1984), 195–6.

[53] T. Burke, *A Catholic History of Liverpool* (Liverpool, 1910), 216–18.

out of an electorate of 60,000) to abstain from voting. Ramsay then changed his tune and promised to support an enquiry. But this worried the Liberal leaders, who did not favour Home Rule, and delighted the Conservatives who stimulated anti-Home Rule opinion and won the contest.[54]

This lesson was not lost on Liberal candidates in the general election, none of whom openly espoused Home Rule. They had little need to do so in current electoral circumstances: it was said that the Irish Catholics supported Liberal candidates in most of the constituencies where their voting strength was important. Conservatives might appeal to Catholic educational interests, as happened at Glasgow and Bradford, but this made little impact on voters mainly concerned with Home Rule.[55] Conservatives had to struggle against pronouncements such as that made by the president of the Glasgow Home Rule Association against 'the evil Minister who has given a watchword of hatred against Ireland as a war cry to his party'.[56] There were branches not only of the Home Rule Confederation of Great Britain but also of the Irish National Land League, as well as Irish Electoral Committees, urging Irish electors in British constituencies 'to see that gentlemen were elected who would promise in every respect to do justice to Ireland'.[57] Irish voters had to be content, however, to support such as Gladstone, who strongly sympathized with most Irish grievances but declined to support Home Rule. Sometimes one Liberal candidate in a constituency was preferred to another because he made more satisfactory promises. The one Catholic candidate in Great Britain, Lord Edmund Talbot, a Conservative, was accused by Home Rulers of representing a Tory stratagem to divide Catholic electors and weaken the Liberal, and the Liberal kept the seat.[58]

Anti-Catholicism also figured in the election, some ultra-Protestant societies intervening in the contests. The Dundee Protestant Association, a flourishing body inaugurated in September 1879, appointed a deputation to interview local candidates. Seven questions were asked of them— whether they would support a bill for the inspection of convents, for example—and their varying replies were printed in the local papers for electors to digest. A speaker at one of this Association's meetings stressed that 'Protestant representation' should be secured as far as possible, even at the cost of having to desert a party political allegiance. A Liberal candidate for Caithness said he hoped to enter Parliament

---

[54] Rossi, *Transformation* 112–15; P. J. Waller, *Democracy and Sectarianism: A Political and Social History of Liverpool, 1868–1939* (Liverpool, 1981), 33–4.

[55] Lloyd, op. cit. 53; Catriona Levy, 'Conservatism and Liberal Unionism in Glasgow, 1874–1912', Ph.D. thesis (Dundee, 1983), 77–81; W. D. Ross, 'Politics and Opinion in Bradford, 1880–1906, with Special Reference to Parliamentary Elections', Ph.D. thesis (Bradford, 1977), 87–8.

[56] *Scotsman*, 17 Mar. 1880, p. 7.

[57] Meeting organized by Dundee branch of the Irish National Land League, 14 Mar.; *Dundee Advertiser*, 15 Mar. 1880, p. 6. Also ibid. 22 Mar., pp. 4,5; 24 Mar., p. 7.

[58] Kilmarnock Burghs election; *Scotsman*, 25 Mar. 1880, p. 7; Rossi, 'English Catholics', 418; L. G. Rylands, *Correspondence and Speeches of Mr Peter Rylands, MP* (2 vols., Manchester and London, 1890), i. 283–4.

'to raise again out of the dust the standard of the Reformation at home'.[59] Anti-Ritualism accompanied anti-Romanism. The Church Association council called on branches to ensure that 'no candidate be supported who will not uphold the principles of the Reformation . . . or who will not endeavour to secure by legislation, if needful, obedience to the law on the part of the clergy'. Electors were directly urged in the same sense.[60] But anti-romanist and anti-Ritualist declarations by candidates were very rare. Most Ritualists may well have been inclined to vote Liberal because of their dislike of the Public Worship Regulation Act.[61]

If the Liberals obtained Home Rule support in Britain without promising Home Rule, they also won Nonconformist support without promising disestablishment. In both cases they profited from Conservative opposition to the reforms. How to treat disestablishment in the election was an important and vexing question for voluntaries. Suppression of the issue during the campaign might assist a Liberal victory, but purveyors of other 'crotchets' (notably temperance) did not want to share the silence. Moreover, if a Liberal Government was returned it might say that disestablishment had not been an issue in the election and therefore did not need to be dealt with. The voluntary dilemma was shown in discussions before the election. Henry Richard said at the annual meeting of the Liberation Society council in May 1879 that, while they were anxious to get rid of the present Government, 'we must not consent to have our great question shunted aside altogether'. But this meeting passed a very mild resolution from which electoral threats were entirely absent.[62] Electoral action was again debated at a Liberation Society conference held in London on 10 December 1879, and it was clear that the dilemma continued. A resolution acknowledged that Liberal divisions should be avoided, but said that voluntary candidates should be obtained. This dual position was reflected by advice issued to supporters by the Society's Electoral Committee. Voluntaries should not 'divide the Liberal party, of which they form an integral part', but they should also ensure that ecclesiastical questions were discussed and pay close attention to the choice of candidates.[63] A joint meeting of the Liberation Society and Dissenting Deputies in January 1880 decided to ask Liberal candidates' opinions on various matters, but disestablishment they were merely asked to support 'as soon as public opinion is sufficiently advanced to justify such a change'.[64]

In the campaign the Liberation Society was content to play an unobtrusive part and, though spending £1,000 and circulating some propaganda, refrained

---

[59] *Dundee Protestant Association: First Annual Report* (Dundee, 1880); Lamb Collection, 188 (12), Dundee Local History Library; *Dundee Advertiser*, 29 Mar. 1880, p. 5, 31 Mar. p. 6, 12 Mar. p. 5.

[60] *Dundee Advertiser*, 11 Mar., p. 6; *T*, 23 Mar. 1880, p. 8.

[61] Cf. Malcolm MacColl to Gladstone, 11 Mar. 1880; Russell, *Malcolm MacColl*, 64.

[62] Hamer, *Electoral Pressure*, 149.

[63] Ibid. 150.

[64] LS, 5 Jan. 1880; A/LIB/6, 220–2; Manning, op. cit. 397–8; Rossi, *Transformation*, 109. Cf. Dale, *Dale*, 387.

from issuing an address to electors. The *Nonconformist* emphasized the loyalty
of Dissenters to Liberal electoral unity, even declaring on 18 March that 'the
whole Nonconformist body' was prepared to vote for a Liberal candidate
'without asking whether he will support disestablishment and disendowment or
no'. The Liberal party, said Guinness Rogers, was no longer in its sad state of
1874: Dissenters were now 'Liberals first, Nonconformists afterwards'.[65] While
voluntary electors would obviously have preferred to support a candidate who
was decidedly for disestablishment, they were ready to support one who was
not. They put their faith in the Liberals' future consideration of the topic, and
especially in Gladstone's praise of the voluntaries, in a speech at Marylebone,
for their self-sacrifice in subordinating their question.[66] Whether quietness
would serve the voluntaries better than clamour only the future would show.

The clearest sign of the new unity between Nonconformity and the Liberal
party was the joint successful candidature at Bradford of Forster, author of the
1870 Education Act, and Illingworth, Baptist treasurer of the Liberation
Society. Such a combination could only have occurred because of the minor
importance of disestablishment in the election, the decline of the education
controversy, and the strong urge for Liberals to unite.

The current low profile of the Liberation Society meant that the Church
Defence Institution also played only a small part in the election, though, unlike
its rival, it did issue an address to electors. This urged them to oppose all
candidates who wanted 'to undermine our present Constitution in Church and
State'.[67] Several Conservative candidates were keen to advertise themselves as
Church defenders, and gave the voluntary question an emphasis it did not get
from Liberal candidates. At least one Liberal, G. J. Goschen, said that, though
supporting equality over burials, he could not countenance disestablishment.
Henry Fowler, a Wesleyan who stood as a Liberal at Wolverhampton, refused
to pledge himself to support disestablishment: he would first have to see the
mode in which it was proposed.[68] Many Conservative candidates were content
to support the Church-State bond and denominational education, but some
stressed the importance of Church reform. Richard Cross reminded the South-
West Lancashire electors that as a Cabinet Minister he had done all he could 'to
strengthen our National Church'. A former Liberal Minister, H. C. E.
Childers, said that the relief of Dissenters had strengthened the establishment,
and he hoped 'to see reforms in her government and in the administration of her
property vigorously taken in hand'.[69]

  [65] Hamer, op. cit. 150–1; J. Guinness Rogers, 'A Nonconformist's View of the Election', *Nineteenth Century*, vii (Jan.–June 1880), 629, 635.

  [66] *T*, 13 Mar. 1880, p. 8; Hanham, *Elections and Party Management*, 124.

  [67] M. J. D. Roberts, 'Pressure-group Politics and the Church of England: The Church Defence Institution, 1859–1896', 573; *T*, 17 Mar. 1880, p. 13.

  [68] *AR* cxxi (1879), 130; *T*, 12 Mar. 1880, p. 10; Edith H. Fowler, *The Life of Henry Hartley Fowler, First Viscount Wolverhampton* (London, 1912), 108–9.

  [69] *T*, 10 Mar. 1880, p. 8; 13 Mar. pp. 8, 10; 15 Mar., pp. 8, 11; 16 Mar., p. 8; *Dundee Advertiser*, 13 Mar., p. 5.

In Wales, disestablishment did not have the political prominence which it later obtained, but was significant in one or two of the contests. In Montgomeryshire the sitting Conservative, Charles W. W. Wynn, lost the seat—the first time a member of the powerful Wynn family of landowners had not succeeded in the constituency since 1799. The victor by 191 votes was an English (and Anglican) radical, Stuart Rendel, who held out hopes for the future prospects of disestablishment and met considerable opposition from Church defenders. Another exciting contest was in Caernarvonshire, where the Liberal and voluntary, Watkin Williams (late MP for the Denbigh Boroughs), easily wrested the seat from the Conservative.[70]

In Scotland the demand for disestablishment was stronger than in Wales or England, and there was sharper conflict between moderation and militancy in the voluntary approach to the election. A public meeting held in Dundee on 2 November 1879, attended by Carvell Williams, resolved that disestablishment 'ought to be part of the avowed policy of the Liberal party' and that the meeting should take 'every legitimate means to return members favourable to that policy'. Even in Scotland, however, moderation held sway during the election.[71] Gladstone's efforts to maintain party unity despite the question were supported by Liberal candidates. Many of these omitted disestablishment from their addresses altogether; others took the Gladstonian line and said that opinion would have to mature on the subject before Parliament undertook to deal with it. The Scottish Disestablishment Association published an election address boldly stating that 'the election of 1880 will be the great point of departure for the question of Scottish Disestablishment', but then descended into meandering vagueness. Forty Liberal addresses did not mention the topic, thirteen gave no decided opinion, and only four favoured disestablishment without qualification.[72]

The usual Liberal approach, then, was to evade the issue, either by silence or by advocating postponement. Captain Heron Maxwell, who was returned for Kirkcudbrightshire, said that disestablishment was a matter for further consideration; R. Preston Bruce, successful in Fife, said the time was not ripe for trying to resolve the question, but disestablishment was 'eventually necessary, and just in principle'; J. C. Bolton, returned for Stirlingshire, was a member of the Church of Scotland but could nevertheless 'contemplate Disestablishment and disendowment without misgiving'. A. Asher, who stood unsuccessfully for Glasgow and Aberdeen Universities, said the issue could not be dealt with until the county franchise had been widened. Stephen Williamson, returned for St Andrews Burghs, complained that Principal

[70] Kenneth O. Morgan, *Wales in British Politics, 1868–1922*, 2nd ed. (Cardiff, 1970), 39–40; *Carnarvon and Denbigh Herald*, 27 Mar. 1880, p. 1.

[71] Newspaper cutting, 3 Nov. 1879, Lamb Collection, 176 (11), Dundee Local History Library. Cf. C. J. Murray, 'Midlothian and Gladstone', MA Hons. thesis (Dundee, 1982), 67–70.

[72] *Scotsman*, 19 Mar. 1880, p. 6; J. G. Kellas, 'The Liberal Party and the Scottish Church Disestablishment Crisis', *EHR* lxxix (1964), 33.

Tulloch, the well-known Church Liberal, was pressing him unduly over disestablishment. He had pledged himself to support it but only when the country wanted it; he denied four times at one meeting that he was connected with the Liberation Society.[73]

The prevaricating Liberal approach encouraged hostile heckling. Sir Donald Currie, who was returned for Perthshire, was asked by a Church of Scotland minister whether he wanted disestablishment all round; it took two further questions from the same person before Currie said that, as a Free Churchman, he did not wish to disestablish 'merely as a disestablisher' but would 'go with the public voice'. General Sir George Balfour, successful in Kincardineshire, was pressed five times for his view on disestablishment before he said he wanted 'a free Church' if the people also wanted it. A much more direct (if questionable) assertion came from Charles Tennant, a Church of Scotland member who was returned for the counties of Peebles and Selkirk: 'The question of Disestablishment is one which the Liberal party have agreed to sink'.[74]

The Liberal statements generally followed Gladstone's approach, which he explained at length to some of his Midlothian constituents at Gilmerton on 22 March. The Church of Scotland would be fought 'fairly and in good humour', because, unlike its former Irish counterpart, it was indigenous and popular. Being founded on the wishes of the people, it should only have to change its established position through the people's clear and decisive desire. He even said that 'so far as at present he could see the question had not been before the people of Scotland, and he saw no likelihood that it would be'.[75] This was pushing conciliation of Church Liberals to extremes and many Dissenting followers of Gladstone must have felt their loyalty severely tested. But the method was successful in maintaining Liberal unity. An example of harmony achieved was in the Edinburgh and St Andrews Universities constituency. Principal Tulloch supported the Liberal member Dr Lyon Playfair, being well satisfied with his views on the church question. Voluntaries were initially alarmed at this, but after inquiry they too said they were satisfied with Playfair, who was returned.[76]

The Liberal *Scotsman* claimed that if disestablishment was raised at all in the election it was 'due solely to the Conservatives, who are manifestly annoyed to find their favourite opening in the Liberal armour so determinedly closed and rivetted against them'.[77] Gladstone alleged that the issue was 'merely being brought forward by the Tories . . . to make a party cry'.[78] So clear was Liberal neutrality on the question that it was difficult for the Tories to make a party cry

[73] *Scotsman*, 8 Mar. 1880, p. 6, 11 Mar., p. 1; *Dundee Advertiser*, 16 Mar., p. 1, 19 Mar., p. 6.
[74] *Dundee Advertiser*, 31 Mar., p. 7, 1 Apr., p. 6; *Scotsman*, 23 Mar., p. 1.
[75] *Dundee Advertiser*, 23 Mar., p. 5 (also leading article, p. 4). Cf. *Scotsman*, 23 Mar., p. 4 (leading article).
[76] *T*, 13 Mar., p. 4.
[77] 23 Mar., p. 4.
[78] *Dundee Advertiser*, 22 Mar., p. 5.

of it. But many Conservative candidates made what they could of the issue by declaring themselves firm defenders of the Church-State connection. Some took the opportunity of condemning Gladstone and other Liberal leaders for being mere 'puppets of the people' over the question. Colonel Drummond Murray, who was unseated in Perthshire, accused Gladstone and Hartington of re-enacting a scene in *Pickwick Papers* and supporting 'the loudest mob'.[79] Colonel David Williamson, the unsuccessful Conservative candidate for Perth city, revived the contentious matter of concurrent endowment as his preferred means of solving the Scottish Church problem. The Conservative candidate who succeeded in North Ayrshire said that the Church of Scotland had raised large sums and built numerous churches since 1873, and he refused to injure such a flourishing institution. Conservatives sometimes linked defence of the establishment with opposition to secular education, sometimes with opposition to Home Rule, and sometimes with support of Presbyterian reunion.[80]

The Liberals proved successful with their electoral tactic of requiring self-abnegation from voluntaries, and they used the economic depression and colonial policy to good effect. They did far better than they had anticipated. An overall Conservative majority of fifty was turned into a Liberal one of fifty-four; 353 Liberals, 238 Conservatives, and sixty-one Home Rulers were returned.[81] Only four Conservatives were returned for Wales (out of thirty-three seats), and only seven for Scotland (out of sixty). Eight Nonconformists were among the Welsh members returned, and about eighty-five out of all the members were Dissenters.[82] It was claimed that about 139 MPs were in favour of disestablishment—a higher number than ever before— and the Liberation Society was understandably delighted.[83] The landowning element in the House of Commons was clearly in retreat. Over half the House consisted of businessmen, and 232 Liberal members obtained their income mainly from a business or profession.[84]

The election seemed a radical triumph, and this was alarming to Whigs and Church defenders. Even county franchise extension did not command the support of all Liberals: G. J. Goschen refused to join the new ministry because he could not support this cause. 'Ere long', said Bishop Magee, 'and certainly in the next Parliament, the effacement of the old Whigs will be complete . . . their party will then be Radical, pure and simple, and headed by Gladstone. Then comes the last struggle between Church and Democracy, and there's no doubt which will win'. Principal Tulloch thought that, since Gladstone would be

[79] *T*, 10 Mar., p. 8; 13 Mar., p. 10; *Scotsman*, 12 Mar., p. 1, 13 Mar., p. 1, 15 Mar., p. 1; *Dundee Advertiser*, 31 Mar., p. 7.

[80] *Dundee Advertiser*, 17 Mar., p. 1; *Scotsman*, 1 Mar., p. 5, 23 Mar., p. 7; *Dundee Advertiser*, 10 Mar., p. 6, 18 Mar., p. 7; Levy, op. cit. 67, 71.

[81] Hanham, *Elections and Party Management*, 232.

[82] Morgan, op. cit. 40; Bebbington, *Nonconformist Conscience*, 12.

[83] Mackintosh, *Disestablishment and Liberation*, 231; LS, 12 Apr. 1880; A/LIB/6, 247–52.

[84] Griffiths, 'Origins', 149.

premier 'or at least the governing spirit' in the new ministry, 'the existence of the Church of Scotland will be before the constituences before three, or at the utmost five years'.[85] Indeed it seemed unavoidable that disestablishment and other causes would come forward again to challenge Liberal unity.

[85] Rossi, *Transformation*, 125; Magee to J. C. MacDonnell, 2 Apr. 1880; MacDonnell, *Magee*, ii. 128; Principal John Tulloch to Revd W. W. Tulloch, 3 Apr. 1880; Oliphant, *Tulloch*, 363–4.

CHAPTER IV

Liberal Government, Voluntaryism, and Home Rule Crisis, 1880–1886

I. INTRODUCTORY

T H E acclaim he had won in the country, and his own readiness to return to high office, might have singled out Gladstone as the obvious head of a new Liberal Government following Beaconsfield's resignation on 21 April. But the Queen had taken a marked dislike to Gladstone and would have preferred to appoint Hartington or perhaps Granville, who were joint official leaders of the party. It was only after they had pressed Gladstone's claims that she reluctantly appointed the People's William as premier on the 23rd.[1]

In his cabinet appointments Gladstone, anxious to strengthen the fragile unity of the party, seemed much more desirous of conciliating Whigs than radicals. No fewer than eight of the eleven new Cabinet ministers were Whigs: it was remarked that the Cabinet was three-fourths Whig but the Liberal party three-fourths radical.[2] Despite the studied moderation of radicals at that juncture—Chamberlain was grateful for his office and said it was 'encouraging for Radicals'[3]—it seemed that the bitter internal conflicts of 1870–4 would be revived. Indeed there was plenty of scope for this in the continued differences over policy, especially land reform and disestablishment.[4] If radicals fretted about the lack of satisfactory reforms by the new Government—it was four years before franchise extension was enacted—Whigs disliked reforms which were introduced, such as the Irish land measures, and began to slip away from the party. The problem of keeping the Whigs in the Liberal party was a serious one for Gladstone well before 1886.

The confident constructiveness which the ministry's large majority seemed to encourage was hampered by lengthy and debilitating Parliamentary conflict over two questions. One was Charles Bradlaugh's claim as an atheist to be allowed to take his seat, which provided Conservatives with a constant means of

---

[1] T. A. Jenkins, 'Gladstone, the Whigs, and the Leadership of the Liberal Party, 1879–1880', *HJ* xxvii (1984), 352–60; D. Southgate, *The Passing of the Whigs, 1832–1886*, 362–3; R. Blake, *Disraeli*, 716–18.

[2] B. Holland, *The Life of Spencer Compton, Eighth Duke of Devonshire* (2 vols., London, 1911), i. 280.

[3] Chamberlain to Dilke, 18 May 1880; CP, JC5/20/33.

[4] Southgate, op. cit. 364 ff.; D. E. Fletcher, 'Aspects of Sheffield Liberalism, 1849–1886' Ph.D. thesis (Sheffield, 1972), 174–6.

attacking Ministers. The other was Irish nationalism, now greatly strengthened and expressing itself in relentless obstruction in the House of Commons as well as in violent agitation in Ireland and group organization in this country. The Irish National League of Great Britain, replacing the Home Rule Confederation, was formed in September 1883 with T. P. O'Connor as president. With a membership consisting mostly of labourers, the league had 127 branches by the end of 1884 and 630 by 1890, and registration committees in many constituencies.[5] The contrasting policies of land legislation and coercion were proffered to Ireland and split Government opinion, and attempts to resolve Irish problems met with some drastic setbacks. There were initial colonial disasters for the Government, and the operations in Egypt in 1882 divided Liberals and drove Bright from the Cabinet. Liberals were bitterly disunited again over the matter of Gordon's rescue in the Sudan in 1884–5. Gladstone described his troubled ministry to his wife as 'a wild romance of politics with a continual succession of hair breadth escapes and strange accidents pressing upon one another'.[6]

Religious issues continued during this ministry, concerning Catholicism, Ritualism, education, and disestablishment. Most British Catholics supported Irish nationalism, but a National Catholic Conservative Association opened its first branch at Sheffield in August 1882.[7] Catholics acted to defend their voluntary schools. The Catholic Union appointed a committee for this purpose and issued a circular which deplored the financial disadvantage suffered by the schools;[8] and the Bishop of Salford, Herbert Vaughan, founded the Voluntary Schools Association to defend Catholic schools in 1884. In some of his appointments Gladstone showed a wish to conciliate Catholics and soften the impression made on them by his *Vatican Decrees* pamphlet. Lord Ripon became Viceroy of India and Lord Kenmare chamberlain of the Queen's household. But there was prolonged ultra-Protestant reaction to these appointments. Meetings were held at Liverpool, Bristol, Glasgow, Dundee, and elsewhere, those in Liverpool being particularly crowded and excited. The Scottish Reformation Society protested to the Queen, the British Reformation Society to Gladstone; the Free Church presbytery of Dundee petitioned the Queen and Parliament, and there were numerous other petitions.[9] But the impulse to protest could conflict with the principle of religious equality. Amongst United Presbyterians in Edinburgh a motion praising the appointments for showing

[5] E. P. M. Wollaston, 'The Irish Nationalist Movement in Great Britain, 1886–1908', MA thesis (London, 1958), 5.

[6] 1 May 1885; A. Tilney Basset (ed.), *Gladstone to his Wife* (London, 1936), 246.

[7] Fletcher, op. cit. 164.

[8] 15 Mar. 1883; Manning Papers. Cf. H. E. Manning, *Is the Education Act of 1870 a Just Law?* (London, [1882]), 19.

[9] L. Wolf, *Life of the First Marquess of Ripon* (2 vols., London, 1921), i. 319; *Dundee Protestant Association: First Annual Report*, 1880 (Dundee, 1880), 12. Cf. Edinburgh Free Presbytery Minutes, 12 May 1880, CH3/111/30, 102–3.

that religion was not a test for civil office was defeated by twenty-seven votes to sixteen in favour of a motion to take no decision on the matter.[10]

There were also hostile expressions from Protestant societies against convents, the increase of priests and chapels, and especially against Irish nationalist agitation. The Phoenix Park murders in Dublin in 1882 caused anti-Catholic riots in Camborne (Cornwall) and Brighouse, Yorkshire, and contributed to an attack on the Irish quarter in Tredegar, Monmouthshire.[11] Rioting between Orangemen and Catholics occurred at Coatbridge, Lanarkshire, in August 1883. On 12 July 1884 the Orange procession at Cleator Moor, a mining centre in west Cumberland, was attacked; one of the assailants was shot dead and many others were wounded.[12] In 1881 the Government commissioned an unofficial envoy at Rome (George Errington, a Catholic and moderate Home Rule MP for Co. Longford) to try and persuade the Pope to discourage clerical support for violent nationalist agitation.[13] T. P. O'Connor's reminiscences inform us that Errington's efforts caused the Pope's condemnation (by a rescript of 10 May 1883) of a testimonial fund for Parnell. But this papal intrusion was resented by many Irish Catholics: the amounts given for Parnell sharply mounted (from £7,000 to £38,000) and his political hold was strengthened.[14]

The Liberal election victory required renewed attention to Church defence. The annual meeting of the Church Defence Institution central council on 25 June 1880 called for 'increased exertions'.[15] But recent events had made Church divisions worse than ever, and many Churchmen saw Conservatives as anything but satisfactory champions. To the outrage of High-Churchmen, one of Beaconsfield's last acts as premier was to appoint the pronounced Evangelical J. C. Ryle as first Bishop of Liverpool. 'Canon Ryle Bishop of Liverpool!', exclaimed Charles Wood to H. P. Liddon, 'I rejoice beyond expression . . . that we have got rid of Lord Beaconsfield, Lord Cairns and all their works . . . The Radicals may be bad, but at least they don't sin against light. I declare I prefer Bradlaugh to Lord Beaconsfield'.[16] Liddon was anxious that Gladstone and not Granville or Hartington should become premier, 'for these are Whigs of the least lovely kind, with the traditional suspicion and dislike of the Church—making the most of her fetters, and stinting her means of self-expression in all

[10] Edinburgh UP Presbytery Minutes, 6 July 1880; CH3/111/36, 95–6.
[11] Wollaston, op. cit. 5.
[12] AR cxxv (1883), Chronicle, 30; cxxvi (1884), Chronicle, 24.
[13] Lord Edmond Fitzmaurice, The Life of Granville Leveson Gower, Second Earl Granville (2 vols., London, 1905), ii. 284–92; D. Bahlman (ed.), The Diary of Sir Edward Walter Hamilton (2 vols., Oxford, 1972), ii. 226; Carnarvon to Salisbury, 22 Aug. 1882; SP; S. Gwynn and Gertrude Tuckwell, The Life of the Rt. Hon. Sir C. W. Dilke (2 vols., London, 1917), i. 374–5.
[14] T. P. O'Connor, Memoirs of an Old Parliamentarian (2 vols., London, 1929), i. 373–6.
[15] CDI Central Council Minutes, vol. 206; Cf. M. J. D. Roberts, 'Pressure-group Politics and the Church of England: The Church Defence Institution, 1859–1896', JEH xxxv (1984), 573–4.
[16] Wood to Liddon, 17 Apr. 1880; J. G. Lockhart, Viscount Halifax (2 vols., London, 1935–6), i. 249. Cf. M. L. Loane, John Charles Ryle, 1816–1900 (London, 1953), 47, 50.

possible ways'. Granville, he noted, had supported the Public Worship Regulation Act, had introduced a 'very mischievous' burials bill, and had been reluctant to support Gladstone over the Balkan question.[17]

High-Churchmen did gain satisfaction from the new ministry's Church appointments. There had been no pronounced High-Church appointments under Beaconsfield, but High-Churchmen promoted by Gladstone in his second Government included Ernest Wilberforce as first Bishop of Newcastle, E. W. Benson as Archbishop of Canterbury, G. H. Wilkinson to the Bishopric of Truro in succession to Benson, and Edward King to Lincoln; also Henry Scott Holland as a canon of St Paul's and Malcolm MacColl as a canon of Ripon. Some of these appointments worsened Gladstone's already poor relations with the Queen, and since most of the new Bishops were Conservatives they did not strengthen his position in the Lords.[18] Gladstone's private secretary, Edward Hamilton (son of a High-Church Bishop) repeatedly noted that Gladstone's appointments favoured High-Churchmen. 'The section which has really received scant favour has been the Evangelical School', he stated; 'the fact being that there are so few men of eminence among the Low Churchmen.'[19] The replacement of Evangelical by High-Church influence was a matter of general comment.[20] When a non-High-Churchman was appointed in 1885 he was a well-known Broad-Churchman, Frederick Temple, who was translated from Exeter to London.

Apart from ecclesiastical appointments, however, there was little to please High-Churchmen during Gladstone's Government. Several lawsuits against Ritualist clergy had commenced in 1879. Three of these resulted in imprisonment of the clergy—T. Pelham Dale, R. W. Enraght, and S. F. Green—after they had refused to recognize Lord Penzance's jurisdiction and defied his monitions. S. F. Green, Vicar of St John's, Miles Platting, Manchester, was kept behind bars for eighteen months from March 1881, despite protests from the English Church Union.[21] Mackonochie also experienced legal reverses, but avoided imprisonment. He was suspended from his benefice by Penzance for three years from November 1879, and this judgment was finally confirmed by the House of Lords on appeal in April 1881. Mackonochie agreed, after a correspondence with Archbishop Tait while the

[17] Liddon to William Bright, 12 Apr. 1880; J. O. Johnston, *Life and Letters of Henry Parry Liddon* (London, 1904), 271–2.

[18] O. Chadwick, *The Victorian Church* (London, 1970), ii. 338; D. Bahlman, 'The Queen, Mr Gladstone, and Church Patronage', *VS* iii (1959–60), 363–79. Cf. id. 'Politics and Church Patronage in the Victorian Age', *VS* xxii (1979), 258–60; Charles Wood to Gladstone, 9, 12, 23 Jan. and 2 Feb. 1885; GP, 44187, fos. 68–79.

[19] Hamilton's diary, 7 Aug. 1884; Bahlman, *Diary*, ii. 668.

[20] e.g. R. E. Bartlett, 'The Church of England and the Evangelical Party', *CR* xlvii (1885), 65–82.

[21] P. T. Marsh, *The Victorian Church in Decline: Archbishop Tait and the Church of England, 1868–1882* (London, 1969), 264–7, 275–6; *AR*, cxxiv (1882), 50; R. T. Davidson and W. Benham, *The Life of Archibald Campbell Tait, Archbishop of Canterbury* (2 vols., London, 1891), ii. 457–64.

latter was on his deathbed, to resign his living at St Alban's Holborn on 1 December 1882,[22] and instead was appointed Vicar of St Peter's, London Docks. But in a further judgment by Penzance in the Court of Arches in July 1883 he was barred from all ecclesiastical promotions in the province of Canterbury. The Ecclesiastical Commissioners ceased to pay his stipend from the date of the judgment, and Mackonochie resigned St Peter's on 23 December.[23] He returned to live and work unofficially at St Alban's. Guinness Rogers took the opportunity of saying in the *Congregationalist* that the real injustice in Mackonochie's case was the State's authority over the Church. This could only be righted by the grant of full spiritual authority through disestablishment.[24]

High-Churchmen could take some comfort from Tait's earnest appeals for conciliation in the last years of his life.[25] But High-Church grievances remained. In 1881 and 1882 a bill passed the Lords for easing the release of imprisoned clergy, but both bills were 'counted out' in the Commons as under forty members were present.[26] Most MPs, tired out by arduous debates on critical questions, had not enough energy left for the imprisoned clergy. After considering and discussing other possibilities of conciliation, Tait adopted a suggestion of John Gilbert Talbot (an MP for Oxford University) that there should be a Royal Commission on ecclesiastical courts. Tait put this to Gladstone and Lord Chancellor Selborne on 3 January 1881 and obtained their support for proposing such a commission in the Lords.[27] Tait also obtained the agreement of Beaconsfield, having told him that a commission would have a much needed 'tranquillizing effect'.[28] Salisbury also approved, but thought that the body would not provide a conclusive solution; he placed more faith in authoritative action by the Bishops.[29]

In March the Lords accepted Tait's proposal, and the Royal Commission was appointed on 16 May. Gladstone had selected twenty-five members with widely differing views on Ritualism. Tait presided over the commission until his death, when the next Archbishop, Benson, succeeded him in the chair. Members with such contrasting opinions could not agree on their report, and only a minority signed it without reservation. Presented in August 1883, the report was quite gratifying to High-Churchmen. It proposed that the Public Worship Regulation Act should be repealed and new courts set up. But conclusions so disputed within the commission could hardly serve as a solution.

---

[22] Davidson and Benham, op. cit. ii. 475–80; Marsh, op. cit. 284–5.
[23] *AR* cxxv (1883), Chronicle, 30, 53; M. Reynolds, *Martyr of Ritualism: Father Mackonochie of St Alban's, Holborn* (London, 1965), 241.
[24] *Congregationalist*, xiii (1884), 158–62; cf. ibid. xii (1883), 48–57.
[25] Marsh, op. cit. 267 ff.
[26] Ibid. 277–9.
[27] See ibid 268–75; Davidson and Benham, op. cit ii. 431, 445.
[28] Tait to Disraeli, 1 Feb. 1881; DP, B/XII/F/19.
[29] Salisbury to Tait, 5 Feb. 1881; Davidson and Benham, op. cit. ii. 448–50.

None of the recommendations was enacted, and the controversy continued.[30] Pusey's final pamphlet had condemned secular courts for presuming to regulate spiritual matters and protested against the Church Association's attacks on Ritualists. Peaceful toleration should be cultivated in the Church, he insisted, so that Churchmen could combine more effectively to counter unbelief.[31] When Pusey died in September 1882 both the Liberal and Conservative leaders, Gladstone and Salisbury, united to honour his memory.

The prosecution of Ritualists was proving to be a failure. Attempts to suppress Ritualism seemed only to encourage it. Evangelicals were taking differing attitudes to the question. The *Rock* newspaper softened its tone somewhat; the *Record* took a fairly tolerant view and rejected the methods of the Church Association.[32] But the desire to prosecute remained: members of the Church Association still wanted to discipline 'law-breaking, wafer-worshipping' members of their own communion.[33]

The *Church Reformer*, a High-Church paper, was premature in proclaiming in July 1884 'the utter collapse of the Church Association and all its works'.[34] The next year a group of laymen complained about thirteen distinct ceremonial acts performed in the communion service by the Revd James Bell Cox, Vicar of St Margaret's, Liverpool. Bishop Ryle had discouraged a prosecution of Bell Cox by the Church Association in 1881, but he allowed new proceedings and the case was referred to Lord Penzance. Bell Cox refused to heed Penzance's monition and was imprisoned for sixteen days in May 1887, until the Court of Queen's Bench quashed his conviction on a technicality. This judgment was confirmed by the House of Lords in 1888. But it was not the end of Bell Cox's tribulations, and by this time the Church Association was encouraging the prosecution of Edward King, Bishop of Lincoln.[35]

There was no lack of anti-Ritualist propaganda and outcry. In 1884 the National Protestant Church Union published a pamphlet by Walter Walsh, an Anglican journalist developing a notable anti-Ritualist career. Walsh listed 600 livings 'in the gift of bishops', held by 'Romanizing' clergymen whose names were given. Bishops who thus used their patronage to advance Ritualists, he said, were practically certain to veto their prosecution.[36] The introduction of

[30] Marsh, op. cit. 287–8; A. C. Benson, *The Life of Edward White Benson, Archbishop of Canterbury* (2 vols., London, 1899), ii. 67–8; R. S. M. Withycombe, 'The Development of Constitutional Autonomy in the Established Church in Later Victorian England', Ph.D. thesis (Cambridge, 1970), 82 ff.

[31] E. B. Pusey, *Unlaw in Judgments of the Judicial Committee, and its Remedies: A Letter to the Revd H. P. Liddon, DD* (Oxford, 1881), 32, 39–41, 56–9, 63–71.

[32] G. R. Balleine, *A History of the Evangelical Party in the Church of England*, 3rd edn. (London, 1951), 231–2; Anne Bentley, 'The Transformation of the Evangelical Party in the Church of England in the Later Nineteenth Century', Ph.D. thesis (Durham, 1971), 165–7.

[33] Cf. J. Bateman, *The Church Association: Its Policy and Prospects Considered*, 3rd edn. (London, 1880).

[34] *Church Reformer*, 15 July 1884; ii. 7, 146.

[35] J. Bentley, *Ritualism and Politics in Victorian Britain* (Oxford, 1978), 115–17; Loane, op. cit. 50–2.

[36] Walter Walsh, *Episcopal Patronage in the Church of England: How it is Exercised* (Market Rasen, 1884), viii. For particulars of Walsh see *Free Church Chronicle*, i (1899), 57–8.

Ritualist services by the Revd G. C. Ommanney, appointed to the Crown living of St Matthew's, Sheffield, in 1882, led to 'hooting and uproar in the church' in the following year.[37] During a service at St Paul's cathedral in London on Easter Eve 1883, a well-dressed man jumped on the altar and dashed the cross, candles, and flowers to the floor. Shouting 'Protestants to the rescue', he was seized by Canon Robert Gregory and others and handed to the police.[38]

Nonconformists equalled the Ritualists in their pleasure at Gladstone's return to power. The Congregational Union, at its annual meeting in May 1880, carried unanimously (with an instruction that a copy be sent to Gladstone) a resolution of gladness at the election result and the return of 'many members, including a considerable number of Congregationalists, who are earnest advocates of religious equality'. While 'heartily approving of the reserve maintained by Nonconformists at the late election in regard to their peculiar questions', continued the resolution, it was desirable that the new Parliament should promptly redress the remaining Dissenting grievances.[39] The following month, however, an article in the *Congregationalist* flatly denied that Nonconformists had supported Gladstone because they thought he would disestablish the Church in return. Their action had been more disinterested: 'we admire the integrity, the high-mindedness, the nobility as well as the genius of the man'.[40]

Indeed Dissenters seemed ready to remain fairly quiet over disestablishment, regarding the subject as one of patient preparation and persuasion before it would be ready for political execution. The Liberation Society's triennial conference in June 1880 demonstrated anew the current solidarity of voluntaries with the Liberal party.[41] Dissenting leaders and organizations showed repeated marks of reverence for Gladstone at this period. In 1881 the Primitive Methodist Conference sent him a message 'recognizing his self-denying efforts to promote national welfare'.[42] Spurgeon addressed him as 'honoured Chief', wrote him congratulatory letters, and said he was quite overcome when Gladstone attended a service in his Tabernacle in January 1882. The Conservative *Saturday Review* sardonically claimed that 'Mr Spurgeon is worth in point of votes at least two bishops'.[43]

If disestablishment was not regarded as a matter for immediate action, related Dissenting concerns received decisive attention. During the Government's first two years, the disendowment of the Churches of England and

---

[37] F. G. Belton (ed.), *Ommanney of Sheffield: Memoirs* (London, 1936), 67–85; *Primitive Methodist Magazine*, NS vi (1883), 382.

[38] H. P. Liddon to Charles Wood, Easter Eve 1883; Lockhart, *Halifax*, i. 249–50.

[39] *Congregational Year-book* (1881), 54.

[40] *Congregationalist*, ix (1880), 451.

[41] D. A. Hamer, *The Politics of Electoral Pressure* (Hassocks, Sussex, 1977), 152–3.

[42] R. F. Wearmouth, *Methodism and the Struggle of the Working Classes, 1850–1900* (Leicester, 1954), 227.

[43] Patricia S. Kruppa, *Charles Haddon Spurgeon: A Preacher's Progress* (New York and London, 1982), 351–2.

Scotland in Ceylon was set in motion; college headships and fellowships were released from clerical restrictions; and the lengthy burials controversy was, for the most part, laid to rest.

II. BURIALS INTERRED?

On 14 May 1880, at the Congregational Union's annual assembly, a motion of Guinness Rogers was unanimously carried, rejoicing at the prospect of an early burials settlement but also asserting that the equitable demands of Nonconformists on this subject would admit of no compromise.[44] Burials legislation figured in the Queen's Speech on 20 May. But the Government trod delicately in the matter. It was proposed to introduce the measure first in the Lords. The bill was initially in the hands of Lord Chancellor Selborne, who was a zealous defender of the Church-State connection.[45] Selborne asked for Tait's opinion on 7 May, saying that Ministers wanted a settlement to take place 'with as much concurrence as possible from those who best understand, and are most desirous to promote, the true interests of the Church'.[46] Tait replied that he thought Harrowby's amendments of 1877, providing for either a silent burial or one with a Christian service, offered a fair solution. But he also wanted two safeguards for clergy to be included: punishment for disorderly or obstructive conduct at the burial, and permission to refuse to read the burial service over the bodies of scandalous evil-livers. Selborne told him that the bill would take the form he wanted, with the addition that obstructive incumbents would be subject to punishment as well as disorderly attenders.[47]

The bill might have satisfied Tait but it was disliked by radical Dissenters because it did not allow non-Christian funerals in churchyards, thus failing in religious equality. Both the Liberation Society and the Dissenting Deputies wanted this restriction to be removed.[48] The *Congregationalist* said that 'loyalty to right' compelled Nonconformists to 'espouse the cause of the unbeliever'.[49] Some High-Churchmen condemned the measure, and these included Archdeacon Denison who saw its intrusion into private property as 'the dawn of communism'. But other High-Churchmen were ready to yield to the bill as the most favourable likely to be obtained from their point of view.[50] Charles Wood, president of the ECU, took this line and carried his council with him. But he acted against a resolution carried by a large majority at the Union's annual

[44] *Congregational Year-book* (1881), 55.

[45] Marsh, op. cit. 257.

[46] Davidson and Benham, op. cit. ii. 392.

[47] Tait to Selborne, 10 May 1880; Selborne to Tait, 18 May; Marsh, op. cit. 258; Davidson and Benham, op. cit. ii. 392–3.

[48] LS, 31 May, 21 June, 13 Sept. 1880; A/LIB/6, 268, 286, 306–9.

[49] *Congregationalist*, ix (1880), 852.

[50] Marsh, op. cit. 258–9.

meeting on 9 June, and many members resigned in protest at his attitude.[51] The Conservative leadership decided against complete resistance to the bill, but nevertheless favoured putting up a fight, and Beaconsfield asked Bishop Christopher Wordsworth to lead the opposition to the measure in the Lords.[52]

Selborne introduced the bill in the Lords on 27 May. Wordsworth moved to reject it, presenting himself as the spokesman for nearly 16,000 clergy who had signed a petition against the bill. He was supported by Viscount Cranbrook (formerly Gathorne Hardy) and others. If the bill became law, said Wordsworth, it would be 'an Act for the burial of the Church of England . . . as a national establishment of religion'. Tait argued, to the contrary, that the concession would only strengthen the Church by undermining opposition. But he had to maintain this view against a storm of clerical protest. Archbishop Thomson of York and six Bishops (including three Welsh) supported Tait, five supported Wordsworth, and the second reading passed by 126 votes to 101.[53] In committee an important amendment was carried by the Earl of Mount Edgecumbe, supported by Thomson and many other Bishops. This made the bill inoperative in a parish which possessed (either in churchyard or cemetery) any unconsecrated ground. But it was bound to meet strong resistance. The third reading passed after Bishop Magee had eloquently opposed it, though he had written that he really wanted the bill to pass.[54] Magee's opposition brought a heated rejoinder from Tait in an 'unepiscopal' and 'unseemly' altercation.[55]

In the Commons the second reading was moved by Osborne Morgan on 12 August and passed by 258 votes to seventy-nine. Beresford Hope and A. J. Balfour spoke against, but sixteen Conservatives (including Lord Randolph Churchill) voted for the bill.[56] In committee Mount Edgecumbe's clause was struck out with the Government's consent. There was also a strenuous attempt to remove the limitation on services to Christian ones. But the Government stood firm on this, announcing that it would withdraw the measure rather than see the alteration made, and the effort failed by a majority of three. After passing the Commons the bill returned to the Upper House on 3 September. Against the arguments of Beaconsfield and Archbishop Thomson, the Lords agreed by a majority of thirty-five to accept the removal of Mount Edgecumbe's clause, and the bill passed into law on 7 September in its original form.

[51] Lockhart, i. 240; ECU Minutes (general), 9 June 1880 (CU dep. 4, 235); G. B. Roberts, *The History of the English Church Union 1859–1894* (London, 1895), 235–6.

[52] Ibid. 259.

[53] Davidson and Benham, op. cit. ii. 393–400; Marsh, op. cit. 259; H cclii. 1013–70; *AR* cxxii (1880), 95–6.

[54] Magee to J. C. MacDonnell, 27 May 1880; J. C. MacDonnell, *The Life and Correspondence of William Connor Magee* (2 vols., London 1896), ii. 130–1; Davidson and Benham, op. cit. ii. 401–3.

[55] MacDonnell, op. cit. ii. 133–4; Nancy E. Johnson (ed.), *The Diary of Gathorne Hardy, Later Lord Cranbrook* (Oxford, 1981), 454.

[56] H cclv. 989–1076.

Archdeacon Denison blamed most of the Bishops and said the Act 'proclaims the absolute Indifference of both Houses of Parlt. to all forms of faith, which Indifference is the plague-spot of Century XIX'. Four strong opponents among the Bishops—Wordsworth, Magee, Ellicott, and Woodford—decided not to consecrate additions to churchyards or cemeteries. A report of the ECU council in 1881 strongly advised closing all churchyards and creating private burial grounds which could be consecrated for exclusive use of the Church. Some clergy told Tait that they could not conscientiously allow the new Act to be applied in their parishes; one said he would 'rather resign . . . than assist God's enemies to rob Him . . . To what an awful state we have come when the Church's own Bishops assist her enemies to destroy her'. Tait could only repeat, in his visitation charge at Dover on 7 September, that he hoped the bill would 'strengthen the Church by removing a most painful cause of controversy'. Despite hostility the Act was operated smoothly, partly because not many Nonconformists made use of it.[57]

The Burials Act technically removed almost the only remaining practical grievance of Dissent. But like some other solutions—marriages in Nonconformist chapels, and the University Tests Act—the burials settlement left irritating relics to be contested and resolved by further decisions. These remains displayed 'the slowness with which every approach to religious equality has been won in practice, even after it has been conceded in theory'.[58] Disputes involved refusals to bury or to register burial, and the charging of fees by incumbents who did not conduct the burial service. One of the cases, that of Llanfrothen in Caernarvonshire in 1888, helped to launch the young Baptist lawyer David Lloyd George on his Parliamentary career.[59] Nonconformists particularly wanted to abolish the distinction between consecrated and unconsecrated ground in public cemeteries. Hopes for an Act providing this were disappointed on several occasions. It was only in 1900 that, following the report of a Select Committee, a Burial Grounds Act satisfied the Dissenting Deputies and the Liberation Society. This measure, while not abolishing the distinction, provided that consecration would be no longer obligatory, that chapels would not be reserved for one denomination, and that there would be equality over the payment of burial fees.[60] This settlement came two years after a Marriage Act which satisfied a more protracted Nonconformist demand by

[57] Davidson and Benham, op. cit. ii. 405–12; *AR* cxxii (1880), 74–5, 96; MacDonnell, op. cit. ii. 143–4, 146–7; Blake, *Disraeli*, 727–31; Marsh, op. cit. 260–2; W. H. Mackintosh, *Disestablishment and Liberation* (London, 1972), 280–1; G. A. Denison, *The Burials Act: Meeting at Leicester, 30 September 1880* (Oxford and London, 1880), 4; ECU Minutes (general), 25 Mar. 1881 (CU dep. 4), 239. Cf. *Correspondence on the Burials Bill Between the Lord Archbishop of Canterbury, the Lord Chancellor Selborne, and the Revd F. C. Hingeston-Randolph* (London, 1880).

[58] B. L. Manning, *The Protestant Dissenting Deputies* (Cambridge, 1952), 322 ff. (cases illustrating these problems are noted here).

[59] P. Rowland, *Lloyd George* (London, 1975), 60–4; W. R. P. George, *The Making of Lloyd George* (London, 1976), 153–8. Cf. S. Maccoby, *English Radicalism, 1886–1914* (London, 1953), 488–9.

[60] Manning, op. cit. 330.

declaring that a registrar would no longer have to be present at weddings in Dissenting chapels.[61]

The Burial Laws Amendment Act of 1880 has been called 'the last major political victory of militant Dissent in England';[62] and so it was, appropriately occurring just about the time that the relative numerical decline of Nonconformity commenced. But this situation was by no means immediately obvious. Apart from the fact that the removal of the 'last' Nonconformist disability left minor disabilities to be removed, the Burials Act was feared to widen disestablishment prospects as much as it was hoped that the settlement would close them. Tait had said in the Lords that the bill should shore up the Church's position and 'recall the Dissenting bodies to that better mind which they showed in former times'. The Earl of Derby, supporting him, said he thought the concession would lessen support for disestablishment.[63] John Bright had said in the Commons that the bill's passing would not influence disestablishment one way or the other.[64] After the bill had passed Guinness Rogers (amidst assembled Congregationalists) expressed conciliation towards and indeed admiration of the Church of England without losing sight of the disestablishment goal.[65] On the other hand it was stated that burial reform had whetted Nonconformist appetites and cleared the way for disestablishment.[66] In retrospect it does appear that the removal of practical grievances lessened the interest of Dissenters in political aims of their own and therefore weakened the voluntary cause. But the weakening was only gradual, and a few years after 1880 disestablishment seemed to receive a fresh boost from the attainment of a wider Parliamentary franchise.

III. THE BRADLAUGH AFFAIR

The burial settlement was concerned with a familiar controversy and provided little fresh interest. Even before the 1880 bill was introduced, however, much religious excitement was being aroused by a new issue—Charles Bradlaugh's claim, as an atheist, to be allowed to sit in the House of Commons. This produced a long succession of Parliamentary and legal involvements which enthused the Conservative Opposition by dividing the Liberals afresh and effectively obstructing the career of a supposedly powerful ministry.

It was hesitancy by the Speaker, Sir Henry Brand, that allowed Bradlaugh's

[61] Ibid. 282–5.
[62] Marsh, op. cit. 262.
[63] H cclii. 1024, 1047–8. These views were also expressed by A. Barry, 'The Burials Bill and Disestablishment', *Nineteenth Century*, viii (Sept. 1880), 501; and, from a different angle, by Revd Henry Holland, *The Opening of the National Graveyards to Nonconformists* (London, n.d.).
[64] H cclv. 1057.
[65] *Congregational Year-book* (1881), 59. Cf. J. Guinness Rogers, 'The Probable Results of the Burials Bill', *Nineteenth Century*, viii (Dec. 1880), 1026, 1028.
[66] *The Burials Question further Examined, From a Layman's Point of View* (London, 1880).

claim to become a major Parliamentary shuttlecock. Bradlaugh, already well known as a militant propagandist of atheism and birth-control, was returned for Northampton in the general election. After the opening of Parliament he presented himself at the swearing-in of members with a written claim to make an affirmation or declaration of allegiance instead of taking the oath. The Parliamentary Oaths Act of 1866, he stated, gave the right to affirm to anyone permitted by law to do so; and, he claimed, he was such a person. But the Speaker, instead of allowing him to affirm and warning him of possible legal consequences, referred the claim to a Select Committee which, after tying at eight votes to eight, decided against Bradlaugh by a casting vote. A party division had already developed, all the Conservatives on the committee voting against Bradlaugh and all the Liberals (except one, who later changed his mind) voting for. Bradlaugh then attempted, against his convictions, to take the oath. Ironically he was opposed over this by the secularist doyen G. J. Holyoake, who could not agree that an athiest should try to take a sacred oath. Bradlaugh declared, in a letter published in *The Times,* that he would not regard himself as bound by the letter of the oath, but only 'by the spirit which the affirmation would have conveyed had I been permitted to use it'.[67]

Determined attempts to prevent Bradlaugh, as a professed atheist, from taking the oath were then commenced by the 'Fourth Party', a Conservative ginger group. Indeed the Bradlaugh case was the making of the Fourth Party as a body wishing to give a much sharper edge to the Opposition than was provided by the Conservative leader in the Commons, Sir Stafford Northcote— 'a scholar and a gentleman', noted A. J. Balfour long afterwards, 'but, when it came to a fight, no more a match for Mr. Gladstone than a wooden three-decker would be for a dreadnought'.[68] The little group comprised Lord Randolph Churchill, Sir Henry Drummond Wolff, John Gorst, and Balfour—though Balfour avoided the Bradlaugh controversy, perhaps because his reputation as a 'philosophical' Christian would cause embarrassment if he became involved in it. Lord Beaconsfield said that respectable Conservatives—among whom he did not number himself—viewed Lord Randolph and his Bashi-Bazouks 'with more repugnance than they do the Fenians'.[69]

The extent of the group's religious motivation in the issue, and especially that of Churchill, has been debated. It is impossible to be sure about this matter. But Churchill, who had a religious family background and considerable theological knowledge, and took a serious interest in ecclesiastical issues, may well have had religious reasons amongst others for what he was doing.[70] But it does seem that

[67] W. L. Arnstein, *The Bradlaugh Case* (Oxford, 1965), 34 ff.; *AR* cxxii (1880), 57–71.

[68] Arthur James, First Earl Balfour, *Chapters of Autobiography,* ed. Mrs E. Dugdale (London, 1930), 141.

[69] Ibid. 148.

[70] See R. E. Quinault, 'The Fourth Party and the Conservative Opposition to Bradlaugh, 1880–1888', *EHR* xci (1976), 316–24; R. F. Foster, *Lord Randolph Churchill: A Political Life* (Oxford, 1981), 66–7.

party political motives are the main explanation for Conservative resistance to Bradlaugh's claim. Otherwise it is difficult to account for the almost unanimous opposition to Bradlaugh of a party which had substantially contributed to the admission of Catholics and Jews to Parliament. Moreover, if politicians had wanted to exclude an atheist simply because they were Christians, then most Liberals would have joined most Conservatives in opposing Bradlaugh, and he would have had only a handful to support him. Instead his claim was supported by most Liberals, including Gladstone, Bright and others who professed to be consciously and continuously guided by religious motives. Instead of forming a united ground on the case, religious arguments were used to support both sides.

The first Parliamentary division on Bradlaugh's claim, on 24 May 1880, was a success for the ministry: a motion by Wolff to stop Bradlaugh taking the oath was defeated, after much excited debate, by 289 votes to 214. A second Select Committee was appointed, and reversed the decision of the first by deciding on 16 June that Bradlaugh could not take the oath but could make an affirmation subject to any statutory penalties. Henry Labouchere, Bradlaugh's radical fellow-member for Northampton, moved on 21 June that Bradlaugh be allowed to affirm, but was defeated by Sir Hardinge Giffard (later Lord Halsbury) who moved a successful amendment that Bradlaugh be permitted neither to swear nor to affirm. The division in Giffard's favour was 275 to 230, and a voting pattern appeared which was often repeated as the case went on. The Opposition had the best of the party struggle because they took more support from the other side than they lost to it, and more Liberals than Conservatives abstained. Whereas 218 Liberals opposed Giffard's amendment and 210 Conservatives supported it, thirty-four Liberals voted for it and only two Conservatives against. Moreover, no fewer than eighty-eight Liberals abstained. Irish Home Rulers began to reflect the predominant Catholic opposition to Bradlaugh's claim by dividing thirty-one to ten for Giffard's amendment.

The Conservatives were naturally delighted with the embarrassment caused to the Government. After Bradlaugh had been committed for a night to the Clock Tower because he had not obeyed the Speaker's order to withdraw from the House, Gladstone carried a resolution on 1 July by 303 votes to 249 that Bradlaugh and other non-believers could affirm instead of taking the oath. Only three Liberals opposed the resolution, and only one Conservative voted in favour. But more Home Rulers opposed (twenty-two) than voted for (fifteen). Bradlaugh them made a solemn affirmation, took his seat and kept it until March 1881. During this period, however, a lawsuit proceeded against him for sitting and voting without having taken the required oath.[71]

'An analysis of the Liberal vote in thirteen key roll calls', it has been shown, 'indicates that 69 per cent of the party's members tended generally to vote in favour of Bradlaugh's admission, 23 per cent tended to abstain, and 8 per cent

[71] Arnstein, op. cit. 49–82; AR cxxii (1880), 71–7; H cclii. 187–223, 333–422, ccliii. 443–514, 550–624.

tended to oppose his admission'.[72] Crucial in deciding the results were the absentee Liberals: had they voted for Bradlaugh, motions in his favour would easily have succeeded. Bradlaugh was strongly supported by some Whigs and heartily opposed by a few radicals. Nonconformists voted on opposite sides; the Wesleyan Henry Fowler and the Congregationalists Samuel Morley and Sir Charles Reed were against the claim. Some Liberals opposed or abstained 'because they feared their constituents would not distinguish between atheism and the just treatment of an atheist'.[73] Cross-voting produced some peculiar bed-fellows. Newdegate and most Catholic MPs agreed at last by opposing Bradlaugh, and Newdegate rejoiced in the 'bond of union between myself and the Roman Catholic members of this House'.[74]

On 7 March 1881 Bradlaugh argued his own case in the Court of Queen's Bench. But the verdict, upheld on appeal, was that he had been sitting and voting illegally as he had no right to affirm. The Parliamentary contest started afresh. Gorst moved that Bradlaugh's seat was vacant and that a writ be issued for a new election at Northampton. Bradlaugh won the consequent by-election on 9 April, against fierce resistance, by a reduced majority of 132. Many Liberal voters seem to have abstained. On 26 April he tried to take the oath but Northcote intervened and moved to disallow him. The Conservatives issued a strong whip, the Government declined to make the question a party one, and after a hot debate the Conservatives won with fifteen Liberals and eleven Home Rulers voting with them. Bradlaugh was then ordered to withdraw several times. He refused, and had to be physically compelled to leave. Next day he appeared again, with the same result. The Government tried to introduce a bill permitting affirmation but were not allowed to bring it in. Bradlaugh again entered the House to take the oath on 10 May, but withdrew quietly. He then tried to bring popular pressure to bear on the House, and by the beginning of August petitions signed by 150,000 had been submitted in his favour. But when, on 3 August, he entered the Commons he was forcibly removed by ten policemen.

The 1882 session began with Bradlaugh trying once more to take the oath but being stopped by a vote of 286 to 228 on 7 February. Thirty-nine Home Rulers and twenty-five Liberals voted in the majority, but seventy-six absent Liberals again decided the question. Undeterred, Bradlaugh administered the oath to himself and, amid cries of outrage, took his seat. The House had to look to its authority. Many supporters of Bradlaugh would not condone infringement of the rules, and Northcote's motion to expel him for contempt succeeded by 297 votes to eighty on 22 February. Gladstone abstained, Bright was absent through illness, and Chamberlain was the only Cabinet minister to vote against

[72] Arnstein, op. cit. 144.
[73] Ibid. 146.
[74] Speech on 3 May 1883; H cclxxviii. 1738; Arnstein, *Protestant versus Catholic in Mid-Victorian England: Mr Newdegate and the Nuns* (Columbia and London, 1982), 208.

expulsion. Bradlaugh consequently went again to the electors of Northampton, and won their endorsement by a further reduced majority of 108 after receiving verbal support from some Nonconformist ministers.

Anticipating another attempt on the oath by Bradlaugh, Northcote carried a resolution (with the help of twenty-five Home Rulers and fourteen Liberals) preventing him from taking the oath. Bradlaugh did not try to take his seat during the remainder of the session, but he obtained many more signatures for petitions in his favour than his opponents obtained against him. Lord Redesdale introduced a bill in the Lords providing that no one could sit in that House unless he declared his belief in an almighty God. But Shaftesbury, Granville, Salisbury, Argyll, and the Bishop of London argued against the proposed declaration on the grounds that it would be irritating without being effectual, and the bill was withdrawn. Argyll then introduced a bill allowing affirmation, but this measure was condemned by Carnarvon and Tait and thrown out.[75]

1883 in the Bradlaugh saga was concerned with the Government's Affirmation Bill. The Cabinet decided to try and pass enabling legislation in Gladstone's absence but with his later reluctant assent. He had previously argued that the matter should be decided by the Law Courts. Bradlaugh, ignorant of the Cabinet decision, held a huge radical meeting in Trafalgar Square on 15 February in support of his next attempt to take the oath. The gathering was adjourned while he went to the House of Commons. He emerged an hour later with the news that the Government would introduce an affirmation bill next day.

But the ministry's effort failed. There was considerable verbal skirmishing in the House before the bill—called the Parliamentary Oaths Act Amendment Bill—was introduced, and the Opposition were in a determined mood to resist. Extensive debates on the second reading began on 23 April. Gladstone, in one of his most highly praised speeches, asserted that religion was being damaged through association with unjust exclusion. He had 'no fear of Atheism in this House': firm application of 'every principle of justice and equity is the best method we can adopt for the preservation and influence of truth'. Unbelief was attracting unwanted sympathy, and this threatened to cause impairment of religious faith, 'the loss of which I believe to be the most inexpressible calamity which can fall either upon a man or upon a nation'. Churchill made the chief Opposition reply on 30 April. He contended that respectable and religious people opposed the change, while 'its supporters [presumably including Gladstone] were the residuum and scum of the population, who scoffed at all restraints, moral or religious'. He distinguished Jewish admission from atheist exclusion by pointing out that Jews and Christians believed in the same God. He referred to Beaconsfield's views about the spiritual debt which Christianity

[75] Arnstein, *Bradlaugh Case*, 92–140; *AR* cxxiii (1881), 138–47, cxxiv (1882), 15–34; H cclx. 1183–251, cclxvi. 92–6, 1234–65, 1314–48, cclxvii. 190–223, 1624–47, cclxxi. 1354–81; Bahlman, *Diary*, i. 134, 159, 219–20, 227–8, 231.

owed to Judaism, and looked forward to a time when Jews would recognise the doctrine of the Trinity. He also claimed that public opinion was heavily against the bill: the signatures on petitions against it exceeded by almost four times the signatures on petitions in favour. R. A. Cross said that petitions against had been signed by 514,000 people.

There were many other speeches, for and against. Beresford Hope said that atheism was rampant in France, and 'England is only 21 miles from France, even without a Channel tunnel'. Arthur O'Connor, a Home Ruler, also opposing said the bill must logically lead to disestablishment, for a Parliament which abandoned an official requirement to believe in God could hardly maintain a national Church. In the division on 4 May the bill was defeated by three votes: seventeen Liberals and thirty-six Home Rulers voted against. Cardinal Manning said the rejection had 'saved the House of Commons from an offence against God, and the country from a shame and endless danger'.

Thereafter Bradlaugh was again prevented, on Northcote's motion, from taking the oath. During the summer Bradlaugh campaigned in the country. Meetings were held in many towns, culminating in two London gatherings, one in St James's Hall in July and the other in Trafalgar Square on 5 August.[76]

Bradlaugh tried to administer the oath to himself at the beginning of the 1884 session. But at length, after considerable confusion during which Bradlaugh voted in divisions, Northcote's motion that he be disallowed from taking the oath was carried by 280 votes to 167; forty-two Home Rulers and twenty Liberals voted against Bradlaugh, but Liberal abstentions decided the outcome. Labouchere, supporting Bradlaugh in the debate, had said (though professedly a Christian himself) that the words of the oath were 'just the same superstitious incantation as the trash of any Mumbo-Jumbo among African savages', a phrase which brought shocked protests from F. H. O'Donnell and W. E. Forster.[77] After further wrangles a writ was issued for a third Northampton by-election. Bradlaugh disappointed any hopes that he would be defeated by increasing his majority to 368.

Bradlaugh's long fight was now being rewarded by a swing of public opinion in his favour, not least in the Press.[78] But the problem was still unresolved. He tried to take the oath again in July 1885, but a motion of Sir Michael Hicks Beach disallowing this action was carried. At length a new Parliament provided the opportunity to settle the dispute. On 13 January 1886 the new Speaker, Arthur Peel, allowed Bradlaugh to take the oath: 'It is not for me . . . it is not for the House, to enter into any inquisition as to what may be the opinions of a Member when he comes to the Table to take the Oath'. There were some

[76] Arnstein, op. cit. 153–5, 189–235; AR cxxv (1883), 12–31, 86–94; H cclxxviii 915–88, 1167–222, 1439–511, 1598–665, 1725–825; Bahlman, op. cit. ii. 426, 430–1; Manning to Northcote, 4 May 1883; Iddesleigh Papers, Add. MS 50041, fo. 185.
[77] Quoted Arnstein, op. cit. 278; AR cxxvi (1884), 26–7.
[78] Arnstein, op. cit. 286–92.

protests in the Press, but Conservative MPs had lost interest in the struggle. Churchill supported an Affirmation Bill in 1887, and this was passed on its reintroduction in 1888.

An observer noted in July 1881 that there was 'a strong feeling out of doors' against Bradlaugh and 'only a limited feeling in his favour'.[79] Public opinion seems to have grown more favourable to Bradlaugh. In June 1883 he complained to Gladstone that the London Press was exaggerating the feeling against him, and listed several large provincial meetings where the declarations were unanimous in his favour. He was sure that 'the manufactured majority of petition signatures' did not represent the real feeling of the country.[80]

The Bradlaugh question caused differences within all parties; it also divided all the leading denominations. Bradlaugh's support for disestablishment helped to explain the ecclesiastical divisions over his claim. Anglican opinion seems to have been mostly against him, and included in the majority were many keen defenders of the establishment. The Church Defence Institution passed resolutions, sponsored meetings and urged every Anglican clergyman to sign petitions against the Affirmation Bill. More than 13,000 clergy (probably a majority) obliged by signing. The bill was also opposed by many diocesan conferences, and by the Lower House of the Convocation of Canterbury. The evangelical *Rock* was firmly against Bradlaugh's claim, as was his brother W. R. Bradlaugh who led an Anti-Infidel League.[81] The High-Church *Guardian*, on the other hand, supported Bradlaugh. The High-Churchman Malcolm MacColl and the Ritualist Stewart Headlam—founder in 1877 of the Guild of St Matthew, dedicated to the conversion of secularists to Christianity—were strongly in his favour. He was also supported by the Revd D. Williams, Vicar of Coalville, Leicestershire, who wrote *Reasons for the Affirmation Bill becoming Law (Though Involving Bradlaugh Sitting)*.

Official opinion in the Church of Scotland was heavily weighted against Bradlaugh. In 1881 the Church of Scotland General Assembly resolved by 177 votes to nineteen to petition against an affirmation bill. Presbyteries of this Church also resolved, either unanimously or by large majorities, to petition against the bill of 1883.[82] Even the Dissenting United Presbyterians produced only one petition for Bradlaugh—but none against him.[83]

Among Nonconformists, there was some difference over the case between denominations in which there was considerable political conservatism and those in which voluntaryism and radical politics prevailed. Most Wesleyan ministers

[79] Bahlman, op. cit. i. 151.

[80] Bradlaugh to Gladstone, 11 June 1883; GP, 44111, fos. 134–5.

[81] E. Royle, *Radicals, Secularists, and Republicans: Popular Free Thought in Britain, 1866–1915* (Manchester, 1980), 300–1.

[82] Arnstein, op. cit. 160–72; Minutes of Edinburgh Church of Scotland Presbytery, 21 Mar. 1883; CH2/121/29, p. 70; Abertarff C. of S. Presbytery, 27 Mar. 1883; CH2/7/8, 434; Dingwall C. of S. Presbytery, 28 Mar. 1883; CH2/92/12, 177.

[83] H cclxxviii. 1204–5.

and laity, it was said, wished to keep Bradlaugh out of Parliament; but this was denied by Wesleyans who favoured Bradlaugh.[84] The Wesleyan Conference protested against Bradlaugh's admission to Parliament in 1881, and the Edinburgh presbytery of the Free Church resolved (on the motion of James Begg) to petition against the Affirmation Bill in 1883. But Congregationalists, Baptists, Primitive Methodists, and Unitarians were generally in Bradlaugh's favour. The committee of the Congregational Union petitioned for the Affirmation Bill, and the Union's assembly recorded its 'extreme regret' at the bill's failure, while R. W. Dale defended the bill as a means of avoiding profanation of the oath. The *Primitive Methodist Magazine* said that anyone who opposed affirmation identified religion with injustice and oppression, and the *Nonconformist* said that resistance to the bill harmed religion and made Bradlaugh a hero. There were, however, exceptions even in the more radical Dissenting bodies. Most, but not all, Baptist MPs supported Bradlaugh. A Baptist minister, the Revd J. T. Almy, opposed him in a rather ambiguously titled pamphlet, *Almighty God or Bradlaugh*. Another Baptist minister opposed the claim in *Should Christians Support Mr Bradlaugh?*[85] Samuel Morley, a Congregational MP though not a voluntary, swung to oppose Bradlaugh.[86]

Similarly, there were differences among Catholics over the issue. Cardinal Manning campaigned zealously against the Affirmation Bill, and the *Tablet* was anti-Bradlaugh. 'For the first time we are asked to comprehend unbelief and explicit denial of the existence of God and His Law', wrote Manning to Northcote in 1882.[87] But Cardinal Newman favoured the Affirmation Bill, and he had considerable Catholic support, including a minority of Home Rule MPs.[88] Newman wanted the compulsory oath to be abandoned because he thought it a sham: 'Christianity had ceased to be the religion of Parliament for many years', he wrote.[89] The anti-Bradlaugh attitude of most Home Rule MPs may have been influenced partly by their own religious feeling, partly by a need to please the Catholic hierarchy, and partly by their desire to embarrass the Government and their readiness to ally with the Conservatives.[90]

Bradlaugh's ultimate success in entering Parliament in 1886 set the seal on a lengthy tendency to relax the religious restrictions on admission. Probably because of Bradlaugh's case the National Secular Society temporarily increased its membership and branches in the early 1880s.[91] The case was argued in

[84] Ibid. 1173, 1469, 1500–1, 1758–9.

[85] F. W. Hillier, *Should Christians Support Mr Bradlaugh?* 3rd edn. (Exeter and London, 1883), 8.

[86] Arnstein, op. cit. 60, 134, 159–61; Edinburgh Free Presbytery Minutes, 28 Feb. 1883; CH3/111/30, 227; *Congregational Year-book* (1884), 3; A. Peel, *These Hundred Years*, 296; R. W. Dale, *Oath or Affirmation?* (Birmingham, 1883); *Primitive Methodist Magazine*, NS vi (1883), 383; *Nonconformist and Independent*, 5 Apr. 1883, p. 301.

[87] Manning to Northcote, 22 Feb. 1882; Iddesleigh Papers, 50041, fos. 88–9.

[88] Arnstein, op. cit. 83, 174–82, 202 ff.

[89] Newman to MacColl, 16 Apr. 1883; G. W. E. Russell (ed.), *Malcolm MacColl: Memoirs and Correspondence* (London, 1914), 305.

[90] Cf. Arnstein, op. cit. 201–24.   [91] Royle, op. cit. 29–30, 36.

anything but a political vacuum: reactions to this issue were affected by party interest and rivalry. In its turn the case affected other political questions—perhaps helping, for example, to divert attention from disestablishment.

IV. DISESTABLISHMENT AND THE RADICAL PROGRAMME, 1880–1885

In spite of the Liberal victory in 1880 and the success over burials, voluntaryism was rather muted in the early 1880s. The desire of many Nonconformists for integration with the Liberal party continued. Guinness Rogers said in January 1882 that Nonconformists 'simply took their place in the ranks of Liberalism'.[92] While seeking to do this, however, voluntaries also wanted the Liberal party to adopt disestablishment principles. They were encouraged by the inclusion of disestablishment in Chamberlain's campaign of speeches and articles beginning in 1883. But there was growing Whig revulsion from the strengthening radical tendency, and as long as Whiggism remained important in the party disestablishment would be strongly contested among Liberals. At the Liberation Society's triennial conference in 1884, Carvell Williams noted the presence of 'a far greater number of representatives of Liberal associations . . . than we have ever had before', but his claim that 'we are fast becoming the Liberal party' seemed unduly optimistic.[93]

While often tactically quiescent at this time, the Liberation Society did not ignore new opportunities for propaganda. The growing agitation against tithes caused the Society to hold a small conference which resolved to aid the protesters.[94] It was desired to draw more Wesleyans into the Society.[95] Confidence in the ultimate success of voluntaryism was voiced, for instance, by the chairman of the Congregational Union in 1882, by John Bright at a Liberation Society meeting at the Metropolitan Tabernacle in 1883, and by Chamberlain at Bright's silver jubilee as an MP for Birmingham.[96]

In July 1883 the Liberation Society laid plans for local conferences during the coming autumn and winter to support three intended Parliamentary motions for disestablishment in England, Wales, and Scotland respectively. Rejection of another deceased wife's sister bill in the Upper House, partly by episcopal votes, prompted the Society to renew its call for the removal of Bishops from the Lords.[97] William Willis, a Baptist and Liberal MP for Colchester, gave notice of a motion to effect this. The three disestablishment motions were strongly supported at a large conference at Leicester in February

[92] Hamer, *Electoral Pressure*, 153.

[93] Ibid.

[94] LS, 1 Mar. 1880, 3 Jan. 1881; A/LIB/6, 239–40, 337.

[95] *Congregationalist*, xii (1883), 722.

[96] *Congregational Year-book* (1883), 38; K. Robbins, *John Bright* (London, 1979), 247–8; *AR* cxxv (1883), 139–40.

[97] LS, 2, 16, 30 July 1883; A/LIB/7, 28–41.

1884. These motions were also the main point of discussion at the joint Parliamentary breakfast held by the Dissenting Deputies and the Liberation Society at the opening of the session, and petitions were presented in their favour.[98] Alfred Illingworth had given notice in the Commons of an amendment to the Cathedral Statutes Bill: until disestablishment gave self-rule to Anglicans, the House should not be 'occupied in considering piecemeal changes in the regulations that now govern the Established Church'.[99] The amendment indicated the tactics to be used by some Nonconformists in face of growing attempts to pass legislation to reform the Church of England.

Willis's motion to remove Bishops from the Lords, couched in exactly the same terms as a successful Commons resolution of March 1641, was defeated in a small House by eleven votes on 21 March 1884. Dissenters, radicals, and some Home Rulers supported the motion. Harcourt opposed it on behalf of the ministry but most members of the Government abstained.[1] The disestablishment motions did not obtain a place in the Parliamentary timetable. The *Congregationalist* said that Welsh disestablishment should have priority: English disestablishment was not yet a matter of practical politics, and the Scots electorate should decide the best time for raising Scottish disestablishment. The Welsh case was 'more urgent and pressing' than the others, for the established Church in Wales was an 'alien' minority like the former Irish establishment.[2]

Henry Richard said in the *Contemporary Review* of August 1883 that adequate reform of the Church of England could come only through self-government after disestablishment. Parliament was not competent to deal with ecclesiastical questions.[3] But the Church Defence Institution had quite different ideas: Church reform must be achieved while the establishment was maintained. At a private conference with Archbishop Tait at Lambeth Palace in March 1881, a CDI spokesman said that voluntaryism was 'a movement against . . . property' pervaded by a 'strong current of communism and socialism'; Bishop Thorold of Rochester said voluntaries were 'Jacobins' heralding a new age of atheism; and Lord Salisbury said those who wanted to save the Church of England must be ready to put up a fight.[4] The CDI central council resolved at its annual meeting in July 1881 that, in view of 'strenuous and persistent efforts now being made to prejudice the public mind against the National Church', it was essential that Churchmen 'without distinction of religion or political party' should take all needful steps to tell the country the truth about the Church of

---

[98] Ibid. 84–9; Manning, *Dissenting Deputies*, 398; Glasgow United Presbyterian Presbytery Minutes, 11 Mar. 1884; CH3/147/I, 287–8. Cf. Hamer, op. cit. 154.

[99] LS, 18 Feb., 24 Mar. 1884; A/LIB/7, 84–6, 93.

[1] H cclxxxvi. 50–1; H. Townsend, *The Claims of the Free Churches* (London, 1949), 229; Bahlman, op. cit ii. 581–2; *Congregationalist*, xiii (1884), 414–16.

[2] *Congregationalist*, xiii (1884), 412–14.

[3] *CR* xliv. 247–8. Cf. *Primitive Methodist Magazine*, NS v (1882), 255.

[4] Roberts, 'Pressure-group Politics', 573–5.

England.[5] The Institution's journal, *The National Church*, accused voluntaries of not really wanting to remove Church abuses but to retain them as weapons against the establishment.[6]

Church defence was voiced by Lord Randolph Churchill in a speech at Birmingham in April 1884: The Church of England was 'an immense and omnipresent ramification of machinery working without cost to the people, and daily and hourly lifting the masses . . . from the dead and dreary level of the lowest and most material cares of life, up to the comfortable contemplation of higher and serener forms of existence and of destiny'.[7] The deceased wife's sister bill of 1883, having passed first the Commons and then the second reading and committee in the Lords, was opposed by Lord Randolph's father, the Duke of Marlborough, on the ground that it would sever the law of the land from the law of the Church and 'would be a step towards destroying the union of Church and State'.[8] The bill was narrowly rejected on the third reading. Church defence was also linked with specific suggestions for improvement. When asked for their views on reform, 128 branches of the English Church Union advocated a voice for the clergy and lay communicants in the appointment of Bishops; the governing of dioceses with the advice of synods; and greater representation of parish clergy in the Convocations.[9] An unsuccessful bill was introduced in 1881 to allow clergy of the Church of England to sit in the Commons; Beresford Hope, opposing the measure, conjured up a fearful picture of parsons canvassing in their cassocks.[10]

Reform of Church patronage continued to be urged. In October 1881 the Bath and Wells diocesan conference resolved unanimously to suggest this reform to Ministers.[11] In the previous March Edward Leatham had once again raised the matter in the Commons, asserting that the 'enormous traffic' in livings required 'remedial measures of the most stringent and radical character'. He condemned 'the shameful auctions . . . at which the cure of souls is knocked down to the highest bidder', and remarked on 'the glowing descriptions of the piggeries and shrubberies at the rectory; of the paucity of labour and the plenitude of pay; of the real county society; of the propinquity of admirals and baronets; and the abundance of trout and rooks'.[12] Gladstone praised Leatham's disinterestedness, as a Nonconformist, in seeking reform of an establishment which could be more easily assailed if its abuses were left intact.[13] Leatham's motion was withdrawn, as also (after debate) was a bill of the Hon.

[5] CDI Central Council Minutes, 6 July 1881 (vol. 206).

[6] *The National Church*, July 1882; xi. 157–8.

[7] Quoted J. F. C. Harrison (ed.), *Society and Politics in England, 1780–1960* (New York and London, 1965), 362.

[8] *AR* cxxv (1883), 138.

[9] G. B. Roberts, *The History of the English Church Union, 1859–1894* (London, 1895), 238–9.

[10] H cclxi. 230–46.

[11] Bishop of Bath and Wells (Lord Arthur Hervey) to Gladstone, 22 Oct. 1881; GP, 44207, fos. 275–6.

[12] H cclx. 178, 195.

[13] Ibid. 207.

Edward Stanhope, a Conservative, to prevent the sale of next presentations. Further bills brought in by Stanhope and Leatham in 1881 and 1882 were dropped. Another bill of Leatham in 1884 passed its second reading, but did not get through committee in the time available.[14] So the already well-worn question remained to be pressed again by those, such as Albert Grey, Harcourt, and Stewart Headlam, who thought there ought to be 'a recognition of the right of popular election of the clergy'.[15]

The Welsh Sunday Closing Act of 1881 was the first example of separate legislation for Wales, and many saw it as a precedent for Welsh disestablishment.[16] But this question remained fairly quiet for some time. In the autumn of 1883 meetings on disestablishment were held in Swansea, Caernarvon, Cardiff, Aberystwyth, Llandudno, and elsewhere. In that year the Liberation Society appointed two Welsh Councils, one for the North and one for the South. but most Welsh Liberal MPs took little interest in these developments. Stuart Rendel and Thomas Gee felt that a clear lead from Chamberlain, as a Cabinet Minister, would greatly assist the cause, and Chamberlain visited Wales in October 1884, speaking at Denbigh and Newtown.[17] However, the cause was obstructed by the need to preserve a façade of Liberal unity at the election of 1885 and by the Liberal split over Home Rule in 1886.

Welsh Church defence, in the mean time, was centred on the need to strengthen the Church's popular appeal, not least by appointing Welsh speakers to Bishoprics and other leading posts.[18] The Archbishop of Canterbury, E. W. Benson, wrote to Gladstone in July 1883: 'Welsh must be regarded as a permanent language for not less than a century to come, and . . . in the desire to hasten its departure, grave mistakes are made which alienate the people from the clergy. I find there are 7 or 8 magazines and penny newspapers published in Welsh and all Nonconformist. There is *one* Welsh *Church* newspaper and it dies this week.'[19] An Oxford University Association for the Defence of the Church in Wales was founded, and the council of the Church Defence Institution resolved in 1884 that 'the Principality of Wales especially should be thoroughly and effectually organised for Church defence purposes'. A year later the council expressed satisfaction with Church defence efforts in Wales.[20]

---

[14] H cclx. 845–6, 973–91; cclxix. 47–62; cclxxxix. 723–69.

[15] F. G. Bettany, *Stewart Headlam: A Biography* (London, 1926), 114–15; *Church Reformer*, 15 Aug. 1884 (iii. 8, 178–9).

[16] W. R. Lambert, 'The Welsh Sunday Closing Act, 1881', *WHR* vi. 2 (1972), 174–5.

[17] G. V. Nelmes, 'Stuart Rendel and his Contribution to the Development of a Distinctly Welsh Political Programme Within the Liberal Party Between 1880 and 1895', MA thesis (Wales, 1977), 92 ff.; F. E. Hamer (ed.), *The Personal Papers of Lord Rendel* (London, 1931), 227; J. W. Roberts, 'Sir George Osborne Morgan, 1826–1897', MA thesis (Wales, 1979), 51.

[18] e.g. Revd Robert Williams, Vicar of Holyhead, to Bishop of Chester, 21 Dec. 1882; GP, 44218, fos. 235–8; Lord Aberdare to Gladstone, 24 Dec. 1882; GP, 44087, fos. 151–8.

[19] Benson to Gladstone, 23 July 1883; GP, 44109, fo. 40.

[20] Sir A. Griffith-Boscawen, *Memories* (London, 1925), 68; CDI Central Council Minutes, 7 July 1884, 19 June 1885 (vol. 206).

At the same time the council extended its sympathies to 'the Scottish establishment under the attack that is being made on it'.[21] Even in Scotland, however, the disestablishment movement was slow to develop in the early 1880s. There remained some difference of view between the pure voluntaries (United Presbyterians and some other Dissenters) and the Free Church disestablishers led by Rainy who opposed the existing establishment because it was not spiritually independent of the State.[22] In current circumstances, however, the difference was slight and it did not prevent Rainy and Dr John Cairns, a leading United Presbyterian, from addressing public meetings together on disestablishment. In 1881 the Scottish Council of the Liberation Society gave full support to its president, J. Dick Peddie (Liberal MP for Kilmarnock Burghs and an elder of the United Presbyterian Church) who tried to raise the question in Parliament.[23] This council also drew up a practical scheme for disestablishment and disendowment. The Liberation Society's Parliamentary committee, on the other hand, would not support the introduction of a motion for Scots disestablishment in 1881;[24] and despite other attempts Peddie did not succeed in introducing a bill until October 1884.[25] Even then this bill, drawn up after consultation with the Liberation Society and proposing to disestablish the Church of Scotland from 1 January 1887, did not receive a debate.[26]

In the Scottish Liberal Association, formed in July 1881, voluntary efforts by radicals were resisted by Whigs; and Rainy's attempts to obtain Liberal party commitment to Scots disestablishment were evaded by Gladstone.[27] One Liberal MP, George Armitstead (member for Dundee and close friend of Gladstone), excused himself from attending a disestablishment meeting in 1882 on the ground that he had pledged himself in the last election not to stir the question in the ensuing Parliament.[28] Gladstone told the Queen in 1883 that he thought the question had not made much progress recently;[29] and it is true that persistent voluntary efforts (for example the resolutions and activities of Dissenting presbyteries) were now being met by resolute Church defence.

[21] CDI Central Council Minutes, 19 June 1885 (vol. 206). But cf. *Church Reformer*, 15 Feb. 1884 (iii. 2, 32).
[22] Cf. D. W. Bebbington, *The Nonconformist Conscience: Chapel and Politics, 1870–1914* (London, 1982), 42; P. Carnegie Simpson, *The Life of Principal Rainy* (2 vols., London 1909), ii. 21–4; R. Rainy, 'Disestablishment in Scotland', *CR* xli. (Mar. 1882), 421–34; *Congregationalist*, xi (1882), 924–5.
[23] *Fourth Annual Report of Scottish Council of Liberation Society, 1880–1881* (Edinburgh, 1881), 9–14.
[24] LS, 14 Mar. 1881, p. 353–4.
[25] A. L. Drummond and J. Bulloch, *The Church in Late Victorian Scotland, 1874–1900*, 113–14.
[26] Ibid. 115.
[27] J. G. Kellas, 'The Liberal Party and the Scottish Church Disestablishment Crisis', *EHR* lxxix (1964), 33; Simpson, op. cit. ii. 16; Mrs M. Oliphant, *A Memoir of the Life of John Tulloch* (Edinburgh, 1888), 368; Hamer, *Liberal Politics in the Age of Gladstone and Rosebery* (Oxford, 1972), 89–90; LS, 8 Jan. 1883; A/LIB/6, 519.
[28] Newspaper extract in Lamb Collection, 176 (11), in Dundee Local History Library.
[29] Gladstone to Queen Victoria, 8 Jan. 1883; J. Morley, *Life of W. E. Gladstone* (3 vols., London, 1903), iii. 102.

Principal Tulloch and the *Scotsman* newspaper were among the contributors to Scottish Church defence. Some local defence committees were formed by presbyteries and other groups.[30] On 2 June 1882 the General Assembly of the Church of Scotland decided, on Tulloch's motion, to form a Church Interests Committee for defence purposes. Tulloch, a Liberal, and Lord Balfour of Burleigh, a Conservative politician, were both conveners of this body. The General Assembly also resolved to issue a pastoral letter to Church members, 'reminding them of the many blessings which, under Divine Providence, the Church of Scotland, as by law established, has conferred on this land'.[31] At the end of 1882 an elaborate National Church Society was founded as another defence organ: it was to have an elected 'sectional council' for each parish and other bodies representing presbyteries and synods.[32] The society was not a success, but Church defenders remained resolute.[33] It was suggested that tighter links should be formed between the Church of Scotland and the Free Church minority which held strongly to the establishment principle.[34] Even some United Presbyterians were beginning to stand forth as defenders of the establishment, as was shown when a Church protection association was founded in Dundee in February 1882.[35]

Conservative politicians tried to make the most of the Scots disestablishment threat in order to gain party support as Church defenders. Sir Stafford Northcote and Lord Salisbury both visited Scotland towards the end of 1882 and stressed the need to support the established Kirk. Salisbury, who had family connections with leading Scottish Conservatives, later told Richard Cross: 'you should work the question of the Scottish Church Establishment if you have the opportunity. In many parts of Scotland that is certainly a telling factor.'[36]

Amid all the competing clamour over disestablishment the still small voice of Scots Presbyterian reunion was there for those who wanted to listen. On 24 November 1884 a small public meeting in the Oddfellows' Hall, Edinburgh, appointed a steering committee to consider steps towards reunion. This held weekly meetings during December and proposed that an association be formed, with a representative committee. The committee consisted of twenty-one members drawn equally from the Church of Scotland, the Free Church, and the United Presbyterian Church. By June 1885, however, the committee had to admit that there 'did not appear to be sufficient ground' to hold further

[30] e.g. Dingwall C. of S. Presbytery Minutes, 30 Nov. 1881; CH2/92/12, 154.

[31] Oliphant, op. cit. 397–403, also 418–22.

[32] *United Presbyterian Magazine*, Feb. 1883; NS xxvii. 63–5.

[33] Oliphant, op. cit. 414.

[34] J. Kennedy, *The Disestablishment Movement in the Free Church* (Edinburgh, 1882); Abertarff C. of S. Presbytery Minutes, 27 Dec. 1882; CH2/7/8, 424–5.

[35] Extract dated 28 Feb. 1882, in Lamb Collection, 176 (11). Cf. Glasgow North UP Presbytery Minutes, 13 Feb. 1883; CH3/147/1, 176.

[36] Salisbury to Cross, 30 Oct. 1883; Cross Papers, Add. MS 51263, fo. 76; *United Presbyterian Magazine*, NS xxvii (1883), 38–9; *Congregationalist*, xii (1883), 10.

meetings, as there was 'no reasonable probability as yet . . . of effecting a union between the Churches in the present state of ecclesiastical relations in Scotland'. None the less it was hoped that 'a way may be opened for entering into consideration of the subject of union in more favourable circumstances'.[37] Thus was recognized the current importance of the disestablishment struggle in Scotland, in which it was difficult to make fruitful progress towards reunion.

About the current state of the disestablishment question in England and Wales there were differing views. Edward Hamilton, Gladstone's private secretary, said in October 1884: 'the general question instead of advancing is receding. It is certainly further off maturing than it was 10 or 15 years ago . . . The fact is, the Church . . . has disarmed serious opposition. I doubt if the question be seriously raised for many a long day.'[38] Guinness Rogers, on the other hand, firmly denied that disestablishment was dying: There was a 'steady advance of public opinion in favour of the principles of the Liberation Society', and 'Nonconformity . . . has not been so powerful a force in the nation since the days of the Long Parliament as it is today'.[39] A book entitled *Disestablishment* by Henry Richard and Carvell Williams, published in 1885, conjured up 'a great tidal wave of opinion sweeping over the face of the nations, directed against civil establishments of religion'.[40] Wishful thinking undoubtedly played a part in such statements, but, particularly after the Reform Acts of 1884–5, it was clear that disestablishment would be a prominent question at the next election, and an awkward one for the Liberal leadership.

Voluntaries were encouraged by the extension of the county franchise in 1884 and the creation of more equal constituencies by the Redistribution Act of 1885. The introduction of single-member constituencies as the norm was expected to boost radicalism by ending the practice of running a Whig and a radical in partnership. Conservatives also hoped to gain from redistribution, as this would give more political weight to the 'villa toryism' of urban constituencies, and Salisbury enthusiastically agreed to this change in compensation for franchise extension. Malcolm MacColl had warned Salisbury in a personal interview not to force a dissolution over the franchise bill: this would only push unwelcome questions forward, including disestablishment.[41] The Liberation Society, in contrast, hoped the reforms would lead to instalments of disestablishment just as the 1867 Act had been followed by Irish disestablishment.[42] The Franchise Act, it was noted, gave the vote 'to a large portion of the community among

---

[37] *Report of the Proceedings of the Scottish Presbyterian Union Association, During its First Session, Ending 10 June 1885* (Edinburgh, 1886), 3–6; Earl of Aberdeen, 'Union of Presbyterian Churches', *FR* xxxvii (Jan.–June 1885), 717–23; Aberdeen to Rosebery, 31 Mar. 1885; RP, 10082, fos. 189–90.

[38] Bahlman, op. cit. ii. 715.

[39] *Congregationalist*, xiii (1884), 1017–21.

[40] H. Richard and J. Carvell Williams, *Disestablishment* (London, 1885), 14.

[41] Russell, *Malcolm MacColl*, 103.

[42] *The Case for Disestablishment: A Handbook of Facts and Arguments*, Liberation Society (London, 1884), 1.

whom the Society has for hears past assiduously laboured'; and the Redistribution Act 'created numerous new constituencies . . . of the kind most likely to return Disestablishment candidates'. Further, the forbidding of corrupt practices by an Act of 1883 and the extension of polling hours 'will tell in the same direction. The opportunity is an unprecedented one.'[43] Now was the time to press disestablishment 'upon Parliament, upon the constituencies, and upon the country at large'.[44]

The Society was quite subdued before the election, however, continuing its passive role of 1880 in an effort to maintain Liberal unity. In 1885 Dick Peddie's bill for Scots disestablishment did not go to a second reading because of the pressure of Government business, and the vitality of Scottish Church defence was shown by the 688,195 signatures appended to petitions against the bill.[45] Voluntaries found more hope in Chamberlain's unauthorized campaign, which culminated in the appearance of *The Radical Programme* at the end of July. This was a collection of essays published in the *Fortnightly Review* over the past two years, covering such themes as free education, land and local government reform, manhood suffrage, Ireland, and religious equality.[46] The introduction to the *Programme* emphasized the prospects opened to radicalism by the Acts of 1884 and 1885. A chapter on 'Measures' said it was 'impossible that, so long as the Establishment exists, there should be anything like complete religious liberty'; disestablishment was, 'some day or other', inevitable. Some of the establishment's funds would be useful for social purposes, and 'it is social legislation which will afford a field for the energy and constructive skill of Radical statesmen in the future'.[47] The essay on religious equality by John Morley said that the diverse religious composition of Parliament 'has reduced the theory of a State Church to a gross farce, an unseemly mockery, and a truly repulsive scandal'.[48] The 'great army of political clergy', thundered Morley, 'has never lost a great opportunity of taking the side of tyranny against freedom, of privilege against equality, of stagnation against improvement'—he ignored the fact that only one Bishop (Ellicott) had voted against the 1884 Franchise Bill. The great extent of voluntary giving to the Church of England indicated that, if disestablished, she would be well able to provide for herself.[49]

The *Radical Programme* with its wide range of proposals was intended to be a campaign document for the forthcoming election. It seemed a recipe for Liberal disunity, however, and was condemned by Gladstone and other Liberals.

[43] LS, 27 Apr. 1885; A/LIB/7, 177.
[44] Ibid. 29 Sept. 1884; A/LIB/7, 147.
[45] Kellas, op. cit. 35; LS, 1 June 1885; A/LIB/7, 185; Dundee C. of S. Presbytery Minutes, 6 May, 1 July 1885; CH2/103/23, 248–9, 256–7; Edinburgh C. of S. Presbytery Minutes, 29 Apr. 1885; CH2/121/29, 237; Edinburgh Free Presbytery Minutes, 13 May 1885; CH3/111/30, 321; Oliphant, op. cit. 444 ff.
[46] *The Radical Programme*, ed. Hamer (Brighton, 1971).
[47] Ibid. 43, 44, 61.
[48] Ibid. 128.
[49] Ibid. 135, 149–50; Bahlman, 'Politics and Church Patronage', 263.

Whigs especially disliked its suggestions, and the programme took the Liberal party to the brink of disruption before Home Rule usurped its role and placed Chamberlain on the same seceding side as the Whigs.

Before the election a minority Conservative ministry took office on 24 June after Conservatives and Home Rulers had combined to defeat the Government (many Liberals abstaining) on an amendment to the budget. Parnell had given his support to the Conservatives after Churchill had promised that coercion would be abandoned by a Conservative ministry. Home Rule was becoming a pressing political question, Parnell being willing to accept the concession from either party. Lord Carnarvon, Irish viceroy in the new Government, favoured the concession of Home Rule.[50] He had several conversations with Justin McCarthy and a famous secret one with Parnell on 1 August. But he denied that he gave Parnell any promise or assurance on the subject.[51] Salisbury knew of the intended conversation with Parnell before it took place, and Carnarvon told him what passed in it immediately afterwards. But only a Disraeli might have persuaded many Conservatives to perform the *volte face* of adopting Home Rule, and instead of Disraeli the party was now led by the more cautious and conservative Salisbury. The Government carried an Irish land purchase bill in October, but to have adopted Home Rule without lengthy preparation would have risked a major revolt. Nevertheless Parnell hoped that Conservatives might be prodded into taking up this policy, for they had the crucial advantage over the Liberals of controlling the House of Lords and were therefore likelier to get a Home Rule bill through. As a secondary alternative, by allying with the Conservatives Parnell could bring much greater pressure on the Liberals to take up the question.

V. THE ELECTION OF 1885

Parliament was prorogued on 14 August, and there followed three and a half months of intensive electioneering. The issues included economic recession and unemployment, foreign policy, and the need for 'fair trade'. Conservatives blamed Liberals for unemployment and a 'weak' foreign policy, and Conservatives drew confidence from Liberal by-election losses and the support of Parnell. The newly enlarged franchise, however, was the greatest force in the election, and all parties made gains from it.

Disestablishment figured largely in the campaign. The Liberation Society hoped that the new franchise would cause the return of more voluntary MPs. But the Liberal party was still as far from adopting disestablishment as it had

[50] Carnarvon to Salisbury, 5 Feb. 1885; SP; memo by Carnarvon, early June 1885; Carnarvon Papers, 60760, fos. 42–5.

[51] Morley, op. cit. iii. 229–30; Lady Gwendolen Cecil, *Life of Robert, Marguess of Salisbury* (4 vols., 1921–32) iii. 151–64; *AR* cxxx (1888), 107–8; L. P. Curtis, jun., *Coercion and Conciliation in Ireland, 1880–1892* (Princeton, 1963), 39–53; F. S. L. Lyons, *Charles Stewart Parnell* (London, 1977), 282–8. Cf. E. J. Feuchtwanger, *Democracy and Empire: Britain, 1865–1914* (London, 1985), 180–1.

been before the 1880 election, and the leaders still wished to minimize the controversial issue. It was in their interest to insist that Conservatives were emphasizing the question in order to divide the Liberals and gain advantage for themselves. Similarly it was in the Conservatives' interest to deny this and say that the Liberals were only asserting it in order to conceal their own divisions.

The Liberation Society inaugurated a policy for the election at the end of 1884, but did so in quite a relaxed way. Electoral conferences were held in the Memorial Hall in London in January and March.[52] While it was important to have voluntaries chosen as Liberal candidates, it would not be essential to have a voluntary standing in every constituency, and support could be given to Liberal candidates who were not committed to disestablishment.[53] Efforts should be made to influence local Liberal associations in the choice of candidates, and to persuade these associations to try and get disestablishment included in the programme of the National Liberal Federation. As in 1880 voluntaries wished to work with the Liberal Party rather than independently of it, and forebore to insist on a pledge of support for disestablishment if this would encourage a Conservative victory. Alfred Illingworth suggested that a commitment only to Scottish and Welsh disestablishment should be asked of candidates.[54] The *Congregationalist* said that disestablishment should not be immediately urged at the cost of Liberal division: the issue should preferably be postponed to the Parliament after next.[55] The prominence of disestablishment in the election owed less to the Liberation Society than to Chamberlain's initial outspokenness and the fervour of Scottish voluntaries.

The progress of Liberal fragmentation is shown by the fact that in at least forty-two constituencies Liberals fought each other for the same seat, most of these constituencies being in Scotland. According to estimates by the Liberation Society, the *Record*, and the *Guardian*, an overwhelming number of Liberal candidates favoured disestablishment while all Conservative candidates opposed it.[56] But many Liberal candidates gave only conditional support, and there seems no doubt that 'only a small minority were hard-core Liberationists'.[57]

The political difficulties of the voluntary question are reflected by Chamberlain's tergiversations. He began in the summer with speeches and a published letter strongly advocating disestablishment. He then tried half-heartedly in mid-September to temper voluntary enthusiasm with practical restraint. But at a meeting of the radical National Liberal Federation on 1 October, which resolved for disestablishment, he reverted to a bold statement

---

[52] Mackintosh, *Disestablishment and Liberation*, 233.
[53] Hamer, *Electoral Pressure*, 154–5.
[54] Ibid. 155–6. Cf. Bebbington, op. cit. 22.
[55] *Congregationalist*, xiv (Sept. 1885), 694–5.
[56] A. Simon, 'Church Disestablishment as a Factor in the General Election of 1885', *HJ* xviii (1975), 794–5; Mackintosh, op. cit. 234; *AR* cxxvii (1885), 154–5; Bahlman, op. cit. 264–5.
[57] Simon, op. cit. 794.

that the new voters would be 'in favour of . . . freeing religion from the control and influence of the State'. He told Gladstone on 7 October, however, that he regarded disestablishment as 'lying in the remoter distance', and announced on 14 October that Liberals were not committed as a party to 'any attack upon the Established Church' and that no one believed there was any chance of a final settlement of the issue in the coming Parliament. Finally on 7 November, after repeating this statement, he spoiled its effect by saying that disestablishment and disendowment appealed not merely to Dissenters but 'to the whole nation and especially to the working classes in respect of their material interests'. By this he meant that surplus Church funds could be used for his cherished social improvements. After this, having done more than anyone else recently to stir up the issue and make life difficult for numerous Liberal candidates, he said no more about it in the remaining fortnight of the campaign.[58]

Liberal unity was certainly strained by the question. While radicals and Nonconformist leaders advocated disestablishment (finding sometimes an enthusiastic reception, and sometimes a cool one),[59] many Whig peers such as Grey, Halifax, Selborne, and Somerset declared themselves strongly against it.[60] Hartington, it was said, was 'anathematizing the Liberationists with more vigour than the Archbishop of Canterbury'.[61]

While Chamberlain, in the interests of party unity, veered from one statement to another, Gladstone with the same object picked out a delicate if complex *via media* which pointed to indefinite postponement of the issue.[62] Gladstone informed Chamberlain on 14 September that disestablishment, along with free education and the powers of the House of Lords, should not be placed in the immediate Liberal programme. Chamberlain was reluctantly prepared to follow him. He told Dilke that 'if we chose to go into direct opposition we might smash him but the game is not worth the candle'. [63]

Gladstone received support from many Liberals in his desire to shelve awkward questions. Granville told a Liberal meeting at Shrewsbury that English disestablishment could not be a practical question in the new Parliament, and at Bristol he said that 'not one of his colleagues of the late Cabinet considered it possible that that immense question could be practically

[58] Ibid. 797–9, 800–1, 804, 808; P. C. Griffiths, 'The Origins and Development of the National Liberal Federation to 1886', 183–4; Gladstone to Granville, 8 Oct. 1885; Morley, op. cit. iii. 225.

[59] e.g. Arch, *The Autobiography of Joseph Arch*, ed. J. G. O'Leary (London, 1966), 136; J. Guinness Rogers, *An Autobiography* (London, 1903) 214–15; F. A. Channing, *Memories of Midland Politics, 1885–1910* (London, 1918), 24. Cf. Ernest Parke, *What Shall I Do With My Vote?* (London, 1885).

[60] e.g. Henry, Third Earl Grey *et al.*, *The Agitation for Disestablishment* (n.p., 1885), 1–3. Cf. K. Robbins, *Sir Edward Grey* (London, 1971), 20; Gathorne Hardy's diary, 6 Nov. 1885 in Nancy E. Johnson (ed.), *The Diary of Gathorne Hardy, Later Lord Cranbrook* (Oxford, 1981), 479.

[61] *Pall Mall Gazette*, 19 Nov. 1885, p. 1.

[62] Simon, op. cit. 795–6; Gladstone to Bosworth Smith, 31 Oct. 1885; D. C. Lathbury, *Correspondence on Church and Religion of William Ewart Gladstone* (2 vols., London, 1910), i. 184–6.

[63] J. Chamberlain, *A Political Memoir, 1880–1892*, ed. C. H. D. Howard (London, 1953), 127; Chamberlain to Dilke, 20 Sept. 1885, copy; CP, JC5/24/428. Cf. Chamberlain to Gladstone, 20 Sept. 1885, copy; Dilke Papers, Add. MS 43887, fos. 175–6.

dealt with in the next Parliament'.[64] W. E. Forster, who was returned for Bradford Central, said that disestablishment could only happen when the majority of electors wanted it; and the Hon. Reginald Brett, standing at Plymouth, said he would favour disestablishment if it were a definite popular demand, but 'there were many strong Liberals who were convinced that the overthrow of the State Church would be a national disaster'.[65] Herbert Cozens-Hardy, a Free Methodist who was returned for North Norfolk, said he supported disestablishment but would only vote for it as a Government measure.[66] Lord Derby said at the Liverpool Reform Club that Liberal disagreements should not be exaggerated: 'the two great Constitutional questions of the future—the question of the Established Church and the question of a Second Chamber—it was agreed on all hands to postpone . . . They had plenty to do on which they were all heartily agreed.'[67] Malcolm MacColl told Rosebery that Liberals would damage their electoral interests by putting forward voluntary candidates: for his part, he was 'getting sick of the way in which the demos is being flattered and bribed with impracticable promises . . . It is like a rivalry of Sophists playing on the ignorance of the multitude'.[68] MacColl and his like would have been comforted by the words of the Liberal *Dundee Advertiser:* 'Disestablishment is being thrown out of the immediate programme of the Liberal party all round. It is not now a question of practical politics.'[69]

If Liberals wanted to put disestablishment out of politics, Conservatives wished to put it back again. Liberal unity demanded suppression of the issue, so Conservatives wanted to magnify the question in order to keep Liberals divided. 'Disestablishment means for the Liberal party complete disruption', said the Conservative *Standard.*[70] The zeal of Conservative politicians for Church defence mirrored that of a great many Churchmen—not all, however, as there were some outspoken 'radical parsons' and a Church Disestablishment League. The League's election manifesto wanted popular representation on Church bodies, the removal of Church government from Parliament, and the abolition of private patronage, and called on Churchmen to vote only for voluntary candidates.[71] Another manifesto, signed by 200 Anglican curates, gave twelve reasons for supporting disestablishment.[72] More typical was the popular activity of the Church Defence Institution, which saw its subscriptions

[64] *Glasgow Observer,* 7 Nov. 1885, p. 5.
[65] *AR* cxxvii (1885), 138, 142.
[66] C. Binfield, *So Down to Prayers: Studies in English Nonconformity, 1780–1920* (London, 1977), 136.
[67] *Dundee Advertiser,* 2 Nov. 1885.
[68] MacColl to Rosebery, 26 Oct. 1885; RP, 10084, fos. 60–7; also 8 Nov. 1885; ibid. 135–44.
[69] *Dundee Advertiser,* 5 Nov. 1885, p. 5.
[70] Quoted Simon, op. cit. 806.
[71] *Church Reformer,* 15 Oct. 1885 (iv. 10, 223).
[72] *Pall Mall Gazette,* 16 Nov. 1885, p. 3.

nearly treble to £12,886 in 1885 compared with the previous year, and employed thirty-three lecturers, sponsored 260 meetings, and issued 2,750,000 pamphlets in the election period of September to November.[73]

It was proposed that, as offshoots of the CDI, Churchmen's Leagues should be formed in every parish. But Archbishop Benson and other influential persons discouraged this on the grounds that, as the Institution was virtually a Tory body, the Church already looked partisan and it would be unwise to emphasize this further. The plan was abandoned.[74] But some local gatherings were held—for example, a conference of clergy and laity at Canterbury—at which disestablishment was condemned.[75] Bishop Magee, in a published speech to the Peterborough diocesan conference in October, said disendowment would harm the poor as the Church of England was 'the largest philanthropic institution in the country'.[76] Benson, when visiting Wales in October to lay the foundation stone of the Canterbury Buildings at St David's College, Lampeter, said the established Church in Wales must be defended.[77] John Wordsworth, newly appointed Bishop of Salisbury, said in a pastoral letter that disestablishment would 'involve an enormous loss to moral stability and the religious character of the whole Empire'.[78] Two Bishops urged Churchmen to demand that candidates for their constituencies should disavow support for disestablishment. Lord Arthur Hervey, Bishop of Bath and Wells, complained of 'an infidel, democratic and socialist upheaval against religion and against our Lord Christ', and other Bishops made similar statements.[79]

Demands for Church reform often accompanied Church defence. A memorial to the two Archbishops from some members of Cambridge University Senate in November urged the removal of 'evils' from Church administration. The memorial called especially for the admission of all classes of laymen to a substantial say in Church affairs.[80] The *Church Reformer* hedged about its own position on voluntaryism but was certain that 'vigorous sweeping democratic reforms' were needed in order to avert disestablishment.[81]

Added to these episcopal, organizational, and journalistic efforts (and, if reports are to be believed, exhortations in sermons), was the strong Church

[73] Roberts, 'Pressure-group Politics', 575. Cf. P. J. Waller, *Democracy and Sectarianism: A Political and Social History of Liverpool, 1868–1939* (Liverpool, 1981), 56.

[74] Roberts, 'The Role of the Laity in the Church of England, c.1850–1885', D.Phil. thesis (Oxford, 1974), 62–3.

[75] *Pall Mall Gazette*, 11 Nov. 1885, p. 10.

[76] W. C. Magee, *The Danger and the Evils of Disestablishment, and the Duty of Churchmen at the Present Crisis*, CDI (London, 1885).

[77] A. C. Benson, *The Life of Edward White Benson, Archbishop of Canterbury* (2 vols., London, 1899), ii. 407.

[78] *Pall Mall Gazette*, 14 Nov. 1885, p. 8.

[79] Simon, op. cit. 804–5.

[80] A. Westcott, *Life and Letters of Brooke Foss Westcott, Sometime Bishop of Durham* (2 vols., London, 1903), 1. 414–15.

[81] *Church Reformer*, 15 Sept. 1885; iv. 9, 193–4.

defence line taken by leading Conservative politicians. Salisbury was foremost
in proclaiming resistance to the disestablishment threat which, he insisted, was
imminent despite Liberal denials. He emphasized discrepancies between
statements of Gladstone and statements of Chamberlain, and the disunity of the
Liberal party as a whole. The Liberals were simply 'not a party', and Anglican
Liberals should put their Church before party considerations. His defensive
attack, launched in Newport, Monmouthshire, on 7 October, culminated in a
speech and an open letter on 21 November.[82] Through disendowment,
Salisbury said on 7 October, 'the Church would be stripped and bare. In every
part of the land the machinery by which God's Word has been upheld . . .
would be put an end to . . . It is a matter of life and death to us.'[83]

Many of Salisbury's colleagues, including Churchill, Cross, and Hicks
Beach, also stressed the danger to the establishment from supposed Liberal
policy.[84] They defended denominational schools against the threat to provide
free education in the board schools, and said the State should give more aid to
voluntary education.[85] Their attempts to alarm and win over moderate Liberals
were thought to be quite successful, to the extent that Conservatives perhaps
hoped to 'ride back into office on the Church question'.[86] Liberal leaders,
realizing that Conservatives had an important advantage over this issue, could
only deny any immediate commitment to disestablishment and assert that their
opponents were using the question as a political weapon.

The voluntary controversy was only 'academic' in England, said Gladstone at
the end of September, but was 'rising' in Wales and 'real' in Scotland.[87] The
Liberation Society held election conferences for North and South Wales in
October, and Henry Richard wanted Gladstone to announce that the question
was for the Welsh people to decide.[88] The recent enfranchisement greatly
increased voluntary political strength in Wales. The question was prominent in
candidates' addresses, and all but one of the thirty Liberal MPs returned from
Wales (out of a total of thirty-four) were for disestablishment.[89] But the issue
was still 'rising' in Wales, and reached full controversial strength a few years
later with the aid of nationalist feeling. In 1885 Gladstone had no difficulty in
finding reasons why the matter should not be brought to a head. The election

[82] Simon, op. cit. 802 ff.; *AR* cxxvii (1885), 181–3.
[83] *AR* cxxvii (1885), 169.
[84] Simon, op. cit. 805.
[85] *Pall Mall Gazette*, 31 Oct. 1885, p. 1; Gillian Sutherland, *Policy-making in Elementary Education, 1870–1895* (Oxford, 1973), 263.
[86] *Dundee Advertiser*, 9 Nov. 1885, p. 4. Cf. *Pall Mall Gazette*, 31 Oct. 1885, p. 1; Simon, op. cit. 807.
[87] Gladstone to Sir W. Farquhar, Bt., 27 Sept. 1885; Lathbury, op. cit. i. 183.
[88] LS, 19 and 26 Oct. 1885; A/LIB/7, 208, 210; Richard to Gladstone, 7 Aug. 1885; Henry Richard Papers 14022E, fo. 238.
[89] Kenneth O. Morgan, *Wales in British Politics, 1868–1922*, 2nd edn. (Cardiff, 1970), 65–6; addresses in, e.g. *T*, 23 Nov. 1885, p. 7, *Western Mail*, 20 and 23 Nov.; *Carnarvon and Denbigh Herald*, 31 Oct.; LS, 14 Dec. 1885; A/LIB/7, 217–18; J. W. Roberts, 'Sir George Osborne Morgan 1826–1897', MA thesis (Wales, 1979), 52–3, 95.

would probably declare Welsh opinion on the subject; for him to say anything before opinion had clearly emerged would be 'premature', and would 'tend seriously to disorganize the action of the Liberal party in the country generally'.[90]

The issue was more pressing in Scotland, and that country tended to become the main hub of the matter for the whole of Great Britain. Salisbury said in July that it was 'in Scotland that the battle of the State Church will be fought'.[91] Pleas for Scottish Presbyterian union, such as were made in 1885 by the Earl of Aberdeen and Sir Charles Tennant (Liberal candidate for Peebles and Selkirk) were lost amid the conflicts of voluntaryism and Church defence.[92] Resolutions were carried such as those in the Aberdeen and Dundee United Presbyterian presbyteries urging all voluntaries to vote only for candidates who would promise to support disestablishment and disendowment.[93] Working-class voters were urged to support disendowment so that surplus Church funds could be used to give their children free education.[94] Some of Chamberlain's expressions, particularly in a published letter to Taylor Innes (a leading Free Churchman) on 28 September, whipped up the enthusiasm of Scots disestablishers.[95] A manifesto for disestablishment from 1475 Scottish ministers was presented to Gladstone (341 Free Church ministers and sixty-four United Presbyterians, however, did not sign);[96] and about seventy Parliamentary candidates in Scotland were said to have openly declared themselves for religious equality.[97]

Church defence efforts, whether by 'Church Liberals' or Conservatives, were equally to the fore. An English Congregational student at Glasgow University, Charles Silvester Horne (later a prominent minister and an MP), wrote home: 'It is, I suppose, quite impossible to go to an Established Church now without hearing the sermon devoted to Disestablishment'.[98] The General Assembly of the Church of Scotland in May 1885 recommended that 'Church interests' committees should be established in all presbyteries of the Church.[99] The great majority of presbyteries formed these committees, which were expected to aid

[90] Gladstone's views given by Lord Richard Grosvenor to Henry Richard, 11 Aug. 1885; quoted Morgan, op. cit. 63.
[91] *T*, 4 July 1885; quoted Simon, op. cit. 795.
[92] Earl of Aberdeen, 'Union of Presbyterian Churches', *FR*, May 1885 (xxxvii. 717-24); speech of Tennant, *Scotsman*, 28 Oct. 1885, p. 8.
[93] Dundee Minutes, 6 Oct; CH3/19/9, 166; Aberdeen Minutes, 13 and 26-7 Oct.; CH3/2/15, 201-2, 209-10.
[94] Anon., *Disestablishment and Free Education: An Address to the Working men of Scotland, by a Layman* (Glasgow, 1885), 7-8.
[95] Simon, op. cit. 799-800.
[96] Simpson, *Rainy*, i. 30; Drummond and Bulloch, *The Church in Late Victorian Scotland*, 119.
[97] *Congregationalist* (Oct. 1885), xiv. 778-9.
[98] Horne to his mother, 16 Nov. 1885; W. B. Selbie, *The Life of Charles Silvester Horne, MA, MP* (London, 1920), 12-13.
[99] J. F. McCaffrey, 'Political Reactions in the Glasgow Constituencies at the General Elections of 1885 and 1886', Ph.D. thesis (Glasgow, 1970), 65.

parish associations.[1] Many Church defence meetings were held—one in Perthshire was chaired by an Episcopalian, 'a minister of a disestablished Church'.[2] At Dundee a Church Establishment Association was formed with the special object of obtaining the return of pro-establishment MPs for the city, 'irrespective of party'.[3] This association co-operated with the Church interests committee of the local presbytery in defending the establishment, for example by advising ministers to hold congregational meetings on the subject. Liberal candidates should only be opposed if they were definitely pro-disestablishment or if they prevaricated on the question. The most favoured candidates were those such as Edward Jenkins at Dundee (now a Conservative) who 'had pledged himself to vote against any Motion for Disestablishment'.[4]

Church defence arguments also appeared in periodical and newspaper articles by Lord Balfour of Burleigh and others; and in the speeches and published addresses of many candidates, not all of whom were Conservative.[5] Balfour of Burleigh shared a platform with the Duke of Argyll at a large anti-voluntary meeting at Glasgow on 20 October.[6] Stafford Northcote (now Earl of Iddesleigh), told an audience at West Calder, Midlothian: 'if you want to defend your Established Church, now is the time to stand up for it'.[7] On 5 November the Free Church minority held a conference at Inverness which declared strong opposition 'to the disestablishment movement at present conducted, as subversive of the principles of the Reformed Church of Scotland'.[8] Church defenders, like voluntaries, wooed working-class voters: a pamphlet entitled *Disestablishment: What Will It Put in My Pocket?* reminded them that the establishment existed to provide religious services for all, not only for those who could afford to pay voluntary contributions.[9]

Scottish Liberals were seriously split by the Church question. In July, 173 prominent Liberals formed a committee in Edinburgh with the object of preventing the selection of disestablishment candidates.[10] The Liberal press was divided, and on 15 September a new political organization, the National Liberal Federation of Scotland, was founded by radicals who were discontented with the Whig-dominated Scottish Liberal Association. The new body gave

[1] D. C. Savage, 'Scottish Politics, 1885–1886', *SHR* xl (1961), 122; *Dundee Advertiser*, 5 Nov. 1885, p. 3.
[2] e.g. Aberdeen C. of S. Presbytery Minutes, 7 July 1885; CH2/1/23, 306; *CR* xlviii. 251.
[3] Lamb Collection, Dundee Local History Library, 176 (15).
[4] Dundee C. of S. Presbytery Minutes, 4 Nov. 1885; CH2/103/23, 307–16; *Dundee Advertiser*, 21 Oct. 1885.
[5] Lord Balfour of Burleigh, 'Church and State in Scotland', *FR* xxxviii (Aug. 1885), 277–85; D. Fraser, 'The Church Problem in Scotland', *CR* xlviii (Aug. 1885), 249–55; address 'to the people of Scotland' issued by Committee of the General Assembly on Church Interests (Edinburgh, 1885); *Dundee Courier and Argus*, 15 Oct. 1885; *Scotsman*, 20–4 Oct. 1885; McCaffrey, op. cit. 113–15.
[6] *Scotsman*, 21 Oct., p. 6.
[7] Ibid. 6 Nov., p. 5.
[8] *Dundee Advertiser*, 6 Nov. 1885.
[9] Anon. (Glasgow, 1885).   [10] Drummond and Bulloch, op. cit. 118.

overwhelming support to disestablishment.[11] Voluntaries sought to take over the Scottish Liberal Association as well. A great many of them attended the Association's meeting at Perth on 16 October. A resolution of Lord Aberdeen advocating postponement of the Church question was overturned, and disestablishment was supported by the huge majority of about 400 votes to seven. This caused Lord Fife to resign as president of the Association.[12] A Liberal peer presided at the Church defence meeting in St Andrew's Hall, Glasgow, on 20 October, and many other Liberals attended.[13]

The divisive Church issue, together with land and labour questions, made the Scots elections particularly confused. At one time no fewer than six Liberal candidates sought election in the Glasgow Bridgeton constituency, and in the College and Central constituencies of Glasgow Church Liberals unsuccessfully resisted the selection of voluntary candidates.[14] Voluntaries, for their part, unsuccessfully opposed the return of Peter McLagan (Liberal MP for West Lothian) because he would not immediately give his support to disestablishment.[15] The Hon. Arthur Elliot, Liberal MP for Roxburghshire, was criticized by voluntaries among his constituents for announcing that, while supporting religious equality, he would not vote on disestablishment during the next Parliament.[16] Elliot was doing his best, amid difficulties, to keep his seat. He was asked by the local Church of Scotland presbytery to state his position on establishment, and temporarily satisfied that body by saying: 'as Disestablishment has not been put before the country by the Liberal leaders, I think the next Parliament ought not to give legislative effect to that policy, and I shall, therefore, if I am returned to the next House of Commons, not support a Disestablishment Bill'.[17] This caused further complaints from voluntaries, and another statement by Elliot brought complaints from Churchmen.[18] But Elliot had only a Conservative opponent at the polls, and was comfortably returned. A voluntary newspaper, the *North British Daily Mail*, claimed that forty-nine Scottish Liberal candidates supported disestablishment, thirty said they would follow the lead of a Liberal Government on the subject, and nine were definitely against disestablishment. The number 'against', however, was probably considerably greater than claimed.[19]

---

[11] Kellas, 'The Liberal Party in Scotland, 1876–1895', *SHR* xliv (1965), 6–7.

[12] Ibid. 8; G. W. T. Omond to Rosebery, 22 Oct. 1885; RP, 10084, fos. 50–3; Kellas, 'The Liberal Party and the Scottish Church', 36; Savage, op. cit. 118–29; McCaffrey, op. cit. 68–79.

[13] Kellas, op. cit. 35; Catriona Levy, 'Conservatism and Liberal Unionism in Glasgow, 1874–1912', Ph.D. thesis (Dundee, 1983), 111–12.

[14] McCaffrey, op. cit. 55, 99–106.

[15] James Steel to Rosebery, 31 July 1885; RP, 10083, fos. 184–5; P. McLagan to Rosebery, 13 Aug.; ibid. fos. 209–10.

[16] Revd J. W. Pringle to Elliot, 3 Aug. and 7 Sept. 1885; Arthur Elliot Papers.

[17] Revd John Fergusson to Elliot, 8 and 15 Oct.; ibid.

[18] William Hilson to Elliot, 20 Oct.; David Cairns to Elliot, 23 Oct.; Revd Robert Fordyce to Elliot, 3 Nov.; Revd John Fergusson to Elliot, 9 Nov.; ibid.; *Scotsman*, 24 Oct., 11–12.

[19] Kellas, op. cit. 36–7.

In at least twenty-seven Scottish constituencies Liberal candidates fought each other.[20] But these contests were over a variety of issues. Of six 'Crofter' candidates sponsored or supported by the Highland Land League, five were returned. In thirteen contests the split between Liberals was over disestablishment. In Kilmarnock Burghs J. Dick Peddie, the Voluntary MP, was opposed by Viscount Dalrymple; neither succeeded and the Conservative squeezed in. In Inverness Burghs R. B. Finlay defeated a radical, W. S. Bright McLaren, nephew of John Bright. In St Andrews Burghs a Church Liberal challenge by Sir Robert Anstruther to the voluntary member (Stephen Williamson) resulted in a tie vote of 1256 each and Anstruther being awarded the seat.[21]

Not the least important feature of the Scottish Church question was Gladstone's role as MP for a Scots constituency. His public pronouncements on the issue were eagerly awaited for their bearing on the question south of the border as well as in Scotland, and especially for their effect on Liberal unity. Gladstone told the Revd Dr G. C. Hutton (a leading United Presbyterian) on 28 July that he held to Lord Hartington's Scottish declaration in 1877.[22] The decision must emerge in time from the matured sentiments of the Scottish people, and (as in 1880) it should not be forced on in the coming election. 'It is a Scottish question and ought to be decided by the people of Scotland', he said in a letter in the *Daily News* on 11 September. It should not be thought essential to hold an election on the question.[23] Gladstone's references to disestablishment in his manifesto in mid-September enlarged this approach, and have been described as 'almost a copy-book exercise in the art of facing both ways'.[24] While the subject had been 'more fully probed and unfolded in Scotland than elsewhere', it was 'obvious that so vast a question cannot become practical until it shall have grown familiar to the public mind by thorough discussion'.[25] From this it appeared, *The Times* said, that he did not think disestablishment would come soon, and was 'glad that he will not have to take a side'; his statement was 'more than usually oracular'.[26] But the statement was also politically astute, being intended above all to maintain Liberal unity. Clearly, in the leader's view, the election should not be fought on disestablishment.

This opinion was contrary to the Scottish radical wish to make disestablishment a test for candidates in the election, but Gladstone maintained his declared views and prominent Liberals agreed with him. Leading ministers tried to pull him from both sides. Robert Rainy urged him in a letter of 27 October to declare

[20] Cf. Savage, op. cit. 118.

[21] Kellas, op. cit. 36; William Robson to Rosebery, 25 Aug. 1885 and enclosure; RP, 10083, fos. 228–30; William Burns to Rosebery, 24 Aug., ibid., 222–5; *Scotsman*, 26 Oct., p. 4; *Dundee Advertiser*, 2 Nov., pp. 5, 7, 5 Nov., p. 3.

[22] Lathbury, *Correspondence*, i. 182.

[23] Simon, op. cit. 796.

[24] Ibid.

[25] Ibid.

[26] *T*, 19 Sept. 1885, p. 9 (quoted Simon, op. cit. 796–7).

for disestablishment, but Gladstone replied that he must leave it to the Scottish people.[27] Tulloch and other Church of Scotland ministers set out to canvass every elector in Gladstone's Midlothian constituency, and after a few days had results from nearly all the parishes. Out of 9,341 electors, 5,992 (or 64 per cent) opposed disestablishment. Next day, 10 November, the results were handed to Gladstone, who was staying at Lord Rosebery's home at Dalmeny on the eve of another Midlothian campaign.[28]

The effect can only have strengthened Gladstone's intention to dampen the controversy. On 11 November he announced, in a seventy-minute speech to a restless and disapproving audience in the Free Church Assembly Hall in Edinburgh, that disestablishment could not be made a test question in the election. It was not such a question in England, though the Tories dearly wanted to make it so in order to embarrass the Liberals. Equally it could not be such a question in Scotland: the effects would spread to England and would have serious consequences for British Liberalism.[29] He firmly relegated the matter to 'the end of a long vista'.[30]

Gladstone's treatment of the issue in Scotland dampened it even more decisively in England. All that the Conservative leaders could now say was that, on the basis of Gladstone's fairly rapid conversion to Irish disestablishment twenty years before, his 'long vistas' could turn out to be quite short.[31] But Gladstone, though accused of reneging, had not repudiated his previous declaration that the question should be dealt with when Scottish opinion had ripened. He had merely stressed the current need to suppress the issue for the sake of Liberal unity. He did not exclude continued consideration of the question and possible Liberal adoption of disestablishment in the future.

Scottish Voluntaries, however, expostulated at Gladstone's words. Gladstone might harp on the need for Liberal unity, but Sir John Kinloch had said at Dundee a few days previously that this unity 'could be purchased at too great a price' if it meant giving up disestablishment.[32] The Whig *Scotsman* praised Gladstone's stand, as did the *Dundee Advertiser*, a radical paper which gave priority to Liberal unity;[33] and Malcolm MacColl told Rosebery that the Edinburgh speech was 'worth at least thirty seats to the Liberals'.[34] But complaints came from the Scottish Disestablishment Association, the National

[27] Simpson, op. cit. ii. 30–5.
[28] Drummond and Bulloch, op. cit. 120–1; Kellas, op. cit. 37.
[29] Gladstone to Rosebery, 5 Nov. 1885; RP, 10023, fos. 108–9; Gladstone to Chamberlain, 6 Nov., J. Chamberlain, *Political Memoir*, 134; Chamberlain to Gladstone, 7 Nov.; GP, 44126, fos. 121–2; Simon, op. cit. 810.
[30] Kellas, op. cit. 37; Simpson, op. cit. ii. 36–9; *AR* cxxvii (1885), 175–7; Simon, op. cit. 812.
[31] Speech of Churchill, 13 Nov.; L. J. Jennings (ed.), *Speeches of the Rt. Hon. Lord Randolph Churchill, MP, 1880–1888* (2 vols., London, 1889), i. 338–9.
[32] Extract dated 2 Nov. 1885, in Lamb Collection, 176 (11).
[33] *Scotsman*, 12 Nov., p. 4; *Dundee Advertiser*, 12 Nov., p. 5.
[34] MacColl to Rosebery, 12 Nov.; RP, 10084, fo. 161.

Liberal Federation of Scotland, and the Liberation Society committee.[35] A large meeting at Kilmarnock on 16 November, addressed by Rainy and Hutton, unanimously expressed regret at Gladstone's attitude; and two days later the Free Church Commission of Assembly affirmed its commitment to disestablishment, on Rainy's motion, by seventy-two votes to eighteen.[36]

Conservatives realized that Gladstone was trying to block one of their lines of attack, but in turn accused him of blatant expediency. He was treating disestablishment, said Churchill, 'not from the standpoint of a great and experienced statesman, but from the debased and degraded level of a common election agent'.[37]

Gladstone repeated his call to neutrality in further important speeches in Midlothian, and there was a growing air of resignation among voluntaries. A conference of delegates from Scottish Liberal associations on 17 November reluctantly agreed to support Gladstone by trying to soften Liberal divisions in the constituency.[38] None the less, these divisions remained a prominent feature in the election.

Gladstone had said on 11 November that Liberals needed unity in order to obtain an independent majority so they could deal with the Irish question. Ireland, he said, should be given a generous degree of self-government provided imperial unity was maintained. Probably Gladstone had decided privately that Home Rule was desirable; and he realized that, preferable though it might be for the Conservatives to deal with the matter, the Liberals would have to settle it if they gained the majority they wanted. But Gladstone's public hints on the subject fell far short of Parnell's demand that the Liberals should go to the polls with a Home Rule policy.[39] Ten days after Gladstone's Edinburgh speech Parnell gave his fateful advice to Irish Home Rulers in Great Britain to vote against the Liberals.

It had been clear, in fact, that Home Rule would be at least as important as disestablishment in the election, for the Reform Acts of 1884 and 1885 strengthened Parnell's party even more obviously than they strengthened the voluntaries. In order to give force to Parnell's policy of gaining Home Rule by playing off one major party against the other, it was important both to return a stronger body of nationalist MPs from Ireland and to marshal Irish voters in Britain to the best effect. The Irish National League of Great Britain was well organized for this purpose, having numerous branches in areas of comparatively high immigrant population. The League branches had ward committees which

---

[35] Simpson, ii. 39–42; *AR* cxxvii (1885), 177; LS, 16 Nov.; A/LIB/7, 214–15; *Dundee Advertiser*, 13 Nov., pp. 4–5, 18 Nov., p. 3; Revd J. W. Pringle to Hon. A. Elliot, 21 Nov. (Elliot Papers).
[36] *Dundee Advertiser*, 17 Nov. p. 7, 19 Nov. p. 3.
[37] L. J. Jennings, op. cit. 338–9. Cf. Salisbury to T. G. Murray, 19 Nov.; GP, 44116, fos. 182–3; Simon, op. cit. 812–14.
[38] *Pall Mall Gazette* 14 Nov., p. 7, 18 Nov., p. 1.
[39] *AR* cxxvii (1885), 178.

canvassed Irish electors and sought (apparently with success in most cases) to persuade them to vote as the League wished.[40]

At the end of October a letter in the *North British Daily Mail* alleged that Irish Catholics in the College division of Glasgow had already been told to vote for the Conservative candidate, and had unanimously agreed to do so.[41] At the annual convention of the Irish National League, held at Glasgow on 31 October with over 200 branches represented, John Redmond (a Home Rule MP) said the Irish in Britain should keep their voting decisions secret until the last minute, and then 'vote as one man'. They should 'use the Whig party when the Whig party served their turn, and use the Tory party when the Tory party served their turn'. The meeting resolved by acclamation that League members should not promise support to candidates but should 'wait the advice of the Executive of the National League . . . [and] stand by that advice when given'.[42] Many Irish Catholic electoral meetings were held in British towns, and in mid-November Parnell encouraged the campaign in Liverpool.[43] At a large meeting of the Irish inhabitants of Dundee on 19 November, chaired by a dean with seven priests and many leading Catholic laymen on the platform, appeals were made 'to await instructions from the Irish parliamentary party as to the . . . candidates they should vote for on election day. Instructions are expected daily.'[44]

John Redmond was responsible for seeing that branches in Scotland observed the League's policy; John Barry was responsible for London and T. P. O'Connor for Lancashire.[45] The League executive issued an order on 14 November detailing the methods of distribution for the manifesto which was to appear the following week.[46] The manifesto, to be signed by Parnell and T. P. O'Connor (president of the League), would be sent 'to each branch of the League where a branch exists, and to some leading and well-known Irish electors where no branch exists'. These branches or individuals should have the advice drawn up in a circular, to be delivered by post or by hand to local Irish electors (of whom every branch should have a list), and bills might also be distributed at church doors. Irish electors should pay no attention to British parties' efforts to mislead them. Each branch should keep its room open throughout the polling day in order to assist voters, and any Irish elector in doubt on any point should 'seek information from the branch, and from that alone'. Special care should be taken to observe the Corrupt Practices Act of 1883, and nothing in the way of bribery should be offered to electors.[47]

---

[40] *Glasgow Observer*, 21 Nov. 1885, p. 3.
[41] McCaffrey, op. cit. 165.
[42] *Glasgow Observer*, 7 Nov., p. 6.
[43] L. W. Brady, *T. P. O'Connor and the Liverpool Irish* (London, 1983), 79 ff.
[44] *Dundee Advertiser*, 18 Nov., p. 7.
[45] C. H. D. Howard, 'The Parnell Manifesto of 21 November 1885, and the Schools Question', *EHR* lxii (1947), 41; Brady, op. cit. 78.
[46] Wollaston, 'Irish Nationalist Movement', 91.   [47] *Glasgow Observer*, 21 Nov., p. 6.

The manifesto 'to our countrymen in England and Scotland', drafted by O'Connor on Parnell's authority and signed by seven leading Home Rulers, was issued on 21 November. It was a fierce attack on 'the Liberal or Radical party' for having, in its last Government, 'betrayed' Ireland. Electors who had been urged in 1880 to oppose Disraeli as they would oppose 'the mortal enemy of their country and their race', were now warned against supporting a party 'so perfidious, treacherous, and incompetent' as the Liberals. A few sterling exceptions, however, would be made of Liberal candidates who had consistently opposed coercion. Parnell named these in a speech at Liverpool on 23 November as Joseph Cowen (Newcastle upon Tyne), Samuel Storey (Sunderland), Thomas Thompson (Durham City), and Henry Labouchere (Northampton), and a notice from the National League added Lloyd Jones (Chester-le-Street). But 'in every other instance', continued the manifesto of 21 November, 'we earnestly advise our countryman to vote against any men who coerced Ireland, deluged Egypt with blood, menaced religious liberty in the school, freedom of speech in Parliament, and promise to the country generally a repetition of the crimes and follies of the last Liberal Administration'.[48]

This advice could have considerable electoral effect. It was true that Irish voters in Britain were estimated at only 150,000, and in only one constituency (the Scotland division of Liverpool) was a Home Ruler, T. P. O'Connor, returned. But the splitting of boroughs into single-member divisions by the Redistribution Act gave increased power to the Irish vote, and 'the Irish were strong in precisely those areas, such as London and industrial Lancashire, where the parties were most evenly balanced and where the outcome of a general election was most likely to be decided'.[49] In such areas the Conservatives were undoubtedly helped. Parnell told large gatherings at Liverpool that Irish Catholics should normally vote Conservative in the election.[50] This was in spite of the Conservative party having given no pledge to Home Rule. Those Conservative candidates who mentioned the Irish question merely promised to oppose coercion and support some extension of local self-government. Home Rule leaders realized that, if the boroughs alone were considered, their electoral recommendations might give the Conservatives so large a majority that they could ignore Irish nationalism. However, when it was remembered that the newly enfranchised county electors were likely to vote Liberal, the policy of the manifesto was allowed to stand.[51]

The Parnellite appeal to Irish electors is sufficient to explain the willingness of many of them to vote Conservative. But this tendency was reinforced by Catholic fears that the demand for free education, revived in the *Radical*

---

[48] *T*, 23 and 24 Nov.; J. Denvir, *The Irish in Britain From the Earliest Times to the Fall and Death of Parnell* (London, 1892), 317; T. P. O'Connor, *Memoirs of an Old Parliamentarian* (2 vols., London, 1929), ii. 7–9.

[49] Howard, op. cit. 42–3.

[50] Burke, *Catholic History of Liverpool*, 246.

[51] Denvir, op. cit. 320.

Programme, would threaten denominational education. It was claimed that, if Chamberlain and his followers had their way, the State would provide free education only in board schools, and voluntary schools could not afford to provide it themselves. Subscribers to voluntary education, who already contributed to rate aid for board schools, might have to pay more tax in order to finance free education in these schools—and would help to present the already dangerously expanding rival system with a large additional attraction.[52] Defence of Catholic voluntary schools meant at least as much to the clergy as Home Rule, and large numbers of laity supported the clergy wholeheartedly over education. Herbert Vaughan, Bishop of Salford, issued a circular to his clergy in October saying that elementary education was 'a question of life and death to the souls of millions'.[53] Manning, who privately opposed Home Rule at this time, gave advice to electors in an article printed in Catholic newspapers and republished as a pamphlet. 'The saving of the Christian education of the people', he said, was a most vital necessity. All who believed this should ask candidates two questions: would they do their utmost 'to place Voluntary schools on an equal footing with Board schools', and strive 'to obtain a Royal Commission to review the present state of education in England and Wales'?[54] 'Insist upon a clear answer to each of these questions', Bishop O'Reilly of Liverpool urged his flock. 'If the answer be favourable, give [the candidate] . . . your vote and all the support you can command . . . the calls of conscience are above those of party'.[55] A Father Cavalli told a Catholic meeting at Cardiff on 18 November that, in view of 'the desire of the Radicals to destroy Voluntary Schools and religious education', he had to 'advise all good Catholics to record a solid vote for the Conservative candidate'.[56]

A printed circular was also issued on 31 October, signed by Manning and the fourteen Catholic Bishops in England and Wales, protesting against existing and potential injustice to voluntary schools and saying they could only place confidence in a candidate who would promise 'to do his utmost to protect liberty of conscience and to redress the present glaring inequalities by providing for the just maintenance and multiplication of Christian and voluntary schools as the growth of the people shall require'.[57] The editor of the *Tablet* sent Manning's two questions on education to all candidates for London constituencies: all except three of the Conservative candidates gave satisfactory answers, but only about two-fifths of the Liberals. A similar result followed in other towns.[58] Conservatives also seemed to have gratifying intentions when Sir Richard Cross

[52] Cf. *Glasgow Observer*, 29 Aug. 1885, pp. 4, 6.
[53] J. G. Snead-Cox, *The Life of Cardinal Vaughan* (2 vols., London, 1910), ii. 100.
[54] H. E. Manning, *How Shall Catholics Vote at the Coming Parliamentary Election?* (London, 1885), 13–14; Howard, op. cit. 45.
[55] Burke, op. cit. 242–3.
[56] *Western Mail*, 20 Nov. 1885.
[57] Manning Papers; Snead-Cox, op. cit. ii. 101.
[58] Howard, op. cit. 45. Cf. Lord Henry Lennox to Manning, 15 Nov. 1885; Manning Papers.

announced at Widnes, Lancashire, on 11 November that the Government had decided to appoint a Royal Commission on education, which would enquire into the position of the voluntary schools. The commission was appointed the following January, and supporters of denominational education were in the majority. The difficult subject was considered for two years but diverse conclusions were reached and further controversy resulted.[59]

The advice of Catholic Bishops and nationalist politicians was that Catholic electors should generally vote Conservative. Thus the education and Home Rule causes managed to coincide in their electoral interests. In Glasgow a Catholic Electoral Association was founded by Archbishop Eyre. The new body co-operated with the National League in the city, the Association being responsible for defending denominational education in school board elections and the League for municipal and Parliamentary elections.[60] Catholic priests and bishops 'would rather have the Tory party attempt the solution of the Home Rule problem, owing to the fact of the Conservatives being in favour of Denominational Education', noted Michael Davitt in a letter of early October which was significantly intimated to Herbert Gladstone.[61] Many Catholics were willing to vote Conservative despite the support of some Conservatives for the compulsory inspection of convents and monasteries.[62]

Parnell's electoral strategy met some Home Rule opposition, however, not least because of his insistence (owing to the circumstances of his private life) that the Liberal Captain O'Shea should be supported as a candidate for Liverpool Exchange. O'Shea was only fifty-six votes short of winning. In some constituencies Irish voters refused to oppose the Liberal.[63] But circumstances differed between constituencies. Sir Robert Cunliffe, defeated as a Liberal in the Denbigh Boroughs, said the Irish Catholic voters 'went quite solid against me', thanks to strong efforts by their priest. Similarly D. Crawford, a Liberal who succeeded in North-East Lanarkshire, said the Catholic electors 'went solid against me, except a mere sprinkling . . . who I gained over in spite of their priests'.[64] In a Glasgow division Catholic electors vocally resented being expected to support a Conservative who was 'not only a prominent anti-Catholic but also a Grand Master of the Orange Lodge in Scotland'; but their request for an exception was refused and the candidate in question was praised in the Catholic press.[65] Ironically, Conservatives in these elections were looking for both Catholic and ultra-Protestant support.

[59] Snead-Cox, op. cit. ii. 102.

[60] Wollaston, op. cit. 19–20. Cf. Glasgow Observer, 29 Aug. 1885, p. 6.

[61] Davitt to Labouchere, 9 Oct. 1885, copy; Herbert Gladstone Papers, Add. MS 46015, fo. 38.

[62] McCaffrey, 'Political Reactions', 111; P. J. Waller, Democracy and Sectarianism: A Political and Social History of Liverpool, 1868–1939 (Liverpool, 1981), 55.

[63] Howard, op. cit. 48–50; Denvir, op. cit. 318–19; O'Connor, op. cit. ii. 10; Labouchere to Rosebery, 25 Nov. 1885; RP, 10041, fos. 18–19.

[64] Cunliffe to A. Elliot, 12 Dec.; Arthur Elliot Papers; Cunliffe to Rosebery, 29 Nov.; RP, 10084, fos. 211–12; Crawford to Rosebery, 2 Dec.; ibid. fos. 219–20.

[65] McCaffrey, op. cit. 167–8; I. Wood, 'Irish Immigrants and Scottish Radicalism, 1880–1906', in I. MacDougall (ed.), Essays in Scottish Labour History (Edinburgh, 1978), 72; A. O'Day, The English Face of Irish Nationalism, 1880–1886 (Dublin, 1977), 110–11.

The election results fell short of Parnell's highest hopes. None the less they gave him a position of unprecedented strength. The Liberals lost much ground in the boroughs but gained in the new county divisions where 'enfranchised Hodge', captured by Chamberlain's agrarian schemes and voluntary propaganda, voted heavily in their favour.[66] The Liberals obtained 335 seats, the Conservatives 249, and the Home Rulers exactly held the balance with eighty-six. This meant that if Parnell managed to marshal all his Parliamentary strength he could just about prevent a Liberal ministry from governing. Liberal losses in the towns occurred for various reasons, including the swing of middle-class voters to Conservatism which the new urban divisions made more effective; the call for 'fair trade' to relieve commercial depression; dislike of the Government's Egyptian policy or the treatment of General Gordon; the efforts of Church defenders against voluntary candidates; and Parnell's advice to the Irish voters which (both Chamberlain and T. P. O'Connor estimated) gave at least twenty-five seats to the Tories.[67] But the Irish vote was small overall, and rarely had much effect. In spite of the aid presumably given to Conservatives by many Irish voters in Glasgow, all seven seats in that city went to the Liberals.[68] In Birmingham also the Liberals won all seven seats, and in Edinburgh all four. In Liverpool, on the other hand, eight of the nine seats were won by Conservatives; and in Manchester Conservatives won five of the six seats. There may have been a certain amount of unaccustomed Liberal voting by electors largely motivated by anti-Catholicism in reaction to Parnell's strategy. But such voters probably still felt that their interests lay more clearly with Conservatism, and the Conservative victories in large towns perhaps owed more to Protestant fervour than Catholic.

Voluntaryism received a numerical boost in the Commons from the election results. The Dissenting Deputies and the Liberation Society executive estimated that more MPs than ever before were now pledged to disestablishment; 171 Liberal MPs, the Society claimed, favoured disestablishment throughout Britain, others advocated it for Scotland or Wales or both, and only twenty-nine Liberals were against it.[69] Several voluntaries, including Dick Peddie, had lost their seats, but others such as Carvell Williams and Joseph Arch were returned for the first time. So even if the results were disappointing for the Liberals they were more than enough to keep the voluntary flag waving. The results also encouraged Bradlaugh's aim to take his seat, following his return again for Northampton.[70]

Radical politicians differed, however, about the expediency of keeping voluntaryism to the fore. Chamberlain was already looking to the time when he

---

[66] Garvin and Amery, *Chamberlain*, ii. 124–5.
[67] *Christian World*, 26 Nov. 1885, p. 895; *Pall Mall Gazette*, 19 and 27 Nov. 1885; memo in BP, 49688, fos. 94–5.
[68] McCaffrey, op. cit. 176–7.
[69] Manning, *Dissenting Deputies*, 399; Mackintosh, *Disestablishment and Liberation*, 234.
[70] Arnstein, *Bradlaugh Case*, 299–306.

could 'go for the Church'. He said at Leicester on 3 December that disestablishment would very likely be prominent in a future election. But Dilke and Morley disliked this emphasis, and Dilke noted in his diary early in December: 'J. Morley and I and Lefevre sat on Chamberlain about the Church and made him drop it'.[71] This suggests that not even Chamberlain was convinced that disestablishment was politically attractive or unifying enough to remain a prominent part of the radical programme.

It was arguable, indeed—at least as regards the boroughs but not the county seats—that the countervailing efforts of Church defence had lost support for the Liberals in England. The *Record* somewhat hyperbolically claimed success for 'the charges of more than a score of Bishops, the sermons in thousands of pulpits, the Church Defence meetings, the lectures, the tract distribution and all the other efforts of tens of thousands of English laymen rallying to the support of their Church'.[72] But the Church must continue fervently to defend and reform itself against renewed attack.[73] The *Church Reformer* urged the complete abolition of patronage.[74] The *Record* believed particularly that Convocation, a 'sleepy creature of a bygone age', must be 'metamorphosed into an organization that can breathe . . . the sharp keen air of the nineteenth century, the chief component element in which is the due representation of the whole Church, clergy and laity'.[75] This desire was only partially realized when the first House of Laymen in the Canterbury Convocation met in February 1886 (followed by one at York in 1892), for this was not widely representative and was not consulted about matters of faith and doctrine.

In Scotland and Wales disestablishment was likely to remain a powerful political force. In England its future was much less certain: the numerical weakening of Nonconformity relative to the population began to reduce the strength of the cause, and questions of social reform were coming to distract attention from disestablishment. Certainly the established status of the Church in England was never again a prominent feature in a general election. Moreover, the intervention of Home Rule as the immediate political issue postponed voluntaryism as a practical proposition in all three countries. It is likely that the contrasting fates of voluntaryism in England and Wales would have been the same without this intervention, but it is far less easy to say this about Scotland.

The vital position now occupied by Parnell's party in British politics forced both parties to decide their position on Home Rule. Gladstone had not obtained the separate majority he wanted in order to 'meet in an independent and imperial spirit any demands which Mr. Parnell might make'.[76] In order to obtain a clear majority he would have to translate his private inclination into

[71] Simon, op. cit. 815–16.
[72] Quoted ibid. 816. Cf. *Record*, 27 Nov. 1885, p. 1201.
[73] Benson, *E. W. Benson*, ii. 62, 64.
[74] *Church Reformer*, 15 Dec. 1885; iv. 12, p. 266.
[75] *Record*, 4 Dec., p. 1226.
[76] *Dundee Advertiser*, 1 Dec. 1885, p. 4.

overt policy, and try and get his party to accept Home Rule. If the Conservatives tried to stay in office they would, as Carnarvon told Salisbury, have to 'govern by and through the Irish . . . unless we are ready to come to some understanding with them they will play us off against the Liberals and reduce us to the sorest difficulties'.[77] But Carnarvon's suggestion that Home Rule be considered was rejected by the Cabinet on 15 December.[78] Gladstone, understandably in view of his own formidable party problems over Home Rule, told his son Herbert on 10 December that the question should be settled by the 'allied' forces of Tories and Home Rulers.[79] But Herbert, a keen Home Ruler himself, had other ideas. Hoping to strengthen his father's political hand and jolt the Liberals into unity behind him, he indiscreetly informed Wemyss Reid (editor of the Liberal *Leeds Mercury*) that Gladstone was a convert to the cause. On the following day Herbert's intimation became public knowledge. Gladstone denied the accuracy of the Press statement but did not specifically renounce a Home Rule solution.

VI. HOME RULE CRISIS, 1886

It can have been no great surprise that a statesman who had already performed a striking act of constitutional separation in the ecclesiastical sphere in 1869 should contemplate adopting a similar separation in the secular realm. But it was immediately clear that a Home Rule policy by Gladstone would cause great disturbance among Liberals. 'Mr. G's Irish scheme is death and damnation [and] we must try and stop it', wrote Chamberlain to Dilke on 17 December. But he added: 'the Whigs are our greatest enemies and we must not join them if we can help it'.[80] The separation of Ireland from Britain, he wrote a few days later, would lead to Irish attempts at Protection and finally to 'a War in which Ireland would have the support of some other power—perhaps America or France . . .Certainly I will not join a Government pledged to such a mad and dangerous proposal . . . I would sooner the Tories were in for the next 10 years than agree to what I think the ruin of the country'.[81] Arthur Elliot said that Home Rule was bound to plit the party: if the leaders proposed it, the Liberals 'may resign all hope of governing the country for the next quarter of a century'.[82]

Gladstone was not yet officially committed to Home Rule, there were still

---

[77] Carnarvon to Salisbury, 6 Dec. p. SP.

[78] Sydney H. Zebel, *Balfour: A Political Biography* (Cambridge, 1973), 50.

[79] Morley, *Gladstone*, iii. 258. Cf. Rosebery to Gladstone, 12 Dec., copy; RP, 10023, fos. 129–33; Gladstone to Rosebery, 13 Dec., ibid. 136–8; Gladstone to Hartington, 17 Dec.; Gwynn and Tuckwell, *Dilke*, ii. 208; Balfour, *Chapters of Autobiography*, ed. Mrs Dugdale (London 1930), 208 ff.

[80] CP, JC5/24/454; part quoted Gwynn and Tuckwell, op. cit. ii. 197.

[81] Chamberlain to Dilke, 26 and 27 Dec. 1885; CP, JC5/24/457–8; Gwynn and Tuckwell, op. cit. ii. 199–201.

[82] Elliot to A. C. Sellar, 18 Dec.; Elliot Papers. Cf. Albert Grey to Elliot, 23 Dec.; ibid.

differences among Conservatives on the question of Irish government, but conciliation ceased between the Government and Home Rulers. The Queen's Speech on 21 January 1886 indicated that Ministers intended to reintroduce coercion and would do nothing to establish a separate Parliament for Ireland. On 27 January the Government was defeated on an agrarian amendment to the Address by Jesse Collings, and the following morning Salisbury resigned. The Home Rule MPs had voted with Gladstone against the Government in the division, but eighteen Liberals—including Hartington, Goschen, and Sir Henry James—voted with the Conservatives, and seventy-six Liberals abstained. This was a warning of gathering Liberal opposition to a Gladstonian Home Rule policy.

By 3 February Gladstone had formed his third Government, with an enthusiastic Home Ruler, John Morley, as Chief Secretary for Ireland. Gladstone had informed those to whom he offered a Cabinet post that he proposed to examine whether it was practicable to establish a separate Irish legislature. Hartington, Goschen, and James refused to join the ministry on these terms. Chamberlain accepted office, though dubiously. On 16 March, when the Home Rule Bill was being discussed in Cabinet, he told R. W. Dale that there was no hope of his being able to support Gladstone's policy.[83] On 26 March Chamberlain, George Trevelyan, and some non-Cabinet ministers resigned.

Before Gladstone brought his Home Rule scheme into the Commons in April, Welsh and Scottish disestablishment were discussed in that House. In Wales the trebling of the county electorate by the 1884 Reform Act and the return of several leading Nonconformists as MPs encouraged the democratic expression of the Dissenting majority. Welsh disestablishment was urged less in accordance with the general scriptural and social arguments of the Liberation Society and more on grounds of nationalist aspiration.[84] 'I think the national spirit is gradually rising in Wales', wrote the young radical Tom Ellis on 6 April; a few days later he wrote that it was 'rising by leaps and bounds'.[85]

On 9 March Lewis Dillwyn, MP for Swansea, moved in the Commons that 'as the Church of England in Wales has failed to fulfil its professed object as a means of promoting the religious interests of the Welsh people, and ministers only to a small minority of the population, its continuance as an Established Church in the Principality is an anomaly and injustice which ought no longer to exist'. Dillwyn based his motion on the allegation that the establishment represented only a seventh of the Welsh population, and added that 'Wales is practically a separate nationality'. Henry Richard, seconding him, acknowledged the recent striking improvements in the Church in Wales, but said they

[83] Chamberlain to Dale, 16 Mar. 1886; CP, JC5/20/55.
[84] Cf. Morgan, *Wales in British Politics*, 64–7.
[85] T. E. Ellis to D. R. Daniel, 6 and 17 Apr. 1886; D. R. Daniel Papers, NLW 309.

had come 'too late'. Albert Grey, Liberal member for Tyneside and an ardent Church reformer, proposed as an amendment that the Welsh Church, rather than requiring disestablishment, needed to become adapted 'more efficiently to the religious needs and wishes of the Welsh people'. The people could be brought back into the established fold if they were given more say in the running of church services: 'let them introduce the principle of self-government; let them nationalize the Church; . . . let them make it not only the Church of the clergy and of the wealthy minority, but the Church of the people, governed and controlled by the people in each parish'.

In the complicated voting which followed the debate it was difficult to estimate the support for Welsh disestablishment. But it was clear that the House wanted neither Dillwyn's motion nor Grey's amendment. By 241 votes to 229 it was decided that the motion should be amended. In the large minority were many (including forty-five Home Rulers) who favoured Dillwyn's motion. But probably there were also many (including Harcourt, who emphasized his opposition to the motion) who would not have supported it in a straightforward division. It was then decided by 251 votes to 152 that Grey's words should be inserted in the motion. Finally, however, the amended resolution was thrown out by 346 votes to forty-nine, the majority including both Conservative Erastians and Welsh voluntaries.[86] Thus there was still a majority against Welsh disestablishment, but radicals were pleased that the attempt had apparently gained much more support than the forty-five votes obtained by the previous motion in 1870.

The Scottish disestablishment movement was still flourishing; but efforts were also being made to encourage the reunion of Presbyterians. It was hoped that a guarantee of spiritual independence for the Church of Scotland would bring about reunion. R. B. Finlay, a member of that Church who was Liberal MP for Inverness Burghs, introduced on 22 January a bill declaring that the Church courts had 'the sole and exclusive right to regulate, determine, and decide all matters spiritual within the said Church'. The expression 'matters spiritual' included all matters relating to worship, discipline, and government.[87] The reaction from embattled Church defenders was lukewarm, but there was some official support in the establishment. The General Assembly's Committee on Church Interests suggested that the next Assembly in May should, if the bill became law, commence 'friendly conference' with the other Presbyterian churches in order to attain 'one National church'.[88] But Free Church opinion was divided. A conference of Free Church ministers and office-bearers opposed to disestablishment declared its support for the bill at

---

[86] H ccciii. 305–67; *AR* cxxvii (1886), 66–7.
[87] Finlay to Rosebery, 21 Dec. 1885; RP, 10084, fos. 275–7. Bill printed in *United Presbyterian Magazine*, Feb. 1886; NS iii. 89.
[88] Dundee C. of S. Presbytery Minutes, 3 Mar. 1886; CH2/103/23, 335–6.

Edinburgh on 16 February. But a pamphlet by Taylor Innes opposed the measure as providing inadequate relief from State control in civil matters.[89] Free Churchmen and United Presbyterians went to London to remonstrate against the bill. The second reading was defeated in the Commons on 17 March by 202 votes to 170. The Government was against the bill, most of the support came from Conservatives, and the opposing majority consisted of Liberals and Home Rulers. The Scottish MPs voted thirty-four to thirteen against, a few Scottish Liberals being in the minority.[90]

The Commons then proceeded, as anticipated, to vote against Scots disestablishment. Dr Charles Cameron's motion, which he based on the minority position of the established Church in Scotland, was defeated on 30 March by 237 votes to 125.[91] The Government had generally opposed the motion. Gladstone said he could not support it as the question had not been put to the country at the last election;[92] but three Cabinet ministers—Chamberlain, Campbell-Bannerman, and Trevelyan—voted for the motion. The division was mainly on party lines, all the supporters being Liberals and all except twenty-one of the opponents being Conservatives; twenty-three Scots MPs voted for, and fifteen against. Five Scottish Liberals voted against, including Sir Donald Currie (a Free Churchman) who had moved an unsuccessful amendment that no disestablishment proposal should be considered until the wishes of the Scottish people had been ascertained.

Although defeated on this occasion, disestablishment remained very much alive in Scotland. Voluntary resolutions continued to be made and Parliamentary motions introduced. In May 1886 a joint Disestablishment Council for Scotland was created by three voluntary bodies; J. Dick Peddie was chairman of the Council, which met for the first time in September. For several years disestablishment continued to overshadow the attempts to secure Presbyterian reunion by the alternative means of spiritual independence for the establishment.[93] It was thirty-five years before the principle of Finlay's bill was enacted.

There was no motion for English disestablishment in 1886. This matter continued to be urged, however, under the recent stimulus of the general election, and Church defence and reform were urged in resistance to it. Increased lay participation in church government and the reform of patronage were advocated. High-Churchmen, though tending to approve of the latter, had

---

[89] *The Claim of Right, with the draft of Mr Finlay's Bill and the Report of a Conference to Promote It* (Edinburgh, 1886); *The Free Church Conference and its Resolutions;* Free Church Defence Association Tracts, no. 4 (Edinburgh, 1886); A. Taylor Innes, *Mr Finlay's Bill and the Law of 1843* (Edinburgh, 1886). Cf. W. G. Blaikie, *Ought the Free Church to Resume Connection with the State?* (London and Edinburgh, 1886).

[90] Kellas, 'The Liberal Party and the Scottish Church Disestablishment Crisis', 39; Simpson, *Rainy*, ii. 63; LS, 15 Mar. 1886; A/LIB/7, 246.

[91] H ccciv. 293–355; *AR* cxxviii (1886), 67–8.

[92] H ccciv. 341–8.

[93] Simpson, op. cit. ii. 51–8, 67.

strong reservations about the former.[94] Bishop Magee spent 'two weary days' in February considering Church reform in a small committee of the two Archbishops and four Bishops. He noted how 'the question of disestablishment at every turn in the discussion seemed to break in, and sway to and fro, according as the speaker did or did not believe it imminent'.[95] One of the matters they dealt with was a Church Patronage Bill, which sought to establish a joint lay and clerical council in each diocese to supervise the movement in preferment. The bill was introduced in the Lords by Archbishop Benson and passed its second reading on 13 May. But it did not get as far as debate in the Commons owing partly to the dissolution in June.[96] A patronage bill which Benson thought a slight one compared with his own was introduced in the Commons and passed a second reading but was later dropped. Trenchant Church reformers like Frederick Temple (now Bishop of London) wanted complete abolition of the sale of patronage.[97] Better fortune was enjoyed by a bill to extend the hours for solemnization of marriages, which passed in April;[98] and by a bill for the redemption of extraordinary tithe, which passed the Commons on 17 June and the Lords a few days later.[99] Both of these measures pleased Dissenters.

But the dominant issue of the session was Home Rule, which shattered the Liberal strength on which voluntaries depended for any hope of success. Preponderant radical support for Gladstone's Irish policy was shown by the agreement of the National Liberal Federation and its Scottish counterpart, and eventually of all the local Liberal associations. But some leading radicals, many of them Nonconformists from a wide range of denominations, opposed Home Rule: Chamberlain, Bright, E. A. Leatham, Dale, Spurgeon, Newman Hall, Henry Allon, Henry Calderwood, Arthur Mursell, and (temporarily) Thomas Gee. Among Nonconformists papers the *Baptist*, the *Christian World*, and others were against Home Rule.[1] Even Lloyd George might have joined Chamberlain if he had gone on the right day to one of his meetings.[2] The Liberal Unionists were mostly a Whig body, and the radical element, centred in Chamberlain's National Radical Union, was only a small section. Dissenting Unionists such as Dale and Chamberlain retained their voluntary principles, but in alliance with Conservatives they were even less likely to realize them than when under Gladstone's leadership.

A reason frequently given both by Conservatives and Liberals for opposing Home Rule was the fear that the Protestant minority in Ireland would be

[94] Roberts, *History*, 285–6.
[95] Magee to MacDonnell, 10 Feb. 1886; MacDonnell, ii. 221.
[96] H cccv. 879–94; Benson, op. cit.ii. 74.
[97] E. G. Sandford (ed.) *Memoirs of Archbishop Temple* (2 vols., London, 1906), ii. 11–12.
[98] H ccciii. 1448–54.
[99] H cccvi. 1756, cccvii. 187; Maccoby, *English Radicalism, 1886–1914*, 484–5.
[1] *Christian World*, 27 Mar. 1886, p. 439; A. Porritt, *More and More of Memories* (London, 1947), 76.
[2] P. Rowland, *Lloyd George* (London, 1975), 53.

unfairly treated by a Parliament dominated by Catholics. On this issue Irish Protestants sought the support of Protestants in Britain, and the matter caused rioting in Glasgow.[3] Chamberlain championed the liberties of Protestants in Ulster, and Churchill declared that repeal of the Union would mean 'the most bitter and terrible oppression of Protestants by Catholics'. There were similar if less pungent declarations by other Unionists, and there is no doubt that still powerful no-popery feelings were receptive to such assertions.[4] But their validity was denied by Liberal Home Rulers and Parnellites.[5] When Gladstone introduced his bill on 8 April he said that the measure specifically prohibited a Church being established by a Home Rule Parliament. This condition was by no means liked by all Catholics, as it would restrict clerical influence in a self-governing Ireland. But it was enough to reassure most Protestants in this country (though not in Ireland), and a great many Protestants showed their indifference to the papist scare by supporting Home Rule.

If some Protestants feared intolerant effects from Home Rule, some Catholics denounced Unionist organizations. William Bagshawe, Catholic Bishop of Nottingham, forbade his flock to join the popular Primrose League founded in 1883 in memory of Disraeli. But his attitude was opposed by other prelates such as Manning and Vaughan.[6]

'I suppose the party must go to smash and the Tories come in', wrote Chamberlain to Dilke on 21 May.[7] His prophecy was soon fulfilled. On 8 June, ninety-three Liberals voted in the majority of thirty against the bill's second reading. Twenty-three Nonconformists voted against the bill, and eighty-one for.[8] Gladstone decided to go to the country, and another general election came only eight months after the last. The country clearly opted for Unionism. Only 191 Liberals (i.e. Gladstonians) were returned, and eighty-five Parnellites, against 316 Conservatives and seventy-eight Liberal Unionists. The net Conservative gain was sixty-seven.[9] Liberals were reduced to a small minority of the representatives from England, but Scotland and Wales returned sixty-six Liberals between them. Hence the causes of Scotland and Wales had more weight in the Liberal party than before. But Scotland returned seventeen

---

[3] McCaffrey, 'Political Reactions', 241, 247.

[4] Foster, *Churchill*, 254–7; Bebbington, *Nonconformist Conscience*, 90, 101; *The Bulwark*, xv (1886), 92–3; Lord Robert Montagu, *Home Rule—Rome Rule* (London, 1886), 8; J. K. Lindsay, 'The Liberal Unionist Party until December 1887', Ph.D. thesis (Edinburgh, 1955), 184; D. C. Savage, 'The General Election of 1886', Ph.D. thesis (London, 1958), 238–41.

[5] e.g. Malcolm MacColl, *Reasons for Home Rule* (London, 1886), 68; J. Guinness Rogers, *The Ulster Problem* (London, 1886); A. Webb, *The Opinions of Some Protestants Regarding their Irish Catholic Fellow-countrymen*, 3rd edn. (Dublin, 1886).

[6] Janet H. Robb, *The Primrose League, 1883–1906* (New York, 1942), 198.

[7] Gwynn and Tuckwell, op. cit. ii. 223.

[8] T. W. Heyck, *The Dimensions of British Radicalism: The Case of Ireland, 1874–1895* (Urbana, Illinois, 1974), 253–4.

[9] *AR* cxxviii (1886), 254–5.

Liberal Unionists and twelve Conservatives, Wales only six Conservatives and three Liberal Unionists (two of whom shortly returned to Gladstone). Wales therefore appeared more strongly Gladstonian than Scotland, and this gave Welsh disestablishment more political force than Scottish.

Home Rule of course dominated the sometimes riotous contest. Gladstonian candidates received strong support from Catholic clergy and the Irish National League of Great Britain.[10] But anti-Catholicism was linked with opposition to Home Rule because of repeated warnings by Chamberlain and other candidates that a Dublin Parliament might set up a Catholic establishment.[11] In Liverpool there was strong preaching in favour of Ulster Protestants during the contest.[12] The 'Catholic establishment' argument was meant to persuade voluntaries and others to turn Unionist. But it did not prevent most voluntaries from supporting Home Rule while urging disestablishment at the same time. Such radicals emphasized that Home Rule must be enacted before other reforming aims could be achieved. Tom Ellis, standing sccessfully in Merioneth, said that after Ireland had obtained 'the right and power to govern her own affairs, by her own sons, on her own soil', Wales could expect to obtain disestablishment and educational, land, and temperance reforms.[13] Ellis was appealing to Welsh nationalism as well as defending Irish, and common aspirations over land and nationhood gave the Welsh a strong affinity with Ireland. Irish nationalists such as Parnell and Dillon spoke in support of Welsh radical candidates. The Irish vote in Britain of course swung back to the Liberals, in so far as it had moved in 1885. But this was insufficient to regain for Liberals more than a handful of seats in face of the tendency of many Liberals to vote Unionist.

Disestablishment, though urged by the usual denominational and inter-denominational bodies, was mentioned in the addresses of only a few candidates. Herbert Henry Asquith, who was returned for East Fife, told electors at Tayport that he was 'opposed upon principle to Established Churches in whatever country they might be found'.[14] Some other candidates who avowed support for this cause said it was unlikely to be a practical issue in the new Parliament.[15] Gladstone ignored the subject in his Midlothian speeches, concentrating wholly on Ireland. Several Liberal Unionists such as Chamberlain stressed that they were still voluntaries; but Liberal Unionism, far from aiding voluntaryism, strengthened the barrier in its path. The secretary of

[10] Lord Beauchamp to Manning, 29 June 1886; Manning Papers; *Dundee Advertiser*, 15 June, p. 5.

[11] C. W. Boyd (ed.), *Mr Chamberlain's Speeches* (2 vols., London, 1914), i. 274–5; *Justice*, 10 July 1886, p. 2; *Dundee Advertiser*, 7 July, p. 5; *Scotsman*, 2 July, p. 1, 3 July, p. 2; J. L. Sturgis, *John Bright and the Empire* (London, 1969), 171–2.

[12] Waller, *Democracy and Sectarianism*, 75.

[13] R. R. Thomas, 'The Influence of the "Irish Question" on Welsh Politics, 1880–1895', MA thesis (Wales, 1973), chap. II, p. 25. Cf. address of Thomas Lewis, Liberal candidate for Anglesey; *Carnarvon and Denbigh Herald*, 2 July 1886, p. 1.

[14] *Dundee Advertiser*, 2 July, p. 7.

[15] Ibid. 21 June, p. 1, 1 July, p. 5.

the Liberal Unionist Association spoke more than he realized when he said that Liberal Unionists 'were not the Dissenters, they were the true Church'.[16]

The Liberation Society believed that 150 candidates favourable to disestablishment were returned, compared with 171 in 1885.[17] But the Conservative victory and Liberal split meant that circumstances were far more opposed to disestablishment than this figure suggested. The Conservative rule was to last for over nineteen years, apart from a brief and struggling Liberal return between 1892 and 1895; and during the long period of Conservative ascendancy the prospect of disestablishment was postponed and interest in it diverted to other objects.

Yet the fortunes of general disestablishment were probably not fundamentally altered by the events of 1886. Except in the case of Wales and perhaps of Scotland, disestablishment was in a dubious political position before 1886. The Liberal divisions over Home Rule had been anticipated, to a large extent, by differences over disestablishment;[18] so disestablishment had been a dangerous topic for the strong pre-1886 Liberal party to handle, even though less dangerous for the weakened party after the split. The beginnings of proportional numerical decline among Nonconformists, the pressure of social questions for political and public attention, and a tendency for some Nonconformists to vote Conservative, would have exerted an important transforming influence without the changes caused by Home Rule. Therefore the ultimate results of the voluntary campaigns in England and Wales, perhaps even in Scotland, might have been the same without the intervention of Home Rule.

[16] Quoted J. F. McCaffrey, 'The Origins of Liberal Unionism in the West of Scotland', *SHR* l (1971), 54.

[17] LS, 19 July 1886; A/LIB/7, 277.

[18] See W. C. Lubenow, 'Irish Home Rule and the Great Separation in the Liberal Party in 1886: The Dimensions of Parliamentary Liberalism', *VS* xxvi (1982–3), 169.

CHAPTER V

Conservative Ascendancy and Liberal Struggle, 1886–1895

I. INTRODUCTORY

ON 21 July 1886 Gladstone resigned, and the Queen sent for Salisbury. Salisbury asked Hartington to try and form a coalition of Conservatives and Liberal Unionists, in which he undertook to serve himself. But Hartington refused the request. Chamberlain had advised him that such a course would mean 'ceasing to be or [to] call yourself a Liberal', and Hartington told Salisbury that many Liberal Unionists would not support such a venture: 'They have represented themselves to their constituencies as Liberals, and nothing will induce many of them to act with Conservatives in general opposition to Liberals'. Salisbury had said that Chamberlain should not be included in such a Government, and Hartington thought this would make a 'coalition' too obviously Conservative. Chamberlain had also advised Hartington that 'we must all give a loyal support to the Conservatives provided that they do not play the fool either in foreign policy or in reactionary measures at home'; and Hartington promised Salisbury 'an independent but friendly support . . . I think that I can rely on the assistance of Mr. Chamberlain.'[1] Salisbury formed a purely Conservative administration which could rely on general Liberal Unionist support as long as Home Rule remained predominant and Chamberlain's broad conditions regarding policy were observed.

In order to emphasize their continued Liberalism, the Liberal Unionist leaders took their seats on the front Opposition bench. Both Hartington and Chamberlain stressed that Liberal reunion might be achieved, but only when Home Rule was abandoned. Plans were made at the end of 1886 for a Round Table conference between Gladstonians and Liberal Unionists, and negotiations lasted for two months early in 1887. But at the end of February there was published a letter of Chamberlain, replying to one of Gladstone, denouncing Home Rule as an obstacle to reform in Britain—'32 millions of people must go

---

[1] Chamberlain to Hartington, 16 July 1886; B. Holland, *The Life of Spencer Compton, Eighth Duke of Devonshire* (2 vols., London, 1911), ii. 168–9; Hartington to Salisbury, 24 July; ibid. 169–71; Hartington to Goschen, 24 July; ibid. 171; Hartington to the Queen, 6 Aug.; ibid. 173 and ff.; Chamberlain to Sir Henry James, 22 July; (J. L. Garvin and J. Amery, The Life of Joseph Chamberlain (4 vols., London, 1933–51), ii. 259, 264; *AR* cxxviii (1886), 256.

without much needed legislation because 3 millions were disloyal'. This brought the conference to an end, and the prospect of formal reunion faded though individual Unionists trickled back to the Liberals. Chamberlain had a friendly but fruitless secret conversation with Gladstone in April. The coercion policy of that year caused brief opposition from Chamberlain and a few other radical Unionists but did not alienate them from the Tories. Thereafter the bond between Conservatives and Liberal Unionists, including the Chamberlainite 'cave', became firmer in spite of significant personal, political, and electoral differences. Chamberlain was pleased by the introduction of elective county councils in 1888, free elementary education in 1891, and Irish reforms; and he was increasingly alienated from Gladstone as the old man pressed his Home Rule shibboleth with sustained vigour.[2]

The annual meeting of the Church Defence Institution in August 1886 welcomed the increased strength of the Church of England in Parliament.[3] Not a little of the enhanced Anglican power in political affairs came from the dispersal of Nonconformist strength into rival factions over Home Rule. It was a painful split which placed fellow-voluntary campaigners like Dale and Guinness Rogers in opposite political camps and caused Dale, after taunts about his 'Toryism' at a Congregational Union assembly in 1888, to avoid future Union meetings.[4] Gladstone said that disestablishment could only come after Home Rule, Chamberlain that support of Home Rule would mean postponing disestablishment indefinitely.[5] Most Liberal Unionists acknowledged the leadership of Whigs who were opposed to voluntaryism. But there were many Nonconformists among the Liberal Unionists; indeed there were Nonconformists (and perhaps a growing number) who were Conservative—a minority of leading Wesleyan ministers and laymen were notable among these. A survey in 1887 of Wesleyan laymen who had been elected to their denominational Conference since 1878 suggested that thirty per cent opposed Home Rule; and a survey of London Congregational deacons in 1894 indicated a similar percentage of Unionists. Both of these groups, however, had little representative value—they were, for example, of relatively high social status— and probably contained a considerably larger proportion of Unionists than Nonconformity as a whole.[6]

While Conservative Dissenters were not disestablishers, many Nonconformists who had become Liberal Unionists tried to retain their voluntary principles even though it was impossible to achieve disestablishment through

---

[2] Cf. M. C. Hurst, *Joseph Chamberlain and West Midland Politics, 1886–1895*, Dugdale Society (Oxford, 1962), 6–7, 35, 43, 46; id. 'Joseph Chamberlain, the Conservatives, and the Succession to John Bright, 1886–1889', *HJ* vii (1964), 64–93; id. *Joseph Chamberlain and Liberal Reunion: The Round Table Conference of 1887* (London, 1967), 284 ff.; Garvin and Amery, *Chamberlain*, ii. 292–3, 414–23.

[3] CDI Central Council Minutes, 3 Aug. 1886 (vol. 206).

[4] A. W. W. Dale, *The Life of R. W. Dale of Birmingham* (London, 1898), 583–8.

[5] Chamberlain to Thomas Gee, 16 Apr. 1890; Gee Papers, 8305D, 17.

[6] D. W. Bebbington, 'Nonconformity and Electoral Sociology, 1867–1918', *HJ* xxvii (1984), 640–5.

alliance with Conservatives. Joseph Chamberlain, although he left the Liberation Society in 1887, insisted that he had not forsaken his voluntaryism.[7] This and other signs of continued radicalism on his part caused some Liberal Unionist alarm when he succeeded Hartington as leader of the party in the Commons early in 1892. The candidature of his son Austen (who held his father's views) at a by-election in East Worcestershire that year caused conflict with local Conservatives, who tried to insist that Austen promise to abandon disestablishment and threatened to run a rival candidate if he did not. But the *contretemps* was resolved and Austen was returned unopposed.[8] Chamberlain's voluntaryism was naturally constrained by his Conservative alliance. In 1892 he told Balfour that he was ready 'to go on voting for disestablishment so long as such a vote is inoperative and to stay away so soon as it becomes dangerous'; and in 1894 he called his principle an 'abstract' one.[9]

There were further signs that adherence to Unionism, among other reasons, weakened voluntaryism in the later 1880s and 1890s. In Scotland even some United Presbyterians, supposed champions of pure voluntaryism, became Unionists and perhaps lost much of their voluntary opinion in consequence. Some United Presbyterians joined the Laymen's League, formed in 1890 from persons of different denominations who accepted the national establishment of religion and sought to promote reunion. In 1891 members of several UP congregations in the Edinburgh area petitioned that the disestablishment agitation be ended, though counter-petitions came from larger numbers in the same congregations and from others.[10] There was still formidable opposition to reunion through compromise over establishment, and the prospect remained at the discussion stage.

In London the Unionist convictions of a group of eleven Nonconformists led to the foundation of the Nonconformist Unionist Association at the Cannon Street Hotel on 17 April 1888. This body acted especially as a link between Irish Protestant non-episcopalian ministers and British Unionism. The Association was active but tenuous, being maintained for many years chiefly by the single-minded and almost single-handed efforts of Sir George Chubb (later Lord Hayter), a Wesleyan Conservative who was managing director of Chubb and Son's Lock and Safe Company for seventy-four years until he died, near his century, in 1946. The body was significant in demonstrating the increasing

[7] Examples of his statements in A. Mackintosh, *Joseph Chamberlain: An Honest Biography* (London, 1906), 419. Cf. J. Chamberlain, *A Political Memoir, 1880–1892*, ed. C. H. D. Howard (London, 1953), 307.
[8] Garvin and Amery, ii. 536–7; Chamberlain to Balfour, 18 Jan. 1892; BP, 49773, fos. 22–7; Sir Charles Petrie, *The Life and Letters of the Rt. Hon. Sir Austen Chamberlain* (2 vols., London, 1939–40), i. 42–53.
[9] Balfour to Salisbury, July 1892, copy; BP, 49690, fo. 58; Mackintosh, op. cit. 419. Cf. Chamberlain to Craig Brown, 5 July 1887; CP, JC6/6/A/3.
[10] Edinburgh UP Presbytery Minutes, 1 Apr. and 7 Oct. 1890, 3 Mar. and 7 Apr. 1891; CH3/111/38, 238–9, 280–1, 340–1. Cf. W. L. Calderwood and D. Woodside, *The Life of Henry Calderwood* (London, 1900), 309 ff.

heterogeneity of Nonconformist political opinion, and thereby giving confidence to Unionist leaders. Salisbury declared at a banquet held by the Association in November 1888: 'there is nothing in Nonconformist opinions which is necessarily or even in any degree hostile to a sympathy for the union of these kingdoms or the integrity of the Empire'.[11]

But most Nonconformists, even most Wesleyans, were Gladstonians and supported Home Rule, sometimes with crusading zeal. The Coercion Act of 1887 aroused great hostility among Nonconformists and encouraged Gladstone once more to court Dissenting moral ardour and dilate on the scriptural rightness of Home Rule. The radical Wesleyan Hugh Price Hughes said in 1888 that Home Rule was 'simply applied Christianity'.[12] As in the later 1870s, however, Nonconformists had their own political objects to urge in the Gladstonian partnership, and they relied on Gladstone's statements that their particular demands would be attended to when Irish nationalism had been assuaged.

After the 1886 election radicals provided over seventy per cent of the Parliamentary Liberal party, and most of these radicals were Nonconformists.[13] Voluntaryism was much stronger in the truncated Liberal party than it had been in the larger one, though the party still contained many who would be reluctant to accept disestablishment. Gladstone well realized the greater pressure now exerted in his party by radicalism, and not least Scottish and Welsh demands. In regard to disestablishment, the 'long vista' which Gladstone had presented to Scottish Liberals in 1885 seemed to grow shorter in the new position of Liberalism.

The Home Rule dispute had stirred up anti-Catholicism, and this was quite prominent in the next few years in association with the continuing Home Rule debate. Chamberlain said at Plymouth in October 1889 that Irish Protestant fears 'that a Roman Catholic Parliament would not rest until it had secured a dominant religious supremacy' could not be entirely discounted. Salisbury said at Exeter in February 1892 that if Home Rule succeeded 'England, the great Protestant State of the world, would be creating in Ireland an ultra-clerical State, under the government of Archbishops Croke and Walsh. It would be . . . giving power to all that was unprogressive over all that was enlightened.'[14]

The Scottish Protestant Alliance and the Scottish Reformation Society tried to obtain support for conventions and commemorations, for example those in association with the tercentenary of the defeat of the Spanish Armada and the bicentenary of the Revolution settlement, both of which fell in 1888.[15] A

---

[11] D. W. Bebbington, *The Nonconformist Conscience: Chapel and Politics, 1870–1914* (London, 1982), 93–6; *T*, 15 Nov. 1888, p. 6.   [12] Quoted Bebbington, op. cit. 98–9.
[13] T. W. Heyck, *The Dimensions of British Radicalism: The Case of Ireland, 1874–1895* (Urbana, Illinois, 1974), 154–6.   [14] *AR* cxxxi (1889), 208; cxxxiv (1892), 11.
[15] Dundee UP Presbytery Minutes, 7 Dec. 1886, 6 Mar. 1888; CH3/9/91, 244, 310; Dundee C. of S. Presbytery Minutes, 7 Mar. 1888; CH2/103/24, 16–17; Aberdeen C. of S. Presbytery Minutes, 27 Mar. 1888; CH2/1/23, 509.

Dunfermline minister, the Revd Jacob Primmer, claimed there were held in Scotland no fewer than '11 great open-air Protestant Demonstrations' between July and September 1890, 'attended by about 160,000 persons', and '29 Protestant Demonstrations in Halls' from January to April 1891, 'attended by about 14,000 persons'.[16] In Liverpool the Home Rule issue brought a notable rise in sectarian violence, thirty instances of rioting occurring between 1886 and 1889; there were also contests between Orangemen, Catholics, and 'Anglican' candidates in school board elections, and quarrels between Orangemen and the Conservative Constitutional Association which was accused of 'truckling to Catholics and Ritualists'.[17]

A London conference at Exeter Hall in June 1889 established the Protestant Churchmen's Alliance with Lord Grimthorpe as president, absorbing the Protestant Association and the Protestant Education Institute. After a further union the Alliance became the National Protestant Church Union in 1893—a body which eschewed a litigious approach and sought to proceed by educative influence, 'speaking the Truth in Love'.[18] A National Protestant Congress was inaugurated in London in 1890, and met at Brighton in October 1891.[19] At the Church Association spring conference at Great Yarmouth in March 1892, the chairman welcomed 'a new departure in the shape of a Protestant van, the gift of a lady, but they still wanted subscriptions to purchase the horse'.[20] Meanwhile the Irish National League of Great Britain was establishing new branches, and at a League meeting in London in May 1890 Parnell called for better organization of the Irish vote.[21]

There was Protestant opposition to any attempt to establish diplomatic relations with the Vatican. According to an overture by the Edinburgh Free presbytery, this would 'endanger the spiritual liberties of this country, and would ignore the whole teachings of history, as to the malign influence of Romanist priestcraft on the prosperity of nations'.[22] Also strongly resisted was a proposal in August 1889 by Balfour, Irish Chief Secretary, to give greater State encouragement to university education for Catholics in Ireland—a proposal which had some potential advantages for the Conservatives but also some drawbacks, and was withdrawn.[23] A relief bill allowing Catholics to hold the

---

[16] Dundee C. of S. Presbytery Minutes, 6 May 1891; CH2/103/24, 369–70.

[17] P. J. Waller, *Democracy and Sectarianism: A Political and Social History of Liverpool, 1868–1939* (Liverpool, 1981), 92–9; cf. Janet H. Robb, *The Primrose League, 1883–1906* (New York, 1942), 196–9.

[18] G. R. Balleine, *A History of the Evangelical Party in the Church of England*, 3rd edn. (London, 1951), 232–3.

[19] *The Rock*, 16 Oct. 1891, p. 4.

[20] *T*, 11 Mar. 1892, p. 11.

[21] *AR* cxxxii (1890), 143.

[22] Edinburgh Free Presbytery Minutes, 28 Mar. 1888; CH3/111/30, 417.

[23] E. Larkin, *The Roman Catholic Church and the Fall of Parnell, 1888–1891* (Liverpool, 1979), 110–35; protest at autumn meeting of Congregational Union, 3 Oct. 1889; *Congregational Year-book* (1890), p. 27, and at Baptist assembly, 10 Oct. 1889; *Baptist Handbook* (1890), pp. 73–4; *AR* cxxxi (1889), 249–50.

Lord Chancellorship of England and the Viceroyalty of Ireland was defeated in the Commons in February 1891.[24]

In 1887 Alexander Mackonochie, doyen of Ritualists, his mind apparently knocked askew by endless litigation, met a tragic death in a Highland snowstorm. But Ritualist controversy continued to attract much attention.[25] Charles Wood, now Viscount Halifax, told the English Church Union in his presidential address in 1886 that 'the crown and completion of the Catholic revival which has transformed the Church of England within the last fifty years is the reunion of Christendom'. This caused the *Bulwark*, the Scottish Reformation Society journal, to comment that 'under the plea of union, the design . . . is nothing short of a full surrender to Romanism'.[26] The ECU might be divided over the modernist theology of *Lux Mundi*, which appeared in 1889, but in some other matters it was united. In 1887 its annual meeting resolved unanimously, in connection with the Bell Cox case, to present a memorial to the Archbishops and Bishops defending the ancient ritual of the English Church and 'vindicating the Church's inherent and constitutional right to decide freely on all matters affecting her Spiritual interests'.[27]

Legal cases had become less frequent, but the most celebrated suit commenced in 1888 when the Church Association for the first and only time encouraged prosecution of a Bishop. Archbishop Benson was petitioned to try Edward King, Bishop of Lincoln, for illegal ritual acts including the use of lighted candles on the altar, the ceremonial mixing of water and wine, concealment of the manual acts during consecration, use of the eastward position, and the sign of the cross. Benson was reluctant to take action but the Judicial Committee of the Privy Council said he should hear the case. In July 1889 the hearing took place at Lambeth Palace by five episcopal assessors and Benson as judge. The trial began in February 1890. Benson's judgment in November went generally in favour of King, though the ceremonial commixture and the sign of the cross were condemned, and he was criticized for concealing the manual acts. The judgment ended with a plea for peace and tolerance in the Church. The Church Association appealed against the judgment to the Judicial Committee, but this court upheld Benson's conclusions in August 1892.[28] Meanwhile the Church Association had also failed to prevent Bishop Temple of London vetoing a suit against the dean and chapter of St Paul's cathedral for allowing the erection of an elaborate reredos

---

[24] *H* cccxlix. 1733–802; Sir Herbert Maxwell, *Life and Times of the Rt. Hon. W. H. Smith, MP* (2 vols., Edinburgh, 1893), ii. 297–301.

[25] e.g. G. G. Perry, 'The Grievances of High-Churchmen', *Nineteenth Century*, xxvi (Sept. 1889), 500–8; articles by Principal A. M. Fairbairn in *CR* lvii. 387–411, lix. 210–37; E. V. Bligh, *Lord Ebury as a Church Reformer* (London, 1891), 209–12.

[26] *The Bulwark, or Reformation Journal*, July 1886; xv. 108.

[27] ECU Minutes (general), 16 June 1887; CU dep. 5, 18.

[28] E. R. Norman (ed.), *Anti-Catholicism in Victorian England* (London, 1968), 113–20; Benson, ii. 324–9, 347–74.

with a large crucifix in the centre.[29] After these unsuccessful efforts the Church Association relaxed its policy of prosecution. High-Churchmen rejoiced at the results, ECU membership continued to grow, and increased High-Church confidence no doubt contributed to the spread of ritual. But this in turn brought renewed resistance.

The Liberal party, with its concentration on Home Rule and acceptance of disestablishment in Wales and Scotland, revived strongly through by-election victories after its defeat in 1886. But a threat from the Left was beginning to pose a challenge to the Liberal party and the issues which mainly concerned it. This was the growth of Labour unrest and organization, seen in the unemployment riots in London in 1886 and 1887; in a vast increase in trade union membership and consolidation in the late 1880s and 1890s; in the holding of some celebrated strikes, including the London Dock Strike of 1889 and the Manningham Mills strike at Bradford in 1891; in the growth of popular Socialist journalism, particularly the papers edited by Robert Blatchford; and in the foundation of political groups, most notably the Independent Labour Party in January 1893, led by the Congregationalist Keir Hardie. Socialists were concerned with reforms which would benefit the working class as a whole. Though many of them were Nonconformists, they regarded some of the traditional aims of radical Liberals—and particularly disestablishment—as promoting working-class division and having a low priority among their broader social aims. Anti-Ritualism and anti-romanism were of even less relevance to them, though most Socialists wanted to place all schools under public control. Hence the emergence of the Labour movement emphasized the role of social reform in displacing ecclesiastical questions from the centre of politics.

II. THE GOVERNMENT AND CHURCH REFORMS, 1886–1892

One religious question was resolved under the new Government. Though opposed by the Protestant Alliance and Cardinal Manning, the Parliamentary Oaths Bill was passed in 1888. In the majority of 250 to 150 which passed the second reading, 140 Liberals were joined by forty-five Liberal Unionists, thirty-five Conservatives, and thirty Home Rulers. Only 148 Conservatives opposed. The Act extended to all MPs the facility already enjoyed by Quakers and Jews of being able to affirm rather than take the oath. A Home Ruler, Alfred Webb, was the first to use the new provision in March 1890, and after the 1892 election over forty members opted to affirm, either because they had no religion or because the taking of an oath conflicted with their religious beliefs.[30]

---

[29] O. Chadwick, *The Victorian Church* (London, 1970), ii. 352–3; cf. E. G. Sandford (ed.), *Memoirs of Archbishop Temple* (2 vols., London, 1906), ii. 112–14.
[30] W. L. Arnstein, *The Bradlaugh Case* (Oxford, 1965), 315; E. Royle, *Radicals, Secularists, and Republicans*, 267–8; *AR* cxxx (1888), 51–2.

Nothing occurred so swiftly in connection with the efforts to reform and strengthen the Church of England. 'We look upon the creation of a Conservative majority', said the *Record*, 'as an opportunity of carrying out wise reforms, not as an excuse for relapsing into utter stagnation'.[31] From this viewpoint the Conservative Government was disappointing to established Churchmen. Benson, not the most effective Parliamentarian himself, naturally became frustrated when repeated attempts to pass Church reforms were blocked by Government concern with other business.[32] Improvements in Church government seemed to have become a no man's land, the Church itself not being allowed to achieve them and the State not wanting to do so. Lord Randolph Churchill might have been showing piety of his own but was giving little encouragement to the Church when he said: 'Church reform which is the product of a Cabinet checked and controlled by party Whips and guided by House of Commons lobbies is surely in its nature a monstrosity, possibly a profanity, certainly a farce'.[33] Many Churchmen would have agreed with this, not least members of the English Church Union who wanted a larger role for Church assemblies in ecclesiastical legislation. But, under existing constitutional practice, Church reform had to come from Parliament. If it did not do so the Church would become more vulnerable to its voluntary critics.

It was small comfort to be sure that Conservatives and most Liberal Unionists were Church defenders when they were taking few practical steps to defend the Church. One reason for their apathy might have been that the Liberation Society was becoming less affluent and less active. The Church Defence Institution at last exceeded it in annual subscriptions after 1886.[34] The weakening of voluntary attack made defence less pressing. Perhaps another reason was that political Church defenders did not wish to offend Nonconformist Unionists whose support they were trying to retain. A further factor was that, though Salisbury and some other politicians were zealous Church reformers, the bills they proposed were not thought important enough to rank highly in Government business yet were too controversial to slip through in the short time made available to them.[35]

The fate of another patronage bill in 1887 made it look as though this subject was being consigned to the same hopeless limbo as deceased wife's sisters. Introduced by Benson, who said that the evils 'although not very wide . . . were very gross', and were 'most effective in the hands of the enemies of the Church', the bill did not try to abolish the sale of patronage but placed sales and presentations under the supervision of the Bishop and specially appointed

---

[31] *Record*, 9 July 1886, p. 685.

[32] e.g. Viscount Chilston, *W. H. Smith* (London, 1965), 286–7. Cf. Archbishop C. Garbett, *Church and State in England* (London, 1950), 109–11.

[33] Quoted P. T. Marsh, *The Discipline of Popular Government: Lord Salisbury's Domestic Statecraft, 1881–1902* (Hassocks, Sussex, 1978), 165–6.

[34] M. J. D. Roberts, 'Pressure-group Politics and the Church of England', 576.

[35] Marsh, op. cit. 166–7.

councillors. Lord Grimthorpe moved to reject the bill, but it was supported by Temple, Magee, and Selborne though Salisbury had some detailed objections. The measure passed the Lords after amendment.[36] But time was not found to consider it in the Commons, and another bill on the subject was not introduced for six years.

It proved no less difficult to stiffen clerical discipline. In 1888 Benson introduced a bill to ease the removal of 'criminous clerks' by ecclesiastical courts and so rid 'the parsonage, the parish church, and the parishioners from the mercies of an immoral or disgracefully neglectful pastor'. Like the patronage bill, this measure passed the Lords but was not introduced in the Commons. Grimthorpe disputed some details of the bill as giving too much power to clergy and thereby introducing 'the thin end of the High Church wedge'. Archbishop Thomson objected to the legal provisions, and Bishop Ryle singled out the Bishop's veto power for complaint.[37] Benson introduced much the same bill in 1890, when it was read a first time in the Lords but then dropped through pressure of business, and in 1891, when the bill was sent down to the Commons. Benson said in the Lords in March 1891 that the measure would prevent an immoral clergyman from residing in his parish during a period of suspension from office: he could 'point to a case where a man has been suspended for extreme and shameless debt, but he persists in residing . . . [and] insists upon presiding at every vestry'. He had the full support of the two Convocations and of W. C. Magee, newly appointed Archbishop of York.[38]

But opposition was expected in the Commons from some Welsh Liberal members, also from Henry Fowler and J. A. Picton—'those who are desirous of hampering the Church', Benson wrote to Gladstone.[39] W. H. Smith, leader of the House, hoped that Harcourt could restrain these radical malcontents on Gladstone's behalf. Gladstone was anxious for the change but Lloyd George and other young Welsh radicals were determined to prevent it. After Goschen had moved the second reading in the Commons on 29 July, Samuel Evans, a Congregationalist who was member for Mid Glamorgan, moved the adjournment of the debate. The motion was defeated, but Lloyd George managed to prolong the debate and procure its adjournment. 'It will probably come on tonight again', he told his wife on the 30th. 'We will however defeat the concern by sheer obstruction. I don't see why we should be bothered with a confounded ecclesiastical bill when the session is already so late and there is so much essential work to be got rid of'. The following day he reported that further discussion of the bill had been disallowed;[40] and the measure was withdrawn.

[36] A. C. Benson, *The Life of Edward White Benson, Archbishop of Canterbury* (2 vols., 1899), ii. 74–5; H cccxi. 678–89, 1027–49, cccxii. 336–48, 1127–31.

[37] H cccxxiii. 1239–54, cccxxvi. 1807–18.

[38] H cccli. 202–21; Benson, op. cit. ii. 78–82.

[39] Benson to Gladstoone, 8 July 1891; GP, 44109, fos. 197–8, also 10 July; ibid. 202–3.

[40] Kenneth O. Morgan (ed.), *Lloyd George Family Letters, 1885–1936* (Cardiff and London, 1973), 43.

Benson resolved to try again next session. In October he told A. J. Balfour, now leader of the Commons, 'how anxiously and confidently we look to the Government for the fulfilment of the promise to take the Clergy Discipline Bill early next Session in the Commons and to carry it . . . Discipline and Patronage are the two subjects in which the strength of the Disestablishers lies.'[41] In 1892 the bill passed quickly through the Lords, appeared as a Government measure in the Lower House, and was read a first time there on 24 March. Again, however, the bill met anti-Erastian opposition from both High-Churchmen and Nonconformists. A meeting of the ECU on 22 March unanimously resolved that, while wanting stringent discipline 'against criminous and immoral clerks', it would resist this bill 'or any measure which professes to confer spiritual powers by authority of Parliament'.[42] No less anxious to rid the Church of its Parliamentary toils was Lloyd George, one of a small band of Welsh radical MPs who took every chance to oppose the bill. These greatly annoyed not only Gladstone and John Morley but also Stuart Rendel, the Welsh Liberal leader, who thought they were doing the voluntary cause no good. Their action was a foretaste of the 'Welsh revolt' two years later.

Lloyd George and his colleagues created much stir but had no success. Their position was weak because their opponents could accuse them of trying to stop the Church reforming itself in order to strengthen the disestablishment campaign. Their real object, as Lloyd George stated, was quite different: it was to emphasize the need for disestablishment so that a secular Parliament would not have to deal with such matters as clerical discipline. He was supported by radicals at home in Wales and by some High-Churchmen. A 'Prominent High Churchman', he said, had told him that he preferred disestablishment to this bill: 'Fancy High Churchmen approving of my conduct . . . I think we are playing a very astute game as we are winning the support of the Ritualists.' He intended to 'overwhelm the bill with amendments'.[43]

On 28 April Balfour moved the second reading, and Lloyd George moved that it was not the function of the State to attend to spiritual discipline, arguing that the Church should be disestablished so that it could regulate itself. Gladstone replied that both he and Lloyd George supported Welsh disestablishment but that this was no reason to prevent the Church of England obtaining a reform it sorely needed. Gladstone received support from some Nonconformist members, but his speech utterly failed to quell the Welsh rebels. The second reading passed easily, by 193 votes to forty-one. But the bill was referred to the Standing Committee on Law, of which Lloyd George and Samuel Evans were members and to which Gladstone had himself specially appointed. The two Welshmen engaged in thoroughgoing 'Parnellite' obstruction, delaying proceedings very efficiently with their endless amend-

---

[41] Benson, op. cit. ii. 84.
[42] G. B. Roberts, *The History of the English Church Union, 1859–1894* (London, 1895), 350–3.
[43] Lloyd George to his wife, 30 Mar. 1892; Morgan, op. cit. 46–7.

ments. Gladstone, realizing that his replies only encouraged their tactics, relapsed into silence save for the eloquence of 'his terrible eye'. Rendel was exasperated by 'the madness of Wales in slapping John Morley and Mr. Gladstone in the face'.

At length the bill emerged from committee, and its third reading was debated on 2 June. Lloyd George, Evans, and others moved numerous amendments, most of which were crushed. The third reading was carried by 145 votes to seventeen, and after the Lords had accepted the Commons' amendments the bill passed. Those who had said that 'no Church Bill could ever pass Parliament again' were wrong, and Benson's faith in the Government as Church reformers had at last been justified.[44]

Welsh voluntaryism made a leading contribution to anti-tithe agitation in the years 1885–91. As agricultural profits declined the tithe became a heavier burden on farmers, yet it was more important for the clergy to receive it as their incomes were dropping as well. There was some resistance to the tithe rent-charge by farmers in the South-East of England, where agriculture was particularly troubled, but much more resistance in Wales, where farming was doing better and tithe was lighter but where voluntaryism was strongest. The example of Irish land agitation had some influence, and especially speeches given in Wales by the Irish nationalist Michael Davitt. Local societies were formed—Lloyd George was secretary of the South Caernarfonshire Anti-Tithe League—and a co-ordinating Anti-Tithe league for Wales was formed at Ruthin, Denbighshire, in September 1886 to encourage refusals to pay and demonstrations against the sale of distrained goods. 'Few tithe sales took place without the attendance of hostile crowds. Heckling, hooting and hissing made the auctioneer's task particularly unpleasant and onerous ... Farm-hands released bulls in the midst of court bailiffs.'[45]

The demonstrations thus threatened to become riots, and police and soldiers were brought in to protect bailiffs and auctioneers engaged in sales organized by the Ecclesiastical Commissioners.[46] The most noted riot occurred in June 1887 at Mochdre in Denbighshire—a county in which militant agitation had originated in December 1885, where the first distraints had taken place in August 1886, and where the Anti-Tithe League had been formed on the initiative of the Revd Thomas Gee, an influential Calvinistic Methodist

[44] H, 4th ser., iii. 1585–640, v. 464–518; Morgan, op. cit. 48–52; Morgan, *Wales in British Politics*, 117; P. Rowland, *Lloyd George* (London, 1975), 97–8; J. Grigg, *The Young Lloyd George* (London, 1973), 109–10; Benson, op. cit. ii. 89–92; Samuel T. Evans Papers, 41 and 43.

[45] D. Richter, 'The Welsh Police, the Home Office and the Welsh Tithe War of 1886–1891', *WHR* xii. 1 (1984), 57. See also J. P. D. Dunbabin *et al.*, *Rural Discontent in Nineteenth-century Britain* (London, 1974), 211–31, 282–96; Morgan, op. cit. 84 ff.; R. Morris, 'The Tithe War', *Denbighshire Historical Society Transactions*, xxxii (1983), esp. 66 ff.

[46] G. F. A. Best, *Temporal Pillars: Queen Anne's Bounty, the Ecclesiastical Commissioners and the Church of England* (Cambridge, 1964), 470–4; D. W. Howell, *Land and People in Nineteenth-century Wales* (London, 1977), 84–5; J. P. Dunbabin, 'The Welsh Tithe War, 1886–1895', in A. Charlesworth (ed.), *An Atlas of Rural Protest in Britain, 1548–1900* (London, 1983), 177–9; Richter, op. cit. 50–75.

journalist and veteran voluntary. 'I rejoice to hear that the Anti-Tithe Agitation is spreading and gaining ground', a correspondent had told Gee in October 1886.[47] The tithe war was 'a form of the awakening of Wales', wrote Tom Ellis;[48] though the illegality of tithe resistance caused disapproval of the activity among some radicals. At Mochdre fifty civilians and thirty-four police were injured. Several questions were asked in Parliament by Welsh MPs—Tom Ellis, for instance, asked if the Home Secretary would prepare a correct Welsh translation of the Riot Act—and a Government inquiry was conducted into the affair.[49] Early in 1888 the Ecclesiastical Commissioners and the Clergy Defence Association commenced a drive to recover all outstanding tithe, and there were many more sales of goods, more riots, and more arguments in Parliament. But the tension relaxed somewhat in 1889 and 1890.

Five attempts were made in these years to reform the tithe system, and the last one succeeded in 1891. Salisbury's bill of 1887 proposed to transfer the charge from the tenant to the landowner, from whom the amount would be recoverable as a personal debt. The bill passed the Lords, but only received a first reading in the Commons and was withdrawn. The next year two bills introduced by Salisbury attempted, in combination, a similar change; but these met the same fate as their predecessor despite receiving considerable support from Churchmen. A bill of 1889 did not initially deal with responsibility for payment, and when the Attorney-General proposed to insert an amendment allocating payment to the landowner, the Speaker said a new bill would have to be introduced. In March 1890 Sir Michael Hicks Beach brought another bill into the Commons making the landlord directly responsible for payment. J. A. Picton, member for Leicester and an Anglican, moved to reject the measure and strongly advocated the Welsh Dissenting case against tithe. Samuel Evans, Stuart Rendel, and others stressed Nonconformist dislike of having to contribute to the established Church, and called on that Church to become as self-supporting as Nonconformity. Rendel said the main object of the bill was 'to give a lingering life to the Church Establishment in Wales'. The second reading passed by 289 votes to 164, but various meetings in the country had shown wide opposition to the bill. Other Government business was regarded as more pressing, and the bill was withdrawn.[50]

Finally, the Government introduced a revised bill in November 1890 with the sole object, as before, of requiring payment from the landowners. Most of these were Churchmen and therefore, it was hoped, more willing to meet their

[47] Ellis J. Griffith to Gee, 11 Oct. 1886; Gee Papers, 8306D, fo. 94.
[48] Ellis to D. R. Daniel, 1 Oct. 1886; quoted Morgan, op. cit. 85.
[49] H ccccxvi. 419–20, 554–6, 767–9, cccxvii. 80–1.
[50] 1887 bill: H cccxii. 1451–63, cccxiv. 168–78, cccxv. 823–52, cccxvii. 3–11; 1888 bills: AR cxxx (1888), 102–3; CDI Council Minutes, 5 July 1888 (vol. 206); 1889 bill: A. G. Gardiner, The Life of Sir William Harcourt (2 vols., 1923), ii. 108–10; Henry, Third Earl Grey, 'The Government and the Tithes', Nineteenth Century, xxvii (Jan.–June 1890), 150–72; 1890 bill: H cccxliii. 39–124; AR cxxxii (1890), 87–91.

obligations than Nonconformist farmers. This bill passed its second reading on 1 December by 224 votes to 130 after opposition from Rendel, Osborne Morgan, and others; the Welsh MPs voted against it by twenty-five votes to five. The bill then had to face a stream of amendments from Lloyd George and Sam Evans—both of whom, however, privately approved of the bill—and about a third of these amendments were accepted. 'Wales practically monopolised the attention of the House for fully three weeks', Lloyd George told the absent Tom Ellis, and Evans told Thomas Gee: 'it is acknowledged on all sides of the House that this has been the toughest and best-sustained fight ever made by the Welsh party'. The pair repeated their performance the following year, over the Clergy Discipline Bill. Harcourt opposed the third reading of the tithe bill on 12 February 1891, but the bill was easily carried. The measure then went fairly smoothly through the Lords, but there was considerable debate over amendments between the Houses before it was enacted on 26 March.[51]

The settlement proved quite effective despite some further Welsh disturbance until 1895. The Tithe Rent-charge Recovery and Redemption Act lessened the grievance of farmers by making the tithe payable by the landlord, and pleased tithe-owners because landlords were readier to pay. Farmers had to pay more rent, however, and there was further agitation against the rent-charge in the depression of the 1920s and 1930s. As a result the Tithe Act of 1936 abolished the rent-charge.

The efforts to settle tithe were expected to help the establishment. The council of the Church Defence Institution in May 1890 had trusted that 'no effort will be spared' to pass the tithe bill.[52] Another aspect of Church defence was support of the voluntary schools. In 1888 the majority report of the Cross Commission revived education controversy by advocating rate aid for voluntary schools. This was opposed by much Nonconformist opinion, for example at a conference held at Exeter Hall by the Liberation Society on 20–21 November, attended by delegates from 170 bodies.[53] A new body, the National Education Association, was formed to champion unsectarian education on the lines of the old National Education League. Some Wesleyans, however, were anxious to maintain denominational schools, including their own; and Chamberlain and Dixon had abandoned their wish to abolish these schools.[54]

Roman Catholics were generally in favour of receiving rate aid for their schools. But Anglicans were divided on the matter, some fearing that rate aid would lead to public control, and the National Society refused to accept rate aid

---

[51] H cccxlix. 241–331, cccl. 500–21; *AR* cxxxiii (1891), 16–19; Rowland, op. cit. 91–2; Gardiner, op. cit. ii. 111–12; Morgan, op. cit. 89; Evans to Gee, 6 Feb. 1891; Gee Papers, 8305D, 60.

[52] CDI Council Minutes, 14 May 1890 (vol. 206).

[53] LS, 8 Oct., 3 Dec. 1888, pp. 417, 426.

[54] Garvin and Amery, *Chamberlain*, ii. 428; Chamberlain to Dale, 28 May 1888; CP, JC5/20/65.

in November 1888.[55] Lyulph Stanley, a radical champion of board schools, told Cardinal Manning that he hoped Liberals would be enabled 'to draw a distinction between you [i.e. Catholics] and the ordinary denominationalists'.[56] If this could be achieved through Catholic schools' acceptance of some public control, education might not weaken the alliance between Liberals and most Catholics over Home Rule. Indeed by 1890 the Liberal front bench made clear that they were prepared to give public support to sectarian schools intended only for a section of the population, such as Catholics. But against this there remained the problem of Nonconformist opposition.[57] Salisbury, for his part, had to admit in January 1889 that legislation to introduce rate aid for voluntary schools would be 'too strong for the stomachs of our Liberal-Unionist contingent'.[58]

Rate aid for voluntary schools was left to the future, but more immediate attention was given to free elementary education, which was still championed by Chamberlain and the radical Unionists. Conservatives had no doubt that free education should be provided in voluntary as well as board schools in order to maintain the former, and should not be left to a Liberal Government. Apart from Conservative desires to uphold the Church, there is some evidence that the Conservative vote was higher where there was a greater proportion of denominational school enrolment.[59] Chamberlain accepted Salisbury's policy. In 1889 the removal of school fees in Scotland created an important precedent for England and Wales. In November of that year, Salisbury surprised his Cabinet colleagues by telling the Conservative National Union at Nottingham that 'assisted' education should be given to the needy. In March 1890 he told Tory Bishops and lay peers at the Carlton Club that if Conservatives dealt with the question 'you may put the voluntary schools into a position from which no future hostile majority can dislodge them'. Several of his Cabinet colleagues were reluctant to adopt free education, however, and Salisbury eventually agreed that legislation should not be attempted in 1890. But a bill was promised for the following year. 'Assisted' education appeared in the Queen's Speech at the opening of the 1891 session, and in Goschen's budget speech in April.[60] On 30 May the Cabinet agreed to bring in a bill. This was introduced on 8 June and proposed to make an additional grant of ten shillings (50p) per head for scholars

[55] Benson to Sir Francis Sandford, 5 Nov. 1888; Sandford to Manning, 6 Nov.; Manning to Sandford, 7 Nov.; C. H. Alderson to Manning, 1889 (all in Manning Papers); Marjorie Cruickshank, *Church and State in English Education, 1870 to the Present Day* (London, 1964), 58–60; J. Murphy, *Church, State, and Schools in Britain, 1800–1970* (London, 1971), 78–9.

[56] Hon. E. Lyulph Stanley to Manning, 11 Oct. 1885; Manning Papers.

[57] M. Barker, *Gladstone and Radicalism: the Reconstruction of the Liberal Party in Britain, 1885–1894* (Hassocks, Sussex, 1975). 101–2. See also the controversy in *AR* cxxxii (1890), 42–7.

[58] Salisbury to Cranbrook, 12 Jan. 1889; quoted Gillian Sutherland, *Policy-making in Elementary Education, 1870–1895* (Oxford, 1973), 268.

[59] P. F. Clarke, 'Electoral Sociology in Modern Britain', *History*, lvii (1972), 46.

[60] Sutherland, op. cit. 284–9; Marsh, op. cit. 169–70; Garvin and Amery, ip. cit. ii. 427–8; Lady Gwendolen Cecil, *Life of Robert, Marquess of Salisbury* (4 vols., London, 1921–32), iv. 156–8.

between the ages of five and fourteen, so that fees could be abolished or reduced by that amount.

Opposition could be expected from both Conservatives and radicals. On 15 June the National Liberal Federation adopted a resolution demanding public control of all schools receiving public money. This demand also came from Alfred Illingworth and the Liberation Society, but many Dissenters such as R. W. Dale and Guinness Rogers accepted the scheme because it did at last bring free education. Chamberlain was naturally delighted with the development. He had already written to Dale: 'I have in the last five years seen more progress made with the practical application of my political programme than in all my previous life. I owe this result entirely to my former opponents.'[61] On the other hand Sir H. H. Howorth, a Conservative MP, wrote to *The Times* that the Conservative proposal of free education 'might have been taken from the catechism of Socialism'. The *Standard* opposed the plan but most leading Conservative papers supported it, as did the Catholic *Tablet*.[62]

In the Commons there was only minority opposition from either side. During the three-day debate on the second reading there was considerable radical Nonconformist criticism of the bill because it did not establish popular control. Not all of these critics opposed the bill, though Lloyd George condemned it as 'the further endowment of the Church of England in Wales': free education should be 'free of denominational trammels'. A Conservative, G. C. T. Bartley, moved to reject the bill because it was over-generous, did not ensure increased educational efficiency, and endangered 'the continuance of voluntary and denominational schools' because popular control would be its natural consequence. The measure was 'an attack on the voluntary schools . . . and through these schools an attack on the Established Church'. He received some support in the debate from members of his own party, but one Conservative said he was sure that 'the interests of the voluntary schools would be safeguarded under the measure, and this view was echoed by others. In the division there were only ten votes for Bartley's motion and 318 against, so the second reading was carried overwhelmingly.[63]

Four days were spent in committee. Henry Fowler, a Wesleyan and Liberal MP, moved that in single-school districts where the school was a voluntary one, the election of local representatives to help manage it should be a condition of receiving the fee grant. Chamberlain opposed this motion, admitting the arguments for popular control but saying 'the voluntary schools were too strong for any Government to force it at the present time'. The motion was negatived, by 267 votes to 166. Another, to prevent the teaching of any religious catechism

---

[61] Chamberlain to Dale, 1 May 1891; CP, JC5/20/73, also 2 May; ibid. 74.

[62] Barker, op. cit. 105; LS, 15 June 1891; A/LIB/8, 110–12; Bebbington, *Nonconformist Conscience*, 134; Dale, *Dale*, 579–81; *Congregational Year-book* (1893), 8–9; Minutes of Wesleyan Conference (1899), 312–13; *AR* cxxxiii (1891), 96–7; Roberts, op. cit. 341; J. G. Snead-Cox, *The Life of Cardinal Vaughan* (2 vols., London, 1910), ii. 106–8.

[63] H cccliv. 1099–157, 1216–303, 1315–59; Rowland, op. cit. 92.

or formulary in schools receiving the grant, was also defeated. An amendment of
Lloyd George, supported by Harcourt, to exclude from the grant schools in
Wales and Monmouthshire whose managers required any teacher to belong to a
particular religious denomination, met the same fate. In a brief debate on the
third reading on 8 July, Bartley still opposed the measure, Harcourt prophesied
'the ultimate downfall of the denominational system', and Jesse Collings
described the bill as the greatest measure of the present Parliament. The
reading passed without division amid cheers from both sides of the House. In
the Lords there was considerable support for the voluntary schools. An
amendment inserted by Bishop Temple gave them additional financial benefit,
but much of this amendment had to be removed before the Commons would
accept the altered bill.[64]

The measure, though welcome to many reformers, could not of course end
the education controversy. The question of rate aid for denominational schools
had been widely aired, but many were determined that only if the schools
became unsectarian and accepted public management should they receive such
aid. The Baptist Union autumn assembly, for example, resolved in 1891 to
continue agitating until voluntary schools in single-school areas 'are placed
under the control of representatives of the ratepayers, and made thoroughly
unsectarian alike in government and instruction'.[65] The question of voluntary
schools, the aid they should receive and the control to which they should be
subject, remained an important matter of religious and political dispute.

Balfour claimed at Plymouth in August 1891 that the introduction of free
education had 'saved the whole system of voluntary and religious education',
and that 'a policy more consistent with the general attitude of the Unionist party
never could have been adopted by a Unionist Government'.[66] The Tithe Act
and Clergy Discipline Act, moreover, had been intended to make the
establishment less vulnerable to attack. The protracted issue of Church
patronage was still unsettled, but otherwise the Government had, after a
considerable wait, achieved a certain amount to satisfy Church reformers.

III. THE LIBERALS AND DISESTABLISHMENT, 1886–1892

The Liberals enjoyed a steady revival from 1887 to 1890, shown in numerous
by-election victories. To some of these the Irish vote made an important
contribution.[67] Harcourt confidently claimed at a banquet at the National
Liberal Club in July 1890 that 'the Government were crumbling to pieces . . . A
process of reunion of the Liberal party, unhappily shattered, had long been

---

[64] *AR* cxxxiii (1891), 141–3; H ccclv. 633–80, 1329–89; Sutherland, op. cit. 301–8.
[65] *Baptist Handbook* (1892), 71.
[66] *AR* cxxxiii (1891), 165.
[67] E. P. M. Wollaston, 'The Irish Nationalist Movement in Great Britain, 1886–1908', M.A. thesis
(London, 1957), 205–11.

going on.'[68] Unhappily for the Liberals this euphoria did not last long, as the O'Shea divorce case in November distracted and weakened them again.

One good result of the Liberal Unionist secession, said Gladstone in 1889, was 'to shift the centre of gravity in the Liberal party in the direction of radical opinions'.[69] The Liberal split had temporarily weakened disestablishment, but this cause revived within the Gladstonian Liberal party where it exerted more influence than before. Even Irish Home Rulers anxious to maintain denominational schools voted for disestablishment as an expression of their alliance with British radicals. Ironically, however, the Liberation Society was now declining into relative inactivity, not least because a formerly healthy financial condition had become one of falling subscriptions, unsuccessful appeals for funds, and permanent indebtedness. There were sporadic resolutions to increase the number of meetings, but financial stringency cramped the Society's efforts and lessened its influence. Some Nonconformists began to say the Society was dead. Its central mirage of English disestablishment was disappearing and being replaced partly by the urge to build a moral Jerusalem. The demand for disestablishment elsewhere, especially in Wales, generally eluded the Society's influence because other groups and organizations were more directly concerned.[70] A unanimous resolution of the Congregational Union assembly in October 1889 for disestablishment in Wales and Scotland recognized the fading of English voluntaryism and the flourishing health of Welsh and Scottish.[71]

Both Scottish and Welsh disestablishment were clearly adopted by the Liberal party after its 1886 defeat, but the Welsh claim edged into the prior position. This arose from the greater numerical pressure for disestablishment among the Welsh MPs; the increasing urgency with which the cause was voiced, especially by young radicals entering the Commons between 1886 and 1890; and the fact that disestablishment was strongly bound to the developing Welsh nationalism of the *Cymru Fydd* (Young Wales) movement. Bishop Edwards of St Asaph declared at the Church Congress at Rhyl in October 1891 that Nonconformists were only some fifty per cent of the Welsh population. But Lloyd George, at a Dissenting meeting in the same town in November, denied Edwards' claim and its implication that half the population belonged to the Church.[72]

There was some constitutional recognition of a separate Welsh identity in the passage of special legislation for Wales—an Intermediate Education Act in 1889 following the Sunday Closing Act in 1881—and voluntaries hoped that this tendency would include disestablishment of the Church in Wales. National

[68] *AR* cxxxii (1890), 176–7.
[69] *AR* cxxxi (1889), 247.
[70] Bebbington, op. cit. 25; D. A. Hamer, *The Politics of Electoral Pressure* (Hassocks, Sussex, 1977), 158–9; LS, 18 Mar. 1889; A/LIB/7, 443.
[71] *Congregational Year-book* (1890), 25.
[72] *AR* cxxxiii (1891), 194–5.

assertiveness was seen in a desire to remove Welsh disestablishment from the lengthy tutelage of the Liberation Society. It was hoped that Welsh disestablishment would gain in popular strength and political thrust by becoming more distinctively a Welsh national concern, and would have more chance of success through separation from the question of the Church in England.[73]

Two Liberal Federations, one for North Wales and one for South, were formed in December 1886 and January 1887 respectively. A Welsh National Liberal Council was founded in October 1887 to link the two. These bodies, in association with Welsh Liberal MPs, expected to take control of voluntary activity from the Liberation Society. Stuart Rendel, who became the first president of the National Council and succeeded Henry Richard as leader of the 'Welsh parliamentary party' in 1888, expounded at length to Carvell Williams in March 1887 his belief that Welsh disestablishment would do better as a clear reflection of Welsh national aspirations: 'It is the ballot and household suffrage that has [sic] got us under way. It is the united breath of Wales that has filled our sails and not at all the mere sailing orders of the [Liberation] Society, useful as they may have been . . . There seems to me no reason why Wales should not, if it be more to her benefit, assume the direction of her own affairs instead of becoming in fact a branch of the Liberation Society.' He hoped that the Society henceforth would not make any arrangements for Wales 'without first communicating with us as a body of Welsh Liberal representatives and giving us ample opportunity to act as we may collectively or individually think best'.[74]

In a circular of 12 March 1887 to his fellow-Welsh Liberal MPs, Rendel wrote that complete identification with the Liberation Society would hamper Welsh disestablishment by linking it firmly with English. 'What is the main argument against us? It is that the Establishment in England and Wales is one and indivisible. To this we have no reply so long as we are Liberationists; for so long we must admit that, in destroying the Establishment in Wales, we are seeking to undermine it in England.'[75] 'The time *must* come', he told Thomas Gee a few days later, 'when the Liberation Society ought to stand aside and leave us to fight the battle in our own way'. But John Morley advised greater caution in dealing with the Liberation Society. He did not think 'the formal administration of a douche' would be expedient.[76] Links with the Society were maintained, and prominent Welsh politicians such as Ellis, Gee, and Lloyd George sat on its executive committee. None the less the Welsh disestablishment campaign stood increasingly on its own two feet.

Rendel was anxious to have Welsh disestablishment fully adopted as part of

---

[73] Cf. Morgan, op. cit. 77–8; P. M. H. Bell, *Disestablishment in Ireland and Wales* (London, 1969), 226–9.

[74] Rendel to Carvell Williams, Mar. 1887; Rendel Papers, 19458E, 19.

[75] Printed letter, 12 Mar. 1887; Gee Papers, 8319E, fo. 2.

[76] Rendel to Gee, 18 Mar. 1887; ibid. 8308D, fo. 257; Morley to Rendel, 17 Mar.; Rendel Papers.

the Liberal programme, and this was shortly attained through the resolutions of successive conferences. Earl Spencer, when attending the opening of the Welsh National Liberal Council at Aberystwyth in early October 1887, was convinced by some of the speeches that the more extreme delegates would prove 'some real danger if we do not adopt Welsh disestablishment as part of our programme after Ireland'. The National Liberal Federation annual conference opened at Nottingham on 19 October, and Rendel and his colleagues had a strong disestablishment resolution ready from the National Council. Welsh disestablishment became part of the official party programme at the conference, Gladstone himself sanctioning it, while advocates of the same status for Scottish disestablishment were told they must wait. Gladstone said that 'the Welsh have been a little beforehand with the Scotch', and that Scotland should try and draw closer to Wales in the return of pro-disestablishment members.[77] Similar success was won by Welsh disestablishment resolutions at later NLF conferences. When a motion on the subject was introduced in Parliament in 1889 it had the formal backing of the Liberal party.

The new elective county councils established in 1888 gave another boost to Welsh radical confidence. The first elections in January 1889 returned a large majority of middle-class Liberals who inflicted severe defeat on the landed gentry, and Thomas Gee became the first chairman of Denbighshire county council.[78] On 14 May the veteran Lewis Dillwyn moved another disestablishment resolution in the Commons. Although the Church in Wales was gaining ground, he said, Nonconformists were in a large majority, and (with reference to the tithe riots) 'the feeling against the Church is increasing in bitterness and strength'. Osborne Morgan, an Anglican like Dillwyn, seconded the motion, accusing the Church in Wales of being as political as Dissenters: 'half the vicarages in Wales are political camps and centres at election time'. A Conservative, Byron Reed, opposing the motion, insisted that the Church in Wales could not be treated separately from the Church of England: only 'as a whole' could the establishment question be settled. Statistics showed, he claimed, that the Church in Wales was growing while Dissent was declining. The resolution was defeated, by 284 votes to 231.[79]

Gladstone was absent from the debate, to the great disappointment of Nonconformists. But he clearly supported both Welsh and Scottish disestablishment in a speech at St Austell, Cornwall, a month later. In England the question was unripe for settlement, and (he said no doubt thankfully) 'naturally at my time of life such a subject is placed beyond all reasonable possibility of contact with myself'. But in Wales and Scotland there had been a clear expression of opinion in favour of the change, and 'when the question is brought

[77] Barker, op. cit. 121–2; Schnadhorst to Rendel, 15 Oct. 1887 (Rendel Papers); *NLF Proceedings in Connection with the 10th Annual Meeting* (London, 1887), 8–9, 18–20, 74; Morgan, op. cit. 80–1.
[78] Ibid. 107.
[79] H cccxxxvi. 70–120.

forward again with respect to the one country or the other I shall be ready to render a distinct account of my opinions', which—it could safely be presumed—would be affirmative.[80] Such a speech in Methodist Cornwall may have been partly designed to win Wesleyans over to Home Rule, to which many of them were opposed.

Gladstone's declaration was gratifying to voluntaries. But the executive committee of the North Wales Liberal Federation, meeting on 13 December 1889, wanted 'an explicit undertaking authoritatively made' that Welsh disestablishment would be adopted by the next Liberal Government.[81] On 23 June 1890 Thomas Gee tried to obtain a clear statement from Gladstone about his intentions on disestablishment, particularly in regard to priority between the Scottish and Welsh issues. Gladstone replied that no priority could be decided at present, 'either as between them, or as among the various measures to which the Liberal party is variously pledged': it was 'only when we have come much nearer to the period of action that the order of action can be usefully considered'. In the mean time the only priority lay with the Irish question, which 'disturbs and obstructs all progress whatever'. But the letter did confirm Gladstone's commitment to Welsh and Scottish disestablishment. 'I trust that you do not doubt Mr. Gladstone's being with us any more than I do', wrote Rendel, a personal friend of Gladstone, to Gee. 'His letter to you does not only pledge him to the principle [of disestablishment]. It pledges him to the opinion that the principle can be realized without serious difficulty and that there are competent persons living who can give it effect.'[82] Tom Ellis, however, while noting that Gladstone was being 'gradually forced on', and that he no longer stressed the difficulty of separating the Welsh case from the English, lamented that he had said nothing about the Church in Wales being 'a sore angry grievance'.[83]

Soon after this interchange, on 17 July, a deputation from the Welsh National Council, including most of the Welsh MPs, met a committee of the National Liberal Federation. The committee said it would urge the Liberal leaders to include Welsh disestablishment in the programme for the next election, in the hope of gaining a mandate to deal with the question in the next Parliament. At the NLF annual meeting at Sheffield in November, one of the successful resolutions (moved by Bernard Coleridge, an Anglican MP) stated that the disestablishment and disendowment of the Church in Wales, and the application of Welsh tithes to public purposes, should be dealt with in the next Parliament as soon as Home Rule had passed. Lloyd George, supporting the

---

[80] *AR* cxxxi (1889), 134–6.

[81] Rendel Papers, 19446E, V. 1, 4.

[82] Gee to Thomas E. Ellis, 26 June 1890; Gee Papers, 8306D, fo. 78; Gladstone to Gee, 2 July 1890; ibid. 91; part quoted Hamer, *Liberal Politics in the Age of Gladstone and Rosebery*, (Oxford, 1972), 130–1; Rendel to Gee, 3 July; Gee Papers, 8308D, fo. 262; Rendel to Gee, 7 July ibid. 263; part quoted Morgan, 90.

[83] Ellis to D. R. Daniel, 12 July; D. R. Daniel Papers, 367.

resolution, said that 'Home Rule must come first, and Wales wanted the question of disestablishment to be placed second on the programme of the Liberal party'.[84] The passing of the resolution gave Welsh disestablishment this place, and the position was confirmed at the next annual meeting at Newcastle in 1891.

Thus Welsh voluntaryism had made impressive political steps, but Church defence had also become very active in Wales. The pressure for disestablishment in the near future was all the greater when a Calvinistic Methodist theologian could write of the established Church in South Wales: 'The strides it has made in the last 15 years is [*sic*] amazing, and unless it be soon disestablished we shall not be able to urge *numbers* against it'.[85] Lord Randolph Churchill and Archbishop Benson gave strenuous aid to the Welsh establishment. Churchill said at Plas Machynlleth in Montgomeryshire in September 1889: 'to the disestablishment of the Church, whether in Wales, in Scotland, or in England, the Tories were bound to oppose an inflexible resistance . . . [in Wales] before another generation had passed away, the Church would have enormously increased her popular strength, and would, perhaps, largely if not altogether have removed the disparity of numbers between herself and her opponents.' Two years before, at Sunderland, he had publicly accused Gladstone of using disestablishment as a bribe to gain support for Home Rule. The growth of the Church in Wales and the need to defend and reform it, were emphasized at the Church Congresses held significantly at Cardiff in 1889 and Rhyl in 1891. Benson attended the latter and made a strong speech. In May 1891 the annual meeting of the Church Defence Institution passed a firm resolution to maintain the Church in Wales as 'an integral part of the National Church'.[86] By now there seemed a slight possibility that, if the momentum of Church growth and Church defence continued, Welsh Voluntary pressure might be rebutted in the end.

In Scotland the picture was similar but more complicated. The established Church was growing in numbers and confidence against a still flourishing voluntary movement. The origin and nature of the Church of Scotland prevented voluntaryism becoming harnessed to national consciousness as it was in Wales. Some Dissenters were turning to support the maintenance of an establishment and the strong backing for Unionism in 1886 had dented voluntary ardour. Liberal organization was unified when the radical National Liberal Federation of Scotland joined with the Scottish Liberal Association in December 1886, but there were still disputes in the enlarged body between

---

[84] *NLF: Proceedings in Connection with the 13th Annual Meeting, Held in Sheffield, 20–1 November 1890* (London, n.d.), 9, 31, 60–3; Rendel to Gee, 26 Dec. 1890; Gee Papers, 8308D, fo. 265.

[85] J. Cynddylan Jones to Gee, 4 Mar. 1887; Gee Papers, 8306D, fo. 122 (quoted Morgan, op. cit. 83). Cf. *Letters from Wales*, repub. from *T* (London, 1889), 10.

[86] *AR* cxxxi (1889), 185, 189–90; L. J. Jennings (ed.), *Speeches of the Rt. Hon. Lord Randolph Churchill, MP, 1880–1888* (2 vols., London, 1889), ii. 234; Benson, *E. W. Benson*, ii. 410; CDI Council Minutes, 14 May 1891 (vol. 206), also 5 July 1888 (ibid.).

radicals and moderates over disestablishment. By October 1887 radicals had persuaded the executive council to send delegates to the NLF conference at Nottingham in order to urge Scottish disestablishment. At that conference Gladstone said, as already mentioned, that Scotland should return to Westminster as large a proportion of Home Rulers (and disestablishers) as Wales. If that happened 'I have not the least doubt that when the day of competition comes Scotland will be able to hold her own'. Several Liberal gains were made at Scottish by-elections, and Morley said at Dundee in December 1889 that 'it would be impossible when a Liberal majority came into power to maintain a Scottish Establishment'.[87]

Voluntary propaganda was largely stimulated by the Disestablishment Council for Scotland, a federation formed in 1886, and as in Wales the Liberation Society found itself overtaken by regional organization. By October 1892 the Society had little contact with the Disestablishment Council, which collected subscriptions hitherto paid to the Society and would only send 'vague and inadequate' information about its activities to London.[88] The Liberation Society was having to retreat from the most vital areas of voluntaryism.

While Scots voluntaries sought to tighten their organization Church defence remained active. There was a multitude of defence committees in the Church of Scotland, many even on the parish level. In March 1887 it was reported that twenty out of the thirty parishes in the Dundee presbytery had defence committees, that in six parishes the committee had lapsed but could be easily revived, and that in only three parishes had no committee been appointed.[89] Lord Balfour of Burleigh stressed, in a *Contemporary Review* article of December 1887, the current expansion of the Church of Scotland which was strengthening its arm against voluntaryism. The establishment's opponents now feared that 'unless her destruction be effected soon, it will never be effected at all'. A reply to this article said that disestablishment would enable Scottish Presbyterians, who had the same creed, form of worship and government, to reunite with ease.[90]

The Liberals were becoming the party of disestablishment. In Parliament a second Scots disestablishment motion by Dr Charles Cameron in June 1888 received 208 votes from Liberals and Irish Home Rulers and was defeated by fifty-two—a marked reduction of the majority of 112 against him in 1886. The Scots MPs voted two to one for the motion, and no Scots Liberal member voted

[87] J. G. Kellas, 'The Liberal Party in Scotland, 1876–1895', *SHR* xliv (1965), 11–13; *AR* cxxix (1887), 161–2, cxxxi (1889), 253–4; *Disestablishment Banner*, Oct. 1890 (special no.).

[88] Bebbington, 'The Nonconformist Conscience: A Study of the Political Attitudes and Activities of Evangelical Nonconformists, 1886–1902', Ph.D. thesis (Cambridge, 1975), 43.

[89] Dundee C. of S. Presbytery Minutes, 2 Mar. 1887; CH2/103/23, pp. 471–2. Cf. C. N. Johnston, *Handbook of Scottish Church Defence*, 2nd edn. (Edinburgh, 1894), 160–1.

[90] Lord Balfour of Burleigh, 'The Attack on the Scottish Church', *CR* lii (1887), 878; Walter C. Smith, 'The Scottish Church Question', ibid. liii. 289–90. Cf. *United Presbyterian Magazine*, vi (1889), 545–9.

against.[91] Nearly a year later Gladstone committed himself to Scottish disestablishment together with Welsh in his St Austell speech. 'If he lives, how low will he go?' asked the Conservative Lord Cranbrook.[92] In November 1889 Gladstone told Rosebery that two sizeable majorities of Scots members voting for Cameron's motions in separate Parliaments were an adequate declaration of Scottish opinion for disestablishment—in fact he did not think the Scots establishment had 'a rag of a case'.[93] The NLF council, meeting at Manchester in December 1889, reaffirmed its repeated declarations for disestablishment and disendowment of the Churches in Wales and Scotland, but gave priority to the Welsh claim, saying that 'Welsh disestablishment and disendowment should be dealt with as soon as Home Rule is attained'. The same priority was maintained at Sheffield the following year.[94]

Gladstone voted for Cameron's third motion on 2 May 1890, after saying he did not think there ever was a country 'where the question of disestablishment is so simple as in Scotland, or where it could be introduced so entirely without shock or serious trouble'. Presbyterian reunion, he believed, would come from disestablishment. Cameron's main opponent in the debate, J. A. Campbell, a Conservative member (and brother of Henry Campbell-Bannerman), stressed the Church of Scotland's growth and the opposition of many Free Churchmen and even United Presbyterians to disestablishment. But the result was pleasing to voluntaries not only because Gladstone spoke and voted for them but because the majority against the motion shrank to thirty-eight. The number of Scots MPs voting in favour was slightly higher than in 1888; sixty-two Irish MPs voted for, twenty-six Welsh, and four English Liberal Unionists including Chamberlain. Only one Scots Liberal MP (Peter McLagan) voted against, though some abstained.[95] The Church Defence Institution passed a resolution of sympathy with the Church of Scotland.[96] Soon after this division, however, in July 1890, growing opposition to voluntaryism and increasing support for Presbyterian reunion among Scots Dissenters was shown by the formation of the Laymen's League—described by the *Disestablishment Banner* as 'the expiring attempt of Tories and Whigs to revive a dying cause'.[97] There was also criticism amongst United Presbyterians of their Synod's Disestablishment Committee. In 1891 over a thousand UP members petitioned that this

[91] H cccxxvii. 1060–107; Kellas, 'The Liberal Party and the Scottish Church Disestablishment Crisis', *EHR* lxxix (1964), 41.

[92] Nancy E. Johnson (ed.), *The Diary of Gathorne Hardy, Later Lord Cranbrook* (Oxford, 1981), 737.

[93] Gladstone to Rosebery, 10 Nov. 1889; RP, 10023, fos. 276–7; part quoted Hamer, *Liberal Politics*, 139.

[94] *NLF: Proceedings in Connection with the 12th Annual Meeting* (London, n.d.), 127; 13th Annual Meeting (London, n.d.), 9–11.

[95] D. Nicholls (ed.), *Church and State in Britain since 1820* (London, 1967), 79; H cccxliv. 62–120; *AR* cxxxii (1890), 133–4; *Disestablishment Banner*, xvii (May 1890).

[96] CDI Council Minutes, 14 May (vol. 206).

[97] No. xxii (Oct. 1890), 8.

committee be discharged, but the Synod voted by 415 to thirty-eight to maintain it.[98]

The Church of Scotland redoubled its efforts to spread propaganda, hold meetings, and encourage the formation of Church defence committees in as many parishes as possible. On the other hand a large meeting in favour of disestablishment addressed by Rainy, Cameron, R. B. Haldane, the Earl of Elgin, and others, was held on 16 October 1890 in Edinburgh; special satisfaction was expressed with Gladstone's declared commitment to disestablishment, which the Liberal leader soon repeated in speeches in Midlothian.[99] The battle over Scots disestablishment continued fiercely for the next few years. Gladstone's election agent in Midlothian told him in July 1890 that the next general election in Scotland would, 'so far as our opponents can make it do so, turn upon the Scotch Church question'.[1]

Before the election, however, Home Rule and the Liberal party were shaken by the O'Shea divorce case. The prospect of a striking Liberal victory, partly owing to Parnell's triumph in the Pigott forgeries case, faded in November 1890 when the public learned what some politicians knew already about Parnell's relations with Mrs O'Shea. The disclosure of adultery by a political leader was just the kind of issue to arouse the crusading moral protests of Nonconformists—and indeed of many others of widely varying religious connections, for in this matter Nonconformists probably represented a broad public consensus. The 'Nonconformist conscience', Guinness Rogers claimed, was 'simply the Christian conscience', though not all Christians would have agreed.[2]

Out of moral outrage and political interest the cry arose that Parnell must resign as leader of the Home Rule party. For Liberals to have acquiesced in Parnell's continuance as leader might have been worse for them than insisting he resign, not least because many Nonconformists might have withdrawn support from Home Rule. As Morley put it, 'electoral calculation and moral faithfulness were held for once to point the same way'.[3]

Nonconformists were not unanimous in their reactions to the revelations. Alfred Illingworth was in favour of Parnell's remaining as leader,[4] and there was hesitancy by others before they took a decided stand. But there was no doubt about the gathering opposition of Nonconformist leaders and apparently of many of their followers to Parnell's retaining his post. Dr John Clifford, a leading Baptist minister, wrote to The Times the day after the verdict that 'men

---

[98] Kellas, op. cit. 42.

[99] Dundee C. of S. Presbytery Minutes, 3 Sept., 5 Nov. 1890, 4 Feb. 1891; CH2/103/24, 292–5, 317, 336–8; *What Would the Taxpayer Gain by Disestablishment?;* Church Interests Committee of Church of Scotland (Edinburgh, n.d.); *Disestablishment Banner,* xxii (Oct. 1890).

[1] P. W. Campbell to Gladstone, 18 July 1890; GP, 44116, fo. 176.

[2] J. Guinness Rogers, 'Nonconformists in Political Life', *CR* lxi (Jan.–June 1892), 503.

[3] J. Morley, *The Life of W. E. Gladstone* (3 vols., London, 1903), iii. 433–4.

[4] I. Sellers, *Nineteenth-century Nonconformity* (London, 1977), 87.

legally convicted of immorality will not be permitted to lead in the legislation of the Kingdom'.[5] The same day the Revd Joseph Parker, a well-known Congregationalist, insisted that Parnell must go. W. T. Stead in a published manifesto, H. J. Wilson before the National Liberal Federation meeting in Sheffield, above all the Wesleyan Hugh Price Hughes in sermons and in his paper the *Methodist Times,* called for Parnell's resignation. 'What is morally wrong', said Hughes, 'can never be politically right'.[6] Lloyd George told his wife on 1 December that he had been to hear 'another awful onslaught on Parnell' by Hughes at his West London Mission chapel, where 'there were loud cheers'.[7]

Gladstone refused to express moral censure on Parnell, but he was convinced by developing Nonconformist opinion that, in the interests of Liberal and Home Rule cohesion, Parnell should resign.[8] On 24 November he sent Morley a letter, published the following day, advocating Parnell's resignation: 'notwithstanding the splendid services rendered by Mr. Parnell to his country, his continuance at the present moment in the leadership would be productive of consequences disastrous in the highest degree to the cause of Ireland'. If Parnell continued, Gladstone's own leadership, linked so closely to Home Rule, would become 'almost a nullity'.[9]

The Irish Home Rule MPs unanimously re-elected Parnell as leader on 25 November, but the publication of Gladstone's letter later that day caused a marked change of opinion among them. Another meeting was convened, beginning on 1 December. On 6 December Parnell was opposed by forty-four votes to twenty-nine, the majority (together with some absentees) forming the 'anti-Parnellite' party led by Justin McCarthy. Parnell then strove to resist this conclusion and retain his leadership until he died in October 1891.

The Nonconformist reaction against Parnell influenced the Catholic. W. T. Stead intended his attack on Parnell to appeal to 'Catholic Ireland' as well as 'Nonconformist England'. He visited Cardinal Manning, who was initially cautious but soon declared that Parnell should go.[10] On 19 November Manning wrote two letters to Archbishop Walsh of Dublin, saying in the first that he hoped Parnell would resign and in the second that English feeling, especially among Nonconformists, was rising rapidly against the Irish leader. On 21 November Manning urged Gladstone to persuade Parnell to retire. Michael Davitt, an ex-Fenian convict, wrote to Walsh on 20 November that, if

---

[5] Quoted Bebbington, *Nonconformist Conscience,* 100. Cf. J. Kent, 'Hugh Price Hughes and the Nonconformist Conscience', in G. V. Bennett and J. D. Walsh (eds.), *Essays in Modern English Church History in Memory of Norman Sykes* (London, 1966), 189–90.

[6] Quoted H. F. Lovell Cocks, *The Nonconformist Conscience* (London, 1943), 7.

[7] Bebbington, op. cit. 100–1; Morgan, *Letters,* 39.

[8] J. F. Glaser, 'Parnell's Fall and the Nonconformist Conscience', *Irish Historical Studies,* xii (1960–1), 119–38.

[9] Morley, op. cit. iii. 437. See C. C. O'Brien, *Parnell and his Party, 1880–1890* (Oxford, 1957), 283 ff.

[10] Morley to Gladstone, 19 Nov. 1890; GP, 44256, fos. 79–80.

Parnell insisted on remaining, 'there is no more hope of Home Rule being won at the General Election than there is of the Queen sending for me to form a Cabinet'. If Parnell was re-elected leader of the party it was 'goodby for *this* generation to Home Rule, and God help Ireland'.[11]

The Irish Catholic Bishops were shocked by the divorce verdict and their leaders soon joined in the call for Parnell's resignation. One of them wrote: 'I can but look forward with dismay to our interests, religious as well as civil, being placed under the guidance of a convicted adulterer'. They opposed the initial inclination of the Home Rule MPs, and doubtless hoped to increase their influence in the party as Manning urged them to do.[12] Archbishop Croke of Cashel thought at first that a temporary withdrawal by Parnell from Parliament might suffice as a compromise. Walsh strove to persuade Parnell to retire but without success. On 29 November Croke stated in a telegram to Justin McCarthy that, if Parnell did not retire, the party would be seriously damaged, the alliance between Home Rulers and Liberals destroyed, and Home Rule indefinitely postponed. On 3 December the standing committee of Irish Catholic Bishops issued a pronouncement against the fitness of Parnell, on moral and political grounds, to remain as leader.[13]

The tendency of Irish Catholic opinion in Great Britain was also against Parnell. An overwhelming majority of the Irish National League branches opposed him, and loyalty to McCarthy's leadership was affirmed at local conventions. But dissidents formed a Parnellite League which, although weak, developed a few branches and removed some support from the main nationalist organization.[14]

The crisis had important political effects. It strengthened clerical influence in the Home Rule party and endorsed Nonconformist influence in the Liberal party. It depressed the Liberals—'we are as low in our luck as we well can be', noted one Liberal in April 1891; and heartened the Unionists—'it is extraordinarily amusing while it lasts', A. J. Balfour said of the upheaval, which Unionists saw as an opportunity to win more Nonconformist support.[15] With the Home Rule forces in disarray, Lloyd George thought the chance had come for Welsh disestablishment to be urged as the main Liberal policy. This cause received encouragement on 20 February 1891, when a motion by Pritchard Morgan was defeated by another reduced majority of only thirty-two. Gladstone, supposedly under Rendel's persuasion,[16] for the first time spoke and

[11] Larkin, *Roman Catholic Church*, 211–12, 217.

[12] Ibid. 214–16, 222, 229.

[13] M. Tierney, *Croke of Cashel: The Life of Archbishop T. W. Croke, 1823–1902* (Dublin, 1976), 236–8; P. J. Walsh, *William J. Walsh, Archbishop of Dublin* (Dublin and Cork, 1928), 406 ff.

[14] Wollaston, 'Irish Nationalist Movement', 65–7. Cf. I. Wood, 'Irish Immigrants and Scottish Radicalism, 1880–1906', in I. MacDougall (ed.), *Essays in Scottish Labour History* (Edinburgh, 1978), 75.

[15] R. C. Munro Ferguson to Rosebery, 27 Apr. 1891; RP, 10017, fo. 234; Larkin, op. cit. 227.

[16] D. Cregier, *Bounder from Wales: Lloyd George's Career before the First World War* (Missouri, 1976), 47.

voted in favour. The Church in Wales, he said, was expanding most creditably, but Nonconformists formed the majority of the Welsh people. Chamberlain, six other Liberal Unionists, and forty-eight Irish Home Rulers voted for the motion.[17]

The recent twists in the Home Rule saga had shaken the Liberals, and party leaders could not agree on details of Home Rule policy.[18] But this question kept its priority among Liberal aims, and Liberal by-election victories continued. It was noted at the NLF meeting in October 1891 that Liberals had gained twenty seats, and lost only one, since the 1886 election.[19] This meeting placed Home Rule at the head of the large, diverse compendium of reforms which became known as the Newcastle Programme and on which the Liberals intended to fight the next general election. Second on the list was Welsh disestablishment. Scottish disestablishment had to be content with inclusion in a more general resolution.

The Welsh voluntaries had been encouraged by the small majority against their cause in the Commons. A Campaign Committee was formed, which appealed for support in a May manifesto and conferred with Carvell Williams at Shrewsbury in August about arranging meetings in England in co-operation with the Liberation Society.[20] Conversely, a letter of the Church Defence Institution in October called for immediate counteraction by means of speeches and leaflets. 'On the events of the next twelve months will largely depend the future of the National Church. The attack is directed against the Established Church not only in Wales but in England.'[21] Chamberlain, however, accurately predicted the fate of the Voluntary proposals: 'Scotch disestablishment and Welsh disestablishment like a pair of disconsolate sisters must wait unconsoled in the lobby'. He himself thought the Church would do better without bondage to the State and hoped that Churchmen would come to agree with this, but he accepted that Unionists would not take up the question and advised the Welsh to concentrate more on social reforms.[22]

In 1892 a motion for Welsh disestablishment was lost in the Commons by forty-seven votes on 23 February, and one for Scots disestablishment by fifty-six on 24 May. Samuel Smith, the Presbyterian MP for Flint who moved the first of these, said that 'every argument that justified the Disestablishment and Disendowment of the Church in Ireland holds equally good in Wales'. Lloyd George claimed that Nonconformity had never been so prosperous and influential in Wales, and Harcourt said establishment was a source of weakness to the Church. But one opponent insisted there was a steady flow towards the

[17] H ccl. 1241–318; AR cxxxiii (1891), 39–41.
[18] Barker, Gladstone and Radicalism, 74.
[19] NLF: Proceedings in Connection with 14th Annual Meeting (London, n.d.), 29.
[20] Pamphlet dated 27 May 1891, in Rendel Papers, 19446E, fo. 33, also ibid. V. 5; LS, 21 Sept. 1891; A/LIB/8, 128.
[21] From printed report in Benson Papers, vol. 149, fos. 3–4.
[22] Garvin and Amery, Chamberlain, ii. 519; T, 14 Oct. 1891.

Church in Wales, and Balfour said the voluntary desire was not disestablishment so much as the removal of Church endowments.[23] The Scottish motion, proposed by Cameron, supported by Campbell-Bannerman, and opposed by Balfour, was countered by an amendment of R. B. Finlay that Scots Presbyterian union should take place within a national Church. Finlay's motion succeeded at the expense of Cameron's.[24] The Liberation Society looked forward to increased support from the general election results.[25] At the end of June Salisbury advised the Queen to dissolve Parliament, and the election was held in July.

Home Rule, being still the main political question, was the leading issue of the contest. Unionists tried to win over Nonconformists and others by stressing once again the supposed threat of Roman Catholic domination in Ireland to the civil and religious liberties of Protestants. Salisbury, Chamberlain, and others played this 'Orange' card as much as the Government's social reform record, and Catholic Unionists like the Duke of Norfolk were accused of association with an anti-Catholic campaign.[26] Chamberlain tried especially to influence Nonconformists, as did the Irish Protestants whether in the Ulster Convention of 17 June or in an appeal sent by non-episcopal Protestant ministers to every Nonconformist minister in Great Britain. This appeal said that the Catholic hierarchy was determined 'to compel obedience . . . in temporal as well as in spiritual matters'. An Irish Parliament would threaten Protestant religious liberties, for most of its members would be 'elected on the nomination of the Roman Catholic priests'.[27]

Protestant and Unionist bodies in Britain were not slow to take up this theme. The Scottish Reformation Society addressed Scots electors on the great need 'to take an active, resolute, and prayerful part' in the coming contest, in order to resist 'the insidious designs of the Papacy, especially in Ireland'. A speaker at a Protestant Alliance meeting said 'at least eighty constituencies might be represented in the new House of Commons by good, sound Protestants if the men and the money could be got'. The Liverpool Protestant Alliance tried to put 'Protestantism before politics' and questioned candidates on their attitude to Ritualism as well as Roman Catholicism. Sir George Chubb chaired a London Unionist meeting where speakers called on more Nonconformists to vote against Home Rule.[28]

Firm denials of course came from Liberals and Irish nationalists that popish persecution would follow Home Rule. T. P. O.Connor told a Liberal meeting

    [23] H, 4th ser., i. 1033–125.
    [24] Ibid. v. 1735–83.
    [25] LS, 7 Mar. 1892; A/LIB/8, 158.
    [26] Glasgow Observer, 21 May, p. 4; Bebbington, Nonconformist Conscience, 95, 102.
    [27] AR cxxxiv (1892), 98–9. Cf. H. M. Bompas, 'Nonconformists and Home Rule', FR lii (July–Dec. 1892), 6–12.
    [28] Scotsman, 2 July, p. 2; The Rock, 27 May, p. 11; Waller, Democracy and Sectarianism, 126; Bebbington, op. cit. 102.

at Chester that there was no danger of religious intolerance. An ex-chairman of the Congregational Union said, in a *Daily News* article, that the Liberal party would only accept a Home Rule measure which safeguarded Protestant rights and forbade a religious establishment. Gladstone also, addressing a gathering of leading Nonconformists at Guinness Rogers' house on 18 June, denied the claims of the Ulster appeal but said that 'clerical power is too great in Ireland, and great fears consequently arise'.[29] Harcourt, speaking at a Liberal demonstration in Manchester, could see no danger from anti-Protestant intolerance, but if it did occur the authority of the imperial Parliament would check it. A reply from Nonconformist ministers to the Ulster address, signed by Hughes, Clifford, and others, said 'the idea of a homogeneous Roman Catholic Parliament in Ireland bent on the Oppression of Protestants appears to us simply an ugly dream'. They were indeed Protestants, but their Protestantism made them zealous for the independence of subject nationalities.[30]

The organization of the Irish Catholic vote in this country to the maximum advantage was the aim of the Irish National League of Great Britain. In May the League's central executive urged all branches to try and poll 'every Irish vote' and assist in the general Liberal canvass. Every branch area should be divided into sub-districts, 'to each of which there should be allotted a good man, who would so devote himself to it . . . that on the day of the election he would be able to bring up every possible voter'. All Irish electors were advised to vote for the official Liberal candidate, but this advice caused local objections if the candidate was not thought satisfactory.[31] The Catholic *Glasgow Observer* indicated the advantage of returning a large Liberal majority. A small majority would indeed make Liberals more dependent on the Irish vote and rivet them to Home Rule, but the largest possible support for a Home Rule bill was needed in the Commons in order to contend with opposition in the Lords.[32]

Catholic political divisions should be prevented or minimized. The League's annual convention at Bradford on 4 June discussed whether the Parnellite minority in the Home Rule party should be conciliated or crushed, but came to no decision. Labour questions, the *Glasgow Observer* agreed, were important to the mainly working-class Catholics, but they must put Home Rule first. This paper would not support 'the selfish and inopportune action of those who seek at this juncture to sacrifice the welfare of a nation to the caprice of a class'. Irish anger at Labour intervention was understandable, for it could help the Unionists by removing votes from Liberals. The *Glasgow Observer* also advised that the need to preserve and strengthen denominational education, important though it was, should not deflect Catholics from voting Liberal. Any attempt at

---

[29] *DN*, 20 June, pp. 7–8, 27 June, p. 4; *AR*, cxxxiv (1892), 102–3.

[30] *DN*, 22 June, p. 5; 29 June, p. 5; also 28 June, p. 5. Cf. L. W. Brady, *T. P. O'Connor and the Liverpool Irish* (London, 1983), 136.

[31] *Glasgow Observer*, 21 May, p. 3, 14 May, p. 3, 11 June, p. 8; *DN*, 1 July, p. 3.

[32] *Glasgow Observer*, 28 May, p. 5.

such deflection was 'a Tory device, no matter from what direction it proceeds', 'a red herring across the path of the Catholics of this country'.[33]

The *Rock* newspaper said that candidates should be asked whether they were against disestablishment as well as Home Rule, for disestablishment (it alleged) would benefit Rome in this country just as Home Rule would benefit Rome in Ireland. Disestablishment in Wales and Scotland played a large part in the election, although it was generally recognized as secondary to Home Rule. Gladstone's address to the Midlothian electors said that the 'public sense' in Scotland and Wales had 'constitutionally declared itself against the maintenance of the respective religious Establishments'. A meeting of the London Nonconformist Council on 13 June urged disestablishment first in Wales and Scotland and subsequently in England; and other Nonconformist bodies passed similar resolutions. As early as September 1890 the Liberation Society executive had noted that 199 Liberal candidates favoured general disestablishment and eighty-two more favoured disestablishment in Scotland or Wales or both. Only thirteen opposed disestablishment. The Society prepared nearly 300,000 copies of publications for the election. But no definite electoral stretegy was put forward, and in any case funds were running too low to make such a strategy very effective.[34]

An Anglican who stood unsuccessfully as a Liberal candidate at Christchurch, Hampshire, said that in England disestablishment was 'not ripe', while in Wales and Scotland it was 'just and right'.[35] This appears, from electoral addresses, to have been the attitude of many Liberal candidates although some advocated English disestablishment. The Welsh voluntary campaign had intensified. Chamberlain and other Unionists had no success in an attempt to persuade Welshmen to abandon Gladstone even though many of them were impatient with the priority given to Home Rule. This impatience was perhaps reflected in the revolt of Lloyd George, Samuel Evans and others against Gladstone's wishes over the Clergy Discipline Bill in June. Despite the official primacy of Home Rule, disestablishment seems to have absorbed most electoral attention in Wales.[36] All the Liberal addresses upheld disestablishment, most placing it second to Home Rule but six putting it first. Eight Nonconformist Unionist candidates sponsored by Chamberlain advocated disestablishment.[37]

The Scottish elections were also much influenced by this question, though there was effective resistance from Church defenders. Within the Free Church the conflict over establishment was heightened by theological differences. A Declaratory Act was finally adopted by that Church in 1892 which, though

[33] Ibid. 11 June, pp. 4, 6–8, 18 June, p. 4, 14 May, p. 5; Catriona Levy, 'Conservatism and Liberal Unionism in Glasgow, 1874–1912', Ph.D thesis (Dundee, 1983), 242, 245–6; Wood, op. cit. 78.

[34] *Rock*, 17 June, p. 9; *DN*, 24 June, p. 5, 14 June, pp. 5–6, 16 June, p. 3: LS, 22 Sept. 1890; A/LIB/8, 53, 30 May 1892; ibid. 180; *AR* cxxxiv (1892), 110; Hamer, *Electoral Pressure*, 159–60.

[35] *DN*, 22 June, p. 6.

[36] R. R. Thomas, 'The Influence of the "Irish Question" on Welsh Politics, 1880–1895', chap. IV, 1–8; *DN*, 20 June, p. 7; *AR* cxxxiii (1891), 228–9.

[37] Morgan, *Wales in British Politics*, 118.

acceptance of its provision was not compulsory, said that the Church did not regard the Confession of Faith (the Westminster Confession) as teaching predestination. The Act drew opposition from the Free Church minority which opposed disestablishment; there was a small secession to form a Free Presbyterian Church, but most of the opponents stayed in the Free Church. During the election several Liberal candidates, including Gladstone, Campbell-Bannerman, and Asquith, said they were for disestablishment. 'In 1890 I fell into the ranks behind Dr. Cameron, and in those ranks I remain', said Gladstone.[38]

But there was strong opposition. Some candidates (not all of them Unionist) supported the establishment, sermons were given in favour of Church defence and church collections were raised for it. The Church Interests Committee of the Church of Scotland emphasized the strength and conciliation of that Church and condemned the attempt to 'smuggle' disestablishment through Parliament 'under the cover of Home Rule'. The question should be put to the Scottish people separately from the Irish issue. The Laymen's League urged electors to use their voting power to support the establishment and encourage the formation of 'a reunited National Presbyterian Church'. The Dundee Church Establishment Association issued a circular to each elector in the city, asking him to vote for candidates who were against disestablishment. A crowded assembly of the Free Church minority in Ross opposed disestablishment as violating the principle of national recognition of religion.[39] Asquith, standing in East Fife, found 'the Kirk [of Scotland], who is a vigorous old lady, scratching and kicking at me like a muscular virago'.[40]

Religious attitudes were prominent in this election because of the tensions between Unionist and Irish organizations over Home Rule and because of disestablishment, temperance, and other issues. Nonconformist ministers sat on Liberal platforms, and in Scotland, according to one radical account, 'every parish manse has been a Tory Committee room; very many pulpits have been turned into Conservative platforms; collections at the church doors have been taken practically on behalf of Tory candidates'.[41] Adherence to disestablishment, and to Home Rule, no doubt assisted some Liberal candidates and hindered others. The loss of Roxburghshire to a Liberal was attributed to disestablishment. It was suggested that R. B. Finlay lost Inverness District because voluntaries made 'a special set' at him. On the other hand, Church defence was a major explanation given for the remarkable fall in Gladstone's

[38] Dundee Advertiser, 1 July, p. 7, 6 July, p. 6.
[39] To the People of Scotland: Address by the Committee on Church Interests of the General Assembly of the Church of Scotland (Edinburgh, 1892); The Laymen's League and the General Election; Laymen's League Office (Edinburgh, 1892); Arthur Elliot to James Melrose, 29 Apr. 1892; Elliot Papers; Scotsman, 1 July, pp. 1, 10, 2 July, p. 5, 12; Dundee C. of S. Presbytery Minutes, 27 June; CH2/103/24, p. 507; Dundee Advertiser, 4 July, pp. 5–6.
[40] Quoted G. I. T. Machin, 'Voluntaryism and Reunion, 1874–1929', in N. Macdougall (ed.), Church, Politics, and Society: Scotland, 1408–1929 (Edinburgh, 1983), 227.
[41] The People's Journal (Dundee), 16 July.

majority in Midlothian from 4,631 in 1885 (when he was last opposed) to 690.[42]
In Wales and Monmouthshire the six Liberal gains were probably mainly
attributable to disestablishment. The Irish vote, however, was an important
explanation for at least twenty Liberal gains throughout Great Britain. 'The
Romanists and Socialists', said *The Rock*, 'have between them given Mr.
Gladstone his majority'.[43]

The combination of 269 Conservatives and forty-six Liberal Unionists
returned in the election easily exceeded the 274 Liberals. But the latter were
able to form a Government with the support of eighty-one Irish nationalists
after the Salisbury ministry had fallen in the new Parliament on a no confidence
motion on 11 August.[44] The Liberals were committed to introducing Home
Rule despite a majority of seventy-one returned from England (and sixteen
from Great Britain) against it. They were also committed to Welsh
disestablishment, and perhaps to Scottish. Thirty-one of the thirty-four seats in
Wales and Monmouthshire were now held by Liberals, though Bishop Edwards
pointed out that this bore no relation to the total votes cast: of the registered
electors, 145,818 had voted for Gladstonian candidates, 86,883 for Unionists
(and 81,839 had abstained). Several Liberal gains in Scotland (all except one
from Liberal Unionists) gave the Liberal party fifty out of the seventy-two seats
there, compared with forty-three in 1886. Twenty-two of the Welsh MPs were
Nonconformists, and 177 of the MPs throughout Great Britain (compared with
ninety-five in 1886); 173 members were said to be favourable to disestablishment in general, eighty-nine to disestablishment in Wales and Scotland.[45]

The Liberation Society expressed pleasure at the results, but they cannot
have been nearly so pleasant to Gladstone. Embarrassing and divisive demands
were now being pressed on him, and his majority of forty was not large enough
to allow him to satisfy them in face of the House of Lords. Not surprisingly, the
Unionists showed relief at the result. 'The person most to be pitied is Mr.
Gladstone', wrote Chamberlain to Balfour. 'What a task he has before him!'[46]

IV. LIBERALS IN OFFICE, 1892–1895

Less than three years after Gladstone formed his fourth ministry in August
1892 the Government of his successor, Lord Rosebery, relinquished its difficult
existence and the Unionists resumed their ascendancy for ten years. The
Liberals during their brief period of Government were more noted for failure

[42] James Brunton to Arthur Elliot, 14 July; Elliot Papers; E. R. Wodehouse to Elliot, 20 July (ibid.);
P. W. Campbell (election agent) to Gladstone, 20 July (quoted Kellas, 'The Liberal Party and the
Scottish Church', 42–3).

[43] Wollaston, 'Irish Nationalist Movement', 214–15; *Rock*, 22 July, p. 8.

[44] *AR* cxxxiv (1892), 120.

[45] Morgan, op. cit. 119; A. G. Edwards, *A Handbook on Welsh Church Defence*, 3rd edn. (London,
1895), 21; Heyck, *Dimensions of British Radicalism*, 264; P. Carnegie Simpson, *The Life of Principal
Rainy* (2 vols., London, 1909), ii. 148; W. H. Mackintosh, *Disestablishment and Liberation* (London,
1972), 301.   [46] 19 July; BP, 49773, fo. 54.

than success, sections of their supporters being disappointed by the fall of a Home Rule bill, Welsh and Scots disestablishment measures, and Local Veto bills to limit the drink trade. The return of the Unionists in 1895 promised there would be no early success for these aims.

By 1892 the Evangelical Free Church council movement was beginning to give a greater interdenominational co-ordination to Nonconformity than it had ever possessed. Beginning in Hampshire in the late 1870s, the formation of Free Church councils representing local Dissenting chapels spread slowly at first but later very rapidly. There were only four councils in 1889, but about 125 more by March 1895 and a total of about 600 by 1899. The councils differed enormously in strength, the smallest representing perhaps only two village chapels, but they all formed the groundwork on which were built county federations, annual congresses, and a National Council. In the late 1880s prominent Nonconformists such as Hugh Price Hughes, Percy Bunting and J. B. Paton began to advocate the foundation of a national federation. In 1890 Hughes invited Guinness Rogers, a Congregationalist, to suggest in the *Methodist Times* the holding of an annual Free Church Congress to parallel the Church Congress of the establishment. A London Nonconformist Council was founded in June 1891, and by the autumn of that year plans were afoot for a national Free Church congress. The first annual Congress was held at Manchester in November 1892; members of nearly all orthodox Dissenting denominations were present but the highest proportion was Congregationalist. A second congress was held at Leeds in 1894 and a third at Birmingham in 1895. Large financial contributions, especially from the Quaker George Cadbury and his brother Richard enabled a permanent organization, the National Council of the Evangelical Free Churches, to be established at the Nottingham congress in 1896. The Revd Thomas Law, a minister of the United Methodist Free Churches, became the Council's enthusiastic organizing secretary.

The movement was an important expression of Dissenting strength, and the insistence on 'Free Churchmanship' reflected a desire for a more positive image than was provided by the negative title of 'Nonconformist'. Current ecumenical tendencies and the wish for social and moral improvement were forceful contributions to the movement, as was the desire to stress the religious beliefs of Evangelicalism and support for disestablishment and the board schools. Many conservative Wesleyans and others did not wish the Free Church Council to become another political organ advocating disestablishment, but they were opposed by radical Wesleyans led by Hughes and by many Congregationalists and Baptists, and the Council tended to become such an organ until about 1910.[47]

Anti-Ritualism, it was said, helped the growth of the Free Church council

[47] Bebbington, *Nonconformist Conscience*, 61–74; E. K. H. Jordan, *Free Church Unity: A History of the Free Church Council Movement, 1896–1941* (London, 1956), 20–51; Gardiner, *The Life of George Cadbury* (London, 1923), 174–87; J. S. Drummond, *Charles A. Berry, DD: A Memoir* (London, 1899), 112–18.

movement. A more pointedly anti-Ritualist society, the National Protestant Church Union, was formed in May 1893 and had local branches and its own magazine. It aimed to provide a rallying point 'for those who, without resorting to litigation, desire to use all possible means to maintain in the Church of England the principles of the Reformation'. The Union's objects included the election of Protestant Churchmen as MPs and members of Convocation, Houses of Laymen, and other Church bodies, and resistance to 'all attempts to deprive the Constitution and Institutions of the country of their Protestant character, and the laity of their rights'.[48] A National Protestant Congress met at Edinburgh in October 1894; and Walter Walsh, editor of the *Protestant Observer*, produced a work entitled *The Secret Work of the Ritualists* from a lecture he had given in Edinburgh in March that year under the auspices of the Protestant Truth Society. The work indicted the Ritualist societies and called on all Protestants to resist their 'gigantic conspiracy'.[49] An example of the use of anti-Ritualism to promote disestablishment was shown by a resolution of the Synod of the Presbyterian Church of England in 1894 'to protest against the continuance of the Church of England in connection with the State while propagating errors it was established to oppose'.[50]

Lloyd George thought the new 'broken-winded' ministry was 'a combination of ineptitudes'. But Rendel was pleased that Gladstone supported his proposal of a bill to prevent the creation of new interests in the Welsh Church. Rendel wanted this to be a Government measure in order to bind the ministry to Welsh disestablishment. He hoped to follow the Irish precedent of 1868, when the rejection of a suspensory bill by the Lords had led to a general election and a decisive majority for disestablishment. The move would also 'give priority to Wales over Scotland', recognizing the much greater national pressure behind the Welsh demand.[51] At a meeting on 1 December and another on 6 February the Welsh Liberal MPs decided there would be no compromise over disestablishment. Similar sentiments were expressed at the NLF meeting at Liverpool on 19 and 20 January.[52] On the side of Church defence Bishop Edwards summoned English aid by warning in a speech at Shrewsbury that the Welsh disestablishment demand was 'an attempt to attack the Church of England as a whole and to shatter her power by disintegration'.[53]

[48] *Monthly Record of the National Protestant Church Union*, no. 6 (June 1893), no. 16 (Apr. 1894).
[49] Walter Walsh, *The Secret Work of the Ritualists*, Protestant Truth Society (London 1895), 44. Cf. Revd W. H. Carwithen, *Is Ritualism in the Church of England Popular Among the Masses?* (London, 1894).
[50] *Digest of the Proceedings of the Synod of the Presbyterian Church of England, 1876–1905* (London, 1907), 600–1.
[51] Morgan, op. cit. 122–3; Lloyd George to S. T. Evans, 19 Aug. 1892 (W. R. P. George, *Lloyd George, Backbencher* (Llandysul 1983), 99–100); Rendel to Gee, 3 Oct.; Gee Papers, 8308D, fo. 274; quoted G. V. Nelmes, 'Stuart Rendel and his Contribution to the Development of a Distinctively Welsh Political Programme Within the Liberal Party Between 1880 and 1895', MA thesis (Wales, 1977), 121; Rendel to Gee, 4 Nov.; Gee Papers, 8308D, 275.
[52] *NLF: Proceedings at 15th Annual Meeting* (London, 1893), 32, 44, 66–74.
[53] George, op. cit. 118; *Oswestry and Border Counties Advertiser*, 18 Jan. 1893.

The very long 1893–4 Parliamentary session was dominated by protracted debates on the Home Rule Bill. Fears were expressed inside and outside Parliament about the 'inadequate' securities for the Protestant minority.[54] The Lords, containing still fewer Liberals than before 1886, trounced the bill by 419 votes to forty-one, and Gladstone expressed his disgust that no Bishop had voted for it.[55] Amid the clamour little hearing was obtained for the Welsh Suspensory Bill. This was brought into the Commons on 23 February 1893 by the Home Secretary, Asquith, who admitted it was a first step towards disestablishment and disendowment. He was sharply attacked by Lord Randolph Churchill who, ailing as he was, seemed momentarily to have regained his old vigour. Churchill accused the Government of introducing the measure merely to gain voters for Home Rule, and his speech provoked Gladstone into defending the bill more vigorously than had been expected. The bill passed its first reading by a substantial majority of fifty-six, partly owing to the abstention of Chamberlain and some other Liberal Unionists.[56]

The Queen reacted strongly after reading the report of the debate, especially Asquith's speech. She complained to Gladstone that he was taking 'the *first step towards* the *disestablishment* and *disendowment* of the *Church* of England!! . . . this measure is *in reality directed against* the *whole Church*'. Gladstone must pause before trying to disestablish part of a Church 'of which *she* is the *Head*'. This produced Gladstone's comment (sent not to the Queen but to Asquith, along with Victoria's letter) that 'the Queen's studies have not yet carried her out of the delusive belief that she is still by law the "head" of the Church of England'. To the Queen he said that Asquith assured him he had used no language which treated the bill as being a first step towards disestablishment of the Church of England.[57]

Forceful protests also came from petitioners (370,005 allegedly in Wales alone);[58] from a circular issued by the Duke of Westminster, the Earl of Selborne, and others; and from meetings in Wales and Manchester, Chichester, and Tynemouth, and a great gathering at the Albert Hall on 16 May, chaired by Archbishop Benson and attended by over 8,000 clergy and laity. Benson, encouraged by Salisbury, had succeeded in getting ten churchwardens from each Archdeaconry to attend this meeting, which was addressed to great applause by Selborne, the Duke of Argyll (a Church of Scotland member) and

[54] *AR* cxxxv (1893), 107–44, 157–63; Waller, op. cit. 138.

[55] Gladstone to Rosebery, 11 Sept.; RP, 10027, fo. 43; Gladstone to MacColl, 12 Sept. (G. W. E. Russell (ed.), *Malcolm MacColl: Memoirs and Correspondence* (London, 1914), 259–60).

[56] H, 4th ser., ix. 204–87; D. R. Brooks, 'Gladstone's Fourth Ministry, 1892–1894', Ph.D. thesis (Cambridge University, 1975), 144–5; Sir A. Griffith-Boscawen, *Fourteen Years in Parliament* (London, 1907), 25; Eluned Owen, *The Early Life of Bishop Owen* (Llandysul, 1958), 142–3; Morgan, op. cit. 133 ff.

[57] P. Guedalla (ed.), *The Queen and Mr Gladstone* (2 vols., London, 1933), ii. 465–6; P. Magnus, *Gladstone* (London, 1954), 410; Gardiner, *Harcourt*, ii. 233–5; Morgan, 135.

[58] Owen, op. cit. 149.

Bishops Temple of London and Westcott of Durham.[59] The Albert Hall meeting was held to promote opposition before a possible debate on the bill in the Lords, but no time was found to go beyond the first reading in the Commons, and the bill was formally withdrawn on 18 September.

Opposition in Parliament was later shown particularly by the Church Parliamentary Committee or 'Church Party' (or the 'Black Brigade' to its opponents). This was formed in November 1893 to defend the Church establishment, support Church reforms, and protect the voluntary schools from the unfriendly administrative pressure allegedly placed on them by A. H. D. Acland, vice-president of the Council with responsibility for education. The immediate reason for the Church party's formation was the Local Government Bill of 1893, which established elective parish councils and reduced the age-old influence of the Church in local government. To the delight of the new group its original provisions were greatly modified in the Lords.[60] Although officially non-aligned in a party political sense, the Church party consisted of back-bench Tory MPs (and a few Liberal Unionists) numbering altogether about sixty. The first chairman was Sir Richard Webster and the second (from 1895 to 1899) was Viscount Cranborne, Salisbury's heir.[61]

Welsh radicals were anxious that the abortive Suspensory Bill should not be the Government's sole step towards disestablishment. A memorial drafted by Lloyd George, dated 26 June and signed by thirty Welsh Liberal MPs (only one refusing) was sent to Gladstone. It aimed to ensure that Welsh disestablishment would be 'the first measure of any magnitude dealt with by the Government after Home Rule' and that other measures would not creep in to displace it. If the policy were suppressed, it was said, several seats in Wales and probably several in strong Nonconformist areas in England would be lost to the Liberals.[62] Gladstone said he could not give a definite reply at present, as the Home Rule Bill was absorbing his attention, but Welsh disestablishment remained an essential part of Liberal plans. 'I don't care for the nature of the reply and we must press him hard', Lloyd George told his wife. 'He will try to get out of it if he can.' Rendel wrote again to Gladstone on 28 July, hoping that he would place in the forefront of next session's programme 'a final and complete measure' of Welsh disestablishment. The premier replied affirmatively, but in terms so circumlocutory that they were almost a self-parody. Lloyd George's still distrustful comment was that 'the old boy refused to pledge

[59] T, 15 Mar., p. 10, 20 Mar., p. 7; AR cxxxv (1893), 164; Defence of the National Church: Report of Proceedings in Albert Hall, 16 May 1893 (London, 1893); Benson, E. W. Benson, ii. 528; A. Westcott, Life and Letters of Brooke Foss Westcott, Sometime Bishop of Durham (2 vols., London, 1903), ii. 171–4; Benson to Salisbury, 17 May 1893; SP.
[60] AR cxxxv (1893), 254–6; Benson, op. cit. ii. 69–70; LS, 30 Apr. 1894; A/LIB/8, 295.
[61] A. I. Taylor, 'The Church Party and Popular Education, 1893–1902', Ph.D. thesis (Cambridge, 1981); Griffith-Boscawen, Memories (London, 1925), 70–5; K. Rose, The Later Cecils (London, 1975), 95–102.
[62] Copy of memorial in S. T. Evans Papers, 185.

himself'.[63] But Lloyd George, though soon to become a rebel himself, would not support a move to separate the Welsh Liberals immediately from the main party, and a meeting of Welsh Liberal MPs rejected this by fourteen to seven on 1 September. The same meeting carried a more moderate motion by Lloyd George, seconded by Ellis (now a Government whip) that the Welsh members would reconsider their position if a Welsh disestablishment measure were not favourably placed in next session's ministerial programme. The Government was soon preparing a full disestablishment and disendowment measure, and Asquith consulted Gladstone on the subject.[64] By 30 November a bill had been drafted, and Lloyd George's opinion of Gladstone had changed. 'The old man has himself taken the business in hand . . . He is full of it. That is a good sign that the Government are really in earnest.'[65]

Gladstone was also disposed to try and carry Scots disestablishment, which was less strongly demanded than Welsh but had the advantage of touching much less directly the establishment in England. Early in 1893 the Queen's Speech expressed ministerial intentions to introduce a suspensory bill for Scotland, but this was not done. Dr Cameron brought in another private bill, which was supported or opposed by petitions from Scottish Church bodies and passed its first reading by sixty-six on 9 May, Gladstone voting in favour. But Rainy declared that only a Government bill would satisfy him, and Cameron's measure made no more progress.[66]

The 1894 session took the question no further. Because of the Queen's opinions, the Government again expressed vague though favourable intentions towards Scots and Welsh disestablishment on 12 March. On the Scots question only another private bill was introduced by Cameron, supported by Ministers and obtaining the expected mixed reception in Scotland. Rosebery, successor to Gladstone who had resigned on 3 March, spoke for disestablishment in Edinburgh on 17 March. But he trod warily, presenting the subject purely as a matter of political expediency. The State was as entitled to maintain an established Church as a standing army, but 'seeing that nearly every manse of the Established Church had become an agency for the Tory party, he was compelled to own that the continuance of the Establishment and of the Liberal party in Scotland, side by side, was coming to be inconsistent'.[67] Rainy called this a 'great speech', but strong protests came from Liberal Church of Scotland ministers against Rosebery's representation of the Church as Tory. Cameron,

[63] Grigg, *The Young Lloyd George*, 134–5; Gladstone to Rendel, 5 July 1893, copy; GP, 44549, fo. 101; Lloyd George to his wife, 5 July and 7 Aug.; Morgan, *Letters*, 60–1; Rendel to Gladstone, 28 July; S. T. Evans Papers, 185; Gladstone to Rendel, 8 Aug. ibid.; Gladstone to Carvell Williams, 14 Aug., GP, Letter-books, 44549, fos. 114–15.

[64] Morgan, op. cit. 140; Grigg, op. cit. 135–6; Cregier, *Bounder from Wales*, 49; T. E. Elliss to D. R. Daniel, 3 Sept.; Daniel Papers, 41b; G. V. Nelmes, op. cit. 130. Asquith's notes on preparation of the bill, and a printed draft of the measure, are in AP lxiv.

[65] Lloyd George to William George, 24 Nov.; George, op. cit. 122; Morgan, op. cit. 140–3.

[66] Kellas, op. cit. 43; Gladstone to Cameron, 17 Apr.; GP, 44549, fo. 81; *AR* cxxxv (1893), 237.

[67] *AR* cxxxvi (1894), 78.

whose bill did not reach a second reading, told Rosebery it was important for the Government to commit itself to a definite disestablishment measure otherwise its general support would be condemned as 'mere kite-flying'.[68]

Despite these hopes at the end of 1893, disappointment was the lot of the Welsh radicals in 1894 and Lloyd George was getting rebellious. In January he persuaded the Liberation Society executive to issue a circular to electors in the Horncastle (Lincolnshire) by-election, urging them not to vote for H. J. Torr, an Anglican Liberal and Church reformer who would not pledge himself satisfactorily to disestablishment. 'We mean to beat this fellow and humble Church insolence', he told his brother. 'They treat Nonconformity as if it were a footstool to power.'[69] The Liberal leaders were annoyed by the Society's action, and Carvell Williams was embarrassed. Torr was defeated, but as the Liberal vote slightly increased the Society's intervention apparently had little effect.[70]

When several Welsh MPs saw Harcourt, leader of the Commons, on 16 March they were told that a disestablishment bill would be introduced and that he thought it could be passed through the lower House that session. This reply was considered fairly satisfactory. But, perhaps impressed by a large drop in the Liberal majority in a Montgomeryshire by-election at the end of March, when a candidate he thought too moderate squeezed home, Lloyd George became decidedly militant and talked of breaking loose from Liberal toils. He told a receptive meeting of his Caernarvonshire constituents on 14 April that Harcourt had declined to give a definite pledge that disestablishment would be carried through all its stages in the Commons that session. The Welsh radical MPs must 'stand on the ground of independency and tell the Government that they would not receive Welsh support to break their pledges to Wales'. In a remark perhaps aimed at stirring up Asquith (a lapsed Congregationalist) he said that the Cabinet contained a few who were originally Nonconformists but who 'left their Nonconformity behind them immediately they came in contact with the atmosphere of London society'. A motion of support for Lloyd George was carried almost unanimously at the meeting, and next day he gave Tom Ellis notice that he, Frank Edwards, and D. A. Thomas would refuse the party whip. Herbert Lewis soon decided to join them, and by early May the brief 'Welsh revolt' had taken shape. But, despite much Press support, it remained 'a revolt of the Four'—the majority of Welsh Liberal MPs isolated them by remaining loyal to the Government. The independent Welsh party on Irish lines which Lloyd George had said he wanted to create before the next election was not to

---

[68] Rainy to Rosebery, 19 Mar. 1894; RP, 10148, fo. 20; Revd Alexander Macleod to Rosebery, 20 Mar.; ibid. fos. 22–3; Revd J. C. Carrick to Rosebery, 20 Mar.; ibid. 24–7; Cameron to Rosebery, 16 June; ibid. 39–40. Cf. Revd Benjamin Martin to Rosebery, 28 June; ibid. 49–50; Revd David Mitchell to Rosebery, 17 July; ibid. 55–6.

[69] Lloyd George to William George, 4 Jan. 1894; George, op. cit. 130.

[70] Hamer, *Electoral Pressure*, 160–1; Bebbington, op. cit. 23; Morgan, op. cit. 65–6.

be, though he and his associates inspired the founding of many branches of a new nationalist *Cymru Fydd* (Young Wales) League.[71]

Meanwhile the Government measure had been redrafted four times during April and, emerging similar to the Irish disestablishment bill of 1869, was introduced by Asquith on the 26th. The Church in the Principality and Monmouthshire would be disestablished from 1 January 1896, Welsh Bishops would be excluded from the Lords and Welsh Bishops and clergy from Convocation. Tithe would be vested in the county councils and put to public and charitable use. The new parish councils would take control of parish burial grounds. Property given to the Church since 1703 would remain in the Church's hands. The bill was necessary, said Asquith, because the Church in Wales was 'not accepted as a national institution by the vast bulk of the people, by whom it is regarded as an aggressive sectarian power'. Hicks Beach, opposing, said the measure was only justifiable if Wales could be considered a separate nation, and he believed Wales had no historical claim to be so considered. Lloyd George, speaking on 30 April, of course took the opposite view, saying the Welsh Church was 'thoroughly anti-national'.[72] The debate was long and the bill was strongly opposed by Bishops and other Church defenders outside Parliament. But the result was an anticlimax. The bill did not reach a second reading and in July the Government withdrew it for the session. Rosebery promised in August that Welsh disestablishment would have first place in the ministerial programme for 1895.[73]

1895 saw further attempts at both Welsh and Scottish disestablishment, and the Government again gave priority to the former. During the autumn of 1894 and until Parliament reopened in February 1895, Rosebery was repeatedly urged by United Presbyterians and Free Churchmen that Ministers should introduce a Government measure of Scots disestablishment. Rainy, the Revd David Mitchell (on behalf of the Disestablishment Council for Scotland), and the Revd Benjamin Martin (on behalf of the United Presbyterian committee on disestablishment) tried to persuade the premier to take this course, prophesying as an alternative the weakening or even the breaking up of Scottish Liberalism. But their efforts gained little reward.[74] Welsh disestablishment was included in

[71] Lloyd George to his wife, 3 May 1894; LGP, NLW 20412C, fo. 425; Grigg, op. cit. 146–9; Rowland, *Lloyd George*, 102–6; Cregier, op. cit. 52–4; *Report of Speeches Delivered at Bangor, 16 May 1894, Reprinted from Carnarvon and Denbigh Herald* (Caernarvon, 1894).

[72] H xxiii. 1455 ff., 1698.

[73] Morgan, op. cit. 145–9; Grigg, op. cit. 149–55; Cregier, op. cit. 51; W. P. Eyton to Rosebery, 1 May 1894, with extract from *Standard*, 30 Apr., on debate in Upper House of Convocation of Canterbury; RP 10094, fos. 10–11; Benson, op. cit. ii. 569, 573; *T*, 19 July 1894, p. 4; L. T. Dibdin, 'Proposed Overthrow of the Church in Wales', *Nineteenth Century*, xxxvi (July–Dec. 1894), 100–10.

[74] Mitchell to Rosebery, 3 and 11 Oct. 1894; 9, 12, and 15 Jan. 1895; RP 10148, fos. 99–100, 108–9, 148–9, 152–5, 158–9; Martin to Rosebery, 16 Oct., 8 Nov., 21 Dec. 1894; ibid. 110–11, 121, 132–3; Martin to Sir John Leng, 1 Nov.; ibid. 116–7; Rainy to Rosebery, 13 Nov. 1894, 15 Jan. 1895; ibid. 125–6, 156–7; Rosebery to Mitchell, 6 Oct. 1894; ibid. 105, 9 Jan. 1895, draft; ibid. 150; Campbell-Bannerman to Rosebery, 16 Jan. 1895; RP, 10003, fos. 53–4; Lord Tweedmouth to Rosebery, 16 Jan.; RP, 10101, fos. 125–7.

the Queen's Speech, Scots disestablishment was not, and Scottish voluntaries were naturally displeased. Rosebery did, however, give his approval to Cameron's bill, and say that shortly the Government would bring in a Scots disestablishment measure. But Sir George Trevelyan, the Scottish Secretary, made clear that the available time would not allow this to happen.[75] Cameron reintroduced his bill on 1 March, but Harcourt stated on the 25th that Ministers could not give facilities for it, and eventually it was announced in June that the bill had been dropped.

In 1894 further discussions had been taking place in Scotland on Presbyterian reunion. Some informal meetings were held between representatives of all the main Churches, but although there was growing desire for a general reunion satisfactory conclusions could not be reached.[76] Greater success was gained by more limited moves to unite the Free and United Presbyterian Churches. These moves recommenced in 1894, encouraged by the already extensive co-operation which had developed between the two Churches. The initiative seems to have been taken by a meeting of the Dundee Free Church laity, members of the office-bearers' union, on 6 March. The chairman spoke of the 'great waste of men and means' and of 'dishonour done to Christianity by a needless and sinful separation', and a motion in favour of union was unanimously adopted.[77] A committee was appointed to take the matter further, and there was a similar move in Glasgow. A *Plea for Union* issued by the Dundee Free Church office-bearers in 1895 urged 'this first step towards the larger union of all Scottish Presbyterians'. It was denied that the aim was to strengthen the disestablishment campaign, which did not have full support in either Church.[78] The question of amalgamation between the two Churches was an important issue until union was achieved in 1900. Although some advocates of union denied the importance of disestablishment in the negotiations, this issue was still a main reason for the opposition of the Free Church minority to union. Opposition was first moved at this time in the General Assembly of 1895, but only forty-two votes were given in support and the motion was easily defeated.[79]

After Rosebery's declaration that there would be an early ministerial measure for Welsh disestablishment had been welcomed by the NLF at Cardiff in January, the Queen's Speech announced the intention to bring in a bill. On 25 February Asquith moved for leave to introduce a measure practically identical

[75] *AR* i (1895), 6; Simpson, op. cit. ii. 151–2; Rosebery to Rainy, 4 May; RP, 10148, fos. 169–71.
[76] Revd James Robertson to A. J. Balfour; BP, 49790, fos. 114–20. Cf. letter of 5 May 1894 in Balfour of Burleigh Papers, bundle 12; Simpson, op. cit. ii. 193.
[77] *Dundee Advertiser*, 7 Mar. 1894.
[78] *A Plea for Union Between the United Presbyterian Church and the Free Church of Scotland, Addressed by the Dundee Free Church Office-bearers to their Brother Office-bearers* (Dundee, 1895). Cf. Dundee Free Presbytery Minutes, 14 Mar. 1894; CH3/91/6, 40–1; D. Woodside, *The Soul of a Scottish Church: Or the Contribution of the United Presbyterian Church to Scottish Life and Religion* (Edinburgh, [1918]), 305–6.
[79] Simpson, op. cit. ii. 195.

to that of 1894. The proposed date of disestablishment was 1 January 1897. There was considerable debate on Asquith's request, alarm being repeatedly expressed by Church defenders that disestablishment in Wales would lead to disestablishment in England. Hicks Beach led the opposition and emphasized that the matter was unreal as far as Parliament was concerned: the attitude of the Lords meant there was no prospect of such a bill getting through.

The measure was read a first time on 28 February, and the second reading passed on 1 April by 304 to 260 after five nights' debate. Asquith and James Bryce, Harcourt, and G. W. E. Russell were among the chief speakers for the bill and Hicks Beach, Goschen, and Balfour took a leading part against. The arguments over disestablishment not only in Wales but, by implication, in England were widely expounded. Some Irish Home Rulers supported the bill, as did Chamberlain, and sixteen Liberal Unionists abstained.[80] Very slow progress was made in committee against determined Unionist opposition. On 20 May Lloyd George moved that a Welsh national council be appointed to redistribute the Church revenues after disestablishment. But this motion was opposed by Asquith; Unionists supported it to embarrass the government, and Lloyd George voted against his own amendment to stop it being carried against Ministers. The motion was lost by ten votes. Gladstone withdrew his pair because he disliked some of the disendowment provisions. The bill was getting into still deeper trouble when the distracted and struggling ministry resigned on 24 June after a narrow defeat on the minor question of cordite supplies for the army.[81]

Within the Church of England, support for Welsh disestablishment came from Liberals such as John Percival, appointed Bishop of Hereford in February 1895. Percival denied that establishment and endowment were essential to the spiritual life of the Church, stressing also the distinct nationality of the Welsh and their clear demand for disestablishment.[82] But Church defence was far more typical of Anglican reactions, whether expressed in a resolution passed against the Welsh bill at a large Oxford meeting in May 1895 or in a pamphlet by the Revd Hensley Henson saying that establishment inflicted no hardship and conferred popular benefits.[83]

Benson did not wish Church defence to be too closely associated with Conservative party interests, and thought a wider and fresher organization than the Church Defence Insitution was needed. After a meeting at Lambeth Palace

[80] H xxx. 1487–551, xxxi. 83–126, 1574–663, 1698–748, xxxii. 49–130, 180–264, 610–99; Morgan, op. cit. 150–1; Garvin and Amery, *Chamberlain*, ii. 603.

[81] Morgan, op. cit. 151 ff.; P. Stansky, *Ambitions and Strategies: The Struggle for the Leadership of the Liberal Party in the 1890s* (Oxford, 1964), 158 ff.; Cregier, op. cit. 55 ff.; Rowland, op. cit. 110–11; Griffith-Boscawen, *Fourteen Years in Parliament*, 60–72; Sir Richard Temple, *The Story of My Life* (2 vols., London, 1896), ii. 293–8.

[82] W. Temple, *The Life of Bishop Percival* (London, 1921), 118–20.

[83] *The Rock*, 24 May 1895, p. 5; H. Hensley Henson, *The Real Aspect of Disestablishment: An Open Letter to Samuel Smith, MP* (London, 1895), 5.

on 5 May 1894, attended by Salisbury, a letter signed by Benson and Archbishop Maclagan of York appeared in *The Times* in July, proposing not a new society but 'the Church acting upon itself for the purpose of extending instruction, information, and encouragement'. The method suggested seemed very like a vast new society, however, with committees of laymen, diocesan and ladies' committees, and, most notably, a committee in every parish open equally to men and women and representing all social classes. It seemed like Benson's answer to the Free Church councils. The work was 'distinct from, but in harmony with, the Church Defence Institution'.[84] Members of the central committee of the new organization included Selborne and Cranbrook, Halifax and Cross, Cranborne and Wolmer, Bishop Edwards, J. G. Talbot, and A. Griffith-Boscawen—displaying a preponderance, it could be alleged, of Conservative interests. Lord Egerton, chairman of the CDI, was among the members of that body who were on the new central committee. Egerton said the new organization was intended to supplement and not supplant the CDI, and to make the latter 'more perfect': there was 'no antagonism whatever between the two bodies'.[85] The CDI and Benson's organization, which was known as the Church Committee for Defence and Instruction, united after considerable controversy in 1896. By February 1895 it was reported that as many as 2,230 parish committees had been formed in connection with the new body.[86]

Church defenders were naturally pleased by the failure of the disestablishment bills, but those who wanted Church reform saw no progress over the question of patronage. Benson's bill to effect certain reforms without removing the right of private patronage was passed by the Lords in May 1893 but made no headway in the Commons. An article in the *Fortnightly Review* condemned the bill as an attack on ancient property rights, 'a sad precedent for those who are aiming at the entire Disestablishment of the Church'.[87] A similar bill, approved by the Bishops and clergy in both Convocations, was read a second time in the Commons in May 1894. It received some Dissenting support in the debate, but went no further. In 1895 a bill designed to prevent the appointment of unfit clergy by giving more power to the Bishops passed its second reading in the Commons in April, but there its progress ceased. Another bill of Benson to reform patronage, resembling the measures of 1893 and 1894, was read a second time in the Lords in May, but petered out after being amended in committee.[88]

V. ELECTION OF 1895

Salisbury formed a coalition ministry when the Liberals resigned. Five Liberal Unionists joined his Cabinet, though some friction still continued, electorally

[84] *T*, 19 July 1894, p. 4; Benson, op. cit. ii. 546–9, 574. Cf. printed leaflet in Benson Papers, vol. 149, fos. 14–15, and Roberts, 'Pressure-group Politics' 578–9.
[85] CDI Central Council Minutes, 22 Nov. 1894 (vol. 206).
[86] Report of 12 Feb. 1895 in Benson Papers, 149, fos. 52–6.
[87] H x. 162–75; R. C. Jenkins, 'The New Patronage Bill', *FR* liii. 543–6.
[88] H xxxii. 843–73, xxxiii. 1141–55, 1686–702.

and otherwise, between the two parties.[89] The new Government sought the backing of the voters and within three weeks a general election commenced. Ministers had no difficulty in overcoming, by a wide margin, the weak resistance of the Liberals who had a diverse and not very popular programme. In 110 seats (excluding Ireland and the universities) no Liberal candidate opposed a Unionist, compared with forty in 1892.[90]

Anti-romanism and anti-Ritualism, disestablishment, education, and Church defence were among the issues figuring in the contests. The interest of Anglo-Catholics such as Lord Halifax in reunion with Rome was causing Protestant alarm. Anti-Ritualist sentiments had recently been aired in the Welsh Church debate in Parliament, when Samuel Smith said that disestablishment would be brought about in the end not by Nonconformists but by the sacerdotalism within the Church.[91]

The Catholic Church appeared to be gaining much confidence in the country. The laying of the foundation stone of a Catholic cathedral at Westminster on 30 June was said by the *Glasgow Observer* to signify that 'the Church has definitely, and for ever, left the obscurity which for so long was her portion, and has come out into the full blaze of day'.[92] The Liberal *Methodist Times* might regard the appointment of the Duke of Norfolk to the ministry as a sign that 'the alliance between Romanism and Conservatism is complete', but anti-Catholic journals usually called on Protestants to vote Conservative in order to frustrate the Liberal-Home Rule alliance. The *Rock* claimed that 'an enormous number of voters view with undisguised alarm the steady growth of Vatican influence in the counsels of the nation. In every constituency our friends must make themselves felt.' The executive committee of the National Protestant Church Union issued an address saying that disestablishment would assist the spread of Ritualism, not prevent it. A manifesto signed by the Orange Grand Master in England called on Orangemen to support only candidates who upheld the Protestant constitution and opposed Home Rule, disestablishment, and 'Romish or Ritualistic education'. A resolution passed at a Protestant Alliance gathering in May wanted electors to require all candidates to pledge themselves against applying national funds to aid Roman or Ritualist teaching. During the election at Blackburn the police had difficulty in preventing physical conflict 'between the Irish and a large body of Tories'.[93]

Irish Catholic electors in Britain were generally urged to support Liberal candidates because of Home Rule. There were fears that they might be won

---

[89] Cf. J. R. Holding, 'An Examination of the Third Salisbury Cabinet, 1895–1902', B.Litt. thesis (Oxford, 1979), 2–3; Henry Chaplin to Chamberlain, 17 Apr. 1895; CP, JC5/13/5; George Peel to Chamberlain, 17 Mar. ibid. JC6/6/1F/9; *AR* i (1895), 121.

[90] E. J. Feuchtwanger, *Democracy and Empire: Britain, 1865–1914* (London, 1985), 221.

[91] H xxxii. 663.

[92] *Glasgow Observer*, 29 June 1895.

[93] *Methodist Times*, 18 July 1895 (quoted É. Halévy, *Imperialism and the Rise of Labour*, trans. E. I. Watkin, 2nd edn. (London, 1951), 189 n.); *The Rock*, 5 July, pp. 8–9; *DN*, 6 July, p. 8, 16 July, p. 7; *Dundee Advertiser*, 6 July, p. 5; *T*, 17 May, 10.

over by the social programme of Labour candidates or the education policy of
Conservatives. The *Glasgow Observer* warned its readers that 'it is Home Rule
or no Home Rule. There are two sides only.'[94] The division between
anti-Parnellites and Parnellites was another complication. A large meeting of
Irish Home Rulers at Newcastle upon Tyne protested at the decision of local
Parnellites to oppose a Liberal candidate, John Morley (who lost his seat).[95]

Disestablishment was again an issue to which radicals were committed in the
contests, though the issue was not, generally speaking, as strong as it had been.
A greater number of Nonconformists, it was stated, voted Unionist.[96] The
Liberation Society executive none the less insisted that 'the tendencies of the
times' were in favour of voluntaryism: advancing democracy was not in keeping
with an 'autocratic' established Church.[97] English disestablishment was
scarcely mentioned by candidates, but Welsh and Scottish were advocated in
numerous Liberal electoral addresses and opposed by many Conservatives.

In Scotland some Unionists said they wanted Presbyterian reunion. Liberals
showed exasperation with the Lords for obstructing their policies: R. B. Haldane told the electors of East Lothian that the Lords were 'little more than a vast
and irresponsible committee of the Conservative party'. To a Conservative
candidate for Pembroke, disestablishment was one of the 'revolutionary
proposals of the Radical Party'. But social questions were also frequently raised
in the election, sometimes in direct competition with disestablishment. The
Labour candidate for Newcastle said that 'the condition of the poor was more
important than such middle class frivolities as disestablishment', and Lloyd
George made clear that social reform was of interest to him as well as
disestablishment and Welsh devolution.[98]

Against voluntary efforts the Church Committee issued a notice advising
parochial and other committees to question the candidates on disestablishment
and circulate their answers throughout their constituencies. It was stressed,
however, that the Church Committee wished to stand outside party politics.[99]
Bishop Edwards, in an article published in July, pointed out that (according to
Nonconformist year-books) only forty-seven per cent of the total Welsh
population was Nonconformist, so 'the Church in Wales is immediately and
directly charged with the whole spiritual provision for more than half the
population'.[1] Similarly the Church Interests Committee of the General

[94] *Glasgow Observer*, 6, 13, 20, and 27 July; Levy, 'Conservatism and Liberal Unionism', 296.
[95] *DN*, 9 July, p. 7.
[96] Bebbington, *Nonconformist Conscience*, 93.
[97] LS, 1 July; A/LIB/8, 363; *DN*, 3 July, p. 5. Cf. Manifesto of Scottish Disestablishment Council;
Dundee Advertiser, 3 July, p. 5.
[98] Haldane Papers, 5904, fo. 41; Parliamentary Election Papers, NLW, 5 July 1895; E. I. Waitt,
'John Morley, Joseph Cowen, and Robert Spence Watson: The Divisions of Liberalism in Newcastle
Politics, 1870–1902', Ph.D. thesis (Manchester, 1972), 439; George, op. cit. 179.
[99] Benson Papers, vol. 149, fos. 138–40; 26 June 1895. Cf. Revd Richard Smith to Cranborne, 8 July
1895; SP, S/4, Box 6; Morton Smith to Cranborne, 10 July; ibid.
[1] *Nineteenth Century*, xxxviii. 124.

Assembly of the Church of Scotland issued an electoral appeal to the Scottish people, stating that the establishment had more churches and 144,000 more members than the Free Church and United Presbyterians combined.[2]

More aid to the voluntary schools was a policy of the Unionist Government, and recent events helped to make education a controversial issue in the election. Disputes had developed in the London School Board over the specifically Christian content of religious instruction in board schools. In March 1894 the board had adopted a circular drawn up by Athelstan Riley, a noted Anglo-Catholic, which provided that teachers should affirm orthodox Christian doctrines in their instruction if they could conscientiously do so. So strong were the protests from teachers and much of the Press, however, that the board decided in April not to add the circular to its official code, though the circular was not withdrawn. The dispute long continued. Anti-romanism played a part in it, and it affected the London School Board election in November. The Nonconformist *Christian World* said this election would 'go a long way to decide whether the England of the future is to be a Protestant nation or a fief of the Papacy', and the *British Weekly* said that growing Ritualist influence must be fought. The London Nonconformist Council issued a manifesto against the 'sacerdotal' party on the board, and viewed with grave concern 'the advance of sacerdotal teaching in the Anglican Church'. The voluntary schools had become a major area in the conflict over Ritualism. The denominationalists lost support in the school board election (though they still had a majority) and the circular was not enforced.[3]

Denominationalists, anxious for relief of the great financial strain suffered by voluntary schools, placed their hopes on Unionist victory in the general election. This was seen, for example, in the electoral activity of the National Association of Voluntary Teachers. Salisbury said at Limehouse in March that it was more probable that 'the church school would eat up the board school than that the board school would eat up the church school'. The Nonconformist *British Weekly* feared that the educational results of a Unionist victory would be 'nothing short of a new establishment and endowment of the Church of England'. The executive committee of the National Education Association said that electors should only support candidates who would maintain the board school system and make public local management a condition of further grants of public money.[4]

Catholics wanted rate aid for their schools, and they were advised by Cardinal Vaughan, by their Bishops and some priests, to put education before Home Rule and vote Conservative. This caused Catholic support to be divided

[2] Dundee Advertiser, 16 July, p. 5.

[3] J. E. B. Munson, 'The London School Board Election of 1894', *British Journal of Educational Studies*, xxiii (1975), 7–17; *T*, 9 Oct. 1894, p. 3; Bishop Frederick Temple to Salisbury, 25 July 1894; SP; Bebbington, op. cit. 134 ff.; J. C. Carlile, *My Life's Little Day* (London, 1935), 109–12; Cruickshank, *Church and State in English Education*, 63–4.

[4] *AR* i (1895), 90; *British Weekly*, 4 July 1895; *DN*, 6 July, p. 8.

between Liberal and Conservative, strained the Nonconformist-Catholic political alliance and threatened some Liberal seats. The Catholic League of South London asked candidates in that area whether they would try and obtain further financial aid for Catholic schools, and received affirmative replies from many but negative replies from some.[5]

The Unionists achieved a sweeping victory in the election. Their majority was 152. There were 340 Conservatives and seventy-one Liberal Unionists against 177 Liberals and eighty-two Irish Home Rulers, but the Home Rulers were bitterly divided and in only precarious alliance with the Liberals. The majority was the largest won by any party since 1832, and the net Liberal loss was about ninety. But the swing of votes to the Unionists in Great Britain was only about three per cent.[6] In Wales the Unionists gained six seats, and in Scotland they gained eight including Sir Charles Cameron's.[7] But the Liberals kept a large majority in Wales, a slim one in Scotland, and could take further consolation from the failure of the Labour threat on their left. Nearly all the former Liberal Ministers who were returned held Scottish or Welsh seats, and perhaps several seats remained Liberal by dint of Irish support.[8]

Many factors contributed to the Liberals' defeat. Some of their measures were widely unpopular, such as the Local Veto Bill;[9] and there was some reduction of Nonconformist support which might have shown decreasing interest in disestablishment. Certainly the Unionist victory meant there was no hope of passing a disestablishment measure for several years, though no one would have foreseen that the Unionists would stay in power for a decade. The Liberals had deliberately tried to pass disestablishment bills on inadequate foundations, having only a small majority in the lower House and a large opposition in the upper. After their electoral defeat they were so weakened in the Commons that it would scarcely be worth while to introduce similar bills in that House for an indefinite period. One local Church defence association, while warning against backsliding into inactivity, rejoiced that the election result would ensure to the Church 'a period of comparative peace'.[10]

---

[5] Bebbington, op. cit. 103; Wollaston, 'Irish Nationalist Movement', 132–7, 219–20; *Glasgow Observer*, 13 July; *DN*, 15 July, p. 7; W. D. Ross, 'Politics and Opinion in Bradford, 1880–1906, with Special Reference to Parliamentary Elections', Ph.D. thesis (Bradford, 1977), 240–1.

[6] Feuchtwanger, op. cit. 221; Garvin and Amery, *Chamberlain*, ii. 641.

[7] *AR* i (1895), 155–6.

[8] Wollaston, op. cit. 220.

[9] Cf. E. Dicey, 'The Rout of the Faddists', *Nineteenth Century*, xxxviii (July–Dec. 1895), 188–98.

[10] Leaflet in Benson Papers, 13 Aug. 1895; vol. 149, fo. 151.

CHAPTER VI

Unionist Rule and Religious Strife, 1895–1905

I. INTRODUCTORY

RADICAL aims such as Home Rule and disestablishment were very far from attainment in the decade from 1895. The Unionist coalition was firmly in power with a large majority, but it proved legislatively weak and failed to pass a major education bill in 1896. This failure was redeemed in 1902, but the ministry enacted few other important social reforms and there was little before the Boer War to enliven a dull political scene.

The Liberal Opposition fell into serious disarray over policy and leadership. Irish Home Rulers continued to be riddled with divisions, but a United Irish League was formed in 1898 (the British Home Rule organization later adopting this name) and Home Rulers officially reunited in 1900 under John Redmond's leadership.[1] The link between Home Rulers and Liberals weakened. Most Liberals probably continued to support Home Rule, but some (including Nonconformists, especially Wesleyans) opposed it and favoured imperial unity. By 1899 the Liberal leaders no longer regarded Home Rule as an immediate party aim. Some Irish voters supported Tory candidates at by-elections, or at least did not vote for Liberals, because Conservatives championed voluntary schools. Other Irish voters were reluctant to support a Liberal who was uncertain on Home Rule.[2] Welsh nationalism fared no better. Lloyd George's attempt to develop a strong Welsh Home Rule movement was defeated in January 1896 when the South Wales Liberal Federation, jealous of its regional independence and mindful of the economic interests of its area, refused to join the North Wales Federation and the Cymru Fydd Leagues in a national organization. Cymru Fydd disintegrated as a result. Welsh Liberal organization was in decay and Welsh radical MPs were demoralized.[3] In 1899 Lloyd George failed to persuade the Welsh Liberal MPs to declare themselves an autonomous branch of the Liberal party.

The position of Nonconformity was ambivalent for ten years or more from 1895. In general a transparent decline in church members had not yet begun, as

[1] F. S. L. Lyons, *The Irish Parliamentary Party, 1890–1910*, new edn. (Westport, Conn., 1975), 38 ff.

[2] H. W. McCready, 'Home Rule and the Liberal Party, 1899–1906', *Irish Historical Studies*, xiii (1962–3), 316 ff.; R. W. Perks to Rosebery, 20 Jan. 1898; RP, 10050, fos. 14–18; Wollaston, 'The Irish Nationalist Movement in Great Britain, 1886–1908', M.A. thesis (London, 1957), 97–9, 220–8.

[3] Morgan, *Wales in British Politics, 1868–1922*, 3rd edn. (Cardiff, 1980), 167–9, 190.

it was to do about 1906. The prosperity of Nonconformists continued to rise. Their social position was becoming more assured, and their ministers more educated. There was a superfluity of applicants to become ministers, and Nonconformists claimed that as a whole they were statistically ahead of the establishment. In the Free Church councils Nonconformists had a new forum to conduct missions and press their causes—an object which was also served by the Nonconformist Political Council formed in 1898 to organize support in the country for Dissenting Parliamentary efforts.[4] Some of these causes were successful. The Marriages Act of 1898, passed with inter-party agreement on the initiative of the Wesleyan Robert Perks, a Liberal MP and president of the Nonconformist Political Council, removed the need for a civil registrar at weddings in Nonconformist and Catholic churches.[5] The Burial Grounds Act of 1900 removed other surviving grievances.

On the other hand, the Nonconformist Political Council proved short-lived, dissolving amid differences over the Boer War in 1900. The lack of any realistic hope of obtaining English disestablishment was displayed in 1897 when, for the first time since 1873, the issue was raised in Parliament. A motion by Samuel Smith on 9 February to disestablish and disendow the Church both in England and Wales was defeated by 204 votes to eighty-six. Some Irish nationalists supported the motion; no Liberal opposed, but over half the Liberals (including the party leaders) declined to vote. Smith's claim that disestablishment was inevitable, especially because of the growth of Ritualism in the Church of England, had brought a weak response: Balfour, opposing the motion, could point to the empty Liberal benches.[6] The Liberation Society had issued a whip for the division, but this had obviously failed and Liberals showed no desire to make disestablishment a definite party aim. A motion by Herbert Lewis in February 1899 to remove Bishops from the House of Lords was defeated by 200 votes to 129, and in that year a bill granting generous rate relief to clerical tithe-owners was carried despite strong Nonconformist protest.[7] When, on 12 June 1899, a deputation from the Liberation Society asked Campbell-Bannerman, the new Liberal leader, to adopt disestablishment as official policy, he made no immediate reply. He obtained from colleagues opinions which were unfavourable to the request, though some of these colleagues were personally inclined to disestablishment, as he was himself. When pressed to declare himself he said in a letter of 1 August that it was 'highly inexpedient for the Party at present to take

    [4] Cf. C. Binfield, *So Down to Prayers: Studies in English Nonconformity, 1780–1920* (London, 1977), 172; K. D. Brown, 'Ministerial Leakage in the Nineteenth Century: An Explanation?', *Journal of the United Reformed Church History Society*, iii. 3 (1984), 94 ff.; J. E. B. Munson, 'A Study of Nonconformity in Edwardian England as Revealed by the Passive Resistance Movement Against the 1902 Education Act', D.Phil. thesis (Oxford, 1973), 34 ff.; Bebbington, *The Nonconformist Conscience: Chapel and Politics, 1870–1914* (London, 1982), 74 ff.; W. Evans and W. Claridge, *James Hirst Hollowell and the Movement for Civic Control in Education* (Manchester, 1911), 56–7.

    [5] H lix. 329–58, lxiii. 1103–10, lxiv. 253–5, 437–41, 618, 633.

    [6] H xlvi. 27–64; Bebbington, op. cit. 24.

    [7] H lxvii. 113–75; *AR* i (1899), 129–43; *T*, 27 June 1899, p. 9; LS, 3 July 1899 (A/LIB/9, p. 77).

up any positive and definite line'. The matter could be no more than an 'open question' among Liberals. The National Liberal Federation conference in 1899 paid little attention to disestablishment, and it did not seem that party loyalty would help voluntaries to reach their goal.[8]

The Liberation Society was indeed in a weak position to make such requests. It was continually in debt, and had no lasting success in its efforts to revive. More meetings were held by the Society in 1897–8 than in either of the previous two years. But veteran leaders like Carvell Williams were not being adequately supplemented by youth, since many of the younger Nonconformist ministers and laymen were indifferent to or even against disestablishment. It seemed that Nonconformists, having lost their more material and mundane grievances, were less willing to support disestablishment on the ground of pure voluntary principles. Dr Joseph Parker, addressing the Congregational Union assembly as chairman in April 1901, said the Liberation Society needed 'copious new blood': 'A strong infusion of Lloyd Georgeism would do us a world of good; and by Lloyd Georgeism I simply mean high spirit, hopeful courage and invincible determination . . . I want the Liberation Society to magnify at the beginning of the brightest of the centuries the religious and spiritual aspects of Nonconformity.'[9] Carvell Williams said at the Liberation Society meeting at Sheffield in October 1901 that a fresh campaign was needed; a Young People's Liberationist League was launched, only to disappear in a short time.[10] The current advance of Ritualism in the Anglican Church enabled voluntaries to claim that such a Church should be disestablished as it did not meet national Protestant requirements.[11] But any hopes of voluntary revival did not impress Beatrice Webb, who noted in January 1901 that the demand for disestablishment was practically dead.[12]

Support for disestablishment was declining in Scotland as well as England. Only in Wales was there much realistic hope of some day attaining the object, and even there the greater numerical advance of the establishment compared with Nonconformity at the turn of the century challenged any assumption of ultimate success. Welsh disestablishment was eventually raised again in Parliament on 4 February 1902. William Jones, member for Arfon (Caernarfonshire) then moved a resolution which was supported in speeches by Harcourt and Asquith. Harcourt said that Welsh disestablishment could be considered and carried independently of the English question. C. T. Ritchie, the Home

---

[8] D. A. Hamer (ed.), *The Politics of Electoral Pressure* (Hassocks, Sussex, 1977), 162–3; Bebbington, op. cit. 25; *AR* i (1899), 70–1; memo by Herbert Gladstone (Liberal chief whip), 14 June 1899 (quoted Hamer, *Liberal Politics in the Age of Gladstone and Rosebery* (Oxford, 1972), 299–300); LS, 18 Sept. 1899 (9, p.89).

[9] LS, 6 June 1898; A/LIB/9, 9; *British Weekly*, suppl., 25 Nov. 1897; *Congregational Year-book* (1902), p. 19.

[10] *T*, 2 Oct. 1901, p. 5; Bebbington, op. cit. 25.

[11] e.g. *Free Church Chronicle*, i (1899), 40–1.

[12] Diary, 15 Jan. 1901; Beatrice Webb, *Our Partnership*, ed. Barbara Drake and Margaret Cole (London, 1948), 208.

Secretary, claimed the opposite. The resolution failed by the surprisingly small majority of 218 votes to 177, many Irish Home Rulers voting for the motion. But the fairly narrow defeat was partly owing to the absence of ministerialists who apparently did not consider the matter very serious. There was full Liberal support for the motion, the Liberation Society noted with pleasure.[13]

The established Church's position was strengthened by the Unionist victory in 1895, but Church defenders were conscious of the need to keep up their activity. There was extension and enlargement of the defence. Benson, as before, was disappointed by Conservative lukewarmness towards Church reform, and recalled the cordial relations he had enjoyed with Gladstone over Church appointments, if not over Welsh disestablishment.[14] Against considerable resistance Benson succeeded, by a two-thirds majority on 30 June 1896, in ending the independent existence of the CDI and amalgamating it with his Church Committee in the interests of wider representation and more efficient organization. The united body, the CCDI (Church Committee for Defence and Instruction) held its first meeting on 24 July. Selborne, Cranborne, and Boscawen were among the members of the executive committee. By March 1898 the body was believed to represent nearly 7,000 ruri-decanal and parochial committees, and a committee in every parish was the goal.[15] The CCDI made proposals for Church reform, and this was also the concern of the Church Reform League, founded at Church House, Westminster, in November 1895 with the Liberal H. J. Torr as secretary. This League's object was the development of self-government by Church assemblies at all levels from parochial to national, and the adoption of reforms in order to avoid disestablishment and encourage the return of Nonconformists to the Church. Patronage should cease, and elected diocesan boards should appoint the clergy; Bishops should be freely elected by cathedral chapters, and should not sit in the Lords by right; more Bishops, and an Archbishop of Wales, were needed.[16] Lay representation on Church bodies and lay participation in Church administration were crucial aims, in accordance with views expressed, for example, in *Essays in Aid of the Reform of the Church* (edited by Charles Gore and published in 1898), or stated thus in a *Contemporary Review* article in 1896: 'In the parish, in the diocese, in the Church at large, the consent of the laity to all that is done ought formally to be obtained. No clergyman ought to be appointed to a parish

[13] H cii. 379–420; *AR* i (1902), 52; LS, 3 Feb. 1902 (9, p. 223).

[14] A. C. Benson, *The Life of Edward White Benson, Archbishop of Canterbury* (2 vols., London, 1899), ii. 99–103; A. I. Taylor, 'The Church Party and Popular Education, 1893–1902', Ph.D. thesis (Cambridge, 1981), 127–32.

[15] M. J. D. Roberts, 'Pressure-group Politics and the Church of England: The Church Defence Institution, 1859–1896', *JEH* xxxv (1984), 579–81; Selborne to Benson, 24 Aug. 1895; Benson Papers, 149, fos. 159–64; also resolutions on amalgamation adopted at a conference of diocesan representatives of the CC, 6 Feb. 1896; ibid. fos. 259–60; CDI Central Council Minutes, 30 June 1896 (vol. 206); Rules for amalgamated body, adopted 16 July 1896; Benson Papers, 149, fos. 414–16; Minutes of CCDI, 24 July, 20 Nov. 1896, 28 Mar. 1898, 30 Mar. 1906 (vol. 34, pp. 2 ff., 8–12, 30, 96–8).

[16] Minutes of Council of Church Reform League, 27 Nov. 1895, 10 Jan. 1896; CRL/1.

without their consent. No parochial or diocesan affairs should be administered without their co-operation.'[17]

A leading aspect of Church defence was support and extension of denominational education, as recommended by a report of the Archbishops' Voluntary Schools Committee early in 1895. This, in association with other facets of educational reform, was a major controversial theme throughout the Unionists' decade in power. Defence of voluntary schools caused determined support of board schools by Nonconformists and others. The dispute involved the question of disestablishment since it concerned endowment for Church purposes, but it was more significant than the voluntary controversy because Government and not Nonconformity took the initiative in the schools issue. Educational reform could be enacted whereas disestablishment could not, and Nonconformists appeared stronger in resisting Government measures then in pressing their own.

In September 1895, Balfour (first lord of the Treasury in his uncle's ministry) wrote to his cousin Cranborne, chairman of the Church Parliamentary Committee, that he was anxious to relieve the 'almost intolerable strain' on voluntary school supporters. The letter was published in *The Times*.[18] Amongst Anglicans the movement for rate aid, rather than increased central Government assistance, was growing in strength although discouraged by Benson. A conference of leading Churchmen, convened by Benson on 7 October 1895, narrowly rejected rate aid in favour of more State aid. A request for State aid and other claims was then embodied in a memorial presented to Salisbury and Devonshire (Lord President of the Council, with official responsibility for education) by a large and influential deputation on 20 November. Sympathetic concern for the position of the voluntary schools and anxiety to alleviate it was shown in Salisbury's reply, though not in Devonshire's.[19] The Congregational Union indicated the Nonconformist opposition which would be expected by unanimously resolving on 3 October to resist any further endowment of sectarian schools from rates or taxes and to demand the extension of school boards throughout the country. The Wesleyan Conference resolved in similar vein, although there were still many Wesleyan voluntary schools and Wesleyan opinion was divided.[20] On the other hand a Voluntary Schools Defence League was formed in Birmingham in November.[21]

[17] J. J. Lias in *CR* lxx (1896), 415; G. L. Prestige, *The Life of Charles Gore* (London, 1935), 187–90.
[18] *T*, 20 Sept. 1895, p. 5; quoted J. R. Fairhurst, 'Some Aspects of the Relationship Between Education, Politics, and Religion from 1895 to 1906', D.Phil. thesis (Oxford, 1974), 55.
[19] Fairhurst, op. cit. 58–9; Benson to Salisbury, 29 Oct. and 19 Nov. 1895; SP; *AR* i (1895), 196–8; Benson, op. cit. ii. 663–4; W. Temple, *The Life of Bishop Percival* (London, 1921), 178–80.
[20] *Congregational Year-book* (1896), 14; *T*, 5 Oct. 1895.
[21] Rt. Revd E. A. Knox, *Reminiscences of an Octogenarian, 1847–1934* (London [1935]), 186.

In December a Cabinet committee began to draft a bill. But differences within the Unionist coalition were soon displayed when Chamberlain, writing to Devonshire, condemned some proposals from outside the committee as 'the maddest I have ever seen . . . They would absolutely break down in the interest of the Church and the Roman Catholics the so-called compromise of 1870. They would impose local rates for voluntary schools without direct popular representation and would infallibly raise the old Church Rates difficulty in the most acute form.' He went on to say that, although he had abandoned disestablishment 'as outside practical politics', he could not 'hold up his head for a day' if he agreed to rate aid for voluntary schools without public control. This point might have appealed to Devonshire's Whig preference for undenominational education, but was contrary to Salisbury's wish to promote schools under Church control.[22] To Balfour, Chamberlain wrote that 'the mere introduction of such a Bill as proposed would do more to reunite a solid Liberal Opposition and to shatter the Unionist majority, than could possibly be accomplished by any other means'.[23]

Chamberlain's protests prevailed. Rate aid gave way to increased State aid in the Government proposals, in spite of pressure for rate aid from an Anglican lobby headed by Cranborne and concentrated mainly in Lancashire. Plans to abolish the school boards and transfer their duties to county and borough councils were greatly modified. The bill (for England and Wales) emerged by February as an untidy compromise which left the Cabinet unenthusiastic, denominationalists dissatisfied, and Nonconformists angered. Voluntary schools (and necessitous board schools) were to receive increased State money, and voluntary schools were relieved of having to pay rates. Under the controversial Clause 27 'reasonable arrangements' for denominational instruction would be permitted in both board and voluntary schools. County and county borough councils could take control of secondary and technical education, and could also assume some control of school boards.[24]

The bill, regarded as the main measure of the session, was introduced on 31 March 1896 by Sir John Gorst, vice-president of the council, the Minister with most direct responsibility for education. As a measure fully satisfying no section of opinion the bill was attacked from all sides—a familiar fate for an education bill in a country so divided on such matters. Supporters of undenominational board school education condemned the increased aid to voluntary schools, attacked Clause 27, and feared that local councils would swallow up the school boards. While the English Church Union supported the bill's main principles,

[22] Chamberlain to Devonshire, 16 Dec. 1895 (quoted J. L. Garvin and J. Amery, *The Life of Joseph Chamberlain* (4 vols., London, 1933–51), iii. 153); George Dixon to Chamberlain, 4 Jan. 1895; CP, JC5/27/9; J. S. Sandars to Balfour, 15 and 19 Dec. 1895; BP, 49760, fos. 34–6; *AR* i (1895), 198; P. T. Marsh, *The Discipline of Popular Government: Lord Salisbury's Domestic Statecraft, 1881–1902* (Hassocks, Sussex, 1978), 250–2.

[23] Memo of 16 Dec. 1895; BP, 49773, fo. 88.

[24] J. Murphy, *Church, State, and Schools in Britain, 1800–1970* (London, 1971), 79 f.

opposition was voiced by the Liberation Society and by assemblies of Baptists and Congregationalists, Presbyterians and Primitive Methodists; and there were complaints that the extension of denominational teaching to board schools would weaken the voluntary schools. Objections came from teachers who feared that the threatened spread of denominational instruction would mean religious tests for more teaching posts.[25] Strong opposition came from some Labour orgaizations wanting purely secular education and public control of schools.[26] The Baptist John Clifford's characteristically trenchant criticism was that the bill was 'as bad as it is specious, as damaging to education as it is to religion, as partial and reactionary as it is clerical and anti-democratic'.[27] Anti-Ritualism and anti-romanism played a notable part in the opposition.[28]

The long and complicated bill had to contend with fierce criticism from the Opposition, and received only lukewarm support if not hostility from the Government benches.[29] The huge majority of 267 obtained for the second reading, perhaps the largest since the Ecclesiastical Titles Bill in 1851, was a very unreal reflection of enthusiasm for the measure. When the committee stage began the session was quite far advanced, and no fewer than 1,238 amendments were tabled. Conservative divisions over the measure were revealed, not least when Major Banes, Tory member for West Ham (South), attacked the bill for extending clerical influence: 'I never have a parson on my platform. If I see one there, I put him off.'[30] The Cabinet considered holding an adjourned session, perhaps extending to March 1897, to accommodate the bill. But instead it was decided to withdraw the measure, as Balfour announced in the Commons on 22 June. He hoped that the recent debates would be 'buried in the unfathomable bog of "Hansard", never again to see the light'.[31]

The episode was a disaster for the ministry. Harcourt wrote elatedly to his wife that he had 'never known a Government so soon and so completely discredited'. Griffith-Boscawen, a supporter of the ministry, later wrote that the diminutive Opposition had 'compelled the strongest Government of modern times to drop the principal measure of their first session'.[32] The debates had shown opposition to the Government scheme not only from Liberal Unionists (especially Nonconformist ones) but also from Conservatives.[33] On the other

[25] Cf. J. E. B. Munson, 'The Unionist Coalition and Education, 1895–1902', *HJ* xx (1977), 616 ff.

[26] B. Simon, *Education and the Labour Movement, 1870–1920* (London, 1965), 160–1.

[27] Sir James Marchant, *Dr John Clifford, CH: Life, Letters, and Reminiscences* (London, 1924), 119. Cf. J. Clifford, 'Primary Education and the State', *CR* lxix (1896), 441–56.

[28] e.g. A. M. Fairbairn, 'The Policy of an Education Bill', *CR* lxix (1896), 766–7; R. F. Horton, 'The Doomed Board Schools', *FR* lx (1896), 110 ff.

[29] H xxxix. 526–80, xl. 555 ff.; M. J. Wilkinson, 'Educational Controversies in British Politics, 1895–1914', Ph.D. thesis (Newcastle upon Tyne, 1978), 117–20.

[30] Sir A. Griffith-Boscawen, *Fourteen Years in Parliament* (London, 1907), 105.

[31] Quoted Wilkinson, op. cit. 129.

[32] A. G. Gardiner, *The Life of Sir William Harcourt* (2 vols., London, 1923), ii. 405; Griffith-Boscawen, op. cit. 106.

[33] Memos in BP, 49769, fos. 84–111.

hand, differences between Liberals and Irish nationalists had been emphasized: sixty-two Home Rule MPs had voted for the second reading, and Irish support for the measure made some Nonconformists cooler towards Home Rule.[34]

The measure had given Nonconformists and other radicals a renewed cause on which to fight the Government. Apart from the involvement of the Free Church councils in the question, new bodies were founded specifically to protect and extend unsectarian education. These included a powerful Northern Counties Education League with the Baptist Alfred Illingworth as chairman and Hirst Hollowell, a Congregational minister, as the extremely active secretary.[35] These organs had a comparatively slight measure to attack in the following year, when the Government introduced a bill to help the voluntary schools by simpler means. Balfour made speeches in July 1896 signalling this intention, and Salisbury told the Queen that the next educational effort would be much smaller. Balfour took charge of the preparation. After Chamberlain's reluctant support was won with the promise of another measure to aid needy board schools, a bill of only three clauses emerged. This gave more State aid to voluntary schools and exempted them from paying rates. The schools would be grouped into associations for the better allocation of the grant.

Balfour introduced the 'Voluntary Schools Bill' as a financial resolution in committee on 1 February 1897, and three days later it went before the full House. Balfour used various means, including the closure, to push the bill through rapidly against somewhat limited opposition. The Liberals first wanted aid for needy board schools in the same bill, and when a separate bill was promised for this purpose they urged that only necessitous voluntary schools should receive extra grant. The second reading passed on 16 February by a majority of 205 with the help of thirty-eight Home Rulers. At the committee stage the Welsh radicals were particularly active in attack. Herbert Lewis moved that the bill should not apply to Wales, but was heavily defeated. Six closures prevented 161 amendments being considered, and the third reading passed the Commons on 25 March, one Liberal Unionist (George Dixon) voting against and twenty being absent. The bill passed quickly through the Lords and became law on 8 April. A Necessitous Board Schools Bill, providing a much smaller amount, was later passed. Balfour's firm conduct of the Voluntary Schools Bill had done much to restore the Government's standing amongst its followers. But the Opposition complained of bias in favour of denominational education, and other educational reformers including Conservatives were disappointed by the lack of administrative reorganization.[36]

The Act was clearly a stopgap. The *Tablet* saw it as 'a new vantage ground for fresh agitation',[37] and it was not far wrong. The consciousness of British

[34] Bebbington, op. cit. 103.   [35] Evans and Claridge, op. cit. 48–9.

[36] *AR* i (1897), 29–34, 40–5, 67–75, 98–9; H xlv. 926–1019, 1084–172, 1314–415, xlvi. 203–50, 415–94, 534–611, xlvii. 971–83, 1329–424, xlviii. 1–81, 360–79; Wilkinson, op. cit. 160 ff.

[37] J. G. Snead-Cox, *The Life of Cardinal Vaughan* (2 vols., London, 1910), ii. 122–5.

educational shortcomings compared with some foreign countries was as strong as ever. The quest for national efficiency continued, and the broader considerations aired in 1896 remained to be tackled again. Balfour, Cranborne, and Gorst favoured rate aid for voluntary schools. Benson was perhaps inclining to this in the autumn of 1896 just before his death, and certainly his successor Frederick Temple had come to favour the prospect. The Convocation of York voted in June 1896 by forty-three votes to eight for rate aid, together with some public control provided this did not impair the schools' religious character. Temple presided at a widely representative gathering organized by the National Society on 30 October. This recommended that voluntary schools in school board districts should receive rate aid, with public inspection taking place but not public representation on the managing bodies. This demand was endorsed at a London conference on 6 November attended by representatives of the National Society and by delegates from the Convocations, Houses of Laymen, diocesan conferences, and diocesan boards of education.[38]

After 1896 only minor education measures were passed for several years, for example the establishment of a Board of Education in 1899. But argument continued over the rival merits of board and voluntary schools, the question of rate aid for the latter, and the need for control by county and borough councils. Protests came from Baptist, Congregational, and Primitive Methodist assemblies against State-supported denominational schools and the revived proposal to establish with Government aid a Catholic university in Ireland.[39] The Northern Counties Education League and similar bodies intervened in by-elections and school board contests, and the Parliamentary committee of the Trades Union Congress championed an unsectarian public-controlled system. Lloyd George moved a resolution against State support for voluntary schools in March 1899 but was heavily defeated. On 28 April that year Samuel Smith condemned the 'Roman practices' being taught in some Anglican schools.[40] In July 1899 the Cockerton judgment stating that board schools should not provide secondary education added to the fire. In April 1901 the appeal court judged against the London School Board for providing such education; and in that year a bill was passed enabling county and county borough councils to empower school boards to provide 'higher elementary' teaching for one year. But the Act was opposed on the ground that it subordinated school boards to other authorities, and in any case it seemed to herald a new attempt at

[38] Fairhurst, op. cit. 88–9; Murphy, op. cit. 79; *AR* i (1896), 129, 195–7; F. D. How, *Bishop Walsham How: A Memoir* (London, 1898), 333–4; J. E. Gorst, 'The Voluntary Schools', *Nineteenth Century*, xl (1896), 709–10.

[39] Baptist Spring Assembly, 27 Apr. 1898; Baptist Handbook (1899), p. 122; J. E. B. Munson, 'A Study of Nonconformity in Edwardian England as Revealed by the Passive Resistance Movement Against the 1902 Education Act', D.Phil. thesis (Oxford, 1973), 68–9; F. A. Channing, *Memories of Midland Politics, 1885–1910* (London, 1918), 206–9.

[40] *AR* i (1899), 66–7, 98–9; H lxx. 830–919.

comprehensive reorganization.[41] When this came in 1902, after a false start in 1901, the rival forces were well prepared for battle.

Greater security for voluntary schools was one way of assisting the Church of England. Another was the long-demanded reform of patronage. Bills to modify patronage were introduced annually in the mid-1890s. Cranborne's private bill of 1896 became long and complex through amalgamation with another measure regarding unfit incumbents. The bill, abolishing the sale of next presentations, prohibiting exercise of patronage within a year of a sale, and enabling Bishops to refuse institution to unfit clergy, passed its second reading in the Commons by a large majority in March. But although it was supported by many Churchmen considerable opposition had been shown. Henry Foster, Conservative MP for Lowestoft, said the bill gave too much power to Bishops at the expense of patrons, though he was opposed by many Anglican clergy in his constituency. Nonconformist MPs were divided in their reactions: Perks supported the bill because it aimed to purify the clergy, Carvell Williams and others opposed because it was not thorough enough. After the Standing Committee on Law had amended the bill, Foster moved to reject it on 3 June, saying he did not want larger powers to be given 'to the sacerdotal or any other party in the Church'. Carvell Williams called for disestablishment so that the Church itself could regulate clerical appointments. Foster's motion was defeated. But the bill fell into misfortune, being talked out on 10 June, refused special status as a Government measure, and finally abandoned. Benson, who had pleaded fruitlessly with Salisbury and Balfour to make the bill a Government one, died in October, disappointed in the ministry and in the hope of seeing this cherished reform carried.[42] He might have seen the episode as vindicating his previous comment that Ministers would be so confident of the church's support that they would not bother to reform it.

Temple, the new Archbishop of Canterbury, saw Balfour in January about the prospects for another bill in 1897, and was told that, though Balfour was personally favourable, he could hold out no hope of Government help that session.[43] Chamberlain hoped that 'no encouragement will be given to the Archbishop to expect Government assistance during the present or even next Session'.[44] Nevertheless, the Archbishop of York introduced a bill in the Lords which passed that House in July but made little progress in the Commons.[45]

[41] Evans and Claridge, op. cit. 51–3; Simon, op. cit. 190 ff.
[42] H xxxviii. 673–713, xli. 370 ff.; *AR* i (1896), 137–8; Canon C. D. Lawrence to Cranborne, 9 Mar. 1896; SP, S(4), Box 7; Benson, op. cit. ii. 94–5; Benson to Balfour, 5 May 1896; BP, 49788, fos. 6–7; Benson to Salisbury, 12 June, enclosing memorial from Archbishops and Bishops to Salisbury, June 1896; SP; Salisbury to Benson, 16 June; Benson Papers, 350, fos. 348–9; Benson to Balfour, 22 June; BP, 49788, fos. 8–11; Balfour to Benson, 1 July; Benson Papers, 150, fos. 356–7; Bishop E. S. Talbot to Balfour, 1 July; BP, 49789, fos. 64–5.
[43] Memo by Balfour, 16 Jan. 1897; BP, 49788, fos. 26–7.
[44] Chamberlain to Balfour, 17 Jan., copy; CP, JC5/5/69.
[45] H xlix. 465–6, l. 1444–7, 1604.

1898, however, saw Ministers take the matter in hand and a measure for partial patronage reform reach the statute book. Both a Government bill and one sponsored by the Church Parliamentary Committee were introduced; differing only in small details, both were read a second time and then amalgamated into a single measure, the Benefices Bill. A new threat to the bill's progress was the intervention of anti-Ritualism, which reached a height in that year both inside and outside Parliament and injected some life into what *The Times* called 'the dullest and least interesting' session in memory.[46] There was much difference of opinion, for example among Nonconformists, and some opponents of the bill claimed it would encourage Ritualism. This it would do by giving more power over appointments to Bishops who allegedly protected Ritualists.

At the report stage on 16 June Henry Foster moved to reject the combined measure because it gave patrons no compensation for loss of private rights and paid no attention to the ritual problem. Samuel Smith and Harcourt made vigorous anti-Ritualist speeches in support of Foster's motion, and Balfour accused them equally vigorously of being irrelevant. The motion was defeated by 220 votes to seventy-five. A motion by Smith on 21 June to insert an anti-Ritualist amendment was also lost (215–103). The bill went on to pass the Commons and then, after amendment, the Lords. The Commons accepted most of the Lords' amendments and the bill was enacted.[47]

The Benefices Act forbade the sale of next presentations, and the sale of advowsons by auction except on certain conditions. Bishops were given wider grounds to refuse institution of a presentee. Bonds of resignation, whereby a presentee undertook to resign at some time in favour of another, were abolished; as also were donatives—a small number of livings where the patron could institute a presentee without reference to the Bishop. The Act was a significant first step in patronage reform after twenty-eight years of effort—a period as long as it had taken some Nonconformist claims to be met. The reform was welcomed by Archbishop Temple even though he wished it had forbidden the sale of advowsons. It was not quite as long until further steps occurred after the Church of England had secured a degree of self-government by the Enabling Act of 1919. An Act of 1923 prevented a clergyman who was also a patron from presenting himself, and abolished the sale of advowsons (with certain exceptions) after two vacancies in the benefice from July 1924. An Act of 1931 gave the parochial church council some influence over the appointment of incumbents.[48]

The desire for self-government in the Church was expressed particularly in

[46] Quoted J. R. Holding, 'An Examination of the Third Salisbury Cabinet, 1895–1902', B.Litt. thesis (Oxford, 1978), 81.

[47] H liv. 355–419, 856–96, lix. 452–532, 963–1075, lxi. 88–127; Griffith-Boscawen, op. cit. 141–2.

[48] O. Chadwick, *The Victorian Church*, ii (1970), 213 n.

Church Reform League meetings throughout the country.[49] The difficulty in getting measures of clerical discipline and patronage reform through Parliament had shown, Bishop Westcott of Durham told his diocesan conference in October 1897, that 'Parliament . . . is not able to deal effectually in ordinary debate with questions of Church reform. It no longer represents Church feeling, has not the time for ecclesiastical legislation.' The Church must obtain more power to govern itself while remaining in partnership with the State. Self-government in the Church of Scotland justified 'the extension of like power to the Church of England'. To obtain such power the Church must acquire a body more widely representative, especially of the laity, through which opinions could be expressed and legislative recommendations made to Parliament.[50] Increased lay representation was also advocated by the Church Committee.[51]

Following opinions published by Charles Gore and others in 1898,[52] the Bishop of London, Mandell Creighton, said at the Church Reform League annual meeting on 25 May 1900 that the laity should be given more representation in the Convocations through the incorporation of the Houses of Laymen with those bodies. He was seconded in speeches by the evangelical Sir John Kennaway and the High-Church Lord Hugh Cecil. Earlier that day the League's central representative council had adopted a resolution that the Convocations should obtain from Parliament the power to reform their own constitutions, to incorporate representative Houses of Laymen as parts of themselves, and to enable these to sit with the Convocations as a united national synod to ease the conduct of business. These proposals were contained in a draft bill brought into Parliament in 1900 but then given only a first reading.[53] Not only Houses of Laymen but grass-roots parochial church councils were advocated, by H. J. Torr and Bishop Percival for example, in order to involve the laity further in Church government. But there were differing views on whether Nonconformists and women should be allowed to sit on these.[54]

A member of the council of the Church Reform League wrote: 'If Churchmen are to wait until Parliament has time to carry out the most necessary reforms in Church matters, they may have to wait for two centuries or more . . . unless some principle of devolution of ecclesiastical business be adopted, Churchmen may sigh for improvements in vain'.[55] But the League's

[49] Revd Lucius G. Fry to Cranborne, 4 Mar. 1897; SP, S(4), Box 8.

[50] A. Westcott, *Life and Letters of Brooke Foss Westcott, Sometime Bishop of Durham* (2 vols., London, 1903), ii. 249.

[51] CCDI Minutes, 13 Oct. 1899 (vol. 34, pp. 65–6, 76).

[52] Charles Gore (ed.), *Essays in Aid of the Reform of the Church* (London, 1898). Cf. Charles Gore, 'The English Church Union Declaration', *CR* lxxv (1899), 468–9.

[53] *T*, 26 May 1900, pp. 10, 11. Cf. *Quarterly Chronicle of the Church Reform League*, I. i (July 1900), *et seq.*

[54] H. J. Torr in Gore, *Essays*, op. cit.; Temple, *Percival*, 171; E. G. Sandford (ed.), *Memoirs of Archbishop Temple* (2 vols., London, 1906), ii. 334.

[55] Revd J. J. Lias in *T*, 4 Sept. 1900, p. 5.

objects had many critics among Churchmen. Some of these critics—including the members of the Churchmen's Liberation League—preferred disestablishment. Others had alternative views of Church reform: one of them thought that self-government by diocesan bodies representative of clergy and laity was preferable to self-government through the Convocations.[56]

A bill to reform the Convocations was again brought into Parliament in 1901. The Upper House of the Canterbury Convocation unanimously agreed to the bill in May 1901, and the London diocesan conference welcomed it in June. But opposition came from G. W. E. Russell as chairman of the annual meeting of the Churchmen's Liberation League on 23 May, and from the Bishop of Sodor and Man (Norman Straton) at his diocesan conference in February. Russell said that only disestablishment would give the Church sufficient freedom, Straton that the scheme would take too much power from Parliament, the representative body of the people (though not the people of Man), and give too much power to the much less representative Convocations.[57] Even *The Times*, though favourable to Church reform, said 'the whole question bristles with difficulties', not least the question of qualifications for the lay franchise. The scheme was at present 'too vague . . . to be the basis of so serious a change in the constitution of the Church of England'.[58]

The bill was introduced by Temple in the Lords, and was read a second time on 13 June after Archbishop Maclagan and Lord Salisbury had spoken in support. Temple said the object was to remove all doubt that the Convocations were able, under licence from the Crown and with its consent, to change their constitutions and correct the gross under-representation of the clergy. The bill also provided that the Convocations could sit jointly in one assembly.[59] The measure passed the Lords but did not get beyond a first reading in the Commons.

The vociferous call for more Church self-government continued, especially in the Church Reform League.[60] But there were differences over the question of lay representation in synods and over the powers of members elected to the Representative Church Council of Bishops, clergy, and laity. This was formed in accordance with resolutions in the Convocations and Houses of Laymen and met for the first time in July 1904.[61] The Council adopted a constitution in 1905, providing for Houses of Bishops, Clergy, and Laity, enabling the House of Laity to take part in all decisions, and conferring an indirect franchise on communicants of the Church of England who did not belong to any other

[56] *T*, 24 May 1901, p. 10; Revd W. A. Mathews to Harcourt, 26 July 1898; HP, 236, fos. 233–8.
[57] Sandford, op. cit. ii. 329–30; *T*, 5 June 1901, p. 7, 24 May, p. 10, 12 Feb., p. 11.
[58] *T*, 14 Feb., p. 9.
[59] H xcv. 217–19.
[60] e.g. annual meeting of League, 10 June 1902, 12 May 1903; *T*, 11 June 1902, p. 6, 14 May 1903, p. 11.
[61] ECU Minutes, 25 Nov. 1903 (CU dep. 5, 200–1), 16 June 1904 (ibid. 207).

religious body. For women voters a household qualification was added.[62] The
Council could not decide questions of doctrine and had no legislative powers,
but was meant to present 'the mind of the Church' to Convocations and
Parliament. Encouraging though this step was to reformers, the Council failed
to absorb the Convocations as was hoped, and had too little representation and
powers to satisfy the demand for change.

III. THE RITUAL QUESTION, 1895–1905

Church reform and consolidation were hampered throughout this decade by
fierce disputes over ritual, which took place on three main levels—a
proliferation of books, articles, and letters to the press; Parliamentary debates,
some on measures directly concerning ritual and others not; the interruption of
church services, the holding of meetings, and the conduct of anti-Ritualist
missions.

There was much variety in Anglican Ritualist practice and its extent was
easily exaggerated. But it has recently been stated that the number of churches
in which eucharistic vestments were used increased from 336 in 1882 to 2,158 in
1901, and the number in which incense was used from nine to 393 in the same
years.[63] The figures may have begun to diminish by 1901 because of episcopal
warnings,[64] but the increase had been rapid. This, along with the failure of the
prosecution of clergy and the Government's encouragement of voluntary
schools (some of which were Roman Catholic, others subject to Anglo-Catholic
influence) produced growing anti-Ritualist feeling from the mid-1890s. At this
time there was tension between some Bishops and their Ritualist clergy.[65]
There was also Protestant alarm at the warm interest shown by Lord Halifax,
president of the English Church Union, and others such as Gladstone in
corporate reunion with the Roman Church—until this hope was quashed, at
least for a time, by Pope Leo XIII's bull of September 1896 declaring Anglican
Orders null and void.[66]

Many publications in the later 1890s illustrated what was often called 'the
crisis in the Church'.[67] Perhaps the most widely read contribution was Walter
Walsh's best-selling volume, *The Secret History of the Oxford Movement*, a

---

[62] *AR* ii (1905), 33.

[63] N. Yates, *The Oxford Movement and Anglican Ritualism*, Historical Association (London, 1983),
32. Cf. similar figures given by Lord Kinnaird in Lords, 9 Feb. 1899; H lxvi. 278; Yates, *The Oxford
Movement and Parish Life: St Saviour's, Leeds, 1839–1929*, Borthwick Papers, no. 48 (York, 1975), 23–4.

[64] Cf. Chadwick, op. cit. ii. 357.

[65] Cf. How, op. cit. 289–90.

[66] J. G. Lockhart, *Viscount Halifax* (2 vols., London, 1935–6), ii. 38–78; Snead-Cox, op. cit. ii.
141–223; Benson, op. cit. ii. 589–622; A. MacCormack, *Cardinal Vaughan* (London, 1966), 244–60;
J. D. Holmes, *More Roman than Rome: English Catholicism in the Nineteenth Century* (London, 1978),
218–23; Duke of Norfolk to Wilfrid Ward, 2 Dec. 1894 (Wilfrid Ward Papers).

[67] Cf. G. I. T. Machin, 'The Last Victorian Anti-Ritualist Campaign, 1895–1906', *VS* xxv
(1981–2), 282–4.

historical exposure of Anglo-Catholic beliefs, practices, and societies, particularly in connection with the desire for reunion with Rome. First published in 1897, praised by the *Primitive Methodist Quarterly Review*, and condemned by the *Church Times* as absurd, irreligious, and untrue, the book reached its fifth edition by January 1899. Also not lacking in readers were the Wesleyan J. H. Rigg's *Oxford High Anglicanism* (1895; enlarged edition 1899), an indictment of the 'Popish flavour and influence' now to be found in High-Churchmanship; *England's Danger* (1898) by the Congregationalist R. F. Horton, a collection of anti-Catholic sermons with titles like 'Romanism and National Decay' which rapidly reached a seventh edition and was attacked by the Catholic *Universe;* and two books by W. E. Bowen (an Anglican clergyman), *The Crisis in the English Church* (1900) and *Contemporary Ritualism* (1902). Many periodical articles and published addresses gave a similar message. John Clifford's address of 1895, *The Renewal of Protestantism*, said the growth of Ritualism was 'the most notorious fact of the day'. Samuel Smith also called for Protestant revival in *The Claims of Rome* (1896). An article by Francis Peak in the *Contemporary Review* (January 1899) said that, since 'it is entirely vain to rely upon the bishops', the first need in dealing with the 'sacerdotal heresy' was to abolish the episcopal veto on prosecutions granted by the Public Worship Regulation Act. Parishioners should have an unhindered right to prosecute clergy who did not strictly observe the law of the Prayer Book. Cornelia, Lady Wimborne, sister of the late Lord Randolph Churchill, warned in a *Nineteenth Century* article in 1898 (reprinted as *The Ritualist Conspiracy*) that 'our Church is suffering from a deadly disease which threatens its very existence'.[68]

There were also directories listing the names of supposedly ritualist clergy. The 1902 edition of the Church Association's *Ritualistic Clergy List* contained 9,600 names (out of about 25,000 Anglican clergy) and was accused of indiscriminatory inflation.[69] A *Protestant Dictionary* prepared by the Protestant Reformation Society in 1904, was intended to 'enable Protestant preachers, lecturers, and Christians unversed in the Romish controversy . . . to testify in a spirit of love against all Romish errors'.[70]

Apart from publications, another means of anti-Ritualist protest was the holding of numerous meetings by the many ultra-Protestant societies. These ranged from well-established bodies such as the Protestant Reformation Society, the Protestant Alliance, the Scottish Reformation Society, and the Church Association, to more recent organizations (some of which were produced by the current anti-Ritualist wave) such as the National Protestant Church Union, the Welsh Protestant League, the Ladies' League for the

---

[68] Lady Wimborne, 'The Ritualist Conspiracy', *Nineteenth Century*, xliv (1898), 531–44.

[69] *Guardian*, 2 Apr. 1902, p. 462. Cr. J. E. B. Munson, 'The Oxford Movement by the End of the Nineteenth Century: The Anglo-Catholic Clergy', *Church History*, xliv (1975), 388.

[70] C. H. H. Wright and C. Neil (eds.), *A Protestant Dictionary* (London, 1904).

Defence of the Reformed Faith of the Church of England, and the Imperial
Protestant Federation (secretary, Walter Walsh) which was joined by many
Protestant societies. Examples of large rallies were a Grand United Protestant
Demonstration held by the Protestant Alliance in April 1897 at the Queen's
Hall, London; a National Protestant Congress at Folkestone in October 1898;
and great Albert Hall gatherings in January 1899 and January 1900. Anti-
Ritualism was linked in these public protests with anti-romanism, and some of
the opposition was to Roman Catholic objects such as a State-aided Catholic
university. This object was supported by some leading politicians of both
parties but withdrawn after a substantial Commons debate in February 1898
and defeated after another in March 1900.[71] The Senate of Cambridge
University in May 1898 refused to recognize a Catholic hall, following
opposition expressed partly in the *Cambridge Anti-Popery Gazette*.[72]

Denominational assemblies added their protests. The Congregational Union
assembly in May 1898 called for disestablishment because of 'the alarming and
widespread revival of mediaeval superstitions' in the supposedly Protestant
Church of England, and said that any attempt to create a denominational
university was 'needless, retrograde, and mischievous'. The Baptist assembly in
October 1897 unanimously resolved that 'priestly pretensions and sacramentar-
ian superstitions' were 'inconsistent with the Gospel testimony that salvation is
the direct work of God's spirit on the believing soul'.[73] Bishop Percival of
Hereford, a Broad-Churchman, disapproved of a travelling Church Association
van in his diocese but stated nevertheless that Ritualism was 'very liable to
deteriorate into an emotional worship, which satisfies a mood, but does not
regenerate and sanctify the life'.[74]

Meetings of the English Church Union often defended ritual as signifying
only an attempt to make services more picturesque and appealing. Ritualists
denied the charges of idolatry and crypto-romanism so often made against
them. But belief in doctrines symbolized by the ritual was not denied.
Confession in the Church of England was supported, for, instead of being the
breaker of family ties as was frequently alleged, it was often 'the occasion for
healing domestic discord, and pressing upon Husband and Wife, upon Parents
and Children, the Christian duties of sympathy, of affection, and of
self-sacrifice'.[75] Canon MacColl, a moderate High-Churchman who said that
he was not attracted to elaborate ritual and had heard confession from only two
people in his life, produced a characteristically voluminous defence of the

[71] H liii. 754–835, lxxxi. 202–300; Perks to Rosebery, 22 Feb. 1898, 4 Feb. 1899; RP, 10050, fos.
21–2, 31–2; *Proceedings of the Third National Free Church Council* (London, 1898).
[72] V. A. McClelland, *English Roman Catholics and Higher Education, 1830–1903* (Oxford, 1973),
417–23.
[73] *Congregational Year-book* (1899), 5; *Baptist Handbook* (1898), 131.
[74] Temple, op. cit. 143–9.
[75] Revd J. P. F. Davidson, *Confession in the Church of England* (London, [1898?]), 11–12.

Ritualists in 1899 and saw this go into a tenth edition by 1901.[76] Nonconformist ministers praised Ritualist clergy for their useful and self-sacrificing lives: Guinness Rogers said that Protestant sentiment would not combine in support of a disciplinary measure 'which would turn out of the Church a large body of the clergy, numbers of whom have commended themselves by their devotion to their work'.[77]

Ritualism became more of a Parliamentary question in the later 1890s than it had been since 1874, and remained an important political concern for several years. As a public controversy it lasted until 1928 and beyond. Parliamentary debates often dealt with Ritualism even when they were ostensibly about something else. In the debate on disestablishment in 1897 Samuel Smith said that 'a large section within the Church was now calling for Disestablishment that it might carry sacerdotal doctrines still further; and a much larger section outside the Church demanded Disestablishment that it might free the nation from complicity with these doctrines'.[78] He launched into a strong condemnation of sacerdotal beliefs and practices in the establishment: '. . . the Confessional . . . and the Mass, and the invocation of saints, and prayers for the dead, and other practices which were forbidden by the law of the Church, were observed without let or hindrance by most of the Bishops'. The national Church had broken its compact to be a Protestant body, so must be disestablished.

As already noted, Smith and Harcourt strongly and extensively intervened in the debate on the Benefices Bill in June 1898, disregarding the bill's purpose and concentrating purely on the alarming growth of Ritualism in the churches and schools, despite interventions from the Speaker and complaints from Balfour and others that they were being irrelevant. Smith moved an amendment that Bishops be enabled to refuse institution to Ritualist priests, but was opposed by both Liberals and Conservatives and lost his motion by 215 votes to 103. He was supported in this division by Harcourt, Campbell-Bannerman, Asquith, Lloyd George, and Carvell Williams, and opposed by Herbert Gladstone, Chamberlain, R. B. Haldane, and Michael Davitt. Harcourt brought the ritual question into an education debate on 17 June, and the Liberal Earl of Kimberley raised it in the Lords' debate on the second reading of the Benefices Bill on 7 July. The question figured in the Commons in February 1899 when the removal of Bishops from the Lords was debated; in discussion on the bill to relieve tithe-owning clergy from paying half their rates; and in the debate on a motion of Lloyd George in March 1899 against the voluntary schools. In the last of these Samuel Smith made another lengthy anti-Ritualist onslaught and Henry Foster said that Nonconformists and Evangelical Anglicans should keep together against Ritualism and not be divided by other

---

[76] Malcolm MacColl, *The Reformation Settlement Examined in the Light of History and Law* (London, 1899); id. 'Protestantism and Sacerdotalism', *FR* lxiv (1898), 288.

[77] 'The Archbishops and the Ritualists', *CR* lxxvi (1899), 313.

[78] Cf. LS, 10 Apr. 1899 (9, p. 66).

issues. There was also a complaint in Parliament about services with illegal ritual at an army chapel maintained by the Government, and in June 1900 Smith was again attacking the Ritualist 'take-over' of education.[79] More substantially, there were efforts to pass legislation in order to banish Ritualist 'excesses' from the Church.

A number of figures were prominent in anti-Ritualist campaigns outside Parliament, mainly Harcourt, Lady Wimborne, John Kensit and his son, and George Wise. These represented a wide social spectrum, illustrating the fact that anti-Ritualism, like Ritualism itself, was supported by people of all social classes.[80] As a foremost politician and leader of the Liberal party, Harcourt's efforts in the Benefice Bill debates brought congratulations and encouragement from many Protestant bodies. The committee of the Manchester Protestant Thousand, a society composed of 'clergymen, ministers and laymen of various evangelical churches and of all political parties', assured him of wide support.[81] Harcourt developed his role as a Protestant champion in a series of nineteen letters to *The Times*, starting on 16 July 1898 and lasting until the end of the year. The *Guardian* also published the letters and they were reprinted as a book, *Lawlessness in the National Church*.[82] The letters denounced an organized effort supposedly afoot to subvert Reformation principles, attacked the Bishops for failing to keep better discipline, and sought to deprive them of their veto over prosecutions. Against High-Church wishes to be free from Parliamentary regulation, Harcourt took the Erastian line that Parliament had full power to decide the doctrine, discipline, and ceremonial of the Church of England. His proposed remedy that Bishops who could be trusted to enforce strict observance of the Prayer Book should be appointed, dissatisfied some anti-Ritualists who thought that only more stringent legislation would suffice.[83] But no anti-Ritualist could deprecate his eagerness to form a wide popular movement by marshalling 'the irresistible force of a well informed public opinion', expressed through organizations in each diocese to report on clerical indiscipline to the Bishops and press for action. To Harcourt anti-Ritualism should be a means of Liberal progress towards democracy: it was through the popular voice that Ritualism would be overthrown.

Harcourt received a great many notes of congratulation for his letters. Lady Wimborne congratulated him, and J. H. Rigg sent him a copy of his book. Harcourt thanked Rigg in return for 'a careful and impartial study of the growth of this unwholesome fungus'. Walter Walsh thanked Harcourt for quoting from

[79] H xlvi. 27–38, lix. 469–85, 513–23, 613–15, 1025–76, lxi. 121–2, lxvii. 122, lxviii. 62–116, lxxii. 1137–8, lxxxiv. 45–128; S. Smith, *My Life Work* (London, 1902), 320 ff.

[80] Cf. Chadwick, op. cit. ii. 311–12, 317.

[81] Resolutions of 24 June 1898; HP, 235, fos. 81; similar resolutions ibid. 236, fo. 2 ff.; Henry Miller to Harcourt, 20 June; ibid. 235, fos. 77–8.

[82] Sir W. V. Harcourt, *Lawlessness in the National Church* (London, 1899), 34, 63, 76 ff., 80, 83, 139–42; *AR* i (1898), 199–201; Gardiner, *Harcourt*, ii. 481 ff.

[83] e.g. Bishop of Sodor and Man to Harcourt, 5 Dec. 1898; HP, 239, fos. 27–8.

his book in *The Times*, which had assisted sales; later he described Ritualists to Harcourt as 'ecclesiastical anarchists'. At the seventy-second annual meeting of the Protestant Reformation Society Harcourt was thanked for the great public service rendered by his 'unanswered and unanswerable letters'. One correspondent told him that the actions of a new incumbent had driven him to attend a Congregational church; another, a Conservative, said Harcourt's stand was tempting him to vote Liberal; a third alleged that 'Romish practices' were not confined to the Anglican Church but were 'also pervading the Presbyterian Churches of Scotland'.[84] One Colonel Alfred Porcelli said that, as a long-standing Conservative, he was so disgusted with the 'pro-popish leanings' of Salisbury and Balfour that he would never again support their party.[85]

Harcourt also had many critics, some of whom were Liberals. Malcolm MacColl, who engaged in epistolary contest with Harcourt in *The Times*, said his position was 'politically absurd' and injurious to his party, for he was an anti-Ritualist who was also a Home Ruler appealing for Irish Catholic support.[86] It could hardly be believed, said MacColl, that Harcourt's 'truculent rhetoric' represented his true feelings; but the sincerity of his intentions was beyond doubt, for 'he is a convinced Whig-Erastian, the most loveless form of religion, if he will forgive me for saying it, in the repertory of human beliefs'.[87] Sincerity was emphatically denied to Harcourt, however, by one of his correspondents: 'We can only hope that the time will come when you will regret your abominable lies, told merely for the sake of playing to the Gallery; and we can at any rate be thankful that it will be impossible for you to lead the Liberal Party as Prime Minister. To a radical Priest like myself the "come down" from Mr Gladstone to you, is too awful for words.'[88]

Harcourt was one of several aristocratic denouncers of Ritualism. John Kensit, of more plebeian stock, took a more novel line than Harcourt in clamorously interrupting church services in order to denounce ritual acts taking place, and in despatching his young 'Wycliffe preachers' on the 'Kensit crusade' to different parts of the country. The Wycliffe preachers had had some predecessors in recent years.[89] There were thirty Wycliffe preachers by 1903, Kensit's son John Alfred being conspicuous among them, and in that year they visited 441 places and held 2,561 meetings. The 'evangelistic vans' of the

---

[84] Lady Wimborne to Harcourt, 29 Jan. 1899; HP, 240, fos. 180–1; J. Telford, *The Life of James Harrison Rigg, DD, 1821–1909* (London, [1909]), 319; W. Walsh to Harcourt, 14 Nov. 1898; HP, 238, fo. 35, 6 Mar. 1903; ibid. 244, fo. 13; *72nd Annual Report of Protestant Reformation Society* (London, 1899), 10; William Long to Harcourt, 6 Nov. 1898; HP, 238, fos. 1–2; V. J. Auber to Harcourt, 4 July 1898; ibid. 236, fo. 32; John Drummond to Harcourt, 8 Jan. 1899; ibid. 240, fos. 81–2.

[85] Porcelli to Harcourt, 15 Aug. 1898; HP, 237, fos. 8–9.

[86] MacColl to Balfour, 28 June 1898; BP, 49790, fos. 63–4; MacColl to Salisbury, 29 July 1898, 15 Jan. 1899 (G. W. E. Russell (ed.), *Malcolm MacColl: Memoirs and Correspondence* (London, 1914), 218–21).

[87] MacColl, 'Protestantism and Sacerdotalism', *FR* lxiv (1898), 288.

[88] Revd G. N. Whittingham to Harcourt, 30 June 1898; HP, 235, fos. 82–3.

[89] J. Kent, *Holding the Fort: Studies in Victorian Revivalism* (London, 1978), 302.

Church Association, numbering eleven by 1902, also visited a great many parts.[90] Kensit *père,* an Anglican bookseller in the City of London who had started the Protestant Truth Society, felt compelled to intervene personally against what he saw as an ever-encroaching evil. Already of some note, he came to wide public attention when he tried to read a protest at the confirmation of Mandell Creighton as Bishop of London in January 1897, partly on the ground that Creighton wore a mitre. Later he complained to Creighton about Ritualist services at St Ethelburgh's, Bishopsgate, and was eventually assured that, after alterations, the services there conformed with the Prayer Book.

In Holy Week 1898 Kensit was particularly active in different parts of London. At St Mark's, Marylebone Road, he rose from his seat and protested against 'this monstrous service, which is not in the Book of Common Prayer', and disorder ensued. On going to St John the Devine, Kennington, to make a protest he found the doors locked against him but addressed people outside. On Good Friday at St Cuthbert's, South Kensington, he was removed by police after he and his wife had vociferously objected to a service in which the congregation kissed a crucifix, and was fined but successfully appealed against this punishment. On 8 May he interrupted a service at St Michael's Shoreditch, and again had to go to court, finding a welcoming crowd outside after the hearing. He tried unsuccessfully to prosecute the curate of St Michael's for assault on the ground that he had sprinkled holy water over the congregation.

Kensit promised to suspend his disturbances for two months when Bishop Creighton agreed to present a petition from him to Convocation. The petition, debated on 11 May, deplored the growth of Catholic beliefs and practices in the Church, especially the Real Presence and sacramental confession; condemned a list of vestments, ornaments, and ceremonies as unlawful; and called for firmer episcopal control, since 'the long neglect of the Ordinaries themselves has been the cause of the confusion and disorder which now exists'. After the two months' peace Kensit or members of his family were active in churches again: in July Lord Halifax attended a service at St Michael's, Shoreditch, where 'the Misses Kensit and thirteen myrmidons were put out'.[91]

Kensit's church protests were noticed in Parliament, Samuel Smith declaring on 16 June that they were 'the beginning of a great revolution'. Kensit was much in demand as a speaker and addressed a demonstration of the Protestant Alliance on 3 May, the Church Association annual meeting next day, an audience in the Christian Institute at Glasgow on 6 September, and many other gatherings.[92] The Wycliffe preachers were active from the summer of

[90] Munson, 'The Oxford Movement', 385.

[91] Machin, op. cit. 285–8; *Guardian,* 13 Apr. 1898, p. 547, 18 May, p. 747; *Daily Graphic,* 3 May, p. 10, 10 May, p. 8; Louise Creighton, *Life and Letters of Mandell Creighton* (2 vols., London, 1913), ii. 215, 288–97, 351 ff.; Lockhart, op. cit. ii. 132–4.

[92] *The Protestant Alliance: Verbatim Report of Speeches Delivered at the Great Demonstration, 3 May 1898* (London, 1898); account of Kensit's speech at Glasgow in *Bulwark,* Oct. 1898, pp. 117–18; *The Rock,* 2 Sept., p. 563.

1898, and a 'Kensit Protestant crusade' demonstration was held in Exeter Hall, London, in October 1899.[93]

In 1900 Kensit and some Wycliffe preachers toured the Midlands and North of England. They visited Belper in Derbyshire on 13 and 14 January and were ejected from a church when they commenced a protest, Kensit making a speech in the street. At St Matthew's, Sheffield, where the Ritualist G. C. Ommanney was vicar, a protest was made by Kensit and his son on 30 January, with a similar result. On 12 March Kensit and several Wycliffe preachers removed some ornaments from a church at Womersley, South Yorkshire. Apparently intending to send the ornaments to the Archbishop of York, they were pursued to a railway station by the vicar, churchwardens, and policemen, and the ornaments were returned. At Wakefield two days later the Kensitites encountered an inimical crowd, and on visiting the village of Hickleton on Lord Halifax's estate on 3 April they were rendered inaudible by unfriendly noises while Lord and Lady Halifax looked on. Later it was alleged that some Kensitites returned to Hickleton and destroyed a memorial cross erected by Halifax, but this was denied.

On Good Friday 1900, Kensit supported by some forty companions protested against 'blasphemous idolatry' in a service at St Mary Magdalene, Munster Square, London; again there was ejection and an address by Kensit outside the church. In mid-May he protested at East Retford, Nottinghamshire; in June he denounced the ordination of a deacon at St Paul's Cathedral; and that summer the Wycliffe preachers addressed crowds at Scarborough and Whitby and visited towns in County Durham and elsewhere.[94] On 9 July the Archbishop of York drew the Lords' attention to 'a gang of disorderly persons going about the country' and was assured by Lord Chancellor Halsbury that legal punishments existed to deal with them.[95] In September at the Church Congress Kensit attacked the Archbishops and Bishops for abusing their trust by allowing gross indiscipline in the national Church.[96]

Whether or not Lady Wimborne was known as 'Kensitina', as Halifax alleged, she was certainly a female counterpart of Kensit and Harcourt in anti-Ritualist zeal. Apart from helping to spread the widely current (but strongly denied) rumour that Ritualist priests conducted part of their Palm Sunday service seated on a donkey,[97] Lady Wimborne was founder and president of the Ladies' League for the Defence of the Reformed Faith of the Church of

[93] *T*, 28 Oct. 1899, p. 13.

[94] Machin, op. cit. 288–9; *Guardian*, 17 Jan. 1900 p. 110, 7 Feb. p.212, 21 Mar., p. 422, 11 Apr., p. 522, 18 Apr., p. 552, 13 June, p. 840; *AR* ii (1900), 8; F. G. Belton (ed.), *Ommanney of Sheffield: Memoirs* (London, 1936), 124–5; Lockhart, op. cit. ii. 135; *The Rock*, 17 Aug., p. 13, 2 Sept., p. 563, 9 Sept., p. 578; *Church Times*, 7 Sept. 1900, p. 235.

[95] H lxxxv. 928–31.

[96] Revd J. C. Wilcox, *John Kensit, Reformer and Martyr: A Popular Life*, Protestant Truth Society (London, [1902]), 48–51; Sandford, *Temple*, ii. 311–12.

[97] Machin, op. cit. 289–90; *Guardian*, 3 Jan. 1900, p. 6, 10 Jan., p. 40: *T*, 13 Feb. 1899, p. 12; H. H. Maughan, Some Brighton Churches (London, 1922), 61.

England. Commencing in 1899, this body had nearly 4,500 members and twenty-nine branches by May 1901, and united with the National Protestant Church Union in 1906 to become the National Church League. When the *Ladies' League Gazette* began in March 1900 it linked imperialism and Protestantism, 'the strongest national forces'. The Boers were trying to throw off the Queen's supremacy, the Ritualists that of the Privy Council—'both alike proclaim their independence of constituted authority'.[98] The young Liverpool barrister F. E. Smith (later Earl of Birkenhead) accepted the paid post of organizing secretary for the Ladies' League in the North of England. His appointment was soon terminated on the motion of the league's zealous treasurer William Joynson-Hicks (later Lord Brentford and president of the National Church League), though it is most unlikely that this occurred because, as was later retailed, he thoughtlessly hung pictures of the Virgin Mary in the society's rooms.[99] At any rate Smith kept the reputation of a Protestant stalwart by defending anti-Catholic propagandists and prosecuting their attackers in the law courts.

Anti-Ritualist agitation was rife in Liverpool, still a hotbed of sectarian politics where long-standing anti-romanism readily produced anti-Ritualism. This was supported in that city by Orange lodges and the powerful Working-men's Conservative Association led by Archibald Salvidge (who ironically had a Roman Catholic wife). It was also championed by the Laymen's League formed in July 1898 and led by George Wise and Austin Taylor; this produced a Church Discipline Bill, drafted by the League's solicitor Mr Frodsham and presented annually in Parliament by Liverpool Unionist MPs.[1] George Wise, a propagandist resembling Kensit and later a city councillor and pastor of an independent congregation, led processions of protest to Anglo-Catholic churches, at one of which the vicar, the Revd John Wakeford, was an outspoken High-Church champion.[2] In November 1900 Wise stood in the school board election as the nominee of the British Protestant Union (which he had founded) and headed the poll, obtaining twice as many votes as his nearest rival.[3] He gained even more popular support in the next few years.

The English Church Union agreed in June 1898 that it would give all possible support to the Bishops in settling liturgical problems. There were continual complaints—for example from the Earls of Portsmouth and Kimberley and Lord Kinnaird in the Lords early in 1899—that Bishops had condoned the spread of Ritualism by vetoing prosecutions. Archbishops and

[98] *Guardian*, 29 May 1901, p. 726; *Ladies' League Gazette*, I. i. 4–5, also 5–8.

[99] H. A. Taylor, *Jix, Viscount Brentford* (London, 1933), 67–72; J. Campbell, *F. E. Smith, First Earl of Birkenhead* (London, 1983), 93–5.

[1] Campbell, op. cit. 86–8; S. Salvidge, *Salvidge of Liverpool: Behind the Political Scene, 1890–1928* (London, 1934), 29–31; *T*, 4 Jan. 1899, p. 6.

[2] *T*, 1 Apr. 1899, p. 5, also 14 Apr. 1900, p. 3.

[3] Ibid. 17 Nov. 1900, p. 10; P. J. Waller, *Democracy and Sectarianism: A Political and Social History of Liverpool, 1868–1939* (Liverpool, 1981), 188.

Bishops for their part claimed that the veto had been little used and insisted they were trying to contain indiscipline by non-litigious means.[4] When the two Archbishops constituted themselves a tribunal to assess the ritual problem, Portsmouth said the tribunal had no legal basis and would not be able to enforce its decisions.[5] Proceedings began at Lambeth Palace on 6 May 1899 and four days later the Commons adopted a resolution that legislation would be necessary if episcopal efforts were not successful.[6]

The archiepiscopal decision was announced on 31 July that the use of incense and processional lights was illegal, though Temple envisaged possible relaxation of this rule 'when our toleration of one another had risen to a higher level'.[7] Harcourt welcomed the judgment but it was regarded as inadequate by many anti-Ritualists because it did not deal with other matters such as confession. Among Ritualists reactions differed widely. There was considerable disposition to obey the decision but also much resistance. Halifax declared at an ECU meeting in October that the decision was not acceptable, and thereafter vigorously condemned it. An abrasive protest signed by 13,794 communicants was handed to Temple by a deputation in January 1900, and Temple in reply defended the decision. On 30 January Lord Portsmouth deprecated the judgment at the Albert Hall demonstration. Temple made a further pronouncement in May, discouraging the practice of reserving the Sacrament, and in January 1901 a letter was issued by the Archbishops and Bishops to the clergy calling on them to submit to the decisions. These efforts had some quietening effect, but by no means brought the disputes to an end.[8]

Harcourt might say that he only wanted to stir the Bishops into more effective action, but many anti-Ritualists wanted to carry a stringent new law against Ritualist practice. This demand embarrassed the Government because of differences among its members and followers over ritual, and because it was trying to appeal to Irish Catholics by encouraging denominational education and social reform. Both parties, indeed, were divided over Ritualism. The Liberals, being in opposition, might have found it easier than the Government to take an anti-Ritualist position, and Harcourt's stand caused many anti-Ritualists, including Walsh and Kensit, to say they would transfer their vote to the Liberals. But there were differences among Liberals on the subject. Whereas Campbell-Bannerman, Asquith, and Lloyd George supported Smith and Harcourt in Parliament, and Lloyd George described Ritualism at a Baptist

[4] ECU Minutes, 16 June 1898 (CU dep. 5, 145); H lxvi. 265–309, lxvii. 1166–78; G. K. A. Bell, *Randall Davidson, Archbishop of Canterbury* (2 vols., London, 1935), i. 331–40.

[5] H lxix. 96 ff.

[6] See below, p. 245–6.

[7] Sandford, op. cit. ii. 294–302.

[8] Ibid. ii. 302–6; Lockhart, op. cit. ii. 128; *AR* i (1899), 175–6, 236–7 i (1900), 17–18, ii (1900), 3; *Guardian*, 24 Jan. 1900, pp. 141–3, 7 Feb., pp. 211–12; *T*, 12 Oct. 1900, p. 5; Bishop Davidson of Winchester to Harcourt, 25 Aug. 1899; Bell, op. cit. i. 341; M. MacColl, 'The Lambeth Decision and the Law', *FR* lxvii (1900), 224–42; J. B. Atlay, *Life of the Rt. Revd Ernest Roland Wilberforce* (London, 1912), 262–73; Creighton, op. cit. ii. 377.

Union assembly as 'a system of salvation by haberdashery', Herbert Gladstone voted on the other side.[9] In any case the Liberals were still officially committed to Home Rule, though in fact divided over this policy, and many of them were struggling to preserve an alliance with Irish Catholics. It was very difficult to avoid offending Roman Catholics by attacks on Anglo-Catholic ritual, although anti-Ritualists claimed they were assailing only Anglican practices which infringed the law of the establishment. Roman Catholic MPs such as William Redmond sometimes showed offence during debates on Ritualism.[10] Many Liberals might have thought that the support of Catholics, who in any case inclined to support the Conservatives over education, could be dispensed with if it were compensated by the recapture of Liberal Unionists and the gain of Conservative voters. But the question placed the Liberals in a dilemma and many wanted to retain the Home Rule alliance.[11]

The Liberal leaders had no agreed line on Ritualism, and any support the anti-Ritualists gave them was welcome so long as it did not mean having to adopt a definite attitude. But for the Government it was more necessary to have a general policy. The introduction of new legislation was seriously considered by the Cabinet at the end of 1898, and a discipline bill was included in the Government programme for 1899 but then deleted.[12] Attempts to impose a new law might only worsen the troubles and hasten the disruption of the Church. Conservative leaders consequently tried to play down the agitation and encourage a settlement by means of episcopal persuasion. Devonshire tried to brush off 'these silly ecclesiastical squabbles', and the attitude of Salisbury and Balfour was similar if more serious. Salisbury, a High-Churchman who was anxious to maintain the strength and stability of the Church of England, said 'the Ritualists are a great evil . . . on account of the anarchy they have introduced into the Church'. They were indeed 'idiots', but the agitation against them was 'very superficial'. Balfour's broad philosophic approach to religion had been displayed in his *Defence of Philosophic Doubt* (1879) and *Foundations of Belief* (1895), and he was personally very remote from, as he stated, the 'abhorrent subject' of violent liturgical quarrels which 'filled the world with the noise of unprofitable controversy'. Both Salisbury and Balfour, addressing meetings in the winter of 1898–9, said the Bishops should be left to restore order. Balfour, who was strongly anti-Erastian, said Parliament should only intervene if episcopal action failed.[13]

---

[9] Voting on Smith's amendment, 21 June 1898; H lix. 1073 ff. and *Protestant Alliance Official Organ* (Aug. 1898), 86–7; J. Grigg, *The Young Lloyd George* (London, 1973), 215.

[10] Speech of William Redmond, with denials by Samuel Smith, 9 Feb. 1899; H lxvi. 418–26.

[11] Duncan Basden to Harcourt, 2 Dec. 1898; HP, 239, fo. 7; J. W. Mellor to Harcourt, 7 Dec.; ibid. 49–54.

[12] J. R. Holding, 'Third Salisbury Cabinet', 88–9.

[13] Earl of Durham to Harcourt, 12 Jan. 1899; HP, 240, fo. 106b; Salisbury to MacColl, 1 Aug. 1898, 9 Feb, 1899; Russell, *Malcolm MacColl*, 219; *AR* i (1898), 202, i (1899), 9–10; Balfour to Devonshire, 26 Sept. 1900, copy; BP, 49769, fos. 187–8; Balfour to George Talbot, 16 Feb. 1899; Blanche Dugdale, *Arthur James Balfour, First Earl of Balfour* (2 vols., London, 1936), i. 277–8; Balfour to Revd J. W. Adams, 22 June 1900, copy; BP, 49853, fos. 210–11.

Thus, although some Liberals and some Conservatives advocated anti-Ritualist legislation, neither side supported it as a party. Leading politicians did not want the increased trouble in the Church which such a policy would cause, and anti-Ritualism did not become powerful enough to change this attitude. Many Church discipline bills were introduced but none was successful.

In March 1898 a bill to strengthen Church discipline received a first reading in the Commons but went no further. Ritualism was debated extensively in the 1899 session. An amendment to the Address by Samuel Smith on 9 February, asking that 'some legislative steps should be taken to secure obedience to the law' drew opposition from a wide range of religious opinion in Parliament and was heavily defeated.[14] The House preferred a more general resolution which did not seek new legislation. A motion on 11 April by Sydney Gedge, a Conservative MP, deplored a recent memorial of the English Church Union and hoped that Ministers would give preferment only to clergymen whom they believed would obey the ecclesiastical law. The motion was withdrawn, but an amended version by C. G. T. Bartley, omitting the specific reference to the ECU was carried by 200 votes to fourteen.[15]

On 10 May 1899 the first of a series of Church discipline bills drafted by the Liverpool Laymen's League was brought into the Commons for a second reading. The bill sought to abolish the episcopal veto; to establish a new civil method of trying ritual cases; and to impose deprivation of living, rather than imprisonment, on recalcitrant clergy. The bill received much support from Protestant societies and meetings, but not all the Conservative or Liberal Unionist MPs for Liverpool fully agreed with it. Walter Long, President of the Board of Agriculture, held that as a Cabinet Minister he could not support a bill which might bring about disestablishment, and this led to his not standing again for the West Derby division of Liverpool at the next election. 'Poor Long', wrote Archibald Salvidge, 'I am afraid he will have to quit West Derby.' Before the debate Salvidge and Austin Taylor spent two days seeking the support of MPs for the bill.[16]

Balfour had anticipated this debate with 'grave anxiety'. It would be 'disastrous' for him, he wrote, to sanction the measure on behalf of the Government, but he could at least defend the Protestant nature of the establishment.[17] The Government intervened with a compromise. Charles McArthur, MP for Liverpool Exchange, introduced the bill, saying it was necessary because the laity did not have confidence in the Bishops. But the Attorney-General, Sir Richard Webster, condemned the bill's harshness and moved an amendment that, if the current efforts of Archbishops and Bishops

[14] H lxvi. 344–460; Augustine Birrell, *Things Past Redress* (London, 1937), 146, 293–304.
[15] H lxix.787–872.
[16] *T*, 11 Jan. 1899, p. 7, 12 Jan., p. 8, 14 Apr., p. 12, 3 May, p. 3, 8 May, p. 11, 10 May, pp. 12, 13; *Guardian*, 25 July 1900, p. 1052; Salvidge, op. cit. 31–3; P. J. Waller, *Democracy and Sectarianism: A Political and Social History of Liverpool, 1868–1939* (Liverpool, 1981), 174–6.
[17] Balfour to Arthur Elliot, 8 May 1899; Elliot Papers, 20.

were not speedily effectual, legislation would be required. Harcourt, attacking the Bishops, gave substantial support to the bill; Sir John Kennaway, an Evangelical Churchman, opposed the measure but supported the amendment; Lord Hugh Cecil opposed both bill and amendment; and Balfour beseeched the House to throw the bill out—existing law as administered by the Bishops would, he believed, be sufficient. The second reading was rejected by 310 votes to 156; some Home Rulers and one or two Liberals supported Conservatives in the majority, and the minority comprised 119 Liberals, thirty-three Conservatives, and four Liberal Unionists.[18] The amendment was then carried without division.

On 1 February 1900 Balfour said in reply to a question in the Commons that the Government would not bring in disciplinary legislation that session. Next day another 'Liverpool' Church discipline bill was introduced but did not go beyond the first reading.[19] With the exception of 1902, similar bills were brought in every year until 1911. Only in 1903, however, did the bill reach a second reading, and even then made no further progress. Had a measure passed it is highly unlikely that peace would have come to the Church. Fiercer conflict, perhaps even schism, would have ensued. The example of the Public Worship Regulation Act was not encouraging.

The relative political weakness of anti-Ritualism was shown in election results. This was not through lack of preparation by anti-Ritualist leaders and organizations. The Church Association said in July 1898 that the Protestant vote should be marshalled and used to the best effect, and the Association announced in 1900 that 'after the war is over the great question for the Hustings at the General Election will be the suppression of the Mass and the Confessional in the Church of England'. Kensit, visiting Leeds in July 1899, suggested that a Protestant Electors' League should be formed there.[20] Anti-Ritualism figured in by-elections in 1898 and 1899, but the results were no more than equivocal. Anti-Ritualist support may have assisted the return of a Liberal candidate, C. P. Trevelyan, at Elland (Yorkshire) in March 1899; and was significant at Southport in both August 1898 and May 1899, members of the Liverpool Laymen's League intervening to help the successful Liberal candidates.[21] But at Oldham in July 1899 Winston Churchill and James Mawdsley, the Conservative candidates, were defeated although they had agreed to support the Church discipline bill and Churchill had publicly noted his kinship with Lady Wimborne. Two Liberals who did not support the bill were returned.[22] In the same month a Liberal who had promised full support for the bill was

[18] H lxxi. 231–300; *AR* i (1899), 100–1.
[19] H lxxviii. 293–4, 416. Cf. S. Smith, *Ritualism in the Church of England in 1900* (London, 1901).
[20] Machin, op. cit. 295.
[21] *T*, 22 Feb. 1899, p. 11; C. P. Trevelyan Papers, 35 (press cuttings); Waller, op. cit. 174–5, 176–7; Salvidge, op. cit. 33–4; *AR* i (1899), 112, 133.
[22] *AR* i (1899), 134–5; R. R. James (ed.), *Winston S. Churchill: His Complete Speeches* (8 vols., New York, 1974), i. 36–45.

unsuccessful at Osgoldcross, Yorkshire, and a Conservative was returned for East St Pancras, London, although he had 'spurned the Church Association'.[23] Other questions complicated the issue in these contests, but taking the group as a whole anti-Ritualism did not yet seem to possess great political weight. Malcolm MacColl of course wanted to minimize the importance of anti-Ritualism and his assessment was premature. Nevertheless he was not too far from the mark in telling Salisbury that the results showed 'that the agitation . . . has never touched the masses and that the Church Association and the Protestant Laymen's League are a negligible quantity in the electorate'.[24]

Attempts to organize the Protestant vote were being made well ahead of the 'Khaki' general election. The secretary of the Church Association, Henry Miller, told Harcourt in June 1898: 'we are issuing Books daily for various constituencies for the enrolment of voters, Liberal and Conservative, who will use their votes at the next Election for the Protestant Cause before all else'. The council of the Imperial Protestant Federation decided in July 1899 to issue 'electoral rolls', including a declaration to be signed by electors that they would vote only in accordance with decisions on how best to secure 'the return of a Protestant party to the House of Commons, powerful enough to counteract the voting power of the Roman Catholic and Ritualistic parties in Parliament'.[25] The National Protestant League employed fifteen agents to obtain pledges to vote in accordance with presumed Protestant interests. It was hoped to form Protestant groups and electoral councils in each constituency.[26] The object was to return MPs who would vote for a discipline bill. This was against the advice of Salisbury. He replied on 16 July to Lord Portsmouth, who urged in the Lords the need for fresh legislation, that patience and persuasion should be maintained. Legislation would be counter-productive, and 'all arts other than those which depend upon litigation' should be tried.[27]

Chamberlain and other Ministers had urged an election since mid-summer because of victories in the war. Salisbury was reluctant to agree, but yielded in mid-August. Parliament was dissolved in September and most of the polling took place in early October.[28] The *Annual Register* stated that, with the exception of imperial policy, Ritualism was pressed harder on candidates than any other question. Certainly the Church Association, Protestant Imperial Federation, Calvinist Protestant Union, Scottish Reformation Society, and other bodies were assiduous in circulating test questions to candidates based on

[23] *AR* i (1899), 134–5.
[24] MacColl to Salisbury, 17 July 1899; Russell, op. cit. 222–3.
[25] H. Miller to Harcourt, 20 June 1898; HP, 235, fos. 77–8; *Imperial Protestant Federation: Report for 1899–1900* (London, [1900]), 21. Cf. Austin Taylor, 'The Ritualists and the Electorate', *CR* lxxvi (1899), 488.
[26] *DN*, 20 Sept. 1900, p. 5; *The Disruption of the Church of England by More than 9,000 Clergymen*, Church Association (London, 1900), app.
[27] H lxxxvi. 10–36.
[28] E. J. Feuchtwanger, *Democracy and Empire: Britain, 1865–1914* (London, 1985), 240.

the Church discipline bill, the coronation oath, and opposition to a Catholic university. The Protestant Women's Institute said its members should be 'up and doing in the matter of circulating Protestant literature'. Lord Portsmouth (a Liberal about to become a Liberal Unionist) tried to insist on 'Protestantism before politics', urging support for candidates of any party who favoured new disciplinary steps. The English Church Union responded vigorously, advising electors to support a radical disestablishment candidate rather than a Conservative who advocated a discipline bill.[29] In Liverpool the Liberals put up a weak resistance to the dominant Unionists, but these differed over Ritualism. Walter Long left his seat for one at Bristol. Another local member, J. H. Stock, annoyed Salvidge and his Conservative Working Men's Association by reneging on his support for the discipline bill, but changed his mind again and kept his seat. He had 'surrendered to the wire pullers', said the *Church Times* disgustedly.[30]

Disestablishment was another election issue, largely in reaction against a National Church said to be succumbing to the Ritualists. Lady Wimborne called on Conservatives who defended the establishment to be decidedly anti-Ritualist, lest their seats be lost to pro-disestablishment anti-Ritualist Liberals.[31] The Liberation Society issued tracts and a circular urging the electoral importance of disestablishment and the opportunity given to it by anti-Ritualism. Carvell Williams argued in a memorandum of 9 July that, since the Liberals were certain to lose the election, voluntaries had no need to support non-voluntary Liberal candidates: voluntaries should insist that their principle be adopted by Liberals. But the Society's executive committee decided against this contentious strategy and voluntaryism played a fairly muted role in the election though it was consistently advocated by Campbell-Bannerman. The Liberal manifesto made only a passing reference to the need for 'complete religious equality'.[32]

Home Rule was also a minor issue in the contest. Under the presidency of T. P. O'Connor, the new United Irish League of Great Britain (successor to the INLGB) supported Liberals who were friendly to Home Rule, but most Liberal candidates treated this as a dormant question and had no intention of pledging themselves on it. A Liberal candidate in a Glasgow division was denounced as a traitor to Home Rule and Irish voters were urged to support his

[29] *AR* i (1900), 202–3; *T*, 1 Oct. 1900, p. 9, 2 Oct., p. 8; *The Rock*, 21 Sept., p. 8; *Bulwark*, Sept. 1900, p. 196, Nov 1900, p. 243; *The Protestant Woman*, Oct. 1900, p. 220; *Church Times*, 21 Sept., p. 285, 28 Sept., p. 310; *Ladies League Gazette*, i. 8, 144–5.

[30] *T*, 19 Sept. 1900, p. 8; *DN*, 19 Sept., p. 7, 21 Sept., p. 8, 22 Sept., p. 8, 25 Sept., p. 5; *Church Times*, 28 Sept., p. 310.

[31] Lady Wimborne, 'Ritualism and the General Election', *Nineteenth Century*, xlviii (1900), 547–8. Cf. LS, 10 Sept. 1900; A/LIB/9, p. 137.

[32] LS, 10 Sept. 1900 (9), p. 137; CCDI Minutes (executive committee), 3 Aug., 21 Sept., 2 Nov. 1900 (vol. 35, pp. 364, 368–70, 376–8); *DN*, 21 Sept., p. 5, 22 Sept., p. 5; *Dundee Advertiser*, 2 Oct., p. 7, 5 Oct., p. 6; Hamer, *Electoral Pressure*, 163–4; F. W. S. Craig (ed.), *British General Election Manifestos, 1900–1974* (London, 1975), 4–6.

Unionist opponent, Andrew Bonar Law. The wishes of the Catholic hierarchy were to be opposed. Catholic Bishops and the *Tablet* advised Catholics to vote Conservative in order to defend their schools and support the proposed Catholic university, but T. P. O'Connor insisted that Home Rule should be the main question for Irish voters.[33] So the latter, like the Liberals, were in a state of unhappy division.

Not much headway was made in the election by anti-Ritualists who wanted new legislation. It was later claimed that in nine constituencies the 'Protestant roll' was responsible for the defeat of the sitting member, in some cases a Conservative and in others a Liberal, but it is impossible to verify this supposition.[34] Liverpool, where only three of the nine seats were contested, consolidated its position as the anti-Ritualist capital by returning eight Unionists (seven Conservatives and a Liberal Unionist) who supported the discipline bill. There was nothing like this anywhere else, though it has been suggested that anti-Ritualism in the addresses of Liberal candidates in East Anglia and Lincolnshire was partly responsible for relative Liberal success in that region.[35] Kensit decided rather late to stand as a 'Protestant' at Brighton, in an area of intense Ritualist dispute. Although defeated he gained a fairly satisfactory 4,693 votes. Benjamin Nicholson, chairman of the Protestant Alliance, also stood as a Protestant at Ashford, Kent; he obtained both Anglican and Nonconformist support but failed by a long way to dislodge a Conservative who would not support a discipline bill. At Tunbridge Wells another Conservative, Griffith-Boscawen, was returned against ultra-Protestant opposition. Balfour gave a negative answer to a deputation from three Protestant bodies asked him to promise fresh legislation, but was returned for East Manchester with a much enlarged majority. Lord Hugh Cecil, son of Salisbury, obtained an increased majority at Greenwich though he had been criticized as a Ritualist sympathizer.[36]

The results showed the Unionists had gained over fifty per cent of the votes, more than in 1895, though their overall majority was eighteen below the figure in that year. 334 Conservatives and sixty-eight Liberal Unionists were successful. The appeal of war success had overcome a recent Liberal revival in by-elections and disappointment with the Government's social reform record

[33] *DN*, 1 Oct., p. 5, 2 Oct., pp. 3, 5; *Dundee Advertiser*, 29 Sept., p. 6, 2 Oct., pp. 5, 6; *T*, 2 Oct., p. 9; *AR* i (1900), 198; I. Wood, 'Irish Immigrants and Scottish Radicalism', in I. Macdougall (ed.), *Essays in Scottish Labour History*, 80–1; Catriona Levy, 'Conservatism and Liberal Unionism in Glasgow 1874–1912', Ph.D. thesis (Dundee, 1983), 347–9; W. D. Ross, 'Politics and Opinion in Bradford, 1880–1906 with Special Reference to Parliamentary Elections', Ph.D. thesis (Bradford, 1977), 285; L. W. Brady, *T. P. O'Connor and the Liverpool Irish* (London, 1983), 163; Snead-Cox, *Vaughan*, ii. 126–7.

[34] *T*, 10 Nov. 1903, p. 11.

[35] H. Pelling, *Social Geography of British Elections, 1885–1910* (London, 1967), 104–5, 226–7, also 157.

[36] Machin, op. cit. 296–7; *T*, 3 Oct. 1900, p. 9, 5 Oct., p. 8, 8 Oct., p. 9; *Church Times*, 5 Oct., pp. 343, 347; *Dundee Advertiser*, 1 Oct., pp. 4, 6 (for Balfour's reply).

to give a strong endorsement to Ministers. Conservatives did particularly well in urban constituencies, and Chamberlain said the large majorities obtained by many Unionists denoted a sizeable transfer of votes. The Liberals, bitterly at odds over imperialism and the war, had put up a weak opposition and left 143 Unionist seats uncontested (excluding Ireland and the universities) as against 110 in 1895.[37] Only 186 Liberals were returned, nine more than in 1895. Liberals did well in Wales, winning twenty-eight of the thirty-three seats and regaining some ground lost five years before; but badly in Scotland, where the Unionists' thirty-eight seats won the first non-Liberal majority since 1832. The removal of Irish Catholic support was given by some candidates as a reason for the Liberal failure.[38] Disestablishment had been at a discount, though the Liberation Society had tried to use anti-Ritualism to advance it and could note without despair that 114 Nonconformists had been returned, sixty-one of whom belonged to the Society.[39] By no means all the Nonconformists returned were Liberals, but Nonconformists were probably not far short of half the Liberal representation. Anti-Ritualism, while obviously effective in several constituencies, had not made a great impact on an electorate which was mainly concerned with imperial war.

But efforts to make anti-Ritualism strong and popular were by no means over. 'We are only now making a beginning', the chief registrar of the National Protestant League had said in September. 'At the next election, I hope our power will be manifest.' The English Church Union pointed to the defeat of several anti-Ritualists of both parties. The moderate *Guardian* tended to play down the effects of anti-Ritualist efforts, and the high *Church Times* said that any apparent successes gained by anti-Ritualism were really owing to imperialist fervour. But the *Rock* was pleased by the anti-Ritualist showing. It said that Liberals had gained Hastings and Torquay because of the Protestant vote, and that 188 seats had been won by candidates pledged to support the Church discipline bill in contests with candidates who were against it. Certainly MacColl was engaging in wishful thinking when he claimed that Kensit's crusade was 'practically dead'.[40] Balfour was visited by an anti-Ritualist deputation from Liverpool, and in December he told Temple that 'the inevitable battle over ritualistic excesses' would be renewed in the next Parliamentary session. He hoped the Bishops' efforts to check ritual could show definite results, otherwise the demand for stringent legislation might strengthen.

Balfour did receive letters from Bishops saying that disobedience to the

[37] Feuchtwanger, op. cit. 249; *DN*, 10 Oct., p. 2.

[38] Campbell-Bannerman to Herbert Gladstone, 19 Oct. 1900; HGP, 45987, fo. 123, and 22 Oct. (quoted A. Davey, *The British Pro-Boers, 1877–1902*, Tafelberg, SA, 1978, 178).

[39] LS, 29 Oct. 1900; A/LIB/9, 43; *T*, 1 Nov. 1900, p. 9. Cf. S. Koss, *Nonconformity in Modern British Politics* (London, 1975), 227.

[40] *DN*, 20 Sept. 1900, p. 5; *Ladies' League Gazette*, i. 8, 145; *Church Union Gazette*, 3 Nov., p. 293; *Church Times*, 12 Oct., pp. 383, 385; *Rock*, 12 Oct., p. 3, 19 Oct., p.8; *Record*, 12 Oct., p. 982; Russell, op. cit. 224

Lambeth decisions was rare among their clergy. Despite the statement of one of Balfour's secretaries that the Archbishop was 'too senile to notice anything less than a knock-down blow', a strong hint from Balfour to Temple produced a letter from the Archbishops and Bishops to their clergy, dated 16 January 1901. The letter called for wider submission to the Lambeth rulings, and it probably had some effect.[41] When Edmund Knox became Bishop of Manchester in October 1903 his predecessor told him that only two incumbents out of 600 were refusing to obey his instruction to stop wearing the chasuble.[42] As well as admonishing, the Bishops could punish persistently disobedient clergy by refusing to carry out confirmations in their churches, to license curates for them, or to grant them money from diocesan funds. When questioned in Parliament, Balfour said in February that episcopal efforts seemed to be establishing better discipline.[43]

Although Balfour and the Bishops insisted that the problem was receding, anti-Ritualists claimed otherwise and the struggle continued. Balfour was pressed to introduce Government legislation. Lady Wimborne and others continued to write against Ritualism, numerous meetings were held against it, and lectures by Kensit and others continued to provoke, or serve as a pretext for physical clashes between Catholic and Protestant.[44] Anti-Ritualism still provided an argument for disestablishment. The Synod of the Presbyterian Church of England, for example, resolved in 1903 that 'the present connection between Church and State in England . . . involves the denial of Reformation principles and a tacit approval of the Sacerdotalism which is rapidly romanizing England'.[45] There was strong but unavailing opposition by the Church Association to the appointment of Charles Gore, a noted High-Churchman, as Bishop of Worcester in 1902. This showed, claimed a pamphlet of the Association, 'the steady determination of the Prime Minister to Romanize the Church of England through the bishops'.[46] Kensit also objected to the appointment of Winnington-Ingram as Bishop of London in April 1901.

There was anti-Ritualist opposition to the creation of new dioceses at Southwark and Birmingham, on the ground that Church discipline should be assured before new sees were created. This project was opposed by many

[41] Balfour to Temple, 15 Dec. 1900; Dugdale, Balfour, i. 282–3; Sydney Parry (a private secretary of Balfour) to Bishop Davidson, 15 Dec. 1900; ibid. i. 278–81; Parry to J. S. Sandars, 31 Dec.; BP, 49853, fos. 243–4; Bishop E. S. Talbot to Balfour, 9 Jan. 1901; BP, 49789, fos. 121–4; letters in BP, 49854, fos. 30–43; memo of Parry to Balfour, 22 May 1901; ibid. 111–12; AR i (1901), 50. Cf. Bishop Randall Davidson to Harcourt, 20 Sept. 1900; HP, 242, fo. 91.

[42] Knox, Reminiscences, 222.

[43] H xc. 86–9.

[44] Lady Wimborne, 'Rome or the Reformation', Nineteenth Century and After, lvi (July–Dec. 1904), 543–58; H. Macleod, Class and Religion in the Late Victorian City (London, 1974), 73.

[45] Digest of the Proceedings of the Synods of the Presbyterian Church of England, 1876–1905 (London, 1907),

[46] Prestige, Life of Charles Gore (London, 1935), 228–36; Lord Salisbury's Nomination to the Bishopric of Worcester, Church Association (London, [1901]), 1, 8.

Nonconformists. It also seemed threatened with obstruction from some Conservatives who disliked episcopal opposition to Government policy on public-house licences, 'Chinese slavery' in South Africa, and other matters. But the plan was finally sanctioned by Parliament in 1904.[47] Anti-Ritualists also opposed current efforts to soften the declaration against transubstantiation to be made by a new sovereign. Attempts were made to alter the declaration when Edward VII ascended the throne in 1901.[48] But the efforts were not successful. They met opposition not only from anti-Ritualists but also from High-Churchmen who thought the alteration insufficient and from Roman Catholics who wanted to abolish the declaration altogether.

A deputation of no fewer than 100 MPs called on the new Archbishop of Canterbury, Randall Davidson, on 11 March 1903 to urge stricter clerical discipline. Davidson said that illegal practices were slowly disappearing, and that further efforts at improvement should be left to the Bishops. To another deputation in May, Davidson said that a few disobedient clergy might have to be treated with 'firm and drastic action'—a statement which seemed to imply their suspension from duty or even expulsion from the Church.[49] In February 1903 Balfour expressed profound gloom about the persistently fractious state of the Church of England.[50]

Continued disturbances in Liverpool centred on Orange-Catholic clashes and the actions of George Wise and Kensit's Wycliffe preachers. In September 1902 J. A. Kensit (junior), leader of the preachers, was imprisoned in Liverpool for refusing to obey a court order to abstain for a year from addressing open-air meetings in the city. Kensit senior visited his son in Walton Gaol and attacked romanism in a lecture at Birkenhead. After the lecture he was struck by an iron bar and died in Liverpool infirmary (perhaps from other physical causes) on 8 October. Kensit's end was thus similar to that of William Murphy, another well-known anti-Catholic agitator, thirty years before. An Irish youth, John McKeever, was charged with Kensit's murder, F. E. Smith being crown prosecutor, but he was acquitted and carried in triumph through the streets.[51] Kensit's death caused renewed determination to continue his movement:

[47] P. S. Morrish, 'The Struggle to Create an Anglican Diocese of Birmingham', *JEH* xxxi (1980), 59–88; H cxxxiv. 397–460; Bishop Talbot to Salisbury, 8 July 1901; SP; Talbot to Balfour, 26 Feb. 1904; BP, 49789, fos. 218–19; Balfour to Talbot, Feb. 1904; ibid. 220–1, 18 July 1904; ibid. 226–7; Prestige, op. cit. 253–4; Sir. A. Fitzroy, *Memoirs*, 5th edn. (2 vols., London, n.d.), i. 206.

[48] H xcvi. 1104–33, xcvii. 1264–94, cxxiv. 494–530, cxxxvii. 268–314; *T*, 14 Feb. 1901, p. 10, 21 Feb., p. 10, 29 Mar., p. 14; Walter Walsh, *A Defence of the King's Protestant Declaration*, Imperial Protestant Federation (London, 1901); Snead-Cox, op. cit. ii. 241 ff.; Duke of Norfolk to Cardinal Vaughan, 2 and 7 Mar. 1901; Vaughan Papers, v. 1/5; Lockhart, *Viscount Halifax*, ii. 193–7; Minutes of United Presbyterian Presbytery of Edinburgh, 17 Sept. 1901; 111/42, 94–5; Ripon to Norfolk, 8 July 1903, copy; Ripon Papers, 43638, fos. 160–1.

[49] *AR* i (1903), 55: Lockhart, op. cit. ii. 141–2.

[50] Balfour to Bishop Talbot, 6 Feb. 1903; Dugdale, op. cit. i. 284–5.

[51] Wilcox, *John Kensit*, 66–9, 88 ff.; Waller, op. cit. 192.

Walter Walsh said Kensit's son was ready to take his place, and J. A. Kensit did so with vigour.[52]

In 1903 George Wise was also imprisoned and this led to further disturbances. But many Protestants recoiled from the anti-papist crudity of some of Wise's speeches, especially concerning the supposed private lives of priests, and from the mob warfare which was replacing religious argument. Faction fights developed between Conservatives and 'Protestants' in the 1903 municipal elections. Some Protestant candidates, including Wise, defeated Conservatives and Archibald Salvidge repudiated Wise for his disruptive extremism. Further cracks among Protestants were caused by the Tariff Reform movement. Austin Taylor, a firm Free Trader, deserted Conservatism for the Liberals. Thus the Liverpool Protestant campaign fell into internal dispute and disintegration. Wise remained active, becoming pastor of his own Protestant Reformers' Memorial Church, where he had the city's largest congregation, containing many reformed drunkards and conducting generally peaceful marches. But sectarian rioting remained endemic in the city for several years. In 1905 the police had to take special measures for preserving the peace on 223 occasions.[53]

Anti-Ritualism was sustained by the Government Education Bill of 1902 granting rate aid to Roman Catholic schools and Anglican ones believed to be influenced by Ritualism. The 'Liverpool' Church discipline bill obtained a second reading for the only time in 1903, and Ritualism then received its first sustained Parliamentary debate since 1899. Austin Taylor moved the second reading on 13 March, and the debate largely concerned the effectiveness or otherwise of the Bishops in restoring liturgical order. Harcourt condemned the futility of the Lambeth decisions but Balfour (now Prime Minister) opposed the bill and defended the Bishops. The second reading was carried by fifty-one, Campbell-Bannerman and Asquith voting in favour, but the bill petered out in committee.[54] Halifax said at an English Church Union meeting, which petitioned against the measure, that if the bill passed it would simply double the membership of the ECU and 'meet with the same ignominious failure as that which befell the Eccleciastical Titles Act [and] the Public Worship Regulation Act'.[55] A competing measure in 1903, introduced by C. A. Cripps, aimed at a different solution by increasing the power of the Bishops. This bill attracted different support, and like its rival passed its second reading but proceeded no further.[56] Protestant frustration at the lack of legislative initiative by the

---

[52] *Free Church Chronicle*, iv (1902), 295–6.

[53] Waller, op. cit. 200 ff.; Salvidge, op. cit. 43–7, 63–6; Campbell, *F. E. Smith*, 117; B. D. White, *A History of the Corporation of Liverpool* (Liverpool, 1951), 192; *T*, 4 Oct. 1902, p. 10, 27 Apr. 1903, p. 9, 28 Apr., p. 10, 30 Nov., p. 7.

[54] H cxix. 733–808.

[55] ECU Minutes, CU dep. 5, 183–4.

[56] H cxxi. 502–24.

Government on the question is said to have contributed to Liberal by-election gains, notably one at Brighton in April 1905.[57]

The Government tried to defuse the conflict by holding an official inquiry. A Parliamentary Select Committee was suggested, but High-Churchmen objected to attempted regulation by a body which might contain elements hostile to the Church's interests, and they had the support of Archbishop Davidson. 'To ask the Church to appear before a tribunal of her enemies is a gross insult and indignity', wrote Lord Hugh Cecil. The Bishops would accept a Royal Commission, however, as being more detached from the political fray, and it was more likely that its recommendations would be respected. So it was decided to issue a Royal Commission into Ecclesiastical Discipline, and its fourteen members were appointed in April 1904. They represented different sections of the Church but included no extreme anti-Ritualists.[58]

The Commission was strongly opposed by anti-Ritualists. On 20 April, after Balfour had announced the Commission's membership and its terms of reference, Austin Taylor moved the adjournment of the House, saying that legislation was needed and not a mere inquiry. He was seconded by Charles McArthur, who objected to the presence of two Bishops and the relative lack of 'Church Protestants' on the Commission. The inquiry was an attempt to shelve the question, 'a political expedient intended to tide over the next general election'. Another supporter of the motion said 'the intention of the Commission was to block the way to legislation'. But there were differences on the matter, even among the Liverpool Unionist MPs. Balfour said the Commission was adequately representative and the motion was lost. Many Nonconformists voted with Taylor in the minority, but Joseph Chamberlain and the Wesleyan Arthur Henderson, a Labour MP, opposed the motion.[59]

Beginning in early May 1904, the Commission held 118 sessions and examined 164 witnesses representing diverse opinions. The inquiry was strongly criticized for considering evidence of law-breaking only since May 1903.[60] Several times during 1905 Balfour was asked in Parliament when the report would appear. Austin Taylor asked in February whether it would be issued before the general election, but Balfour said he did not know when either event would take place.[61] The report eventually appeared in June 1906, five months after the election. While the Commission's proposals were awaited, the

---

[57] *AR* i (1905), 101. Cf. *78th Annual Report of Protestant Reformation Society for 1904* (London, 1905), 8; Churchill to Campbell-Bannerman, 15 May 1905; CBP, 41238, fo. 39.

[58] Cecil to Balfour, Mar. 1904; BP, 49759, fos. 43–6; Davidson to Balfour, 4 Mar. 1904; ibid. 49788, fos. 240–3; Lockhart, op. cit. ii. 141–4; Prestige, op. cit. 253; Bell, *Randall Davidson*, i. 454–61; Sir W. Joynson-Hicks, *The Prayer Book Crisis* (London, 1928), 89 ff.; R. Lloyd, *The Church of England, 1900–1965* (London, 1966), 138–9.

[59] H cxxxiii. 757–82.

[60] M. J. F. McCarthy, *Church and State in England and Wales, 1829–1906* (Dublin and London, 1906), 595–6.

[61] H cxli. 780.

anti-Ritualist agitation died down somewhat. But the continuing tension was such that the proposed reforms could easily cause a revival of open antagonism.

IV. SCOTS PRESBYTERIAN CHURCHES: UNION AND CONTENTION, 1895–1905

The prospect of union of all three major Presbyterian Churches in Scotland suffered a setback in the mid 1890s, but the union of most of the Free Church with the United Presbyterians progressed steadily towards attainment from 1897 to 1900. Informal conferences between members of the three Churches in 1894 and 1895 had agreed that the State should recognize the Church and respect its spiritual independence, and provide facilities for religious education, but had not agreed on the question of establishment which remained the major stumbling-block to union. The Church of Scotland General Assembly of 1896 decided to withdraw from co-operation with the other two Churches in producing a hymn-book. Although this decision was reversed the next year, bitterness had been created and the question of a threefold union was temporarily postponed as it seemed impractical.[62] This development strengthened the prospect of a more limited twofold union, which was supported however by many of those hoping for a wider combination.

In 1896 the United Presbyterian Synod invited the General Assembly of the Free Church to discuss union between their Churches. Robert Rainy advocated a cautious response, moving at the General Assembly that the invitation should be considered by the Assembly's Committee and brought before the next general meeting in 1897, the whole Church being asked in the mean time to give earnest consideration to the matter. The motion was accepted, and at the 1897 Free Church Assembly another motion of Rainy to proceed with union negotiations was overwhelmingly carried. Committees of the two Churches held frequent joint meetings, and their harmonious preparations were clouded only by the possibility of legal action by the Free Church minority opposed to union and by the consequent adverse effects on the property of a united Church. But of three leading legal opinions obtained, only one was unfavourable and the others were largely favourable to the union. Rainy told the Free Church Assembly in May 1900 that 'the Church should always be ready . . . to go forward under the conviction that God would take care of their property as well as other interests'.[63]

The Free Church Assembly of 1898 decided (with a minority opposing) that the establishment issue was no bar to union, as the original Free Church attachment to the principle of establishment was not part of the Church's subscribed formula. The practical details of union were thereafter agreed on,

[62] J. H. S. Burleigh, *A Church History of Scotland* (Edinburgh, 1960), 398–9; P. Carnegie Simpson, *The Life of Principal Rainy* (2 vols., London, 1909), ii. 197–204.
[63] Ibid. ii. 234.

but a Free Church Defence Association spoke for the opposing minority and campaigned against union.

The 1899 Free Church Assembly accepted the plan of union and, in accordance with constitutional practice, sent it down for decision by the presbyteries. Of these only four out of seventy-five (Dingwall, Inveraray, Lochcarron, and Skye) rejected the plan, though Inverness accepted it by only one vote. The Uniting Act was adopted by a huge majority in the Free Church Assembly in May 1900, and was also sent down to presbyteries. The Act was adopted unanimously by the Synod of the United Presbyterian Church in May, and was accepted by all its twenty-nine presbyteries, though fifteen of its kirk sessions (out of 539) opposed it and another fifteen were uncertain.[64] On 30 October the Act was passed in the Free Church Assembly by 643 to twenty-seven. Next day the union was formally effected in the presence of 6,000 people when the first Assembly of the United Free Church met in Waverley Market, Edinburgh. Rainy became first Moderator of the new Church. The tiny Free Kirk minority, however, reconstituted the Assembly which the large body of unionists had left. They elected a Moderator (the Revd C. A. Bannatyne) and resolved to continue as an independent Free Church.[65]

One of the main points of discussion was the union's effect on disestablishment. No official stand on the subject was taken by the new Church, where it was an open question. Rainy trusted, as he said in his moderatorial address, that 'a larger Presbyterianism for Scotland' would come out of the union, 'very friendly I hope to the civil authority, very serviceable to the welfare of the nation, but free from the temptations and the risks of a statutory connection with the State'.[66] This seemed a denial of any wish for establishment. Some claimed indeed that the union would bring a revived threat to the established status of the Church of Scotland, a question considerably neglected in the recent general election.[67] On the other hand, perhaps many Free Churchmen who joined the union, and even some United Presbyterians, were not opposed to establishment provided safeguards for spiritual independence could be obtained.[68] Disestablishment did remain an object of many in the United Free Church, and pronouncements in its favour were made for some years. But developments arose to remove attention from any fresh voluntary campaign and thereby to weaken indirectly the disestablishment cause.

The little Free Church remnant, whose members and adherents totalling perhaps 50,000 were largely in the Highlands and Islands, challenged its big rival over property rights as had been threatened before the union.[69] Over

[64] Dundee UP Presbytery Minutes, 8 Feb. 1899; CH3/91/13, 321–2.
[65] Simpson, op. cit. ii. 188 ff.; A. Stewart and J. K. Cameron, *The Free Church of Scotland, 1843–1900: A Vindication* (Edinburgh and Glasgow, [1910]), 103–14.
[66] Simpson, op. cit. ii. 252. Cf. W. Wallace, 'The Future of Church and Creed in Scotland', *FR* lxix (1901), 1055 ff.
[67] *T*, 4 Sept. 1900, p. 4; *Disestablishment Banner*, lix (Dec. 1900), 4–5.
[68] Cf. *British Weekly*, 20 Sept. 1900, pp. 425–6.
[69] Stewart and Cameron, op. cit. 130–1.

ninety congregations remained with the Free Church, which had initially only twenty-five ordained ministers. In many cases the buildings remained in the hands of a minister who had joined the United Free Church wth a minority of his congregation, so the problem of physical property was a severe one for the Free Kirk.[70] Since it was not offered a satisfactory share of the property, the Free Kirk proceeded to claim the entire temporalities of the pre-1900 Church. Its reasons were that those who had taken part in the union had abandoned the principle of establishment and the doctrine of predestination and therefore did not represent the Church of the 1843 Disruption. Only the Free Church remnant, it was held, maintained these tenets, and therefore only this was entitled to hold the 'whole lands, property and funds' of the larger pre-1900 Church which had held the property on the basis of those principles. A summons of the civil Court of Session was issued on 14 December 1900 to all the general trustees of the former Free Church and all the members of the union Assembly.

A bitter confrontation developed. In the main legal action the Free Church claimed all the property, but an alternative claim (to be pressed if the first one failed) held they were entitled to at least a proportionate share. In 1904 the 'Wee Frees' obtained a remarkable victory. On 1 August the House of Lords by a majority of five to two, after the leading opinion had been delivered by Lord Chancellor Halsbury, overturned the Court of Session's unanimous judgment of 4 July 1902 that the establishment principle was not fundamental to the pre-1900 Church. The whole amount, including trust money of some £2 millions, was judged to belong to the Free Church.[71] There was widespread astonishment and protest. The Free Church could scarcely enter fully into its inheritance as its twenty-eight ministers would have to manage about 700 churches and numerous overseas missions, as well as providing fifteen professors for three divinity colleges. 'The minority', wrote one protester, Samuel Smith, 'is almost as much to be sympathized with as the majority owing to the incredible burden of business laid upon them.'[72] Indeed the Free Church was prepared to transfer most of the property to the Government after providing comfortably for its own needs.[73]

The surrender of church buildings to the Free Kirk by legal process began in the autumn of 1904 and by mid-December eleven churches had been taken over. But there was a call from Church leaders and politicians for arbitration on the problem, and Free Churchmen welcomed Parliamentary intervention to dispose of the property after due inquiry. *The Times* and Asquith said that legislation might be necessary; Campbell-Bannerman suggested a committee

[70] *Dundee Advertiser*, 20 Sept. 1900, p. 4.

[71] Stewart and Cameron, op. cit. 119 ff.; Simpson, op. cit. ii. 300 ff.; *AR* i (1904), 235–7; R. B. Haldane, *An Autobiography* (London, 1929), 70–4; J. M. Sloan, 'The Scottish Free Church Case', *FR* lxxvi (1904), 450–61; *British Weekly*, 4 Aug. 1904 (leader).

[72] S. Smith, MP (ed.), *The Scotch Church Crisis: Articles and Letters to the Press* (London, [1904]), 5.

[73] Stewart and Cameron, op. cit. 268, 284.

be appointed to recommend a fair division of property between the two Churches.[74] The Secretary for Scotland, Graham Murray, suggested to both Churches that a Royal Commission should investigate the matter and propose action, and that another commission should make interim arrangements for the use of property. This proposal was accepted. The appointment of the three Royal Commissioners was announced on 13 December; and on 19 April 1905 they recommended that Parliament appoint an Executive Commission to take control of the property and divide it in a way intended to be liberal to the Free Church without being grossly illiberal to the United Free Church.

With Scottish Church legislation in prospect the Church of Scotland wished to gain something from it. Its General Assembly intervened with a unanimous request that the Government bill should contain a clause allowing the Church to draw up, independently of the State, a new formula to be subscribed by its ministers on ordination. This request was agreed to by Ministers, and the contentious Clause 5 of the bill, looking out of place among the other provisions, proposed to give the desired permission.[75]

The Churches (Scotland) Bill, introduced by Lord Advocate Scott Dickson on 7 June 1905, proposed to enact the Royal Commission's recommendations. An Executive Commission of five would allocate churches to the Free Kirk where its congregations equalled at least one-third of the pre-Union figure. Campbell-Bannerman generally welcomed the measure but strongly objected to the tacking on of Clause 5. 'You are not going in a casual way like this to give the Church of Scotland a new constitution in the expiring days of an expiring Parliament . . . the introduction of . . . this extraneous adventitious element into the Bill is a fatal course.'[76] Dislike of clause 5 was expressed by the Free Church and by some presbyteries in the UF Church. Both Churches objected to the plan for dividing property, the UF Church complaining that it was too generous to the Free Church and the latter that it was not generous enough.[77]

The second reading was debated on 4 and 12 July, particular attention being given to clause 5. Scott Dickson, defending the clause, said the Church of Scotland should have as much liberty as the UF Church on such matters, and Balfour supported the clause because he wanted the bill to assist all Scots Presbyterians and help their reunion. Campbell-Bannerman said the clause was

[74] *AR* i (1904), 238; Rainy to Campbell-Bannerman, 1 Nov. 1904; CBP, 41242, fos. 29–31; Stewart and Cameron, op. cit. 284. Cf. T. Shaw, *The Church Difficulty: A Way Out*, 2nd edn. (Edinburgh, 1904), 10 ff.; resolution of Congregational Union autumn assembly, 27 Sept. 1904; *Congregational Year-book* (1905), 9; resolution of Baptist autumn assembly, 4 Oct. 1904; *Baptist Hand-book* (1905), 246–7; W. T. Stead, *Are There Any Free Churches? An Examination of the Strange True Story of the Free Church of Scotland in the Light of the Recent Decision of the House of Lords* (London, 1904); Smith, *Ritualism*, 13 ff.

[75] *AR* i (1905), 241–3; Stewart and Cameron, op. cit. 297–304.

[76] H cxlvii. 972–80; Revd Dr James Robertson to Balfour, 15 June 1905; BP, 49790, fos. 168–73.

[77] Minutes of Edinburgh UP Presbytery, 20 June 1905; CH3/111/42, pp. 468–9; Stewart and Cameron, op. cit. 305–10. Cf. James Denney to Robertson Nicoll, 15 Sept. 1906 (W. Robertson Nicoll (ed.), *Letters of Principal James Denney* (London, 1920, 72–3); *Ar* i (1907), 261–2.

an 'undesirable alien' which should be dealt with in a separate bill. He was supported by English and Scottish Nonconformists who said that a Church should not have the freedom now desired without relinquishing its established status. But a defender of the clause said it was inconsistent with Liberalism to oppose such a liberating provision.

An amendment to exclude clause 5 was defeated by 203 votes to sixty-three (fifty-four Scots members out of seventy-two voting against), and the bill was read a second time.[78] Before the committee stage began on 18 July a motion by J. H. Dalziel, a Scottish Liberal MP, to divide the bill, leaving clause 5 as a separate measure, was supported by Campbell-Bannerman, Lloyd George, James Bryce, and others. Lloyd George invoked the danger of similar liberty being bestowed on the Church of England, which might then be turned by Ritualist pressure into 'a Catholic Church'. The motion was supported mainly by Nonconformist votes and defeated by 100. Some minor amendments were made in committee. Austin Taylor, like Lloyd George, wanted to avoid a precedent which might aid Ritualism in the Church of England, but he was heavily defeated. On 26 July clause 5 was challenged again by George White, a Baptist, on voluntary grounds. But the clause was endorsed on a division of 270 to 157, Liberals comprising the minority, and the bill was read a third time.[79] It passed through the Lords after some interesting debate and became law on 11 August.[80]

The Free Church regarded the measure, because of clause 5, as an unholy compact between the UF Church and the Church of Scotland.[81] Clause 5 was disliked by Free Churchmen because of its intention to allow the terms of subscription to become more liberal. In 1910 the Church of Scotland adopted a new relaxed formula akin to that already possessed by the UF Church. Their formula assisted the union negotiations then in progress between the two Churches, but gave no encouragement to the Free Church to join in them.

Debates on the 1905 measure had been largely on a matter separate from the property quarrel, namely the independent rights of the Church of Scotland, and this had been disputed partly on grounds which concerned the Church of England. If clause 5 had not been included there would have been little argument over the bill, as it was generally supported by both parties. But clause 5, though extraneous to the main issue, was very important for enhancing the spiritual self-government of the Church of Scotland. The *United Free Church Magazine* welcomed the clause as altering 'the whole relation of the Church to the State'.[82] The alteration encouraged moves for a wider Presbyterian union,

[78] H cxlviii. 1003–70, cxlix. 415–70.
[79] H cxlix. 1089–137, 1209–58, cl. 369–410.
[80] H cl. 840–2, cli. 231–9.
[81] Stewart and Cameron, op. cit. 304 ff.
[82] *UF Church Magazine*, Sept. 1905, p. 2.

even though the eventual result of these moves was not the disestablishment which some Scottish supporters of clause 5 said they wanted.[83]

The property dispute probably helped to discourage Scots disestablishment. If the new UF Church had not been compelled to give its energies to this problem; if it had not been unwise for it to urge disestablishment when the Free Church was challenging its right to property on that very issue; and if an alliance had not been formed between the established Church and UF Churchmen to pass the bill, there might have been more pressure for voluntaryism from the UF Church. There were also broader reasons for the voluntary recession, such as common interest among the Churches in social reform, common growth of theological liberalism, and common concern about the decline of Church membership relative to population growth—all of which helped to lower the barriers between establishment and Dissent.[84] There was in fact very little discussion of disestablishment in the presbyteries of the UF Church. A Liberal candidate in a St Andrews Burghs by-election in September 1903 said Scots disestablishment was not currently a matter of practical politics. A commentator suggested in 1903 that the next electoral contest would give short shrift to a socially nondescript issue like disestablishment, for this contest would be a struggle 'between bourgeoisie and proletariat'. This was not the case, but even so the election of a Liberal Government did not stimulate a fresh wave of voluntaryism.[85]

V. EDUCATION CRISIS AND NONCONFORMIST PRESSURE, 1902–1905

Nonconformists and the Liberal party as a whole were bitterly divided over the Boer War,[86] and another cause of division was Home Rule. But the Government's renewed education initiative after the 1900 election provided a means for Liberals partially to reunite, and it allegedly regained for them the support of many Nonconformist Liberal Unionists. It was complained that Ministers had not mentioned education during the election and that far fewer Nonconformists would have voted Unionist had they known what was in store for them. As in 1896, an unpalatable Government policy gave Nonconformists an object to fight against. Dependence on ministerial action of this kind was not very favourable to the long-term political prospects of Nonconformists, but at least the response to the resistance call showed they had still considerable force to use.

---

[83] H cl. 381 (Monro Ferguson), 388–9 (R. B. Haldane).

[84] Cf. R. Sjölinder, *Presbyterian Reunion in Scotland, 1907–1921* (Edinburgh, 1962), 86–90.

[85] Anon. art. in *FR* lxxiv (1903), 864–8; *T*, 11 Sept. 1903, p. 4. Cf. Lord Sands, *Dr Archibald Scott and his Times* (Edinburgh and London, 1919), 208.

[86] Bebbington, *Nonconformist Conscience*, 106, 122–3; S. Koss, *Nonconformity in Modern British Politics* (London, 1975), 32–3; H. McLeod, *Class and Religion in the Late Victorian City* (London, 1974), 178; Waller, *Democracy and Sectarianism*, 182.

Government members were not united on the details of education policy. But there was a desire among many of them to abolish school boards and transfer control of elementary schools to county and municipal councils, developing secondary education also within the council system. Sir John Gorst and his rising secretary Robert Morant were keen on these reforms and they were supported by a Fabian pamphlet, *The Education Muddle and the Way Out*. After a contentious bill of 1901 establishing new education authorities was withdrawn, a temporary measure was passed permitting school boards to provide some secondary education for a year if county and county borough councils agreed.[87] Ministers then prepared for next session a measure even bolder than that of 1896.

In anticipation of the measure the National Free Church Council campaigned for universal school boards, the Liberation Society issued statements defending the boards, and the Congregational Union said there should be no rate aid for voluntary schools without public control.[88]On the other hand, the council of the Church Committee and other Anglican bodies resolved on comprehensive reform of education and public support of all public elementary schools.[89] Bishops tried to persuade Cabinet members to meet the Church's wishes.[90] A conference of the joint Convocations of Canterbury and York and the 'Church party' in Parliament agreed as a compromise that there should be public representation on the managing committees of voluntary schools in return for rate aid.[91]

During preparation of the bill Devonshire was persuaded to give full support to compulsory rate aid for voluntary schools, Salisbury also yielded to this prospect, and perhaps Morant partially overcame Chamberlain's reluctance to countenance this aid. Chamberlain accepted that councils should be permitted, but not compelled, to take control of both board and voluntary schools and finance them from the rates. Balfour agreed to this compromise for the sake of the unionist alliance, but there was still ministerial dispute over the bill until its form was finally settled on 21 March, only three days before the measure was to be introduced in the Commons.[92]

---

[87] *AR* i (1901), 123–5, 144–6, 169–72; *Free Church Chronicle*, iii (1901) 141–2.

[88] Munson, 'Unionist Coalition', 630; Bebbington, op. cit. 141–2; LS, 25 Nov. 1901 (9), p. 214; R. W. Perks to Rosebery, 6 Dec. 1901; RP, 10050, fo. 194.

[89] CCDI Minutes, 4 Dec. 1901 (vol. 34, p. 124); *AR* i (1901), 212–13.

[90] Bishop Randall Davidson to Selborne, 25 Nov. 1901; Selborne Papers, 88, fos. 52–4; Bishop E. S. Talbot to Salisbury, 4 Dec. 1901; Gwendolen Stephenson, *Edward Stuart Talbot, 1844–1934,* (London 1936), pp. 142–3; Salisbury to Talbot, 7 Dec. 1901; ibid. 143–4; Lord George Hamilton to Cardinal Vaughan, 17 Dec. 1901; Vaughan Papers, v. 1.

[91] Taylor, 'The Church Party and Popular Education', 311–13.

[92] Munson, op. cit. 624 ff.; Taylor, op. cit. 329–57; Fairhurst, 'Education, Politics, and Religion', 204 ff.; Wilkinson, 'Educational Controversies', 265–82; Devonshire to Balfour, 6 Dec. 1901; BP, 49769, fos. 201–2; Marjorie Cruickshank, *Church and State in English Education, 1870 to the Present Day* (London, 1964), 75–8; Holding, 'Third Salisbury Cabinet', 156–61; Chamberlain to Cardinal Vaughan, 10 Dec. 1901; Vaughan Papers, v. 1; Fitzroy, *Memoirs*, i. 63 ff.; Dugdale, *Balfour*, i. 322–4; R. F. Mackay, *Arthur James Balfour: Intellectual Statesman* (Oxford, 1985), 90 ff.

The bill was brought in by Balfour and read a first time on 24 March. It proposed to enable committees of the county, county borough, and other councils to take over the work of school boards. The new local authorities were to develop secondary education and had the option of giving rate aid to voluntary schools in return for supervising their secular teaching and appointing two out of their six managers. The bill was read a second time on 11 May after four days' debate and a division of 402 to 165 on party lines, many Irish Home Rulers voting with the Government (and three Liberal Unionists and two Conservatives voting against). On 2 June the bill entered a marathon committee stage (including 276 divisions) which needed a special autumn session and frequent help from the 'guillotine' to reach a conclusion on 20 November. After a third reading on 3 December by a majority of 152, the bill was rushed through the Lords and became law on 18 December, nine months after its introduction. It had been debated on fifty-seven days, compared with the twenty-two days given to its important predecessor, the Education Bill of 1870.[93]

Strong Nonconformist opposition soon greeted the measure because it threatened school boards and allowed rate aid to voluntary schools without bringing them under full public control and permitted them to retain religious tests in the appointment of head teachers. Nonconformist resistance, to which the main exception was a minority of Wesleyans, was seen in large rallies and demonstrations, in the activities of Free Church councils and the Northern Counties' Education League, and in resolutions by the Liberation Society and denominational assemblies.[94] Sympathetic protests also came from Scots Dissenters. A deputation arranged by the National Free Church Council saw Balfour on 12 June; Principal Andrew Fairbairn read an address containing their objections, but Balfour would make no concessions and the campaigning gathered in intensity.[95] John Clifford, who coined the emotive phrase 'Rome on the rates', and Hirst Hollowell were the most prominent and determined leaders of Dissenting protest. A series of letters by Clifford in the *Daily News* drew a published reply from Balfour, answered in turn by Clifford in a powerful retort.[96] As a new religious endowment, rate aid to voluntary schools produced calls for a new disestablishment campaign, supplementing anti-Ritualism which itself provided arguments against voluntary schools. Rarely had

[93] H cv. 846–966, cvii. 638–763, 809–936, 953–1020, 1097–220, cviii. 1130 ff., cx. 317 ff., cxi. 130 ff., cxii. 138 ff., cxiii. 97 ff.; *AR* i (1902), 137–42, 186–90, 222–7, 231–5; Simon, *Education and the Labour Movement*, 220.

[94] e.g. *Free Church Chronicle*, iv (1902), 85; resolutions of Congregational Assembly, 13 and 15 May 1902; *Congregational Year-book* (1903), 6–8.

[95] LS, 20 June 1902 (9), p. 244; *T*, 8 May 1902, p. 11; *AR* i (1902), 168–9; W. B. Selbie, *The Life of Andrew Martin Fairbairn* (London, 1914), 273–7; E. K. H. Jordan, *Free Church Unity: A History of the Free Church Council Movement, 1896–1941* (London, 1956), 80.

[96] Marchant, *Clifford*, 114 ff.; May Lloyd, 'Baptist Political Attitudes, with Special Reference to the Late Nineteenth Century', M.Phil. thesis (Leeds, 1974), 121–8; Evans and Claridge, *Hirst Hollowell*, 84 ff.

Dissenting effort been so fully concentrated on a single issue, and similar cases of concerted effort had usually also been over education.

Nonconformists carried almost the entire Liberal party with them in the dispute, and the Education Bill proved a catalyst for Liberal reunion. Liberal imperialists and anti-imperialists managed to overcome their differences for a time in opposition to the bill, Rosebery agreeing with Harcourt and Sir Edward Grey with Lloyd George.[97] Some Liberal leaders, including Rosebery, were not immediately against the bill. Even Lloyd George liked it, except for the 'weak' optional clause, perhaps until he realized that religious teaching in voluntary schools would not be under public control. At any rate, his role of radical Nonconformist champion would not permit any other line but outright opposition. Lloyd George became Balfour's leading Parliamentary antagonist over the bill, speaking about 160 times in committee and winning Balfour's tribute that he was 'an eminent parliamentarian'.[98] 'For the sake of teaching dogmas to children who cannot understand them', said Lloyd George, 'we in the midst of our difficulties and the rocks that surround us, propose to put the chaplain on the bridge . . . It is a mad proposal.'[99]

Nearly all leading Liberals came to oppose the bill, R. B. Haldane being an exception with his belief 'that neither the Church nor the Nonconformists must rule, but that education must come first'.[1] On 26 April the party leader, Campbell-Bannerman, gave to a Nonconformist deputation a pledge of strong opposition both inside and outside the Commons to 'a mere Church bill in disguise', and the National Liberal Federation meeting in May carried a firm resolution against the proposals.[2]

Several alterations were made as the bill went through committee. The main ones were the removal of the optional clause on 9 July by 271 votes to 102, and the introduction of lay control over religious teaching in voluntary schools. Deletion of the optional clause relating to the councils' control of elementary education antagonized Nonconformists further because it entailed the abolition of all school boards in England and Wales and the bestowal of rate aid on all voluntary schools. For the same reasons it pleased the Catholics and most Churchmen.[3] Chamberlain had suffered an accident and was unable to attend the Commons at the time, but he may well have been aware of Balfour's plans on this matter. His son Austen opposed the change but his veteran supporter Jesse

[97] Cf. H. C. G. Matthew, *The Liberal Imperialists* (Oxford, 1973), 95–7.

[98] Lloyd George to his wife, 24 Mar. 1902 (Kenneth O. Morgan (ed.), *Lloyd George Family Letters, 1885–1936* (Cardiff and London, 1973), 131–2); Grigg, *Lloyd George: The People's Champion, 1902–1911* (London, 1978), 25–30, 32–4; W. R. P. George, *Lloyd George, Backbencher* (Llandysul, 1983), 355.

[99] Grigg, op. cit. 34.

[1] Haldane to his mother, 8 May 1902; Haldane Papers, 5967, fo. 136.

[2] J. A. Spender, *The Life of Sir Henry Campbell-Bannerman* (2 vols., London, 1923) ii. 64; *NLF: Proceedings of 24th Annual Meeting* (London, 1902), 6.

[3] Snead-Cox, *Vaughan*, ii. 128–37; D. R. Pugh, 'The Church and Education: Anglican Attitudes, 1902', *JEH* xxiii (1972), 219 ff.

Collings voted in favour of it. Chamberlain was quite bitter about this development as it contravened the understanding on which he had agreed to support the bill. None the less he wanted to stay in alliance with the Conservatives and remained on cordial terms with Balfour, who became Prime Minister in July. In October Chamberlain even managed to persuade a meeting of Birmingham Liberal Unionists to pass resolutions in favour of the bill. One of these resolutions, however, demanded a majority of local authority nominees on the boards of voluntary schools, and this concession Chamberlain failed to obtain.[4]

On the other hand Balfour agreed to an important alteration to Clause 8 which made all the managers instead of the clergyman alone responsible for religious teaching in each voluntary school. The religious teaching should be in accord with the provisions of the school's trust-deed. This amendment was seen, with considerable justice, as a move to contain Ritualism. It was not openly sponsored by Balfour, but he may have agreed to it beforehand and he spoke strongly for it.[5] It was moved by Colonel William Kenyon-Slaney, Conservative MP for North Shropshire, who held Evangelical sympathies. He said his proposal was intended to make Ritualistic excesses more difficult. The motion passed on 31 October by 211 votes to forty-one. The majority was composed of Liberals and Conservatives and the Irish Home Rulers stood aloof. Strong opposition was shown by Lord Hugh Cecil and other members of the Church party and by a Catholic MP, Lord Edmund Talbot; but another opponent, Sir John Kennaway, was an Evangelical. The amendment caused some bitter resentment. One protester told Kenyon-Slaney it was 'the greatest betrayal since the Crucifixion', and Bishop Gore strongly denounced it.[6] Chamberlain's concern, on the other hand, was somewhat relieved by the amendment which was welcomed by Nonconformist sentiment.[7] But attempts at a more general compromise over popular control, suggested by Temple, Percival, Gore, and others did not succeed.[8]

In contrast to the general approval of the bill by Catholic and most Anglican Bishops was the hostility of most Nonconformist leaders to the measure. Rate aid for denominational schools was condemned as an affront to the Nonconformist conscience, a revived version of church rates, despite accusations of inconsistency on the grounds that Nonconformists who earned

---

[4] Taylor, op. cit. 371–6, 390–3; J. Sandars to Balfour, 9 Oct. 1902; BP, 49761, fos. 53–6.

[5] Wilkinson, op. cit. 351.

[6] Cf. MacColl to Balfour, 23 Dec. 1902, 1 Jan. 1903; BP, 49790, fos. 70. 76.

[7] Taylor, op. cit. 396–403; H cxlii. 1311–62; Griffith-Boscawen, *Fourteen Years in Parliament*, 246–7; W. Durnford (ed.), *Memoir of Colonel the Rt. Hon. William Kenyon-Slaney MP* (London, 1909), 80–4; Pugh, op. cit. 228–31; B. Sacks, *The Religious Issue in the State Schools of England and Wales, 1902–1914* (Albuquerque, New Mexico, 1961), 38–41; Cruickshank op. cit. 83–4.

[8] Pugh, 'The 1902 Education Act: The Search for a Compromise', *British Journal of Educational Studies*, xvi (1968), 164–78; Wilkinson, op. cit 323 ff.; Chamberlain to Balfour, 4 Aug. 1902; BP, 49774, fos. 7–12; Chamberlain to Balfour, 31 Aug., copy; CP, JC11/5/8; Balfour to Chamberlain, 3 Sept.; ibid. 11/5/7; D. C. Lathbury, 'The Clergy and the Education Act', *Nineteenth Century*, liii (1903), 1–13.

enough already paid tax to maintain voluntary schools; that Anglicans and Catholics had to pay rates to maintain board schools; and that the bill was arguably an extension of religious equality.[9] The most striking of innumerable protest meetings and demonstrations was a huge gathering in a strong Nonconformist district, on Woodhouse Moor, Leeds, on 9 September. This was said to be attended by 70,000 people, speeches being delivered from six platforms by sixteen MPs and others. Hirst Hollowell composed a special song for the occasion.[10]

Protests continued long after the bill was enacted, partly because a London Education Bill with similar provisions was passed in 1903, also because it was hoped to defeat Ministers on the issue at the next general election.[11] Several Liberal by-election gains in 1902 and 1903 were attributed to the bill. Bury (Lancashire) was gained in May 1902. North Leeds was won in July by a Baptist who overturned a large Conservative majority, mainly on the education issue. The same question dominated in August at Sevenoaks (Kent) where another Baptist, though not gaining the seat, greatly reduced the Conservative majority.[12] The Liberals also gained Devonport in June 1904 after dispute between Irish voters on the question of Home Rule versus education.

Apart from some Fabian supporters of the bill, the Labour movement joined in opposition to it. But reasons for this differed between groups. The Independent Labour Party was under considerable Nonconformist influence, but the Social Democratic Federation was independently secular in its attitude to education. 'Religious belief is, and must be, a private matter', said an SDF manifesto of 11 October 1902, 'and, to have any kind of religious teaching in our public [i.e. State] schools is an infringement of religious liberty.' Fellow-workers must beware of supporting 'one or other of the capitalist parties. Nothing is further from their consideration than the cause of education.' The Federation's organ, Justice, accused the Liberal party, divided and 'morally bankrupt' as it was, of increasing the strife over education merely to regain 'its lost position'.[13]

The most distinctive expressions of Nonconformist resistance to the 1902 Act were the personal refusal to pay rates to support denominational schools and the refusal by some county councils to provide funds for these schools. The former method, known as 'passive resistance', was familiar to Nonconformists who recalled old battles over church rates. It was intended to be a witness to conscience and democratic conviction, and could be used by persons of any or no denomination. The old secularist leader G. J. Holyoake, who had forfeited an eight-day clock in 1855 in lieu of church rates, now lost a picture as a passive

---

[9] Sacks, op. cit. 38; H. M. Bompas, 'The Education Bill', FR lxxii (1902), 441–7.

[10] Evans and Claridge, op. cit. 85; Munson, 'A Study of Nonconformity', 175–6; Ross, 'Politics and Opinion in Bradford', 302–3.

[11] Free Church Chronicle, v (1903), 201–2.

[12] Simon, op. cit. 222; Bebbington, Nonconformist Conscience, 146; T, 18 Aug, 1902, p. 4.

[13] Simon, op. cit. 225–34.

resister.[14] A few Evangelical Anglicans refused to pay rates to support the inculcation of 'false doctrines . . . contrary to the teaching of the Bible and the Book of Common Prayer'.[15] But the campaign, denounced by High-Churchmen and Roman Catholics, was generally a Nonconformist one.

George White, a Baptist and Liberal MP, first advocated a possible 'no rate' campaign even before the Education Bill was introduced. Following White's lead, Robertson Nicoll, Presbyterian editor of the *British Weekly*, called for passive resistance in his paper on 3 April 1902 and in subsequent issues.[16] He was echoed by Hugh Price Hughes and Joseph Parker and received strong support from assemblies of Baptists, Congregationalists, Primitive Methodists, United Methodists, Bible Christians, and the Methodist New Connexion, also from various denominational magazines. But objections came from many Nonconformists, including Guinness Rogers, and some of these stressed the need to obey the law. Wesleyans were especially divided in their attitudes. Robert Perks championed passive resistance but some Wesleyans were grateful for the aid given to their 450 schools by the Act. The Wesleyan Conference of 1903, while expressing sympathy for passive resisters, refused to pronounce for or against their actions.

The National Free Church Council was hesitant and confused in its reaction to the policy, despite the declared willingness of most local Free Church councils to enrol the names of passive resisters. The council at Bradford formed a 'solemn league and covenant' to include the enrolled names.[17] In December 1902 the National Free Church Council decided not to lead the movement itself but to place the organization of resistance in the independent hands of a National Passive Resistance Committee chaired by John Clifford. This interdenominational body eventually had forty-six members. Already some local resistance groups, called Citizens' Leagues or Passive Resistance Leagues, had been formed. As many as 648 of these were eventually founded, overlapping a good deal with Free Church councils. The leagues advised their members how much of the rate to withhold. The *Crusader* magazine was commenced in November 1902 to help publicize the cause.

Rate refusals commenced after the Act began to operate in April 1903. The first prosecution for non-payment began in the Derbyshire village of Wirksworth in May. After a court appearance (perhaps before a magistrate who was a resister himself) the goods of resisters could be distrained and auctioned in order to meet the amount of rate withheld plus costs. Often, in a process that Winston Churchill called pantomime martyrdom, the articles were bought back by friends on behalf of the offenders and perhaps distrained again after a fresh

[14] E. Royle, *Radicals, Secularists, and Republicans, 1866–1915* (Manchester, 1980), 314.

[15] Munson, op. cit. 137.

[16] G. W. Lawrence, 'William Robertson Nicoll, 1851–1923, and Religious Journalism in the Nineteenth Century', Ph.D. thesis (Edinburgh, 1954), 165 ff.

[17] W. D. Ross, 'Politics and Opinion in Bradford', 304.

refusal. Clifford kept two silver trowels for repeated distraints. But it was not only well-wishers who met the debt. At Bradford a 'Passive Resisters' Anti-Martyrdom League' was formed to pay amounts legally claimed in order to undermine the movement. Refusal to allow distraint, or the lack of goods to distrain, could result in imprisonment. By March 1906, it has been estimated, 70,880 summonses had been issued (many of these being 'repeats' to the same people for separate offences), 568 auctions had been held, and 176 defaulters had been to gaol. These figures only scratched the surface of potential support.

Primitive Methodists, who as a substantially rural denomination were particularly subject to the 'single school' grievance, contributed more imprisonments than any other denomination despite their relatively small numbers—sixty of them up to February 1907, compared with forty-eight Baptists, forty Congregationalists, fifteen Wesleyans, and twenty-seven others. Loss of a vote in elections was imposed on some resisters, until this was ruled out of order in September 1904. Resistance went on for many years, and Clifford appeared forty-one times in court before the First World War.[18]

But the zeal of individuals and the repeated support of denominational assemblies were no compensation for widespread indifference. The movement was hampered by doubt and division from the first. It lost its enthusiastic impetus even before the Unionists left office and a Liberal Government attempted a new educational solution. The campaign eventually petered out without repealing the Act of 1902. It did help, however, to keep Nonconformist aims before the public and in the Liberal programme.

Passive resistance was far less of a worry to the Government than the reaction of some county councils and other authorities against the Act. This reaction was fiercest in Wales, where there was a Nonconformist majority and a widespread 'single school' grievance—also, under the Welsh Intermediate Education Act of 1889, a comparatively flourishing secondary education system which made the benefits of the Act less obvious than in England. Lloyd George, in a manifesto to the Welsh people on 17 January 1903, advised that, instead of a flat refusal by councils to pay, advantage should be taken of a loophole in the Act. The Act did not specifically declare that rate aid must be granted under any circumstances, so it should be withheld from voluntary schools unless their trustees accepted full public control of the funds allocated to them and abandoned all tests on the appointment of teachers. He bluntly expounded his plan of campaign in a speech at Cardiff four days later. 'For popular control—cash and cash down. No popular control—no cash.' In other words, the spirit if not the letter of the Act was to be defied in the interests of local democracy. Most of the Welsh

---

[18] Bebbington, op. cit. 142–5; James, *Churchill: Speeches*, i. 160; Munson, op. cit. 157–299; Jane T. Stoddart, *William Robertson Nicoll, Ll D: Editor and Preacher* (London, 1903), 145 ff.; Jordan, op. cit. 81–96; J. Scott Lidgett, *My Guided Life* (London, 1936), 185–6; Cruickshank, op. cit. 87; G. M. Morris, 'Primitive Methodism in Nottinghamshire, 1815–1932', Ph.D. thesis (Nottingham, 1967), 271–2.

county councils—the only exceptions being Brecon and Radnor, which had
Unionist majorities—agreed with the scheme. Lloyd George saw it as a means
of reviving Welsh radicalism: the Act, said his manifesto, 'had presented Wales
with its greatest political opportunity'.[19]

It was typical of Lloyd George, however, that as well as issuing firm public
challenges he also tried a conciliatory approach to the other side. He had struck
up an incongruous friendship with Bishop Edwards of St Asaph, one of the
most determined defenders of the Welsh Church establishment. Edwards no
doubt wanted a compromise in the hope of lessening opposition to a Church
threatened with disestablishment. Prolonged negotiations took place (some of
them on the golf course) between Edwards and Lloyd George about a possible
'concordat'. There was agreement among county council delegates at
Llandrindod Wells on 27 February 1903, and further discussion on 24 March in
London between representatives of the Welsh county councils and of the
voluntary schools in Edwards' diocese, on a solution for all rate aided schools.
This was based on the teaching of an agreed syllabus for religious instruction in
school hours and denominational teaching out of school hours. But because of
episcopal objections it did not seem that the Church would accept it. So Lloyd
George resumed his public aggression. 'Our business', he told the North
Staffordshire Liberal Federation in June, 'is to snatch the key [of education]
from the girdle of the priest and hand it to the people', and on 11 June he spoke
at a vast rally against Government education policy in the Albert Hall.[20]

The Government tried to cool the dispute by postponing enforcement of the
Act in Wales until 1 February 1904. But the controversy only increased. At the
beginning of March the Welsh county council elections, including those in
Brecon and Radnor, returned strong majorities for Lloyd George's scheme.[21]
Balfour remained intransigent. On 26 April the Government introduced an
Education (Local Authority Default) Bill, to empower the Board of Education
to support denominational schools over the head of a stubborn authority and
deduct the amounts from the Parliamentary grant to councils. Lloyd George
replied to this proposal, called by the *Daily News* the Coercion of Wales Bill, by
threatening to empty church schools by withdrawing the children of
Nonconformists and establishing new voluntary schools for them. However, in
spite of united Liberal opposition and a walk-out of all Liberal MPs from the
Commons at one point,[22] the bill became law on 15 August. In the same session

---

[19] Morgan, *Wales in British Politics*, 187 ff.; Grigg, *The People's Champion*, 39–42; P. Rowland, *Lloyd George* (London, 1975), 170–1; *AR* i (1903), 3 ff.

[20] Grigg, op. cit. 42–4; Cregier, *Bounder from Wales: Lloyd George's Career before the First World War* (Missouri, 1976), 81–3; George, op. cit. 372–8; Eluned Owen, *The Later Life of Bishop Owen* (Llandysul, 1961), 37–44 and ff.; Bishop A. G. Edwards, 'Educational Concordats', *Nineteenth Century and After*, lv (1904), 46.

[21] John Owen, Bishop of St David's, to Balfour, 15 Apr. 1904; BP, 49790, fos. 36–8; Morgan, op. cit. 191–2.

[22] *AR* i (1904), 114–15.

Bishop Edwards failed, because of the opposition of Churchmen, to pass a bill embodying the concordat proposals of 1903.

Thereafter the Evangelical revival of 1904–5 in Wales, led by the ex-miner Evan Roberts, heartened Nonconformists politically as well as spiritually. The membership of Nonconformist Churches increased by some 82,000. No comparable benefit was reaped by the established Church, and recent Dissenting despondency about establishment growth was removed.[23] The revival proved disappointingly transient, but the increase in Nonconformists' confidence caused them to carry on defying the Government. In October 1904 Lloyd George addressed a convention of Welsh county council representatives at Cardiff, attended by Clifford and other English Free Churchmen, which resolved that if the Default Act was put into operation Nonconformist parents should be called on to withdraw their children from Church schools.

When the Ministry resigned at the end of 1905 the penalties of the Default Act had been imposed on the authorities of Merioneth, Montgomery, Glamorgan, Barry, and Mountain Ash, but only in Merioneth had a substantial number of children been withdrawn from Church schools.[24] In England, Cambridgeshire County Council had refused rate aid on the same principles. The West Riding County Council had withheld part of the salaries of head teachers in voluntary schools but this was declared illegal. The East Ham Borough Council threatened not to administer the 1903 Act after May 1905 because it placed too heavy a burden on ratepayers.[25] The search for a compromise had continued. Balfour privately suggested such a scheme in March 1904 and said he was giving it 'such stray fragments of reflection as I can at present find time for'.[26]

A Unionist victory at the polls might have broken the Welsh revolt by exhausting its financial resources. Since the Unionists were resoundingly defeated and the new Government did not apply the Default Act the revolt enjoyed a temporary success. But this was short-lived. Although, in anticipation of reform by the Liberal Government, the recalcitrant counties began to observe the provisions of the 1902 Act, their hopes of reform were not realized. In 1843 Nonconformists protests had persuaded a Conservative Government to withdraw an education bill; in 1902 and after, similar protests could not even produce amendment of the Act by either a Unionist or a Liberal ministry. No doubt the contrast reflected the difference between a rising political and social force and one beginning to weaken.

---

[23] R. Currie, A. Gilbert, and L. Horsley (eds.), *Churches and Churchgoers: Patterns of Church Growth in the British Isles since 1700* (Oxford, 1977), 142, 149, 178; C. R. Williams, 'The Welsh Religious Revival, 1904–1905', *British Journal of Sociology*, iii (1952), 242–59; *The Religious Revival in Wales, 1904, by Awstin and Other Special Correspondents of the 'Western Mail'* (n.p. 1905); B. Hall, 'The Welsh Revival of 1904–5: A Critique', in G. J. Cuming and D. Baker (eds.), *Studies in Church History*, viii (Cambridge, 1972) 291–301.

[24] Grigg, op. cit. 43–7; George, op. cit. 397–9; *AR* i (1904), 202–3.   [25] *AR* i (1905), 142.

[26] Balfour to Lord Hugh Cecil, 29 Mar. 1904; BP, 49737, fos. 20–1; quoted Munson, op. cit. 304–5.

The numerical support for Nonconformity might indeed have indicated incipient weakening, but the education quarrel revived the old cause of disestablishment, and not only in Wales. Ritualism in the Church of England had provided a reason for attacking its established status, and the Education Acts of 1902 and 1903 gave a more direct reason because they could be seen as a new Church endowment. The bill's 'complete public endowment of denominational schools', said Asquith in St James's Hall in November 1902, 'was nothing more nor less than a fresh endowment of the Church of England'.[27] 'The struggle over the Education Acts has really gathered round the central idea of a State Church', wrote Guinness Rogers. 'The practical issue of the Government policy has been not only to grant a new endowment to the State Church, but also to give a fresh legislative sanction to the State Church principle.' Nonconformists were 'resisting the establishment of a State Church School as an annexe to the existing State Church'.[28]

The Liberation Society showed fresh signs of hope, increased its meetings by 1904 to the highest annual number since 1875, and planned a disestablishment conference at Westminster on 16 December 1902 to inaugurate a new campaign. The meeting, chaired by H. J. Wilson, a Congregationalist and Liberal MP for Holmfirth, attracted 200 representatives and condemned an established Church as 'a standing obstacle to . . . a really national system of Education'. Wilson planned to tell the meeting that 'the State Church is really at the bottom of, and the strength of, the mis-named Education Act'. Although two Liberal MPs, James Bryce and Robert Perks, declined the presidency of the Society, Clifford accepted the post and Lloyd George joined Carvell Williams as a vice-president. The Anglican *Guardian* feared that the Society, 'which of late years has shown signs of diminished vitality, is to be reanimated by the infusion of the unadulterated vigour of Dr. Clifford and Mr. Lloyd George'; and that a voluntary 'foreward movement' would not be easier as the mass of Free Church councils provided an important propaganda channel.[29] On 22 December the Society's committee trusted that the new Education Act would 'convince the electorate in increasing numbers of the necessity for the disestablishment and disendowment of the State Church'.[30] Several large urban meetings were held during 1903, and it was noted in May that a total of 4,669 lantern lectures had now been held by the Society. Augustine Birrell, addressing a gathering of the Society in 1903, said the disestablishment cause did not rest on opposition to Ritualism but on broader concepts: the union of Church and State was 'hurtful to religion, and most injurious to the sincerity of the citizen'. He was pleased, he added, that 'this great society . . . has entered upon a new course, and that it will go on holding up the flag of a free Church in a

---

[27] J. A. Spender and C. Asquith, *Life of Herbert Henry Asquith* (2 vols., London, 1932) i. 166.

[28] Guinness Rogers, *An Autobiography* (London, 1903), 289–90.

[29] 31 Dec. 1902, p. 1877.

[30] LS, 17 and 24 Nov., 22 Dec. 1902 (9), pp. 264, 266, 270–2; Notes for a speech in H. J. Wilson Papers, MD 2613.

free State until the hour of victory'.[31] In 1905 the separation of Church and State in France gave another boost to British voluntary morale.

By autumn 1903 the Liberation Society was planning to press disestablishment as part of a general election campaign. Meetings were to be encouraged, 'especially in places where resistance to the payment of Education rates has been most vigorous'. The co-operation of the working classes should be sought through trades councils, and a tract should be issued showing that the time spent on bills favouring the Church was 'a hindrance to industrial legislative progress'.[32] An electoral manifesto was adopted, wanting not only the fundamental amendment of the Education Acts but also the return of firm Voluntaries to Parliament.[33] The Society's executive committee suggested in July 1904 that disestablishment be moved in Parliament the following year, but Lloyd George discouraged this as being likely to revive Liberal disunity when it was otherwise diminishing.[34]

After a suggestion by Silvester Horne, a prominent Congregational minister, that 100 Free Churchmen should stand as Liberal candidates, negotiations took place between Thomas Law, secretary of the National Free Church Council, and Herbert Gladstone the Liberal chief whip, over seats which Nonconformists might contest. Gladstone was encouraging, but there were complaints from Dissenters that he exploited their inexperience and gave them '25 hopeless constituencies'.[35] Nevertheless he gave a firm promise that the first task of a Liberal Government would be to amend the Education Acts.[36] Thereafter the Free Church organizations were kept on electoral alert, and success was claimed at the Brighton by-election in April 1905 when a Liberal defeated the sitting Conservative.[37] Denominational resolutions such as a Congregational one in October 1903 echoed this electoral policy: only candidates who supported public control of schools and no religious tests for teachers should be supported.[38] Nonconformist objects were prominent in municipal elections. Church candidates were successfully opposed in London County Council elections in February 1904. For local contests in the rest of England in November 1903 the National Free Church Council issued a manifesto and the Church Committee engaged in counter-propaganda. Education was pre-eminent in the contests in several large towns.[39]

Over education the Unionists had much Catholic support, but there was an

---

[31] LS, 9 Mar., 6 and 7 Apr., 25 May 1903 (9), pp. 284–5, 289–90, 292, 295–6; T, 7 May 1903, p. 11; D. Nicholls (ed.), *Church and State in Britain since 1820*, 111–14.

[32] LS, 21 Sept. 1903 (9), pp. 309–10.

[33] Ibid. 313 (5 Oct.).

[34] Ibid. 358 (11 July 1904).

[35] Perks to Rosebery, 23 Sept. 1903; 2nd letter; RP, 10051, fos. 134–5; Bebbington, op. cit. 76–7; Koss, *Nonconformity in Modern British Politics*, 59. Cf. *The Liberator*, May 1904.

[36] Bebbington, op. cit. 77.

[37] Ibid.

[38] *Congregational Year-book* (1904), p. 12.

[39] T, 3 Nov. 1903, p. 4; CCDI executive committee Minutes, 22 Sept. 1903 (vol. 34, pp. 38–42), 28 June 1904; ibid. 176.

inclination among Nonconformist Unionists to abstain or to vote Liberal, and
the Liberals probably gained more benefit than the government from the
dispute. Catholic MPs generally followed their official Church line on the
question, to the extent of providing some votes for the Default Bill against
county councils. Michael Davitt firmly rejected this approach, however, and
there was a noted lack of enthusiasm by Home Rule MPs at some stages in the
debates of 1902 and even opposition to one clause in the bill.[40] Lord Ripon, a
Catholic Liberal and advocate of disestablishment, was still hoping that an
educational bridge could be built between Catholics and Nonconformists by
detaching Catholic educational interests from Anglican.[41] About the Unionist
losses Chamberlain complained to Devonshire in September 1902: 'I told you
that your Education Bill would destroy your own party. It has done so. Our best
friends are leaving us by scores and hundreds, and they will not come back.'[42]
This may have exaggerated the situation, but repeated statements about the
losses appear in correspondence, including a detailed prophecy of the reduced
support (even among Conservatives) which could be expected at the next
election in Devon.[43] It may therefore be reasonably assumed that losses did
occur and harmed the Unionists at elections.

Although Liberal differences over Home Rule and imperialism continued,
the education controversy gave most Liberals a common cause and helped to
restore party confidence. This tendency was enhanced by Chamberlain's tariff
reform campaign, launched in May 1903 and perhaps owing something to his
sense of frustration over the education issue and consequent need for
innovation. His new departure combined the Liberals in defence of Free Trade
and divided his own Unionists. Radical attitudes on education, Home Rule and
other matters prevented a proper alliance between Liberal and Unionist Free
Traders. Campbell-Bannerman and Herbert Gladstone suggested that a
compromise might be reached on education in order to ease the way for such an
alliance, but John Clifford said that a Unionist Free Trader of the Lord Hugh
Cecil stamp could never be supported by Nonconformists.[44] However, some

[40] Pugh, 'The 1902 Education Act', 175. For Catholic differences cf. Wollaston, 142 ff.;
F. Sheehy-Skeffington, *Michael Davitt* (London, 1967), 177.
[41] Bryce to Ripon, 4 Dec. 1902; Ripon Papers, 43542, fos. 21–2; Ripon to Bryce, 7 Dec.; ibid. fos.
23–4; Bryce to Ripon, 30 Dec. 1903; ibid. 43542, fos. 29–30; Ripon to Bryce, 1 Jan. 1904, copy; ibid.
43542, fos. 31–2; Ripon to Mr Anderton, 20 Dec. 1903, copy; ibid. 43638, fos. 164–7; Ripon to
Campbell-Bannerman, 18 Oct. 1903, copy; ibid. 43518, fos. 21–2; Munson, op. cit. 347–8, 353–5.
[42] Quoted P. Fraser, *Joseph Chamberlain: Radicalism and Empire, 1868–1914* (London, 1966), 223.
Cf. Chamberlain to Balfour, 4 Aug. 1902; BP, 49774, fos. 7–12; Balfour to Chamberlain, 3 Sept.; CP,
JC11/5/7; E. H. H. Green, 'Radical Conservatism: The Electoral Genesis of Tariff Reform', *HJ* xxviii
(1985), 687–8.
[43] Letter of 15 Aug. 1902 from Edward Windeatt to an agent, sent by Chamberlain to Balfour, 22
Aug.; BP, 49774, fos. 15–16.
[44] Richard A. Rempel, *Unionists Divided: Arthur Balfour, Joseph Chamberlain, and the Unionist Free
Traders* (Newton Abbot, 1972), 83; A. Sykes, *Tariff Reform in British Politics, 1903–1913* (Oxford,
1979), 75.

Unionist Free Traders such as Churchill became Liberals and consequently changed their attitude to the education question.[45]

By-election results continued to run generally against Ministers, and there were other boosts for the Opposition—'Chinese slavery' in South Africa and the Licensing Bill of 1904. The latter, although relatively harmless, aroused the opposition of Anglicans as well as Nonconformists and Lloyd George declared that 'the arm of the Most High is uplifted' against it.[46] Liberals even reached a near-compromise over Home Rule, in the shape of Campbell-Bannerman and Asquith's shaky 'step by step' policy, by November 1905.[47] But Rosebery's misinterpretation and public denunciation of this policy led Balfour to see, in continued Liberal disunity, some chinks of hope for shortly regaining office. It was with this slender possibility in mind that he resigned on 4 December 1905 so that Liberal divisions might spoil his opponents' chances in a general election.

The education crisis had administered a powerful dose of *sal volatile* to the decaying strength and drooping spirits of Nonconformity. From the encouragement which it gave to disestablishment, few would have predicted in 1902 that the education conflict was 'the last great battle in the war of the English sects'.[48] Such it proved to be, with the possible exception of renewed struggle over Welsh disestablishment several years later. Out of the 'last great battle' Nonconformist hopes were not to be realized. But when a Liberal Government took office at the end of 1905 and won a great electoral victory, Dissenting hopes of success in their educational and perhaps even their voluntary aims stood quite high.

[45] Rempel, op. cit. 77 ff.; Lord Hugh Cecil to Devonshire, 29 June 1903 (B. Holland, *The Life of Spencer Compton, Eighth Duke of Devonshire* (2 vols., London, 1911), ii. 373–4); Campbell-Bannerman to Herbert Gladstone, 22 Dec. 1902; HGP, 45988, fos. 71–2; Rempel, 'Lord Hugh Cecil's Parliamentary Career, 1900–1914: Promise Unfulfilled', *Journal of British Studies*, xi. 2 (May 1972), 117–18; Matthew, *Liberal Imperialists*, 106–7.

[46] Grigg, op. cit. 71.

[47] McCready, 'Home Rule and the Liberal Party, 1899–1906', *Irish Historical Studies*, xiii (1962–3), 336–48.

[48] H. F. Lovell Cocks, *The Nonconformist Conscience* (London, 1943), 67.

CHAPTER VII

Church Issues in Peace and War, 1905–1921

I. ELECTION OF 1906

The Liberal ministry which Campbell-Bannerman agreed to form on 5 December 1905 needed an election victory to secure itself in office. Nonconformist hopes for educational relief and other aims were likewise focused on the polls. But Liberalism and Nonconformity were far from coextensive, as the election results were to show. The Cabinet of nineteen contained more members of Nonconformist background, and probably more who remained practising Dissenters, than any previous Cabinet. The new premier was a Scots United Free Churchman who favoured disestablishment and did not want to encourage extreme Ritualism. James Bryce was a Baptist, Sir Henry Fowler a Wesleyan. Lloyd George was a Baptist who delighted in singing Welsh hymns and attending rousing sermons, but his personal views were allegedly unorthodox. Asquith was an ex-Congregationalist, now an Anglican. Augustine Birrell, President of the Board of Education, was an ex-Baptist inclined to Deism but retaining (so he repeatedly claimed) a strong respect for Nonconformity. R. B. Haldane, also of Baptist background, had become sceptical of religion.[1]

Such a Cabinet could hardly be described as strongly Nonconformist; rather it perhaps illustrated the once great but now declining hold of Evangelical Nonconformity on society. But the Cabinet was undoubtedly in favour of satisfying Nonconformist claims, for, in addition to the Dissenting members, the Anglican and other members generally supported them. Lloyd George assured his Caernarfon constituents just after his appointment as President of the Board of Trade: 'of the nineteen men who constitute the Cabinet, nineteen are in favour of [Welsh] disestablishment'.[2]

The Government faced the January election more united than its opponents in both policy and organization. Tariff Reform was the dominant issue, encouraging Liberal unity in defence of Free Trade but displaying Unionist

[1] P. Rowland, *Lloyd George*, 30–1; K. Morgan (ed.), *Lloyd George Family Letters, 1885–1936* (Cardiff and London, 1973), 7; C. Binfield, 'Asquith: The Formation of a Prime Minister', *Journal of United Reformed Church History Society*, ii. 7 (Apr. 1981), 204 ff; D. Sommer, *Haldane of Cloan: His Life and Times, 1856–1928* (London, 1960), 47.
[2] J. Grigg, *Lloyd George: The People's Champion, 1902–1911* (London, 1978), 95.

divisions.[3] Education, among other questions such as drink licences, 'Chinese slavery', and Home Rule, was also prominent.

Over education in particular there was intense and lively Nonconformist campaigning. A Free Church Council pamphlet, *Organizing for the Elections*, said that 'the vital amendment of the Education Acts is of primary importance both to the Free Churches and to the English nation'. Candidates should be persuaded to pledge themselves publicly to give first place to this matter.[4] Election tours were organized by Thomas Law, secretary of the Free Church Council, and leading ministers visited different areas in early and unreliable motor cars. The Free Church Council reached its climax of political activity in this campaign. A manifesto of 3 January demanded a national education system under effective public control, countering the widespread defence of the 1902 Act by political opponents. On Law's initiative large demonstrations were held and local Free Church councils were advised to establish election funds and obtain satisfactory pledges from candidates.[5]

Forty per cent of the Liberal candidates, sixty-six per cent of the Labour Representation Committee candidates, and fifteen per cent of the Unionists were Nonconformists.[6] These candidates appealed to about a million Free Church voters among others. The candidates were aided by ministers, some of whom took the chair at Liberal and Labour meetings. The theological examinations of Primitive Methodist students were postponed to enable them to campaign for the Liberals and their Labour allies, and a Primitive Methodist circular called on members of that Church to make every effort 'to secure the emancipation of National Education from the power of the priest and from the tyranny of reactionary politicians'.[7] Liberal politicians spoke for educational reform, including Churchill who said at Manchester that public control and religious equality should govern a national education system. 'I am told', he said, 'that I described passive resisters as pantomime martyrs. I admit I said so. It was a stupid thing to say [laughter].'[8] Asquith said at Huddersfield that 'corrective' educational legislation would be the ministry's first task.[9]

On the other side the Church Committee issued questions to be asked of

[3] Cf. M. Craton and H. W. McCready, *The Great Liberal Revival, 1903–1906* (London, 1966), 15 ff.

[4] Copy in LGP (House of Lords Record Office), A/2/3/1.

[5] D. W. Bebbington, *The Nonconformist Conscience: Chapel and Politics, 1870–1914* (London, 1982), 77–8; E. K. H. Jordan, *Free Church Unity: A History of the Free Church Council Movement, 1896–1941* (London, 1956), 101: H. Jeffs, *Press, Preachers, and Politicians: Reminiscences, 1874 to 1932* (London, 1933), 113–14; A. K. Russell, *Liberal Landslide: The General Election of 1906* (Newton Abbot, 1973), 183–4; S. Koss, *Nonconformity in Modern British Politics* (London, 1975), 69–74.

[6] Russell, op. cit. 62.

[7] Jordan, op. cit. 103; R. F. Horton, *An Autobiography* (London, 1917), 259; R. Currie, A. Gilbert, and L. Horsley (eds.), *Churches and Churchgoers: Patterns of Church Growth in the British Isles since 1700* (Oxford, 1977), 111; G. M. Morris, 'Primitive Methodism in Nottinghamshire, 1815–1932', Ph.D. thesis (Nottingham, 1967), 273–4; *Aldersgate Primitive Methodist Magazine*, nsv (1906), 80–1.

[8] R. R. James (ed.), *Winston S. Churchill: His Complete Speeches* (8 vols., New York, 1974), i. 537; P. F. Clarke, *Lancashire and the New Liberalism* (Cambridge, 1971), 267.

[9] *Dundee Advertiser*, 9 Jan. 1906, p. 6.

candidates on education and disestablishment, and leaflets on these subjects
were distributed to speakers.[10] Balfour's address said the new Ministers
intended to carry 'Home Rule, disestablishment, the destruction of voluntary
schools, and the spoliation of the Licence-holder'.[11] Anglican defence of the
1902 Education Act was not unanimous among clergy, as the views of Bishop
Percival, Canon Hensley Henson and others showed, but it was generally
pervasive in their ranks. Even George Lansbury, a Socialist standing for
Middlesbrough, had some sympathy as an Anglican with the 1902 Act and did
not press secular education like most of his Labour colleagues.[12]

For the Roman Catholics Archbishop Francis Bourne of Westminster and
the Duke of Norfolk defended the 1902 Act. Catholic Bishops and associations
asked candidates whether they would protect Catholic education, and varying
responses were received.[13] But Catholic attitudes sharply differed. Michael
Davitt and the United Irish League of Great Britain urged Catholic voters to
support the Liberals for the sake of Home Rule and in the hope of obtaining
special treatment for Catholic schools in a Liberal reform scheme. Archbishop
Bourne's manifesto, said the pro-Labour Davitt, might just as well have been
'drafted by Arthur Balfour in the interests of the Unionist candidates'. The
League said the best way for Catholics to protect their schools was to strengthen
the party in favour of Home Rule. Unionists, seeking Catholic votes, said this
was nonsensical; but there were some indications that Liberals were ready to
consider Catholic educational wishes favourably, however offensive such a line
may have been to many of their followers. The Irish League's widespread
electoral influence was used in the Liberal interest, even against some pro-
Home Rule Labour candidates who were fighting Liberals. The League's
action was probably more effective than the pro-Unionist line of Norfolk and
the Catholic Bishops, and the Liberal landslide was probably assisted by most of
the 200,000 Irish Catholic votes in the country.[14]

Disestablishment was not a major issue in the campaign. Even in Wales it was
less prominent than previously. Unionist candidates in England and Scotland
were more vocal in opposition to disestablishment than Liberal candidates were
vocal in its favour, and the Church Committee spoke out against it.[15]

[10] Minutes of CCDI executive committee, 16 Nov., 18 Dec. 1905 (vol. 36, pp. 154, 156–8); *Guardian*,
3 Jan. 1906, p. 18.
[11] F. W. S. Craig (ed.), *British General Election Manifestos, 1900–1974* (London, 1975), 8.
[12] A. W. Purdue, 'Parliamentary Elections in North-East England, 1900–1906: The Impact of
Labour', M.Litt. thesis (Newcastle upon Tyne, 1974), 248.
[13] Bourne Papers, Box 1/49; E. P. M. Wollaston, 'The Irish Nationalist Movement in Great Britain
1886–1908', MA thesis (London, 1957), 108–9, 153–5; E. Oldmeadow, *Francis, Cardinal Bourne* (2
vols., London, 1940–4), i. 272–7.
[14] Russell, op. cit. 186–91; F. Sheehy-Skeffington, *Michael Davitt* (London, 1967), 190–200;
meeting of United Irish League of Great Britain, 30 Dec. 1905; *Dundee Advertiser*, 1 Jan. 1906, p. 7;
I. Wood, 'Irish Immigrants and Scottish Radicalism, 1880–1906', in I. MacDougall, (ed.), *Essays in
Scottish Labour History* (Edinburgh, 1978), 83–4.
[15] Morgan, *Wales in British Politics, 1868–1922*, 3rd edn. (Cardiff, 1980), 216; *Scotsman*, 3 Jan., p. 10,
4 Jan., p. 7; *Dundee Advertiser*, 8 Jan., p. 9, 10 Jan., p. 1, 19 Jan., p. 8, 22 Jan., p. 9; *Guardian*, 3 Jan.,
p. 18.

W. G. Black, Unionist candidate for Aberdeen South, opposed disestablishment but advocated reform of the Church of Scotland in order to encourage the return of Dissenters to it.[16] Lloyd George, addressing the annual convention of the Welsh National Liberal Council, confirmed on the premier's authority that Welsh disestablishment was still an essential part of the Liberal programme. The Liberation Society interpreted this as a call for a mandate from the electors and urged strong support for Welsh disestablishment at the polls. On the other hand the Bishop of Liverpool, F. J. Chavasse, said that 'the Church in Wales was an integral part of the Church of England, and . . . it was slowly but surely recovering its ancient spirituality and vigour, and gathering its once alienated people into the fold'.[17]

Churchill said that disestablishment was clearly needed in Wales, but not in England where he thought it was hardly an issue in the election. However, in oblique reference to the Ritualist dispute, he said that disestablishment and disendowment might come in England if there was 'a great schism in the Church on doctrinal matters'.[18] There were other references to Ritualism in the same connection. Augustine Birrell argued that disestablishment would be better than statutory Church discipline for the Church of England.[19] Protestant societies, such as the flourishing Church Association with its 371 electoral councils, were active in the election.[20] Orangemen, who put the Anglo-Irish Union foremost, were happy to support the Conservatives. But disillusion was shown by ultra-Protestants because the Tories had not successfully combatted Ritualism, and party ties were eschewed or little regarded.

Ultra-Protestant efforts hampered Unionist candidates who were trying to get Catholic support on the education issue. The Conservative who unsuccessfully challenged T. P. O'Connor in Liverpool (Scotland) appealed for Catholic support over education and Protestant support over anti-Catholicism.[21] Many successful candidates gave an anti-Ritualist undertaking, either firm or vague.[22] But the only candidate to stand under the name of 'Protestant' was J. A. Kensit at Birkenhead, where his father had been assaulted. He obtained 2,118 votes against the successful Labour candidate, who also had Conservative opposition but not Liberal. The *Bulwark* said Kensit would have done better if Free Trade had not been so important in the area.[23] The elections indicated that anti-Ritualism had not become a strong popular cause and that, except in Wales, disestablishment was a dying topic.

---

[16] *Dundee Advertiser*, 15 Jan., p. 8.

[17] Ibid. 3 Jan., p. 3, 5 Jan., p. 3; Russell, op. cit. 110–11.

[18] Speech at Manchester, 9 Jan.; James, op. cit. i. 540.

[19] *Dundee Advertiser*, 9 Jan., p. 6.

[20] Russell, op. cit. 188; P. J. Waller, *Democracy and Sectarianism: A Political and Social History of Liverpool, 1868–1939* (Liverpool, 1981), 227.

[21] Russell, op. cit. 188.

[22] e.g. F. E. Smith at Liverpool, Walton constituency (J. Campbell, *F. E. Smith, First Earl of Birkenhead* (London, 1983), 125–6); N. Briggs Constable, Unionist candidate for West Fife (*Dundee Advertiser*, 17 Jan., p. 9). [23] *Bulwark*, Feb. 1906, p. 36.

The Liberals won an unexpectedly large majority, the biggest since 1832. With 400 seats (including the 'Lib-Labs') they had an overall majority of 132. The Unionist MPs shrank to 157; several of their leading lights, including Balfour and his cousin Lord Hugh Cecil, lost their seats. In Wales all thirty-four constituencies returned Liberals, except one which returned Keir Hardie; twenty-five of the Welsh members were Nonconformists.[24] Results in other strong Nonconformist areas suggested a swing from Liberal Unionism among Dissenting voters. In Suffolk four of the five seats were Liberal gains, in Essex five of the eight; in the West Riding there were fifteen Liberal or Labour gains among the thirty-eight seats. The only comfort for the Unionists was a much higher proportion of votes than seats: despite the huge difference in seats won the total Liberal vote was only 306,400 above the Unionist.[25]

Radical Nonconformist euphoria contributed to that of Liberals overall. The total number of Nonconformist MPs, which had reached a previous peak of some 117 in 1892, was now about 210. Of these about 180 were Liberals and twenty Labour; sixty-three of the Liberals were Congregationalists and twenty-seven Wesleyans.[26] Most of the Nonconformist Unionists lost their seats. Herbert Gladstone's predictions of probable or possible Liberal Nonconformist victories were considerably exceeded, and Nonconformists had won most of the 'hopeless' seats he had given them to fight.[27] More Dissenters than Tories had been returned, noted Silvester Horne in the *Christian World* (though a few of the Dissenters were Tories), and this journal somewhat prematurely rejoiced that 'the last dark years' had ended.[28]

The Nonconformist returns, though impressive, gave Dissenters only about the same proportion of Liberal returns as in 1900, though higher than in 1892. Nonconformists were still in a minority of the Liberal MPs and the success of their aims depended on their non-Dissenting colleagues. It was noted that the overall Liberal majority made the Ministers independent of Irish Home Rule support.[29] It cannot be said they were independent of Nonconformist support, for a substantial Nonconformist defection would have lost them their overall majority. But there remained the old question of how likely such a defection was if it meant lending support to the Conservatives.

Nonconformists were not in a totally commanding position after the election, even within the Liberal ranks. The results, it has been stated, 'reflected the social composition of Liberalism rather than the power of Nonconformity'.[30]

[24] Morgan, op. cit. 219–20.
[25] Cf. W. L. Arnstein, 'Edwardian Politics', in A. O'Day (ed.), *The Edwardian Age: Conflict and Stability* (London, 1979), 70.
[26] Koss, op. cit. 288.
[27] Ibid. 74.
[28] *Christian World*, 1 Feb. 1906, pp. 10, 11. .
[29] *Bulwark*, Feb. 1906, p. 36.
[30] J. F. Glaser, 'English Nonconformity and the Decline of Liberalism', *American Historical Review*, lxiii (1957–8), 361.

Doubtless some of the Nonconformists returned were only nominal ones. Robertson Nicoll claimed in 1907 that only eighty-three Dissenting MPs were taking their Free Church responsibilities seriously. A correspondent of the *Baptist Times* said in 1910 that the number of real Nonconformists in the 1906 Parliament was 'vastly over-rated': 'many who were claimed as such were Nonconformists only in name, and during the whole four years took absolutely no part in helping the work of the Nonconformist [Parliamentary] Committee'.[31] While a rosy prospect could be presented for Nonconformist aims in January 1906, it could also be prophesied that they would find it hard to succeed.

II. LABOUR AND THE CHURCHES

The return of thirty MPs sponsored by the Labour Representation Committee (now renamed the Labour Party), and a further twenty-three trade union MPs under the Liberal banner, was a striking victory for the Labour movement. 'The workers have crossed the Rubicon', proclaimed Robert Blatchford's *Clarion*;[32] and though it was unclear what Rubicon they had crossed the returns gave good reason to assess Labour's attitudes to current political questions, including ecclesiastical ones. There had been a 'sudden outcrop of the Labour vote', noted the Church of England *Guardian*. But it was not particularly despondent, going on to say, emotively but with considerable prescience: 'The representatives of Labour are by no means certain to commit themselves to the programmes of those who now claim them as allies, and they are likely to be free from many of the prejudices of the sects, which as a rule are less in touch with them than we are . . . we are not prepared to take it for granted that the Church must necessarily suffer from the extension of democracy'.[33]

The British Labour movement, bearing both Christian and Marxist impressions, reflected a very wide and not easily reconcilable diversity of influences. The movement's motivation was partly religious, springing from the experiences obtained by many of its members as Sunday school pupils and teachers, lay preachers, and attenders at church services and meetings. The Churches were by no means always sympathetic to the aims of Labour, but they became more so as questions of social reform demanded and received their attention. The idea of the 'social gospel' obtained abundant support among Church members, whatever political party might be seen as the likeliest instrument for realizing it—the Labour party proclaiming Socialism, the Liberals 'progressive' collectivism, or the Conservatives increased prosperity from Tariff Reform. Gradually increasing support for Socialism seems to have come from Church members, though there was also decided opposition to it

[31] Koss, op. cit. 78, 88.
[32] *Clarion*, 19 Jan. 1906.
[33] *Guardian*, 24 Jan., p. 140.

among them, shown for example by the Nonconformist Anti-Socialistic Union and a stand against Socialism by many Catholics who were conscious of the bitter continental battles between Socialism and their Church.[34]

There were numerous small denominational Socialist societies such as Stewart Headlam's Anglican Guild of St Matthew commenced in 1877; The Church (of England) Socialist League formed in 1906; the Socialist Quaker Society in 1898; the Wesleyan Sigma Club in 1909; and Catholic Socialist societies founded in Glasgow, London, Liverpool, and elsewhere despite episcopal opposition. Attempts were also made to establish interdenominational groups, such as the Christian Socialist Society which lasted from 1886 to 1892 and the Free Church Socialist League founded in 1909. 'Sacramental Socialism' was a distinctive Anglo-Catholic idea, holding that the common reception of sacramental grace bound men together in brotherly social bonds which should promote Socialist policies.[35]

Supporters of Socialist groups included clergy and ministers of both established and non-established Churches. The cautious Fabian group was the preferred channel for Socialist-inclined clergy and ministers. The Socialist but non-Marxist Independent Labour Party had Nonconformist leadership in Keir Hardie, Philip Snowden, and Arthur Henderson, and some clerical support including the Revd R. J. Campbell and the Revd James Barr, a Scots United Free Churchman.[36] One or two sects, in particular the Primitive Methodists, were largely working-class, and many Primitives inclined to Socialism though there were differences in the denomination over the question.[37]

It was common for Labour politicians to have a denominational allegiance. This was often though by no means exclusively Nonconformist, no doubt reflecting the comparatively democratic government of Nonconformist denominations although there were reactions against the domination of employers and managers in some Dissenting chapels.[38] The oratory of Philip Snowden showed Wesleyan revivalism used on behalf of Socialism: 'Come with us and call to the man with the muckrake, and tell him to lift his eyes from the earth and to grasp the heavenly crown above his head. Come with us and help us

[34] E. R. Norman, *Church and Society in England, 1770–1970* (Oxford, 1976), 221 ff.; Bebbington, op. cit. 158–9.

[35] P. d'A. Jones, *The Christian Socialist Revival, 1877–1914* (Princeton, 1968), 5–27, 85 ff., 225 ff.

[36] Cf. *Church Reformer*, vii. 1 (Jan. 1888), 18; F. Bealey and H. Pelling, *Labour and Politics, 1900–1906* (London, 1958), 8–9; K. D. Brown, 'Nonconformity and the British Labour Movement', *Journal of Social History*, viii (1975), 116 ff.; G. J. Mayhew, 'The Ethical and Religious Foundations of Socialist Politics in Britain: The First Generation and their Ideals, 1884–1931', D.Phil. thesis (York, 1981), 499 ff.

[37] Morris, op. cit. 168–71, 252–3; E. J. Hobsbawm, *Primitive Rebels* (Manchester, 1959), 135–42; R. F. Wearmouth, *Methodism and the Struggle of the Working Classes, 1850–1900* (Leicester, 1954), 175–207; J. Kent, *Holding the Fort: Studies in Victorian Revivalism* (London, 1978), 189; *Primitive Methodist Conference Minutes, 1913* (London, 1913), 7–8.

[38] D. B. Rees, *Chapels in the Valley: A Study in the Sociology of Welsh Nonconformity* (Upton, Wirral, 1975), 148–50, 168.

to remove poverty, sin, and suffering, and to bring hope and health and joy and brotherhood to every child of our Common Father'.[39] Henderson was a Wesleyan lay preacher; Ben Tillett, Will Crooks, and George Barnes were Congregationalists; Ernest Bevin and J. H. Thomas were Baptists. George Lansbury was president of the Church Socialist League, Clement Attlee and Stafford Cripps were Anglo-Catholics, and John Wheatley a Roman Catholic. Out of about 250 Labour MPs surveyed in 1929, it was claimed that only eight were declared agnostics or atheists.[40]

But there was also a vocal anti-religious element in British Socialism. To Belfort Bax, Socialism was 'atheistic Humanism': 'The establishment of society on a Socialistic basis would imply the definite abandonment of all theological cults, since the notion of a transcendant God or semi-divine prophet is but the counterpart and analogue of the transcendant governing-class'.[41] *Justice*, the organ of the Social Democratic Federation, was perhaps more anti-clerical than anti-Christian in berating the 'intolerant, persecuting spirit of clericalism' and stigmatizing Rome as 'a tremendous reactionary power'.[42] But Edward Aveling, a leading SDF member and son of a Congregational minister, wrote pamphlets on *The Wickedness of God* and *A Godless Life the Happiest and Most Useful*.

Labour politicians were often from the artisan section of the working classes, which was much more influenced than the labouring mass by traditional religious forms. Despite the assiduous working-class missions of late Victorian times, the labouring majority of workers remained notoriously detached from the Churches, owning perhaps to a personal Christianity but otherwise ostensibly indifferent.[43] Churches were regarded as symbols of privilege and social respectability.[44] This was the common view particularly of the Church of England, to a lesser extent of the Church of Scotland, and usually of Nonconformist Churches as well, though some of the latter escaped it and the Catholic Church certainly did so. Though they probably sent their children to Sunday school, most working men shunned both church and chapel. This was a vital political fact, for the extension of the franchise established a working-class majority in the electorate; and this majority, being indifferent to the Churches as religious bodies, was also generally indifferent to the Churches' political aims. This was true not least because the working-class majority was markedly interested in social improvement as a political object. The growing pressure of

[39] Quoted Clarke, 'British Politics and Blackburn Politics, 1900–1910', *HJ* xii (1969), 307.

[40] Hobsbawm, op. cit. 141–2.

[41] E. Belfort Bax, *The Religion of Socialism*, 3rd edn. (London, 1891), 81.

[42] *Justice*, 18 Feb. 1899, p. 6; Mayhew, op. cit. 164–76. Cf. Lord Snell, *Men, Movements, and Myself*, 2nd edn (London, 1938) 126 ff.

[43] K. S. Inglis, *Churches and the Working Classes in Victorian England* (London, 1963), 322–36 and *passim*.

[44] Cf. G. Haw (ed.), *Christianity and the Working Classes* (London, 1906), 23, 51, 76, 119 (contains essays by Will Crooks, Arthur Henderson, and George Lansbury).

social questions helped to diminish the role of ecclesiastical questions in politics.

Socialism tended to sit uncomfortably with formal religion, and some Christian Socialists proclaimed the Churches' uselessness to their end. 'Christianity', wrote Tom Mann, 'is made part and parcel of the national commercialism, and wholly subservient to the individualistic acquisitiveness of the age . . . the Socialist agitator and the Trade Union organiser is doing far more than the preachers and the Christians, the Missionary Societies and the Bible Societies, to make Christ's gospel prevail.'[45] Probably only a minority of British Socialists wished to divorce their opinions entirely from Christianity, and even some who did, such as Bruce Glasier, talked of Socialism being a 'religion' in itself.[46] To George Edwards, an agricultural trade unionist, Primitive Methodist lay preacher, and MP, the Labour movement was 'always a most sacred thing . . . try how one may, one cannot divorce Labour from religion'.[47]

Some Socialists saw a need to link religion more clearly and exclusively to the objects of the Labour movement by forming special institutions.[48] Thus from 1891 there developed the Labour Churches, and their offshoots the Socialist Sunday schools. In 1893 a Labour Church Union was formed at Manchester by delegates from seventeen Labour churches. The object of John Trevor, the Unitarian founder of the movement, was to assert God's presence in the Labour movement but not in a Christian form. The religion taught in Labour churches was strongly ethical and undogmatic: membership seemed to depend on religious 'feeling' rather than definite faith. It could easily have been thought that religion was being subordinated to Socialism, but this was denied by Trevor whose view was rather that Socialism was an extension of religion and inseparable from it. The Labour churches were actively encouraged by some Christian Socialists. But the movement did not prosper. Although quite influential in Bradford and Manchester it did not spread very successfully. At least 121 congregations were formed, but most of them were short-lived. The movement's newspaper ceased publication in 1901 and only a few of the churches survived the First World War.[49]

The attempt to give Labour a special kind of religion did not succeed. But a Socialist view developed which stressed that religious zeal, through whatever denominational channels it might run, should be directed towards social

[45] T. Mann, A Socialist's View of Religion and the Churches, Clarion pamphlet no. 10 (London 1896), 6.

[46] K. St J. Conway and J. B. Glasier, The Religion of Socialism (Manchester and Glasgow, n.d.); S. Yeo, 'A New Life: The Religion of Socialism in Britain, 1883–1896', History Workshop, iv (Autumn 1977), 5–56.

[47] G. Edwards, From Crow-scaring to Westminster: An Autobiography (London, 1922), 43, 235–6.

[48] Cf. R. A. Bray, Labour and the Churches (London, 1912), 71, 101–12.

[49] H. Pelling, Origins of the Labour Party, 1880–1900 (Oxford, 1966), 132–42; D. F. Summers, 'The Labour Church and Allied Movements of the Late Nineteenth and Early Twentieth Centuries', Ph.D. thesis (Edinburgh, 1958), 311–20.

security and equality. The main political aims of Labour were (in addition to democracy) social welfare and nationalization—a much more emphatic and class-orientated version of the collectivist tendencies of the 'new Liberalism'. This approach did not ignore older radical aims such as disestablishment, but gave more attention to social questions and had the support of many Nonconformists in doing so.[50]

Individual Labour MPs, such as Keir Hardie who represented a Welsh constituency, might emphasize their voluntaryism, and Ramsay MacDonald seconded a disestablishment motion in the Commons in February 1908.[51] Collectively, however, the Labour political groups paid the matter little attention; indeed they were perhaps glad to detach themselves from an issue which caused working-class division.[52] 'One man one job, and every man a job', said Keir Hardie in 1892, 'was a greater question for the unemployed than plural voting . . . and a greater question than disestablishment of the Church'.[53] Hardie, though a Nonconformist, rejected suggestions for a conference between the Labour Representation Committee and the 'stucco saints' of the National Free Church Council, as he called them, in November 1905.[54] In February 1908 Stephen Walsh, Labour MP for Ince (Lancashire) opposed disestablishment in the Commons: 'considering the mass of social reform that both great parties in the State had set themselves to deal with, it could not be thought for one moment that this vast problem of the disendowment and disestablishment of the Church of England—a Church which had deeply rooted itself in the national life—was practical politics'.[55] Most workers indeed, especially town-dwellers, could hardly be expected to take an interest in disestablishment: they did not attend church and suffered no material oppression from the establishment.

The programme of the Social Democratic Federation, published in *Justice* in February 1900, placed 'the disestablishment and disendowment of all State Churches' ninth on the list. The Federation's main object was 'the socialisation of the means of production, distribution, and exchange, to be controlled by a democratic State in the interests of the entire community'. An ILP leaflet of 1904 included an eight-hour working day, full employment, State pensions, and adult suffrage on its list, but not disestablishment.[56] The *Church Socialist* magazine, however, ran a series of pro-disestablishment articles during

[50] Cf. J. Cox, *The English Churches in a Secular Society: Lambeth, 1870–1930* (Oxford, 1982), 154–6, 170–2.
[51] Kenneth O. Morgan, *Rebirth of a Nation: Wales, 1880–1980* (Oxford, 1981), 55; *AR* i (1908), 40–1.
[52] Cf. Bray, op. cit. 52 ff.
[53] Quoted W. D. Ross, 'Politics and Opinion in Bradford with Special Reference to Parliamentary Elections', Ph.D. thesis (Bradford, 1977), 216.
[54] Russell, *Liberal Landslide*, 183.
[55] H clxxxiv. 367.
[56] *Justice*, 3 Feb. 1900, p. 8; *The Independent Labour Party Platform*, leaflets (London, 1901–4); leaflet no. 165.

1912.[57] Other 'sectarian' issues were also little regarded by Socialists. As a solution to the education dispute, secular teaching alone was demanded by the SDF, the ILP, and large majorities at Trade Union Congress and Labour party conferences, though there were strong objections from Catholic delegates such as James Sexton, the Liverpool dockers' leader.[58] On anti-Ritualism, when the Labour candidate for Rochdale in 1900 was asked whether he supported the Protestant Alliance he said that body should 'practise true religion, which is to visit the sick and help the widow and the orphan . . . instead of trying to raise sectarian discussions over bigoted nonsense'.[59] The Labour movement generally wished to avoid divisive religious issues in its quest to achieve social justice, and it strengthened the tendency for social questions to displace ecclesiastical ones in politics. In this way the emergency of Labour indirectly helped to shore up the Church establishment.

III   EDUCATION, RITUALISM, AND DISESTABLISHMENT,
1906–1911

After the Liberal victory Nonconformists looked for satisfaction over education and Welsh disestablishment; over education, however, their aims were not to succeed, and success with Welsh disestablishment was postponed for several years. Because of the divergent views of Nonconformists and Catholics on education the Government was hampered in reaching an acceptable solution. Besides this, educational reform was one of the Liberal policies obstructed by the House of Lords, where Balfour made political use of the huge Conservative majority to counter the huge Liberal majority in the Commons. This tactic was to cause Ministers in turn to limit the Lords' veto over bills passed by the lower House. Welsh disestablishment, as had been shown in the previous Liberal ministry, could hardly expect to succeed unless this limitation was effected.

It was announced in the King's Speech at the opening of the session of 1906 that Ministers would attempt a new education settlement.[60] But the religious differences over the question ensured that the task would be arduous. 'The difficulty', as a writer in the *Fortnightly Review* stated, 'is to find an equitable arrangement that will give . . . satisfaction to Roman Catholics, Anglicans and Nonconformists.'[61] Ministers well realized the difficulty of satisfying Catholics in a measure designed largely to please Nonconformists, since most Catholics

---

[57] *The Church Socialist*, i. 2–9 (Feb.–Sept. 1912).

[58] B. Simon, *Education and the Labour Movement*, 142 ff.; J. E. B. Munson, 'A Study of Nonconformity in Edwardian England as Revealed by the Passive Resistance Movement Against the 1902 Education Act', D.Phil. thesis (Oxford, 1973), 326–8; *Standard*, 12 Sept. 1908, p. 6; *AR* i (1904), 201; B. Sacks, *The Religious Issue in the State Schools of England and Wales, 1902–1914* (Albuquerque, New Mexico, 1961), 147 ff.

[59] *T*, 22 Sept. 1900, p. 11.

[60] H clii. 177.

[61] Anon., 'Sir Henry Campbell-Bannerman's Opportunities', *FR* lxxix (1906), 232.

were anxious to retain denominational education in schools maintained by public funds and most Nonconformists wanted to abolish it.[62]

Augustine Birrell, who as President of the Board of Education was responsible for preparing a measure, received Nonconformist deputations which urged the undenominational view. A Primitive Methodist delegation told him that many children of their Church's members had to attend Anglican schools because they lived in single-school districts.[63] The bill which emerged tried to relieve Nonconformist grievances while also making concessions to Catholics and Anglicans. But for all its good intentions it did not satisfy either side, and proved an unsuccessful attempt at compromise.

Birrell's bill, which he introduced in the Commons on 9 April, proposed to end the dual system of 1902 on 1 January 1908. All voluntary schools wishing to continue receiving public funds would come under the full control of local education authorities. No religious tests would remain for teachers. Undenominational scriptural teaching could be given by the regular staff at the local authority's discretion. Denominational teaching, moreover, might be permitted under Clause 3 by the local authority on two days a week, but had to be given outside school hours and by special teachers. Clause 4 was even more contentious. This offered 'extended facilities', also at the local authority's discretion, for denominational teaching every day at schools in urban areas with over 5,000 inhabitants, if over four-fifths of the parents of children at the school requested it.[64] The clause was intended to assist mainly Catholics. Wales was to have a National Council for Education, apparently on Lloyd George's suggestion.[65]

Amid the ensuing uproar the bill had considerable backing. The onus of opposition, in 1902 so plainly with the Liberals, now shifted to the Tories and Home Rulers. In the Cabinet even Lord Ripon, the one Roman Catholic member, favoured it; and in the Commons large majorities for it came from Government supporters. Nonconformist attitudes, as expressed by the Liberation Society, Free Church Council, and denominational assemblies, were those of qualified support. But most Anglicans and Catholics rejected 'Birreligion': they condemned the measure as undermining denominational education and derided the concessions in clauses 3 and 4 as inadequate.[66] On the other hand, clause 4 was alarming to undenominational education champions,

---

[62] James Bryce to Lord Ripon, 30 Dec. 1903; Ripon Papers, 43542, fos. 29–30; Ripon to Campbell-Bannerman, 13 Dec. 1905, copy; ibid. 43518, fo. 61; Sydney Smith to Lady Primrose, 9 Feb. 1906; CBP, 41239, fos. 37–44.

[63] N. J. Richards, 'The Education Bill of 1906 and the Decline of Political Nonconformity', *JEH* xxiii (1972), 52; *British Weekly*, 12 Apr. 1906, p. 1.

[64] *AR* i (1906), 90–5.

[65] L. W. Evans, 'The Welsh National Council for Education, 1903–1906', *WHR* vi. 1 (1972), 86; Morgan, *Wales in British Politics*, 223–4.

[66] Marjorie Cruickshank, *Church and State in English Education, 1870 to the Present Day* (London, 1963), 94–5; *Guardian*, 2 May 1906, p. 724; Archbishop Francis Bourne in *Nineteenth Century and After*, lix (Jan.–June 1906), 721.

especially Hirst Hollowell whom the clause was said to have made physically ill, and Robert Perks who led a deputation of Nonconformist MPs to protest to Birrell.[67] Clifford, however, was conciliatory, moving in the Baptist Assembly that the bill should be welcomed but significantly amended. The Congregational Assembly in May declared the bill 'a just and statesmanlike measure', but wanted the withdrawal or at least the amendment of clause 4, as also did the Free Church Council.[68]

The bill's second reading passed on 10 May by 410 votes to 204. In the debates Ramsay MacDonald and Philip Snowden called for exclusively secular education, and John Dillon for a large extension of clause 4.[69] Twenty-three Labour party MPs voted for the bill (including MacDonald, Snowden, and Henderson) and only four against. In committee an amendment in favour of purely secular education obtained only sixty-three votes, resembling the figure received by a similar motion in 1870. Clause 4 was modified in the interests of the denominationalists but still did not satisfy them. Joseph Chamberlain moved unsuccessfully to substitute 'universal denominational facilities' for the Cowper-Temple system. The third reading passed easily on 30 July, and the bill went up to face a much harder test in the Lords.

Already the dispute had produced many public meetings and some large demonstrations. A great Catholic gathering at the Albert Hall on 5 May was addressed by Catholic MPs such as Hilaire Belloc, a Liberal, and was said to have been attended by as many as 60,000 inside and outside the building.[70] Lord Ripon tried in the Government's interest to persuade the Catholic Bishops not to reject clause 4 out of hand, and eventually his advice bore fruit: on 18 June the Catholic Education Council decided to appoint a committee to work with the Irish Catholic MPs to obtain amendments to the clause.[71] Anglican dislike of the bill was shown by episcopal propaganda and many protest meetings. Lord Halifax and Bishop Gore, both Anglo-Catholics, were vehement in opposition; Halifax condemned 'backsliding' Tories and Bishops who entertained a compromise.[72] The Evangelical Bishop Knox of Manchester

[67] J. Scott Lidgett, *My Guided Life* (London, 1936), 189; W. Evans and W. Claridge, *James Hirst Hollowell and the Movement for Civic Control in Education* (Manchester, 1911), 121–5; Bebbington, op. cit. 147–8; Perks to Rosebery, 10 and 30 Apr.; 5, 8, 14 May; 3 and 29 June; 22 July; 8 Nov. 1906; RP, 10052, fos. 147–8, 152, 157, 160–7, 174–6, 179, 185–6, 211–13.

[68] *British Weekly*, 12 Apr. 1906, pp. 1–2; *Baptist Handbook* (1907) 218, 226–7; *Congregational Year-book* (1907), 5.

[69] H clvi. 1010 ff., 1065 ff., 1241 ff., 1317 ff., 1504 ff.

[70] *AR* i (1906), 99 f.; Oldmeadow, *Bourne*, i. 298–300.

[71] Cruickshank, op. cit. 96; Ripon to Archbishop Bourne, 18 Apr. (copy), 4 May (copy), 26 May 1906 (copy), Ripon Papers, 43545, fos. 54–6, 67–8, 81; Bourne to Ripon, 26 Apr., 4, 7, and 25 May, 19 June; ibid. fos. 57–64, 69–70, 76–7, 78–9; Ripon to Birrell, 14 and 15 June, 22 July; Ripon Papers, 43542, fos. 58–61, 64; Birrell to Ripon, 24 July; ibid. fos. 66–7; Ripon to S. C. Scrope, 11 May (copy); ibid. 43639, fos. 178–80; Scrope to Ripon, 13 May; ibid. fos. 181–3.

[72] Richards, op. cit. 56; J. G. Lockhart, *Viscount Halifax* (2 vols., London, 1935–6), ii. 156–7; *Church Union Gazette* (supplement), Mar. 1906; ECU Minutes, C.U. dep. 5, 228; CCDI Minutes, 22 June, 5 Nov. (vol. 34, 202, 205); Eluned Owen, *The Later Life of Bishop Owen*, 83 ff.

was active against the measure, reviving the Church Schools Emergency
League and organizing for 8 June a large protest journey of Lancashire
Churchmen to London. They went from about 150 parishes in thirty-two trains
and gathered in the Albert Hall.[73]

Some Liberal Anglicans, however, supported the bill while wishing to amend
it. These included Bishop Percival, Hensley Henson, and Lady Wimborne
(who had become a Liberal over the Free Trade issue). Because of the divisions
over Ritualism some Anglicans were said to support the bill as 'a curb on
Anglican priestcraft'.[74] For the Conservative party, Balfour relentlessly
attacked the measure. He said it was directed against the Church of England
and that clause 4 was only there 'to save the Roman Catholics' for the
Liberals.[75] 'Even a hostile House of Commons', it was said, 'was compelled to
admire his extraordinary skill in taking advantage of the diversities of opinion
and driving wedges between the Government and its supporters'.[76] Party
attacks also came from George Wyndham, Lords Robert and Hugh Cecil,
F. E. Smith, and others.

The bill's success in the Commons was not repeated in the Lords. In the
upper House there were five times as many Unionist peers as Liberals; and the
attitude of the majority to much of the Government's legislation was clearly
displayed in 1906. The Trade Disputes Bill was considered to be in the broad
interests of the working class and allowed to pass. But the Education Bill, it was
claimed, satisfied only a section of Liberals, and this measure was altered so
significantly that Ministers would not accept the changes. Tories were only too
ready to agree with F. E. Smith that the Government 'should get rid of
confounding the Liberal party with the people'.[77]

The battle between the Houses was intensified by the West Riding County
Council's refusal to pay teachers for giving religious instruction in voluntary
schools; the Lords decided against the Council on appeal in December. The
upper House agreed to read the bill a second time on 3 August, and then
proceeded to amend it heavily while demonstrations for and against the measure
continued to take place in the country.[78] Clause 4 was made mandatory on the
local authorities; it was not to be restricted to urban areas, and a two-thirds

[73] Cruickshank, op. cit. 95; Lockhart, op. cit. ii. 158; E. A. Knox, *Reminiscences of an Octogenarian,
1847–1934* ([1935]), 242–5; Charles Gore, *Objections to the Education Bill of 1906* (London, 1906), 3 ff.;
G. L. Prestige, *The Life of Charles Gore* (London, 1935), 287–8.

[74] Beatrice Webb, *Our Partnership*, ed. Barbara Drake and Margaret Cole (London, 1948), 340–1;
Henson, *Retrospect of an Unimportant Life* (3 vols., London, 1942–50), i. 144; W. Temple, *The Life of
Bishop Percival* (London, 1921), 186; Lady Wimborne to Henry Wace, Dean of Canterbury, 4 Feb., 26
Apr. 1906; C. C. Osborne Papers, 46048, fos. 56–7, 70; Wace to C. C. Osborne, 6 Feb.; ibid. fos. 58–61,
also 66 ff.

[75] *AR* i (1906), 160–1.

[76] J. A. Spender, *The Life of Sir Henry Campbell-Bannerman* (2 vols., London, 1923), ii. 281–2. Cf.
Augustine Birrell, *Things Past Redress* (London, 1937), 191.

[77] *AR* i (1907), 23.

[78] e.g. ECU demonstration, Oct. 1906; ECU Minutes, CU dep. 5, 232; Liverpool and Leeds Catholic
demonstrations, Oct. and Nov. 1906; SP, S(4), box 13.

majority of the parents was substituted for four-fifths. It would be possible for denominational teaching to be given in any council school by the regular staff. The proposed Welsh educational council was rejected, one opponent saying it would encourage disestablishment.[79] The third reading passed on 6 December by 105 votes to twenty-eight.[80]

The Government and its supporters opposed the amendments because they would put too much denominational education back into a measure intended to restrict it. There were murmurs about the need to reduce the Lords' veto powers. On 27 November both the Congregational Union and the National Liberal Federation called on the Government to refuse the amendments.[81] On 7 December the Cabinet decided to reject them *en bloc;* and Birrell, who regarded his amended bill as 'a miserable, mangled, tortured, twisted tertium quid', announced the decision to the Commons on the 10th.[82] Two days later the Commons voted by 416 votes to 107 to reject the amendments. Fifty-five Irish Home Rulers now voted in the majority, and only three opposed.[83] Most Home Rule MPs were satisfied with additional concessions to denominational education which Ministers were ready to make, namely an extension of the clause 4 facilities and establishment of parents' committees with a strong voice in the appointment of teachers in Catholic schools. The Home Rulers had reluctant support from Catholic Bishops for their action but annoyed Catholic Unionists, not least the Duke of Norfolk who complained strongly to Archbishop Bourne.[84]

On 17 and 19 December the Lords debated the Commons' resolution, and a compromise still seemed possible. The Earl of Crewe, for the Government, offered even further concessions to heal the breach, and a conference of party leaders was held on the 18th. But the conference failed, allegedly because of Balfour's intransigence and Devonshire's absence.[85] In the Lords the Marquess of Lansdowne, for the Opposition, said the concessions were still inadequate. He carried a motion, which Devonshire opposed, that 'the House do insist on its amendments'.

In reply, Campbell-Bannerman told the Commons on 20 December that, since the Lords aimed to destroy the whole intention of the bill, it was now being dropped. Halifax, who had feared that 'short of a miracle the bill will pass', was immensely relieved.[86] Also relieved were Nonconformists who

[79] Morgan, *Wales in British Politics*, 227–8.
[80] *AR* i (1906), 202–6, 222–32, 239–40.
[81] Ibid. 238; Richards, op. cit. 60; *Congregational Year-book* (1907), 26.
[82] Bebbington, op. cit. 148; Perks to Rosebery, 24 Nov.; RP, 10052, fos. 222–3.
[83] *AR* i (1906), 243–5; Cruickshank, op. cit. 101. Cf. Bourne to Ripon, 8 Dec.; Ripon Papers, 43545, fos. 92–3.
[84] Norfolk to Bourne, 2 Jan. 1907; Bourne to Norfolk, 3 Jan.; Bishop of Salford to Bourne, 6 Jan.; memo of Norfolk, 30 Jan.; Lord Edmund Talbot, MP, to Bourne, 9 Mar.; Bourne to Talbot, 12 Mar.; Bishop of Nottingham to Bourne, 8 Apr.; memo of Monsignor Brown, 13 Feb.; Bourne Papers, box 1/178.
[85] Birrell, op. cit. 191–2; Spender, op. cit. ii. 309–11.   [86] Lockhart, op. cit. ii. 159.

abhorred the concessions offered to denominationalists. But this did not stop them condemning the Lords. The upper House 'stands for the denial of democratic government in England', said the *Baptist Times;* and the *Bible Christian Magazine* said the country could scarcely tolerate the House 'as at present constituted'.[87]

Thus ended the 1906 Education Bill, an unhappy measure from the start. The efforts of Edward VII, Archbishop Davidson, Campbell-Bannerman, and Devonshire to reach a compromise had not succeeded.[88] Balfour had correctly surmised that Ministers would not dissolve Parliament on the issue. But on the larger, looming question of the Lords' power to reject bills passed by the Commons, the premier said: 'the resources of the British Constitution and the House of Commons were not wholly exhausted. A way must, and would be, found by which the will of the people, expressed through their elected representatives in that House, must be made to prevail.'[89]

On the broad constitutional question the Government reached ultimate victory in 1911, via the Lloyd George Budget of 1909. But there was no success for ministerial education efforts. In 1907 a bill permitting marriage with a deceased wife's sister was adopted by the Government and enacted after fifty-eight years' Parliamentary struggle. But Dissenters who had long supported the reform could find little comfort in this concession by the Lords when their educational wishes were still obstructed. Despite the concession of 1907 a man was not officially enabled to marry his deceased brother's widow until 1921; or (for example) his brother's deceased son's widow until 1931. The 1907 Act allowed a clergyman to refuse to celebrate marriages with deceased wife's sisters or to withhold permission for his church to be used for them.[90]

Reginald McKenna, a Congregationalist who had succeeded Birrell as President of the Board of Education, introduced a small one-clause bill on 26 February 1907 relieving local authorities of having to pay for denominational teaching out of the rates. Home Rulers voted against it, Conservatives also generally opposed it as a 'passive resister's' bill, and it was too narrow to satisfy Nonconformists.[91] When asked their opinion by the Government, the

[87] May E. Lloyd, 'Baptist Political Attitudes with Special Reference to the Late Nineteenth Century', M.Phil. thesis (Leeds, 1974), 56; *Bible Christian Magazine*, 6th ser. vi (1906), 465.

[88] See G. K. A. Bell, *Randall Davidson, Archbishop of Canterbury* (2 vols., London, 1935), i. 520–30; Spender, op. cit. ii. 302 ff.; Davidson to Campbell-Bannerman, 28 Nov., 5 and 11 Dec. 1906; CBP, 41239, fos. 161–70, 186–7; J. D. Fair, *British Interparty Conferences: A Study of the Procedure of Conciliation in British Politics, 1867–1921* (Oxford, 1980), 62–74.

[89] *AR* i (1906), 247–50.

[90] *AR* i (1907), 29, 221–3; S. Maccoby, *English Radicalism, 1886–1914* (London, 1953), 486; Lockhart, op. cit. ii. 227–8; Sir A. Fitzroy, *Memoirs*, 5th edn. (2 vols., London, n.d.), i. 331; ECU Minutes, 20 June 1907 (CU dep. 5, 240–2).

[91] Davidson to Balfour, 16 Mar. 1907; BP, 49788, fos. 262–3; CCDI Minutes, 10 May 1907 (vol. 34, p. 216); handbill of Catholic Federation (copy in Runciman Papers, WR 24, 2); Sir A. Chamberlain, *Politics from Inside: An Epistolary Chronicle, 1906–1914* (London, 1936), 61; Oldmeadow, op. cit. i. 329–33.

committee of Nonconformist MPs said they would prefer a more comprehensive bill next year, and in May Campbell-Bannerman announced that McKenna's bill would be withdrawn.[92]

The measure for next year proposed a national system of undenominational education. All schools in 'single school' areas would be transferred to this system. But denominational teachers would have the 'right of entry' to council schools on two days a week outside normal teaching hours. Outside 'single school' areas denominational schools could 'contract out' of the system, receive a Parliamentary grant, and supplement it by charging fees. The bill would revive pre-1902 complaints about 'intolerable financial strain' in voluntary schools, and Lloyd George told McKenna in November that with such a proposal he was 'heading straight for the rocks'.[93]

McKenna introduced his new bill on 24 February 1908. It was criticized especially by Churchmen and Roman Catholics because denominational schools would lose rate support.[94] Another bill was brought in by Bishop Edwards of St Asaph, proposing that all elementary schools should be under public control; denominational teaching could be given in them but not at public cost.[95] Davidson favoured this bill but Halifax and Gore found it unacceptable. It was not taken to a second reading. McKenna's bill passed its second reading on 20 May against the votes of Conservatives and sixty-four Home Rulers, but there its progress stopped.[96]

McKenna had left the Board of Education in April in a ministerial reshuffle following Campbell-Bannerman's resignation. McKenna was succeeded by Walter Runciman, a Wesleyan. Catholic dislike of McKenna's bill contributed, it was said, to Government by-election losses. The Liberal loss of Peckham in March was attributed partly to Catholic defections.[97] Churchill, who was given Cabinet office in April and had to stand for re-election under the practice which ended in 1911, lost North West Manchester by 429 votes because, he alleged, 'those sulky Irish Catholics changed sides at the last moment under priestly pressure'. The 900 Irish electors had been advised to oppose Churchill by the Catholic Bishop of Salford and his clergy who disliked McKenna's bill; also by a local federation of Catholic trade unionists and by John Redmond, who thought that under its new leader (Asquith) the Government would become

[92] Bebbington, op. cit. 149.

[93] Perks to Rosebery, 26 Nov. 1907; RP, 10053, fo. 59 ff.; Cruickshank, op. cit. 104–5; *AR* i (1908), 34–6.

[94] Circular letter from Hon. Charles Russell, chairman of the Catholic Federation of the Archdiocese of Westminster, 25 Feb. 1908; letters to Archbishop Bourne from J. W. Gilbert (6 Mar.), F. R. Anderton (30 Mar.), Tyneside Catholic Teachers' Association (30 Mar.), Liverpool and district Catholic Teachers' Association (5 Apr.), Duke of Norfolk, 8 Apr. (all in Bourne Papers, 1/179); *Tablet*, 29 Aug., p. 349.

[95] *AR* i (1908), 39, 78; H clxxxvii. 1–49.

[96] *AR* i (1908), 107–9.

[97] Oldmeadow, op. cit. i. 360.

even cooler towards Home Rule. But Churchill stressed his own attachment to Home Rule and said the Government would fight on the issue at the next general election. Consequently the local Home Rule politicians advised support for him, and there were other possible reasons for his defeat besides Catholic voting. His successful opponent was Joynson-Hicks who, strangely for a well-known ultra-Protestant but no doubt judiciously, said in his manifesto that McKenna's bill 'breathed enmity against the Church of England and the Church of Rome'.[98]

The same was said by other determined opponents of yet a further attempt to settle the education problem, made by Walter Runciman. He sought agreement from all sides to a compromise solution. He managed to obtain the assent of some Free Church leaders (including, practically, a very reluctant Clifford) to a scheme amalgamating all rate aided elementary schools in a general State system and including 'right of entry' for denominational teachers to ex-voluntary schools. Denominational schools outside single school areas could contract out and receive a Parliamentary grant. This proposal was put to a meeting of 100 Nonconformist MPs on 9 November 1908 and accepted by a majority. A large concession had thus been wrung from naturally unwilling Dissenters. Davidson gave reluctant approval to the plan. But discussions between Ministers and Roman Catholics were inhibited by a recent further deterioration of relations. Out of fear of popular anti-popish disorder, Asquith and Herbert Gladstone (the Home Secretary) had persuaded a reluctant Lord Ripon, as a Catholic, to put pressure on Archbishop Bourne not to permit the consecrated Host to be carried in a street procession at an international Eucharistic Congress in London on 13 September. Ripon's unhappiness with Government behaviour in this affair caused him to resign from the Cabinet (ostensibly on grounds of age and infirmity) immediately afterwards. Catholic indignation over the incident helped to cause the loss of another Liberal seat, at Newcastle upon Tyne on 23 September.[99] It was not fully established until a Relief Act of 1926 that Catholic processions could take place without restriction.

When, as Bourne stated, Catholics believed (however unjustifiably) that Government had 'gone out of its way to wound us in our most cherished religious convictions', they were unwilling to discuss probably disadvantageous educational changes with Ministers. Bourne said he could not participate in

[98] *AR* i (1908), 83–4; R. S. Churchill, *Winston S. Churchill*, ii (London, 1967), 253–61, and companion vol., pt. 2 (London, 1969), 788; H. Pelling, *Winston Churchill* (London, 1974), 110–12; H. A. Taylor, *Jix, Vixcount Brentford* (London, 1933), 85–6.

[99] Bebbington, op. cit. 150; W. B. Selbie, *The Life of Charles Silvester Horne* (London, 1920), 199–202; M. J. Wilkinson, 'Educational Controversies in British Politics, 1895–1914', Ph.D. thesis (Newcastle upon Tyne, 1978), 598; Runciman to Davidson, 9 Nov. 1908; Runciman Papers, WR35, I; Clifford to Runciman, 19 Nov. ibid. 35, II; memo of Committee of Protestant Dissenting Deputies, 26 Nov. ibid. 24, I; correspondence in AP xx. 1–80; G. I. T. Machin, 'The Liberal Government and the Eucharistic Procession of 1908', *JEH* xxxiv (1983), 559–83.

negotiations unless the remaining civil disabilities of Catholics were removed.[1] Thus, although he did have further contact with Bourne on the matter, Runciman was unable to include the Catholics in his 'concordat'—which it was unlikely he could have done in any case. Catholic MPs showed in the debates on the bill that they could not accept it.

Runciman presented the bill on 20 November. The second reading passed easily on the 26th. Most Liberals voted in favour; as did most Labour party members (17–4); Unionists were divided, fifty-six voting against and thirty-six for; and most Home Rulers voted against. Any appearance of agreement behind the scheme was soon dissipated. Objections came from all sides, both inside and outside Parliament. The National Society denounced the bill and Bishop Knox condemned it. At a Representative Church Council meeting on 3 December the Houses of clergy and laity (though not the House of Bishops) rejected the arrangement as undermining denominational education. Even Davidson was unhappy about the measure because the financial support proposed for 'contracting out' schools seemed inadequate.[2] Cabinet decided to withdraw the bill on 4 December, and Runciman had to be content with congratulations for his attempt at educational peace.

Had the compromise got through the Commons it would scarcely have passed the Lords, who could have pointed to the fierce divisions over it. The Government, having in 1908 lost several seats in by-elections and major legislative measures (the education and licensing bills) was in a state of depression from which only the Lloyd George budget and the challenge to the Lords next year relieved it.

The failure to reach an education settlement brought mixed reactions. Nonconformists who had been declaring their impatience with the Government before the last bill was introduced were doubtless no less impatient after its withdrawal. The Primitive Methodist Education Committee, however, was pleased that 'concessions to clericalism' had failed, and said that it could not agree to right of entry, contracting out, or any tests for teachers.[3] But suggestions for a compromise were made in 1910 by an interdenominational Education Settlement Committee, which published a peace plan admitting a high degree of denominationalism in the proposed system. The difficulties in reaching a solution remained, however, even after the Lords' veto power had been limited, because from 1910 the Government majority depended on Catholic Home Rulers who wanted to preserve the 1902 system. Hence the

[1] Bourne to Runciman, 27 Oct. 1908; Bourne Papers, 1/181; Runciman to Ripon, 12 and 18 Nov.; Ripon Papers, 43640, fos. 176–8, 181–2; Bourne to Runciman, 19 Nov.; Bourne Papers, 1/181; Runciman to Bourne, 20 Nov.; ibid.
[2] Wilkinson, op. cit. 606; H cxcvii. 417–523, 707–817; Henson, op. cit. i. 86–7; Lockhart, op. cit. ii. 161; Cruickshank, op. cit. 107, 110; Oldmeadow, op. cit. i. 363; Bell, op. cit. i. 537–9.
[3] Revd J. Hocking to Runciman, 20 Oct. 1908; Runciman Papers, WR 24, 1; Revd T. E. Soddy to Runciman, 21 Oct.; ibid.; Revd J. Pickett (secretary of Primitive Methodist Education Committee) to Runciman, 1 Mar. 1909; ibid. WR 28.

existing system of rate aided council and voluntary schools remained. Resistance to the education rate continued and a centralized Passive Resistance League commenced in 1909 with Clifford as president.[4] But the efforts were fruitless in effecting change.

The education quarrel was linked to the Ritualist dispute. As late as 1914 Balfour complained that 'where ritual is concerned mankind seem more than usually incapable of retaining any sense of proportion'.[5] The report of the Royal Commission on Ecclesiastical Discipline was issued on 21 June and published on 2 July 1906. Searching for a *via media* between opposite attitudes, it steered gingerly between approval of 'elaborate and spectacular ceremonial' and condemnation of all Ritualist practice. The report's basis was the belief that 'the law of public worship in the Church of England is too narrow for the religious life of the present generation', and that 'modern thought and feeling are characterised by a care for ceremonial, a sense of dignity in worship, and an appreciation of the continuity of the Church, which were not similarly felt at the time when the law took its present shape'. 'An extraordinary revival of spiritual life and activity' had taken place but the Church was still 'without that power of self-adjustment which is inherent in the conception of a living Church'. 'Greater elasticity' in worship was recommended—which meant greater, but still restrained, freedom for ritual.[6] To this end, royal letters of Business should be issued to the Convocations so that they could prepare a revised Prayer Book for Parliamentary enactment.

As to the practices themselves, confession and prayers for the dead were deemed permissible. The use of incense was also practically allowed, since it was only slightly discouraged by the statement that it was probably illegal. But 'practices of special gravity and significance' should be prohibited (amongst Anglicans) by Bishops and ecclesiastical courts. These included reservation of the Sacrament under conditions which might lead to adoration, processions with the Sacrament, veneration of images, the invocation of or confession to the Virgin Mary or the saints. Other proposals included the founding of new ecclesiastical courts; a new Court of Final Appeal; repeal of the Public Worship Regulation Act; and abolition, with certain safeguards, of the Bishops' veto in ritual cases.[7]

The report could scarcely end the controversy; indeed it opened a new phase in it. The recommendations were generally well received as a conciliatory basis of possible settlement, but objections were not lacking.[8] Evangelicals were

[4] Cruickshank, op. cit. 111; Jordan, *Free Church Unity*, 116–17; C. T. Dyke Acland to Runciman, 19 Aug. 1909; Runciman Papers, WR 28; G. A. Beck (ed.), *The English Catholics, 1850–1950* (London, 1950), 387.

[5] Balfour to Davidson, 9 Jan. 1914; BP, 49788, fo. 274.

[6] Bell, op. cit. i. 471.

[7] Ibid. i. 470–3; *AR* i (1906), 168–70.

[8] e.g. H. Hensley Henson, 'The Ecclesiastical Discipline Report', pts. I and II, *CR* xc (July–Dec. 1906), 241–57, 408–25.

divided in their reactions: moderates showed considerable satisfaction but the more extreme protested.[9] The Church Association was displeased. Lord Halifax also objected to the report in the Press, and the English Church Union condemned the proposed revision every year from 1908 to 1911.[10] When the Convocations began systematically to discuss liturgical revision in 1907 their debates, reports, and provisional rubrics concerning vestments and reservation of the Sacrament helped to continue the disputes. They did so for a very long time. The difficult proceedings were protracted, partly because of delay during the war, until a revised Prayer Book was finally produced in 1927.[11] The controversy then intensified over the new book. In the mean time Ritualism, considerably encouraged by the 1906 report, became more widespread and the tension continued.

So the prospect of peace in the Church of England was postponed. None the less the controversy became on the whole less open and strident than in the years preceding the Commission, and despite the continuance of markedly anti-Ritualist meetings the agitation tended to become less intense. In Parliament there was little revival of debate on the matter. Bills on 'Church discipline' or 'ecclesiastical disorders' were still presented. They were sponsored by Liberal, Conservative, and Labour MPs, and a spurt of them came late in the summer of 1906 after the report appeared. But none of these in the years 1906–11 received a second reading. There was some spirited debate, however, in February 1908 when C. F. G. Masterman, a junior Minister, made a strong plea for tolerance of divergences within the Church and moved an amendment for disestablishment. Ramsay MacDonald seconded this motion, but another Labour MP (Stephen Walsh) said disestablishment was not within half a century of practical politics when there was so much social reform to be dealt with.[12] After 1911 Parliamentary debate on the ritual question practically ceased until 1927. The hope of forming a Parliamentary phalanx strong and insistent enough to impose effective statutory curbs on Ritualism had not been realized, and for many years ahead concern over the question focused on proceedings in the Convocations.[13]

Anti-Ritualism was still considerably in evidence, and so was anti-romanism. This was shown, for example, by protests from the Reformation Society, Protestant Alliance, and Church Association at the betrothal of Princess Ena of

[9] e.g. views of Lady Wimborne, in *The Nineteenth Century and After*, lx (July–Dec. 1906), 169–81.
[10] P. J. Waller, *Democracy and Sectarianism*, 227–8; Prestige, *Gore*, 297; S. Dark, *Archbishop Davidson and the Church of England* (London, 1929), 162.
[11] Bell, op. cit. i. 647–54; J. W. Walmsley, 'The History of the Evangelical Party in the Church of England Between 1906 and 1928' Ph.D. thesis (Hull, 1981), 17 ff.; Prestige, op. cit. 302 ff., 377. As early as October 1908 Sir George Kekewich asked the Prime Minister in the Commons whether he would impose a time limit on the Convocations' proceedings; H cxcv. 511.
[12] H clii. 523, cliii. 319, clx. 423, 1361, clxi. 418 (1906); clxix. 420, 856–9 (1907); clxxxiii. 540, clxxxiv. 303–80 (1908); 5th ser. i. 334, 1867 (1909); xiv. 354, 1007–9 (1910); xxi. 453, xxv. 2354–61 (1911).
[13] For these see Bell, op. cit. i. 647–54; Walmsley, op. cit.; K. Hylson-Smith, 'The Evangelicals in the Church of England, 1900–1939', Ph.D. thesis (London, 1983).

Battenberg, niece of Edward VII, to the King of Spain because this involved her abjuration of Protestantism; by complaints about a life-sized statue, modelled on one of the Virgin and Child, in St Cuthbert's Church of Scotland in Edinburgh, and about the King's attendance at a requiem mass in February 1908 for the assassinated Portuguese monarch; and by fears about Catholic 'denominationalism' in the National University of Ireland founded by an Act of 1908.[14] The eucharistic procession of September that year was opposed by fifty-one Protestant societies, and after the procession had taken place there were further public expressions of ultra-Protestantism.[15]

There was also opposition, by some Liberal as well as Conservative MPs, to attempts to alter or repeal laws which were unfavourable to Catholics. These were efforts to change the Sovereign's accession declaration against transubstantiation, to open the Lord Chancellorship of England and Lord Lieutenancy of Ireland to Catholics, and to permit outdoor Catholic processions without restriction.[16] 'The King's Declaration must stand as our security against a Popish monarch', said the *Bulwark*. But a change of Sovereign in May 1910 brought new demands for an altered declaration. Against continuing objections from Protestant societies and public meetings, and from both Unionists and Liberals, Parliament passed by the end of July the Accession Declaration Act which removed words particularly offensive to Catholics. A by-election at Liverpool (Kirkdale) was said to have been won by an ultra-Protestant Unionist mainly on this question. The core of the new formula was simply 'I am a faithful Protestant' instead of, as originally drafted, 'I am a faithful member of the Church by law established in England'—this change being made to satisfy Nonconformists and members of the Church of Scotland.[17]

The large radical majority of 1906 had a stimulating effect on voluntaryism. Robert Perks said in January 1907 that he wanted to 'force on' disestablishment.[18] On 27 February that year R. L. Everett, Liberal MP for Woodbridge (Suffolk) moved in the Commons that the Church in England and Wales should be disestablished and disendowed. The motion was based on the argument that the establishment 'had within her pale less than one-half of the

[14] *79th Annual Report of Protestant Reformation Society, 1905* (London, 1906), 9–10; *AR* i (1906), 148, i (1908), 75–7, 101–3, 174–6, ii (1908), 20; Oldmeadow, op. cit. i. 266, 349–51; Edinburgh C. of S. Presbytery Minutes, 9 Oct. 1907, 25 Nov. 1908, 27 Apr., and 29 June 1910; CH2/121/33, pp. 261–2, 363–6; *Scotsman*, 29 June 1910, p. 8; Waller, op. cit. 237–41; H, 5th. ser. vi. 1910–11 (24 June 1909); Clifford to Asquith, 23 Sept. 1908; AP xx. 25–7; *Bulwark*, Oct. 1909, 226–7.

[15] Machin, op. cit. 574.

[16] *AR* i (1908), 231–2; i (1909), 113–15; H iv. 2155–232.

[17] *Bulwark*, Sept. 1908, p. 220; *AR* i (1910), 126–7, 153–4, 195–200; Revd J. Scott Lidgett to Runciman, 21 May 1910 (Runciman Papers, WR, 35); *The Sovereign's Accession Declaration: Resolutions of the Protestant Reformation Society* (London, 1910); *Scotsman*, 6 June 1910, p. 6, 7 June, p. 8, 15 June, p. 9, 5 July, p. 5, 8 July, p. 5, 9 July, p. 9, 11 July, pp. 10, 11, 12 July, pp. 7, 9; *Aldersgate Primitive Methodist Magazine*, Sept. 1910 (NS, ix. 752); Selbie, op. cit. 223–5.

[18] Perks to Rosebery, 7 Jan. 1907; RP, 10053, fos. 1–2.

active religious life of the nation, and probably not much more than one-third of the whole people', and that disestablishment would make the Church more effective. D. F. Goddard, Liberal member for Ipswich, who seconded the motion, claimed that 'the influence of the Established Church as a whole had been against popular progress'. Sir John Kennaway moved, as an amendment, to maintain the established Church: 'never was she so deep in the affections of the people as at the present time'. Austin Taylor said he would support neither the motion nor the amendment, as the only cure for the Church's ills was the removal of Ritualist practice: 'could it be any longer maintained that the Church of England was fulfilling its duty as a trustee of the Protestant religion of this country?' Members of the Government showed hardly any interest in the motion, and all the 'Nonconformists' in the Cabinet, except Birrell, were absent from the debate.[19] The division was largely a party one, the opponents of the motion being mostly Conservatives and the supporters Liberals, Home Rulers, and Labour party members. The motion succeeded by 198 to ninety after the amendment had been lost by 206 to ninety-three.

But no bill was introduced after this success. Nonconformists were currently more concerned with the education problem, but this was related to the voluntary question—the *Guardian* warned that 'the disestablishment of educational trust-deeds' might be 'the first step towards a larger form of disestablishment'.[20] The Liberation Society was still struggling financially, but said it was pleased by the interest shown by some Anglicans in voluntaryism and thankfully noted a unanimous Congregational Union resolution for disestablishment in October 1907. However, some Nonconformist disillusion with politics resulted from the failure to settle the education question; and an anonymous work entitled *Nonconformity and Politics,* published early in 1909 and calling for less political and more spiritual commitment by Dissenters, had considerable influence.[21]

In Scotland disestablishment was still alive but was strongly related to the question of larger Presbyterian reunion. Robertson Nicoll predicted in the *British Weekly* in 1900 that the next attempt at Presbyterian union would involve 'a compromise with the Establishment'.[22] The official view of the United Free Church Assembly was that disestablishment was a pre-condition of reunion. Early in 1907 the Church and State committee of the UF Church appealed to Campbell-Bannerman for disestablishment: 'it is an intolerable thing that an alien institution like the State should be suffered permanently to disrupt and keep asunder two great bodies of Scottish Christians, comprizing

[19]   Perks to Rosebery, 1 Mar.; ibid. fo. 30.

[20]   H clxv. 124–66; *Guardian*, 2 May 1906, p. 724.

[21]   LS, 7 Oct. 1907, p. 26; *Congregational Year-book* (1908), 28; Bebbington, op. cit. 157–8; 'A Nonconformist Minister', 'Nonconformity and Politics: A Word From Within', *FR* lxxxv (1909), 102–22.

[22]   *British Weekly*, 20 Sept. 1900, 425.

between them the vast bulk of the population'.[23] Among the resolutions of the Scottish Liberal Federation in 1908 was one in favour of disestablishment.[24] But many United Free Churchmen were less concerned with disestablishment than with spiritual freedom as an essential condition of reunion. If spiritual independence were guaranteed they might be prepared to accept established status. These were matters on which most Scots Presbyterians were ready to confer, and formal discussion on co-operation and union began to take place.

On 24 April 1907 the Edinburgh presbytery of the Church of Scotland adopted, by thirty-eight votes to three, a motion of Dr Archibald Scott for unreserved discussions on co-operation and union between the Church of Scotland, the UF Church, and the Free Church. The Church of Scotland in May that year did not accept Scott's proposal in full but appointed a large committee with Dr Norman Macleod as convener to consider terms for discussion. In 1908 the General Assembly adopted a proposal of Dr Macleod's committee that the UF Church and the Free Church be invited to confer with the Church of Scotland 'in a friendly and generous spirit' on the ecclesiastical situation, and 'to consider how a large measure of Christian fellowship and co-operation could be brought about so as to prepare the way for union'. In 1909 the UF Church, but not the Free Church, accepted the invitation provided there would be no restriction on the topics for discussion. This was agreed in the Church of Scotland Assembly on 27 May 1909, and consequently the question of establishment was included in the deliberations. Each Church assembly appointed its own committee of 100 members (the 'Hundred') composed equally of ministers and elders. The two committees were 'to enter into unrestricted conference on the existing ecclesiastical situation and on the main causes which keep the Churches apart'. In November, at their first conference, the committees appointed a joint subcommittee—a further testimony to combined seriousness of purpose.[25] Fair progress was made, and in 1910 the Churches were drawn closer when the Church of Scotland adopted a wider form of subscription to its confession of faith, similar to that already in use in the UF Church.

A crucial stage on the road to reunion would be the adoption of a new constitution for the Church of Scotland, to be presented to Parliament for enactment. A proposed general basis of this constitution was prepared by a lawyer, Christopher Johnston, later Lord Sands. After amendment and approval by the Hundred a Memorandum containing the proposals was laid

[23] J. H. S. Burleigh, *A Church History of Scotland* (Edinburgh, 1960), 399. Cf. Prof. J. A. Paterson to Campbell-Bannerman, 29 Nov. 1905; CBP, 41238, fos. 105–7.

[24] *AR* i (1908), 253.

[25] Burleigh, op. cit. 399–400; A. I. Dunlop, 'The Paths to Reunion in 1929', *Records of the Scottish Church History Society*, xx (1980), 166 ff.; Lord Sands, *Dr Archibald Scott and His Times, 1837–1908* (Edinburgh and London, 1919), 229; A. Gammie, *Dr John White: A Biography and a Study* (London, 1929), 140–3; G. F. Barbour, *The Life of Alexander Whyte, DD* (London, 1924), 516–21.

before the General Assemblies in 1912. The broad suggestion was that the Church of Scotland, while remaining established, should have complete spiritual self-government.[26]

Adoption of this proposal required considerable deviation from standpoints in the old conflict over establishment. By no means all the members of either Church were prepared to relinquish long-held opinions; there were still firm Erastians and firm voluntaries who resisted compromise. A UF minister, for example, asserted that any attempt to modify the established Church's constitution while still maintaining the State connection, 'so as to unite Presbyterians within one State Church', would be 'doomed to failure'.[27] Nevertheless by 1913 the Memorandum secured majority approval in both General Assemblies, Archibald Henderson making a persuasive speech in favour at the UF gathering.[28] The Church of Scotland Hundred was instructed to draft a constitution to be placed before the next Assembly, 'with a view to its transmission as a Basis of Union to the Assembly of the United Free Church'. Articles were produced in 1914 and it was decided to send them to the Church of Scotland presbyteries for consideration and decision.[29] But further progress was delayed by the war. In 1915 it was decided to postpone the discussions until armed hostilities ended.

English disestablishment had not revived, having lost any fresh impetus which Nonconformist election success and the education dispute might have given it. Much of the interest formerly given to Scots disestablishment was being transferred to discussions on reunion. Welsh disestablishment remained in increasingly lonely eminence. The long arguments over it seemed tired, but the question was kept alive by the persistently large numerical lead of Nonconformity (after many years of impressive advance the Church in Wales could still claim only twenty-six per cent of church membership in 1905);[30] by the nationalist ingredients which the issue possessed in Wales, unlike England and Scotland; and by the fact that all thirty-four Welsh MPs returned in 1906 were expected to support the demand.

But the Government made no immediate effort to carry Welst disestablishment, which would probably have been rejected by the Lords. It was three years

---

[26] Archibald Henderson to Lord Balfour of Burleigh, 19 Feb., 8 Mar. 1912 (copies); Sands Papers, CH1/10/2; Balfour of Burleigh to Sheriff C. Johnston, 19 and 23 Feb., 8 and 15 Mar., 18 Mar., 29 Apr., 9 and 27 July 1912; ibid.; Johnston to Balfour of Burleigh, 2 May; ibid.; Revd John White to Keir Hardie, Apr. 1914; A. Gammie, op. cit. 146–51; Lady Frances Balfour, *A Memoir of Lord Balfour of Burleigh, KT* (London, 1924), 151–2; *AR* i (1912), 277–8.

[27] *The Liberator*, June 1910; also Sept. 1911, pp. 147–8, Feb. 1913, pp. 24, 29, Mar. 1913, pp. 41–2, June 1914, p. 88; J. A. Paterson to Bonar Law, 19 and 28 June 1913; BLP, 29/5/39; Law to J. A. Paterson, 26 June; ibid. 33/5/38; Arthur Steel-Maitland to Law, 23 June; ibid. 29/5/48.

[28] A. Muir, *John White, CH, DD, Ll D* (London, 1958), 148; W. P. Patterson, 'The Union Problem of the Scottish Church', *CR* civ (1913), 44–51; *AR* i (1913), 264–5; Henderson to Bonar Law, 12 June 1913; BLP, 29/5/24.

[29] *AR* i (1914), 254–5.

[30] H. Pelling, *Social Geography of British Elections, 1885–1910* (London, 1967), 350.

before the Liberals introduced this measure. Bishop Owen of St David's said early in 1906 that Welsh disestablishment would probably be brought into Parliament in 1907, but that it would probably be beaten 'by the help of the Lords'. Sir Alfred Thomas, MP and chairman of the 'Welsh party', publicly claimed he had a guarantee that Ministers would introduce Welsh disestablishment not later than 1908, but Campbell-Bannerman said in Parliament that he was unaware of any such promise. Samuel Evans gave notice of a Suspensory Bill for the Welsh Church in March 1906, but by Government request he abandoned his plan. The Prime Minister assured Evans that 'Welsh disestablishment remains an integral part of the legislative programme of the Liberal party, and will be dealt with at the first available opportunity'.[31]

The Welsh members were themselves divided on the subject. Lloyd George, whose interests were now mainly in social and economic matters, was ready for a compromise solution to the old question. He suggested to Bishop Edwards that there might be 'a very mild and kindly Welsh bill' leaving to the Church all its property except tithe.[32] This suggestion, it has been noted, would have 'instantly forfeited the confidence of Welsh radicals in Lloyd George' if they had known about it.[33] But Ministers' only early action on the matter was to institute a Royal Commission in June 1906 to inquire into the property of the Church in Wales and into the religious work done by all Welsh Churches. Samuel Evans and three other Nonconformists were members, also two Liberal Churchmen understood to favour disestablishment, Lord Hugh Cecil and Archdeacon Evans of Carmarthen who defended the establishment, and Lord Justice Vaughan Williams as chairman.[34] The Commission was far from harmonious. Three of the Nonconformists resigned after objecting to a decision by the chairman, and were replaced by other Dissenters. The Commission's report did not appear until 1910, and only two members signed it without reservation.

Welsh radicals were displeased that their favourite subject had been delayed by an official inquiry.[35] Much impatience was shown, and was often directed at Lloyd George as a prominent Welsh Dissenter in the Cabinet. After the Lords had destroyed the 1906 Education Bill, Lloyd George said at Caernarvon in January 1907 that 'urgent reforms were matters for purely academic discussion' until the Commons could enforce their will in Parliament: if the Government was planning to confront the Lords 'the Welshmen who worry the Government into attending to anything else until the citadel has been stormed ought to be put in the guard-room'. This unhappy phrase was taken to imply that, whatever

[31] Owen, *Bishop Owen*, 80–2; *AR* ii (1906), 4; H clxi. 1055; Sir A. Thomas to Samuel Evans, Mar. 1906; Samuel Evans Papers, 46; Campbell-Bannerman to Evans, 12 Mar. 1906; ibid. 14.

[32] Rowland, *Lloyd George*, 191; Bell, *Randall Davidson*, i. 504.

[33] Morgan, *Wales in British Politics*, 233.

[34] Rowland, op. cit. 191; Morgan, op. cit. 261; Owen, op. cit. 82–3, 88 ff.; *Guardian*, 27 June 1906, p. 1049.

[35] Morgan, op. cit. 233–5.

measures were chosen to lure the upper House into a constitutional ambush, Welsh disestablishment would not be one of them.

Nonconformist and Liberal meetings in Wales showed indignation at the speech, and Welsh MPs protested. Lloyd George, himself a rebel twelve years before against a Liberal ministry over disestablishment, was now a Liberal Minister having to quell an incipient Welsh revolt on the same issue. The *British Weekly* strongly criticized him for 'abandoning' disestablishment, and a speaker at a meeting of Caernarfonshire Congregationalists was loudly applauded when he asked whether Lloyd George would leave a Government 'which insulted his nation and co-relitionists'. The reaction against Lloyd George was significant enough for him to take deliberate steps to reduce it. He sent a conciliatory message to an assembly of the Welsh Congregational Union in June 1907, but this only partly satisfied the audience. As a result of this meeting it was suggested that a Nonconformist League be formed in Wales. A large convention was arranged and resolutions were prepared for it, amounting to a vote of censure on the Government.

Lloyd George unexpectedly obtained nomination as a delegate to this gathering at Cardiff on 10 October. He asked Campbell-Bannerman what he might say at the meeting, and was told he could say that the Government wanted to deal with Welsh disestablishment as soon as possible, but could give no definite promise on it because 'we are face to face with a crisis in the relationship of the two Houses'.[36] At a preparatory meeting of the executive committee on 9 October Lloyd George succeeded in having the resolutions softened. Then he persuaded the main meeting of 2,500 next day that he and the Government were sincere by stressing the obstacle of the Lords' veto and by saying that Welsh disestablishment would be sent up to the Lords by the 1909 session. If Parliament were dissolved Welsh disestablishment would assuredly be placed before the country. His statements were applauded and the speech ended with a declaration of loyalty—'*Duw a wyr mor anwyl yw Cymru lan i mi!*' (God knows how dear to me is my Wales)—which duly overwhelmed the audience, no doubt because it was genuine as well as expedient.[37]

'Cardiff turned out much more satisfactorily than I had feared', Lloyd George told Campbell-Bannerman. 'The government will not be worried much more on the subject of Welsh Disestablishment until the time comes to arrange the programme for 1909.'[38] Moves to resist the expected bill began in autumn 1908, when the publications committee of the Conservative National Union made a small grant for 'the production of Welsh leaflets in Welsh written by a Welshman'. At the Church Congress at Manchester in October, Bishop Owen

---

[36] Lloyd George to Campbell-Bannerman, 5 Oct. 1907; CBP, 41240, fos. 86–7; Campbell-Bannerman to Lloyd George (copy, n.d.); ibid. fos. 88–9.

[37] H. du Parcq, *Life of David Lloyd George* (4 vols., London, 1912–13), iii. 462–74; Rowland, op. cit. 192–3.

[38] 19 Oct. 1907; CBP, 41240, fos. 105–6; quoted Rowland, op. cit. 193; Morgan, op. cit. 237–8.

noted a Government announcement that a bill would be introduced next year.[39] A cabinet committee of six, including Lloyd George, was appointed on 28 October to draft a bill. The Liberation Society, enjoying a modest revival under its new secretary, the Revd David Caird, organized meetings in the bill's favour.[40] Another bill drafted by the campaign committee of the Welsh Free Churches wanted a National Endowment Board to take charge of all the property of the Church in Wales. Nonconformist denominational assemblies applauded the ministerial effort, but the Church Committee (now called the Central Church Committee) unanimously resolved on 'unfaltering determination' to resist Welsh disestablishment and disendowment. 'The Disestablishment movement is dying at its roots from old age', claimed Bishop Owen in April. 'It will wither away if we can only beat off this attack.'[41]

The bill caused little excitement, however, as it was so unlikely to get through Parliament. It was 'merely there for show', said one observer after the King's Speech, and Arthur Henderson (the Labour leader) 'regretted that time should be spent on Welsh disestablishment'.[42] On 21 April Asquith moved for leave to introduce the measure, which was similar to the last bill in 1895 except that a Council of Wales elected by local authorities would administer the secularized endowments from 1915. The four Welsh dioceses would cease to be established on 1 January 1911. A Church Representative Body would take into its hand the church buildings and residences, furniture, plate, closed burial grounds, and all benefactions since 1662. Secularized endowments would be used for public health, education, and other social purposes. By these means 'the Church would gain more than she would lose', said Asquith. Relieved of the trammels of establishment and excessive endowment, she would be much stronger in appealing to the people.[43]

Church defenders were unconvinced. A Conservative, W. C. Bridgeman, seconded by F. E. Smith, moved an amendment that leave to introduce the bill be refused until the Royal Commission had reported. Bridgeman said the issue should be considered 'from the point of view of religion and not . . . party politics'. Smith pointed to a sinister alliance between Welsh voluntaries and Irish Home Rulers to support each other's measures, mentioning a recent speech by John Redmond at Wrexham. Speaking as one 'brought up as a Nonconformist' and 'not a convinced adherent of the Church of England', Smith thought the bill was 'common peculation' and threatened to attack the Church in England after Wales had been dealt with. The Bill was also

---

[39] NUCA executive committee Minutes, 16 Oct. 1908, p. 327 (microfiche); T, 9 Oct. 1908, p. 7; Bishop Owen to A. J. Balfour, 18 Nov.; BP, 49790, fox. 41–2. Cf. CCDI executive committee Minutes, 29 Oct. (vol. 36, p. 364).

[40] LS, 5 Jan., 23 Feb., 2 Mar., 8 June 1909; A/LIB/10, 106.

[41] Guardian, 27 Jan. 1909, p. 124; CCDI Minutes, 24 Mar. 1909 (vol. 34, 250); also executive committee Minutes, 22 Apr. (vol. 36, 406–8), 21 May (ibid. 424); E. Owen, 131–2 and ff.

[42] Fitzroy, Memoirs, i. 375; AR i (1909), 16.

[43] H iii. 1525–38.

condemned by Lord Robert Cecil, Sir John Kennaway, Balfour, and others. Cecil said the measure was merely 'a parade . . . to satisfy the inconvenient protests of a section of the Government supporters'. The amendment was lost by 262 votes to ninety, the division being on party lines with Labour members voting against the amendment. The bill was then brought in and read a first time.[44]

The second reading debate was fixed for a few days later, but time was not found for it amid Government preoccupations over Lloyd George's budget. The bill was dropped in June after promises to the Welsh members that it would have first place among Government measures in 1910.[45] But by then a constitutional crisis had succeeded the financial fracas, and Welsh disestablishment seemed to depend on its outcome.

The People's Budget of 1909 may not have been deliberately planned to provoke the Lords to reject a financial measure and hence to enable Ministers to attack the Lords' veto. But it was aimed to revive the Government's sagging fortunes and strengthen its efforts to press its policies on the Lords. The results were dramatic. The bold array of taxes, generally designed to redistribute income from the rich to the less well off and defended by Lloyd George's provocative polemics, caused fierce resistance and the formation of special protest groups. So strong was Unionist opposition that Balfour decided he would have to support rejection of the budget in the Lords.[46] On 30 November the peers threw out the finance bill by 350 to seventy-five; Archbishop Lang and three Bishops voted for the budget, one Bishop voted against, and twenty Bishops abstained. The Government decided to appeal to the country and polling commenced on 15 January 1910.

The question of restricting or abolishing the Lords' veto permeated the elections, and the *Liberator* said that all supporters of religious equality should vote only for candidates pledged to 'the abolition of the final veto of the House of Lords'. [47] But the contest was not over a specific plan to reduce the Lords' powers, as no such plan had been agreed on. Asquith tried to maintain the loyalty of different sections by assuring them that their particular demands—educational reform, Home Rule, Welsh disestablishment, and others—would be urged forward. The outcome was disappointing to the Liberals. Heavy losses left them with only 275 seats compared with 400 in 1906, and they obtained over 120,000 fewer votes than the Unionists. The latter won 273 seats, a big advance on the 157 of 1906; their gains almost equalled Liberal losses. 103 seats gained from the Unionists by a Liberal or Labour candidate in 1906 returned a Unionist in January 1910. Just over 100 Unionist gains (nearly all the total) were made in the South and Midlands of England; only ten Unionist gains

[44] Ibid. 1538–96.   [45] *DN*, 15 June 1909; *AR* i (1909), 137.
[46] E. J. Feuchtwanger, *Democracy and Empire: Britain, 1865–1914* (London, 1985), 288–90.
[47] *Liberator*, Jan. 1910, p. 179. Cf. LS, 30 Nov. 1909 (vol. 10, 131–4); memo of Liberation Society to Asquith, 26 Nov.; AP xii. 66–7. Cf. *Congregational Year-book* (1910), 28.

occurred in the North of England, three in Ireland, two in Wales, and none in Scotland.[48] About 140 Nonconformists were returned as Liberal or Labour members.[49]

The financial dispute had dominated the contests. Unionists had gained by winning over mainly middle-class opponents of the budget, including many Nonconformists. Tariff reform remained a virile alternative policy to the budget and Free Trade. Demand for extensive social reform also figured in the election, for example in the manifesto of the Church Socialist League; Clifford had described the finance bill as 'a great Christian budget' when addressing a huge Hyde Park demonstration in 1909.[50] Disestablishment was not, generally speaking, a very prominent question, though Archbishop Lang urged that candidates be asked whether they opposed this policy.[51] The National Free Church Council was retreating from its political role, but suggested that all local councils should advertise the importance of the disestablishment, educational, and other aims;[52] and in Wales of course disestablishment remained important in the contests, if somewhat mechanically. Lloyd George assured Nonconformists at a great Queen's Hall demonstration in London on 16 December that the peers were a solid obstacle to their aims;[53] and it was well realized that the Government had to assert its will over the Lords before a Welsh disestablishment bill could pass. English disestablishment was hardly mentioned. In Scotland some Liberal candidates said they favoured disestablishment, but others evaded the topic on the grounds that negotiations for Church union were going on.[54]

Many Irish Home Rule MPs had revolted against the whisky and licence duties in the budget, and the regain their support Ministers had to give firm backing to Home Rule. Asquith's commitment to this policy was welcomed by the United Irish League and enticed the votes of many Irish in Great Britain, but his declared maintenance of Liberal education aims tended to drive them in the opposite direction.[55] Catholic Bishops and priests urged defence of Catholic education and 'the great Act of 1902', even if this meant voting for a Unionist. It was claimed, however, that the Irish vote kept many seats Liberal, usually at the expense of Unionists but sometimes of Labour.[56] Redmond was emphatic that

[48] *McCalmont's Parliamentary Poll Book: British Election Results, 1832–1918*, ed. J. Vincent and M. Stenton (Brighton, 1971), 332–3 and *passim;* Feuchtwanger, op. cit. 293.
[49] LS, 22 Feb. 1910 (vol. 10, 135–6).
[50] P. d'A Jones, *The Christian Socialist Revival*, 267; Sir James Marchant, *Dr John Clifford, CH: Life, Letters, and Reminiscences* (London, 1924), 130; Koss, *Nonconformity in Modern British Politics*, 110, 229.
[51] *AR* i (1910), 24. Cf. N. Blewett, *The Peers, the Parties, and the People: The General Elections of 1910* (London, 1972), 341.
[52] Runciman Papers, WR 28 (newspaper extract).
[53] Du Parcq, op. cit. iv. 717–23; Blewett, op. cit. 344.
[54] *Dundee Advertiser*, 12 Jan. 1910, p. 9.
[55] Blewett, op. cit. 349–50; Oldmeadow, *Bourne* ii. 41; *Tablet*, 1, 4, 15 Jan. 1910 (lxxxiii. 5, 24, 50, 85).
[56] Blewett, op. cit. 351–2; Charles Diamond to Runciman, 14 Feb. 1910; Runciman Papers, WR, 35.

the election was a Home Rule one, and denounced English Conservative Catholics who were distracting their co-religionists over education as 'worse foes of Ireland than the Orangemen of Liverpool'.[57]

Catholic voters might have been torn between Home Rule and education, but Home Rulers won a double victory on these questions. The Liberals, having scarcely any lead over the Unionists, depended on the eighty-three Irish nationalists and the forty Labour party MPs for a sure majority. The Irish nationalists were in a stronger pivotal position than Labour; in fact their position was similar to Parnell's after the 1885 election. Hence Redmond's party was able both to harness the Liberals to Home Rule and to deter them from introducing an unacceptable education reform.[58] Although the Government, urged by Nonconformist organizations, said it intended to bring in a large education bill by 1913, it never did so. Discussions were held between Ministers and leading Nonconformists in 1914, without result. The dispute rumbled on but the 1902 Act survived. The only comfort for Cliffordites was the gradual transfer of many non-Catholic voluntary schools to public control, owing to financial difficulty and, later, agreement over religious teaching. There were 14,238 voluntary schools in England and Wales (accommodating fifty-five per cent of the children) in 1903, and 11,906 (accommodating thirty-eight per cent) in 1923.[59]

After the Government's successful election the Lords passed the contentious budget in April, but Ministers proceeded with plans to reduce the Lords' veto power. By November a protracted Constitutional Conference on the veto between four cabinet Ministers and four leading Unionists terminated without agreement, the Home Rule issue being the main obstacle. It had been reluctantly recognized that a second general election must be held specifically on the constitutional question before the King would agree to create enough new peers to ensure the passage of a veto bill. Asquith therefore again advised dissolution, and the electors trooped once more to the polls in December. There were 163 unopposed returns, compared with seventy-five in January. The Lords question dominated the contests, but Home Rule, Welsh disestablishment, and education were involved since it was hoped these would be settled through reform of the veto.[60]

---

[57] *AR* i (1910), 6.

[58] Cf. *Tablet*, 29 Jan. (lxxxiii. 161).

[59] Bebbington, *Nonconformist Conscience*, 151–2; Morgan, op. cit. 231; Wilkinson, 'Educational Controversies', 672 ff.; Munson, 'A Study of Nonconformity', 377 ff.; Rowland, *The Last Liberal Governments*, (2 vols., London, 1968–71), ii. 212–13; Lord Riddell, *More Pages From My Diary, 1908–1914* (London, 1934), 184–5; T. H. Darlow, *William Robertson Nicoll: Life and Letters* (London, 1925), 383–4; *AR* i (1912), 42; Talbot Baines (secretary of National Society) to Archbishop Bourne, 14 Mar. 1912; Bourne Papers, 1/181.

[60] *Liberator*, Dec. 1910, pp. 333, 341; *Tablet*, 3 and 10 Dec. (lxxxiv. 885, 929–30); Bishop of Leeds to Bourne; Bourne Papers, 1/181; Clifford to Runciman, 13 Mar. 1911; Runciman Papers, WR44: Blewett, op. cit. 353.

There were only minor variations from the January result, and the anti-Unionist majority remained the same at 124: Unionists 273, Liberals 271, Home Rulers eighty-four, Labour forty-two. Of the returned candidates, 304 were said to have declared themselves for Welsh disestablishment as against 286 in January.[61] The result again dampened ministerial hopes of appearing as popular champions against an obstructive peerage, but it remained important to restrict the Lords' veto in order to carry Government policies. A Parliament Bill limiting the veto power was brought in and caused the expected strong Unionist resistance. One of the unsuccessful amendments to the measure was that Home Rule, disestablishment, and licensing reform should be excluded from the bill's scope, and that a general election should be held before a bill on any of these subjects was introduced.[62] With the threat of hundreds of newly created peers hanging over them, most opponents in the upper House gave way amid bitter recriminations and allowed the bill to pass on 10 August 1911. On the final reading thirty-seven Unionist peers and thirteen bishops joined eighty-one Liberal peers in voting for, against 114 diehards (including two Bishops, Williams of Bangor and Yeatman-Biggs of Worcester) who still voted against. 'We have been stabbed in the back by our friends', wrote Selborne to Halsbury, 'and they deserve the eventual estimation of all traitors'.[63]

IV. WELSH DISESTABLISHMENT AND CHURCH DEFENCE, 1911–1914

After the Parliament Act Nonconformists expected Welsh disestablishment just as the Irish expected Home Rule. Unionists were strongly against both reforms, and bills for them were the only ones which encountered the Lords' full power of delay under the recent Act—a maximum of three consecutive Parliamentary sessions in which a bill was passed by the Commons.

The report of the Welsh Church Commission appeared, along with separate memoranda from some of its members, in November 1910. But its depiction of Welsh religion was only an exhaustive presentation of what was generally known, and it left the disestablishment question exactly where it was. Some Church defenders, encouraged by recent falls in Welsh Nonconformist membership compared with the continued small growth of the Church, protested that the issue had become inferior to others in the 1910 elections. This was not really so, however, as disestablishment had been an important if unobtrusive ingredient in the budget and veto controversy.[64] The radical majority in Wales and Ministers' desire to

---

[61] Feuchtwanger, op. cit. 293–8; LS, 16 Feb. 1911 (vol. 10, 46).
[62] Rowland, *The Last Liberal Governments*, ii. 23–4.
[63] 11 Aug. 1911; Halsbury Papers, 56374, fo. 170.
[64] Griffith Roberts (Dean of Bangor), 'Fresh Light on the Church in Wales', *Nineteenth Century and After*, lxx (July–Dec. 1911), 248–9.

vindicate their own constitutional powers ensured that Welsh disestablishment again achieved a foremost place in Government business, with much greater chance of success than before.

The general result was almost a foregone conclusion. But Church defenders put up a strong fight during the last major struggle over the question. It might not be possible in the end to keep the established status of the Church, but much might be done to save the endowments.[65] St David's and St Asaph girded themselves early in 1911. For many months they addressed meetings and called on the aid of English Churchmen (including Liberals) and of Nonconformists who disliked the prospect of disendowing religion in an age of growing secularism.[66] Bishop Owen was only too willing to describe the Welsh bill as 'a flank attack on the Church of England', and cannot have been displeased when, for example, the *Liberator* hopefully proclaimed in September 1911 that 'disestablishment is just as inevitable in England as it is in Wales'.[67] Owen was convinced, he told Balfour, that 'the Church of England . . . will fight the Welsh Bill with all its strength in a way it has never fought any Bill for many generations'.[68] The Central Church Committee became busy in defence, issuing propaganda and stimulating interest at by-elections. A Conciliation Committee was formed, comprizing thirty-two Churchmen and Nonconformists, chaired by the Wesleyan Sir Henry Lunn, but containing no Welshmen. Against much opposition from Dissenters it suggested a generous settlement for the Church over endowments.[69] Opposition to Welsh disestablishment was shown by Church of Scotland bodies, and support for it in the United Free Church. Most English Nonconformists counterbalanced the attitude of Conservative Churchmen by supporting the Welsh Voluntary cause.[70]

The preparation of a disestablishment bill and its passage through the Commons for the first time was slow and contentious, lasting from 1911 to 1913. A Cabinet committee was appointed on 24 October 1911 to consider terms of legislation, and a final draft was approved by Cabinet on 16 April 1912. Asquith told the king it was very generous to the Church; indeed it left the Church with a much larger income than was proposed in the 1909 bill. The four Welsh dioceses could be separated from the Canterbury Convocation. The pre-1662 endowments would be secularized and transferred to the University of Wales and county councils.[71]

---

[65] Selborne to Salisbury, 12 Sept. 1916, copy; Selborne Papers, 6, fo. 186.

[66] Owen, op. cit. 145 ff., 158 ff., 165 ff.

[67] Ibid. 151; *Liberator* (Sept. 1911), 145.

[68] Owen to Balfour, 23 Oct. 1911; BP, 49790, fo. 47.

[69] CCDI executive committee Minutes (vol. 37, pp. 24–6, 44–6, 58, 60, 66–72; Sir. H. S. Lunn, *Chapters From My Life* (London, 1918), 294 ff.; Owen, op. cit. 173; Lidgett, *My Guided Life*, 235–7.

[70] Unanimous resolution at Baptist assembly, Oct. 1911 (*Baptist Handbook* (1912), 295).

[71] See P. M. H. Bell, *Disestablishment in Ireland and Wales* (London, 1969), 248–59 for a comparison of the provisions of Welsh disestablishment bills since 1894.

McKenna moved the first reading on 23 April, a day after Archbishop Davidson had eloquently assured 10,000 Churchment at Caernarfon that he was pledged to resistance. While McKenna was speaking there were 'constant interruptions and howls of mirth', largely from Lords Robert and Hugh Cecil. This led Lloyd George to castigate them as descendants of a family which had profited greatly from the sale of church lands at the Reformation, and therefore should not be complaining about disendowment. After an able debate the first reading was carried by seventy-eight, one Liberal (George Harwood, Bolton) voting against.[72] F. E. Smith, opening the second reading debate on 13 May, said the bill had 'shocked the conscience of every Christian community in Europe', thereby arousing the poetic ridicule of G. K. Chesterton:

> Are they clinging to their Crosses,
> F. E. Smith,
> Where the Breton boat-fleet tosses,
> Are they, Smith?
> Do they, fasting, trembling, bleeding,
> Wait for news from this our city?
> Groaning 'That's the Second Reading!'
> Hissing 'There is still Committee!'
> If the voice of Cecil falters,
> If McKenna's point has pith,
> Do they tremble for their altars?
> Do they, Smith?[73]

Balfour condemned the 'incredibly mean squabbling over pounds, shillings and pence' at a time when religion as a whole was confronted by great intellectual challenges. After Lloyd George had accused the Duke of Devonshire's ancestors of having 'hands dripping with the fat of sacrilege', the second reading passed on 16 May by a majority of eighty-one. But a few Liberals were unhappy with the bill, and two of them, Sir Edward Beauchamp and George Harwood, voted against it.[74] A Liberal Churchmen's Union was formed to oppose the bill, led by Dean T. C. Fry of Lincoln and amply supplied with information by Bishop Owen. Some Liberal MPs, estimated at about twenty and including several Nonconformists, told Asquith they would oppose the third reading unless considerable changes were made in the Church's favour in committee. C. P. Scott, editor of the *Manchester Guardian* and a former Liberal MP, favoured dropping all the disendowment provisions except those relating to tithe.[75]

Ministers had other important measures, including Irish Home Rule, to steer

---

[72] Rowland, op. cit. ii. 165–7; Morgan, op. cit. 263–4; H, 944 ff., 1252 ff., 1371 ff.
[73] S. McKenna, *Reginald McKenna* (London, 1948), 135–40.
[74] Morgan, op. cit. 263; H xxxviii. 801 ff., 981 ff., 1144 ff., 1294 ff.; Owen, op. cit. 176 ff.
[75] Ibid. 181 ff.; Morgan, op. cit. 267, 268–9.

through the Commons, and the committee stage of the Welsh bill did not come on until late in the year. This gave several months for both opposition and support to muster. By 21 July the number of petitioners against the bill in Wales reached a huge 539,000, about thirty per cent of the adult population, and there were about three times as many English petitioners. Among the numerous meetings, a great demonstration of some 10,000 Welsh Churchmen was held in the Albert Hall and Hyde Park on 12 June.[76]

In December commenced the committee stage of the bill. There were further calls from Liberals for more lenient treatment of the Church over endowment. On 13 December two Liberals, G. A. France (MP for Morley, a Wesleyan) and W. G. C. Gladstone (Kilmarnock, grandson of the late premier), proposed to remove only tithe. The Government opposed the amendment but, although it was defeated by 265 votes to 215, the ministerial majority was half its usual figure. Eleven Liberals had voted against the Government which, said the Unionists, had only been saved by the Irish because of Home Rule. Asquith recognized the marked difference of opinion among Liberals, and the Government braved Nonconformist resentment by making more concessions to the Church, including acceptance of an amendment by W. G. C. Gladstone on 10 January 1913 to provide for the commutation of life interests in benefices. The third reading passed by 107 on 5 February. Only one Liberal (Beauchamp) voted against but three others (Gladstone, France, and the Hon. E. Fiennes) abstained. Many Labour members voted for and none against. The Lords proceeded to reject the bill on 13 February by 252 votes to fifty-one; sixteen Bishops voted against and two (Percival and Gore) in favour.[77]

The Welsh bill smoothly negotiated the next stage in its allotted progress, the second reading passing the Commons on 17 June 1913, the third on 8 July, and a second reading being refused by the Lords on 22 July.[78] With equal predictability Nonconformist bodies urged that a halt should be called to concessions, and Church defenders continued to oppose the measure. A meeting of the Central Church Committee's executive on 6 February suggested holding demonstrations, and Davidson and others sought Bonar Law's services in the campaign. Law said the Unionists would repeal a Welsh disestablishment measure if it were carried before a general election was held specifically on it. Viscount St Aldwyn stated in November that if the bill finally passed, as expected, in 1914, it could be repealed if 'the verdict of the country' went

---

[76] Owen, op. cit. 183; *AR* i (1912), 137; letters to Bonar Law from A. Griffith Boscawen (10 Apr. 1912), Revd A. Winnifrith (11 Apr.), Revd H. Biddell (19 Apr.), Revd D. O. Davies (23 Apr.), Revd R. A. Morgan; BLP, 26/2/12, 15, 34, 43, 45.

[77] Morgan, op. cit. 268–9 and refs.; *AR* i (1913), 17–18, 33–6, 44–9; Rowland, op. cit. ii. 183–4, 193–6; D. Nicholls (ed.), *Church and State in Britain since 1820* (London, 1967), 191–9.

[78] H liv. 59–174, 225–348, lv. 243–365, xiv. (House of Lords) 1115–202, 1205–78; Morgan, op. cit. 269–70.

against it in an election. Two hundred open-air demonstrations against the bill were, it was claimed, held in June alone in England and Wales.[79]

In autumn 1913 it was suggested that Unionists might abandon their opposition to the Welsh bill in return for the exclusion of Ulster from the Home Rule provisions. Davidson was aware of the difficulty of trying to stop this happening: 'We can hardly say "Do nothing to prevent Civil War in Ireland, lest, by preventing it, we make Disestablishment in Wales easier".'[80] The danger did not materialize, nor did the opposite possibility that Welsh disestablishment might be dropped in order to persuade Conservatives to accept Home Rule.[81] Church defence efforts continued in 1914, with considerable success. Bishop Owen appealed to 'reasonable Nonconformists' that disestablishment might only encourage secularization. As many as 15,300 Nonconformists in St Asaph diocese ignored the opinion of other Dissenters (including the Liberation Society executive) when they signed a protest against disendowment provisions in the bill. The document was forwarded to Asquith on 14 February. In South Wales a similar protest drawn up by a Cardiff city councillor was launched in the *Western Mail*, and a committee of 100 Nonconformists was formed to support it. More than 103,000 Nonconformists signed protests throughout Wales, as was revealed just before the bill received its second reading in the Commons (for the last time) on 21 April by a majority of eighty-four.[82] The bitterness in the disestablishment issue was lessened by the fact that so many were prepared to be conciliatory.

The bill's third reading passed by seventy-seven on 19 May, France and Gladstone voting in favour. Bishop Owen's hope had been that the Ulster problem would force an election which, by returning a large Unionist majority, would cause defeat of the Welsh bill. He was against allowing a second reading of the bill in the Lords, saying this would weaken the fight to repeal it. On St Aldwyn's motion the Lords appointed on 2 July a select committee of inquiry on some aspects of the Welsh Church question.[83] After the outbreak of war on 4 August, Davidson and Owen protested against the immediate passage of the bill because of the 'staggering blow' which disendowment would inflict on the Church amid wartime difficulties.[84] The Government, however, wanted to

---

[79] *Congregational Year-book* (1914), 6; *Primitive Methodist Conference Minutes* (1913), 252; LS, 13 Apr. 1913 (vol. 11); CCDI Minutes (vol. 37, 186–7); Lord Kenyon to Bonar Law, 26 Feb. 1913; BLP, 29/1/31; Davidson to Bonar Law, 9 May ibid. 29/4/4; *AR* i (1913), 238; Owen, op. cit. 194–200.

[80] Davidson to Bishop Owen, 11 Nov. 1913; Owen, op. cit. 206.

[81] John Massie to Lloyd George, 16 Sept. 1913; LGP, C/9/5/31.

[82] Owen, op. cit. 210–18; LS, 17 Feb. 1914 (vol. 11); *AR* i (1914), 27–8, 78–80. Cf. CCDI executive committee Minutes, 16 July 1914 (vol. 37, 286).

[83] Owen, op. cit. 224 ff.

[84] Davidson to Asquith, 6 and 10 Aug. 1914; AP xiii. 191–2, 201–3; Owen to Asquith, 10 Aug. ibid. 204–5; also Lord Robert Cecil to Selborne, 18 Aug., copy; Selborne Papers, 90, fos. 11–14; Bishop E. S. Talbot of Winchester to Lloyd George, 18 and 28 Aug.; LGP, House of Lords, C/11/2/4, 5; M. and E. Brock (eds.), *Asquith: Letters to Venetia Stanley* (Oxford, 1982), 163–4, 175, 182, 187, 233, 235, 242–5; M. Bentley, *The Liberal Mind, 1914–1929* (Cambridge, 1977), 197–8.

place the Irish Home Rule and Welsh disestablishment bills on the statute book. There was much Unionist dissent, but it was decided to abandon this for the sake of national unity in war at a party meeting at the Carlton Club on 14 September, Lord Hugh Cecil demurring. On 18 September both bills received the royal assent, but their operation was postponed for at least a year (and, it was intended, until peace was signed) by a Suspensory Bill enacted on the same day.[85]

The Welsh Act left to the disestablished Church its cathedrals and churches, glebe-houses, and property worth £102,000 a year. The secularized property was worth £158,000 p.a. The life-interests of incumbents were commutable, but there was no compensation for curates.[86] The bill having been safely enacted, Asquith expressed private satisfaction that 'all the bluffing and outrageous manoeuvring of the Tories has been frustrated'.[87] The postponement of operations, moreover, was not complete, despite Davidson's protests. Welsh Church Commissioners were to perform prescribed duties regarding the territorial composition of the Church. On 19 December 1914 a large Welsh Church conference at Shrewsbury solemnly protested against the Act and then started to make arrangements for appointing a Representative Body for the Church to receive and administer the property allocated by the statute.[88]

V. THE GREAT WAR AND CHURCH QUESTIONS, 1914–1921

The effect of the war on religious belief is difficult to assess. The faith of some might have been lost on account of the monumental slaughter; or, occasionally, ecclesiastical allegiance might have been weakened by the spectacle of Churches apparently abandoning the gospel of peace when the war began and supporting with intense and bellicose patriotism their own countries in the conflict. On the other hand it was suggested that experience of wartime sorrow and sacrifice 'have awakened a fresh interest in the spiritual significance of life, and religion has undoubtedly gained a new value in the thought and experience of many who have not been accustomed to give much heed to it'.[89]

What is clear is that the war did not reverse the gradual overall decline in church allegiance. Decrease in church membership and attendance, well established before the conflict, continued after it (with important denominational exceptions) and might even have been encouraged by the unsettlement

[85] *AR* i (1914), 203–6. The text of the Welsh Act of 1914 is printed in R. P. Flindall (ed.), *The Church of England, 1815–1948: A Documentary History* (London, 1972), 308.
[86] P. M. H. Bell, *Disestablishment in Ireland and Wales*, 258–9.
[87] M. and E. Brock, op. cit. 246.
[88] Davidson to Asquith, 15 Sept. 1914 (2 letters, AP xiii. 212–18); Bell, *Randall Davidson*, i. 640–4; P. M. H. Bell, op. cit. 298–9.
[89] *Liberator*, Jan. 1916, p. 3. Cf. Wilkinson, *The Church of England and the First World War* (London, 1978), 230 ff.

caused by war.[90] Concern was shown about the ignorance of religion shown by vast numbers in the armed forces, but no great missionary effort took place after the war to try and reverse the obvious widespread indifference. The Churches were perhaps too immersed in old disputes and in schemes for internal reform to pay sufficient attention to wider problems.

But the Churches did share in the enthusiasm for further social reform when the war ended; and the desire for greater interdenominational understanding and union, stemming particularly from the World Missionary Conference at Edinburgh in 1910, was another broad aim enhanced by the hope of post-war reconstruction. Some discussion on Methodist union continued during the war, having been stimulated by the formation of the United Methodist Church through the combination of three small denominations in 1907.[91] Conferences were also held to promote Nonconformist federation, and a Federal Council of the Evangelical Free Churches was established in 1917.[92] Hensley Henson attributed a wartime desire for Christian fellowship to 'the remarkable demonstrations of fraternity which have been observed in the vast armies of Englishmen overseas. The blessed contagion of religious fellowship is flowing back from the Front to the parishes at home.'[93] The Lord Mayor of London in 1916 proposed a conference of representatives of all Churches, to form 'a great British Church' with a common basis.[94] 'There is for Christians to-day no more urgent problem than that of the reunion of Christendom', said a publication of 1919; 'we long for unity, and are ready for almost any personal sacrifice to obtain it.' The author then stated some of the formidable difficulties in the way.[95] The Lambeth Conference of Anglican Bishops in 1920 sustained this approach by issuing an 'Appeal to all Christian people'.

Desire for fellowship and the removal of barriers was by no means unlimited, as old divisions persisted. Theological controversy continued during the war, for example over the appointment of the pronounced liberal theologian Hensley Henson to the Bishopric of Hereford in 1917. Controversy over Ritualism was indeed stimulated by the conflict. Among other disputed matters, prayers for the dead became more popular because of the vast number of bereavements, and reservation of the Sacrament increased because it was desired to make it available to the wounded and convalescent.[96] J. A. Kensit attributed a flattering influence to papal diplomacy by saying: 'that the dark sinister hand of

[90] Cf. S. P. Mews, 'The Effects of the First World War on English Religious Life and Thought', MA thesis (Leeds, 1967), 13–17 and ff.

[91] Lidgett, op. cit. 264–5, also 242–7.

[92] Revd J. H. Shakespeare to Walter Runciman, 2 Mar., 27 Apr. 1917; Runciman Papers, WR, 161; J. H. Shakespeare, *The Churches at the Crossroads: A Study in Church Unity* (London, 1918), 2ff.

[93] Henson, *Retrospect*, i. 299; cf. Wilkinson, op. cit. 199 ff.

[94] LS, 26 July 1916 (vol. 11).

[95] Canon H. L. Goudge, *The Catholic Party and the Nonconformists* (London, 1919), 3 and ff.

[96] Knox, *Reminiscences*, 310, 313; Walmsley, op. cit. 58: N. Yates, *The Oxford Movement and Anglican Ritualism*, Historical Association (London, 1983), 34–5.

the Papacy was behind the Central Powers in the Great War is now accepted by all unprejudiced minds'. Also to be feared was 'Rome's army in Great Britain': 958 Roman priests were in the country about 1870, 4,458 in 1918.[97]

A small victory came for religious equality when Lloyd George insisted that Lord Kitchener appoint Dissenting chaplains to the armed forces on equal terms with those of the established Churches. Some passive resisters in the education rate dispute suspended their action until the war ended. But the Passive Resistance League resolved in March 1915 that the well-tried if unsuccessful methods of protest should continue, and a few resisters such as Clifford doggedly continued their action during and after the war.[98] This did not prevent Clifford, Robertson Nicoll, A. T. Guttery, and most other prominent Nonconformists from becoming ardent champions of the war for its whole length. Indeed they led a moral crusade against Germany resembling the anti-Turkish one of the 1870s and later. Sir William Robertson Nicoll said in the widely circulated *British Weekly* that there was 'not a more flagrant iniquity on earth' than the Prussian military system.[99] An article by Nicoll, published in many daily papers on 1 September 1914, said: 'I call on all Nonconformists who can fight to set down their names in the hour of crisis, and to enlist without delay'.[1] Through this and later articles, Nicoll became one of the Government's most useful recruiting agents. The Congregational Union assembly in May 1915 said it respected members of its churches who believed 'war is never justifiable in the light of Christianity', but none the less it held that 'national righteousness' currently demanded a warlike course.[2] Nonconformists indeed, like Liberal and Labour politicians and trade unionists, were passionately at odds over support for the war in general, or over support for compulsory conscription—opposition to which did not imply an anti-war attitude or sympathy for conscientious objectors.[3]

Some Dissenters, notably Nicoll, wanted to push Lloyd George towards the premiership for about a year before he attained it in December 1916. But they can hardly have anticipated the damage to their own political interests caused by

[97] J. A. Kensit, *Rome Behind the Great War*, Protestant Truth Society (London 1918). Cf. *Tablet*, xcix (Jan.–June 1918), 572–3.

[98] Marchant, *Clifford*, 143–4; Jordan, *Free Church Unity*, 123–4.

[99] Quoted Bebbington, *Nonconformist Conscience*, 126.

[1] Also in *British Weekly* (3 Sept. 1914). Cf. J. G. Bowran, *The Life of Arthur Thomas Guttery* (London, 1922), 145–52; K. Robbins, 'The Spiritual Pilgrimage of the Revd R. J. Campbell', *JEH* xxx (1979), 274–5.

[2] A. Peel, *These Hundred Years A History of the Congregational Union of England and Wales, 1831–1931* (London, 1931), 389. Cf. S. P. Mews, 'Neo-orthodoxy, Liberalism, and War: Karl Barth, P. T. Forsyth, and John Oman, 1914–1918', in D. Baker (ed.), *Studies in Church History*, xiv (Oxford, 1977), 361 ff.

[3] Koss, *Nonconformity in Modern British Politics*, 127–34; T. Wilson, *The Downfall of the Liberal Party, 1914–1935* (London, 1966), 23–7; C. Binfield, *So Down to Prayers: Studies in English Nonconformity, 1780–1920* (London, 1977), 242–6; A. Mor-O'Brien, 'The Merthyr Boroughs Election, November 1915', *WHR* xii (1984–5), 538–66; Morris, 'Primitive Methodism in Nottinghamshire', 281–5.

the rift between Asquith and Lloyd George and the latter's dependence as premier on Conservative backing. On the suggestion of the Revd J. H. Shakespeare, prominent Baptist and intimate of the new Prime Minister, Lloyd George tried to still Nonconformist fears about the support for his Government by inviting many Dissenting ministers to a breakfast at Downing Street in October 1917. About seventy ministers attended. Among other assurances Lloyd George said that an education measure had been necessarily postponed but not dropped.[4] But, apart from the implementation of Welsh disestablishment, radical Nonconformists must have wondered just what Lloyd George could now offer them.

By November 1918 a Nonconformist had 'won the war'. But the bitter Liberal division which accompanied his triumph hastened the decline of Dissent as a political force because it deprived Nonconformists of their traditional strong party means of expression. Apart from the achievement of peace through victory, the gains of radical Nonconformity during and after the conflict were almost non-existent. Many Nonconformists were encouraged by official discouragement of alcoholic consumption during the war to hope for prohibition of the drink trade, but this was not obtained. Some hopes were also aired for a general advance of voluntaryism when the war ended, but these expectations faded when it became clear that the trends against them were well established.[5] The Liberation Society experienced further financial difficulty during the war and did not recover satisfactorily after it.

The passage of Welsh disestablishment had been a clear victory for radical Nonconformity, but since its operation was suspended it remained a matter of controversy. The three Commissioners of Church Temporalities in Wales, appointed in September 1914, proceeded to carry out their work during the war, including the allocation of certain parishes either to Wales or to England.[6] The Duke of Devonshire introduced a bill to postpone the date of disestablishment, and the Government responded by bringing in its own Welsh Church Postponement Bill in March 1915 to delay the date from immediately after peace was signed to six months later. The object was to give the Church more time for organization. But strong opposition came from the Welsh Liberal MPs, who had not been consulted. Asquith described them as *moutons enragés*. Supported by the National Free Church Council and the Liberation Society, they denounced McKenna as the Government spokesman, ignored Lloyd George's plea for sympathetic submission to the Welsh Churchmen's request, and procured the withdrawal of the bill by July. A six months' extension would have been long enough, they said, for a Conservative Government to repeal the 1914 Act. Repeal was indeed the stated object of some Church defenders,

[4] Marchant, op. cit. 230–1; Koss, op. cit. 140; Perks to Runciman, 3 Nov. 1917; Runciman Papers, WR, 161.
[5] *Liberator*, Jan. 1916, p. 3.
[6] Ven. C. A. H. Green, *The Welsh Church Act, 1914: A Special Charge* (Newport, Mon., 1914), 9 ff.

including the Central Church Committee and the House of Laymen of Canterbury Convocation.[7] But repeal was practically impossible within the time limit laid down, as Churchmen generally realized, and the Welsh Church continued to prepare for disestablishment. In October 1917 a convention at Cardiff established a Representative Body to govern the Church in Wales, and a constitution was drafted for the Church after disestablishment.[8] On 28 November, however, a meeting of the Central Church Committee's executive and the Welsh Bishops resolved that the proceedings of the Cardiff convention 'in no way implied relaxation of opposition to the Act.'[9]

Church defenders were still hoping for an extension of the postponement after the war and the restoration of endowments. Lord Salisbury said he would not despair 'if we lost the Establishment [in Wales] for good—as distinguished of course from the endowments'.[10] Lord Selborne wrote in January 1917 that Lloyd George, now premier, might 'easily be persuaded' to postpone disestablishment for a year after peace was signed, and if the Unionists did very well in a general election immediately after the war 'we could make what terms we liked for the Welsh Church'.[11] In March 1917 Bishop Owen complained to Bonar Law about 'the outrageous statutory provision' concerning the date of disestablishment. This stipulation was extremely serious for the Church, 'with our leading laymen either serving at the Front or fully occupied in various forms of service connected with the war, and with the mass of Welsh Churchmen between eighteen and forty years of age serving in the Army'. He hoped therefore that Law would be able to obtain a year's postponement for disestablishment after the signing of the peace treaty.

The Central Church Committee in July 1918 wanted the terms of the Welsh Church Act to be reconsidered in a new Parliament. In September, 181 Conservative MPs sent a memorial to Bonar Law denouncing the Act; and in October the executive committee of the National Union of Conservative Associations carried a motion of Lord Selborne for reconsideration of the measure, especially its disendowment clauses.[12] Bonar Law interviewed Bishop Edwards in October, and told Lloyd George that Edwards' desires for the Church were 'very moderate': all he wanted as additional endowment was the Church's glebes, a lump sum of two million pounds, and an income of £10,000 a

[7] LS, 9 and 23 Feb. 1915 (vol. 11); CCDI executive committee, 18 Feb. 1915 (38, p. 10), 11 Nov. (34, p. 338); *Liberator*, Apr. 1915, p. 29; M. and E. Brock, op. cit. 468–80; Morgan, op. cit. 278–9; Selborne to Lord Robert Cecil, 11 Feb. and 19 Apr. 1915; Cecil of Chelwood Papers, Add. MS 51157, fos. 90–7.

[8] Morgan, op. cit. 279; Owen, op. cit. 348 ff.

[9] CCDI, vol. 38; also minutes of 21st annual meeting, 18 May 1917 (vol. 34, p. 356).

[10] Salisbury to Selborne, 18 Sept. 1916; Selborne Papers, 6, fo. 196.

[11] Selborne to Viscount Wolmer, 8 Jan. 1917; ibid. d. 451, fos. 20–1.

[12] Owen to Law, 13 Mar. 1917 (copy sent by Law to Balfour, 17 Mar.; BP, 49790, fos. 57–8); CCDI, vol. 38 (11 July, also 9 Oct., 14 Nov.); memo of 12 Sept. 1918; BLP, 104/3/2 also 3/3, 6, 8; NUCA executive committee Minutes, 8 Oct. 1918, p. 74. Cf. Lloyd George to Bonar Law, 29 Aug. 1918; LGP (House of Lords), F/30/2/45.

year. He also wanted an election statement by Lloyd George that some financial details should be reviewed by the new Parliament.[13]

The election of 14 December 1918 found Nonconformists very divided, and only about 100 of them were returned compared with about 150 in December 1910. Church questions hardly figured at all in a contest which was swept on by demands for a 'just and lasting' peace treaty and generous reconstruction provisions. No mention of Church issues occurred in any of the party manifestos. Sixty-five Nonconformists stood as Asquith Liberals in the election, fifty-nine as Lloyd George Coalition Liberals, and forty-seven for the Labour party; eight of the fourteen Dissenting ministers who stood were Labour candidates. Labour was attracting support from Nonconformists, but most of them probably voted for a Liberal candidate of one section or the other. Asquith Liberals were 'disappointed, discouraged, and dismayed', it was said, 'to see the whilom protagonist of their faith [Lloyd George] bow the head to worship in the heathen temple of the political Rimmon'.[14]

But many Nonconformists, with the influential backing of the *British Weekly* and *Baptist Times*, did support Lloyd George and the Coalition, which was returned with an overall majority of 149; 335 of the successful Coalition candidates were Unionists, 133 were Liberals, and ten Labour. The substantial drop in Nonconformist MPs was largely explained by the rout of the Asquith Liberals, only twenty-eight of whom were returned—a veritable party of 'Wee Frees'. The growth of the Labour representation to sixty-three showed significant progress. Of the Nonconformists returned, at least fifty-two were Coalition Liberals, at least seven Asquith Liberals, and at least twenty Labour.[15]

The Welsh Church question remained to trouble the victorious Coalition. Lloyd George naturally wanted to minimize differences on the subject among his supporters, and his strong conciliatory bent had completely displaced his former militant provocation: he could hardly accuse his own colleagues of 'dripping with the fat of sacrilege'. Disestablishment would take effect when peace was ratified, and Church defenders still wanted a more generous settlement over endowments. They were encouraged by the large Conservative preponderance in the Coalition.

In January 1919 Bishop Edwards suggested new terms to Bonar Law, including retention of the churchyards and glebes and compensation of £1,500,000. He made similar suggestions to Lord Hugh Cecil in February.[16] Bonar Law warned Cecil on 3 August, however, that the Unionists despite their

[13] Law to Lloyd George, 22 Oct.; LGP, F/30/2/51; Bishop Owen to Law, 10 Dec.; BLP, 104/3/14.

[14] B. G. Evans, 'The Premier and the Welsh Elections', *FR* cv (Jan.–June 1919), 239–40; Koss, op. cit. 147 ff.

[15] Koss 231.

[16] Edwards to Law, 9 Jan. 1919; BLP, 104/3/19; Edwards to Lord Hugh Cecil, 18 Feb. 1919; Lord Quickswood Papers, box 6. Cf. LS, 16 Jan., 13 May 1919 (vol. 11); Samuel Hoare to Bonar Law, 27 May 1919; BLP, 194/3/34.

large representation were not technically in power but only part of a coalition. Indeed some of them owed their seats to Liberal votes. They could not therefore be expected to meet former pledges to restore Welsh Church endowments on returning to power. Conservatives remained divided over the terms of settlement, and Lord Robert Cecil had resigned from the Government in November 1918 because he would not be a party to the removal of Church endowments. But leading Welsh Churchmen hurriedly prepared a draft of a Welsh Church Temporalities Bill (known as the Amending Bill) at the end of July 1919, after Lloyd George had returned from peace making at Paris and given his attention to the Welsh Church. Bonar Law told Lord Hugh Cecil that both he and leading Welsh Churchmen wanted this bill to settle the matter.[17]

On 6 August the Central Church Committee executive said that, though disestablishment and disendowment were 'a great moral wrong', they were reluctantly prepared to accept the bill because of its improved financial provisions.[18] By then the measure was already passing rapidly through Parliament. Postponing the date of disestablishment and granting the Church a million pounds from the Treasury, the Temporalities Bill made disendowment a gradual process but did not give the glebes and churchyards to the Church (though it was privately arranged that the Church could buy the glebes back on favourable terms). The bill was attacked by Cecils and others in both Houses, but Griffith Boscawen, who had opposed disestablishment consistently since 1893, accepted it as a compromise. The second reading in the Commons passed by 182 votes to 37, a mixture of Conservatives, Liberals, and Labour voting on each side. In the Lords Archbishop Davidson and Bishops Edwards and Owen supported it. Conservative peers stayed away from the final stages, and the bill became law on 19 August.[19] Disestablishment came into effect on 31 March 1920, and in June Bishop Edwards became the first Archbishop of Wales. The Church continued to flourish and two new Bishoprics were created.

At the end of 1919 Lloyd George claimed in a letter to Bonar Law: 'The Welsh Church . . . [is] an illustration of how an old controversy, which has divided a whole nationality for over fifty years, has at last been settled by common consent to the complete satisfaction of both parties without leaving a trace of bitterness'.[20] There was justice in Lloyd George's claim, and it was appropriate that one who had acted so long and prominently on the question, first as agitator and then as conciliator, should have made it.

While Welsh disestablishment continued to be debated, the question of more

---

[17] Owen, op. cit. 391 ff., 400 ff.; Lord Hugh Cecil to Law, 2 Aug. 1919; BLP, 104/3/50; Law to Cecil, 3 Aug.; Quickswood Papers, box 6; Bishop Edwards to Law, 4 and 6 Aug,; BLP, 194/3/52, 53; Law to Bishop Talbot of Winchester, 18 Aug. copy; ibid. 104/3/60; Viscount Cecil of Chelwood, *All the Way* (London, 1949), 174. Cf. Sir Alfred Mond to Lloyd George, 15 July; LGP, House of Lords, F/36/6/50; memo. of conference of some Coalition Ministers and MPs, 22 July; ibid. F/21/4/7.

[18] CCDI executive committee, 38, 182–4; *Guardian*, 14 Aug. 1919, p. 842 (also 7 Aug., p. 805).

[19] H cxix. 459–510, 1927–63, 1259–66; Morgan, op. cit. 287–90; Owen, op. cit. 391 ff.; P. M. H. Bell, op. cit. 309.   [20] LGP; House of Lords, F/31/1/14.

autonomy for the Church of England was a parallel and related matter for discussion, and an appropriate one amid the talk of postwar reconstruction. On 4 July 1913 the Representative Church Council had passed a resolution which was virtually put into law in 1919. It was resolved that there was 'no inconsistency between a national recognition of religion and the spiritual independence of the Church', and the two Archbishops were asked to consider appointing a committee to suggest changes in Church-State relations which would secure 'a fuller expression of the spiritual independence of the Church as well as of the national recognition of religion'. The Archbishops duly appointed a Committee on Church and State, with the Earl of Selborne, vice-president of the Church Reform League, as chairman and twenty-five other members including Balfour, Lord Hugh Cecil, the Revd William Temple (son of the late Archbishop of Canterbury), Viscount Wolmer (son of Selborne), and the Hon. Edward Wood (son of Halifax).[21]

The committee began meeting in autumn 1914 and held twenty-three daily sessions. Edward Wood resigned in March 1916 because he thought the majority were making inadequate proposals for Church self-government.[22] The committee's report in July 1916 held that change and development in the Church were paralysed by the difficulty of securing Parliamentary legislation. Parliament was unrestricted in religious composition and unrepresentative of the Church, and 'the experience of recent years has shown that it possesses neither time nor inclination nor knowledge for dealing with ecclesiastical affairs'. Out of 217 Church bills brought into the Commons between 1880 and 1913, only thirty-three were passed, one was rejected, and 183 were dropped. A recent important case, the Bishoprics Bill of 1913 establishing new sees of Sheffield, Chelmsford, and St Edmundsbury, had only succeeded through a special arrangement with opposing Nonconformists. It was no wonder that 'the wheels of the ecclesiastical machine creak and groan and sometimes refuse to move'. Church–State relations should be given 'a more elastic and rational basis'—the 'greater elasticity' in liturgy suggested by the 1906 Royal Commission should be extended to Church government as a whole. Anglican Churches overseas already enjoyed spiritual freedom from the State, and the Church of Scotland wanted confirmation of complete spiritual autonomy in order to achieve Church reunion. The Church of England had had a different historical development and did not ask for nearly so much, but none the less wanted a certain amount of liberty. The Church should be enabled 'to regulate its own affairs' without encroaching 'either on the supremacy of the Commons or the rights of Parliament'.[23]

[21] Davidson to Selborne, 26 and 30 Oct., 18 Nov. 1913; Selborne Papers, 88, fos. 71–8.

[22] Bishop Gore to Hon. Edward Wood, 15 Mar. 1916; ibid. fos. 145–6; Wood to Selborne, 29 Mar.; ibid. fo. 161.

[23] *Report of the Archbishops' Committee on Church and State* (London, 1916), 1–38; Viscount Wolmer, 'The Rights of Citizens and the Rights of the Church', *CR* cx (July–Dec. 1916), 574–83; J. R. Cohu, 'Church and State: The Archbishops' Committee Report', ibid. cxii (July–Dec. 1917), 312–19.

Some members of the committee had suggested that only disestablishment could bring adequate spiritual independence, but as a whole the committee wished to continue the Church–State connection. The Church should have more power to legislate, subject to the criticism and veto of Parliament and the veto of the Crown. A representative Church assembly should be set up as a reformed version of the Representative Church Council. This assembly would be the apex of a system based on the annual parochial church meeting, which would be open to those of either sex who had been baptized (not necessarily confirmed, as Anglo-Catholics wanted) in the Church of England.[24] The meeting would elect representatives to the parochial church council, which in turn would elect deputies to ruridecanal and diocesan conferences. Lay representatives of the diocesan conferences would be elected to the national Church Assembly, which would comprize three Houses, of Bishops, clergy, and laity (consisting of the Houses already in or attached to the two Convocations, with a broadened system of representation). The proposed changes would give an altogether new authority to the House of Laymen.

The authority of Parliament and the Crown would be maintained by submitting measures passed by the Church Assembly to an Ecclesiastical Committee of the Privy Council, which would be less open to political pressure than the Cabinet. If a measure was recommended by the Ecclesiastical Committee and was deemed to require Parliamentary sanction, Parliament would decide whether to submit it for royal assent. An Enabling Bill, drafted in an appendix to the report, would need to be passed by Parliament in order to *recognize* (not to constitute) the Assembly established by the Church itself and enable it to carry out its work by the proposed means. 'The State has the fullest right to give, or not to give, its recognition and approval to the institutions that the Church may set up. But it has not the right to impose a government upon the Church, nor even to share with the Church the task of building up such a government.'[25]

To marshal public support for an Enabling Bill both a Church Self-government Association (with Bishop Gore as chairman) and a Life and Liberty Movement were formed and set to work. 'If the Church is to have new life, even if it is to maintain the life which it has, it must have liberty', wrote Bishop Mandell Creighton's widow in a letter to *The Times* in June 1917.[26] Life and Liberty began among discussions held between clergy and laity in the Revd Dick Sheppard's vicarage of St Martin's in the Fields. Sheppard, Wolmer, Temple (who resigned the wealthy living of St James's, Piccadilly, to work full-time for the movement), Cyril Garbett, A. A. David, F. A. Iremonger, R. H. Tawney, and others were the organization's youthful leaders. The

[24] Norman, *Church and Society in England*, 274.
[25] *Archbishops' Committee Report*, 39–64; Bell, *Randall Davidson*, ii. 957 ff.; Lord Hugh Cecil to Viscount Wolmer, 30 Sept. 1916; Selborne Papers (3rd Earl), c. 980, fo. 55.
[26] Quoted Flindall, *The Church of England*, 334.

movement was inaugurated at a large meeting in the Queen's Hall, London, in July 1917. With a single but notable dissentient, Hensley Henson, who objected that the national status and breadth of the Church would be weakened by the proposed changes, a strong resolution was passed advocating spiritual freedom.[27] Halifax, however, thought the committee's report should have demanded complete spiritual freedom for the Church, and the Liberation Society believed that only disestablishment would adequately meet the wish for autonomy.[28]

The prime movers were impatient to spread their ideals, and would not heed Davidson's advice to wait for the end of the war. Temple told his parishioners when he resigned in November 1917 that the war was encouraging plans for institutional reform: 'Men's minds are open now to large ideas. The world has to be rebuilt.'[29] Lord Hugh Cecil, who gave restrained support to the movement, thought that Temple was 'insane' to give up St James's and that 'war fever' was urging on the movement far too quickly. If the desired reform was delayed for ten years, he said, this would not harm the 'spiritual efficiency' of the Church.[30] But Church reformers could have said this was endorsing just the kind of delay they wanted to eliminate. Church reform indeed was catching at this time. In February 1918 the Church Reform League decided to seek the co-operation of the Representative Church Council, the Life and Liberty Movement, and the Church Self-government League in a campaign to obtain a more effective voice for the Church in the appointment of Bishops.[31]

The Representative Church Council, after being addressed by Davidson in favour of the scheme to turn it into a Church Assembly with greater legislative powers, gave its approval to the scheme. The Enabling Bill—or the National Assembly of the Church of England (Powers) Bill—was presented in the Lords by Davidson on 3 June 1919. The Government was neutral over the bill. It was opposed by Lord Birkenhead (F. E. Smith), and by Lord Haldane who argued that it would 'exclude the greater part of the people from effective influence in the affairs of the National Church'. But it was defended by Lords Parmoor (C. A. Cripps) and Salisbury and passed its second reading by ninety-seven. In the Commons in November the second reading passed after the defeat by 304 votes to sixteen of a motion for rejection by Thomas Broad (a Coalition Liberal and Congregational minister), who said that disestablishment was the only

[27] Church Reform League Minutes, 17 July 1916; CRL/5, fos. 116–17; Archbishop C. Garbett, *Church and State in England* (London, 1950), 111–14; W. Temple, *Life and Liberty* (London, 1917); F. A. Iremonger, *William Temple, Archbishop of Canterbury: His Life and Letters* (London, 1949), 220 ff.; R. E. Roberts, *H. R. L. Sheppard: Life and Letters* (London, 1942), 118 ff.; Henson, *Retrospect*, i. 206 ff.; id. *Anglicanism* (London, 1921), 223–9; Mews, 'Effect of the First World War', 256–8; Norman, op. cit. 275–6.

[28] Speech of Halifax, 23 Jan. 1917; ECU Minutes, C.U. dep. 6, 30–2; LS, 26 July 1916 (vol. 11).

[29] Quoted J. M. Winter, *Socialism and the Challenge of War: Ideas and Opinions in Britain, 1912–1918* (London, 1974), 175.

[30] Cecil to Wolmer, 30 Oct. 1917; Selborne Papers, c. 980, fo. 68.

[31] Minutes, 4 Feb. 1917; CRL/5, 187–8.

satisfactory way to free the Church.[32] Outside Parliament, opposition came from the Liberation Society and the Congregational Union, arguing that if a Church remained established Parliament should have undiminished control over it. Bishops Henson and Knox were strong opponents of the measure, Henson arguing in a series of letters to *The Times* that the bill 'scotticized' the English Church.[33]

The bill became law in December and was known as the Enabling Act. It generally granted to the new assembly the legislative powers proposed in the 1916 report, but a successful amendment in the Commons had substituted an Ecclesiastical Committee of both Houses of Parliament for the Privy Council committee originally proposed.[34] A. V. Dicey believed the Act was a clear sign of 'the approaching disestablishment of the Church of England'.[35] This prediction proved wide of the mark, though the Act was a significant step towards spiritual freedom and encouraged further reforms along the same lines. But the results of the Act within the next decade were disappointing to Church reformers. A prime concern of the new assembly was Prayer Book revision, and in 1920 the new body appointed a committee of all three of its Houses to consider the Convocations' proposals. When a Revised Prayer Book was submitted to Parliament, the civil legislature rejected it and thereby clearly demonstrated its continuing supremacy.

While Anglicans were trying to gain more self-governing power, the Church of Scotland wished to gain assurance of much greater autonomy than the Church of England in order to assist union with the United Free Church. After the outbreak of war there was little official discussion of these matters until March 1918, when the Church of Scotland 'Hundred' again convened despite a previous decision to wait until peace came. One minister understandably said that, amid the personal worries caused by war, he could scarcely give his mind to such important topics.[36]

There was still much dispute about a self-governing constitution for the Church of Scotland, including its faith and the nature of its establishment. It was said the differences might even provoke a secession on Erastian grounds.[37] The National Church Defence Association disliked any weakening of the State connection; on the other hand the Disestablishment Council for Scotland lamented that the Kirk would remain established and therefore a cause of social

[32] *AR* i (1919), 72–3, 84–5; H cxx. 1817–96.

[33] D. M. Thompson, 'The Politics of the Enabling Act, 1919', in D. Baker (ed.), *Studies in Church History*, xii (Oxford, 1975), 383–92; *Guardian*, 14 Aug. 1919, p. 842; LS, 25 June, 3 Dec. 1919 (vol. 11); *Liberator*, July 1919, p. 79–85; *Congregational Year-book* (1920), 63–4; Henson, *Retrospect*, i. 301–5; Knox, *Reminiscences*, 318–19; Wilkinson, *The Church of England*, 271–4.

[34] Bell, op. cit. ii. 976–80; Thompson, op. cit.; Garbett, op. cit. 115 and ff.; Nicholls, *Church and State in Britain*, 199–206; J. H. B. Masterman, 'Liberal Churchmen and the Enabling Bill', *CR* cxvi (July–Dec. 1919), 286–90.

[35] Dicey to Balfour of Burleigh, 7 May 1920; Balfour of Burleigh Papers, 47.

[36] Revd D. Macmillan to Revd Dr Williamson, 10 Apr. 1918 (copy); Sands Papers, CH1/10/16.

[37] Prof. James Cooper to Balfour of Burleigh, 7 Mar. 1918 (copy); ibid. 10/5; Cooper to Lord Sands, 15 Mar. 1918; ibid. 10/8; Revd A. Henderson to Sands, 22 Apr.; ibid. 10/9; memo by Sands, ibid. 10/20.

friction. The old arguments over voluntaryism still produced a good deal of passion on both sides.[38] None the less, negotiations proceeded on articles drawn up by Lord Sands and accepted by the Church of Scotland Assembly in 1919. Under these the Church had complete control, independent of civil authority, over its doctrine, worship, and government, but fully accepted the need for national recognition of religion.[39] The articles were receiving wide though not unanimous acceptance in both the Church of Scotland and the UF Church, and the joint committee said in May that under the articles 'the Church . . . would be both national and free'.[40] The Church of Scotland General Assembly sent the articles to be approved or otherwise by the presbyteries, and seventy-four out of eighty-four presbyteries accepted them 'as the basis of an approach to the Government in regard to legislation necessary to promote the cause of Presbyterian Reunion'.[41]

The Church of Scotland Hundred was authorized in December to approach the Government, and delegates of the committee met Lloyd George at Downing Street on 19 March 1920. Bonar Law, an ex-Presbyterian, announced that legislation would be presented, but he was urged to reject the proposed scheme at two meetings he had on 14 May with the National Church Defence Association and the UF Church Association respectively. In October it was still uncertain whether the bill would be a ministerial one.[42] However, the intention to introduce a Government measure was announced in the King's Speech in February 1921. The Church of Scotland Bill, endorsing the articles previously agreed, was introduced by Robert Munro (the Scottish Secretary) in the Commons on 28 April. It was approved by 292 votes to fourteen in the Church of Scotland Assembly and by a large majority in the UF Assembly.[43] Opposition was raised on the second reading debate on 22 June and the third on 11 July. On the former occasion Thomas Johnston (Labour MP and UF Church elder) defended disestablishment, and on the latter Joseph Johnstone (Coalition Liberal MP, UF elder and ex-United Presbyterian) complained that 'the principle of a free Church in a free State' was being abjectly surrendered by the UF Church so that it could 'enter into the establishment fold'. But three-quarters of the Scottish members supported the bill, James Brown (a Labour MP) saying for example that the Churches had never been more active and that union would enable them to 'extend their work still more'. Balfour also spoke in

[38] *Liberator*, Oct. 1918, p. 59, Mar. 1919, pp. 74–5; James Barr, *The Scottish Church Question* (London, 1920) 161–2; J. Hay Thorburn, *Gold May be Bought Too Dear: An Appeal to the People of Scotland* (National Church Defence Association (Leith, [1920]).

[39] W. Mair, *The Scottish Churches, June 1918* (Edinburgh, 1918); Revd A. W. Wotherspoon to Sands, 17 Apr. 1918 and later letters; Sands Papers, 10/18; F. Lyall, *Of Presbyters and Kings: Church and State in the Law of Scotland* (Aberdeen, 1980), 68–71.

[40] Printed statement in Sands Papers, 10/20, fo. 40.

[41] Minutes of Edinburgh C. of S. Presbytery, 30 July 1919; CH2/121/137–8; Thorburn, op. cit. 18.

[42] J. Hay Thorburn to Law, 15 May 1920; BLP, 104/2/12; Robert Munro, Secretary for Scotland, to Law, 9 Oct.; ibid. 104/2/21.

[43] Printed account in Sands Papers, 10/20, fo. 47, p. 13.

favour, and the bill passed through the Commons without division.[44] It sailed smoothly through the Lords, commended by the Lord Chancellor (Lord Birkenhead) and by Haldane and Parmoor, and became law on 28 July.[45].

The Church of Scotland may now have been free as well as established, but questions regarding the transfer of temporalities to the Church had to be dealt with in order to ease union. These matters were settled, though not with unanimous approval, by the Property and Endowments Act of 1925. Therefore, with both its spiritual and temporal position settled, the Church of Scotland could proceed to unite with most of the United Free Church in May 1929.[46] As in 1900, a minority refused to take part in the union, and an independent UF Church loyal to voluntary principles remained in being. None the less the 1921 and 1925 Acts had induced a Presbyterian reunion much larger than that of 1900.

While Welsh disestablishment and the constitutional position of the Church of Scotland had been resolved by 1921, the Ritualist controversy had not been settled, nor had the education dispute. In 1918 two important Education Acts were passed but neither altered the 1902 settlement and therefore left many Nonconformists unsatisfied. The bill for England and Wales, introduced in February and enacted in August, was mainly concerned with raising the minimum school leaving age to fourteen, with part-time continuation schooling thereafter. There were religious objections from the Roman Catholics, who found that the legislation did not adequately recognize their right to provide continuation schooling.[47] Discussions initiated in 1919 by H. A. L. Fisher, President of the Education Board, on possible changes in doctrinal teaching came to nothing. The Act for Scotland, coming into effect in May 1919, established a system similar to that of 1902 in England and Wales. It replaced school boards with county education authorities, and provided equitable rate aid for denominational schools (and equitable salaries for their teachers) while leaving them the right of approving the appointment of teachers on religious grounds. The Catholics, who were the main beneficiaries of these provisions, welcomed the settlement though there were differences over the details of its operation. The Liberation Society protested about public support of denominational education, and Presbyterian bodies regretted that religious education had not been made an essential part of the ordinary curriculum in provided schools.[48]

[44] H cxliii. 1397–469, cxliv. 951–69.
[45] Ibid. cxlv. 1339–64; Muir, *John White*, 203–13.
[46] Dunlop, 'Paths to Reunion', 172–6; Muir, op. cit. 214 ff.
[47] *Tablet*, xcix (Jan.–June 1918), 707–8, 823–5; *AR* i (1918), 66.
[48] J. E. Handley, *The Irish in Scotland*, one-vol. edn. (Glasgow, 1964), 319–20; T. R. Bone (ed.), *Studies in the History of Scottish Education, 1872–1939* (London 1967), 41–64; J. H. Treble, 'The Working of the 1918 Education Act in Glasgow Archdiocese', *Innes Review*, xxxi (1980), 27–44; LS (management committee), 23 Oct. 1918 (vol. 11); C. of S. Edinburgh Presbytery, 21 Aug., 18 Dec. 1918; 121/36, 79/80; I. R. Findlay, 'Sir John Struthers, KCB: A Study of his Influence upon Scottish Educational Development', Ph.D. thesis (Dundee, 1979), 237–304.

Some passive resisters continued to make their protests for a while, but they soon desisted and the 1902 settlement remained. Apart from the education and ritual questions, however, ecclesiastical aims took important steps towards attainment in the hectic three years after the war. Religious issues were leaving politics, but they were going out in style.

CHAPTER VIII

Conclusion

RELIGIOUS issues had been fairly prominent in politics in the years from 1919 to 1921, but did not remain so much longer. The inter-war years were marked rather by the recession of ecclesiastical questions and—certainly in the 1930s— the continued decline of church allegiance taken as a whole but with notable denominational exceptions. The extent of church membership and attendance was the most crucial factor explaining the pressure of Church questions in politics, especially in an age of democratic advance when former limitations on the expression of political aims were being removed or greatly lessened. Membership of a denomination did not guarantee interest in or attachment to political aims held by many in that Church. But it did often signify support for those aims, which were brought to the attention of members if only indirectly. When church membership was growing the political aims connected with it flourished; when it was in decline the aims withered.

This pattern helps to explain the rise and decline of religious issues in British politics between about 1780 and 1920. From the later eighteenth to the later nineteenth century there was a vast growth of denominations outside the established Churches, and many of the ecclesiastical issues in politics were concerned with the aspirations of Nonconformists and Roman Catholics for civil equality. These aims, encouraged by important concessions to Dissenters and Catholics in 1828 and 1829, gained more political strength as democracy began to advance soon afterwards. The Reform Act of 1832 gave a certain amount of encouragement to religious equality by giving rather more political expression to its supporters. The Reform Act of 1867 had a similar effect by extending the franchise further, though the effectiveness of the enlarged vote was severely limited by the distribution of seats which was little altered.

The first redistribution of seats to take place in accordance with something like democratic principles occurred in 1885, as an accompaniment to further franchise extension in 1884. This was the most promising political advance so far for the particular aims of Nonconformists. Even so it was highly doubtful whether Dissent had grown strong enough to gain disestablishment in England, as opposed to Wales and perhaps Scotland, and Dissent was beginning to undergo proportional decrease. In fact the reforms of 1884–5 were followed by little further success for radical ecclesiastical aims in politics, and the political importance of these aims went generally into recession. Catholic nationalist force had gained Irish disestablishment in 1869 with Dissenting electoral aid.

Welsh Nonconformist national force was to achieve Welsh disestablishment in 1920 after a long struggle and deferred hopes. In England, Dissenters obtained relief from their burials grievance in 1880, following similar settlements, over a long period, of their grievances over marriages, church rates, and university tests. But English disestablishment, demanded with generally increasing strength from 1844 to 1885, proved a will o' the wisp never to be caught. Even the formidable pressure mounted for educational reform by a still flourishing and influential Dissent from 1902 to 1908 was not successful. A Scottish disestablishment movement was powerful between 1874 and 1885. But this too later faded, and was edged out by willingness to accept spiritual freedom within an officially established Church. The substantial anti-Ritualist campaign in politics from 1898 to 1906 likewise failed to repeat the success of 1874 and pass a new disciplinary Act.

Various cultural factors helped to explain the change from a period of relative success for such aims to one of relative failure. Among them was the growth of a more ecumenical spirit in place of the rigid division which had promoted determined rivalry on political matters. As well as the positive face presented by ecumenicalism, however, there was also the growth of simple indifference to denominational questions, to church-going, perhaps to religion altogether. Not least, of course, successive victories over religious equality removed long-fought issues from the political scene, and Nonconformity's inferior social position practically disappeared. These successes, however, did not result in the progressive strengthening of Dissent but rather the reverse: it was said in 1922 that 'the old dissidence loses zeal as Dissent ceases to carry penalties'.[1]

Other political changes contributed to the explanation. A decidedly more democratic political system from 1885 could not bring success for radical ecclesiastical objects if these were supported by a declining proportion of the population, which was now beginning to occur. So it was that, in spite of hopes and expectations, democracy could not bring further success for radical ecclesiastical demands because democracy was now exposing the inadequacy of ecclesiastical pressure in politics. To an increasing extent the electorate consisted of non-church-goers, not only because much of the working class was now enfranchised but because church-going was practised less by the middle classes. A largely working-class electorate ensured that politics would be increasingly concerned with the aims of the working class. As only a minority of the working class attended church these aims were far less likely to be ecclesiastical than economic and social.

By the early twentieth century this change was reflected by the greater attention being paid by Liberals to social change through State intervention and by the emergence of a separate Labour party. Secular developments of this kind in party political attitude and realignment had an important effect on religious

[1] A. Porritt, *The Best I Remember* (London, 1922), 27.

issues in politics, just as the rise or fall of support for the Churches affected the priorities of politicians. The Liberal split over Home Rule in 1886 had weakened Dissenting aims by dividing Nonconformists and ushering in many years of Conservative ascendancy sustained by further Liberal divisions over imperialism in the decade from 1895. What seemed a strong revival in 1906 had fairly disappointing results for Nonconformists. A further Liberal split came in 1916 over war policy and weakened what remained of the Nonconformist urge in politics. Thereafter, Conservative ascendancy in inter-war politics, the dominance of economic and social questions, and the insistent intrusion of class division, helped to obstruct the remaining ecclesiastical demands which were dying in any case because of the numerical decline of their support.

Welsh disestablishment in 1920 was of course a success for Nonconformity, but was the delayed culmination of past efforts rather than a reflection of vital current interest. The effects of the Church of Scotland Act of 1921 represented compromise with the establishment idea rather than triumph over it. It was clearer than ever that English disestablishment had insufficient support to secure adoption by a Government, not least because the growing Catholic Church did not take it up. Ecclesiastical aims had gained much political success, but from 1920 economic depression ensured that economic and social issues became even more prominent than before. The old religious aims could now make no headway in politics. By the 1930s the contrast with a century before in this respect could hardly have been greater.

Nevertheless the issues with which we have been dealing did not immediately stop where this book has ended. After the Enabling Act the questions of autonomy of the Church of England from the State, and the desirability of disestablishment to make sure of achieving this, continued and still continue to be debated. The laity was given a more official role in Church government when the General Synod was inaugurated in 1970, and the advance to greater autonomy was renewed. In the 1980s there have been repeated disputes between Churchmen and the State over questions of national policy and Church government. A newspaper article in July 1982 on the Church of England emphasized 'the fundamental tension between church and state'. 'According to its contemporary self-image', said the article, 'the Church of England does not feel itself beholden to the Government, but answerable to no earthly power', yet at the same time 'any real scheme for separating church and state' would be extremely complex, 'upsetting to established patterns of thought' and 'questionable in its appeal to popular opinion'.[2] Thus was restated the dilemma of High-Churchmen for the last 150 years, and the dilemma may continue for another 150. The bonds of State control have been gradually relaxed (if not as much as some Churchmen wish); and, partly as a consequence,

---

[2] Clifford Longley in *T*, 28 July 1982. Cf. ibid. 5 July 1976, 31 Jan. 1983, 18 Aug. 1984 and E. Norman, ibid. 21 Feb. 1983. See also E. R. Norman, *Church and Society in England, 1770–1970* (Oxford, 1976), 453–7.

there remains little sign of a powerful demand for outright disestablishment from within the Church.

From outside the Church this demand has become weaker than from within. The Liberation Society hoped for revival after the First World War but did not attain it. Lack of adequate subscriptions continued to restrict the Society and showed a small and lessening interest in its aims and activities. In June 1921 the full-time organizer had to be given notice on account of financial deficit, and it was decided that fewer numbers of *The Liberator* could be issued.[3] In discussing preparations for a general election in 1922, the executive committee agreed unanimously that 'nothing more ambitious than the questioning of candidates by local supporters of the Society could be attempted on the present financial resources'.[4]

Referring to disestablishment, the Methodist Lord Snowden noted in his *Autobiography* published in 1934: 'It is curious how a political question excites great interest for a time, and then becomes a dead issue. The present generation has never heard of the Disestablishment of the Church of England. This, no doubt, is due to the emergence of social and industrial problems into the sphere of politics.'[5] He was exaggerating, but not unduly. There were still flickers of interest in disestablishment among Nonconformists, but these were rare and led to no sustained revival of concern. In 1935 Lloyd George, casting around for political light in his isolation of that decade, tried to rally Nonconformist support for a Council of Action for Peace and Reconstruction.[6] Based on the Free Church Council framework, this body intervened strongly in the 1935 general election but to little positive effect. The effort was largely unsuccessful in trying to revive forces whose old appeal had been much reduced. Despite Lloyd George's nostalgic hopes, nothing like the powerful education movement of 1902–5 materialized. Nonconformist political effort had long been dispersed into support for different political parties, and the Council of Action could not unite it.

In 1949 Henry Townsend, a member of the Liberation Society's council, published *The Claims of the Free Churches* in which he stated: 'A National Church is a contradiction of itself. Christianity is a universal religion and it is impossible to enshrine the universal in a national institution'.[7] But what was by then undoubtedly a more widely held Dissenting view was stated in a report of a Free Church Federal Council commission, published in 1953 as *The Free Churches and the State*: 'Though Free Churchmen reject State *control* of religion they welcome State *recognition* of religion. We do not desire to see a

[3] LS, 10 June 1921, vol. 11. Cf. S. Koss, *Nonconformity in Modern British Politics* (London, 1975), 156.
[4] LS, 21 Mar. 1922, vol. 11. Cf. ibid. 14 May, 10 June, 23 Nov. 1920.
[5] Philip, Viscount Snowden, *An Autobiography* (2 vols, London, 1934), i. 41–2.
[6] See Koss, op. cit. 187 ff.
[7] H. Townsend, *The Claims of the Free Churches* (London, 1949), 200, 223. Cf. id. *The Liberation Society: A Plea for Free Church Support*, leaflet (n.p., 1946).

secular State in England . . . . It would be easy by ill-considered proposals for disestablishment to jeopardize the existing valuable co-operation between Church and State, in which the Free Churches have come increasingly to share'.[8] If compromise was coming from the side of Free Churchmen who stressed their desire for State recognition of religion, but not for a State-controlled Church, it was also coming from Anglicans who wanted greater freedom from State control but not disestablishment.

The Liberation Society published its last annual report in March 1958, and then went out of existence. After a good deal of success the once confident and prominent organization founded in 1844 had ended almost forgotten with its main object, English disestablishment, unrealized. Its protracted twentieth-century longevity had been the palest reflection of its nineteenth-century buoyancy, for it had ceased to have much influence before 1914. The old cause could come back, however, as was shown when it was suddenly raised in an address by a prominent Socialist politician of Congregational family background in March 1983. Anthony Wedgwood Benn called for a national campaign for disestablishment in order to conclude logically the current relaxation of Church–State bonds and to free the Church from any odour of complicity in current Government policies. The message aroused momentary press comment, but the question immediately died away without further remark. Yet a century before the matter had been at the centre of political contention. Equally illuminating was *The Times'* comment on Benn's speech: so much autonomy had been gained by the Church that 'the introduction of nominal disestablishment would now be of marginal importance to the life of the nation and of the Church'.[9]

Of other issues long contested between Church and Dissent, education remained controversial in the 1920s and after but was much less prominent than before, and the 1944 Education Act maintained the 1902 system of rate aided voluntary as well as rate aided council schools. Payment of tithe was frequently refused in the great depression of the early 1930s, opposition occurring particularly in Denbighshire and East Anglia. The dispute was ended by the Tithe Act of 1936, which abolished the rent-charge and compensated the tithe-owners.[10]

The spiritual autonomy of the Church of Scotland, which continued to be regarded by many Anglicans as a desirable example to follow, had been assured by the Act of 1921. The Act's main object was to encourage union with the United Free Church, and after being further assisted by the settlement of the endowments question in 1925 this was attained in 1929. A small minority of UF Churchmen remained as a separate Church, and this body flourished while in the enlarged Church of Scotland there was quiet consolidation. After this major

---

[8] *The Free Churches and the State*, Free Church Federal Council (London, 1953), 62.

[9] *T*, 3 Mar. 1983.

[10] G. F. A. Best, *Temporal Pillars: Queen Anne's Bounty, the Ecclesiastical Commissioners and the Church of England* (Cambridge, 1964), 476–9.

reunion there was another three years later when, again as the culmination of much discussion, the Methodist Church was formed by the combination of Wesleyans, Primitive Methodists, and the United Methodist Church. Ecumenicalism has remained significant since then, and occasional further unions have occurred.

Since 1921 internal dispute has not been absent in the Church of England, where in addition to doctrinal argument there was liturgical contention still centred on the quarrel over Ritualism. In 1927 the Church Assembly fulfilled the intentions of the 1906 report of the Commission on Ecclesiastical Discipline and produced a Revised Prayer Book. This contained optional alternatives and additions to the old liturgy, including reservation of the Sacrament and a new order of Communion. The new provisions were strongly opposed mainly by anti-Ritualists but also by many Anglo-Catholics who found insufficient freedom in the concessions. In Parliament, the Book easily passed the Lords in 1927 but was rejected in the Commons by 238 votes to 205. After modification the Book experienced the same fate in 1928, failing in the Commons by 266 votes to 220. The State had demonstrated its continuing constitutional control over the establishment and strengthened anti-Erastian feeling in the Church.[11] The ritual issue continued to cause dispute when Convocation resolved to allow the Book of 1928 to be used, at the discretion of the Bishops, and the new provisions were employed without strict legality. A greater sense of mutual toleration eventually developed, but the old tension persists in a weakened form.

Anti-Catholicism also continued to cause tension, though the Irish constitutional settlement in 1921–2 removed one of its familiar means of expression. The persistence of anti-Catholicism in a political form was most evident in Liverpool, Glasgow, and Edinburgh. In Liverpool George Wise had a successor in the Revd H. D. Longbottom, who fought several Parliamentary elections for the Liverpool Protestant Party in the 1930s but obtained only about two per cent of the vote. Ultra-Protestants also contested municipal elections in the city and were still doing so in the 1970s.[12] Ultra-Protestant groups had some political influence in Scotand in the 1930s, and there was some riotous activity. The leader of Protestant Action, John Cormack, won a seat on the Edinburgh city council, and the Scottish Protestant League won seven seats in Glasgow municipal elections.[13] A Catholic procession in the mining village of Carfin in Lanarkshire was banned by the police in 1924 in accordance with a

[11] G. K. A. Bell, *Randall Davidson, Archbishop of Canterbury* (2 vols., 1935), ii. 1335 ff; C. Garbett, *Church and State in England* (London, 1950), 204–10; Hensley Henson, *Disestablishment* (London, 1929); id., *Church and State in England* (London, 1930), 6, 41–2; D. Nicholls, (ed.), *Church and State in Britain since 1820* (London, 1967), 207–11. Cf. Canon N. P. Williams, *The Bishop of Durham and Disestablishment*, Church Self-government League (London, 1929), 24–6.
[12] P. J. Waller, *Democracy and Sectarianism: A Political and Social History of Liverpool, 1868–1939* (Liverpool, 1981), 285 ff., 323 ff.
[13] See T. Gallagher, 'Protestant Extremism in Urban Scotland, 1930–1939: Its Growth and Contraction', *SHR* lxiv (1985), 143–67; J. Cooney, *Scotland and the Papacy* (Edinburgh, 1982), 19–20.

provision in the Catholic Relief Act of 1829, and thus revived memories of the eucharistic procession in London sixteen years before. But the long-awaited recompense now followed. A Catholic Relief Bill was introduced in the Commons in 1926, permitting full liberty for Catholic processions and repealing other archaic Catholic disabilities. Some opposition was voiced, but the bill passed both Houses without a division and became law.[14] After this Catholics were still prevented by public statute from becoming Sovereigns of the country (or their wives or husbands), Lord Chancellors, or High Commissioners of the Church of Scotland.

By the 1920s it was clear that religious issues no longer occupied the large place they had held in politics for about a hundred years. Many of the issues had been resolved, and the few which remained attracted insufficient public interest and sense of urgency to form powerful political questions. Recent party political change had weakened or destroyed traditional denominational attachments to political parties, though some faint traces of them can still be discovered at the present time.[15] Political changes had emphasized the growing importance of economic and social questions and of class divisions in politics. Trade unions displaced Nonconformist denominations as a challenge to the established order.

The political role of the Churches was disappearing; their contribution to social welfare had been largely taken over by the State; their provision for leisure activities was being increasingly supplied by secular bodies.[16] All this meant that the Churches, in terms of general culture, were becoming more and more marginal to society. They were being reduced to their primary functions of teaching and witnessing to religion, and in this capacity they attracted, on the whole, fewer people. It is quite likely that the political role of Churches was important to their numerical prosperity and that they lost support when this role subsided or vanished.[17] But the relative weakening of the Churches, taking them as a whole, commenced in the 1880s when they were still very significant in a political sense. Loss of political significance probably helped at a later stage to continue the decline. 'Numerical decline', of course, has its own limitations when applied to the role of Churches, and in any case it is something which can only be applied to them with care and selectivity. Most Protestant churches in England experienced statistical decline from about 1906, though there have been fluctuations—the 1920s for example seeing something like stability but the

---

[14] Ibid.; W. L. Arnstein, *Protestant versus Catholic in Mid-Victorian England: Mr Newdegate and the Nuns* (Columbia and London, 1982), 219–20; Susan McGhee, 'Carfin and the Roman Catholic Relief Act of 1926', *Innes Review*, xvi (1965), 56–78.

[15] D. Martin, *A Sociology of English Religion* (London, 1967), 49–50, 58; B. R. Wilson, *Religion in Secular Society* (London, 1966), 59–60; R. Blake, *The Conservative Party from Peel to Churchill* (London, 1979), 272.

[16] A. D. Gilbert, *The Making of Post-Christian Britain* (London, 1980), ix ff., 72 ff., 110 ff.; S. Yeo, *Religion and Voluntary Organizations in Crisis* (London, 1976), 169, 321; J. Cox, *The English Churches in a Secular Society: Lambeth, 1870–1930* (Oxford, 1982), 182 ff.; Garbett, op. cit. 100 ff.

[17] Cf. R. Currie, A. Gilbert, and L. Horsley (eds.), *Churches and Churchgoers: Patterns of Church Growth in the British Isles Since 1700* (Oxford, 1977), 107–13.

1930s a sharp decline. Among Protestants in Scotland the experience of numerical decline was generally delayed until the 1950s. In both countries the Catholic Church grew steadily until about 1970. Nevertheless the decrease of formal religious practice is an important twentieth-century British phenomenon. Society and politics have become secularized, religion has tended to become privatized. Decreasing public support for the Churches weakened their political aims, and lessening political significance in turn contributed to their loss of support. Whether these trends will continue in the future is not for the historian to guess.

Bibliography

I   MANUSCRIPTS

Asquith Papers, Bodleian Library.
Balfour (First Earl of) Papers, British Library, Additional MSS 49683–49962.
Balfour of Burleigh Papers (in private hands; courtesy of Scottish Record Office).
Benson (Archbishop) Papers, Lambeth Palace Library.
Bonar Law Papers, House of Lords Record Office.
Bourne (Cardinal) Papers, Archbishop's House, Westminster.
Bright (John) Papers, British Library, Add. MSS 43383–43392.
Campbell-Bannerman Papers, British Library, Add. MSS 41206–41252, 52512–52521.
Carnarvon Papers British Library, Add. MSS 60757–61100.
Cross (Viscount) Papers, British Library, Add. MSS 51263–51289.
Cecil, Lord Hugh (Baron Quickswood) Papers, Hatfield House, Hertfordshire.
Cecil, Lord Robert (Viscount Cecil of Chelwood) Papers, British Library, Add. MSS 51071–51204.
Chamberlain (Joseph) Papers, Birmingham University Library.
Church Defence Institution (later Committee for Church Defence and Instruction): Minutes of Central Council and Executive Committee, Church House, Dean's Yard, Westminster.
Church of Scotland Presbytery Minutes: Aberdeen, Abertarff, Edinburgh, Glasgow, in Scottish Record Office; Dundee, in Dundee District Council Archives.
Church Reform League: Minutes of Council and Executive Committee, Church House, Dean's Yard, Westminster.
Dale (R. W.) Papers, Birmingham University Library.
Davidson (Archbishop) Papers, Lambeth Palace Library.
Dilke Papers, British Library, Add. MSS 43874–43967, 49385–49455.
Disraeli Papers, Bodleian Library.
Elliot (Arthur) Papers, National Library of Scotland.
Ellis (T. E.) Papers, National Library of Wales.
English Church Union Minute Books, Lambeth Palace Library.
Evans (Samuel T.) Papers, National Library of Wales.

Free Church of Scotland Presbytery Minutes: Aberdeen, Edinburgh, Glasgow, Tongue, in Scottish Record Office; Dundee, in Dundee District Council Archives.

Gee (Thomas) Papers, National Library of Wales.

Gladstone (Herbert) Papers, British Library, Add. MSS 45985–46118, 46474–46486.

Gladstone (W. E.) Papers, British Library, Add. MSS 44086–44835.

Haldane Papers, National Library of Scotland.

Halsbury Papers, British Library, Add. MSS 56370–56377.

Harcourt Papers, Bodleian Library.

Hope-Scott Papers, National Library of Scotland.

Hughes (Hugh Price) Correspondence, John Rylands Library, University of Manchester.

Iddesleigh Papers, British Library, Add. MSS 50013–50064.

Lewis (Herbert) Papers, National Library of Wales.

Liberation Society Minutes of Executive Committee etc, Greater London Record Office, County Hall.

Lidgett (Scott) Correspondence, John Rylands Library, University of Manchester.

Lloyd George Papers, House of Lords Record Office and National Library of Wales.

Manning (Cardinal) Papers St Mary of the Angels, Bayswater (Moorhouse Road, London W2); courtesy of Revd Prof. A. Chapeau.

Melly (George) Papers, Liverpool Local History Library.

Murray of Elibank Papers National Library of Scotland.

National Union of Conservative Associations: Minutes of National Executive Committee (on microfiche).

Northcote (Sir Stafford) Papers: see Iddesleigh.

Osborne (C.C.) Papers, British Library, Add. MSS 46402–46408.

Perks (R. W.) Correspondence, John Rylands Library, University of Manchester.

Quickswood Papers: see Cecil, Lord Hugh.

Rendel Papers, National Library of Wales.

Richard (Henry) Papers, National Library of Wales.

Ripon (First Marquess of) Papers, British Library, Add. MSS 43510–43644.

Rosebery Papers, National Library of Scotland.

Runciman Papers, Newcastle upon Tyne University Library

Salisbury Papers (Third and Fourth Marquesses), Hatfield House, Hertfordshire.

Sands Papers, Scottish Record Office.

Selborne (Second and Third Earls of) Papers, Bodleian Library (on deposit by Earl of Selborne).

Tait (Archbishop) Papers, Lambeth Palace Library.

Temple (Archbisop Frederick) Papers, Lambeth Palace Library.

Trevelyan (C. P.) Papers Newcastle upon Tyne University Library.

United Free Church Presbytery Minutes: Aberdeen, Edinburgh, Glasgow, in Scottish Record Office; Dundee, in Dundee District Council Archives.

United Presbyterian Church Presbytery Minutes: Aberdeen, Edinburgh, Glasgow, in Scottish Record Office; Dundee, in Dundee District Council Archives.

Vaughan (Cardinal) Papers, Archbishop's House, Westminster.

Ward (Wilfrid) Papers, St Andrews University Library.

Whitelaw (Alexander) Papers, Glasgow University Library (Archives Dept.).

Wilberforce (Bishop Samuel) Papers, Bodleian Library.

Wilson (H. J.) Papers, Sheffield City Library.

II NEWSPAPERS AND PERIODICALS

Baptist Times
Beehive
Bible Christian Magazine
Bradford Observer
British Weekly
Bulwark, or Reformation Journal
Carnarvon and Denbigh Herald
Catholic Times
Catholic Union Gazette
Christian World
Church Reformer
Church Socialist
Church Standard, or Quarterly Magazine of the National Protestant Church Union
Church Times
Church Union Gazette
Clarion
Companion: Quarterly Journal of the Church of England League
Congregationalist
Congregational Review
Contemporary Review
Daily Graphic
Daily News
Disestablishment Banner
Dundee Advertiser
Dundee Courier and Argus
Fortnightly Review
Free Church Chronicle
Glasgow Free Press
Glasgow Observer
Guardian
Justice
Ladies' League Gazette
Liberator
Methodist New Connexion Magazine
Methodist Recorder
Methodist Times

Monthly Record of the National Protestant Church Union
Monthly Record of the Protestant Churchmen's Alliance
National Church: Monthly Record of Proceedings of the Church Defence Institution
Nineteenth Century and After
Nonconformist (Nonconformist and Independent from 1878*)*
Oswestry and Border Counties Advertiser
Pall Mall Gazette
People's Journal (Dundee)
Primitive Methodist Magazine (later *Aldersgate Primitive Methodist Magazine*)
Primitive Methodist Quarterly Review
Protestant Alliance Official Organ
Protestant Defence Brigade Monthly Record
Protestant Woman
Quarterly Chronicle of the Church Reform League
Record
Rock
Scotsman
Standard
Tablet
The Times
Union Magazine (United Free Church of Scotland)
United Free Church Magazine
United Presbyterian Magazine
Voice of Truth (Monthly Tract Society)
Voice of Warning (Monthly Tract Society)
Wesleyan Methodist Magzine
Western Mail
Yorkshire Post

III REFERENCE WORKS AND PARLIAMENTARY REPORTS

Annual Register
Baptist Handbook
Chronicle of the Convocation of Canterbury

Congregational Year-book

Craig, F. W. S. (ed.), *British Parliamentary Election Results* (London 1974).

—— *British Election Manifestos, 1900–1974* (London 1975).

Dictionary of National Biography

Digest of the Actings and Proceedings of the Synod of the Presbyterian Church in England, 1836–1876 (1877).

Digest of the Proceedings of the Synods of the Presbyterian Church of England, 1876–1905 (1907).

Hansard's *Parliamentary Debates*, 3rd, 4th, and 5th ser.

Journal of the Convocation of York

McCalmont's Parliamentary Poll Book: British Election Results, 1832–1918, ed. J. Vincent and M. Stenton (Brighton, 1971).

Mulhall, M. G., *The Dictionary of Statistics*, 4th edn. (1899).

National Liberal Federation: *Annual Reports* (on microfiche)

Ollard, S. L., G. Crosse, and M. F. Bond (eds.), *A Dictionary of English Church History*, 3rd edn. (London, 1948).

IV BOOKS, PAMPHLETS, AND ARTICLES

(Place of publication is London unless otherwise stated)

Acland, A. H. D. (ed.), *Memoir and Letters of the Rt. Hon. Sir Thomas Dyke Acland* (1902).

Adams, F., *History of the Elementary School Contest*, ed. A. Briggs (Brighton, 1972).

Addison, W. G., *Religious Equality in Modern England, 1714–1914* (1944).

Address to Mr Gladstone by the Scots Liberal Clergy (Edinburgh, 1885).

Addresses of the London Working-men's Council to their Brethren of Great Britain ([1872]).

A Defence of the National Church, by a Free Churchman (1890).

Adelman, P., *Victorian Radicalism: The Middle-class Experience, 1830–1914* (1984).

Akenson, D. H., *The Church of Ireland: Ecclesiastical Reform and Revolution, 1800–1885* (New Haven and London, 1971).

Allen, B. M., *Sir Robert Morant* (1934).

Allon, H., *Religious Reasons for Disestablishmnt* (Bolton, 1872).

Altholz, J. L., 'The Vatican Decrees Controversy, 1874–1875', *Catholic Historical Review*, lvii (1971–2), 593–605.

—— D. McElrath, and J. C. Holland (eds.), *The Correspondence of Lord Acton and Richard Simpson* (3 vols. Cambridge, 1971–5).

Anson, P. F., *Underground Catholicism in Scotland, 1622–1878* (Montrose, 1970).

A Plea for Union Between the United Presbyterian Church and the Free Church of Scotland, Addressed by the Dundee Free Church Office-bearers to their Brother Office-bearers (Dundee, 1895).

Arch, J., *The Autobiography of Joseph Arch*, ed. J. G. O'Leary (1966).

Archbishops' Committee on Church and State: *Report, with Appendices* (1916).

Argyll, Eighth Duke of, *The Patronage Act of 1874: All That Was Asked For in 1843* (Edinburgh, 1874).

—— *Autobiography and Memoirs*, ed. Dowager Duchess of Argyll (2 vols., 1906).

Armytage, W. H. G., *A. J. Mundella, 1825–1897* (1951).

Arnstein, W. L., *The Bradlaugh Case* (Oxford, 1965).

Arnstein, W. L., *Protestant versus Catholic in Mid-Victorian England: Mr Newdegate and the Nuns* (Columbia and London, 1982).

Ashburnham, Earl of, *English Catholics and Home Rule* (1886).

Askwith, G. R., *Lord James of Hereford* (1930).

Atlay, J. B., *The Life of the Rt. Revd Ernest Roland Wilberforce* (1912).

Auld, A., *Life of John Kennedy, DD* (1887).

Auspos, Patricia, 'Radicalism, Pressure Groups, and Party Politics: From the National Education League to the National Liberal Federation', *Journal of British Studies*, xx. 1 (1980), 184–204.

Aveling, E. B., *The Wickedness of God* (1881).

—— *A Godless Life the Happiest and Most Useful* (1882).

Aydelotte, W. O. (ed.), *The History of Parliamentary Behavior* (Princeton, 1977).

Bahlman, D., 'The Queen, Mr Gladstone, and Church Patronage', *VS* iii (1959–60), 349–80.

—— 'Politics and Church Patronage in the Victorian Age', *VS* xxii (1979), 253–96.

—— (ed.), *The Diary of Sir Edward Walter Hamilton* (2 vols., Oxford, 1972).

Baker, D. (ed.), *Studies in Church History*, xii, xiv, xv (Oxford, 1975, 1977, 1978).

Balfour, Arthur James, First Earl, *A Defence of Philosophic Doubt* (1879).

—— *Disestablishment Policy Exposed* (Edinburgh, 1894).

—— *The Foundations of Belief* (1906).

—— *Chapters of Autobiography*, ed. Mrs E. Dugdale (1930).

Balfour, Lady Frances, *A Memoir of Lord Balfour of Burleigh, KT* (1924).

Balfour, W., *The Establishment Principle Defended* (Edinburgh, 1873).

Balleine, G. R., *A History of the Evangelical Party in the Church of England*, 3rd edn. (1951).

Barbour, G. F., *The Life of Alexander Whyte, DD* (1924).

Barker, M., *Gladstone and Radicalism: The Reconstruction of the Liberal Party in Britain, 1885–94* (Hassocks, Sussex, 1975).

Barlow, J., *The Wesleyans and Disestablishment: A Speech Delivered at Bolton*, Nonconformist Association of Bolton and Neighbourhood (Bolton, 1873).

Barr, J., *The Scottish Church Question* (1920).

—— *The United Free Church of Scotland* (1934).

Bassett, A. Tilney (ed.), *Gladstone to his Wife* (1936).

Bateman, J., *The Church Association: Its Policy and Prospects*, 3rd edn. (1880).

Bax, E. Belfort, *The Religion of Socialism*, 3rd edn. (1891).

Bealey, F., and H. Pelling, *Labour and Politics, 1900–1906* (1958).

Bebbington, D. W., 'Gladstone and the Nonconformists: A Religious Affinity in Politics', in D. Baker (ed.), *Studies in Church History*, xii (Oxford, 1975), 369–82.

—— *The Nonconformist Conscience: Chapel and Politics, 1870–1914* (1982).

—— 'Nonconformity and Election Sociology, 1867–1918', *HJ* xxvii (1984), 633–56.

—— 'Baptist MPs in the Twentieth Century', *Baptist Quarterly*, xxxi. 6 (Apr. 1986), 252–87.

Beck, G. A. (ed.), *The English Catholics, 1850–1950* (1950).

Begg, J., *Union on the Proposed Basis Inconsistent with Free Church Principles* (Edinburgh, 1871).

—— *The Principles, Position, and Prospects of the Free Church of Scotland* (Edinburgh, 1875).

—— *Scottish Public Affairs, Civil and Ecclesiastical: A Letter to Lord Beaconsfield* (Edinburgh, 1879).

Beith, A., *To the Men of the North: A 'Letter'* (Edinburgh, 1876).

Bell, G. K. A., *Randall Davidson, Archbishop of Canterbury* (2 vols., 1935).

Bell, P. M. H., *Disestablishment in Ireland and Wales* (1969).

Bellesheim, A., *History of the Catholic Church in Scotland*, (4 vols., trans. O. Hunter Blair Edinburgh and London, 1890).

Belton, F. G. (ed.), *Ommanney of Sheffield: Memoirs* (1936).

Bennett, F., *The Story of W. J. E. Bennett* (1909).

Bennett, G. V., and J. D. Walsh (eds.), *Essays in Modern English Church History in Memory of Norman Sykes* (1966).

Benson, A. C., *The Life of Edward White Benson, Archbishop of Canterbury* (2 vols., 1899).

Bentley, J., *Ritualism and Politics in Victorian Britain: The Attempt to Legislate for Belief* (Oxford, 1978).

Bentley, M., *The Liberal Mind, 1914–1929* (Cambridge, 1977).

Best, G. F. A., *Temporal Pillars: Queen Anne's Bounty, the Ecclesiastical Commissioners and the Church of England* (Cambridge, 1964).

Bettany, F. G., *Stewart Headlam: A Biography* (1926).

Betts, J. A., *Education and Passive Resistance: What is the Fight About?* ([1903]).

Binfield, C., *So Down to Prayers: Studies in English Nonconformity, 1780–1920* (1977).

—— 'Asquith: The Formation of a Prime Minister', *Journal of the United Reformed Church History Society*, ii. 7 (Apr. 1981), 204–42.

Bingham, J. H., *The Period of the Sheffield School Board* (Sheffield, 1949).

Birkenhead, Second Earl of, *F. E.: the Life of F. E. Smith, First Earl of Birkenhead* (1965).

Birks, T. R., *Church and State* (1869).

Birmingham School Board: *Religious Instruction in Board Schools: Report of a Debate, 1872* (Birmingham, 1872).

Birrell, Augustine, *Things Past Redress* (1937).

Blaikie, W. G., *Ought the Free Church to Resume Connection With the State?* (London and Edinburgh, 1886).

Blake, R., *The Unknown Prime Minister: The Life of Andrew Bonar Law* (1955).

—— *Disraeli* (1966).

—— *The Conservative Party from Peel to Churchill* (1979).

Bland, Sister Joan, 'The Impact of Government on English Catholic Education, 1870–1902', *Catholic Historical Review*, lxii (1976), 36–55.

Blewett, N., *The Peers, the Parties, and the People: The General Elections of 1910* (1972).

Bligh, E. V., *Lord Ebury as a Church Reformer* (1891).

Blondel, J., *Voters, Parties, and Leaders* (Harmondsworth, 1967).

Bochel, J., and D. T. Denver, 'Religion and Voting: A Critical Review and a New Analysis', *Political Studies*, xviii (1970), 205–19.

Bogle, A., 'James Barr, DD, MP', *Records of Scottish Church History Society*, xx. 2 (1982), 189–207.

Bone, T. R. (ed.), *Studies in the History of Scottish Education, 1872–1939* (1967).

Booth, C., *Life and Labour of the People in London*, 3rd ser., *Religious Influences* (1902–3).

Boulton, J. T. (ed.), *The Letters of D. H. Lawrence*, i (Cambridge, 1979).

Bourne, F., *The Catholic Attitude on the Education Question* (1906).

Bowen, D., *The Idea of the Victorian Church* (Montreal, 1968).

Bowen, W. E., *The Crisis in the English Church* (1900).

—— *Contemporary Ritualism: A Volume of Evidence* (1902)

Bowran, J. G., *The Life of Arthur Thomas Guttery* (1922).

Boyd, C. W. (ed.), *Mr Chamberlain's Speeches* (2 vols., London, 1914).

Boyle, T., 'The Liberal Imperialists', *Bulletin of the Institute of Historical Research,* li (1979), 48–82.

Braden, C. B., *The Disestablishment of the English Church* (1876).

Bradlaugh, C., *The Radical Programme* (1885).

Bradley, J. F., *The Case against Welsh Disestablishment* (1911).

—— *Nonconformity and the Welsh Church Bill* (1912).

Brady, L. W., *T. P. O'Connor and the Liverpool Irish* (1983).

Bray, R. A., *Labour and the Churches* (1912).

Briggs, J., and I. Sellers (eds.), *Victorian Nonconformity* (1974).

Britten, J., *A Prominent Protestant: John Kensit,* Catholic Truth Society (1898).

Brock, M. and E. (eds.), *H. H. Asquith: Letters to Venetia Stanley* (Oxford, 1982).

Brooks, D., 'Gladstone and Midlothian: The Background to the First Campaign', *SHR* lxiv (1985), 42–65.

Brown, K. D., 'Nonconformity and the British Labour Movement', *Journal of Social History,* viii (1975), 113–20.

—— 'Ministerial Leakage in the Nineteenth Century: An Explanation', *Journal of the United Reformed Church History Society,* iii. 3 (1984), 94–103.

Brown, R., *Our National Church: An Appeal Against Disestablishment* (Edinburgh, 1886).

Buckle, G. E., *The Life of Benjamin Disraeli, Earl of Beaconsfield,* v and vi (1920).

—— (ed.), *The Letters of Queen Victoria, 2nd ser., 1862–85* (3 vols., 1926–8); *3rd ser., 1886–1901* (3 vols., 1930–2).

Budd, Susan, *Sociologists and Religion* (1973).

—— *Varieties of Unbelief: Atheists and Agnostics in English Society, 1850–1960* (1977).

Bullock, A., *The Life and Times of Ernest Bevin,* i (1960).

Burke, T., *A Catholic History of Liverpool* (Liverpool, 1910).

Burleigh, J. H. S., *A Church History of Scotland* (Edinburgh, 1960).

Burt, T., *Thomas Burt, MP: Pitman and Privy Councillor* (1924).

Bury, C. A., *The Church Association* (1873).

Butler, E. C., *The Life and Times of Bishop Ullathorne* (2 vols., 1926).

—— *The Vatican Council, 1869–1870, Based on Bishop Ullathorne's Letters,* ed. C. H. Butler (1962).

Buxton, S., *A Handbook to the Political Questions of the Day,* 9th edn. (1892).

Caird, D., *Church and State in Wales: A Plain Statement of the Case for Disestablishment* (1912).

Cairns, J., *On the Disestablishment of the Church of Scotland* (Edinburgh, 1872).

Calderwood, H., *Disestablishment and Union of the Presbyterians of Scotland* (Edinburgh, 1889).

Calderwood, W. L., and D. Woodside, *The Life of Henry Calderwood* (1900).

Campbell, J., *F. E. Smith, First Earl of Birkenhead* (1983).

Carlile, J. C., *My Life's Little Day* (1935).

Carpenter, S. C., *Winnington-Ingram: The Biography of A. F. Winnington-Ingram, Bishop of London* (1949).

Carter, T. T., *The Position and Duty of Churchmen at the Present Time,* EC publ. (1877).

—— *The Present Movement a True Phase of Anglo-Catholic Church Principles* (1878).

Carwithen, W. H., *Is Ritualism in the Church of England Popular Among the Masses?* (1894).

Cecil, Lady Gwendolen, *Life of Robert, Marquess of Salisbury* (4 vols., 1921–32).

Cecil of Chelwood, Viscount, *All the Way* (1949).

Chadwick, O., *The Victorian Church*, ii (1970).

—— *Hensley Henson: A Study of Friction Between Church and State* (Oxford, 1983).

Chamberlain, Sir A., *Politics from Inside: An Epistolary Chronicle, 1906–1914* (1936).

Chamberlain, J., *The Education Policy of the Government, From a Nonconformist Point of View* (Birmingham, 1875).

—— *The Radical Platform* (Edinburgh, 1885).

—— *Mr Chamberlain's Speeches*, ed. C. W. Boyd (2 vols., 1914).

—— *A Political Memoir, 1880–1892*, ed. C. H. D. Howard (1953).

Channing, F. A., *Memories of Midland Politics, 1885–1910* (1918).

Charlesworth, A. (ed.), *An Atlas of Rural Protest in Britain, 1548–1900* (1983).

Cheyne, A. C., *The Transforming of the Kirk: Victorian Scotland's Religious Revolution* (Edinburgh, 1983).

Chilston, Viscount, *W. H. Smith* (London, 1965).

Church and State in England: Is Their Union Worth Maintaining?, by an English rector (1879).

Church Association: *Annual Reports*

—— *The Report of the Conference of the Church Association held in Willis's Rooms, London, 26 and 27 Nov. 1867* (1867).

—— *Lectures in St James's Hall, London* (1869).

—— *The Disruption of the Church of England by More Than 9,000 Clergymen who are Helping the Romeward Movement in the National Church* (1900).

—— *Lord Salisbury's Nomination to the Bishopric of Worcester: A Protest Against the Nomination of Canon Gore* (1901).

Church Defence Institution: *Annual Reports* (1868–1921).

—— *List of Associations in Union Throughout the Country* (Westminster, 1872).

—— *Minutes of Proceedings at the Church Defence Meeting at Cheam, Surrey, June 1872* (1872).

—*The Church Defence Handy Volume* (1885).

Church of England Working Men's Society: *Constitution and Rules* (1885).

Church of Scotland: *Report of Meeting of Those who are Opposed to the Disestablishment of the Church of Scotland* (Dundee, 1885).

—— *Mr Gladstone's Position on the Church Question* (Edinburgh, 1890).

—— *To the People of Scotland: Address by Committee on Church Interests* (Edinburgh, 1892).

—— *What Would the Taxpayer Gain by Disestablishment?* (1892).

Church Reform League: *Annual Reports* (from 1901).

Churchill, Lord R., *Speeches of Rt. Hon. Lord Randolph Churchill, MP, 1880–1888*, ed. L. J. Jennings (2 vols., 1889).

Churchill, R. S., *Winston S. Churchill*, ii (1967); and companion vol., pt. 2 (1969).

Churchill, W. S., *Lord Randolph Churchill* (2 vols., 1906).

—— *Winston S. Churchill: His Complete Speeches*, ed. R. R. James (8 vols., New York, 1974).

Clark, H., *Disestablishment Necessary for the Well-being of the Church of England*, English Church Union (1871).

Clarke, P. F., 'British Politics and Blackburn Politics, 1900–1910', *HJ* xii (1969), 307–27.

—— *Lancashire and the New Liberalism* (Cambridge, 1971).

—— 'Electoral Sociology in Modern Britain', *History*, lvii (1972), 31–55.

Clay, W. L. (ed.), *Essays on Church Policy* (1868).

Clifford, J., *The Non-attendance of Professed Christians at Public Worship* (1868).

—— *Romanism Judged and Condemned by Jesus Christ* (1876).

—— *The Renewal of Protestantism* (1895).

—— *Socialism and the Teaching of Christ* (1897).

—— *Jesus Christ and State Churches* (1897).

—— *Clericalism in British Politics: Letters on the Education Bill of 1902* (1902).

Cocks, H. F. Lovell, *The Nonconformist Conscience* (1943).

Cockshut, A. O. J. (ed.), *Religious Controversies of the Nineteenth Century: Selected Documents* (1966).

Colman, H. C., *Jeremiah James Colman: A Memoir* (1905).

Colyer, R. J., 'The Gentry and the County in Nineteenth-century Cardiganshire', *WHR* x. 4 (1981), 497–535.

Conway, K. St J., and J. B. Glasier, *The Religion of Socialism* (Manchester and Glasgow, n.d.).

Cooke, A. B., 'Gladstone's Election for the Leith District of Burghs, July 1886', *SHR* xlix (1970), 172–94.

—— and J. Vincent, *The Governing Passion: Cabinet Government and Party Politics in Britain, 1885–1886* (Brighton, 1974).

Cooney, J., *Scotland and the Papacy* (Edinburgh, 1982).

Cornford, J. P., 'The Transformation of Conservatism in the Late Nineteenth Century', *VS* vii (1963–4), 35–66.

Correspondence on the Burials Bill Between the Lord Archbishop of Canterbury, the Lord Chancellor Selborne, and the Revd F. C. Hingeston-Randolph (1880).

Cowan, C., *Reminiscences* (privately publ. 1878).

Cowen, R., *Disestablishment Necessary in the Interest Both of Spiritual Independence and of the Establishment Principle* (Edinburgh, 1877).

Cox, J., *The English Churches in a Secular Society: Lambeth, 1870–1930* (Oxford, 1982).

Cox, J. T., (ed.), *Practice and Procedure in the Church of Scotland*, 6th edn. (Edinburgh, 1976).

Craig, F. W. S. (ed.), *British General Election Manifestos, 1900–1974* (1975).

Crane, D., *The Life Story of Sir R. W. Perks*, (1909).

Cranswick, J. M., *The Romeward Movement in the Church of England* (Stalybridge, 1873).

Crapster, B. L., 'Scotland and the Conservative Party in 1876', *Journal of Modern History*, xxix (1957), 355–60.

Craton, M., and H. W. McCready, *The Great Liberal Revival, 1903–1906* (1966).

Cregier, D., *Bounder from Wales: Lloyd George's Career before the First World War* (Missouri, 1976).

Creighton, Louise, *Life and Letters of Mandell Creighton* (2 vols., 1913).

Crewe, Marquess of, *Lord Rosebery* (2 vols., 1931).

Cruickshank, Marjorie, *Church and State in English Education, 1870 to the Present Day*, (1964).

Currie, R., *Methodism Divided: A Study in the Sociology of Ecumenicalism* (1968).

—— A. Gilbert, and L. Horsley (eds.), *Churches and Churchgoers: Patterns of Church Growth in the British Isles since 1700* (Oxford, 1977).

Curtis, jun., L. P., *Coercion and Conciliation in Ireland, 1880–1892* (Princeton, 1963).

Dale, A. W. W., *The Life of R. W. Dale of Birmingham* (1898).

Dale, Helen P. (ed.), *The Life and Letters of Thomas Pelham Dale* (2 vols., 1894).

Dale, R. W., *The Politics of Nonconformity* (Manchester, 1871).

—— *The Scotch Education Bill* (Birmingham, 1872).

—— *The Bradlaugh Question* (Birmingham, 1882).

—— *Oath or Affirmation?* (Birmingham, 1883).

Dark, S., *Archbishop Davidson and the Church of England* (1929).

Darlow, T. H., *William Robertson Nicoll: Life and Letters* (1925).

Darragh, J., 'The Irish Catholic Population of Scotland, 1878–1977', *Innes Review*, xxix (1978), 211–47.

Daunton, M. J., *Coal Metropolis: Cardiff, 1870–1914* (Leicester, 1977).

Davey, A., *The British Pro-Boers, 1877–1902* (Tafelberg, SA, 1978).

Davidson, J. P. F., *Confession in the Church of England* ([1898]).

Davidson, R. T., and W. Benham, *The Life of Archibald Campbell Tait, Archbishop of Canterbury* (2 vols., 1891).

Davies, A., R. George, and G. Rupp (eds.), *A History of the Methodist Church in Great Britain*, iii (1983).

Davies, H., *Worship and Theology in England*, iv: *From Newman to Martineau, 1850–1900* (Oxford, 1962).

—— *Worship and Theology in England*, v: *The Ecumenical Century, 1900–1965* (Princeton, 1965).

Davis, R. W., *Political Change and Continuity, 1760–1885: A Buckinghamshire Study* (Newton Abbot, 1972).

Day, G., and M. Fitton, 'Religion and Social Status in Rural Wales', *Sociological Review*, NS xxiii (1975), 867–91.

Dearmer, P., *Christian Socialism Practical Christianity*, Clarion pamphlet no. 19 (1897).

Declaration Against Rigid Uniformity of Individual Worship (1874).

Defence of the National Church: Report of Proceedings in Albert Hall, May 1893 (1893).

Denholm, A., *Lord Ripon, 1827–1909: A Political Biography* (1982).

Denison, G. A., *The Church of England in 1869* (London and Leeds, 1869).

—— *The Persecution of 1874, and the Elementary Education Act of 1870: A Visitation Charge* (1874).

—— *The Position, Ecclesiastical and Civil, 1876* (1876).

—— *The Charge of the Archdeacon of Taunton at his Visitaton, April 1877* (Oxford, 1877).

—— *Notes of my Life, 1805–1878* 3rd edn. (Oxford and London, 1879).

—— *The Burials Act:* Meeting at Leicester, 30 September 1880 (Oxford and London, 1880).

—— *Mr Gladstone, with Appendix Containing the Accumulated Evidence of 55 years* (1885).

—— *Mr Chamberlain, June 1886* (1886).

Denison, J. E., *Notes From My Journal* (1899).

Denison, Louisa E. (ed.), *Fifty Years at East Brent: The Letters of G. A. Denison* (1902).

Denvir, J., *The Irish in Britain From the Earliest Times to the Fall and Death of Parnell* (1892).

Dingle, A. E., *The Campaign for Prohibition in England: The United Kingdom Alliance, 1872–1895* (1980).

Disestablishment: An Appeal to Wesleyan Methodist Ministers, by A Minister (Leeds, 1886).

Disestablishment and Disendowment of the Established Churches of England and Scotland: Statement by Committee of Synod of United Presbyterian Church (1873).

Disestablishment and Free Education: An Address to the Working Men of Scotland, by a Layman (Glasgow, 1885).

Disestablishment: Speeches by the Earl of Minto, etc., Scottish Disestablishment Association (Edinburgh, 1876).

Disestablishment: What Will It Put In My Pocket? (Glasgow, 1885).

Downing, S. E., *The Church in Wales: Disestablishment and Disendowment* (1915).

Drummond, A. L., and J. Bulloch, *The Church in Late Victorian Scotland, 1874–1900* (Edinburgh, 1978).

Drummond, J. S., *Charles A. Berry, DD: A Memoir* (1899).

Dugdale, Blanche, *Arthur James Balfour, First Earl of Balfour* (2 vols, 1936).

Dunbabin, J. P. D., 'The Revolt of the Field: The Agricultural Labourers' Movement in the 1870s', *Past and Present*, xxvi (1963), 68–97.

—— 'Parliamentary Elections in Great Britain, 1868–1900: A Psephological Note', *EHR* lxxxi (1966), 82–99.

—— *et al.*, *Rural Discontent in Nineteenth-century Britain* (1974).

Duncan, W., *The Life of Joseph Cowen* (1904).

Dundee: Elections and Disestablishment Meetings, newspaper extracts (1873–95); Lamb Collection, Dundee Local History Library, 18/6–12, 176/11–15.

Dundee Protestant Association: *Annual Reports and Annual Meetings, etc.* (1879–83); Lamb Collection, 100/4.

Dundee Republican Club; newspaper extracts (1871–5); Lamb Collection, 17/13, 118/36.

Dunlop, A. I., 'The Paths to Reunion in 1929', *Records of Scottish Church History Society*, xx (1980), 163–78.

Dunn, J., *The Honesty of our Position* (1878).

Du Parcq, H., *Life of David Lloyd George* (4 vols., 1912–13).

Durnford, W. (ed.), *Memoir of Colonel the Rt. Hon. William Kenyon-Slaney* (1909).

Dutton, D. J., 'The Unionist Party and Social Policy, 1906–1914', *HJ* xxiv (1981), 871–84.

Edwards, Bishop A. G., *A Handbook on Welsh Church Defence*, 3rd edn. (1895).

Edwards, G., *From Crow-scaring to Westminister: An Autobiography* (1922).

Edwards, J. H., *The Life of David Lloyd George* (5 vols., 1913–24).

Edwards, M. L., *Methodism in England, 1850–1932* (1943).

Elliot, A., *The State and the Church* (1882).

Elliott-Binns, L. E., *Religion in the Victorian Era* (1936).

Ellsworth, Lida E., *Charles Lowder and the Ritualist Movement* (1982).

Elton, Lord, *Life of J. Ramsay MacDonald, 1866–1919* (1939).

English Church Union: *Public Worship Regulation Bill: Report of Speeches at English Church Union, June 1874* (1874).

—— *Tourists' Church Guide* (1924).

Enraght, R. W., *My Prosecution Under the Public Worship Regulation Act* (Birmingham, 1883).

Ensor, R. C. K., *England, 1870–1914* (Oxford, 1936).

Escott, H., *A History of Scottish Congregationalism* (Glasgow, 1960).

Evans, J. H., *Churchman Militant: G. A. Selwyn, Bishop of New Zealand and Lichfield* (1964).

Evans, L. W., 'The Welsh National council for Education, 1903–1906', *WHR* vi. 1 (1972), 49–88.

Evans, W., and W. Claridge, *James Hirst Hollowell and the Movement for Civic Control in Education* (Manchester, 1911).

Facts for Electors: A Handbook for Unionist Committee-men, 8th edn. (Edinburgh, 1905).

Fair, J. D., *British Interparty Conferences: A Study of the Procedure of Conciliation in British Politics, 1867–1921* (Oxford, 1980).

Fairbairn, A. M., *Catholicism, Roman and Anglican* (1899).

Feuchtwanger, E. J., *Disraeli, Democracy, and the Tory Party* (1968).

—— *Gladstone* (1974).

—— *Democracy and Empire: Britain, 1865–1914* (1985).

Field, C. D., 'The Social Structure of English Methodism, Eighteenth to Twentieth Centuries', *British Journal of Sociology*, xxviii (1977), 199–225.

Figgis, J. N., and R. V. Lawrence (eds.), *Lord Acton's Correspondence* (2 vols., 1917).

Finlayson, G. B. A. M., *The Seventh Earl of Shaftesbury, 1801–1885* (1981).

Fitzmaurice, Lord Edmond, *The Life of Granville Leveson Gower, Second Earl Granville* (2 vols., 1905).

Fitzroy, Sir A., *Memoirs*, 5th ed. (2 vols., n.d.).

Fleming, J., *A History of the Church in Scotland, 1875–1929* (Edinburgh, 1933).

Fletcher, R., *The Akenham Burial Case* (1974).

Flindall, R. P. (ed.), *The Church of England, 1815–1948: A Documentary History* (1972).

Foster, R. F., *Lord Randolph Churchill: A Political Life* (1981).

Fowler, Edith H., *The Life of Henry Hartley Fowler, First Viscount Wolverhampton* (1912).

Fowler, W. S., *A Study in Radicalism and Dissent: The Life and Times of Henry Joseph Wilson, 1833–1914* (1961).

Fraser, D., *Urban Politics in Victorian England* (Leicester, 1976).

Fraser, P., 'The Liberal Unionist Alliance: Chamberlain, Hartington, and the Conservatives, 1886–1904', *EHR* lxxvii (1962), 53–78.

—— *Joseph Chamberlain: Radicalism and Empire, 1868–1914* (1966).

Free Church Defence Association: *Tract no. 4: Resolutions Adopted at Free Church Conference at Edinburgh, February 1886* (Edinburgh, 1886).

Freeman, E. A., *Disestablisment and Disendowment* (1874).

Fremantle, W. H., *Lay Power in Parishes: The Most Needed Church Reform* (1869).

Fry, Carol, 'The Demographic Status of Methodism in Scotland', *Journal of the Scottish Branch of the Wesley Historical Society*, xii (1979), 3–8.

Gallagher, T., 'Protestant Extremism in Urban Scotland, 1930–1939: Its Growth and Contraction', *SHR* lxiv (1985), 143–67.

Gammie, A., *Dr John White: A Biography and a Study* (1929).

Garbett, C., *Church and State in England* (1950).

Gardiner, A. G., *The Life of George Cadbury* (1923).

—— *The Life of Sir William Harcourt* (2 vols., 1923).

Garvin, J. L., and J. Amery, *The Life of Joseph Chamberlain* (4 vols., 1933–51).

Gathorne-Hardy, A. E., *Gathorne Hardy, First Earl of Cranbrook* (2 vols., 1910).

Gay, P., *The Geography of Religion in England* (1971).

General Conference of Nonconformists: Authorized Report of Proceedings, 2nd edn. (Manchester and London, 1872).

George, W., *My Brother and I* (1958).

George, W. R. P., *The Making of Lloyd George* (London, 1976).

—— *Lloyd George, Backbencher* (Llandysul, 1983).

Gilbert, A. D., *Religion and Society in Industrial England: Church, Chapel, and Social Change, 1740–1914* (1976).

—— *The Making of Post-Christian Britain* (1980).

Gill, Angela, 'The Leicester School Board, 1871–1903', in B. Simon (ed.), *Education in Leicestershire, 1540–1940* (Leicester, 1968), 156–78.

Gladstone, W. E., *The Vatican Decrees in their Bearing on Civil Allegiance: A Political Expostulation* (1874).

—— *Gleanings of Past Years, 1843–1878* (7 vols., 1879).

—— *Political Speeches in Scotland, November–December 1879* (Edinburgh, 1879).

—— *The Scottish Church Question* (Edinburgh, 1882).

—— *Political Speeches Delivered in November 1885* (Edinburgh, 1885).

—— *The Gladstone Diaries*, vii, viii, ed. H. C. G. Matthew (Oxford, 1982).

Glaser, J. F., 'English Nonconformity and the Decline of Liberalism', *American Historical Review*, lxiii (1957–8), 352–63.

—— 'Parnell's Fall and the Nonconformist Conscience', *Irish Historical Studies*, xii (1960–1), 119–38.

Glover, T. R., *The Free Churches and Reunion* (Cambridge, 1921).

Glover, W. B., *Evangelical Nonconformists and Higher Criticism in the Nineteenth Century* (1954).

Gordon, A., *The Life of Archibald Hamilton Charteris, DD, LL D* (1912).

Gore, Charles (ed.), *Essays in Aid of the Reform of the Church* (1898).

—— *Objections to the Education Bill of 1906* (1906).

Gorst, H. E., *The Fourth Party* (1906).

Gosden, P. H. J. H., *The Development of Educational Policy in England and Wales* (Oxford, 1966).

Goudge, Canon H. L., *The Catholic Party and the Nonconformists* (1919).

Gray, R., *Cardinal Manning* (1985).

Gray, W. F. (ed.), *Non-churchgoing* (Edinburgh, 1911).

Green, E. H. H., 'Radical Conservatism: The Electoral Genesis of Tariff Reform', *HJ* xxviii (1985), 667–92.

Green, Ven. C. A. H., *Disestablishment* (Cardiff, 1911).

—— *Disendowment* (Cardiff, 1911).

—— *The Welsh Church Act, 1914: A Special Charge* (Newport, Mon., 1914).

—— *Disestablishment and Disendowment: The Expansion of the Church in Wales* (1935).

Greenall, R. L., 'Popular Conservatism in Salford, 1868–1886', *Northern History*, ix (1974), 123–38.

Grey, A., and W. H. Fremantle (eds.), *Church Reform* (1888).

Grey, Henry Third Earl, *et al.*, *The Agitation for Disestablishment* (n.p., 1885).

Griffith-Boscawen, Sir A., *Fourteen Years in Parliament* (1907).

—— *Memories* (1925).

Grigg, J., *The Young Lloyd George* (1973).

—— *Lloyd George: The People's Champion, 1902–1911* (1978).

—— *Lloyd George: From Peace to War, 1912–1916* (1985).

Grimthorpe, Lord, *Speech at the Opening of the Protestant Churchmen's Alliance* (1890).

Guedalla, P. (ed.), *The Queen and Mr Gladstone* (2 vols., 1933).

Gutzke, D. W., 'Rosebery and Ireland, 1898–1903: A Reappraisal', *Bulletin of Institute of Historical Research*, liii (1980), 88–98.

Gwynn, S., and Gertrude Tuckwell, *The Life of the Rt. Hon. Sir C. W. Dilke* (2 vols., 1917).

Haldane, R. B., *An Autobiography* (1929).

Halévy, É., *Imperialism and the Rise of Labour*, trans. E. I. Watkin, 2nd edn. (1951).

Halifax, Viscount, *Leo XIII and Anglican Orders* (1912).

Hall, B., 'The Welsh Revival of 1904–1905: A Critique', in G. J. Cuming and D. Baker (eds.), *Studies in Church History*, viii (Cambridge, 1972), 291–301.

Hall, C. Newman, *Autobiography* (1898).

Hamer, D. A. *John Morley: Liberal Intellectual in Politics* (Oxford, 1968).

—— (ed.), *The Radical Programme* (Brighton, 1971).

—— *Liberal Politics in the Age of Gladstone and Rosebery* (Oxford, 1972).

—— *The Politics of Electoral Pressure* (Hassocks, Sussex, 1977).

Hamer, F. E. (ed.), *The Personal Papers of Lord Rendel* (1931).

Hamilton, Mary A., *Arthur Henderson: A Biography* (1938).

Handley, J. E., *The Irish in Scotland*, one-vol. edn. (Glasgow, 1964).

Hanham, H. J., *Elections and Party Management: Politics in the Time of Disraeli and Gladstone* (1959).

Harcourt, Sir W. V., *Lawlessness in the National Church* (1899).

Hardie, F., *The Political Influence of Queen Victoria, 1861–1901*, 2nd edn. (1963).

Hardie, J. Keir, *Can a Man be a Christian on a Pound a Week?* ([1901]).

Hardinge, Sir A., *The Life of Henry H. M. Herbert, Fourth Earl of Carnarvon* (3 vols., 1925).

Hargest, L., 'The Welsh Educational Alliance and the 1870 Elementary Education Act', *WHR* x. 2 (1980), 172–205.

Harrison, Frederic, *Autobiographic Memoirs* (2 vols., 1911).

Harrison, J. F. C. (ed.), *Society and Politics in England, 1780–1960* (New York and London, 1965).

Hastings, A., *A History of English Christianity, 1920–1985* (1986).

Haw, G. (ed.), *Christianity and the Working Classes* (1906).

Headlam, S. D., P. Dearmer, J. Clifford, and J. Woolman *Socialism and Religion* (1908).

Helmstadter, R., 'The Nonconformist Conscience', in P. Marsh (ed.), *The Conscience of the Victorian State* (Syracuse, NY, 1979), 135–72.

Henson, H. Hensley, *The Real Aspect of Disestablishment An Open Letter to Samuel Smith, MP* (1895).

—— *Cui Bono? An Open Letter to Lord Halifax on the Present Crisis in the Church of England* (1898).

—— (ed.), *Church Problems: A View of Anglicanism by Various Authors* (1900).

—— *The Education Act and After: An Appeal to Nonconformists* (1903).

—— *Anglicanism* (1921).

—— *Disestablishment* (1929).

—— *Retrospect of an Unimportant Life* (3 vols., 1942–50).

Herbert, S. H., *Auberon Herbert: Crusader for Liberty* (1943).

Herrick, F. H., 'The Origins of the National Liberal Federation', *Journal of Modern History*, xvii (1945), 116–29.

Hervey, Lord Arthur (Bishop of Bath and Wells), *A Contribution to the Settlement of the Burials Question* (1877).

Heyck, T. W., *The Dimensions of British Radicalism: The Case of Ireland, 1874–1895*, (Urbana, Illinois, 1974).

Highet, J., *The Churches in Scotland Today* (1950).

Hillier, F. W., *Should Christians Support Mr Bradlaugh?* 3rd edn. (1883).

Hird, D., *Jesus the Socialist*, Clarion pamphlet no. 46 (1908).

Hirst, F. W., *Early Life and Letters of John Morley* (2 vols., 1927).

Hobsbawm, E. J., *Primitive Rebels* (Manchester, 1959).

Hodder, E., *The Life and Work of the Seventh Earl of Shaftesbury* (1888).

—— *Life of Samuel Morley*, 5th edn. (1889).

Holland, B., *The Life of Spencer Compton, Eighth Duke of Devonshire* (2 vols., 1911).

Holland, H., *The Opening of the National Graveyards to Nonconformists* (n.d.).

Hollowell, J. Hirst, *National Elementary Education: The New Sectarian Demands* (1888).

—— *The Clerical Attack on National Education* (1896).

—— *What Nonconformists Stand For* (1901).

Holmes, J. D., *More Roman than Rome: English Catholicism in the Nineteenth Century* (1978).

Horton, R. F., *England's Danger*, 7th edn. (1899).

—— *For Conscience Sake* (1904).

—— *The Church of England, Established and Free* (1916).

—— *An Autobiography* (1917).

—— and J. Hocking, *Shall Rome Reconquer England?* (1910).

How, F. D., *Bishop Walsham How: A Memoir* (1898).

—— *Archbishop Maclagan* (1911).

Howard, C. H. D., 'The Parnell Manifesto of 21 November 1885 and the Schools Question', *EHR* lxii (1947), 42–5.

Howarth, H., *Auricular Confession and Particular Absolution: A Letter to his Parishioners* (1874).

Howarth, Janet, 'The Liberal Revival in Northamptonshire, 1880–1895', *HJ* xii (1969), 78–118.

Howell, D. W., *Land and People in Nineteenth-century Wales* (1977).

Howie, R., *The Churches and the Churchless in Scotland* (Glasgow, 1893).

Hughes, Dorothea, *The Life of Hugh Price Hughes* (1905).

Hughes, J. J., *Absolutely Null and Utterly Void: An Account of the Papal Condemnation of Anglican Orders* (1968).

Hughes, T., *James Fraser, Second Bishop of Manchester* (1887).

Hume, A., *Some Account of Recent Nonconformist Attacks Upon the Church of England*, CDI (1873).

Hunter, J., 'The Politics of Highland Land Reform, 1873–1895', *SHR* 53 (1974), 45–68.

Hurst, M. C., *Joseph Chamberlain and West Midland Politics, 1886–1895*, Dugdale Society (Oxford, 1962).

—— 'Joseph Chamberlain, the Conservatives, and the Succession to John Bright, 1886–1889', *HJ* vii (1964), 64–93.

—— *Joseph Chamberlain and Liberal Reunion: The Round Table Conferences of 1887* (1967).

—— 'Liberal versus Liberal: The General Election of 1874 in Bradford and Sheffield', *HJ* xv (1972), 669–713.

—— 'Liberal versus Liberal, 1874: A Rebuttal', *HJ* xvii (1974), 162–4.

Hutchings, W. H., *Life and Letters of T. T. Carter* (1903).

Hutchison, I. G. C., *A Political History of Scotland, 1832–1924: Parties, Elections, and Issues* (Edinburgh, 1986).

Hutton, G. C., *State Churchism in Scotland* (Edinburgh, 1875).

Hyndman, H. M., *The Record of an Adventurous Life* (1911).

Illingworth, A., *Fifty Years of Politics* (Bradford, 1905).

Imperial Protestant Federation: *Report* for 1899–1900 ([1900]).

Independent Labour Party: *Report of Tenth Annual Conference* (1902).

—— The Platform (1901–4).

Ingham, S. M., 'The Disestablishment Movement in England, 1868–1874', *Journal of Religious History*, iii (1964), 38–60.

Inglis, K. S., *Churches and the Working Classes in Victorian England* (1963).

Innes, A. Taylor, *The Scotch Law of Patronage* (Edinburgh, 1875).

—— *Mr Finlay's Bill and the Law of 1843* (Edinburgh, 1886).

—— *Chapters of Reminiscence* (1913).

Iremonger, F. A., *William Temple, Archbishop of Canterbury: His Life and Letters* (1949).

Jagger, P. J. (ed.), *Gladstone: Politics and Religion* (1985).

—— 'The Formation of the Diocese of Newcastle', in W. S. F. Pickering (ed.), *A Social History of the Diocese of Newcastle, 1882–1982* (Stocksfield, 1982).

James, R. R. (ed.), *Winston S. Churchill: His Complete Speeches* (8 vols., New York, 1974).

Jay, R., *Joseph Chamberlain: A Political Study* (Oxford, 1981).

Jeffs, H., *Press, Preachers, and Politicians: Reminiscences, 1874 to 1932* (1933).

Jenkins, H., 'The Irish Dimension of the British Kulturkampf: Vaticanism and Civil Allegiance, 1870–1875', *JEH* xxx (1979), 353–77.

Jenkins, R., *Asquith* (1964).

Jenkins, T. A., 'Gladstone, the Whigs, and the Leadership of the Liberal Party, 1879–1880', *HJ* xxvii (1984), 337–60.

Jennings, L. J. (ed.), *Speeches of the Rt. Hon. Lord Randolph Churchill MP, 1880–1888* (2 vols., 1889).

Johnson, M. D., 'Thomas Gasquoine and the Origins of the Leicester Conference', *Journal of United Reformed Church History Society*, ii (1978–82), 345–53.

Johnson, Nancy E. (ed.), *The Diary of Gathorne Hardy, Later Lord Cranbrook* (Oxford, 1981).

Johnston, C. N., *Handbook of Scottish Church Defence* (London, 1892); 2nd edn. (Edinburgh, 1894).

Johnston, J., *The Ecclesiastical and Religious Statistics of Scotland* (Glasgow, 1874).

Johnston, J. O., *Life and Letters of Henry Parry Liddon* (1904).

Jones, D. K., *The Making of the Education System, 1851–1881* (1977).

Jones, E. R., *The Life and Speeches of Joseph Cowen, MP* (1885).

Jones, J. D., *Three Score Years and Ten* (1940).

Jones, P. d'A., *The Christian Socialist Revival, 1877–1914* (Princeton, 1968).

Jones, R. T., *Congregationalism in England* (1962).

Jones, T., *Lloyd George* (1951).

Jordan, E. K. H., *Free Church Unity: A History of the Free Church Council Movement, 1896–1941* (1956).

Joyce, P., *Work, Society, and Politics: The Culture of the Factory in Later Victorian England* (1982).

Joynson-Hicks, Sir W., *The Prayer Book Crisis* (1928).

Kadish, A., *Apostle Arnold: The Life and Death of Arnold Toynbee* (Durham, North Carolina, 1986).

Kellas, J. G., 'The Liberal Party and the Scottish Church Disestablishment Crisis', *EHR* lxxix (1964), 31–46.

—— 'The Liberal Party in Scotland, 1876–1895', *SHR* xliv (1965), 1–16.

Kennedy, A. L., *Salisbury, 1830–1903: Portrait of a Statesman* (1953).

Kennedy, J., *Unionism and its Last Phase* (Edinburgh, 1873).

Kennedy, J., *Disestablishment and Disendowment of the Established Churches* (Edinburgh, 1873).
—— *Letter to the Members of the Free Church in the Highlands* (Edinburgh, 1876).
—— *The Establishment Principle and the Disestablishment Movement* (Edinburgh, 1878).
—— *A Plea in Self-defence* (Edinburgh, 1878).
—— *The Disestablishment Movement in the Free Church* (Edinburgh, 1882).
Kensit, J. A., *Rome Behind the Great War*, Protestant Truth Society (1918).
Kent, J., 'The Role of Religion in the Cultural Structure of the Later Victorian City', Transactions of the Royal Historical Society, 5th ser. xxiii (1973), 153–73.
—— A Late Nineteenth-century Nonconformist Renaissance', in D. Baker (ed.), *Studies in Church History*, xiv (Oxford, 1977), 351–60.
—— *Holding the Fort: Studies in Victorian Revivalism* (1978).
Kent, W., *John Burns: Labour's Lost Leader* (1950).
Kimberley, First Earl of, *A Journal of Events during the Gladstone Ministry, 1868–1874*, ed. Ethel Drus, Camden Miscellany, xxi (1958).
Knox, E. A., *Reminiscences of an Octogenarian, 1847–1934* ([1935]).
Knox, R. B., 'The Relationship Between English and Scottish Presbyterianism, 1836–1876', *Records of Scottish Church History Society*, xxi. 1 (1981), 43–66.
Koss, S., *Nonconformity in Modern British Politics* (1975).
Kruppa, Patricia S., *Charles Haddon Spurgeon: A Preacher's Progress* (New York and London, 1982).
Lambert, W. R., 'The Welsh Sunday Closing Act, 1881', *WHR* vi. 2 (1972), 161–89.
Lancelot, J. B., *Francis James Chavasse* (Oxford, 1929).
Landels, W., *Ritualism* (1873).
Lang, Cosmo G., *The Principles of Religious Education* (1906).
Lansbury, G., *My Life* (1928).
Larkin, E., *The Roman Catholic Church and the Creation of the Modern Irish State, 1878–1886* (Philadelphia and Dublin, 1975).
—— *The Roman Catholic Church and the Plan of Campaign, 1886–1888* (Cork, 1978).
—— *The Roman Catholic Church and the Fall of Parnell, 1888–1891* (Liverpool, 1979).
Lathbury, D. C., *Dean Church* (1905).
—— (ed.), *Correspondence on Church and Religion of William Ewart Gladstone* (2 vols., 1910).
Law, H. W. and I., *The Book of the Beresford Hopes* (1925).
Laymen's League: *The Layman's League and the General Election* (Edinburgh, 1892).
Lenman, B., and J. Stocks, 'The Beginnings of State Education in Scotland, 1872–1885', *Scottish Educational Studies*, iv (1972), 93–106.
Leslie, S. (ed.), *Letters of Herbert, Cardinal Vaughan, to Lady Herbert of Lea, 1867 to 1903* (1942).
Letters from Wales repub. from *The Times* (1889).
Liberation Society: *The Property and Revenues of the English Church Establishment* (1877).
—— *The Case for Disestablishment* (1884).
—— *The Three Disestablishment Motions* (1885).
—— *Hints to Electors in Regard to Ecclesiastical questions* (n.d.).
—— *The General Election* (1885).
—— *Some Facts About the Scottish Establishment* (n.d.).
—— *A Jubilee Retrospect* (1894).
—— *News and Notes*, new ser. (from 1945).
—— (Scottish Council), *Fourth Annual Report* (1881).

—— —— *Scheme of Disestablishment and Disendowment of the State-Church of Scotland* ([1881]).

—— —— *The Church of Scotland, its Position and Work: A Rejoinder* (Edinburgh, 1882).

Liddon, H. P., *The Purchas Judgement* (1871).

—— *The Life of Edward Bouverie Pusey*, ed. J. O. Johnston and R. J. Wilson (4 vols., 1893–7).

Lidgett, J. Scott, *My Guided Life* (1936).

Lloyd, R., *The Church of England, 1900–1965* (1966).

Lloyd, T., *The General Election of 1880* (Oxford, 1968).

Loane, M. L., *John Charles Ryle, 1816–1900* (1953).

Lochhead, Marion, *Episcopal Scotland in the Nineteenth Century* (1966).

Lochore, J., *Union of Scots Presbyterian Churches* (Glasgow, 1890).

Lockhart, J. G., *Viscount Halifax* (2 vols., 1935–6).

London Working-men's Council for Church Defence: *Report for 1875* (1876).

—— *Addresses of the London Working-men's Council to their Brethren of Great Britain* (n.d.).

Lord Salisbury's Nomination to the Bishopric of Worcester ([1901]).

Lorne, Marquess of, *Disestablishment* (1885).

Lubenow, W. C., 'Irish Home Rule and the Great Separation in the Liberal Party in 1886: The Dimensions of Parliamentary Liberalism', *VS* xxvi (1982–3), 161–80.

—— 'Irish Home Rule and the Social Basis of the Great Separation in the Liberal Party in 1886', *HJ* xxviii (1985), 125–42.

Lunn, Sir H. S., *Chapters From My Life* (1918).

Lyall, F., *Of Presbyters and Kings: Church and State in the Law of Scotland* (Aberdeen, 1980).

Lyons, F. S. L., *The Irish Parliamentary Party, 1890–1910*, 1st edn. (1951); new edn. (Westport, Conn., 1975).

—— *The Fall of Parnell, 1890–1891* (1960).

—— *John Dillon: A Biography* (1968).

—— *Ireland since the Famine* (1971).

—— *Charles Stewart Parnell* (1977).

McCaffrey, J. F., 'The Origins of Liberal Unionism in the West of Scotland', *SHR* l (1971), 47–71.

—— 'Politics and the Catholic Community since 1878', *Innes Review*, xxix (1978), 140–55.

—— 'Roman Catholics in Scotland in the Nineteenth and Twentieth Centuries', *Records of Scottish Church History Society*, xxi (1981), 43–66.

McCarthy, M. J. F., *Church and State in England and Wales, 1829–1906* (Dublin and London, 1906).

—— *The Nonconformist Treason, or the Sale of the Emerald Isle* (Edinburgh, 1912).

—— *Home Rule and Protestantism* (Glasgow, 1910).

McClelland, V. A., *Cardinal Manning: His Public Life and Influence, 1865–1892* (Oxford, 1962).

—— 'The Protestant Alliance and Roman Catholic Schools, 1872–1874', *VS* viii (1964–5), 173–82.

—— *English Roman Catholics and Higher Education, 1830–1903* (Oxford, 1973).

Maccoby, S., *English Radicalism, 1853–1886* (1938).

—— *English Radicalism, 1886–1914* (1953).

MacColl, Malcolm, *Lawlessness, Sacerdotalism, and Ritualism*, 3rd Edn. (1875).

—— *Reasons for Home Rule* (1886).

MacColl, Malcolm, *The Reformation Settlement Examined in the Light of History and Law* (1899).
—— *The Education Question and the Liberal Party* (1902).
MacCormack, A., *Cardinal Vaughan* (1966).
McCready, H. W., 'Home Rule and the Liberal Party, 1899–1906', *Irish Historical Studies*, xiii (1962–3), 316–48.
MacDonnell, J. C., *The Life and Correspondence of William Connor Magee* (2 vols., 1896).
MacDougall, I. (ed.), *Essays in Scottish Labour History* (Edinburgh, 1978).
Macdougall, N. (ed.), *Church, Politics and Society in Scotland, 1408–1929* (Edinburgh, 1983).
McDowell, R. B., *The Church of Ireland, 1869–1969* (1975).
MacEwen, A. R., *The Life and Letters of John Cairns, DD, LL D* (1895).
Macfadyen, D., *Alexander Mackennall, DD: Life and Letters* (1905).
Macfie, R. A., *The Scotch Church Question*, 2nd edn. (Edinburgh, 1896).
McGee, Susan, 'Carfin and the Roman Catholic Relief Act of 1926', *Innes Review*, xvi (1965), 56–78.
Machin, G. I. T., *Politics and the Churches in Great Britain, 1832 to 1868* (Oxford, 1977).
—— 'The Last Victorian Anti-Ritualist Campaign, 1895–1906', *VS* xxv (1981–2), 277–302.
—— 'Voluntaryism and Reunion, 1874–1929', in N. Macdougall (ed.), *Church, Politics, and Society in Scotland, 1408–1929* (Edinburgh, 1983), 221–38.
—— 'The Liberal Government and the Eucharistic Procession of 1908', *JEH* xxxiv (1983), 559–83.
Macintyre, A., *Secularization and Moral Change* (Oxford, 1967).
Mackay, R. F., *Arthur James Balfour: Intellectual Statesman* (Oxford, 1985).
McKenna, S., *Reginald McKenna* (1948).
Mackie, J. B., *The Life and Work of Duncan McLaren* (2 vols., 1888).
Mackintosh, A., *Joseph Chamberlain on Both Sides: A Book of Contrasts* (1905).
—— *Joseph Chamberlain: An Honest Biography* (1906).
Mackintosh, W. H., *Disestablishment and Liberation* (1972).
Mackonochie, A. H., *First Principles versus Erastianism* (1876).
Macleod, D., *Memoir of Norman Macleod, DD* (2 vols., 1876).
Macleod, H. *Class and Religion in the Late Victorian City* (1974).
Macphail, I. M. M., 'The Highland Elections of 1884–1886', *Transactions of the Gaelic Society of Inverness*, l (1976–8), 368–402.
McRoberts, D., 'The Restoration of a Scottish Catholic Hierarchy in 1878', *Innes Review*, xxix (1978), 3–29.
—— (ed.), *Modern Scottish Catholicism, 1878–1978* (Glasgow, 1979).
Mactavish, J., *Address to Free Church Members* (Inverness, 1882).
Maehl, W. H., 'Gladstone, the Liberals, and the Election of 1874', *Bulletin of the Institute of Historical Research*, xxxvi (1963), 53–69.
Magee, W. C., *The Danger and Evils of Disestablishment, and the Duty of Churchmen at the Present Crisis*, CDI (1885).
Magnus, P., *Gladstone* (1954).
Mair, W., *The Scottish Churches: The Hope of Union* (Edinburgh, 1909).
—— *The Scottish Churches, June 1918* (Edinburgh, 1918).
Mallet, Sir C., *Herbert Gladstone: A Memoir* (1932).
Mallock, W. H., and Lady Guendolen Ramsden (eds.), *Letters, Remains, and Memoirs of Edward Adolphus Seymour, Twelfth Duke of Somerset* (1893).
Mann, T., *A Socialist's View of Religion and the Churches*, Clarion pamphlet no. 10 (1896).

Manning, B. L., *The Protestant Dissenting Deputies* (Cambridge, 1952).

Manning, H. E., *The Vatican Decrees in their Bearing on Civil Allegiance* (1875).

—— *Is the Education Act of 1870 A Just Law?* ([1882]).

—— *How Shall Catholics Vote at the Coming Parliamentary Election?* (1885).

Marchant, Sir James, *Dr John Clifford, CH: Life, Letters, and Reminiscences* (1924).

Marsh, P. T., *The Victorian Church in Decline: Archbishop Tait and the Church of England, 1868–1882* (1969).

—— *The Discipline of Popular Government: Lord Salisbury's Domestic Statecraft, 1881–1902* (Hassocks, Sussex, 1978).

—— (ed.), *The Conscience of the Victorian State* (Syracuse, NY, 1979).

Martin, D., *A Sociology of English Religion* (1967).

Marx, K., *The First International and After: Political Writings,* iii, ed. D. Fernbach (Harmondsworth, 1974).

Masterman, N., *The Forerunner: The Dilemmas of Tom Ellis, 1859–1899* (Llandybie, 1972).

Matthew, H. C. G., *The Liberal Imperialists* (Oxford, 1973).

—— 'Gladstone, Vaticanism, and the Question of the East', in D. Baker (ed.), *Studies in Church History,* xv (Oxford, 1978), 417–42.

—— (ed.), *The Gladstone Diaries,* vi (Oxford, 1978); vii, viii (Oxford, 1982); ix (Oxford, 1986).

—— *Gladstone, 1809–1874* (Oxford, 1986).

Maughan, H. H., *Some Brighton Churches* (1922).

Maxwell, Sir Herbert, *Life and Times of the Rt. Hon. W. H. Smith, MP* (2 vols., Edinburgh, 1893).

—— *The Life and Letters of George William Frederick, Fourth Earl of Clarendon* (2 vols., 1913).

Mayers, M. J., *Establishments and Voluntaryism Contrasted, in Answer to Mr Miall* (1871).

Mayor, S., *The Churches and the Labour Movement* (1967).

Meacham, S., 'The Church in the Victorian City', *VS* xi (1967–8), 359–78.

—— *Lord Bishop: The Life of Samuel Wilberforce* (Cambridge, Mass., 1970).

—— *A Life Apart: The English Working Class, 1890–1914* (1977).

Melly, G., *Recollections of Sixty Years 1833–1893* (Coventry, 1893).

Mews, S. P., 'Neo-orthodoxy, Liberalism, and War: Karl Barth, P. T. Forsyth, and John Oman, 1914–1918', in D. Baker (ed.), *Studies in Church History,* xiv (Oxford, 1977), 361–75.

Meyer, F. B., *The Religious Basis of the Free Church Position* (1903).

Miall, A., *The Life of Edward Miall* (1884).

Miall, C. S., *Henry Richard, MP* (1889).

Miall, E. *et al., Religious Equality,* Manchester Nonconformist Association (1873).

Miller, D. W., *Church, State, and Nation in Ireland, 1898–1921* (Dublin, 1973).

Mills, W. H., *Grey Pastures* (1924).

Minutes of Proceedings at the Church Defence Meeting at Cheam, Surrey, 29 June 1872 (1872).

Moberley, R. C., *Is the Independence of Church Courts Really Impossible?* (Oxford, 1886).

Montagu, Lord Robert, *Register, Register, Register! An Appeal to Catholics* (1873).

—— *Home Rule—Rome Rule* (1886).

Moore, J. R., *The Post-Darwinian Controversies, 1870–1900* (Cambridge, 1979).

Moore, R. S., *Pitmen, Preachers, and Politics: The Effects of Methodism in a Durham Mining Community* (Cambridge, 1974).

Morgan, Sir G. Osborne, *The Church of England and the People of Wales*, 2nd edn. (1895).

Morgan, Kenneth O., *Wales in British Politics, 1868–1922*, 2nd edn. (Cardiff, 1970); 3rd edn. (Cardiff, 1980).

—— (ed.), *Lloyd George Family Letters, 1885–1936* (Cardiff and London, 1973).

—— *Consensus and Disunity: The Lloyd George Coalition Government, 1918–1922* (Oxford, 1979).

—— *Rebirth of a Nation: Wales, 1880–1980* (Oxford, 1981).

Morley, J., *The Life of W. E. Gladstone* (3 vols. 1903).

Mor-O'Brien, A., 'The Merthyr Boroughs Election, November 1915', *WHR* xii (1984–5), 538–66.

Morris, R., 'The Tithe War', *Denbighshire Historical Society Transactions*, xxxii (1983), 51–97.

Morrish, P. S., 'The Struggle to Create an Anglican Diocese of Birmingham', *JEH* xxxi (1980), 59–88.

—— 'Church Attendance at Ripon: A Contemporary Assessment', *Northern History*, xx (1984), 217–23.

Mr Gladstone's Views on the Scottish Church Question in his own Words (Edinburgh, 1882).

Mudie-Smith, R. (ed.), *The Religious Life of London* (1904).

Muir, A., *John White, CH* (1958).

Munson, J. E. B., 'The Oxford Movement by the End of the Nineteenth Century: The Anglo-Catholic Clergy', *Church History*, xliv (1975), 382–95.

—— 'The London School Board Election of 1894', *British Journal of Educational Studies*, xxiii (1975), 7–23.

—— 'The Education of Baptist Ministers, 1870–1900', *Baptist Quarterly*, xxvi (1976), 320–7.

—— 'The Unionist Coalition and Education, 1895–1902', *HJ* xx (1977), 607–45.

Murphy, J., *The Religious Problem in English Education: The Crucial Experiment* (Liverpool, 1959).

—— *Church, State, and Schools in Britain, 1800–1970* (1971).

National Church League: *Reports* (from 1906).

National Church Union: *Record of Proceedings* (from 1898).

National Free Church Council: *Proceedings of Councils* (from 1896).

National Homage to Christ not Disestablishment, by a Free Church elder (Glasgow, 1875).

National Liberal Federation: *Proceedings Attending the Formation of the National Federation of Liberal Associations* (Birmingham, 1877).

—— *Proceedings in Connection with Annual Meetings* (from 1879).

Nelmes, G. V., 'Stuart Rendel and Welsh Liberal Political Organization in the Late Nineteenth Century', *WHR* ix (1979), 468–85.

Newbold, J. A., *The Revd Hugh Price Hughes and Wesleyan Methodist Educational Policy*, Manchester Tracts on Education, no. 6 (1889).

—— *The Nonconformist Conscience a Persecuting Force* (Manchester, 1908).

Newman, J. H., *A Letter to the Duke of Norfolk on the Occasion of Mr Gladstone's Recent Expostulation* (1875).

—— *The Letters and Diaries of John Henry Newman*, ed. C. S. Dessain and T. Gornall, xxv–xxxi (Oxford, 1973–7).

Nicholls, D. (ed.), *Church and State in Britain since 1820* (1967).

Nicoll, W. Robertson (ed.), *Letters of Principal James Denney* (1920).

Nonconformity and Politics, by a Nonconformist Minister (1909).

Norman, E. R., *The Catholic Church and Ireland in the Age of Rebellion, 1859–1873* (1965).

—— (ed.), *Anti-Catholicism in Victorian England* (1968).

—— *Church and Society in England, 1770–1970* (Oxford, 1976).

—— *The English Catholic Church in the Nineteenth Century* (Oxford, 1984).

Nossiter, T. J., *Influence, Opinion, and Political Idioms in Reformed England: Case Studies from the North-East, 1832–1874* (Brighton, 1975).

Nuttall, G. F., and O. Chadwick (eds.), *From Uniformity to Unity; 1662–1962* (1962).

O'Brien, C. C., *Parnell and his Party, 1880–1890* (Oxford, 1957).

O'Connor, T. P., *Memoirs of an Old Parliamentarian* (2 vols., 1929).

O'Day, A., *The English Face of Irish Nationalism, 1880–1886* (Dublin, 1977).

—— (ed.), *The Edwardian Age: Conflict and Stability* (1979).

Ogilvy, D., *The Present Importance of Free Church Principles* (Edinburgh, 1875).

Oldmeadow, E., *Francis, Cardinal Bourne* (2 vols., 1940–4).

Oliphant, M., *A Memoir of the Life of John Tulloch* (Edinburgh, 1888).

Oliver, A., *Life of George Clark Hutton* (Paisley, 1910).

Ollivant, A., *The Want of Unity in the Church and the Church's Teaching as to Confession* (Cardiff, 1873).

Olney, R. J., *Lincolnshire Politics, 1832–1885* (1973).

Omond, G. W. T., *The Lord Advocates of Scotland*, 2nd ser. 1834–80 (1914).

Ormsby-Gore, W. G. A., *Welsh Disestablishment and Disendowment* (1912).

Orr, R. L., *The Free Church of Scotland Appeals* (1904).

Ostrogorski, M., *Democracy and the Organization of Political Parties*, trans. F. Clarke (2 vols., 1902).

Our Ecclesiastical Difficulties: or, the Alternative of Disestablishment (1876).

Overton, J. H. and Elizabeth Wordsworth *Christopher Wordsworth, Bishop of Lincoln* (1888).

Owen, Bishop J., *The Acceptance of the Welsh Church Temporalities Act* (1919).

Owen, Eluned, *The Early Life of Bishop Owen* (Llandysul, 1958).

—— *The Later Life of Bishop Owen* (Llandysul, 1961).

Oxford and Asquith, First Earl of, *Fifty Years of Parliament* (2 vols., 1926).

Parke, Ernest, *What Shall I Do With My Vote?* (1885).

Parry, J. P., 'Religion and the Collapse of Gladstone's First Government, 1870–1874', *HJ* xxv (1982), 71–101.

—— *Democracy and Religion: Gladstone and the Liberal Party, 1867–1875* (Cambridge, 1986).

Paton, J. L., *John Brown Paton: A Biography* (1914).

Peel, A., *The Free Churches, 1903–1926* (1927).

—— *These Hundred Years: A History of the Congregational Union of England and Wales, 1831–1931* (1931).

—— and J. A. R. Marriott, *Robert Forman Horton* (1937).

Pelling, H., *Origins of the Labour Party, 1880–1900* (Oxford, 1966).

—— *Social Geography of British Elections, 1885–1910* (1967).

—— *Popular Politics and Society in Late Victorian Britain* (1968).

—— *Winston Churchill* (1974).

Perks, R. W., *The Growth of Monastic and Conventual Establishments in Great Britain*, Free Church Council (1905).

—— *The Reunion of British Methodism* (1920).

Petrie, Sir Charles, *The Life and Letters of the Rt. Hon. Sir Austen Chamberlain* (2 vols., 1939–40).

Pickering, W. S. F. (ed.), *A Social History of the Diocese of Newcastle, 1882–1982* (Stocksfield, 1981).

Picton, J. A., *Memorials of Liverpool, Historical and Topographical* (2 vols., Liverpool, 1873).

Popery in the Church of England: A Joint Letter by Five Wesleyan Ministers (1873).

Porritt, A., *The Best I Remember* (1922).

—— *More and More of Memories* (1947).

Potter, S. G., *Of What Religion is Mr Gladstone?* (1873).

'Presbyter Protestans', *The English Church Union Proved From its Official Publications and Other Documents to be a Romanizing Confederacy* (London, 1877).

Prestige, G. L., *The Life of Charles Gore* (1935).

Preston, W., *Seventy-five Objections to the Union of Church and State Analysed* (1874).

Primitive Methodist Conference Minutes (1913).

Proceedings Attending the Formation of the National Federation of Liberal Associations (Birmingham, 1877).

Protestant Alliance: *Verbatim Report of Speeches Delivered at the Great Demonstration, 3 May 1898* (1898).

Protestant Electoral Union: *circular*, i–iv (1866–70).

Protestant Reformation Society: *Annual Reports.*

—— *The Sovereign's Accession Declaration: Resolutions Adopted by the Executive Committee, May 1910* (1910).

Pugh, D. R., 'The 1902 Education Act: The Search for a Compromise', *British Journal of Educational Studies*, xvi (1968), 164–78.

Pusey, E. B., *The Proposed Ecclesiastical Legislation: Three Letters to The Times* (Oxford, 1874).

—— *Public Worship Regulation Bill: A Speech at a Meeting of English Church Union* (1874).

—— *Unlaw in Judgments of the Judicial Committee, and its Remedies: A Letter to the Revd H. P. Liddon, DD* (Oxford, 1881).

Quinault, R. E., 'The Fourth Party and the Conservative Opposition to Bradlaugh, 1880–1888', *EHR* xci (1976), 315–40.

—— 'John Bright and Joseph Chamberlain', *HJ* xxviii (1985), 623–46.

Rainy, R., *Three Lectures on the Church of Scotland* (Edinburgh, 1872).

—— *Disestablishment in Scotland Considered from the Point of View of the Free Church* (Edinburgh, 1874).

—— et al., *Church and State Chiefly in Relation to Scotland* (Edinburgh, 1878).

—— *Disestablishment in Scotland Urgent*, Scottish Disestablishment Association Occasional Papers, no. 1, (n.d.).

Ramm, Agatha (ed.), *The Political Correspondence of Mr Gladstone and Lord Granville, 1876–1886* (2 vols., Oxford, 1962).

—— 'Gladstone's Religion', *HJ* xxviii (1985), 327–41.

Ramsden, J., *The Age of Balfour and Baldwin, 1902–1940* (1978).

Rattenbury, J. E., *Six Sermons on Social Subjects* (1908).

Ravenstein, E. G., *Denominational Statistics of England and Wales* (1870).

Read, D., *The English Provinces, c.1760–1960: A Study in Influence* (1964).

Reardon, B. M. G., *Religious Thought in the Victorian Age: A Survey from Coleridge to Gore* (1980).

Rees, D. B., *Chapels in the Valley: A Study in the Sociology of Welsh Nonconformity* (Upton, Wirral, 1975).

Reid, T. W., *Life of the Rt. Hon. W. E. Forster*, 3rd edn. (2 vols. in one, Bath, 1888).

Reith, G. M., *Reminiscences of the United Free Church General Assembly, 1900–29* (Edinburgh, 1933).

Religious Instruction in Board Schools: Report of a Debate in the Birmingham School Board, 1872 (Birmingham, 1872).

Rempel, Richard A., *Unionists Divided: Arthur Balfour, Joseph Chamberlain, and the Unionist Free Traders* (Newton Abbot, 1972).

—— 'Lord Hugh Cecil's Parliamentary Career, 1900–1914: Promise Unfulfilled', *Journal of British Studies*, xi. 2 (May, 1972), 104–30.

Report of Speeches Delivered at Bangor, May 1894, Reprinted From Carnarvon and Denbigh Herald (Caernarfon, 1894).

Reynolds, M., *Martyr of Ritualism: Father Mackonochie of St Alban's, Holborn* (1965).

Richard, H., and J. Carvell Williams, *Disestablishment* (1885).

Richards, N. J., 'Religious Controversy and the School Boards, 1870–1902', *British Journal of Educational Studies*, xviii (1970), 180–96.

—— 'The Education Bill of 1906 and the Decline of Political Nonconformity', *JEH* xxiii (1972), 49–63.

Richter, D., 'The Welsh Police, the Home Office, and the Welsh Tithe War of 1886–1891', *WHR* xii. 1 (1984), 50–75.

Riddell, Lord, *More Pages From My Diary, 1908–1914* (1934).

Rigg, J. H., *Oxford High Anglicanism and its Chief Leaders*, 2nd edn. (1899).

Robb, Janet H., *The Primrose League, 1883–1906* (New York, 1942).

Robbins, K., *Sir Edward Grey* (1971).

—— *John Bright* (1979).

—— 'The Spiritual Pilgrimage of the Revd R. J. Campbell', *JEH* xxx (1979), 261–76.

Roberts, A. W., 'Leeds Liberalism and Late Victorian Politics', *Northern History*, v (1970), 131–56.

Roberts, G. B., *The History of the English Church Union, 1859–1894* (1895).

Roberts, M. J. D., 'Private Patronage and the Church of England, 1800–1900', *JEH* xxxii (1981), 199–223.

—— 'Pressure-group Politics and the Church of England: The Church Defence Institution, 1859–1896', *JEH* xxxv (1984), 560–82.

Roberts, R. E., *H. R. L. Sheppard: Life and Letters* (1942).

Robertson W., *The Life and Letters of the Rt. Hon. John Bright* (3 vols., 1884).

Robson, R. (ed.), *Ideas and Institutions of Victorial Britain* (1967).

Rogers, J. Guinness, *The Ritualistic Movement in the Church of England, a Reason for Disestablishment* (1869).

—— *Why Ought Not the State to Give Religious Education?* (1872).

—— *The Bennett Judgement and Recent Episcopal Charges* (Manchester, 1873).

—— *Which is Right, the Church of England or the Liberation Society?* (1878).

—— *The Ulster Problem* (1886).

—— *An Autobiography* (1903).

Rogerson, J., *Old Testament Criticism in the Nineteenth Century* (1984).

Rose, K., *The Later Cecils* (1975).

Rossi, John P., 'Lord Ripon's Resumption of Political Activity, 1878–1880', *Recusant History*, xi (1971–2), 61–74.
—— 'Home Rule and the Liverpool By-election of 1880', *Irish Historical Studies*, xix (1974–5), 156–68.
—— 'English Catholics, the Liberal Party, and the General Election of 1880', *Catholic Historical Review*, lxiii (1977), 411–27.
—— *The Transformation of the British Liberal Party, 1874–1880* (Philadelphia, 1978).
Rowell, G., *Hell and the Victorians* (Oxford, 1974).
—— *The Vision Glorious: Themes and Personalities of the Catholic Revival in Anglicanism* (Oxford, 1983).
Rowland, P., *The Last Liberal Governments* (2 vols., 1968–71).
—— *Lloyd George* (1975).
Roxburgh, J. M., *The School Board of Glasgow, 1873–1919* (1971).
Royle, E., *Radicals, Secularists, and Republicans: Popular Free Thought in Britain, 1866–1915* (Manchester, 1980).
Rupp, G., R. Davies and A. R. George (eds.), *A History of the Methodist Church in Great Britain*, ii (1978).
Russell, A. K., *Liberal Landslide: The General Election of 1906* (Newton Abbot, 1973).
Russell, G. W. E. (ed.), *Letters of Matthew Arnold* (2 vols., 1895).
—— (ed.), *Malcolm MacColl: Memoirs and Correspondence* (1914).
—— *Arthur Stanton: A Memoir* (1919).
Rylands, L. G., *Correspondence and Speeches of Mr Peter Rylands, MP* (2 vols., Manchester and London, 1890).
Ryle, J. C., *Yes or No! Is the Union of Church and State Worth Preserving?* CDU (1871).
—— *Disestablishment: What Would Come of It?* (1874).
—— *Shall We Surrender?* (1876).
—— *Church and State* (1877).
—— *Where Does This Road Lead to? A Question about Ritualism* (1879).
—— *Churchmen and Dissenters* (1880).
—— *Principles for Churchmen*, 2nd edn. (1884).
—— *Disestablishment Papers* (1885).
Sacks, B., *The Religious Issue in the State Schools of England and Wales, 1902–1914* (Albuquerque, New Mexico, 1961).
Salvidge, S., *Salvidge of Liverpool: Behind the Political Scene, 1890–1928* (1934).
Sandford, E. G. (ed.), *Memoirs of Archbishop Temple* (2 vols., 1906).
—— *The Exeter Episcopate of Archbishop Temple, 1869–1885* (1907).
Sands, Lord, *Dr Archibald Scott and His Times, 1837–1908* (Edinburgh and London, 1919).
Savage, D. C., 'Scottish Politics, 1885–1886', *SHR* xl (1961), 118–35.
Schreuder, D., 'Gladstone and the Conscience of the State', in P. Marsh (ed.), *The Conscience of the Victorian State* (Syracuse, NY, 1979), 73–134.
Scotland, N., *Methodism and the Revolt of the Field: A Study of the Methodist Contribution to Agricultural Trade Unionism in East Anglia, 1872–1896* (Gloucester, 1981).
Scottish Disestablishment Association: Tract no. 1, *The New Patronage Act and the Scottish Churches* ([1874]).
Scottish Presbyterian Union Association: *Report of Proceedings During First Session, June 1885* (1886).
Selbie, W. B., *The Life of Andrew Martin Fairbairn* (1914).
—— *The Life of Charles Silvester Horne* (1920).

Selborne, First Earl of, *A Defence of the Church of England Against Disestablishment*, (1886).
—— *Memorials Personal and Political* (2 vols., 1898).
Selby, D. E., 'Henry Edward Manning and the Education Bill of 1870', *British Journal of Educational Studies*, xviii (1970), 197–212.
Sellers, I., *Nineteenth-century Nonconformity* (1977).
—— 'A New Town Story: The United Reformed Churches in the Warrington-Runcorn Urban Complex', *Journal of the United Reformed Church History Society*, iii. 7 (1985), 290–307.
Shakespeare, J. H., *The Churches at the Crossroads: A Study in Church Unity* (1918).
Shannon, R. T., *Gladstone and the Bulgarian Agitation, 1876*, 1st edn. (London, 1963); 2nd edn. (Hassocks, Sussex, 1975).
Shaw, G. B. (ed.), *Fabian Essays in Socialism* (1889).
Shaw, R. D., *The True Meaning of Disestablishment* (Edinburgh, 1875).
Shaw, T., *The Church Difficulty: A Way Out*, 2nd edn. (Edinburgh, 1904).
Sheehy-Skeffington, F., *Michael Davitt* (1967).
Simon, A., 'Church Disestablishment as a Factor in the General Election of 1885', *HJ* xviii (1975), 791–820.
Simon, B., *Education and the Labour Movement, 1870–1920* (1965).
—— (ed.), *Education in Leicestershire, 1540–1940* (Leicester, 1968).
Simpson, P. Carnegie, *The Life of Principal Rainy* (2 vols., 1909).
Sjölinder, R., *Presbyterian Reunion in Scotland, 1907–1921* (Edinburgh, 1962).
Skeats, H. S., and C. S. Miall, *History of the Free Churches of England, 1688–1891* (1894).
Smith, B. A., *Dean Church* (1958).
Smith, S., *The Claims of Rome* (1896).
—— *Ritualism in the Church of England in 1900* (1901).
—— *My Life Work* (1902).
—— *The Scotch Church Crisis: Articles and Letters to the Press* ([1904]).
Smith, T., *Memoirs of James Begg, DD* (2 vols., Edinburgh, 1885–8).
Smout, T. C., *A Century of the Scottish People, 1830–1950* (1986).
Snead-Cox, J. G., *The Life of Cardinal Vaughan* (2 vols., 1910).
Snell, Lord, *Men, Movements, and Myself*, 2nd edn. (1938).
Snowden, Viscount, *An Autobiography* (2 vols., London, 1934).
Sommer, D., *Haldane of Cloan: His Life and Times, 1856–1928* (1960).
Southgate, D., *The Passing of the Whigs, 1832–1886* (1962).
—— (ed.), *The Conservative Leadership, 1832–1932* (1974).
Spender, J. A., *The Life of Sir Henry Campbell-Bannerman* (2 vols., 1923).
—— *Life, Journalism, and Politics* (2 vols., 1927).
—— and C. Asquith, *The Life of Herbert Henry Asquith* (2 vols., 1932).
Stansky, P., *Ambitions and Strategies: The Struggle for the Leadership of the Liberal Party in the 1890s* (Oxford, 1964).
Stead, Estelle W., *My Father: Personal and Spiritual Reminiscences of W. T. Stead* (1913).
Stead, W. T., *Blastus, the King's Chamberlain: A Political Romance* (1898).
—— *Are There Any Free Churches? An Examination of the Strange True Story of the Free Church of Scotland in the Light of the Recent Decision of the House of Lords* (1904).
—— *The Revival of 1905* (1905).
Stephen, M. D., 'Gladstone and the Composition of the Final Court in Ecclesiastical Causes, 1850–1873', *HJ* ix (1966), 191–200.
Stephenson, Gwendolen, *Edward Stuart Talbot, 1844–1934* (1936).

Stevens, R., 'The Final Appeal: Reform of the House of Lords and Privy Council, 1867–1876', *Law Quarterly Review*, lxxx(1964), 343–69.

Stewart, A., and J. K. Cameron, *The Free Church of Scotland, 1843–1910: A Vindication* (Edinburgh and Glasgow, [1910]).

Stirling, C., *The Decline of England: An Appeal to the Protestants of the Empire* (1897).

Stoddart, Jane T., *William Robertson Nicoll, Editor and Preacher* (1903).

Sturgis, J. L., *John Bright and the Empire* (1969).

Summerton, N. W., 'Dissenting Attitudes to Foreign Relations, Peace, and War, 1840–1890', *JEH* xxviii (1977), 151–78.

Sutherland, Gillian, *Policy-making in Elementary Education, 1870–1895* (Oxford, 1973).

Swift, R., and S. Gilley (eds.), *The Irish in the Victorian City* (1985).

Swinfen, D. B., 'The Single Judgment in the Privy Council, 1833–1966', *The Juridical Review*, ii (1975), 153–76.

Sykes, A., *Tariff Reform in British Politics, 1903–1913* (Oxford, 1979).

Taylor, H. A., *Smith of Birkenhead* (1931).

—— *Jix, Viscount Brentford* (1933).

Telford, J., *The Life of James Harrison Rigg, DD, 1821–1909* ([1910]).

Temmel, M. R., 'Liberal versus Liberal, 1874: W. E. Forster, Bradford, and Education', *HJ* xviii (1975), 611–22.

—— 'Gladstone's Resignation of the Liberal Leadership, 1874–1875', *Journal of British Studies*, xvi. 1 (1976), 153–75.

Temple, Sir Richard, *The Story of My Life* (2 vols., 1896).

Temple, W., *Life and Liberty* (1917).

—— *The Life of Bishop Percival* (1921).

The Burials Question Further Examined, From a Layman's Point of View (1880).

The Burials Question: What is to be Done? (1877).

The Case for Disestablishment: A Handbook of Facts and Arguments, Liberation Society (1884).

The Church Established in Scotland: A Historical Study (Edinburgh, 1879).

The Church of England, Dissent, and the Disestablishment Policy, by A Member of the Carlton (1873).

The Church of England in her Fourfold Aspect, by A Country Vicar, 2nd edn. (1869).

The Church of England in 1910, by an Old Priest (1874).

The Church of England: Reform or Disestablishment, Which? by One of her Presbyters (1873).

The Claim of Right, with the Draft of Mr Finlay's Bill (Edinburgh, 1886).

The Clerical Ritualistic Who's Who, with an Account of the Ritualistic Conspiracy (1908).

The Confessional in the Church of England: A Full Report of the Meeting Held in Exeter Hall, June 1873, repr. from *The Rock* (1873).

The Distribution and Statistics of the Scottish Churches (1886).

The Free Churches and the State; Free Church Federal Council (1953).

The Geography of Religion in the Highlands (Edinburgh, 1905).

The Increase of the Episcopate: Is it Desirable at the Present time?, by 'Telegonus' (1877).

The Laymen's League and the General Election (Edinburgh, 1892).

The National Church: An Appeal Against Disestablishment (London and Edinburgh, 1878).

The New Patronage Act and the Scottish Churches (n.p., n.d.).

The Religious Revival in Wales, 1904, by Awstin and Other Special Correspondents of the Western Mail (1905).

The Ritualistic Conspiracy, Comprising Lists of Priests Reprinted from The Rock (1877).

Thomas, J. A., *The House of Commons, 1906–1911: An Analysis of its Economic and Social Character* (Cardiff, 1958).

Thompson, D. M. (ed.), *Nonconformity in the Nineteenth Century* (1972).

—— 'The Politics of the Enabling Act, 1919', in D. Baker (ed.), *Studies in Church History*, xii (Oxford, 1975), 383–92.

Thompson, K. A., *Bureaucracy and Church Reform, 1800–1965* (Oxford, 1970).

Thompson, L., *The Enthusiasts: A Biography of John and Katherine Buce Glasier* (1971).

Thompson, P., *Socialists, Liberals, and Labour: The Struggle for London, 1885–1914* (1967).

Thorburn, J. H., *Gold May Be Bought Too Dear: An Appeal to the People of Scotland and a Challenge to the Promoters of the Draft Articles of Union*, National Church Defence Association, (Leith, [1920]).

Tierney, M., *Croke of Cashel: The Life of Archbishop T. W. Croke, 1823–1902* (Dublin, 1976).

Tillett, B., *Memories and Reflections* (1931).

Townsend, H., *The Claims of the Free Churches* (1949).

—— *The Liberation Society: A Plea for Free Church Support*, leaflet (n.p., 1946).

Treble, J. H., 'The Development of Roman Catholic Education in Scotland, 1878–1978', *Innes Review*, xxix (1978), 111–39.

—— 'The Working of the 1918 Education Act in Glasgow Archdiocese', *Innes Review*, xxxi (1980), 27–44.

Tsuzuki, C., *H. M. Hyndman and British Socialism* (1961).

Tuckwell, W., *The Church of the Future* (Birmingham, 1886).

Tulloch, J., *A Political Church, or Short Reflections on the Disestablishment Movement* (Edinburgh, 1874).

—— *Position and Prospects of the Church of Scotland* (Edinburgh, 1878).

—— *A Plea in Self-defence Addressed to Leaders of the Disestablishment Party in the Free Church* (Edinburgh, 1878).

Tyson, T. C., 'The Church and School Education', in W. S. F. Pickering (ed.), *A Social History of the Diocese of Newcastle, 1882–1982* (Stocksfield, 1981), 270–90.

Twelve Reasons for Refusing to Join the English Church Union (1871).

Vincent, J., (ed.), *Disraeli, Derby, and the Conservative Party, 1849–1869* (Hassocks, Sussex, 1978).

Vincent, J. E., *The Land Question in North Wales* (1896).

Vogeler, Martha S., *Frederic Harrison: The Vocations of a Positivist* (Oxford, 1984).

Wace, H., *et al.*, *The Education Crisis* (1907).

Wagner, A. D., *Christ or Caesar? A letter to the Archbishop of Canterbury* (1874).

Walker, D. G. (ed.), *A History of the Church in Wales* (Cardiff, 1976).

Walker, R. B., 'Religious Changes in Liverpool in the Nineteenth Century', *JEH* xix (1968), 195–211.

Walker, W. M., 'Irish Immigrants in Scotland: Their Priests, Politics, and Parochial Life', *HJ* xv (1972), 649–67.

Waller, P. J., *Democracy and Sectarianism: A Political and Social History of Liverpool, 1868–1939* (Liverpool, 1981).

Walsh, P. J., *William J. Walsh, Archbishop of Dublin* (Dublin and Cork, 1928).

Walsh, Walter, *Episcopal Patronage in the Church of England: How it is Exercised* (Market Rasen, 1884).

Walsh, Walter, *The Secret Work of the Ritualists* (1895).
—— *The Secret History of the Oxford Movement*, 5th edn. (1899).
—— *A Defence of the King's Protestant Declaration* (1901).
Ward, W., *The Life of John Henry, Cardinal Newman* (2 vols., 1912).
Ward, W. R., *Victorian Oxford* (1965).
Watts, M. R., ' "The Hateful Mystery": Nonconformists and Hell', *Journal of United Reformed Church History Society*, ii (1978–82), 248–58.
Wearmouth, R. F., *Methodism and the Struggle of the Working Classes, 1850–1900* (Leicester, 1954).
Webb, A., *The Opinions of Some Protestants Regarding their Irish Catholic Fellow-countrymen*, 3rd edn. (Dublin, 1886).
Webb, Beatrice, *My Apprenticeship*, 2nd edn. (1946).
—— *Our Partnership*, ed. Barbara Drake and Margaret Cole (1948).
Weber, M., *The Sociology of Religion* (Boston, Mass., 1963).
Wesleyan Connexional Record and Year-book for 1875 (1875).
Westcott, A., *Life and Letters of Brooke Foss Westcott, Sometime Bishop of Durham* (2 vols., 1903).
What Would the Taxpayer Gain by Disestablishment? (Edinburgh, n.d.).
White, B. D., *A History of the Corporation of Liverpool* (Liverpool, 1951).
Wickham, E. R., *Church and People in an Industrial City* (1957).
Wilcox, J. C., *John Kensit, Reformer and Martyr: A Popular Life*, Protestant Truth Society ([1902]).
Wilkinson, A., *The Church of England and the First World War* (1978).
Williams, Canon N. P., *The Bishop of Durham and Disestablishment*, Church Self-government League (1929).
Williams, C. R., 'The Welsh Religious Revival, 1904–1905', *British Journal of Sociology*, iii (1952), 242–59.
Williams, J. Carvell, *The New Position of the Burials Question* (1878).
Wilson, B. R., *Religion in Secular Society* (1966).
—— (ed.), *Patterns of Sectarianism* (1967).
Wilson, T., *The Downfall of the Liberal Party, 1914–1935* (1966).
Wilson, W., *Memorials of R. S. Candlish* (Edinburgh, 1880).
Wimborne, Lady, *The Ritualist Conspiracy* (1898).
Winter, J. M., *Socialism and the Challenge of War: Ideas and Opinions in Britain, 1912–1918* (1974).
Withrington, D. J., 'Towards a National System, 1867–1872: The Last Years in the Struggle for a Scottish Education Act', *Scottish Educational Studies*, iv (1972), 107–24.
—— 'The Churches in Scotland, c.1870–1900: Towards a New Social Conscience?', *Scottish Church History Society Records*, xix (1975–7), 155–68.
Wolf, L. *Life of the First Marquess of Ripon* (2 vols., 1921).
Wood, I., 'Irish Immigrants and Scottish Radicalism, 1880–1906', in I. MacDougall (ed.), *Essays in Scottish Labour History* (Edinburgh, 1978), 65–89.
—— 'John Wheatley, the Irish, and the Labour Movement in Scotland', *Innes Review*, xxxi (1980), 71–85.
Wood, J., *The Need for Active Church Defence Against the Designs of the Liberation Society*, 2nd edn. (Alfreton, 1871).
Woodside, D., *The Soul of a Scottish Church, or the Contribution of the United Presbyterian Church to Scottish Life and Religion* (Edinburgh, [1918]).

Wright, C. H. H., and C. Neil (eds.), *A Protestant Dictionary* (1904).

Wright, D. G., 'Liberal versus Liberal, 1874: Some Comments', *HJ* xvi (1973), 597–603.

Yates, N., *The Oxford Movement and Parish Life: St Saviour's, Leeds, 1839–1929*, Borthwick Papers, no. 48 (York, 1975).

—— *The Oxford Movement and Anglican Ritualism*, Historical Association (1983).

—— (ed.), *Kent and the Oxford Movement* (Gloucester, 1983).

Yeo, S., *Religion and Voluntary Organizations in Crisis* (1976).

—— 'A New Life: The Religion of Socialism in Britain', *History Workshop*, iv (1977), 5–56.

Zebel, Sydney H., *Balfour: A Political Biography* (Cambridge, 1973).

Zetland, Marquess of (ed.), *The Letters of Disraeli to Lady Bradford and Lady Chesterfield* (2 vols., 1929).

V UNPUBLISHED THESES

Bebbington, D. W., 'The Nonconformist Conscience: A Study of the Political Attitudes and Activities of Evangelical Nonconformists, 1886–1902', Ph.D. thesis (Cambridge, 1975).

Bentley, Anne, 'The Transformation of the Evangelical Party in the Church of England in the Later Nineteenth Century', Ph.D. thesis (Durham, 1971).

Brooks, D. R., 'Gladstone's Fourth Ministry, 1892–1894', Ph.D. thesis (Cambridge, 1975).

Cunningham, H. ST C., 'British Public Opinion and the Eastern Question, 1877–1878', D.Phil thesis (Sussex, 1969).

Fairhurst, J. R., 'Some Aspects of the Relationship Between Education, Politics, and Religion from 1895 to 1906', D.Phil. thesis (Oxford, 1974).

Field, C. D., 'Methodism in Metropolitan London, 1850–1920: A Social and Sociological Study', D.Phil. thesis (Oxford, 1974).

Findlay, I. R., 'Sir John Struthers, KCB: A Study of his Influence upon Scottish Educational Development', Ph.D. thesis (Dundee, 1979).

Fletcher, D. E., 'Aspects of Sheffield Liberalism, 1849–1886', Ph.D. thesis (Sheffield, 1972).

Griffiths, P. C., 'The Origins and Development of the National Liberal Federation to 1886', B.Litt. thesis (Oxford, 1973).

Holding, J. R., 'An Examination of the Third Salisbury Cabinet, 1895–1902', B.Litt. thesis (Oxford, 1978).

Hylson-Smith, K., 'The Evangelicals in the Church of England, 1900–1939', Ph.D. thesis (London 1983).

Lawrence, G. W., 'William Robertson Nicoll, 1851–1923, and Religious Journalism in the Nineteenth Century', Ph.D. thesis (Edinburgh, 1954).

Levy, Catriona, 'Conservatism and Liberal Unionism in Glasgow, 1874–1912', Ph.D. thesis (Dundee, 1983).

Lindsay, J. K., 'The Liberal Unionist Party until December 1887', Ph.D. thesis (Edinburgh, 1956).

Lloyd, May, 'Baptist Political Attitudes, with Special Reference to the Late Nineteenth Century', M.Phil. thesis (Leeds, 1974).

Lyon, D., 'The Eclipse of Christian Religious Assumptions: England in the 1870s', Ph.D. thesis (Bradford, 1976).

McCaffrey, J. F., 'Political Reactions in the Glasgow Constituencies at the General Elections of 1885 and 1886', Ph.D. thesis (Glasgow, 1970).

Mayhew, G., 'The Ethical and Religious Foundations of Socialist Politics in Britain: The First Generation and their Ideals, 1884–1931', D.Phil. thesis (York, 1981).

Mews, S. P., 'The Effect of the First World War on English Religious Life and Thought', MA thesis (Leeds, 1967).

Morris, G. M., 'Primitive Methodism in Nottinghamshire, 1815–1932', Ph.D. thesis (Nottingham, 1967).

Munson, J. E. B., 'A Study of Nonconformity in Edwardian England as Revealed by the Passive Resistance Movement Against the 1902 Education Act', D.Phil. thesis (Oxford, 1973).

Murray, C. J., 'Midlothian and Gladstone', MA Hons. thesis (Dundee, 1982).

Nelmes, G. V., 'Stuart Rendel and his Contribution to the Development of a Distinctively Welsh Political Programme within the Liberal Party Between 1880 and 1895', MA thesis (Wales, 1977).

Newton, J. S., 'The Political Career of Edward Miall', Ph.D. thesis (Durham, 1975).

Phillips, J., 'The Irish University Question, 1873–1908', Ph.D. thesis (Cambridge, 1978).

Pritchard, P. B., 'The Churches and the Liverpool School Board, 1870–1903', Ph.D. thesis (Liverpool, 1981).

Purdue, A. W., 'Parliamentary Elections in North-East England, 1900–1906: The Impact of Labour', M.Litt. thesis (Newcastle upon Tyne, 1974).

Roberts, J. W., 'Sir George Osborne Morgan, 1826–1897', MA thesis (Wales, 1979).

Roberts, M. J. D., 'The Role of the Laity in the Church of England, c.1850–1885', D.Phil. thesis (Oxford, 1974).

Roland, D., 'The Struggle for the Elementary Education Act and its Implementation, 1870–1873', B.Litt. thesis (Oxford, 1957).

Ross, W. D., 'Politics and Opinion in Bradford, 1880–1906, with Special Reference to Parliamentary Elections', Ph.D. thesis (Bradford, 1977).

Savage, D. C., 'The General Election of 1886', Ph.D. thesis (London, 1958).

Summers, D. F., 'The Labour Church and Allied Movements of the Late Nineteenth and Early Twentieth Centuries', Ph.D. thesis (Edinburgh, 1958).

Taylor, A. F., 'Birmingham and the Movement for National Education, 1867–1877', Ph.D. thesis (Leicester, 1960).

Taylor, A. I., 'The Church Party and Popular Education, 1893–1902', Ph.D. thesis (Cambridge, 1981).

Thomas, R. R., 'The Influence of the "Irish question" on Welsh Politics, 1880–1895', MA thesis (Wales, 1973).

Waitt, E. I., 'John Morley, Joseph Cowen, and Robert Spence Watson: The Divisions of Liberalism in Newcastle Politics, 1870–1902', Ph.D. thesis (Manchester, 1972).

Walmsley, J. W., 'The History of the Evangelical Party in the Church of England Between 1906 and 1928', Ph.D. thesis (Hull, 1981).

Welch, A. H., 'John Carvell Williams, the Nonconformist Watchdog, 1821–1907', Ph.D. thesis (Kansas, 1968) (copy in Greater London Record Office).

Wilkinson, M. J., 'Educational Controversies in British Politics, 1895–1914', Ph.D. thesis (Newcastle upon Tyne, 1978).

Withycombe, R. S. M., 'The Development of Constitutional Autonomy in the Established Church in Later Victorian England', Ph.D. thesis (Cambridge, 1970).

Wollaston, E. P. M., 'The Irish Nationalist Movement in Great Britain, 1886–1908', MA thesis (London, 1957).

Wright, D. G., 'Politics and Opinion in Nineteenth-century Bradford, 1832–1880', Ph.D. thesis (Leeds, 1966).

Index